Office 2003
Bible

Office 2003
Bible

Edward C. Willett

WILEY

Wiley Publishing, Inc.

Office 2003 Bible

Published by
Wiley Publishing, Inc.
10475 Crosspoint Boulevard
Indianapolis, IN 46256
www.wiley.com

Copyright © 2004 by Wiley Publishing, Inc., Indianapolis, Indiana

Library of Congress Control Number: 2003101887

Published simultaneously in Canada

ISBN: 0-7645-3949-3

Manufactured in the United States of America

10 9 8 7 6 5 4 3 2 1

1O/RY/QX/QT/IN

About the Author

Edward Willett is the author of more than 20 books, ranging from computer books on a variety of topics to children's nonfiction to young adult science fiction and fantasy. A former newspaper reporter and editor, he writes a science column for newspapers and radio and hosts a weekly TV phone-in show about computers and the Internet. He's also a professional actor and singer. Ed lives in Regina, Saskatchewan, with his wife and daughter.

About the Contributing Authors

Allen Wyatt, an internationally recognized expert in small computer systems, has been working in the computer and publishing industries for almost two decades. He has written almost 50 books explaining many different facets of working with computers, as well as numerous magazine articles. His books have covered topics ranging from programming languages to using application software to using operating systems. Through the written word, Allen has helped millions of readers learn how to better use computers.

Allen is the president of Discovery Computing Inc., a computer and publishing services company located in Mesa, Arizona. Besides writing books and technical materials, he helps further the computer-book industry by providing consulting and production services. Allen also publishes a free weekly newsletter for users of Word and Excel. You can find more information at www.VitalNews.com.

Bill Rodgers is a computing consultant from Newcastle, Australia, with a passion for V8Supercars and Rugby league and Rugby Union football. Bill specializes in Office and Windows systems, collaboration, and advanced technologies. Bill has been a contributing author and technical editor on many Office books for leading international companies and has been awarded the Microsoft MVP (Most Valuable Professional) award for the past four years for his support of and expertise with Microsoft products.

About the Technical Editors

Most of the technical editors of *Office 2003 Bible* have earned the prestigious "MVP" — Microsoft Most Valuable Professional — designation for the topic areas they reviewed in this book. MVPs are recognized by their peers and Microsoft for their active participation in Microsoft technical communities, primarily answering user questions about the products and technologies. Diane Poremsky and Ben Schorr are Outlook MVPs. Echo Swinford is a PowerPoint MVP, and Herb Tyson is a Word MVP. You can read more about the MVP program and these individuals' contributions to the Office community at http://mvp.support.microsoft.com.

Credits

Acquisitions Editor
Jim Minatel

Project Editor
Eric Newman

Technical Editors
Diane Poremsky
Tyler and Rima Regas
Ben M. Schorr
Echo Swinford
Herb Tyson

Copy Editors
Luann Rouff
Kezia Endsley

Editorial Manager
Mary Beth Wakefield

Vice President & Executive Group Publisher
Richard Swadley

Vice President and Executive Publisher
Bob Ipsen

Vice President and Publisher
Joseph B. Wikert

Executive Editorial Director
Mary Bednarek

Project Coordinator
Regina Snyder

Graphics and Production Specialists
Beth Brooks
Amanda Carter
Jennifer Click
Carrie Foster
Michael Kruzil
Kristin McMullan
Heather Pope
Kathie S. Schnorr
Janet Seib

Quality Control Technicians
Laura Albert
John Tyler Connoley
John Greenough
Andy Hollandbeck
Carl William Pierce
Rob Springer
Kathy Simpson

Permissions Editor
Carmen Krikorian

Media Development Specialist
Greg Stafford

Proofreading and Indexing
TECHBOOKS Production Services

This book is dedicated to the two Alices.

Preface

Welcome to *Office 2003 Bible*, your guide to the latest and greatest version of Microsoft's immensely popular suite of office applications. Within these pages you'll find everything you need to know to make immediate, effective use of Word, Excel, Outlook, PowerPoint, Access, and FrontPage. You'll learn how to use each program separately. You'll also learn how to use them together to create integrated documents that draw on the strengths of all these programs to help you do your work better.

Is This Book for You?

If you use, or will soon be using, Office 2003, then this book is for you. Throughout this book you'll find useful tips and step-by-step guides to carrying out the most common Office tasks. Both the excellent index and thorough table of contents can help you find the topics that interest you.

How This Book Is Organized

Office 2003 Bible is divided into nine parts and four appendixes.

Part I: Getting Started

These two chapters cover the Office user interface and offer basic information on such common tasks as saving and printing.

Part II: Using Word

The heart of any office suite is the word processor, and with Word, Microsoft Office has the most popular and powerful word processor in the world. Here you'll learn how to put Word's power to work for you.

Part III: Using Excel

Excel is Office's spreadsheet application, and, like Word, it's pretty much the standard in its field. These chapters show you how to get the most from your worksheets.

Part IV: Using Outlook

Outlook is Office's application for managing e-mail and fax messages, as well as your time. These chapters help you get the most from Outlook's powerful features.

Part V: Using PowerPoint

PowerPoint is Office's presentation software. These chapters demonstrate how to make great presentations that communicate your message clearly and effectively.

Part VI: Using Access

Just as Outlook lets you manage messages and your time, so Access lets you manage data—and use it in other Office applications. These chapters explain how.

Part VII: Office and the Web

FrontPage helps you create professional-looking Web pages and manage them effectively, but you can also create Web pages in other applications. These chapters tell you how to make use of both FrontPage and the main Office applications on the Web.

Part VIII: Collaborating in Office

Office's most powerful attribute is the seamless way all of its applications work closely together to accomplish things none of them could on their own. These chapters explore Office's cooperative capabilities and the tools to make the most of them, including Picture Library and Microsoft Office Document Imaging.

Part IX: Customizing and Automating Office

Get great customizing tips for all of Office's applications and learn how to create your own custom commands with macros in these final two chapters.

Appendixes

Four appendixes include additional valuable information.

   ✦ Appendix A describes the content of the accompanying CD-ROM.

   ✦ Appendix B, "Optimizing Your Office Installation," provides a few tips on using Office Setup.

✦ Appendix C, "International Support and Accessibility Features," details Office's international language support. It also provides tips for those users who could benefit from special accommodations, such as longer key delays, different screen display options, and verbal prompts.

✦ Appendix D, "Finding Office Information on the Web," points you to Web sites where you'll find more information and lots of useful tips, tricks, templates, and more, including additional links.

Conventions Used in This Book

We've made finding your way through this tome easier by including a variety of signposts that point you to useful information. Look for the following icons in the left margin.

Notes highlight something of particular interest about the current topic or expand on the subject at hand.

These icons clue you in to hot tips, or show you faster, better ways of doing things.

If a process holds some risk of losing data, irrevocably altering a document, or annoying the heck out of you, this icon will warn you about it.

This icon points you to another section of the book where additional information on the current topic can be found.

Please note also the following typographical conventions:

✦ When we tell you to use a particular command from a menu, we'll write it like this: Choose File ⇨ New. That tells you to pull down the File menu and select the New command. If there's another level of menu beyond that, it'll look like this: choose View ⇨ Toolbars ⇨ Formatting.

✦ Keyboard commands are written like this: Press Ctrl+A. That means to press the Ctrl key and continue to hold it down while you press the A key.

What You'll Find in Sidebars

Sidebars provide related information, examples, or additional detail about a topic. Generally the information in sidebars, while interesting, isn't critical to understanding how to use an application, so you can skip them if you like. (We'd prefer you didn't, though — after all, we put a lot of work into writing them!)

Where Should I Start?

With such a complete and thoughtfully designed resource (a book as comprehensive as its subject), it may be difficult to decide where to begin. Here are a few helpful hints:

✦ To work with a specific application — Word, Excel, Outlook, PowerPoint, Access, or FrontPage — refer to the pertinent parts and chapters in the book.

✦ To work with a specific topic, let the table of contents or the index be your guide.

✦ To find additional sources of information, refer to Appendix D.

✦ If all else fails, simply turn the page and begin. We're sure you'll find reading this book as enjoyable a process as using Office 2003.

Acknowledgments

Acknowledgment and thanks go to my agent, Djana Pearson Morris; all those who worked on this book at Wiley (my acquisitions editor, Jim Minatel; my project editor, Eric Newman; the book's copy editors, Luann Rouff and Kezia Endsley; and the technical reviewers: Diane Poremsky, Tyler and Rima Regas, Ben Schorr, Echo Swinford, and Herb Tyson); and, as always, my wife, Margaret Anne, for sharing me with my computer.

Contents at a Glance

Contents

Part IV: Using Outlook   437

Part V: Using PowerPoint   531

Part VIII: Collaborating in Office   859

Chapter 42: Building Integrated Documents 861

Part IX: Customizing and Automating Office   1007

Getting Started

Welcome to Your New Office

Welcome to Microsoft Office 2003! It's a powerful, complex suite of applications, but don't let that intimidate you; this book will get you up and running in no time, even if you've never used Office before. If you have used Office before, you'll soon find yourself as comfortable with the new version as you are with the old.

Introducing Office Applications: What Do They Do?

Microsoft Office contains numerous applications, each of which we'll be looking at. The following list briefly describes the programs outlined in this book (you may not have all of these applications installed, depending on what version of Office 2003 you've purchased):

✦ **Word.** A powerful word processor, Word makes it easy to enter text into the computer, format it the way you want, and then print it or post it online.

✦ **Excel.** A versatile spreadsheet program, Excel can be used in countless ways, but its most basic use, like the spreadsheets on paper that inspired it, is as a tool for organizing numbers into rows and columns and manipulating and analyzing them to help with budgeting and planning.

✦ **Outlook.** Outlook is Office's application for managing messages, from e-mail to faxes, and your time. Its powerful calendar function keeps you organized, its Tasks list makes sure you don't forget your day-to-day responsibilities, and its Contacts folder stores all the information you'll ever need about the important people in your life.

✦ **PowerPoint.** Office's presentation application, PowerPoint can help you create vivid onscreen or printed presentations that communicate your ideas clearly and effectively.

✦ **Access.** A database program, Access makes it easy to collect and analyze data—and use it in other Office applications.

✦ **FrontPage.** A powerful tool for creating and managing Web sites, FrontPage is the only Office component entirely dedicated to that task. (You can create Web pages with all Office applications.)

Starting Office Applications

You can open any Office application from the Start menu just as you open any other application: choose Start ➪ Programs, and then find the application you want to start and select it.

Tip   You might find it handy to create shortcuts on your desktop to your most commonly used Office applications. To do so, right-click the program in the Start ➪ All Programs menu and drag it to your desktop. You'll see a shortcut menu offering you two choices: Copy Here or Move Here. If you choose Copy Here, the program remains listed in your Start ➪ All Programs menu, but a shortcut is also added to your desktop. If you choose Move Here, the program appears as a desktop shortcut and is no longer listed in your Start ➪ All Programs menu.

Creating, Saving, and Closing Documents

In all Office applications except Outlook, your goal is to create some kind of "document," whether it's a PowerPoint presentation, a Word document, an Excel spreadsheet, a FrontPage Web site, or an Access database.

Creating documents

You can create Office documents in two main ways:

✦ From within an Office application

✦ Using the Start menu

If you're already in an Office application, the easiest way to create a new document is to choose File ➪ New. This brings up different options depending on the program you're using. For instance, choosing File ➪ New in Word opens the task pane shown on the right in Figure 1-1. You can choose to create a new blank document, Web page, XML document, or e-mail message; create a new document based on an existing document; or create a new document based on a template.

In Outlook, you choose from a different list of options, including Mail Message, Appointment, Contact, Distribution List, Task, Journal Entry, Note, and Fax. Excel's options are similar to Word's, Access's are different again, and so on.

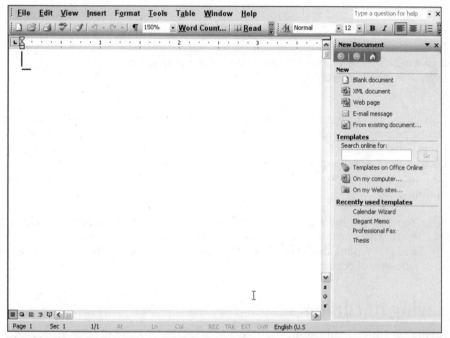

Figure 1-1: Choosing File ➪ New brings up a number of different options, depending on which application you're using. On the right is the New Document task pane.

You can save a step in creating a new document if you already know what kind of document it will be. Instead of first opening an Office application and then creating a new document, you can create a new document and open the application you need at the same time.

You can do that by choosing Start ➪ Programs ➪ Microsoft Office Tools ➪ New Office Document. The New Office Document dialog box is shown in Figure 1-2.

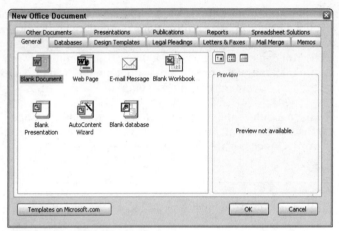

Figure 1-2: The New Office Document dialog box enables you to choose from numerous kinds of Office documents.

This dialog box brings together all the many different types of Office documents that can be automatically created, from a blank Word document, PowerPoint presentation, Excel workbook, Access database, or Outlook e-mail message to specific templates, such as the PowerPoint template for Recommending a Strategy or the Excel template for Loan Amortization. Just click the tab you want and choose from the available options.

Note   You can find more than just templates in the New Office Document dialog box. You'll also find a plethora of useful wizards, such as the Calendar Wizard and Resume Wizard, that take you step by step through the process of creating a specific type of document.

Saving documents

No matter which application you're working in, the process of saving documents (and an important process it is, too!) is much the same: Choose File ➪ Save or File ➪ Save As (the Standard toolbar usually has a Save button on it as well, if you prefer the one-click approach).

The first time you choose Save, or any time you choose Save As, you'll see the Save As dialog box (see Figure 1-3).

This is a relatively standard dialog box that you're probably familiar with from other Windows applications. Type the name you want to give the document into the File name text box, and choose the type of file it is in the Save as type box, using the drop-down list provided. By default, this will be the standard file format used by that program; in the example shown in Figure 1-3, it's the PowerPoint Presentation format, which uses the .ppt extension.

Figure 1-3: The Save As dialog box enables you to specify where, in what format, and with what name you wish to save your Office document.

Other options include template format, which makes the document available for use as a template for future documents; older versions of the standard format for backward compatibility; Web page format, which turns the document into an HTML file suitable for viewing online using a standard Web browser; and, in some applications, XML format, a powerful new feature that makes it easy to create documents that can import and manage data from remote sources and non-Office applications (provided, of course, that they too support XML).

Cross-Reference   For more information about using XML in Office applications, see Chapters 11, 20, and 38.

Once you've saved a document once, choosing Save again doesn't open this dialog box: instead, it overwrites the previous version of the document with the currently open version. If you'd prefer to save the new version of a document without over-writing the previous version, or if you want to save the new version in a different file format, or in a different location, choose File ➪ Save As. This will open the Save As dialog box again, enabling you to give the new version of the file a new name (perhaps for version tracking) and/or a new format or save it in another location, such as to a different folder or to another drive.

Closing documents

To close a document without closing the application, click the closest X in the upper-right corner (just underneath the topmost X, which closes the entire application). Alternatively, choose File ➪ Close. If you haven't saved the current version of the document, the application will ask you if you want to save any changes you made to that file. Choose Yes to overwrite any previous version with the current version, No to keep the currently saved version without preserving any changes you may have made to it, or Cancel to return to the application without saving.

Working with Smart Tags and Task Panes

Smart Tags and task panes, introduced in Office XP and further developed in Office 2003, provide quick access to commonly used commands. Making good use of them can make your Office experience more pleasant and more efficient.

Task panes are windows that appear within an Office application to one side of the workspace. They provide a list of commands you may want to use, depending on what you're trying to do. You've already seen one in Figure 1-1.

Like toolbars, task panes can be made to float or dock against any side of the workspace you prefer. To pull the task pane free of its default location, click and drag the upper-left corner of the task pane's title bar, just to the left of the title, where you see a column of small dots.

Tip   As you use any Office application, you're likely to open a series of task panes. You can move through these task panes just as you'd maneuver through a series of pages you've opened in your Web browser, by using Back and Forward buttons (located in the upper-left corner of the task pane). You'll also see a Home button. Clicking this takes you to the application's most basic task pane, which enables you to open a document or create a new document. The Home task pane also includes a Search box that connects you to Office on Microsoft.com (provided, of course, you are online). To close a task pane, click on the X at the right end of its title bar, or press Ctrl+F1.

Smart Tags are buttons that provide choices for enhancing content or layout in Office applications. You don't call them up yourself; instead, they appear when you need them (or at least when Office thinks you need them—such as when you make a mistake in an Excel formula, or when Word automatically corrects something you've done, or when you paste in data from the clipboard). Clicking the Smart Tag will bring up a small menu offering the options you need to fix the error, reverse the action, or do whatever else might be appropriate.

Figure 1-4 shows a Smart Tag (and a task pane, for good measure) in Excel.

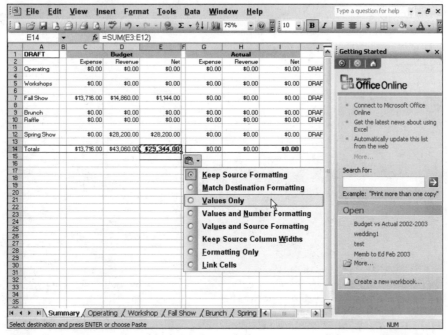

Figure 1-4: Smart Tags and task panes can help you accomplish your Office tasks quickly and easily.

Using Office Search Effectively

Another useful feature in Office 2003 is an enhanced search capability that makes it easy to locate specific documents both on your computer and on the network it's connected to, if any. It will even search through all the messages you've stored in Outlook!

To access Search from any Office application, choose File ➪ File Search. This opens the Basic File Search task pane shown on the right in Figure 1-5.

This task pane contains three text boxes:

✦ In the top text box, Search text:, enter any keywords that might help identify the file. The program will look for files containing those words in the name of the file, in the body of the file, or in any keywords assigned to the file. The more words you enter, the more specific the search. You can also use wildcards. The asterisk (*) can stand for any number of characters. Thus, a search for h*p would return everything from hip and hop to hoop, hyssop, and horsewhip. The question mark stands for any single character; using h?p in your search would return files containing hip, hop, and hep, but not hoop, hyssop, or horsewhip.

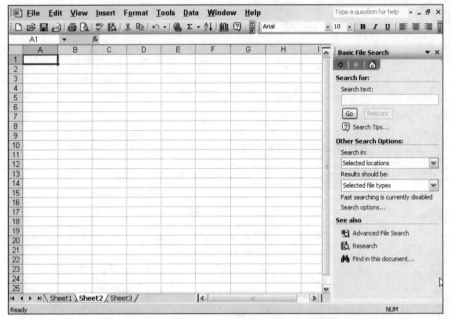

Figure 1-5: The Basic File Search task pane helps you find Office files quickly and easily.

Note   Search looks for all forms of a word you enter in the Search text box. If you enter "run," for instance, it will also find files containing "running" and "ran."

Tip   If you're searching your Outlook mailbox and you're working in English, you can frame your search query using natural language, just as if you were talking to a human being, in other words. For example, you could type "Find all messages received today."

✦ In the Search in: text box, specify at least one place in which Office should search. The proffered list of possibilities includes My Computer, My Network Places, and Outlook. You can narrow the search by specifying only certain folders.

✦ Finally, in the Results should be: text box, specify which types of file to search for: Anything, Office Files, Outlook Items, or Web pages (items with .htm, .html, .mht, .mhtml, or .asp extensions). You can specify which types of Office files to search for and which specific Outlook items (e-mail messages, appointments, contacts, tasks, or notes), to narrow the search.

Figure 1-6 shows some typical results. Office has found two files containing the keyword indicated ("sunset").

Figure 1-6: Results of an Office search

Once results are displayed, you can rest your pointer on the filename to get more information about it, click it to open it, right-click it to see more actions you can perform (such as edit the file, create a new document based on it, or copy a link to it to your clipboard), or click Modify to start a new search.

Click Advanced File Search at the bottom of the Basic File Search task pane to run searches based on document properties, such as author and date modified, and to use logic (i.e., AND/OR) to include or exclude information in your search.

In the Advanced File Search task pane, you first enter a property to search for (there's a long list of possibilities, from Address to Size to Format to Web page), then select a condition for that property (in the case of text properties such as Address, you can choose to search for files that either include the text you enter or precisely match it; other properties offer other conditions), and then set a value to search for — a text string, for instance, or a file size.

Next, click Add to add that value to your search. You can build in additional search parameters by creating additional property/condition/value combinations and clicking either the And or Or radio buttons, depending on whether you want all of the conditions you've specified to be met or if meeting any one of them is sufficient.

Finally, choose the locations to search in and the file types you're interested in, just as you did with the Basic File Search, and click Go.

Getting Help in Office Applications

Office may not give you much in the way of a printed user's manual (which may be why you bought this book!), but it does provide a massive amount of help information on your screen. Because Office presents you with so many complex applications and supporting utilities, the ability to find the help you need and find it quickly becomes a vital skill.

Office's Help tools include three main components: the Office Help system, which links you to a set of files containing help information stored on your local computer; the optional Office Assistant, which offers a small and friendly-to-a-fault gateway to the main Help system; and Office on Microsoft.com, a link to Microsoft's Web-based Office resources.

Using Help

Figure 1-7 shows an Excel help topic.

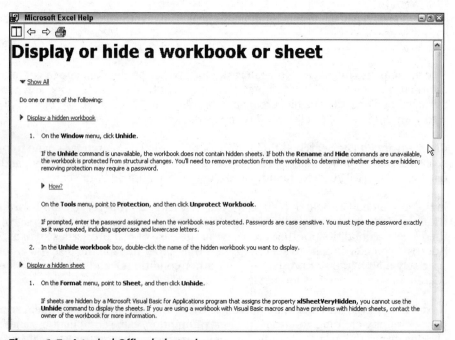

Figure 1-7: A typical Office help topic

You can access Help from an Office application in three ways:

✦ Type your query into the box in the upper-right corner of any Office application (look for the grayed-out text "Type a question for help" inside the box). Enter a question, such as "How do I change text color?" and then press Enter.

✦ Press F1 or choose the menu item for the current application from the top of the Help menu (for example, Help ➪ Microsoft PowerPoint Help). The main Help task pane appears (see Figure 1-8). At the top, in the Assistance section, is a search box; enter keywords related to what you're trying to do and click the arrow to search the help files for information containing those keywords. Alternatively, you can click the Table of Contents link (below the text box) to see a list of all the topics covered by the help files.

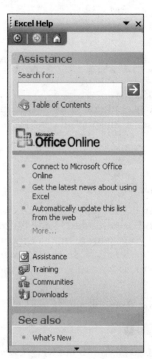

Figure 1-8: Use the Help task pane to find the information you need about any Office application.

✦ If the Office Assistant is enabled (see the following section for Office Assistant options), click it and then type a question into its balloon or click one of the topics it suggests (see Figure 1-9). You're taken to the Help system, which displays the relevant information.

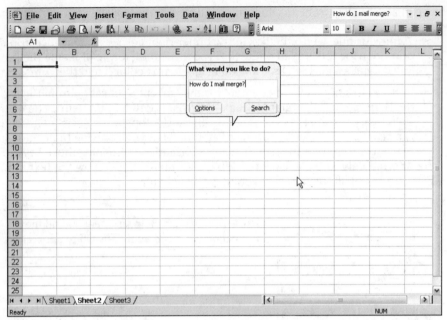

Figure 1-9: The Office Assistant (not shown) presents a "balloon" in which you define your help requests.

Working with the Help task pane

Once you've conducted a search for information, it's displayed in a standard task pane. At the top, once again, you'll see the Back, Forward, and Home buttons. The main part of the task pane displays results from your search; below that is an area labeled "Can't find it?" with a link to tips for better search results. Below that are links to "Other places to look," including Clip Art and Media, Research, and Microsoft Product Support.

Working with the Office Assistant

The Office Assistant is an animated graphic that attempts to answer your questions and offer advice even before you know you want it — even, unfortunately, when you most emphatically *don't* want it. One of the most popular changes Microsoft made when it released Office XP, the previous version of Office, was to make the Office Assistant optional, providing access to its basic functions through the Type a question: box already described.

Obviously, however, enough people actually like the Assistant that Microsoft decided to keep it around. If you're one of those users who enjoy getting information from an animated paperclip, then here's what you need to know:

The Office Assistant performs two main functions:

✦ It offers tips, letting you know about Office features you may be unaware of and pointing you to more efficient ways to accomplish certain tasks. Some of these tips are displayed automatically, as soon as you use a program feature for which the Assistant has a tip — for example, if you type "Dear Mr. Smith" in Word, the Office Assistant notes, "It looks like you're writing a letter" and asks if you'd like help. Sometimes it just lets you know a tip is available by displaying a lightbulb; click on the lightbulb to read the tip.

✦ It provides another way to access the Help system, via its "speech balloon" (refer to Figure 1-9), displayed when you click on the Assistant. You can select from one of the topics that the Assistant thinks you might be wondering about — based on your most recent actions — or type in a question and choose Search.

Taking control of the Assistant

Even if you like the Assistant, it might occasionally annoy you. To dismiss it from the screen, right-click on it and choose Hide.

To alter the Assistant's actions more permanently, choose Options in the Assistant's speech balloon. (You'll need to click the Assistant to open the speech balloon, if it isn't already open; alternatively, you can right-click the Assistant and choose Options from the shortcut menu.) This opens a dialog box (see Figure 1-10).

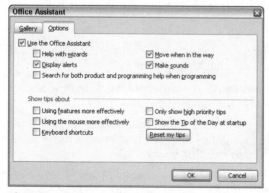

Figure 1-10: Control the Office Assistant from this dialog box.

Select the Options tab to define how the Assistant should work for you. For instance, you can tell the Assistant what sort of tips you want it to display, decide whether it should display alerts or make sounds, and more.

Tip   One good way to learn a little bit more about Office each time you use it is to check the Show the Tip of the Day at startup option in the Office Assistant dialog box. Every time you start the current application, you'll see a new tip. (Once you start seeing tips you've already seen, you can return to this dialog box and turn the Tip of the Day off.)

The Gallery tab enables you to change the appearance of the Assistant — from the default paperclip to an animated cat, or even an animated wizard.

Tip   You can download additional Assistants from the Microsoft Web site.

Deactivating the Assistant

If you decide you don't like the Assistant, you can turn it off altogether. Don't use Help ➪ Hide the Office Assistant — that just hides the Assistant without deactivating it. Instead, right-click the Office Assistant, choose Options... from the shortcut menu, and then uncheck the Use the Office Assistant checkbox in the Office Assistant dialog box. (You can still bring the Assistant back at any time by choosing Help ➪ Show the Office Assistant.)

Summary

This chapter offered a brief introduction to some basic aspects of Office you need to be aware of. For instance:

✦ Office is a suite of applications, each of which is designed to perform specific tasks (although there is some overlap among them).

✦ You can create new Office documents in a variety of ways, but the process of saving them and closing them is the same from application to application.

✦ Office displays useful commands in Smart Tags that become available automatically as you work, while task panes offer ready access to the commands and help you need to accomplish any Office task.

✦ Office Search is a powerful tool for finding documents of any description, using a wide range of criteria.

✦ Everybody needs help sometimes, so Office has made it readily accessible in a variety of ways, from the unobtrusive search box in the upper-right corner of every Office application to the in-your-face-like-a-puppy Office Assistant.

✦   ✦   ✦

Using Office's Menus and Toolbars

Office is a powerful suite of programs that can do a lot of amazing things, but they don't necessarily do them the way you expect them to.

Most people use some menu commands and toolbar buttons all the time and others not at all. Wouldn't it be great if you could put the commands you use the most right where you want them, and tuck the ones you don't use out of sight?

Well, you can. In fact, Office lets you change toolbars and menus at will.

As a means of working more efficiently, you can also record command sequences you use a lot, store them as macros, and play them back with the click of a toolbar button; that's discussed in detail in Chapter 49.

If even the hundreds of commands offered by Office right out of the box don't meet all your needs, you can learn how to create your own complex custom commands (and even separate, specialized applications) using Visual Basic for Applications (VBA), the Office programming language. A discussion of VBA is beyond the scope of this book; a good place to start would be Steve Cummings's *VBA For Dummies,* Third Edition (Wiley Publishing, Inc., 2001).

Creating Customized Menus and Toolbars

If you've used versions of Office before Office 2000, you've probably noticed that there are fewer toolbars at the top of your applications than you might expect.

The usual Standard and Formatting toolbars are still there, but by default they're now on the same level. In addition, they don't display all their buttons all the time—and the buttons they do display aren't always the same ones.

That's because when you first open an Office application, only the commands Office thinks are the most commonly used are visible on the toolbars or menus.

To access all available commands on a docked toolbar, click the Toolbar Options button at the toolbar's right end (it's a narrow, vertical band with two tiny arrows pointing right at the top and a slightly larger downward-pointing arrow underneath).

To see all the items available in any menu, hold your mouse pointer over the menu name for a second or click the chevron at the bottom of the menu.)

Tip   If you prefer to always see full menus, choose Tools ➪ Customize, click on the Options tab of the resulting dialog box, and check the Always show full menus checkbox.

If you don't see the double arrow on the Toolbar Options button, all the toolbar's buttons are already visible. However, on built-in toolbars—those that ship with Office—the Toolbar Options button always shows a single arrow pointing down, even when all buttons are visible. This indicates that you can still access the Add or Remove buttons command (described in more detail in the "The Add or Remove buttons command" section of this chapter).

Whenever you use a command, it's automatically made visible on the abbreviated toolbar or menu, replacing a button or command that hasn't been used for a while. Eventually the abbreviated toolbars and menus display the commands you use most often.

Tip   You can find out what any standard Office button does by holding the mouse pointer over the button for a second or two. In Office, the message that appears is called a *ScreenTip*. If you don't see the ScreenTips, turn them on by checking the Show ScreenTips on toolbars box in the Options tab of the Tools ➪ Customize dialog box.

In a way, then, Office automatically personalizes your menus and toolbars as you work. However, you can override these selections by using a simple drag-and-drop system—as described in the following section.

Customizing toolbars

In Office, a menu bar—although it looks different to the user because its commands appear as text, rather than as graphical buttons—is simply another type of toolbar. That means you can customize toolbars and menu bars in much the same way. You can also put menus onto toolbars, and graphical toolbar buttons onto menu bars.

Note, however, that phrase "in much the same way." There are enough differences between the way in which you customize toolbars and the way in which you customize menus that the procedures are described separately.

Caution   Changes you make to a toolbar or menu can't be reversed with the Undo command used for editing and formatting. If you make a mistake, you'll have to either manually undo the changes you've made or use the Reset command (see "Restoring the original menus and toolbars," later in this chapter).

Displaying and hiding toolbars

Want to see a toolbar that's not currently visible—or hide one that is? Right-clicking any toolbar brings up a shortcut menu that lists most of the available toolbars, with checkmarks beside the ones currently displayed (see Figure 2-1).

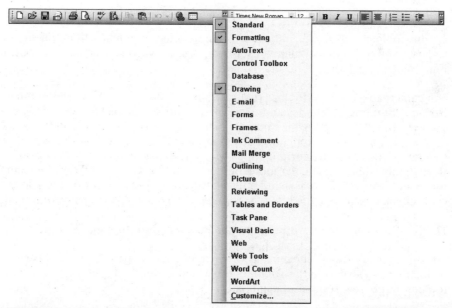

Figure 2-1: Choose from this shortcut menu the toolbar(s) you want displayed.

A few less frequently known and less frequently used toolbars don't appear on this shortcut menu. To see the others, or to show or hide more than one toolbar at a time, choose Customize from the bottom of the menu. The Customize dialog box (see Figure 2-2) enables you to hide, display, create, rename, or delete toolbars, as well as add or remove buttons.

Figure 2-2: PowerPoint's Customize dialog box — it's similar in all Office applications.

Creating your own toolbars

On the Toolbars tab, you'll find a more complete list of toolbars than the one that shows up on the shortcut menu described previously. You'll also see four buttons: New, Rename, Delete, and Reset.

You can create your own toolbar that contains commands you use all the time — perhaps for paragraph styles and/or AutoText entries you use for a particular project — by clicking the New... button. Type a name for the toolbar in the New Toolbar dialog box that appears. The list in the Toolbars tab shows almost all the toolbars available in the current application. However, some toolbars appear in the list only when a particular mode of the program is active. In Word, for example, the Print Preview toolbar is listed only when you're doing a print preview. In any case, check or uncheck the box next to the name of a toolbar to show or hide it.

That's not all you can do with the Customize dialog box, though.

To add a new toolbar to the current Office application, open the Tools ➪ Customize dialog box and switch to the Toolbars tab. Choose New and type a name for the toolbar in the New Toolbar dialog box.

Note

The Word version of the New Toolbar dialog box includes an extra field labeled "Make toolbar available to:". It provides a drop-down list from which you can choose where you want to store your new toolbar. If you want to make it available in all your documents, choose Normal. If you want to use it only in a currently open document, choose the name of that document from the list. (If you want to make it available in all documents based on a particular template, first open that template, create the new toolbar, and then choose the name of that template from the list.)

Cross-Reference

For more information on using templates in Word, see Chapter 8.

Click OK, and a new, completely empty toolbar appears. Now you can add buttons to it just as you would to any other toolbar, as described later in this chapter.

Relocating and deleting buttons

What if you don't like the default arrangement of your toolbar buttons? You can move a button to a new location at any time simply by holding down Alt while you click on the button and drag it to a new location—either elsewhere on the original toolbar or to a new location on an entirely different toolbar.

If the Tools ⇨ Customize dialog box is open, you don't even have to press Alt. You can simply drag buttons around wherever you like. You can also copy them by dragging them while holding down Ctrl. (When the Customize dialog box isn't open, holding down Ctrl and Alt together while dragging allows you to copy buttons.)

To add space between two buttons, press Alt and drag one of the buttons sideways in either direction. To delete a button, press Alt and drag it either into the middle of the window or up onto the title bar. When an X appears below the pointer, release the mouse button, and the toolbar button will vanish.

Tip

You can create more space on some toolbars by narrowing buttons that provide drop-down lists, such as the Font button on the Formatting toolbar. If you open the Tools ⇨ Customize dialog box and click one of these types of buttons (Style and Font Size are other examples), you can change its width by moving the pointer to either edge (it becomes a double-headed arrow) and dragging the edge in either direction. Of course, you may not be able to see the full names of the fonts and styles in those drop-down lists if you do so. Note, too, that this works only with drop-down lists. Some buttons, like Outside Border, have fly-out menus; they can't be resized.

The Add or Remove Buttons command

At the right end of any docked toolbar is a thin Toolbar Options button. Clicking on it displays any of the buttons native to the toolbar that aren't currently visible because there's no room for them; it also offers you the options to Show Buttons on Two Rows (which separates the Standard and Formatting toolbars onto two different rows) or to Add or Remove Buttons. Selecting Add or Remove Buttons opens a pop-up menu that provides alternate access to the Customize dialog box, or a display of all the buttons Office thinks are suitable for the toolbar you're currently working with (see Figure 2-3).

To add any of these buttons to or remove them from the toolbar, just check or uncheck them. The buttons are not permanently deleted from this menu; you can always retrieve any you choose to deactivate—or, for that matter, any you dragged off the toolbar.

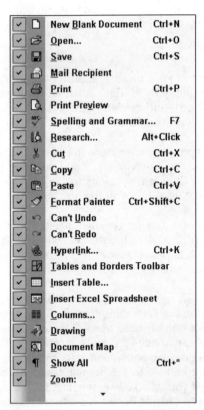

Figure 2-3: The buttons that Office assigns to Word's Standard toolbar

Note   The Toolbar Options button doesn't appear on floating toolbars (see "Will That Be Hidden, Docked, or Floating?" later in this chapter for more details on floating and docking toolbars). Instead, find the small, white down arrow to the far right of the title bar. Click on it to access the Add or Remove Buttons command.

Adding buttons to toolbars

To place new buttons on toolbars, open the Tools ⇨ Customize dialog box. This time, you want the Commands tab (see Figure 2-4). On the left, Office displays a list of various command categories. Choose a category (many of them correspond to the categories you already see on the menu bar), and all the commands in that category are displayed on the right. To add any command to a toolbar, simply click on it and drag it to the toolbar to which you want to add it.

Tip
If you aren't sure what category the command you're looking for belongs to, or you just want to see a complete list of all available commands, choose "All commands" in the category list. The commands are then displayed alphabetically, without regard to their categories.

Note
If a command has an icon associated with it (not all of them do), it will be displayed as an icon on the toolbar to which you drag it. If it doesn't have an icon, it will be displayed as text only (which takes up a lot more space).

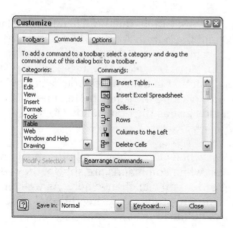

Figure 2-4: Use the Commands tab of the Customize dialog box to add buttons for any command to any toolbar.

The Rearrange Commands command

New in Office 2003 is yet another way to rearrange the buttons on a toolbar — and add new ones or delete old ones. The Customize dialog box now includes a Rearrange Commands button, which opens the dialog box shown in Figure 2-5.

Figure 2-5: The new Rearrange Commands dialog box offers yet another way to personalize your toolbars and menu bars.

Choose the toolbar or menu bar you want to work with at the top. Then use the list of buttons (called *Controls* in this dialog box) and the buttons on the right to customize the toolbar or menu bar as you see fit. Simply highlight the command you want to work with, and then choose Delete, Move Up, Move Down, or Modify Selection (which lets you alter the button's appearance; more on that in a moment). You can also add a command to a toolbar using this dialog box; clicking the Add... button opens an Add Command dialog box that lists commands just as the Commands tab of the Customize dialog box lists them.

Rearranging commands may seem pointless when Office shows only the most commonly used commands by default; however, when commands are shown, they're displayed in a particular order. That's the order you can change here. As well, you'll often find yourself calling up full menus or floating toolbars; using this dialog box allows you to organize those full displays of commands as you see fit.

Customizing individual buttons

Your toolbars and menus are so customizable that you don't even need to have buttons that look like the default ones Office provides. To change the appearance of a button, choose Tools ➪ Customize again. With the Customize dialog box open, right-click any button on a toolbar to open a shortcut menu with a full list of options related to the button's appearance (see Figure 2-6).

Tip   You can see this same list of options by highlighting the command whose icon you want to change in the command list on the Customize dialog box, and clicking the Modify Selection button.

Figure 2-6: Modify any toolbar button's appearance with this shortcut menu.

The options include the following:

✦ **Name.** Even buttons that display as icons have a name; change it here. Obviously, changing the name also changes the text displayed on buttons that include text, or that have only text; it also changes the name that's displayed as a ScreenTip when you hover your mouse pointer over a button.

✦ **Copy Button Image.** If an application has a button image you particularly like that isn't available in another application, you can use this command to make it available. Start in the application that has the button image you like. Open the Customize dialog box and right-click on the button to get this shortcut menu; then choose Copy Button Image. Go to the application that has the command to which you'd like to add that button image, open the Customize dialog box, right-click on the button you'd like to change to the new image, and choose the next command on the shortcut menu.

✦ **Paste Button Image.** Use this option to add the button image you selected from the other application.

Tip

Of course, you can also copy and paste button images within a single application if you wish. In either case, you can use an existing button image as a starting point for another button image. For example, if you've chosen to show the Save As command on a toolbar, you'll see that it has no button image. Copy the image from the Save command's toolbar button, paste it onto the blank Save As button, and then use the button editor (see Figure 2-7) to change its colors or otherwise modify it so you can visually distinguish it from the Save button.

✦ **Reset Button Image.** Changed your mind about having altered the way a button looks? This resets it to its default appearance.

✦ **Edit Button Image.** Want to play around with the button image, or even design your own? Choose this option. This opens the Button Editor, shown in Figure 2-7. In the Picture area, you see an enlarged view of the button image, showing each individual pixel (picture element). Click on a square to toggle that pixel between off (that is, the same color as the background) and the currently selected color from the Colors area. Click the Clear button to erase the entire image. Use the Move buttons to fine-tune the positioning of the image within the Picture area. In the Preview area, you can see a normal-size image of the button you're editing. (Lift the mouse pointer from the enlarged image in order to see your most recent change.)

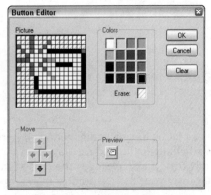

Figure 2-7: The Button Editor is a simple editing tool for button images.

✦ **Change Button Image.** This opens a shortcut menu displaying 42 button images Office already has on hand for you to use or modify.

✦ **Default Style.** This displays only the icon for a particular command (unless it has no associated image, in which case you see text).

✦ **Text Only (Always).** The command is always displayed as text only.

✦ **Text Only (in Menus).** The command is displayed as an icon on a toolbar, but as text only in menus.

✦ **Image and Text.** This displays both the image and the text associated with a command on the toolbar. This is useful if you've added new commands to a toolbar and you're not yet confident you know what their icons look like.

✦ **Begin a Group.** This adds to the left of the selected button one of those little dividers that look like a slight indentation in the toolbar.

✦ **Assign Hyperlink.** This has three sub-options: Open, which creates a link to a Web page or file (so you could, for example, set a button to provide one-click access to a document you refer to frequently); Insert Picture, which creates a link to a graphic file (this is available in Word, PowerPoint, and Excel only); and Remove Link, which returns the button to its usual function.

 Caution

Assigning a hyperlink to a button deactivates its original function, so it's usually best to use this option only with a brand-new button.

 Note

You can't convert a menu or drop-down list button into a hyperlink.

Customizing menus

Menu bars are really just toolbars, and the menus themselves are really just another form of button — one that displays a list of other commands when clicked. Usually, the commands are the same ones you can find on toolbars, although sometimes the command on the menu is yet another menu button, which opens a submenu of some kind.

Because menus are commands like any other, you can move them around exactly as you move toolbar buttons around. This means you can even add one menu to another menu, turning it into a submenu. Similarly, you can move a submenu onto a main menu bar, turning it into a menu.

Menu display options

As noted earlier, by default, Office applications display only the menu commands you've used recently. (Remember, if you'd rather see all the menu commands all the time, open the Tools ➪ Customize dialog box again and check the box labeled "Always show full menus.")

You can find the following other settings relating to menus under the Options tab of the Customize dialog box:

✦ **Show full menus after a short delay.** This is checked by default; it causes the full menu to appear automatically after a couple of seconds, even if you don't click on the down arrows at the bottom of a menu.

✦ **Reset menu and toolbar usage data.** Click here to restore all the menus and toolbars to their default state. This doesn't undo any customizing you've done; it just makes the menus and toolbars display the same set of visible commands in abbreviated format as they did the first time you started Office.

✦ **Menu animations.** If you prefer your menus to appear gradually instead of rudely popping open, choose Random, Unfold, Slide, or Fade from this drop-down list. Try each option to see which one you like.

Note   All these menu display settings are global, meaning they will be applied in all your Office applications, no matter which application you actually change them in.

Creating new menus

If you want to place a new menu on any menu bar or toolbar, first open the Tools ⇨ Customize dialog box, and then click the Commands tab. Scroll down through the Categories list to Built-in Menus and New Menu.

✦ Select **Built-in Menus** to see a list in the Commands box of all the menus and submenus found in that application. Now you can drag any prefabricated menu you like to any toolbar or menu bar and further customize it as you wish.

✦ Select **New Menu** to bring up the New Menu command in the Commands box. Drag this to a toolbar or menu bar to create a new empty menu. Rename it by right-clicking on it and choosing Name from the shortcut menu, and then customize it as you would any other menu or toolbar.

Tip   Most menu names include an underlined character that indicates the keystroke (typically called a shortcut or hot key) that, in combination with Alt, will open that menu. Type an ampersand (&) immediately before the character that you want to use for that purpose in your new menu name. For example, you might type &Web, to indicate the new Web menu you're creating can be opened by pressing Alt+W.

Customizing the shortcut menus

Shortcut menus are the context-sensitive menus that pop up when you right-click on something in Office—and you can customize them, too!

Again, open the Tools ⇨ Customize dialog box. This time you want the Toolbars tab: Scroll down the list of toolbars until you find Shortcut Menus, and switch to the Toolbars tab. Scroll the Toolbars list to find a Shortcut Menus item. Check the Shortcut Menus box, and Office displays a special toolbar for customizing shortcut menus (see Figure 2-8).

Note   For some reason, Excel doesn't have a Shortcut Menus item.

Figure 2-8: The Shortcut Menus toolbar in Access

The Shortcut Menus toolbar groups the shortcut menus for the current application into categories, indicated as special menu buttons on the toolbar. When you find the shortcut menu you want, click on it to display the items on that menu. Now you can work with the shortcut menus just as you did with the regular menus and toolbars, dragging items from one shortcut menu to another or adding items from the Commands list in the Customize dialog box.

Note   You may have to do a lot of repositioning of the Customize dialog box and the Shortcut Menus toolbar to ensure that you can see everything you need to see at the same time.

Restoring the original menus and toolbars

Gone a little overboard on the customization and can't remember what's what? To reset a menu to its default appearance, go back to the Customize dialog box, right-click on the menu you want to restore to its default appearance, and choose Reset from the top of the shortcut menu.

To reset a toolbar to its default appearance, go back to the Customize dialog box, highlight the toolbar you want to reset in the Toolbars: list, and click the Reset button.

Will That Be Hidden, Docked, or Floating?

Every Office toolbar can either be hidden, docked, or made to float. Hidden toolbars can't usually be seen; Figure 2-9 shows the other two types.

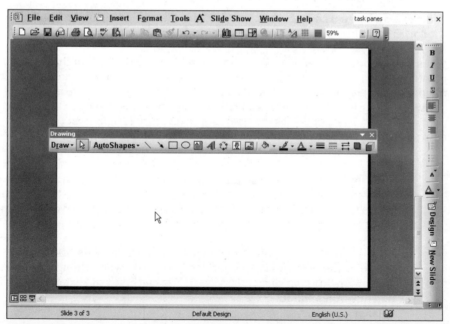

Figure 2-9: Here you can see both floating and docked toolbars, including one docked along the right side of the PowerPoint window.

Displaying and hiding toolbars

To display a hidden toolbar, or to hide one that's visible, right-click anywhere on any toolbar, or choose View ➪ Toolbars; then check or uncheck the toolbars you want made visible. You can also hide a floating toolbar by clicking the little X at the right end of its title bar.

Office also displays some toolbars automatically. In Word, for example, whenever you enter Outline view, the Outlining toolbar appears.

Tip   Something that doesn't appear on the toolbar list is the menu bar; normally, you can't hide it. (It does appear on the list of toolbars in the Tools ➪ Customize dialog box, but you can't uncheck it!) However, in Word and Excel you do have the option of using Full Screen view (choose View ➪ Full Screen), which hides the menu bar and all other toolbars (except for the Full Screen toolbar, which is automatically displayed). You can then display only the toolbars you want by opening them up via the Toolbars tab of the Tools ➪ Customize dialog box. You can temporarily reveal the menu bar by pointing at the top of the workspace.

Docking and floating toolbars

Toolbars can be docked at the top, bottom, left, or right edges of the application window. They can occupy as many parallel rows or columns as you want.

When you point to the vertical bar at the left end of any docked toolbar, your pointer will turn into a four-headed arrow. Now just click and drag, and the entire toolbar will detach from wherever it's docked, allowing you to move it to a new docking spot or let it float. (You can also move it up or down — or to the left or right — within a stack of docked toolbars, or even place it right next to another docked toolbar. Office will shrink both toolbars, hiding some buttons in the process, to enable them to fit.)

Note   Although you can move the main menu bar around and dock it along any edge of the application window, just like any other toolbar, it's the only bar that isn't allowed to share space with any other toolbar. Also be aware that if you dock it on the left or right edges, the text will turn sideways, making it hard to read.

Once a toolbar is floating, you can drag it anywhere you like by its title bar — even outside the application window onto your desktop, if you wish (though if you minimize the window, the toolbar disappears, too). You can also resize it or close it just as you would any other window.

Tip

To instantly turn a floating toolbar into a docked one, or vice versa (provided it has already been both), double-click the toolbar anywhere but on a button or the move handle (although this can be hard to do if the toolbar is chock-full of buttons). The toolbar switches to docked or floating, whichever it currently isn't, in the location where it was the last time it appeared in that form. (Note, however, that this doesn't work on the main menu bar when it's docked.)

Summary

If you don't like the way Office presents its multiplicity of commands and tools to you, change it! There are several ways:

✦ Through the Tools ⇨ Customize dialog box, change the set of tools on any toolbar just by clicking and dragging buttons around.

✦ Create custom toolbars that contain commands you use all the time.

✦ Customize menus the same way you customize toolbars, by clicking and dragging.

✦ Alter the icons and names associated with the various commands.

✦ Modify the context-sensitive shortcut menus that pop up when you right-click on items.

✦ Move toolbars wherever you like, floating them, docking them, or hiding them completely.

✦   ✦   ✦

Using Word

Creating and Working with Documents

A journey of a thousand miles," an old proverb says, "begins with a single step." In Word, a manuscript of a thousand pages begins with the creation of a new document. Word provides you with a variety of tools for beginning and carrying out a new project, some of which can even help you with the look and content of your document.

Creating New Documents

Creating a new document in Word is so easy you don't have to do anything at all: Word automatically presents you with a blank document the moment you start the program (see Figure 3-1).

That doesn't mean you have to restart Word every time you want to create a new document, however. You can also create a new document at any time by choosing File ➪ New. This opens the New Document task pane (see Figure 3-2).

This task pane offers you five options:

✦ **Blank document.** If you're creating an ordinary paper document, choose this option. This will begin a new document based on the Normal template, just as Word normally does when you start it.

Cross-Reference
To learn about the use of templates in Word, see Chapter 8.

Tip
If you want to open a blank document, you don't need to open this task pane at all. Instead of choosing File ➪ New, simply click the New Blank Document button on the left end of the Standard toolbar.

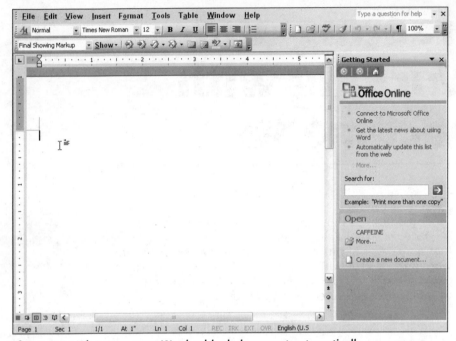

Figure 3-1: When you open Word, a blank document automatically appears.

    ✦ **XML document.** This is new to Office 2003. For the first time, you can use Word to create and edit XML documents.

See Chapter 11 for more information on XML and working with it in Word.

    ✦ **E-mail message.** This opens a form you can use to create and send an e-mail message.

Although you use Outlook to manage e-mail accounts and receive and send e-mail, Word is Office's default e-mail editor.

    ✦ **From existing document.** Use this option to create a new Word document based on an existing Word document. Essentially, it opens a copy of an existing document, which you can then edit and save without having to worry that you're overwriting a document you don't actually want to change. This is particularly useful if the existing document contains macros or other customized items you'd like to use in the new document.

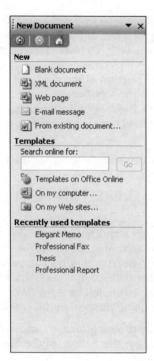

Figure 3-2: You can start a new document from within Word by bringing up the New Document task pane.

You also have the option of basing a new document on a template. The task pane lets you search for templates on Microsoft.com, visit Microsoft's Templates home page, or find templates on your computer or on your own Web site. Obviously, you'll need to be connected to the Internet for some of these options.

Cross-Reference   For more on using Word templates, see Chapter 8.

Navigating in Word

You have several ways to move around your Word document. However, before you set out on a journey, it's important to know where you're starting from. Your current position — the place where text will be entered if you start typing — is called the *insertion point*. It's represented by a flashing vertical bar. Once you know where you are, you can move around your document in many different ways:

    ✦ **Use the mouse.** Inside a document, your mouse pointer appears as a vertical bar with smaller crossbars at the top and bottom, like a capital letter *I*. (This is the flashing vertical bar referred to in the previous paragraph.) Place this wherever you want the insertion point to appear and click once.

Note If you're in Normal view (see the "Word's Views" section later in this chapter), the insertion point can be placed only at the beginning of a blank document. In any other view, you can place the insertion point anywhere within a blank document.

You can move the insertion point only within the portion of the document currently displayed. If the document extends beyond the top, bottom, or left or right sides of the screen, use the scrollbars to see the rest of it. (If you have a mouse with a wheel on it, you can also roll the wheel forward or backward to move up or down.)

- To move up or down one line at a time, click the single arrow at the top or bottom of the vertical scrollbar.

- To move up or down one screen at a time, click in the light-colored area above or below the box-shaped slider.

- To scroll smoothly through the document, click and hold the single arrows or drag the slider up and down. The advantage of using the slider is that as you scroll through your document, pop-up windows show you what page you're on and, if your document is divided into sections, what section you're in (see Figure 3-3). You can navigate left or right through an extra-wide document in similar fashion, using the horizontal scrollbar.

Tip You can avoid having to use the horizontal scrollbar by choosing Tools ⇨ Options ⇨ View and checking the Wrap to window checkbox near the bottom of the View dialog box. This ensures that all text remains visible in your window; however, it also means that what you see on the screen is no longer exactly what you'll see when you print the document, so be sure to turn this option off when you're ready to check for awkward line breaks.

✦ **Use the keyboard.** You can also move through your document using your keyboard. The cursor keys move your insertion point up or down one line at a time, or left or right one character at a time.

- You can move through your document faster by holding down the Ctrl key at the same time: In that case, the left and right cursor keys move you through your document one word at a time, while the up and down keys move you one paragraph at a time.

- Four other keys are also particularly useful for navigation. Home moves you to the beginning of the line that contains your insertion point; End moves you to the end of that line. Ctrl+Home takes you to the top of the document; Ctrl+End takes you to the end. Page Up moves you one screen up in the document; Page Down moves you one screen down.

✦ **Use Find and Replace.** Finally, you can navigate through a Word document by using the Find and Replace dialog box, which you access by choosing Edit ⇨ Find — and which is described in the following section.

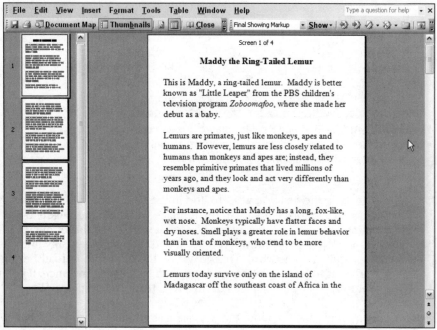

Figure 3-3: The slider in the vertical scrollbar indicates to what part of your document you've moved.

Using Find and Replace

Use the Find and Replace dialog box to locate and move to specific strings of text in the document. Choose Edit ⇨ Find to open the dialog box, and click the Find tab if it isn't already selected. Type the text you want to find in the Find what field, and then click Find Next (see Figure 3-4).

The next instance of the word after the current location of the insertion point is highlighted. (The Find and Replace dialog box automatically repositions itself so as not to hide the highlighted word.) To move to the next instance of the word, click Find Next again.

The Replace tab of the Find and Replace dialog box works similarly, except that it not only finds the word or words you're looking for, it lets you replace them with something else. This is particularly useful if, for example, you've spelled Mr. Remple's name as Mr. Ripple throughout a long document (something I did once when I was a newspaper reporter).

Figure 3-4: The Find and Replace dialog box can take you to the exact point in your document you want to reach, even when you don't know where it is.

As before, type the text you want to find in the Find what field, and then type the text you want to replace it with in the Replace with field (see Figure 3-5). Click Find Next to find the next instance of the chosen text. If you want to replace it with your new text, click Replace; that will replace it and then automatically find and highlight the next instance of the word. This gives you the opportunity to either replace it or click Find Next to leave it as it is and move on to the next instance. If you're sure you want to replace all instances of the given text, click Replace All.

Caution   Think very carefully about the Replace instructions you've issued before clicking Replace All, because it can sometimes have unintended consequences. For instance, simply replacing "her" with "him" could result in words like "thermal" and "heroes" changing to "thimmal" and "himoes." To avoid this problem, click the More button in the Replace dialog box, then check the Find whole words only checkbox.

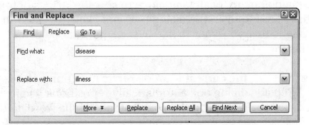

Figure 3-5: Replace lets you act on your second thoughts about some of the words you've used in your document.

You can use Find and Replace to search for and change more than just text. You can also use Find to look for formatting elements such as specific font and paragraph styles, as well as special characters such as tabs, hard returns, and em dashes; and use Replace to replace those special elements and characters with other special elements and characters. For example, you could use Replace to find all the instances of bold text in your document and color it red or to italicize every instance of the title of a book you referred to frequently.

To access these additional capabilities, click More in the Find and Replace dialog box. This increases the size of the box and adds several more controls (see Figure 3-6).

Figure 3-6: The Find and Replace dialog box is an even more powerful navigation and editing tool when you take advantage of its additional capabilities by clicking More.

At the top of this expanded section is the Search Options area, which offers a pull-down menu that lets you choose All, Down, or Up. If you choose All, Find and Replace will search the whole document. If you choose Down, Find and Replace will search down from the insertion point, and ask you if you want to search the rest of the document once it gets to the end. If you choose Up, Find and Replace will search up from the insertion point, and ask you if you want to search the rest of the document once it gets to the top.

The following checkboxes offer more search options:

✦ **Match case.** Checking this box ensures that Word finds only instances of text whose letters match the case of those you entered. For example, it would distinguish between the word "cart" and the acronym "CART" (Championship Auto Racing Teams).

✦ **Find whole words only.** This treats the search text as a whole word, which is important if the search text can also be found as part of other words. If you're searching for every instance of the word "dog," you don't want to locate every instance of the words "boondoggle," "dogwood," and "doggerel" too.

✦ **Use wildcards.** This lets you search for words or phrases that begin or end with specific words or phrases by inserting an asterisk to represent what comes before or after the selected text. The search term "the*end," for instance, would find everything from "the living end" to "the flexible teacher taught the whole class how to bend." Conversely, it wouldn't find "The End" because Use wildcards finds only text that exactly matches the case of the search term.

✦ **Sounds like.** This lets you search for words that sound vaguely like the search text. For example, a search for "cat" with this option selected turned up "quite," "good," "got," and "cut" in one document I tested.

✦ **Find all word forms.** Used "try," "tries," and "tried" when you meant to use "attempt," "attempts," and "attempted"? Choose this option and enter "try" as your search text and "attempt" as your replace text. Word will find all forms of the word and change them.

✦ **Format.** If you want to take formatting into account, click the Format button and choose which formatting options you want to search for (if your insertion point is in the Find what field), or apply (if your insertion point is in the Replace with field).

✦ **Special.** Click this button to search for or insert special characters and other document elements such as tabs, footnote marks, and even graphics. The options in the Special list vary depending on whether your insertion point is in the Find what field or the Replace with field.

Using Go To

Go To, the remaining tab in the Find and Replace dialog box (see Figure 3-7), takes you to a specific area of your document without regard to content.

Tip   You can open the Go To dialog box at any time by pressing Ctrl+G or choosing Edit ➪ Go To.

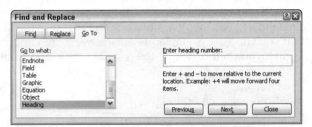

Figure 3-7: The Go To tab of the Find and Replace dialog box can take you to specific areas of your document.

Here you have a whole new series of search criteria:

✦ **Page.** This lets you move to a specific page of your document by entering the page number and clicking Next, or by entering a certain number of pages forward or backward from your current location. Enter *+n* or *-n,* where *n* is the number of pages you want to move.

✦ **Section.** If you've used section breaks (see Chapter 4) in your document, you can move among those sections just as you move among pages, by entering a specific section to go to or the number of sections you want to move forward or backward.

✦ **Line.** Again, you can enter a specific line to move to, or a certain number of lines to move forward or backward.

✦ **Bookmark.** You can insert a bookmark, and give it a name, by choosing Insert ➪ Bookmark. Then you can use Go To to move to a specific bookmark by typing in the bookmark's name or selecting it from the drop-down menu.

✦ **Comment.** This lets you jump to comments entered by any reviewer or by a specific person.

✦ **Footnote.** Use this option to find a specific footnote (by number) or jump a certain number of footnotes forward or backward.

✦ **Endnote.** Use this option to find a specific endnote or to jump a certain number of endnotes forward or backward.

✦ **Field.** Jump to a specific field by selecting the field type from the drop-down list.

✦ **Table.** Jump to a specific table by entering the table number or jump a certain number of tables forward or backward.

✦ **Graphic**. Jump to a specific graphic (by number) or a certain number of graphics forward or backward.

✦ **Equation.** Jump to a specific equation (by number) or a certain number of equations forward or backward.

✦ **Object.** Jump to a specific type of object, chosen from the drop-down menu. These can include such things as embedded sounds and video clips, Excel spreadsheets, PowerPoint slides, and more.

✦ **Heading.** Jump to a specific heading (by number) or a certain number of headings forward or backward.

The navigation tools

Three controls at the bottom of the vertical scrollbar let you browse through your document in the way that suits you best. To use these tools, first click the Select Browse Object button — it's the middle of the three controls. This opens the small graphical menu shown in Figure 3-8.

From this menu, select the type of element you want to use as the basis of your browsing; then use the Previous and Next buttons, above and below the Select Browse Object button, respectively, to move through your document. The twelve options in the Select Browse Object menu are Field, Endnote, Footnote, Comment, Section, Page, Go To, Find, Edits, Heading, Graphic, and Table.

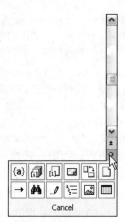

Figure 3-8: Use the graphical menu to select the type of object you want to base your browsing on.

Go To and Find open their respective tabs in the Find and Replace dialog box; once you've entered search text or selected search options in those tabs' fields, the Previous and Next buttons will move you to each occurrence of your selected criteria (enabling you to close the dialog box but continue to search through the document). With the other options, Previous and Next simply move you from instance to instance of the selected browse object — up to the previous location at which you edited text, for instance, or down to the next-occurring graphic.

With so many ways to navigate through your Word document, there's no reason to ever get lost!

Word's Views

Just as Word offers you many ways to move around within a document, so it offers you many ways to view your document. In fact, it offers you seven: Normal, Web Layout, Print Layout, Reading Layout, Outline, Web Page Preview, and Print Preview.

Normal, Web Layout, Print Layout, Reading Layout, and Outline are accessed from the View menu; Web Page Preview and Print Preview are available from the File menu.

Normal view

Normal view, as its name suggests, is the standard view for typing, editing, and formatting text. Because its focus is on text, it simplifies the layout of the page and hides page boundaries, headers and footers, objects with text wrapping, floating graphics, and backgrounds (see Figure 3-9). You can vary this view with the Zoom control box on the Standard toolbar, which lets you specify at what percentage of full size you want the page displayed.

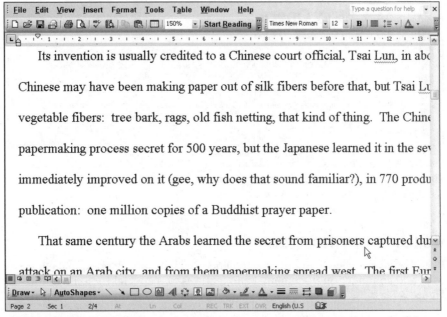

Figure 3-9: The normal view is the easiest view to use when entering and editing text. Here, I've used the Zoom control to boost the text size to 150 percent.

Print Layout view

Print Layout view shows you exactly how text, graphics, and other elements will appear in the final printed document. Print Layout makes it easy to work with elements other than regular text, such as headers and footers, columns, and drawings (see Figure 3-10).

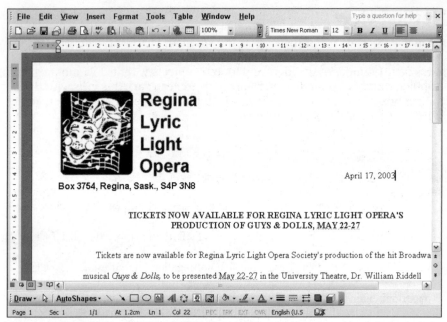

Figure 3-10: Print Layout view shows you more accurately than Normal view what the finished document will look like.

Reading Layout view

Reading Layout view is brand new to Office 2003. It's designed to make it easier to read and comment on documents, and features two special toolbars of its own (see Figure 3-11).

Tip   You can also get to Reading Layout view by clicking the new Read button on the Standard toolbar.

In Reading Layout view, the document is displayed in a format very much like the pages of an open book. These book-like pages are automatically sized to fit your screen and provide maximum legibility.

Note   These screens are not related at all to the actual pages of the document—for example, what's on Screen 9 of the document in Reading Layout view may be on Page 4 of the document in Print Layout view.

You can maneuver through the document using either the Document Map (see Figure 3-12), which displays only the document's headings and provides links to them so that you can instantly jump to a particular section of the document, or thumbnails (visible in Figure 3-11); just click on the thumbnail to which you want to jump.

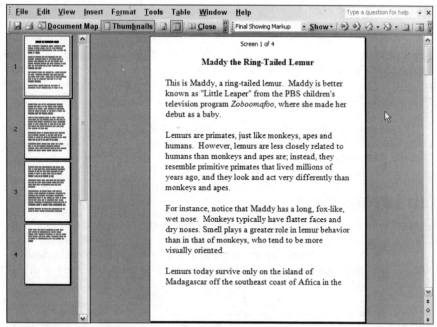

Figure 3-11: Reading Layout view, new in Office 2003, presents documents in an easy-to-read fashion.

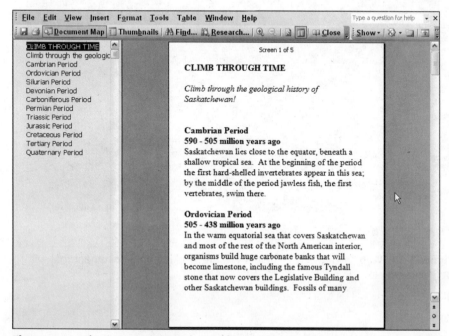

Figure 3-12: The Document Map in Reading Layout view displays the document's headings as links down the left side of the window.

The Document Map and Thumbnails buttons are displayed on the Reading Mode toolbar, along with Find and Research (both of which work the same way they do elsewhere in Word); Increase Text Size and Decrease Text Size, which are self-explanatory; Actual Page, which displays the current document page as it would actually print; Allow Multiple Pages, which toggles the view between two pages (the default) and one page; and the Close button, which returns you to the previous view you were using.

Cross-Reference   The Reviewing toolbar appears by default along with the regular Reading Mode toolbar when you switch to Reading Layout view. The Reviewing toolbar is covered in detail in Chapter 10.

Web Layout view

Use Web Layout view when you're creating a Web page or any other document that's going to be viewed exclusively on a computer monitor, as opposed to on a physical sheet of paper. In Web Layout view, you can see backgrounds, text is wrapped, and graphics are placed as they are in a Web browser (see Figure 3-13).

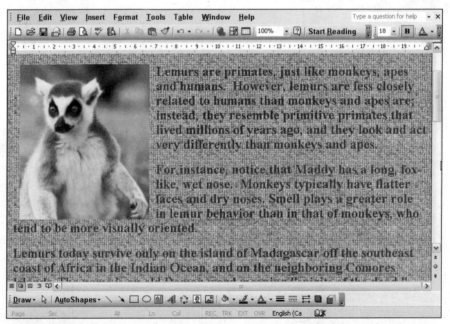

Figure 3-13: Web Layout view is ideal if you are working on a document that will be displayed electronically.

Tip If you're creating an online document, don't use Web Layout view just to check it over when you're done; do your creating in Web Layout view, too. Otherwise, you may find that things don't appear quite where you expect them to when you do switch to Web Layout view.

Outline view

Outline view lets you see the structure of a document and reorganize text simply by dragging headings (see Figure 3-14). If you wish, you can collapse Outline view to see only the main headings.

 Cross-Reference For more detailed information on working with outlines, see Chapter 7.

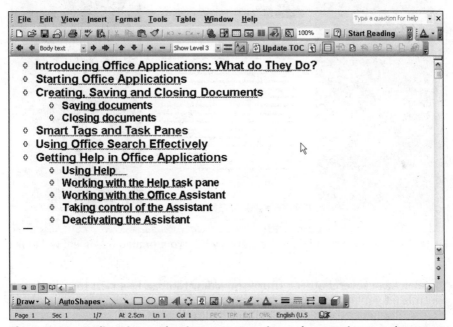

Figure 3-14: Outline view makes it easy to organize and reorganize your document.

Web Page Preview

Web Page Preview (File ➪ Web Page Preview) shows you how your document will appear when viewed online using a Web browser by displaying it with Internet Explorer. You can't edit in this view; it's just a way of checking the final appearance of your work (which should be the same as it was in Web Layout view).

Print Preview

Print Preview (File ➪ Print Preview), similarly, shows you how your document will appear when printed (see Figure 3-15). By default, this view shows you the whole page. By pointing at the document and clicking, you can toggle back and forth between a view of the whole page and a larger view that makes it easier to read the text.

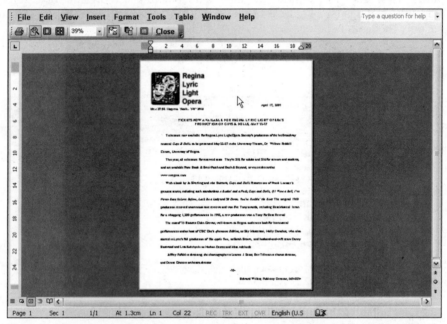

Figure 3-15: Print Preview shows you exactly how your printed document will look.

You also have several other controls on a new toolbar. From left to right, these controls let you do the following:

✦ Print the document

✦ Toggle the magnifying glass pointer on and off (when it's off, you can edit the page as you would in Normal view)

✦ Display one page or, in a larger document, several pages at once (as many as six or more at a time depending on the size of the Word desktop windows and your screen resolution)

✦ Display the page at a specific percentage of full size

✦ Toggle the ruler on and off

✦ Shrink the document by one page so that a small portion doesn't spill onto another page

✦ Toggle Full Screen display (which hides everything except the print preview toolbar and the page you're previewing)

✦ Close the print preview

Word's Wizards

Sometimes you want to create a document from scratch. Other times, you wouldn't mind a little help. As you've seen, Word makes it easy to open a blank document, but it's also standing by with a selection of wizards to guide you in creating your document.

To access the wizards, choose File ➪ New. In the New Document task pane, click the On my computer link in the bottom section, labeled Other templates. This opens the Templates dialog box shown in Figure 3-16.

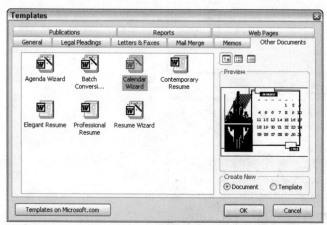

Figure 3-16: Among Word's templates you'll find wizards for many of the most common types of documents.

Now you can choose the type of document you want to create. For example, if you choose Other Documents, you'll see the selection shown in Figure 3-16. Some of these are templates, another excellent tool Word provides to help you design effective, eye-catching documents.

Cross-Reference   Templates are covered in detail in Chapter 8.

However, among the templates, both on this tab and on others in the Templates dialog box, you'll also find several wizards, such as the Calendar Wizard.

To use a wizard, simply double-click its icon. You'll be presented with a screen something like the one shown in Figure 3-17 (obviously, the details will vary depending on what kind of wizard you're using).

Click Next to proceed through the wizard. You'll be asked to choose from a series of options. For example, with the Calendar Wizard, you first choose from one of three styles of calendar: Boxes & borders, Banner, or Jazzy (see Figure 3-18). A thumbnail sketch of each type gives you a good idea of what they'll look like.

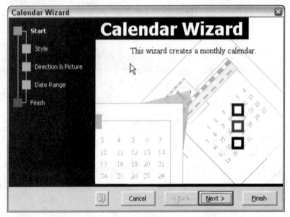

Figure 3-17: Whenever you select a wizard, you'll first see an introductory screen such as this.

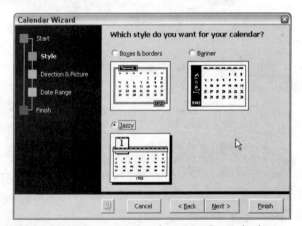

Figure 3-18: In many wizards, you're first asked to select an overall design style for your document.

As the wizard progresses, you're asked to make other choices (such as whether you want to print your calendar with a portrait or landscape orientation, and whether you want to leave room for a picture — and, of course, what date range you want to appear on your calendar).

When you've completed going through the wizard, click Finish. Voilà! Your document is complete (see Figure 3-19).

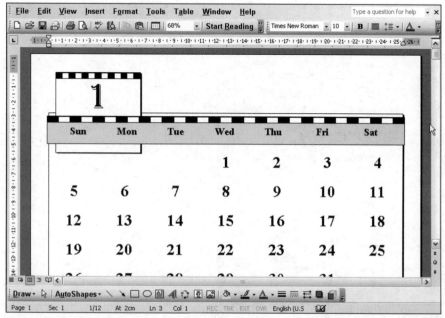

Figure 3-19: Word's Calendar Wizard makes it possible to create this calendar in a matter of minutes.

Note The documents that Word's wizards create are not written in stone; you can edit them and tweak them to your heart's content. For many wizards, such as the Resume Wizard, you still have to add your own words and graphics to complete the document; in others, such as the Calendar Wizard, you may not be entirely satisfied with Word's default creation and want to individualize it. Don't worry, you can!

Tip One extremely useful Word wizard converts batches of files from another format into Word files — or vice versa. This Batch Conversion Wizard, located on the Other Documents tab in the Templates dialog box, lets you choose what format of file you want to convert to or from, and then specify the files you want to convert. It's a great timesaver, especially if you've switched to Word from some other word-processing system.

Using Word's AutoCorrect Features

As you'll see in Chapter 4, Word makes it easy for you to correct and format text once you've entered it. If you want or need it, however, Word also offers help automatically as you enter text.

To access Word's automatic functions, choose Tools ⇨ AutoCorrect Options. This opens the dialog box shown in Figure 3-20, which has five tabs: AutoCorrect, AutoFormat As You Type, AutoText, AutoFormat, and Smart Tags.

Figure 3-20: Word offers a number of automatic functions that can help you create error-free documents more quickly and efficiently.

AutoCorrect

AutoCorrect watches for common typing errors and corrects them as you make them — sometimes before you're even aware you have made them. For example, Word gives you "smart" quotes by displaying the "straight" quote you typed, analyzing its position with regard to adjacent text, and then converting it to the proper left or right "curly" quote. However, often this happens so fast that it looks as if you've actually typed the curly quote.

Choose which errors you would like automatically corrected from the list. If you want it to, Word will automatically correct words or sentences with two initial capitals (a common mistake for fast typists with sluggish keyboards); capitalize the names of days, the first letter of sentences (which it assumes to be any word following a period or other typical sentence-ending punctuation mark) and the first letter of table cells; and correct accidental usage of the Caps Lock key.

If you select Replace As You Type, Word will replace approximations of symbols with actual symbols (e.g., replace (c) with © or (r) with ®), and correct common spelling errors. (For example, if you type "accomodate," Word will automatically change it to "accommodate" as soon as you hit the spacebar to enter the next word.) You can see exactly what AutoCorrect is programmed to correct by scrolling through the list at the bottom of the AutoCorrect tab.

You can teach Word to correct your own most common errors by entering the wrong spelling in the Replace box and the correct spelling in the With box (and choose whether to make formatting an issue by clicking the Plain text or Formatted text radio buttons), and then clicking Add. If you want to remove an existing entry in the AutoCorrect list, highlight it and click Delete. If you'd like Word to automatically replace words it doesn't recognize with suggestions from the spelling checker, check the checkbox at the bottom of the tab.

Sometimes AutoCorrect can be a nuisance. The famous poet e.e. cummings, for example, would have hated it, because he never used capital letters to start his sentences. To tell Word to ignore certain specific usages that look like mistakes but really aren't, click Exceptions. You can teach Word not to capitalize after abbreviations ending in a period (a list of common ones is provided), to ignore certain words that are supposed to have two initial capital letters (such as CDs), and to ignore other words that you can add to a list.

Tip One handy use for AutoCorrect is to speed typing. If there is a word or phrase you're going to use often, you can configure AutoCorrect to recognize an abbreviation of some kind that you select and replace it with the full text: For example, you could set it to enter your full name every time you type your initials.

AutoFormat As You Type

Word can do more than correct mistakes automatically; it can even automatically apply formatting, which can save you a lot of mouse clicking and dragging. To fine-tune this capability, open the AutoFormat As You Type tab of the AutoCorrect dialog box (see Figure 3-21).

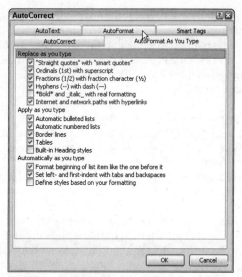

Figure 3-21: The AutoFormat As You Type
options apply formatting automatically, which
can save you a lot of mouse clicking and dragging!

There are three sections to this tab: Replace as you type, Apply as you type, and
Automatically as you type.

Replace as you type

Replace as you type will automatically replace certain items that can be readily
entered via the keyboard with others that can't but might look or work better: For
example, you can ask Word to replace the straight quotation marks on the keyboard
with the curly ones that are usually used in books and magazines. These options
are self-explanatory: Just click their checkboxes to activate them.

Apply as you type

The following five commands format text as you enter it, so you don't have to do it
later:

✦ **Automatic bulleted lists.** Select this and Word will assume you're creating a
bulleted list whenever you type a -, >, or asterisk at the beginning of a paragraph and follow it by a space or tab mark, or type an O (uppercase letter O)
and follow it with a tab mark. The current paragraph will be tagged as a list
item (much like this list item), and subsequent paragraphs will also be tagged
and bulleted as list items until you press Enter twice or press Backspace to
delete the last bullet in the list.

✦ **Automatic numbered lists.** This works exactly the same way as automatic bulleted lists, except it looks for a number or letter, followed by a period, followed by a tab or space, at the beginning of a paragraph.

✦ **Border lines.** Select this and Word will automatically apply a border to your current paragraph if you enter three or more hyphens (for a thin border), underscore marks (for a thick border), or equal signs (for a double-line border).

✦ **Tables.** If this is selected, Word will draw a table if you enter a series of plus signs and hyphens, such as +–+–+. Word will create a column between adjacent plus signs.

✦ **Built-in Heading styles.** If this is selected, Word automatically applies Heading styles 1 through 9 to the headings and subheadings in your document (Word assumes a paragraph is a heading if it doesn't end in a punctuation mark and you press Enter twice after it).

Cross-Reference   For more information on styles, see Chapter 8.

Automatically as you type

There are three options in this section:

✦ **Format beginning of list item like the one before it.** This can save you time when creating lists. If, for example, you want the first word of each list item to be italicized, click this; and once you've formatted the first list item, each subsequent list item will have its first word italicized automatically.

✦ **Set left- and first-indent with tabs and backspaces.** This enables you to use the Tab key to increase left- and first-indents, and the Backspace key to decrease them.

✦ **Define styles based on your formatting.** Select this and Word automatically creates new styles based on the manual formatting you apply to paragraphs in your document. If you want to format subsequent paragraphs in the same way, just apply the style instead of manually formatting again.

Cross-Reference   See Chapter 8 for more information about applying styles.

AutoText

AutoText, the third tab in the AutoCorrect dialog box (see Figure 3-22), tries to figure out what word or phrase you're typing, based on the first four letters, and offers to complete that word or phrase for you. It draws on information entered into the current template.

If you're using the Normal template (which you use by default), for example, and you type the first four letters of any month of the year, a little pop-up tip will show you the complete name of the month. Press Enter or F3, and Word inserts the complete word for you. If you want to ignore the AutoText suggestion, just keep typing.

Figure 3-22: AutoText tries to save you keystrokes by guessing what word or phrase you're typing and offering to insert it automatically.

You can make your own additions to AutoText. To do so:

1. Type a word or phrase you often use and want AutoText to help you with.

2. Highlight it. (Be careful not to highlight any spaces before and after it unless you want them to be part of the AutoText entry.)

3. Choose Tools ➪ AutoCorrect Options.

4. Click the AutoText tab.

5. Type a name for the entry in the Enter AutoText entries here field, and click Add. The next time you type the first four letters of that word or phrase, Word will offer to complete it for you.

To delete an AutoText entry, highlight it and click Delete. Click Insert to insert a high-lighted AutoText entry into the current document. Click Show Toolbar to display a small AutoText toolbar that opens the AutoText dialog box with a single click. This displays a menu of standard AutoText entries so you can insert them with a single mouse-click, without even typing the first few letters.

AutoFormat

AutoFormat, the fourth tab in the AutoCorrect dialog box, has most of the same options as AutoFormat As You Type. The difference is that AutoFormat is applied to the whole document at once, and it takes effect only when you choose Format ➪ AutoFormat. By default, AutoFormat preserves styles you've added to the current document, which is probably what you want, though you can turn that option off if you wish.

Smart Tags

Smart Tags, as I explained earlier, provide easy access to lists of actions Word thinks you're likely to want to perform on certain types of data Word can recognize. For instance, if Word realizes you're typing a person's name, it will provide a Smart Tag that includes actions such as Open Contact, Schedule a Meeting, Add to Contacts, or Insert Address.

The Smart Tags tab of the AutoCorrect dialog box lets you turn Smart Tags on or off for certain types of data — or turn Smart Tags off completely by unchecking the Label text with Smart Tags box. It also provides a link to Microsoft's Web site, where you can find more Smart Tags.

AutoSummarize

AutoSummarize, activated by choosing Tools ➪ AutoSummarize, analyzes your doc-ument to determine the key sentences, and then automatically creates a summary (see Figure 3-23). You can choose how long you want the summary to be (anywhere from 10 sentences to 75 percent of the length of the original), and choose how to present it: as highlighted sentences in the original document, as a separate docu-ment, as an executive summary or abstract at the top of the original document, or by hiding everything except the summary (in that case, a toolbar pops up that lets you show or hide more of the original document as you see fit).

AutoSummarize is just a starting point for an effective summary — you'll undoubt-edly have to edit the result considerably to get what you want — but it can save you a lot of time and effort.

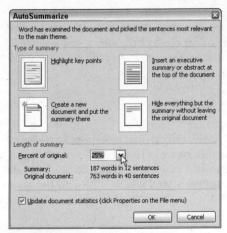

Figure 3-23: AutoSummarize analyzes your document and does its best to boil it down to a few key sentences.

Using Simple Macros

Macros are instructions to Word to perform an action or series of actions. Every command built into Word is a macro; by creating your own, you can automate common tasks that may currently require several steps and several minutes.

You can create a simple macro at any time by recording it: You perform the action you want to turn into a macro, and Word remembers how to do it. The next time you want that action performed, you issue a single command, and Word carries it out much faster than you could.

To record a macro:

1. Choose Tools ⇨ Macro ⇨ Record New Macro. (You can also choose View ⇨ Toolbars ⇨ Visual Basic to call up the Visual Basic toolbar, and then click Record Macro.) This opens the Record Macro dialog box (see Figure 3-24).

2. Give your macro a name.

3. Assign your macro a command. You can create a new toolbar button for your macro by clicking Toolbars, and/or assign your macro a keyboard shortcut by clicking Keyboard. (If you prefer, you can skip this step and assign your macro to a toolbar or keyboard shortcut later by using the same techniques for customizing commands described in Chapter 2.)

Figure 3-24: Assign a name and a command to your macro in the Record Macro dialog box.

4. Decide whether to store your macro in the current template, which means it will be available whenever you create documents using that template, or to store it in the specific document you're creating, which means it will be available only when you're working on that document.

5. Type a description of the macro in the box at the bottom. This is optional, but it can help you remember what that macro does, especially if you label it with a cryptic name like Macro1.

6. Click OK. The Record Macro dialog box disappears, replaced by a much smaller dialog box with two buttons, Stop Recording and Pause Recording, and the image of a cassette appears next to your mouse pointer to indicate you're recording.

7. Carry out the task you want recorded. If you need to do something you don't want recorded, click Pause Recording. (The pause is not recorded and won't be played back when you run the macro.) To resume recording, click Resume Recording (the same button as the Pause Recording tool).

8. When you're finished, click Stop Recording.

Tip

If your macro requires some action to be performed on highlighted text, highlight the text before you open the Record Macro dialog box, because once you've opened it, you can't highlight any text.

To run the macro, click the toolbar button you've assigned or press the keyboard shortcut. You can also choose Tools_ ➪ Macro ➪ Macros, pick your macro from the list, and click Run, but that's cumbersome and rather defeats the purpose of recording a macro in the first place. You can also edit macros from this dialog box.

Cross-Reference

For detailed information on creating and editing macros, see Chapter 49, "Creating Macros."

Saving: Format Options

Once you've created your document, you'll obviously want to save it so you can call it up again in the future for further revision or reference.

To save a document, click the Save button in the Standard toolbar, or choose File ⇨ Save. If the document hasn't been saved before, this opens the Save As dialog box (see Figure 3-25). (If the document has been saved before, this will overwrite the old version with the new version.)

Browse until you find the file folder in which you want to save your new document, and then double-click on the folder to open it. Type a name for your document in the File Name text box, and then, in the Save as type field, select the format in which you want to save the document.

Figure 3-25: Word offers you many different format options for saving your work.

Normally, you'll save your document as a Word document, the default choice, but you can also choose to save it as the following:

✦ **An XML document.** XML stands for eXtensible Markup Language, and is designed to allow diverse applications to more easily share data over the World Wide Web.

Cross-Reference

For detailed information about XML and using it in Word, see Chapter 11.

✦ **A Single File Web Page.** This is just what it says: a Web page saved as a single file, even if it contains graphics, as opposed to...

✦ **A Web Page.** In this format, a Web page that contains graphics will consist of the Web page itself and a new file folder containing the graphics.

✦ **A Web Page, Filtered.** This "cleans up" the Web page, removing Office-specific coding that Office uses to re-create Word formatting in a Web browser but that non-Microsoft browsers might choke on.

✦ **A Document Template.** This is a good choice if you've created the prototype of a document that will serve as the basis of many future documents.

✦ **Rich Text Format.** This is a standard format that preserves a good deal of formatting and can be read by a wide variety of word processors.

✦ **Plain Text.** This is just what it says: plain ASCII text. Essentially, no formatting except paragraph marks survives the translation into plain text, but on the plus size, nearly any program can read it.

✦ **Previous versions of Word.** You can save documents in Word 3.0 for MS-DOS, if you want to. This is useful if you are exchanging documents with someone who doesn't have the latest version of Word.

Caution

If your document contains formatting that wasn't supported by the earlier version of Word, you'll lose that formatting when you save it in the older format. (And for that reason, Word always asks you if you're sure you want to save in that format.) Always double-check your documents after you save them in an older format to ensure that they're both legible and aesthetically acceptable.

✦ **Other word processor formats.** This enables you to exchange documents with friends who may be using WordPerfect or some other word processor, such as WordStar or AmiPro.

To save a copy of a document, or save it in a different format, without losing the original document, choose File ➪ Save As. You can save the copy in a different place with the same name or a different name, under a different name in the same location, and/or in a different file format, as you wish.

Summary

In this chapter, you learned about many of the numerous tools Word provides for creating and working with documents.

✦ The New Document task pane offers you several different ways to start a new document, whether it's a standard blank Word document, a Web page, an XML document, or an e-mail message; you can also base a new document on an existing document or template.

✦ You can navigate through your Word documents using the mouse or keyboard, or you can use the Find and Replace dialog box—which, of course, is also really good at finding and replacing. You can also browse through a document by jumping from object to object—for example, from one table to the next, or from graphic to graphic.

✦ You have seven different ways to view your documents: Normal view, Web Layout view, Print Layout view, the new Reading Layout view, Outline view, Web Page Preview view, and Print Preview view.

✦ Word offers numerous wizards for creating special documents such as calendars and resumes. There's even one for converting batches of documents from one format into a Word format—or vice versa.

✦ Word's powerful AutoCorrect features can keep your most common errors under control, insert frequently used text automatically, and even guess what you're trying to type and save you the trouble of typing it.

✦ If you often use a complicated series of commands to accomplish a particular task, consider recording those commands as a macro—turning the task from a complicated procedure into a simple one-click operation.

✦ You can save your Word documents in many different formats, from straight text to older versions of Word to XML to other word-processing formats.

✦   ✦   ✦

Working with Text

Word's numerous advanced capabilities enable you to create documents containing graphics, tables, bulleted lists, hyperlinks, and more. We'll be looking at all of these elements in the next few chapters. However, above all else, Word is a word processor — a piece of software designed to manipulate text, to make it easy to alter, rearrange, and reformat your words until they deliver your message in the most effective way possible. In this chapter, we'll walk through Word's basic tools for working with text, from entering it and formatting it to adding headers, footers, page numbers, and footnotes.

Entering, Selecting, and Editing Text

Before you can process words, you have to enter them. Generally, whenever you start Word (which automatically opens a blank Word document) or create a new Word document from within Word, you can start entering words immediately: The cursor is already ready and waiting for you in the document area. Just start typing, and your text appears.

Later in this chapter, we'll look at the various formatting options for text. Formatting can be applied either before you begin entering text, by setting options before you start typing, or after text has already been entered — in which case you need to select the text to which you want to apply the formatting.

Editing text

To edit text, you first have to move the cursor to the place in the document where you want to make changes. Recall that inside the document area, your mouse pointer is a vertical bar with two smaller horizontal bars on each end, like a capital *I*. This special pointer enables you to precisely position the cursor within the document. Simply move the mouse pointer to the desired location and click once. The cursor, a solid, flashing vertical line, will appear where you click.

The position of the cursor also marks the position of the insertion point, the point in the document where new text will be entered the next time you start typing. Therefore, if you want to insert new words in an existing sentence, for example, click the mouse pointer at the spot in the sentence where the new words should appear. This moves the cursor to that spot; then type the additional words. You can also move the cursor using the arrow keys.

By default, any text to the right of the insertion point moves over to make room as you add text. If you prefer, however, you can have your new text replace the existing text to the right as you type: Just double-click the grayed-out OVR button in the status bar at the bottom of the document area, or press the Insert key.

Tip If you want to make overtyping Word's default choice for inserting text, choose Tools ⇨ Options, click the Edit tab, and check the Overtype mode box.

Selecting text

To replace an entire phrase or change the formatting of a section of text, you first have to select it. To do so, use the mouse to position the cursor at either the beginning or end of the section you want to select. Then, holding down the left mouse button, drag the cursor backward or forward through the text. The selected text is highlighted: that is, it appears in the reverse of whatever colors you're using — white on black, for instance, instead of black on white (see Figure 4-1).

Once text is selected, you can manipulate it in a number of ways, from simply typing over it (the new text will automatically replace all of the selected text) to moving it, cutting and pasting it, and changing its formatting.

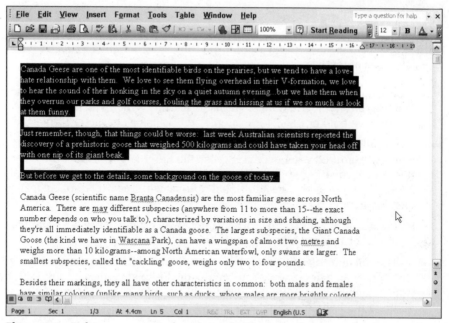

Figure 4-1: Before you can work with text in Word, you have to select it.

Although clicking and dragging is the most common way to select text, there are other methods as well:

✦ Position the insertion point, and then hold down the Shift key and select text using the arrow keys. If you hold down the Ctrl key, too, you can select larger chunks of text at once: one word at a time, if you're using the right or left arrow keys; or one paragraph at a time, if you're using the up or down arrow keys.

✦ You can select an entire word by double-clicking anywhere inside it; you can select an entire paragraph by triple-clicking it.

✦ You can select an entire line by moving the mouse to the left edge of the document until the usual I-beam cursor changes to a right-pointing (as opposed to the usual left-pointing) arrow. Use the arrow to point at the line you want to select, and then click once.

Formatting Text

Word supports four different levels of formatting, which apply to successively larger sections of text:

✦ **Character formatting** applies to all selected characters, or all the characters you type after you've established the formatting. When you make a single word or sentence bold or italic, for example, you're using character formatting.

✦ **Paragraph formatting** applies to all the text between two paragraph marks, which are entered whenever you press the Enter key. You can apply many of the same formatting options that you can apply to characters — e.g., bold or italic — but you also have additional options with regard to spacing, alignment, and indents.

✦ **Page formatting** affects the formatting of every page in the document and includes settings such as page size, tabs, and margins.

✦ **Section formatting** is useful if you want several different types of formats within the same document. You can divide it into several sections, and then format each section individually, with different indents and margins, or even different numbers of columns.

These various kinds of formatting overlap quite a bit: You can make a paragraph bold by using paragraph formatting, for example, but you can also make it bold by selecting all the text in it and using character formatting. Generally, because character formatting is what we use most often, we tend to make it our first choice, but if you're working with a large section of text, remember that other formatting methods may be more efficient.

Formatting characters

As just noted, character formatting is what we use most often in word processing. You see it everywhere: in newspapers, in magazines, and in books, including this one. For example, each level of heading, from the chapter titles to the subhead just above this paragraph, has its own special character formatting: a specific combination of typeface, size, style, and alignment.

If the primary purpose of text is to communicate, then the purpose of character formatting is to help text communicate as effectively as possible, by establishing an overall visual style, enhancing legibility, or emphasizing certain textual elements (again, like the headings in this book).

The Formatting toolbar

The most commonly used character formatting options are available by default on the Formatting toolbar (see Figure 4-2).

Figure 4-2: The Formatting toolbar provides the most commonly used character formatting tools.

Character formatting tools on the Formatting toolbar are as follows (the tools not mentioned in the following list are described in the section "Formatting paragraphs"):

✦ **Styles and Formatting.** This button opens the Styles and Formatting task pane, which provides ready access to Word's styles, a powerful tool for formatting text consistently throughout a document.

✦ **Style.** Existing styles are available in this drop-down list on the Formatting toolbar.

For detailed information on using styles, see Chapter 8.

✦ **Font.** A font is a set of characters that have a common design. Each font has a name, such as Times New Roman or Arial. You can apply any of the fonts installed on your computer to selected text by choosing the one you want from the Font drop-down menu. Office 2003 makes this easier by showing you the name of each font using characters from that font.

✦ **Font Size.** Font size refers to the size of a font as measured from the top of the tallest letter to the bottom of the letters like "p" and "q." Font sizes are measured in points. One point is approximately $\frac{1}{72}$ of an inch, so 72-point characters may be close to an inch tall when printed (depending on the design of the font), 36-point characters are roughly half an inch tall, 18-point characters are roughly a quarter of an inch tall, and so on. (Remember that characters get proportionally wider as they get taller.) You apply a font size to selected text just as you apply a font: Choose the size you want from the Font Size pull-down menu.

✦ **Bold.** Click this button to make the selected text thicker and darker than usual. Many fonts have a specially designed additional set of bold characters; for fonts that do not, Word simulates the bold characters by making the existing letters thicker and/or darker.

✦ **Italic.** Click this button to make the selected text slant to the right. (As with bold, many fonts come with a second set of characters designed to be italic, which means some of them are actually quite different from the standard set—for example, a true italic f looks quite different from a non-italic f. For fonts that don't have a set of italic characters, Word simulates italics by slanting the regular characters to the right.)

✦ **Underline.** Click this button to underline the selected text.

Note

Typically, the Formatting toolbar isn't floating as shown in Figure 4-2; instead, it's docked next to the Standard toolbar. Because there isn't room for all of the buttons on both toolbars to be displayed, many of them are normally hidden and have to be accessed by clicking the Toolbar Options button that appears at the right end of every toolbar. As you use commands from the Toolbar Options box, they're added to the visible toolbar, which grows longer to accommodate them. This can cause the Standard toolbar to get shorter, dropping some of its commands into the Toolbar Options box.

✦ **Highlight.** Highlighting selected text in Word is just like highlighting it with a highlighting pen. Click the downward-pointing arrow to the right of the Highlight button to call up a small menu of possible highlight colors. Choose the one you want, and a strip of that color will overlie the selected text. It's a great way to make important text stand out visually on your monitor.

Tip

If you click the Highlight button before you select any text, you'll get a special cursor that you can use exactly like a highlight pen: Click and drag it over the desired text to apply your selected highlight color. To turn off the highlighter, click the Highlight button again.

✦ **Font Color.** Whereas highlighting text lays a strip of color over it, the Font Color button changes the color of the text itself. Again, click the downward-pointing arrow to the right of the button to see a menu of possible colors. Choose the one you want, and the selected text changes color. Choose more colors to open a dialog box that lets you select from a larger palette.

The Font dialog box

Several additional character formatting options are available that aren't included on the Formatting toolbar. Instead, you have to open the Font dialog box, shown in Figure 4-3, by selecting Format ➪ Font, or by right-clicking and choosing Font from the shortcut menu.

The Font dialog box has three tabs, each of which controls a different aspect of character formatting.

Font

Under the Font tab, you can access most of the character-formatting options available on the Formatting toolbar, sometimes with enhancements. For example, not only can you choose to underline selected text, you can choose what type of underlining you want to use, such as a double underline. You can also choose to use a different color for underlining than you do for text.

You also have additional formatting options, called Effects, which include Strikethrough, Double strikethrough, Superscript, Subscript, Shadow, Outline, Emboss, Engrave, Small caps, All caps, and Hidden. You can see them as you apply them in the Preview area at the bottom of the Font dialog box.

Figure 4-3: The Font dialog box lets you apply many of Word's character formatting options in one step.

Character Spacing

The Character Spacing tab offers a new set of controls (see Figure 4-4); the effects are illustrated in Figure 4-5.

✦ **Scale** adjusts the width of the selected text without affecting its point size. If you adjust this upward, the letters look fat and squat; if you adjust it downward, the letters look tall and skinny. The Preview area at the bottom of the dialog box shows you what your text will look like.

✦ **Spacing** adjusts the amount of space between letters. You select whether you want the text spacing Normal, Expanded, or Condensed; and then you specify the amount of space (in points) you want to add to or subtract from between letters. Again, use the Preview area to get just the effect you want.

✦ **Position** adjusts the location of the selected text relative to the normal baseline for text. You select whether you want the text Normal, Raised, or Lowered, and then you specify how many points you want to raise or lower the text above or below the baseline. This is different from superscript and subscript, which make the raised or lowered text smaller than the normal text; Position doesn't change the size of the moved text. You might want to use this instead of superscripting or subscripting to make the raised or lowered letters more legible.

✦ **Kerning** adjusts the spacing between certain letters to make text as legible and attractive as possible. If you select the Kerning checkbox, Word will automatically adjust kerning in TrueType or other scalable fonts whenever they're equal to or larger than the size you specify.

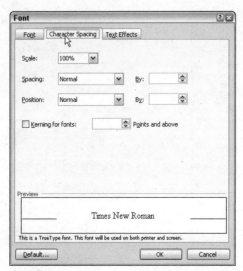

Figure 4-4: Fine-tune your characters with these controls.

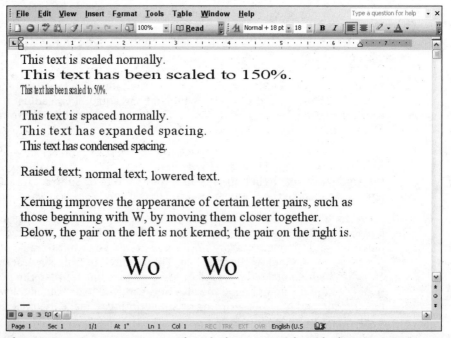

Figure 4-5: Here are some examples of what you can do with character spacing.

Text Effects

The third tab in the Font dialog box, Text Effects (see Figure 4-6), doesn't apply to documents you are preparing for printing, but if your document is going to be read on other computers, you might find that making characters blink, shimmer, or sparkle really makes them stand out!

Caution　Characters that blink, shimmer, or sparkle may also be annoying to anyone trying to read your document, so use these effects sparingly.

To apply any of the text effects, just select the text you want to animate, open the Font dialog box, and then choose the effect you want to apply and click OK. You can check each effect in the Preview area to be sure you've chosen the one you want.

Setting default text

You can also use the Font dialog box to change your default text — for example, from the usual 10-point Times New Roman to 24-point shimmering, bold, italic, blue Arial. Or anything else. Just apply the formatting you'd like to use as the new default, and click the Default button at the bottom of the dialog box. Word will ask you if you're sure; if you are, click Yes. From then on, whenever you start a new document in Word using the same template you're currently using (which, by default, is the normal.dot template), text will automatically have the new formatting.

Figure 4-6: If your readers will be using computers to peruse your document, you can spice it up with one of these snazzy animation effects!

Keyboard shortcuts

You have one other way to apply formatting to selected text: Use the shortcut keys, which some people find quicker to use when typing than reaching for a mouse. The keyboard shortcuts for formatting are shown in Table 4-1.

Tip   One of the most useful shortcuts is Ctrl+spacebar, which removes all character formatting, returning selected text to the default.

Table 4-1	
Keyboard Shortcuts for Character Formatting	
Format	**Shortcut**
Bold	Ctrl+B
Italic	Ctrl+I
Underline (underline words and spaces alike)	Ctrl+U
Word underline (underline words, but not the spaces between them)	Ctrl+Shift+W
Double underline	Ctrl+Shift+D
Subscript	Ctrl+= (equals sign)
Superscript	Ctrl+Shift++ (plus sign)
Small caps	Ctrl+Shift+K
All caps	Ctrl+Shift+A
Change case (from lower to upper, or vice versa)	Shift+F3
Hide text	Ctrl+Shift+H
Remove formats	Ctrl+spacebar
Font	Ctrl+Shift+F
Symbol font	Ctrl+Shift+Q
Point size	Ctrl+Shift+P
Next larger size	Ctrl+Shift+>
Next smaller size	Ctrl+Shift+<
Up one point	Ctrl+]
Down one point	Ctrl+[

Formatting paragraphs

In addition to formatting characters, Word provides tools that enable you to apply formatting to entire paragraphs at a time. Word considers a paragraph to be any section of text that falls between two paragraph marks, which are inserted whenever you press Enter. (The only exception to that rule is the first paragraph of a document, which Word recognizes as being the text from the top of the document to the first paragraph mark.)

To see where the paragraph marks are in your document, click the Show/Hide ¶ button in the Standard toolbar (if you can't see it, you can find it by clicking the Toolbar Options button or floating the toolbar). This will make all the paragraph marks visible (see Figure 4-7).

Paragraph formatting affects the spacing and alignment of all the lines in a paragraph. As with character formatting, you have more than one way to format a paragraph, but all of them begin with your placing your cursor somewhere inside the paragraph you want to format (it doesn't matter where, as long as it's between the two marks that define the paragraph).

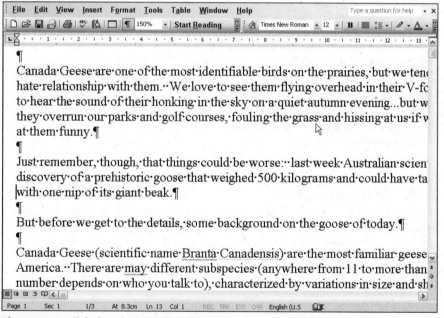

Figure 4-7: Click the Show/Hide ¶ button to see where the paragraphs are in your document.

The Formatting toolbar

The most commonly used paragraph formatting options, as with character formatting, are available on the Formatting toolbar (refer to Figure 4-2), beginning with four buttons that determine the paragraph's alignment:

✦ **Align left.** This aligns all the lines in the selected paragraph flush left.

✦ **Center.** This centers all the lines in the selected paragraph on the page.

✦ **Align right.** This aligns all the lines in the selected paragraph with the right margin.

✦ **Justify.** This adds space between words so that all the lines in the paragraph (except the final one) appear to be the same length and are aligned with both the left and right margins.

Three other buttons on the Formatting toolbar also apply to paragraphs:

✦ **Increase Indent.** Each time you click this button, the selected paragraph is indented an additional one-half inch. (It doesn't matter if you're using a different measurement unit — for example, centimeters, millimeters, picas, or points — clicking this button still indents in half-inch increments.)

✦ **Decrease Indent.** Each time you click this button, any existing indent on the selected paragraph is reduced by one-half inch. If the paragraph isn't currently indented, this button has no effect (it doesn't move the paragraph to the left of the current document margin).

✦ **Border.** Click on the downward-pointing arrow next to this button to see a menu of the possible borders you can add to the selected paragraph. You can enclose the entire paragraph in a border, or simply apply a partial border, with lines along one, two, or three sides. Note that some of these options show an inside border; those apply primarily to tables and can't be used as paragraph formatting. You can also use the Border menu to insert a horizontal line.

The Paragraph dialog box

Several additional paragraph formatting options are available from the Paragraph dialog box, which you open by selecting Format ➪ Paragraph, or by right-clicking on a paragraph and choosing Paragraph from the pop-up menu (see Figure 4-8).

The Paragraph dialog box has two tabs, which are covered in the following sections.

Indents and Spacing

Not only do the controls on the Indents and Spacing tab enable you to apply formatting to a paragraph, they provide valuable information about the current formatting of the paragraph. From this tab, you can change the paragraph's alignment, adjust the indentation with much greater precision than with the Indent buttons on the Formatting toolbar, and adjust the amount of space that appears both above and below the current paragraph. As usual, a Preview area shows you the effects of your formatting choices. The darker text in the middle of the Preview area indicates the currently selected paragraph.

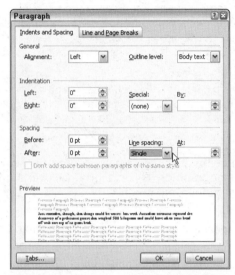

Figure 4-8: The Paragraph dialog box lets you precisely control the alignment and spacing of your paragraphs.

The Paragraph dialog box also gives you control over line spacing (the amount of space between lines). You have six options:

- ✦ **Single.** This leaves a minimum amount of space between lines, just enough that their characters don't overlap. This is relative to the point size, so the actual amount of space between lines increases as the point size increases. However, proportionately it's the same.

- ✦ **1.5.** This leaves one-and-a-half times as much space between lines as Single does.

- ✦ **Double.** This leaves the equivalent of a blank line between lines.

- ✦ **At Least.** When you choose this, Word will automatically adjust line spacing in the paragraph to allow for smaller or larger font sizes or graphics, but it will never leave less space between lines than what you specify.

First-Line and Hanging Indents

One of the indentation controls gives you the option to apply First-Line or Hanging indents. Both align the first line of a paragraph differently from the succeeding lines.

A **first-line indent,** like the one that starts this paragraph, begins the paragraph's first line to the right of the rest of the lines. This is the kind of indent usually used to set off the first line of a paragraph in many books, magazines, and newspapers. Some people use tabs to achieve this effect, but that requires an extra keystroke at the beginning of each paragraph and is also subject to unexpected changes in formatting if a new tab is set, so it's not recommended.

A **hanging indent,** like the one that starts this paragraph, begins the paragraph's first line to the left of the rest of the lines. It's often used to format a list of items.

✦ **Exactly.** When you choose this and enter a value in points, Word will use that line spacing regardless of font size or graphics. This can produce overlapping lines, a cramped look, or other deleterious and unattractive results, so use this option with care.

✦ **Multiple.** This lets you enter line spacing as a multiple of single spacing: 1.6, for example, or 2.4.

Line and Page Breaks

The Line and Page Breaks tab (see Figure 4-9) lets you control the flow of text within a paragraph. It offers several options.

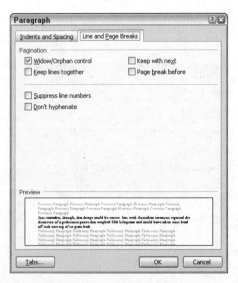

Figure 4-9: Controlling the flow of text with these controls can make your document look cleaner and more professional.

✦ **Widow/Orphan control.** This prevents widows (the last line of a paragraph that appears by itself at the top of a page) and orphans (the first line of a paragraph that appears by itself at the bottom of a page).

✦ **Keep lines together**. This prevents any page break in the middle of a paragraph, even if it doesn't result in a widow or orphan.

✦ **Keep with next.** This prevents a page break from occurring between the selected paragraph and the one that follows. One way in which this is useful is ensuring that headings remain with the text that follows them and don't end up all by themselves at the bottom of a page. (A heading may be a single line, but because it ends with a paragraph mark, it's still considered a paragraph by Word.)

✦ **Page break before.** This inserts a page break before the selected paragraph, useful if you're starting a brand-new chapter or section of a document.

✦ **Suppress line numbers.** If you have line numbering enabled within a document, this option keeps those line numbers from being displayed for the currently selected paragraph.

✦ **Don't hyphenate.** This prevents the selected paragraph from being automatically hyphenated if Hyphenation is enabled. (To enable hyphenation, choose Tools ➪ Language ➪ Hyphenation. In the resulting dialog box, you can choose to Automatically hyphenate document, and whether or not you want to Hyphenate words in CAPS. You can also set the size of the hyphenation zone and limit the number of consecutive hyphens. To check each proposed hyphenation personally, and alter it if necessary, click the Manual button.)

Tabs

In addition to the preceding options, the Paragraph dialog box includes a Tabs button that brings up the Tabs dialog box shown in Figure 4-10. (You can also access this dialog box by choosing Format ➪ Tabs.)

Enter the tabs you want in the box on the left, and then set their alignment using the radio buttons directly underneath. You have several options:

✦ **Left.** If you press Tab, the cursor will go to this spot, and any subsequent text you type will appear to the right of the Tab stop.

✦ **Right.** If you press Tab, the cursor will go to this spot, but any subsequent text will appear to the left of the Tab stop.

✦ **Center.** Press Tab to send the cursor to this spot, and any subsequent text will be centered on the Tab stop.

✦ **Decimal.** This is most commonly used when you're creating a column of monetary amounts and want the figures, such as 139.99 and 5.05, to align vertically, the way readers typically expect to see them. Set the Tab stop where you want the decimal to appear. Press Tab, and then type in the number. The numerals to the left of the decimal will appear to the left of the Tab stop, but once you enter a decimal, subsequent numerals appear to the right of the Tab stop.

✦ **Bar.** This draws a vertical bar at the spot where you insert the Tab stop. It has no effect when you press the Tab key.

In addition to setting Tab stop alignments, you can optionally assign each Tab stop a leader — characters that will be inserted in the tabbed line before the stop. You can use dots, dashes, or underline marks. (On a typewriter, you would have done this by repeatedly pressing the period key until you reached the other side of the page.)

Figure 4-10: Set tabs and their leaders (if any) using the Tabs dialog box.

Keyboard shortcuts

Shortcut keys are also provided for paragraph formatting. They're shown in Table 4-2.

Table 4-2 Keyboard Shortcuts for Paragraph Formatting	
Format	**Shortcut**
Left-align text	Ctrl+L
Center text	Ctrl+E
Right-align text	Ctrl+R

Format	Shortcut
Justify text	Ctrl+J
Indent from left	Ctrl+M
Remove indent from left	Ctrl+Shift+M
Increase hanging indent	Ctrl+T
Decrease hanging indent	Ctrl+Shift+T
Single-space lines	Ctrl+1
Use 1.5-line spacing	Ctrl+5
Double-space lines	Ctrl+2
Add or remove 12 points of space before a paragraph	Ctrl+0 (zero)
Remove paragraph formats not applied by a style	Ctrl+Q
Restore default formatting (reapply the Normal style)	Ctrl+Shift+N
Display or hide formatting marks and nonprinting characters	Ctrl+Shift+*

Using the ruler

You can also set indents and tabs using the ruler:

✦ **Left indent.** Go to the left end of the ruler and click and drag the little square below the two diamond-shaped arrows pointing at each other. Place the arrows however far from the left margin you want the indent to be set, and release the square.

✦ **First-line indent.** Drag the top diamond to the right of the bottom arrow by the amount you want the first-line indent to be.

✦ **Hanging indent**. First set a left indent as above, and then drag the top arrow to the left of the bottom arrow by the amount you want the hanging indent to be.

✦ **Right indent.** To change the right margin of a paragraph, drag the arrow at the right end of the ruler to the left or right.

To set tabs using the ruler:

1. Click the button at the far left of the ruler repeatedly to cycle through the various types of Tab stops. Pick the one you want.

2. Click the ruler at the point where you want the Tab stop to be set.

3. Adjust the Tab stop as necessary by dragging it left or right along the ruler.

4. If you make a mistake, delete the Tab stop by dragging it off the ruler.

Formatting pages

Page formatting controls the appearance of all the pages in the document — page size, orientation, margins, and so on.

To set page formatting, choose File ➪ Page Setup. This opens the Page Setup dialog box, which has three tabs: Margins, Paper, and Layout. We'll look at the first two tabs in this section, and then look at the Layout tab in detail in "Formatting sections."

Margins

The Margins tab (see Figure 4-11) lets you set margins — the distance between the edge of the page and the start of text — all around the page.

Figure 4-11: Set margins with these controls.

Enter the width you want each margin to be in the Top, Bottom, Left, and Right boxes. You can also use the little arrow buttons to the right of each box to adjust the number displayed up or down, one-tenth at a time.

You can also set a gutter margin, either at the left or at the top. Setting this adds that amount of additional space in the margin you've specified. You typically set a gutter margin when your document is going to be bound and you need to leave room for punch holes, spiral binding, or whatever.

These options change slightly if you choose Mirror margins, 2 pages per sheet, or Book fold from the Multiple pages drop-down list in the Pages section of the dialog box:

✦ If you choose Mirror margins (the best choice if you have asymmetrical margins and your document is going to be read book- or magazine-style), the gutter is automatically in the middle, and instead of Left and Right margins, you set Inside and Outside margins, inside being the margin closest to the center of the two-page spread and outside being the margin on the outside edges.

✦ If you choose 2 pages per sheet (because you want to create a booklet that folds down the middle, for instance), you set left and right margins, but the gutter is automatically centered.

✦ The Book fold option is a combination of 2 pages per sheet and Mirror margins.

You can also decide how you want the paper to be oriented: Portrait style (in which the longest dimension is the height) or Landscape (in which the longest dimension is the width). Finally, using the Apply to list box, you can choose whether to apply your page formatting to the whole document, only to those pages that follow the current insertion point, or to the section of text you currently have selected or are in.

Paper

Use the Paper tab (see Figure 4-12) to specify the paper size on which you'll be printing your document. You can choose one of the commonly used sizes (e.g., Letter, Legal, A4) from the Paper size list box, or specify a size of paper using the Width and Height controls. You can also specify how to apply this formatting: to the whole document, just to those pages that follow the insertion point, or just to whatever text you currently have selected — which means you can print half your document on letter-sized paper and half on legal-sized, if you wish!

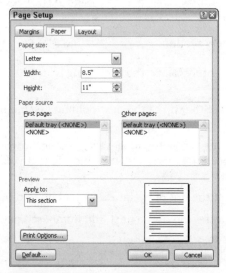

Figure 4-12: Use the Paper tab to set the size and orientation of the paper on which you'll be printing.

The Paper source section of the Paper tab lets you specify which bin of available printer paper you want to use, and whether you want to feed the paper in manually.

You can also choose to have the first page drawn from a bin other than the one used for subsequent pages — an option you might want to use if one bin is loaded with color paper, which you want for the front of your document, and another is loaded with white paper, which you want for your document's interior. Again, you can apply these choices to the whole document, just to the pages that follow the current insertion point, or to selected text.

The Print Options button you see on this tab is detailed in the final section of this chapter, "Printing."

Formatting sections

Word lets you apply different formats to different parts, or sections, of the same document, something you've seen already in each of the Page Setup tabs. This enables you to specify the portions of the document to which you want to apply the page formatting.

A typical use of this capability is to combine text set in columns with text that isn't, or to use different page numbering (Roman numerals, for instance, as used in the frontmatter of books, including this one) in one part of a document.

When you use Page Setup to format part of your document differently from another part, Word creates a new section. To control how Word deals with those sections, open the Page Setup dialog box again by choosing File ⇨ Page Setup, and click the Layout tab (see Figure 4-13).

Word offers you five ways to start each new section:

✦ **Continuous.** The section will immediately follow the preceding text, without a page break.

✦ **New Column.** The section will start at the top of the next column (assuming, of course, that columns are being used).

✦ **New Page.** The section will start at the top of the next page. In other words, this option adds a page break between the preceding text and the text you've just selected to make a new section.

✦ **Even Page.** This starts the section at the top of the next even-numbered page.

✦ **Odd Page.** This starts the section at the top of the next odd-numbered page.

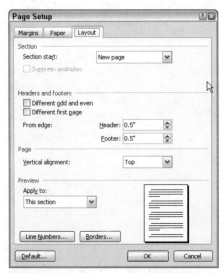

Figure 4-13: Use the Layout tab of the Page Setup dialog box to control the flow of sections within your document, among other things.

You can tell where one section begins and another ends because Word inserts a line in the document space labeled "Section Break."

The Layout tab also contains several other commands:

✦ **Vertical alignment.** Use this drop-down list to control the spacing of the text in your document between the top and bottom of the page. You can align it with the top (the default), align it with the bottom, vertically center it, or vertically justify it (which adds spaces between the lines of full pages to ensure that they extend completely to the bottom margin).

✦ **Line Numbers.** Click this button to open the Line Numbers dialog box shown in Figure 4-14. Check the Add line numbering box to add a number to selected lines. In the Start at box, enter the starting number for line numbering; in the From text box, enter how far to the left of the text you want the numbers to appear; and in the Count by box, enter the increment you want to count by (one, five, ten, etc.). Click the appropriate radio button under Numbering to restart numbering on each page, in each new section, or to make numbering continuous throughout the document.

✦ **Borders.** Click this button to apply borders and shading to your pages using the Borders and Shading dialog box.

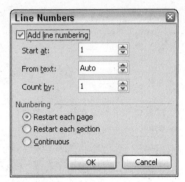

Figure 4-14: Line numbering, controlled from this dialog box, is often used in contracts and other legal documents.

Cross-Reference

For details on using Borders and Shading, see Chapter 9.

You can apply any of these layout options to the whole document, to only those pages that follow the current insertion point, or to selected text.

Headers, Footers, and Page Numbers

A header is copy (typically text, but it can be a graphic) that appears at the top of every page in a document; a footer is copy that appears at the bottom of every page.

To set the distance from the top and bottom that you want any headers or footers to appear, go back to the Layout tab of the File ➪ Page Setup dialog box and enter the distances you want to use with the From edge: controls in the Headers and footers section of the tab.

Note

You will normally set this amount to be less than the amount entered for the top and bottom margins. If a header or footer is too big to fit in the margin, Word will automatically adjust the margins of the page so they fit. To avoid that, enter a hyphen before the Top or Bottom margin setting. Word will then keep the margins of the page constant no matter how big the header or footer gets. (Of course, if either one is too big, it may overwrite part of the main text.)

To create the header or footer itself, select View ➪ Header and Footer. Word automatically switches to the view shown in Figure 4-15, which displays the entire page.

At the top and bottom of the page are fields (dotted boxes) into which you can enter text or graphics for your headers and footers. The Header and Footer toolbar also opens.

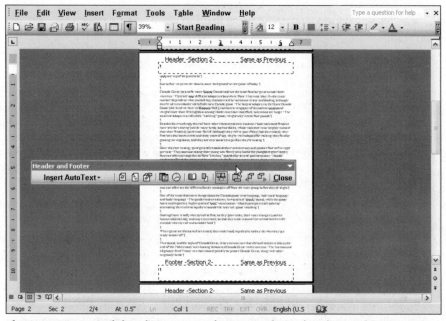

Figure 4-15: Control the placement and content of your headers and footers using the Header and Footer toolbar and this special view of your document.

Type text into the header and footer fields just as you would in the main document. All of the formatting options available for regular text are also available for headers and footers — for example, you can position your header or footer flush left on the page, flush right on the page, or centered on the page.

In addition, you can use the Header and Footer toolbar to automatically add certain features to your headers and footers, including the following:

✦ **AutoText.** Click Insert AutoText to pull down a menu of AutoText items you might want Word to add to your headers or footers, including the date your document was last printed, the date on which it was created, who created it and the filename, and so on. Just select the AutoText item you want to use, and Word automatically adds it to the header or footer you're currently creating.

✦ **Insert Page Number**, **Insert Number of Pages**, and **Format Page Number.** These three options are described in detail in the next section.

✦ **Insert Date.** Click this button to insert the current date into your header or footer. The date is inserted as a field, so it will always display the current date when you open the document.

✦ **Insert Time.** Click this button to insert the current time as a field.

Cross-Reference

For detailed information about using fields in Word, see Chapter 6.

The Header and Footer toolbar also includes several other useful buttons:

✦ **Page Setup.** This opens the Page Setup dialog box, where, under the Layout tab, you can choose to have different headers and footers on odd and even pages, and a unique header and footer for the first page. (Your unique header or footer for the first page can be no header or footer at all.) If you choose those options, place your insertion point on an even page before opening the Header and Footer toolbar in order to create the header and footer for even pages, and then do the same for odd pages and/or the first page.

✦ **Show/Hide Document Text.** Clicking this button hides the document's main text, so you can work on your header or footer without distraction.

✦ **Same as Previous.** This button is active only if you have more than one section in your document. If you do, it makes your header or footer for the current section the same as the header or footer for the previous section.

✦ **Switch Between Header and Footer.** You can get from the header box to the footer box (or vice versa) by scrolling down (or up) the page—or you can simply click this button to instantly switch back and forth between them.

✦ **Show Previous, Show Next.** If your headers and footers are different on odd and even pages, or on the first page, or across sections, you can move from one to the other using these buttons.

Page numbering

One of the most common uses of headers and footers is to add page numbers. To add a page number to either a header or footer, simply place the cursor in the header or footer where you want to place the page number, then click the Insert Page Number button on the Header and Footer toolbar. Several AutoText options also include the page number.

If you want to automatically include the total number of pages in the document, click the Insert Number of Pages button on the Header and Footer toolbar. (The most common usage of that is to insert a phrase like "Page x of y," where you'd type "Page," insert the current page number field for "x," type "of," and insert the total number of pages field for "y.")

Of course, you have more than one way to indicate page numbers. For instance, sometimes you want Roman numerals, and sometimes you want Arabic. That's where the Format Page Number button on the Header and Footer toolbar comes in. Click it to bring up the Page Number Format dialog box shown in Figure 4-16.

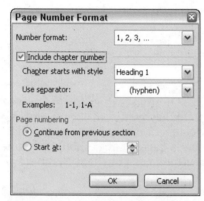

Figure 4-16: Use this dialog box to specify how Word should display your page numbers.

Here, you can choose a format for your page numbers: regular Arabic numerals, Roman numerals (both uppercase and lowercase), or letters (again, both uppercase and lowercase). If you like, you can have Word add a chapter number in front of the page number, and specify the character that will separate the two numbers (e.g., 1-2 or 2:A). You can also specify how Word will recognize the beginning of a chapter, by indicating which style of text is used to start one. Finally, you can have page numbering be continuous from section to section, or start anew at the beginning of each new section — and specify which number page numbers in a new section should start with.

Cross-Reference

For more on styles, see Chapter 8.

If the only element you want in your header or footer is the page number, you don't have to use the Header and Footer toolbar at all. Simply choose Insert ➪ Page Numbers. This opens the Page Numbers dialog box, shown in Figure 4-17.

Figure 4-17: Adding page numbers to your document is a breeze, thanks to the Page Numbers dialog box.

Choose a position for your page numbers (top or bottom of the page—as a header or footer, in other words) and an alignment (right, left, center, inside, or outside—the latter two apply only if you're creating a document that will be bound and have mirrored margins). You can also specify whether a page number should be shown on the first page. Finally, clicking the Format button opens the Page Number Format dialog box already examined.

Creating Footnotes

For scholarly writing, Word offers you the option of placing footnotes directly beneath the text in which they appear, at the bottom of the page on which the reference appears, at the end of a section, or at the end of the document (in which case they're called *endnotes*).

To insert a footnote or endnote, place the insertion point where the footnote reference (usually a superscripted number) will appear, and then choose Insert ➪ Reference ➪ Footnote to open the Footnote and Endnote dialog box, shown in Figure 4-18.

Use this dialog box to specify whether you want to insert a footnote (at the bottom of the page—Word automatically makes room for however many footnotes you want to insert) or an endnote (at the end of the document). If you want, you can have Word automatically number footnotes sequentially (and choose what number you want Word to start with). If you'd prefer to use a symbol of your own choosing, click the Custom mark button instead, and type what you want to use (e.g., an asterisk) in the space provided. If you're looking for a symbol more exotic than anything that appears on the keyboard, click the Symbol button to bring up the Symbol dialog box, shown in Figure 4-19, whence you can select any character from the various fonts installed on your computer. (But don't choose a font that a recipient of the file might not have on his or her computer; that could cause confusion.)

Figure 4-18: The first time you insert a footnote or endnote, this dialog box opens.

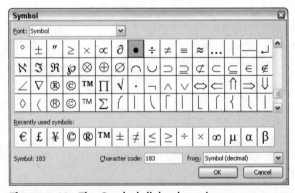

Figure 4-19: The Symbol dialog box gives you access to any character, in various fonts.

You can choose whether you want the numbering to be continuous throughout the document or to restart in each section or on each page. In addition, you can specify whether you want to apply your choices to the whole document or just to the current section.

Once you're happy with your footnote or endnote setup, click Insert. This opens a footnote pane in the bottom portion of the screen (see Figure 4-20). Type your footnote into this pane. You can change its size by dragging the split bar (at its top) up or down. Once you're done entering footnotes, you can close the pane by clicking the Close button; alternately, you can return your insertion point to the main document area and continue typing with the footnote pane open.

Note   In Normal view, footnotes are visible only when the footnote pane is open. However, they're always visible in Print Layout view or Reading Layout view.

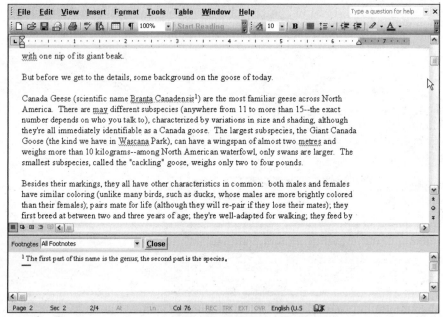

Figure 4-20: When you insert a footnote, the footnote pane opens at the bottom of your screen; type the text for your footnote into it.

As you continue to add footnotes throughout the document, they'll all appear in the footnote pane, where you can easily move through them and edit them as necessary. To move a footnote, simply move its reference mark in the text: Select the reference mark, cut it, and paste it in its new location. Similarly, you can delete a footnote simply by selecting and deleting its reference mark. Word will automatically adjust the numbering of all footnotes as needed.

You can change footnotes to endnotes or vice versa by selecting the notes you want to convert in the footnote pane, and then right-clicking and choosing Convert to Endnote or Convert to Footnote from the shortcut menu.

Printing

It doesn't usually take a lot of extra work to prepare a document for printing in Word; you're generally seeing a good representation of what it will look like on paper, especially if you're using Print Layout view or if you've taken a look in Print Preview.

Cross-Reference See Chapter 3 for more details about these two views.

Once you're ready to print, you have three ways to go about it: by clicking the Print button on the Standard toolbar, by choosing File ➪ Print, or by pressing Ctrl+P.

Clicking the Print button sends the document at once to the last printer you used, and prints it with the last print settings you chose.

Tip Not sure which printer is currently selected? Hover the mouse pointer over the Print button momentarily. The name of the selected printer will be displayed in a ScreenTip.

Choosing File ➪ Print or pressing Ctrl+P inserts one more step into the printing process, opening the Print dialog box (see Figure 4-21).

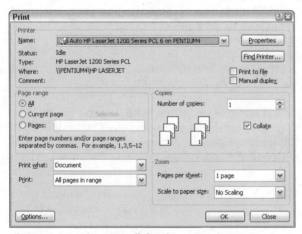

Figure 4-21: The Print dialog box contains many options for printing your document.

The first thing to do here, obviously, is choose an available printer. They're listed in the Name drop-down list (the printer shown here is the one set as your default printer in the Printers folder of your Windows Control Panel). Click the Properties button to change setup options for the current printer (these are the options specific to the particular printer you're using).

Note   "Printers" can include special functions such as faxing and creating a PDF document from a Word document.

In the Page range section of the dialog box, choose the pages you wish to print: All, just the Current page, just the current Selection (if you selected text before opening this dialog box), or specific pages, which you indicate by number.

Caution   The current page is not necessarily the page you can see peeking out from behind the Print dialog box. To Word, the current page is whichever one you left your insertion point on — even if you've scrolled somewhere else . Make sure you know where your insertion point is, and that it's where you want it to be, before choosing to print the current page.

To indicate a sequence of pages, enter the first and last page number, separated by a hyphen — for example, 4-10. To print a selection of individual pages, separate the numbers with commas — for example, 3, 6, 12. You can also combine these. For example, you could print pages 5, 6, 7, and 12, 13, and 14 by entering 5-7, 12-14.

Below the Page range section is a Print what list box. Open it if you want to print something other than the document. You can choose to print the document properties, the document showing any markup you've added (e.g., inserted comments, tracked changes, etc.), a list and descriptions of the styles you used, and even the current key assignments (a great way to get a printed list to refer to if you have trouble remembering key assignments on your own).

Below that is the option to print all pages within your chosen range of pages, just odd pages, or just even pages.

At the bottom of the dialog box is an Options button, which opens the dialog box shown in Figure 4-22 (which you also get when you select the Print tab from the Tools ⇨ Options dialog box). It contains several general printing options, including an option to include with the document other items, such as document properties and field codes.

Figure 4-22: The Options button on the Print dialog box opens this other Print dialog box, which contains additional options for customizing your print job.

On the right side of the main Print dialog box are two more areas, Copies and Zoom. In Copies, you can set the number of copies you want to print; you also have the option to collate. If you leave Collate checked (it's checked by default), each copy of a multiple-page document emerges from the printer in proper page order, ready for paper-clipping or binding — with Collate unchecked, you instead get multiple copies of page 1, then multiple copies of page 2, and so on. However, collating can result in slower printing if the pages are complex — with numerous graphics, for instance — because it takes time for information to be sent to the printer, and it has to be sent repeatedly if you're asking for collation, once for every copy you're making. Conversely, the time lost to the slower printing may very well be less than the time lost to the manual collating effort you'll have to make afterward, so it's probably a trade-off.

Finally, in the Zoom section of the dialog box, you can scale your document to fit a particular size of paper. (This may be useful, for example, if you laid out your document to fit legal-size paper but you have only letter-size available in your printer.) You can also choose to print more than one page per sheet of paper, a great way to both review a draft and save paper. A setting of two pages per sheet generally gives you quite legible text.

When you're happy with your print settings, click OK — and commit your document to paper!

Summary

Word's primary function is the manipulation of text; in this chapter, we looked at its basic tools for inserting, editing, and formatting text in your documents.

 ✦ There are multiple ways to select and move through text once you've typed it in.

 ✦ Word offers separate, multiple formatting tools for characters (especially the Font dialog box), paragraphs, pages, and sections.

 ✦ If you prefer, you can format text using keyboard shortcuts instead of pointing and clicking with the mouse.

 ✦ You can insert text or graphics into headers and footers, and add automatically updated page numbers, the date, the time of day, and more with the Headers and Footers toolbar.

 ✦ You can insert footnotes or endnotes, as you see fit, and number them in a variety of ways.

 ✦ Word will print to the last printer you used at the click of the Print button on the Standard toolbar; you can also give it detailed printing instructions by choosing File ➪ Print.

✦   ✦   ✦

Working with Tables

Tables are among Word's most useful ways of organizing
information to the benefit of both the creator and the
reader. Readers benefit from a clearer understanding of the
relationships among the various items inserted into the table.
Creators benefit from Word's ability to sort, sum, and otherwise manipulate information entered into tables. Recognizing
their importance, Word makes tables easy to set up and use.

Creating Tables

You have more than one way to create a table in Word. In fact,
there are three: a tool on the Standard toolbar and two different menu commands.

The Table tool

The quickest way to create a table is to click the Insert Table
tool on the Standard toolbar. This brings up the small grid
shown in Figure 5-1, which represents the rows and columns
of a table. You can select how many rows and columns you
want simply by moving your mouse pointer over the grid; the
grid squares you've selected turn dark.

Once you've chosen the number of rows and columns, click.
Your table is automatically created.

Figure 5-1: Move your mouse pointer over this grid to choose the number of rows and columns you want in your table.

Draw Table

The second way to create a table is to choose Table ➪ Draw Table. When you choose this command, your view automatically changes to Print Layout, zoomed out so you can see the entire page, and your mouse pointer changes to an image of a pencil, which you can use to draw the rows and columns of your table, just as you might draw a table on a piece of paper with a regular pencil and a ruler. You can make the table as large as you want, and add as many vertical and horizontal lines as you want (see Figure 5-2).

Draw Table is a very powerful command for creating nonstandard tables: tables that have different numbers of columns in different rows, for instance; or tables in which columns and rows are of varying widths and heights. Notice that when you choose Draw Table, you also automatically open the Tables and Borders toolbar. This toolbar provides handy access to tools for applying borders and shading.

Cross-Reference   See Chapter 9 as well as many of the formatting tools for tables discussed in detail later in this chapter.

Insert Table

The third way to create a table is to choose Table ➪ Insert ➪ Table. This opens the Insert Table dialog box shown in Figure 5-3.

In the Table size area, enter the number of rows and columns you want your table to have. In the AutoFit behavior area, choose how columns will respond when you enter information in them. With a fixed column width (which can be set automatically by Word or which you can specify), columns never get wider, only deeper, when data too wide for the current width is entered in them. If you choose AutoFit to contents, columns get wider to accommodate whatever you put into them. If you choose AutoFit to window, the table's width changes to keep it within the margins you have set for the page. (AutoFit is described in more detail in the section "Using automatic formatting with tables" later in this chapter.)

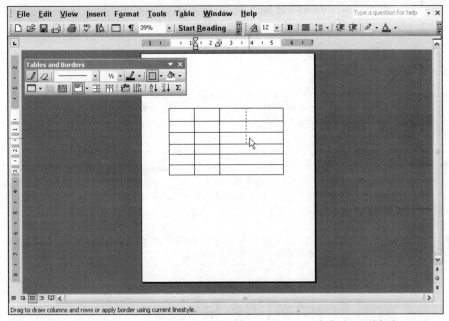

Figure 5-2: This table has six rows, and a column is currently being added.

If the size of table you're creating is one you're likely to use repeatedly, check the Remember dimensions for new tables box before clicking OK.

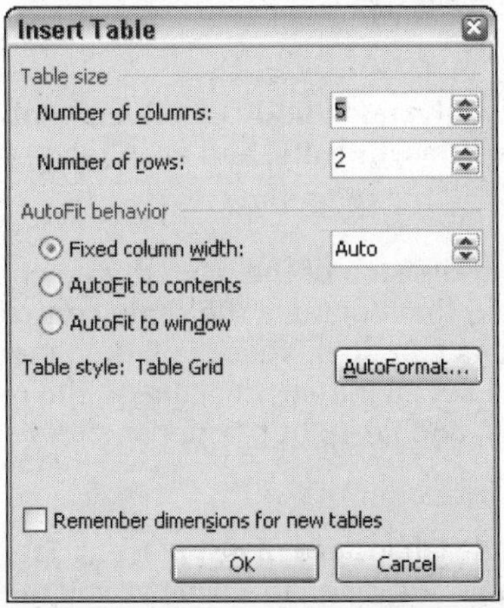

Figure 5-3: Specify the size of the table you want to create in this dialog box.

The other button in this dialog box, AutoFormat, is described in the section "Using automatic formatting with tables" a little later in this chapter.

Adding data

The simplest method of adding data to a table is to type it in. You can think of each cell of the table as a separate little word-processing window; just place your insertion point in the cell in which you want to enter information and type away.

You can also add data by copying it from elsewhere onto the clipboard, and then pasting it into your table cells. If you have a lot of data already in tabular form in another Office application, such as Excel or PowerPoint, you don't have to rely on copy-and-paste or retype it. You can import that table directly into Word as a linked or embedded object.

Cross-Reference   For more information on linked and embedded objects and sharing data among Office's various components, see Chapter 42.

Editing and Formatting Tables

Once you have created your table and populated it with data, you may want to make changes. Editing text in a table is the same as editing text anywhere else in Word. You can copy text from place to place, highlight it and type over it or delete it, and so on.

Cross-Reference   For more details on editing text in Word, see Chapter 2.

You can also format text the same way you do in the main body of a document, with one major difference: You can set individual margins, indents, and even tab stops for each cell in a table.

Whenever you click inside a cell, you'll see a subdivision of the main document area ruler that corresponds to the size of the cell and that contains the same controls as the main ruler. You can use these controls just as you do in your main document, moving the upper triangular slider at the left to set an indent, clicking on the ruler to create a tab stop, and moving the left-bottom and far-right triangular sliders to set margins (see Figure 5-4).

Tip   To use a tab stop within a table cell, press Ctrl+Tab instead of just pressing Tab, as you would if you were not working with a table. Pressing Tab will move you to the next table cell instead of to the tab stop.

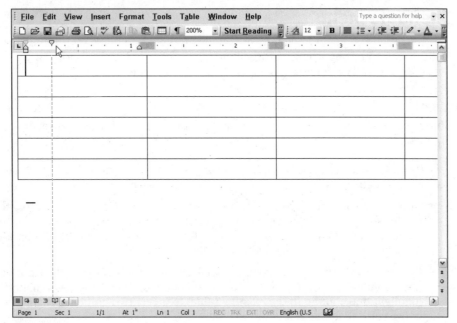

Figure 5-4: You can set the margins, indents, and tab stops individually for each cell in a Word table.

Similarly, you can change fonts and their sizes and styles within each cell just as you do anywhere else in your Word document, using the usual text formatting commands.

Tip　The easiest way to copy the formatting of one cell to another is with the Format Painter. Just highlight the contents of the cell whose formatting you want to use, and then click Format Painter on the Standard toolbar and use it to highlight the contents of the cell you want to apply the formatting to.

In addition to formatting the text within a table, however, you'll probably want to format the table as a whole, to give it a unified look or simply to make the information you've entered into it more easily accessible to your audience.

Word provides many tools for fine-tuning the appearance of a table—most of them, as you might expect, listed under the Table menu.

The Table menu

Choose Table, and you'll find many commands to help you make your table look just the way you want. The first three commands, covered in the following sections, enable you to add or delete cells, rows, columns, or whole tables.

Insert

Choose Table ⇨ Insert, and you're presented with a submenu featuring several options:

✦ **Table.** This inserts a new table into your document, as described in the section "Creating Tables."

✦ **Columns to the left.** This inserts a new column or columns into the table to the left of the column where your cursor is currently located. If you want to insert one column, first highlight one column in the existing table; if you want to insert two columns, highlight two columns, and so on.

✦ **Columns to the right.** This inserts a new column or columns to the right of the column where your cursor is located. Again, to insert one column, first highlight one column in the existing table; to insert two columns, highlight two columns, and so on.

✦ **Rows above.** This inserts a new row or rows above the row where your cursor is currently located.

✦ **Rows below.** This inserts a new row or rows below the row where your cursor is located.

✦ **Cells.** This brings up a small dialog box that asks you if you want to shift cells down or shift cells right when you insert your new cell. If you choose to shift cells down, the new cell will force all the cells below it in its column down one to make room for it. If you choose to shift cells right, all the cells in the new cell's row will shift to the right to make room for it. You can also choose to insert a whole column or a whole row using this menu.

Delete

Choose Table ⇨ Delete, and you're presented with commands that are essentially the opposite of the Insert commands. You can delete the entire table, or just the row or column where your cursor is currently located. If you choose Table ⇨ Delete ⇨ Cells, you'll see a Delete Cells dialog box just like the Insert Cells dialog box, except instead of being asked if you want to shift the other cells in the column or row down or right, you're asked if you want to shift them up or left.

Insert Cells and Delete Cells work a little differently if you use them with multiple cells selected (see the following section, "Select," to learn how to select more than one cell). If you choose to shift cells to the right in the Insert Cells dialog box, Word inserts the same number of cells as you've selected, and shifts the rows in which they appear to the right. If you choose to shift cells down, however, Word doesn't just insert the number of cells you've selected; it inserts a number of rows equal to the number of rows of cells in your selection. In the Delete Cells dialog box, you can choose only to shift cells left; if you choose to shift cells up, Delete Cells deletes the content of the selected cells and moves content from the cells below up, but doesn't actually remove the cells in question.

Select

Table ➪ Select offers you the same four options: Table, Column, Row, and Cell. Click Table to highlight the whole Table for formatting, Column to select the entire column where your cursor is located, Row to select the entire row, or Cell to select the cell where you've placed your cursor.

Tip　You can also select parts of a table with your mouse. To select a cell, triple-click anywhere inside it. To select an entire row, move your mouse pointer to the left edge of the table. Just outside the table boundaries, the pointer will turn into a white arrow pointing back at the row. Click once to select the row. Similarly, to select a column, move your pointer to just outside the table's top edge. Your pointer will turn into a black arrow pointing down at the column. Click once to select the column. You can also select a specific range of cells by clicking and dragging from one cell to another.

The next section of the Table menu lets you merge and split cells, or even split the entire table.

Merge Cells

Suppose you want to create a single headline that runs across the top of your table, or subheads that cover two or three columns farther down inside your table. To do that, you need to combine two or more cells into one larger cell that spans one or more columns or rows.

To combine cells, simply highlight the cells you want to combine into one, and then choose Table ➪ Merge Cells (see Figure 5-5).

Split Cells

Sometimes, of course, you want to do just the opposite: You want to subdivide an existing cell into two or more smaller cells. To do that, select the cells you want to subdivide, and then choose Table ➪ Split Cells. You'll see the Split Cells dialog box shown in Figure 5-6.

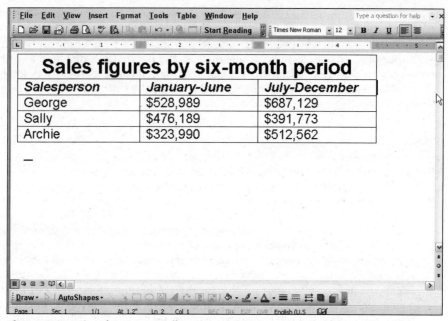

Figure 5-5: Using the Merge Cells command, you can create larger cells within your table's regular grid, as I've done with this table.

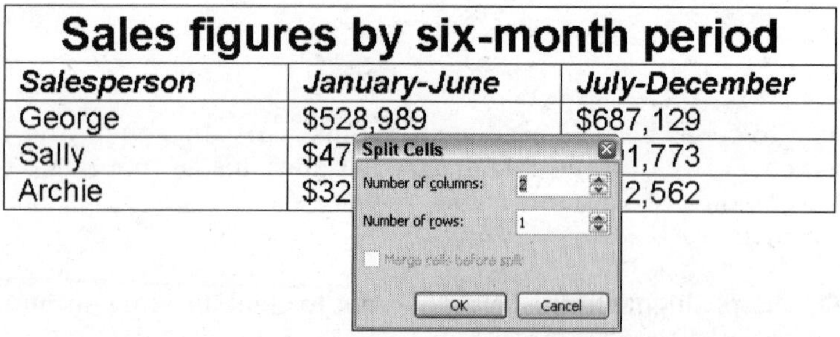

Figure 5-6: You can use the Split Cells command to reorganize part of your table, or even to completely reconfigure it.

Choose the number of rows and columns into which you want to divide the selected cell or cells. You can choose to split each cell you've selected individually into that many rows or columns, or, by checking Merge cells before split, combine all the selected cells into one large cell that is then subdivided into the number of rows and columns you've specified.

Tip You can use the Split Cells command to quickly change the number of rows and columns in your whole table. Choose Table ➪ Select ➪ Table to highlight every cell in your table, and then choose Table ➪ Split Cells. Enter the new number of rows and columns you want in your table, making sure Merge cells before split is checked, and then click OK. Your table will instantly change from whatever it was before to the number of rows and columns you've specified.

Split Table

You can turn a single table into two separate tables with the Split Table command. Just place your cursor in the row that you want to be the first row of the bottom table and choose Table ➪ Split Table. The table will split apart above the row you've selected (see Figure 5-7).

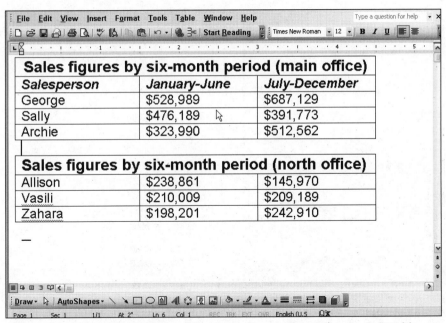

Figure 5-7: Have only one table when you really need two? Use the Split Table command to remedy the situation.

Tip The cursor, after the Split Table command, is between the two tables. This enables you to enter text before the second table. If you've created a table as the first thing in a new document, place your cursor in the top row of the table and use this command to make room for text above the table, if you need it.

Using automatic formatting with tables

Also within the Table menu are several options for applying automatic formatting to tables. Automatic formatting can save you time and effort and ensure a consistent, professional look to your tables.

AutoFormat

AutoFormat automatically applies shading, borders, colors, and other interesting formatting elements to your table. You can apply AutoFormat to a table either when you first create it (by clicking AutoFormat on the Insert Table dialog box) or at any time by placing your cursor anywhere within the table and choosing Table ➪ Table AutoFormat (see Figure 5-8).

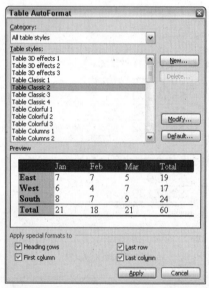

Figure 5-8: The Table AutoFormat dialog box lets you apply all or parts of several pre-designed formats to your table.

Choose the format you want from the Formats scroll-down list; the Preview box will show you exactly what it will look like. You don't have to apply the entire format. Instead, you can choose to apply only those parts that you like by choosing from the Apply special formats to checkboxes at the bottom of the dialog box.

Clicking the New button enables you to create your own table style; clicking the Modify button enables you to alter one of the existing table styles (see Figure 5-9).

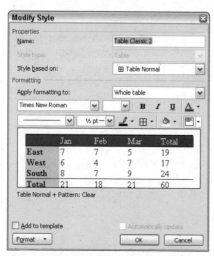

Figure 5-9: Modify an existing table style with the Modify Style dialog box.

Cross-Reference For detailed information on working with the New Style and Modify Style dialog boxes, see Chapter 8.

Once you're happy with your choices, click OK to see your new table.

AutoFit

AutoFit, the next option in the Table menu, determines how rows and columns change to accommodate the text you enter in the cells. AutoFit offers five options:

✦ **AutoFit to Contents.** If you choose this option, your table will automatically adjust itself to wrap snugly around the text entered in cells.

✦ **AutoFit to Window.** If you choose this option, your table will adjust its width to fit within the margins you have set for the page.

✦ **Fixed Column Widths.** If you choose this option, your column widths will remain the same, and text will automatically wrap when it comes to the end of the column, instead of making the column expand.

✦ **Distribute Rows Evenly.** This makes all rows in your table the same height — the same height as the tallest row in your table, which means your table may suddenly get much taller.

✦ **Distribute Columns Evenly.** This makes all columns the same width, by subdividing the width of the column evenly. In other words, whereas Distribute Rows Evenly makes your table higher, Distribute Columns Evenly keeps the column the same width and makes some rows wider and some narrower.

Heading Rows Repeat

This command is useful if your table is going to span more than a single page. To use it, select the top row or rows of your table, and then choose Table ⇨ Heading Rows Repeat. If your table jumps to another page, the top rows you selected will be displayed again as heading rows (provided you're in Print Layout or Reading Layout view or are viewing the printed document).

Other Table menu commands

The remaining commands on the Table Menu are Convert, Sort, Formula, Show/Hide Gridlines, and Table Properties. The following sections describe these commands in detail, beginning with Convert and Show/Hide Gridlines.

Convert

Convert enables you to turn a table into text, or text into a table.

Table to text

To convert a table to text:

1. Select the rows of the table that you want to convert to text. (You must select entire rows; if you leave, for example, the first cell in a row unselected, then Word converts the entire table to text instead of just the cells you selected.)

2. Choose Table ⇨ Convert ⇨ Table to Text.

3. From the dialog box, choose what you want to use to separate the items from the table once it's converted into text (see Figure 5-10): paragraph marks, tabs, commas, or any other character you specify (the default is tabs).

4. If any of the cells in the table you're converting contains a nested table, check Convert nested tables; if you'd like to keep the nested table as a table, don't check it. (If no tables are nested, this option is grayed out.)

5. Click OK.

Figure 5-10: Word lets you specify what character or delimiter you want to use to separate entries from a table when it's converted into text.

Text to table

Convert also enables you to turn text into a table. To do so:

1. Highlight the text you want to convert.

2. Choose Table ➪ Convert ➪ Text to Table.

3. A dialog box almost identical to the usual Insert Table dialog box appears (see Figure 5-11), with one difference: At the bottom, you have to tell Word what character it should look for to figure out how to break the text into table entries. In addition, note that while you can choose the number of columns, you can't choose the number of rows — it's set automatically. That's because the total number of cells created has to match the number of entries that Word will form from the converted text.

4. Click OK.

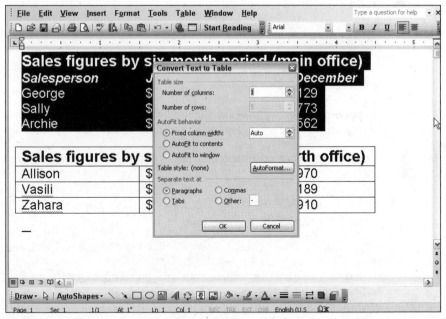

Figure 5-11: You can instantly place text into a table by using the Convert Text to Table command.

Show/Hide Gridlines

This command toggles on and off the gridlines that Word provides to outline your table's cells.

These gridlines are not the same as the borders you can apply to tables (outline borders are used by default on new tables — unless you change these borders, this command will appear to have no effect). Gridlines are visual aids only; unlike borders, they don't show up in the printed document. In addition, this command applies to all tables in the document.

Table Properties

Table Properties, at the bottom of the Table menu, is one of the most powerful commands the menu has to offer. It opens a dialog box that lets you handily specify most of your table's characteristics. The Table Properties dialog box has four tabs.

Table

Use the Table tab to specify three major properties of your table as a whole (see Figure 5-12):

✦ **Size.** Set the preferred width of your table, in inches or as a percent of the page width.

This width may change later as you add or edit entries to the table, depending on your AutoFit choices.

✦ **Alignment.** Set your table against the left margin, centered on the page, or against the right margin, or enter a specific amount for it to be indented.

The Indent from Left command is available only if you choose left alignment.

✦ **Text wrapping.** Choose None if you want text to appear only above or below your table. Choose Around if you'd like text to wrap around the table on the page (this can sometimes improve the look of your page, particularly if your table is small). If you choose Around, click Positioning to specify exactly how you want text to relate to your table: Options include horizontal and vertical positioning relative to margins, columns, paragraphs, or the page as a whole, and how much white space you want to add around the table. You can also specify whether the table should move with the text, or the text should overlap it.

Figure 5-12: The Table tab of the Table Properties dialog box lets you specify your table's size and alignment, and how text wrapping is handled.

Clicking the Options button at the bottom of the Table tab opens a dialog box that enables you to set the top, bottom, left, and right default cell margins of your table, and to add spacing between cells. You can also disable the default option that causes cells to automatically resize to fit their contents.

Cross-Reference Clicking the Borders and Shading button opens the Borders and Shading dialog box; this is covered in detail in Chapter 9.

Row

Use the Row tab (see Figure 5-13) to specify the height of a range of rows (if you've highlighted several of them) or individual rows (if you haven't). Here's how the options work:

✦ **Size.** Word tells you which row or range of rows you're working with. Specify the height you want the row or rows to be. You can indicate whether you want the row(s) to be exactly that height, or if that's a minimum measurement.

✦ **Options.** You can choose to allow or disallow the row to break across pages. If you're working with the first row, you can choose to make it a header row that will repeat on each page the table occupies.

✦ **Previous Row or Next Row.** Click here to adjust the next row above or below the currently selected row or rows.

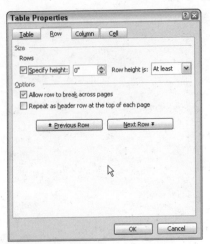

Figure 5-13: The Row tab of the Table Properties dialog box lets you specify the heights of your rows.

Column

The Column tab looks very much like the Row tab and behaves exactly the same way, except you specify width, not height. There are no options for breaking across pages, and you can specify width not only in inches but also as a percentage of the total table width.

Cell

The Cell tab (see Figure 5-14) lets you specify the preferred width for a selected cell or cells. Again, you can specify width in inches or as a percentage of the total table width. Below that, you can choose how to align text within the cell: flush against the top, centered vertically, or flush against the bottom.

Finally, clicking Options brings up a small dialog box in which you can set the cell's margins (or choose to leave them the same as for the rest of the table), and whether to wrap text when it gets too long or to squeeze or widen it to make it fit the width of the cell.

Figure 5-14: Use the Cell tab to specify cell width and vertical alignment within a cell.

Using Sort and Formulas

If you're planning to sort, sum, or otherwise manipulate a lot of data, you're probably better off doing it in Excel than you are in Word. However, if all you need are some simple calculations, or you want to create an alphabetically sorted list of names, then Word's tables can probably do it for you.

Using Sort

To use Sort, select the range of cells you want to sort, and then choose Table ➪ Sort. This opens the Sort dialog box shown in Figure 5-15.

Note　　If you don't select a range of cells, Word automatically selects the entire table.

Figure 5-15: Specify how your table should be sorted using this dialog box.

Word lets you sort your table in three ways: by text, by number, or by date (depending on what type of data is entered). In the Sort by area, you choose which column you primarily want to sort, whether to sort by text, number, or date, and whether to sort in ascending order or descending order. In the two Then by areas, you enter the criteria you want to apply to settle any ties (where the initial criteria are identical for two or more entries). Use the data in one of your remaining columns to decide which of the tied entries comes first. Then choose whether to sort the tied entries in ascending or descending order.

At the bottom, indicate whether your table has a header row or not. If you indicate that it does, the entries in the top row will not be sorted with the others. In addition, columns will be indicated by the entries associated with them in the header row, instead of just being listed as Column 1, Column 2, etc., as they otherwise are.

Click Options to fine-tune the sorting command. For example, you can specify what language Word should use to sort with and whether the sorting order should be case-sensitive.

Using formulas

Formulas enable you to perform calculations on the entries in your table's cells. The calculations aren't limited to the cell in which you place the formula; they can reference other cells in the table or any data in the document (provided you've marked it with a bookmark; to mark a table with a bookmark, simply place your cursor in the first cell in the table, choose Insert ⇨ Bookmark, type a name for your bookmark in the resulting dialog box, and then click Add).

Sorting Tips and Tricks

To sort a single column without affecting the columns on either side of it, first highlight the column (hover the cursor above the top edge of the column until it turns into a black down arrow, then click). Then choose Table ⇨ Sort and click Options. Check the box marked Sort Column Only, and then return to the main Sort dialog box and choose your criteria as usual. Click OK. Only the selected column will be sorted.

You can also sort a text list that isn't in a table with the Table ⇨ Sort command, provided each item in the list ends with a paragraph mark. Highlight the list, and then choose Table ⇨ Sort. A dialog box will open; choose ascending (i.e., A, B, C . . . or 1, 2, 3 . . .) or descending order and whether you're sorting text, numbers, or dates, and then click OK.

Word keeps track of the cells in a table with a simple reference system that combines the column and the row with a colon. B:3, for instance, refers to the third cell down in the second column from the left. You can also reference an entire row or column by using the column letter or row number twice, separated by a colon; B:B would reference the entire second column, and 3:3 would reference the entire third row.

You can devise quite complex formulas in Word tables. For example, you might add all the values of a row in one table, which you've bookmarked Expenses, and then subtract that from the sum of all the values of a column in another table, bookmarked Income. The formula might look like the following:

{=(SUM(Income C:C)) - (SUM(Expenses 4:4))}

Cross-Reference   Formulas are a form of field. For more detailed information on fields, see Chapter 6.

You can enter a formula by typing it directly into a cell, but an easier method is to click in the cell where you want the formula to appear, choose Table ⇨ Formula and use the resulting dialog box (see Figure 5-16) to enter the formula. You can type it directly into the Formula box; the Paste function list box at the bottom of the dialog box provides you with a complete list of all the formula functions available to you. Just click the one you want to have it automatically entered in your formula.

From the Number format drop-down list, select the format in which you wish to display the results of your calculation (e.g., do you want it to appear as a percentage, or in dollars and cents?). If you want to reference a bookmarked table, you'll find all of the ones available in your document listed under Paste Bookmark. Again, just click the one you want to enter it into your formula.

Once your formula is complete, click OK.

Figure 5-16: Formulas are powerful tools for automatically generating new data from data you've already entered in tables.

The Tables and Borders Toolbar

One last thing before we leave this chapter — another, and sometimes easier, way to access the table formatting tools previously discussed.

As mentioned earlier, when you use the Draw Table tool, you also automatically open the Tables and Borders toolbar (see Figure 5-17). (Of course, you can also bring up this toolbar by choosing View ➪ Toolbars ➪ Tables and Borders.) Most of the tools on the bottom half of this toolbar relate to tables, and most of them we've already looked at. From left to right, they are Insert Table, Merge Cells, Split Cells, Alignment, Distribute Rows Evenly, Distribute Columns Evenly, Table AutoFormat, Change Text Direction, Sort Ascending, Sort Descending, and AutoSum.

Figure 5-17: The Tables and Borders toolbar provides one-click access to many of the most useful table-formatting tools.

Cross-Reference

The tools in the top half of this toolbar are discussed in detail in Chapter 9.

The Change Text Direction command

One of the commands we haven't yet looked at is the Change Text Direction command, which is also available by right-clicking inside a cell. Text Direction lets you run text vertically on the page instead of horizontally. To use it, highlight the text to which you want to apply it, or simply place your cursor inside the cell in which you want it to apply, and click the Text Direction button. The text will move from horizontal to vertical, and what was at the left margin is now at the top. Click the button again and the text will remain vertical, but what was at the left margin when the text was horizontal is now at the bottom. Click the button a third time and the text returns to its original horizontal position.

If you choose this command from the right-click pop-up menu instead, you'll get a dialog box that shows you the three positions and illustrates what each looks like to help you make your choice.

Using AutoSum

Another useful command on this toolbar is AutoSum. This calculates and displays the sum of the values in the cells above or to the left of the cell containing the insertion point.

Summary

This chapter covered all the tools Word offers for creating and formatting tables. Major points included the following:

✦ Word gives you three methods to create tables. For a small table, you can click the Insert Table button; for a larger table, you can choose Table ⇨ Insert ⇨ Table; and to create a complex, custom table, choose Table ⇨ Draw Table.

✦ Use the Table menu to add, delete, and format rows, columns, and individual cells.

✦ Why re-create the wheel? Let AutoFormat give your table a sharp, professionally designed look at the click of a button.

✦ Use the Table Properties dialog box to adjust the size of rows, columns, cells, and the table as a whole as you see fit. Specify exactly how you want other text to fit around your table.

✦ Convert text to tables and tables to text by choosing Table ⇨ Convert.

✦ Choose Table ⇨ Sort to organize your table the way you think works best. You can also choose to sort a single column.

✦ Formulas are powerful tools that you can use to generate new data from information you've already entered into tables. You can add entries together, average them, and more.

✦ The Tables and Borders toolbar provides one-click access to the most common table-formatting commands.

✦   ✦   ✦

Forms, Fields, and Merging

Entering information in Word is most often done by typing, but that's not always the best way. Sometimes the information you need isn't at your fingertips and has to be imported from another source. Sometimes the same material needs to be repeated in numerous parts of the document, so typing it repeatedly is extremely inefficient. Sometimes numerical information has to be calculated from other information elsewhere in the document. Sometimes parts of the document remain static over time, while other parts have to be updated regularly. In other cases, the information has to be supplied by the person reading the document. And then, of course, there's the classic form letter, where the text of the letter is always the same, but the address and salutation are personalized. Word has powerful tools that can help you in all of these situations and many more: fields, forms, and merging capabilities.

Using Fields

With fields, you can insert dynamic data—information that changes over time—into your document. The date is a good example of dynamic data. So is the amount of time you've spent working on a particular document. With fields, you can automatically insert either of these bits of data (or your choice of many others) into a header or footer, or anywhere else in the document. Fields are used extensively in Word's templates to automatically insert the date, your address, and other information, so even if you don't insert them into documents you build from scratch, you're likely to run into them.

Page numbers automatically inserted into headers and footers are good examples of fields at work; Word can determine how many pages a document consists of and what page you are on, so that it can insert "page 3 of 10," for example, and keep that information current as the document's content changes. (You have to insert the words "page" and "of" manually.) Word can also use the information in a document to automatically compile an index or a table of contents.

Cross-Reference   For more information on indexes and tables of contents, see Chapter 7.

What can fields do?

You can create your own customized fields, but Word provides more than 70 fields for your use, grouped into categories by general purpose (to see them, choose Insert ⇨ Field). The names of these groups are a pretty good indication of how these fields are used:

Note   What follows here is only a brief introduction to the topic of fields: A complete exploration of all of the fields Word offers, and their options, would make a pretty good-sized book all on its own. However, once you know the basics of using fields, you can experiment with them on your own. How you use them depends on what you need them for and is really limited only by your imagination.

✦ **Date and Time.** Using these fields, you can automatically insert temporal information such as the current date and time; when the document was created, last printed, or last saved; and how much time was spent working on it.

✦ **Document Automation.** These fields enable you to perform tasks such as moving the insertion point, running macros, sending commands to a printer, inserting variables, comparing values, and carrying out conditional branching (i.e., if something has a certain value, print one bit of text; if it has a different value, print a different bit of text).

✦ **Document Information.** These fields insert information about the document itself, such as who created it, its size and name, how many pages it contains, and the comments included in its Summary Info.

✦ **Equations and Formulas.** Carry out calculations on numerical data using these fields. Others in this group enable you to offset the text that follows the field to the left, right, up, or down to make way for the calculated data.

✦ **Index and Tables.** These fields help you automatically construct tables of contents, indexes, and tables of authorities (used primarily in legal documents, a table of authorities is a list of references made within the document to other legal documents).

✦ **Links and References.** Insert AutoText items, graphics (this is useful for inserting graphics that may still be works in progress; as they change, the latest versions are automatically displayed in the Word document), links to files created in other programs, and other objects with these fields.

✦ **Mail Merge.** Most commonly used to personalize form letters, these fields enable you to combine saved data with a template to create individualized documents. (Because this is one of the most common uses of fields, we'll look at merging documents in detail in the section "Using Mail Merge," later in this chapter.)

✦ **Numbering.** Anything to do with numbering can be inserted with these fields, including page numbers, the number of times the document has been saved, the current section number, list elements, and more.

✦ **User Information.** The User Information tab in the Options dialog box (Tools Í Options) enables you to enter your name, initials, and mailing address. These fields automatically insert that information into your document. For example, when you use the Comment feature, the resulting Comment is "stamped" with your name as you entered it into the User Information dialog box.

Viewing fields

Much of the time, most fields are invisible, because what's important is the information they insert into the document, not the fields themselves. However, sometimes you may want to check which fields are at work, or edit them (many fields have options that you can change—for example, to alter how displayed information is formatted).

To see fields in a document, you have to turn them on by pressing Alt+F9. This displays all the fields in the document (see Figure 6-1). Pressing Alt+F9 toggles them off.

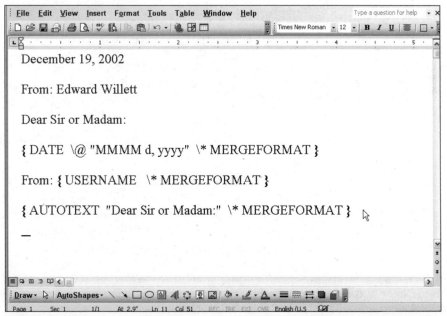

Figure 6-1: The same set of fields has been copied into this document twice. The top three lines show what the document looks like without the fields displayed; the bottom three lines show the fields that generated the top three lines.

To display a single field, place your insertion point inside it and press Shift+F9, or right-click and choose Toggle Field Codes from the shortcut menu. You can also use this method to display a selected group of fields.

Inserting fields

Inserting a field is very much like inserting anything else in Word. To insert a field:

1. Choose Insert ⇨ Field. This opens the Field dialog box (see Figure 6-2).

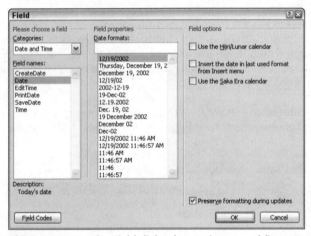

Figure 6-2: Use the Field dialog box to insert and fine-tune all the fields available in Word.

2. Choose the category of field you're interested in. In the figure, the Date and Time category is selected.

3. From the Field names list, choose the field you want to insert—in this case, Date.

4. Specify the field properties. These will differ greatly from field to field. In the case of Date, you have numerous formats from which to choose.

5. Check any field options you want to use from the list on the right.

You can take even greater control of any field by displaying the field code. Click the Field Codes button in the lower-left corner of the Field dialog box to display the code (see Figure 6-3).

Note   Some fields display the field code automatically when you choose them from the Field names list.

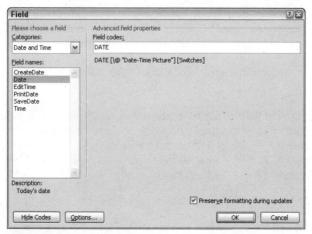

Figure 6-3: For real hands-on control of fields, edit the field code directly.

If you've experimented with field codes a lot, you might feel comfortable simply typing code in this dialog box. A better bet, though, is to click the Options button. This opens yet another dialog box, as shown in Figure 6-4.

Figure 6-4: The Field Options dialog box makes editing field codes much easier.

Field options are usually listed under two tabs, General Switches and Field Specific Switches. The Description area at the bottom of the dialog box provides a brief explanation of the effects of the various options as you click them.

When you're happy with your selection, click Add to Field. If you abruptly change your mind after doing so, there's no need to panic; just click Undo Add (grayed out in the figure because the option has not yet been added to the field).

Finally, click OK to return to the Field dialog box; click OK to insert the field in your document.

Tip   Word uses a backslash (\) in field codes to indicate that what follows is a switch (i.e., a command that sets one of the field's options) of some kind. This can be a problem if you're adding optional information, such as a file path, which uses the backslash character literally. To make a backslash character appear without messing up the field syntax, use it twice: for example, `C:\\Webpages\\FP Web\\index.htm`.

Updating fields

When you first insert a field, and whenever you open a saved document, the information displayed in it is current as of that moment. However, the whole point of fields is that they can display dynamic information, which means that by the time you print your document, the information displayed in the various fields may be out of date. Fortunately, you can update any or all fields at any time:

✦ To update a single field, click on it and press F9.

✦ To update several fields at once, highlight the area of the document that contains the fields you want to update and then press F9.

✦ To update all the fields in the document (except for fields in headers and footers and footnotes and endnotes — you'll have to update those separately), choose Edit ➪ Select All or press Ctrl+A, and then press F9.

This causes all the selected fields to calculate or fetch the latest version of the data they display — for example, the current time.

Tip   You can configure Word to update fields automatically upon printing. To do so, choose Tools ➪ Options and select the Print tab. Click Update fields in the Printing options area, and then click OK.

Formatting fields

As noted earlier, you can preset some field formatting from the Field dialog box — determining whether the date will be displayed as "Wednesday, January 14, 2004" or as "01/14/2004," for example. You can also format fields just as you do any other text, by highlighting them and using the formatting options discussed in detail in Chapter 4.

Tip If you want formatting that has been applied to a field to remain in place even after the content of the field changes because of updating — which it might if the information in the field is drawn from another document whose own formatting may have changed — make sure that the Preserve Formatting During Updates checkbox in the Field dialog box is checked when you insert the field into your document. Checking this box includes the * MERGEFORMAT switch in the field.

Using fields to perform calculations

As explained in Chapter 5, fields can be used to perform calculations on the contents of the cells of a table. They can also be used to perform calculations involving any other numerical data in your document, provided that data is either inserted by another field or has been bookmarked, so that the calculating field knows where to find it.

For example, suppose you've written a report that contains total annual sales figures from two different stores in two different locations in the document. Now you want to calculate the average monthly sales for the operation as a whole and include that figure in your closing paragraph. To do that, you would first have to bookmark the two stores' sales figures as, say, West and East.

Note To insert a bookmark, highlight the text you want bookmarked and then choose Insert ⇨ Bookmark. Type the name of the bookmark and then click Add. To go to a bookmark later, choose Edit ⇨ Go To, select Bookmark from the Go to what list box, and choose from the Enter bookmark name drop-down list the bookmark you want to go to.

Then you could create a field that will add the two and divide them by 12, as follows:

1. Place your insertion point where you want the figure displayed, and then choose Insert ⇨ Field.

2. Select (All) from the list of categories, and = (Formula) from the list of Field names (it appears at the top).

3. Click the Formula button that appears.

4. In the Formula dialog box (see Figure 6-5), enter the Formula in the text box at the top.

5. Choose a number format from the drop-down list. Because this is a monetary figure, I chose the format that includes the $ sign.

6. Click OK. The results of your calculation are displayed.

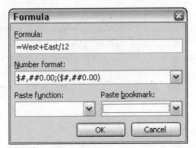

Figure 6-5: The formula entered in the field in the last paragraph adds the figures from the previous two paragraphs and divides the total by 12.

What makes formulas so powerful, in this and other instances, is that if you have to revise the information referenced in the formula, you don't have to recalculate the final result yourself; just update your fields, and the formula field recalculates and displays the new result.

Creating and Using Forms

Forms are documents that use one or more fields to enable you or someone else to easily enter data into the document. A good example of a form is the fax cover letter shown in Figure 6-6, one of the templates that come with Word. The fields in this form enable you to enter your own information in several places, and even to check off checkboxes. Another field automatically enters the date.

Most forms are set up as templates. This makes it easier to, for example, send out invoices that have the same look, while still individualizing the portions that need to be individualized—such as who's being billed, what for, and for how much.

Cross-Reference   For more information on templates, see Chapter 8.

To create a form, first create the information that won't change very often, if at all: the name of the form, the name and address of the company, logos or other graphics, and the like. Then, when you're ready to begin entering form fields, choose View ➪ Toolbars ➪ Forms to call up the Forms toolbar, shown in Figure 6-7. Insert and edit the fields as you see fit, and then save the document as a document template (*.dot) file.

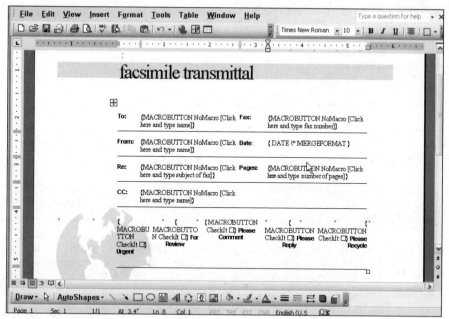

Figure 6-6: This fax template is a good example of a Word form.

Figure 6-7: The Forms toolbar provides all the tools you need to create your own forms.

The Forms toolbar

The Forms toolbar contains the controls you will most often need in order to create forms of any type:

✦ **Text Form Field.** One of the most common elements of a form is a place for the user to enter free-form text. Click this button to create such a field.

✦ **Check Box Form Field.** Checkboxes are also common elements in forms. Click this button to place a checkbox in your document. If the form is being filled out onscreen, a user can check or uncheck this box by clicking it.

✦ **Drop-Down Form Field.** This form field is useful in an onscreen form only. It creates a drop-down list from which the user can make a selection.

✦ **Form Field Options.** This lets you set various options (which we'll look at in detail in the next section of this chapter, "Inserting a form field") for any of the form fields.

✦ **Draw Table.** This opens the Tables and Borders toolbar. You can use this toolbar to create a table into which you can then enter static text or form fields.

Cross-Reference

See Chapter 5 for details about creating tables.

✦ **Insert Table.** This is the same as the Insert Table command, discussed in detail in Chapter 3. It enables you to insert a table of a size you specify.

Note

If you click an existing table and select a column, this button changes to Insert Columns; if you select a table row, it changes to Insert Rows; if you select a cell, it changes to Insert Cells.

✦ **Insert Frame.** This inserts a frame, a handy, resizable box that can be used to contain graphics or text. (It's similar to a text box, but more versatile, in that it can be used to position text or graphics that contain comments, footnotes, endnotes, and — important for forms — certain fields.)

✦ **Form Field Shading.** If you would like all the fields in your document to be shaded, so you can recognize them even when they aren't being displayed as fields, click this button to toggle that shading on (note that this shading appears on the screen only; it doesn't print). Click it again to turn the shading off.

✦ **Protect Form.** If you click this button, users can still enter data into your form fields, but they won't be able to modify the form fields.

Inserting a form field

To insert a text, checkbox, or drop-down form field, place your insertion point wherever in your document you want the field to appear, and then click the appropriate button on the Forms toolbar. Text and drop-down form fields appear as shaded rectangles (assuming you've activated Form Field Shading); checkbox form fields appear as shaded, black-bordered boxes.

Once you've inserted the field, you can fine-tune it by clicking on it and then clicking the Form Field Options button on the Forms toolbar, or simply by double-clicking it.

The Form Field Options dialog box offers different options for each type of form field.

Text form fields

When you insert a text form field, the Text Form Field Options dialog box looks like the one shown in Figure 6-8.

Figure 6-8: Use the Text Form Field Options dialog box to set the size and other specific properties of your text form field.

You have several options here to help you fine-tune your text form field:

✦ **Type.** From this drop-down list, choose what type of text you want entered in this field: regular (free-form) text, a number, a date, the current time, the current date, or a calculated value. Specifying the type of text restricts what the user may enter; for example, a number field will accept numbers only.

✦ **Default Text.** Type whatever you want to appear in the field by default, if any. Note that if you indicate that you want a number or date in the field, this box changes to Default Number or Default Date. If you choose to enter the current time or current date in the field, this box isn't available. If you've associated the field with a calculated value, then this is where you enter the formula that produces that value (see the section "Using fields to perform calculations," earlier in this chapter).

✦ **Maximum Length.** The default is Unlimited, but if you wish, you can specify the maximum length to which the text field can expand, in characters. This is useful in making sure the user enters only as much information as is necessary. For instance, you might set the maximum length of a field where the user enters his or her ZIP code to five digits (you can always add a second four-digit field for the +4 part of the code).

✦ **Text Format.** Use this drop-down list to specify the format for text entered in the text field. The list varies depending on what type of text you've chosen. For regular text, the options are limited to uppercase, lowercase, first capital, and title case; but for numbers and dates, you have many more options from which to choose.

In the next section of this dialog box, entitled Run macro on, you have two options:

✦ **Entry.** You can create macros for your form that will run when a user clicks on certain fields. If you want to associate a macro with a field, choose it from the list here.

✦ **Exit.** This is like Entry, except the macro you choose here runs when the user exits a field by pressing Tab (typically done to move successively through fields) or clicking outside it.

Cross-Reference   To learn more about creating macros, see Chapter 49.

Finally, in the bottom section of the Text Form Field Options dialog box you'll find the Field settings:

✦ **Bookmark.** This assigns a bookmark name to the field. As noted earlier, if you wish to perform calculations based on the input from a field, that field has to be locatable; a bookmark makes it so.

✦ **Fill-in enabled.** Check this box if you want the user to be able to fill in the field onscreen. If you just want it to display a predetermined value, preventing users from entering anything, uncheck this box.

✦ **Calculate on exit.** Check this if you want Word to recalculate the contents of the field once the user leaves it.

✦ **Add Help Text.** Click this button to create your own help messages, which will appear in Word's status bar and/or in a small message box when the user selects the field and presses F1.

Click OK when you're done choosing options.

Checkbox form fields

When you insert a checkbox form field and double-click on it or click the Form Properties button, you get different options in the dialog box (see Figure 6-9).

Figure 6-9: A Check Box Form Field, as you'd expect, has different properties you can specify.

Some of the options are exactly the same as in the Text Form Field Options dialog box: Entry and Exit, Bookmark, Check box enabled (the same thing as Fill-in enabled in the previous dialog box), Calculate on exit, and Add Help Text. However, there are a few differences:

✦ **Check box size.** In this area, you can choose Auto, which automatically adjusts the size of the checkbox to correspond to the size of the surrounding text, or Exactly, which lets you specify a size for the box, in points.

✦ **Default value.** There are two options: Not Checked or Checked.

Drop-down form fields

With drop-down form fields, you can create the same kind of drop-down lists Office itself (and most other Windows software) often presents you with. To create and edit such a list:

1. Place your insertion point where you want the drop-down list to appear and click the Drop-Down Form Field button on the Forms toolbar. The drop-down list initially looks like a text form field.

2. Double-click the form field to call up the Drop-Down Form Field Options dialog box (see Figure 6-10).

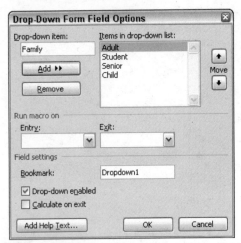

Figure 6-10: Use the Drop-Down Form Field Options dialog box to add whatever options you like to a drop-down list.

3. Type the first option you want in the list in the Drop-Down item text box, and click Add. Repeat this procedure until you've added all the options you want to the list.

4. To move an item up or down within the list — perhaps to place the most likely choice at the top, for instance — highlight it by clicking it, and then click the up or down arrows labeled Move. To remove an item, click on it, and then click Remove.

5. As with text form fields and checkbox form fields, you can assign a macro to run (when the user either clicks on the drop-down list or leaves it) by choosing the macros you want from the Entry and Exit lists. You can also assign a bookmark to the list, set it to perform a calculation when the user exits it, enable or disable it, and assign help text to it.

6. When you're satisfied with your drop-down list, click OK.

Note   You'll notice that as soon as you click OK, your drop-down list doesn't actually look like a drop-down list, and your checkbox doesn't behave like a checkbox (because you can't check it). That's because your form is still in an editable format, so that you can make changes to it. Drop-down lists and checkboxes don't begin acting the way they're supposed to until you protect the document — as described in the next section.

Protecting your form and fields

At the moment, your form is rather useless, because anyone using it is not only free to type in information but is also free to change what goes into text form fields, to fiddle with checkbox form fields, and to alter the list of items in drop-down list form fields. Generally, to make a form work, you have to protect your form — that is, you have to inform Word that only authorized people such as yourself should be allowed to alter the form's properties.

Protecting forms

To protect the forms in your document, click the Protect Form button on the Forms toolbar.

 Cross-Reference You can protect your document in other ways, too, to ensure that unauthorized people can't make changes to it. You can even stop unauthorized people from opening the file in the first place, by attaching a password to it. For more information about protecting your documents, see Chapter 46.

Locking fields

You can't protect the other fields in your document the same way you protect forms. Anyone who can change any other part of the document can change the fields. You can, however, lock individual fields so that they aren't updated when the rest of the fields in the document are. To lock an individual field, click on it and press Ctrl+F11. To unlock it, click on the locked field and press Shift+Ctrl+F11.

Using Mail Merge

"Mail merge" is a misleading term. Although it is probably most commonly used to create individualized form letters, address labels, and the like, it can in fact be used to merge any kind of data with any kind of document to create a single Word file containing a whole series of individualized documents. No matter what kind of document and data you're merging, the basic process is the same:

1. **Create the main document.** This is the "boilerplate," the part of the document that doesn't change regardless of what data is merged with it. If you're creating a form letter, for instance, this will probably include most of the letter's main body.

2. **Create the data that will be merged with the document.** This is the information that will be used to personalize each document — typically, names, addresses, and other data about the individuals for whom the document is intended. You can create this mail-merge data source directly in Word, or take it from an existing database.

3. **Define the merge fields in the main document.** These fields tell Word where to put the data from the data source—the first name after "Dear" in the salutation line, for instance.

4. **Merge the data and the main document.** Word follows your instructions to create a series of individualized documents based on the main document, each containing one set of data from the data source.

5. **Print.** You can print all the documents or a range of them because they're all part of a single Word document file.

It's helpful to know the process, but Word doesn't even require you to remember these steps on your own: It provides a handy Mail Merge Wizard that leads you through them one at a time.

The Mail Merge task pane

To begin a mail merge, choose Tools ⇨ Letters and Mailings ⇨ Mail Merge to open the Mail Merge task pane (shown in Figure 6-11), which takes you through the process of setting up and completing a mail merge step by step.

Figure 6-11: Word takes you though the mail merge process step by step.

Step 1: Select a document type

Select what type of document you are creating:

✦ **Letters.** These are letters in which the address, salutation, and any other information you want are personalized based on the information in your data source. When the mail merge is finished, you have a single Word file containing all the personalized letters. Because each one is its own section and they're separated by page breaks, it's easy to print a single letter, a range of them, or the entire set.

✦ **E-mail messages.** Just like a letter, but intended for electronic delivery; these can still be personalized.

✦ **Envelopes.** You specify the size of envelope you want to use, and then address them from your database.

✦ **Mailing Labels.** You specify the size of label you want to use, and then Word creates a main document for you that consists of a single page of appropriately sized labels. Each label contains the fields you specify. After the merge, you have a single document file consisting of many pages of labels. Unlike the form letters, all the labels are in one section.

✦ **Directory.** Whereas a form letter mail merge creates one document per record in the database, a directory creates one large document containing all the data, forming a list — descriptions and prices of various items for sale in your store, for instance, or a handy reference list of all the addresses to which you've sent letters.

Click Next.

Note | The remainder of this chapter takes you through the process of creating a form letter (because that's probably the most common use of mail merge); however, the differences between using mail merge for a form letter and for the other types of documents listed above are minor.

Step 2: Select a starting document

Now you have to select the method you want to use to set up your form letter. You have three options:

✦ **Use the current document.** You may have already written your letter and just want to insert recipient information, or you may be planning to write your letter from scratch. In either case, use this option.

✦ **Start from a template.** Word offers a number of templates that are ready to use; you just have to customize them. If you choose this option, you'll click the Select template link to locate the template you want to use.

✦ **Start from existing document.** If you've previously set up a mail merge document that you simply want to modify, choose this option. You'll be asked to specify the document you wish to use, of course.

For the purposes of this demonstration, I've chosen to work from the existing document.

Step 3: Select your recipients

Now it's time to specify the data you want to insert into your form letter. Again, you have three options:

✦ **Use an existing list.** If you've already entered the names and addresses of the people to whom you want to send this letter in a database, choose this option; a Browse link enables you to locate the database for Word.

✦ **Select from Outlook contacts.** If you want to send this list to people who are also entered in your Outlook address book, choose this option. You can then browse through your contacts and specify the ones to whom you want to send the letter.

✦ **Type a new list.** If you haven't yet entered into a database the information you want to use to personalize your letter, you can do so by choosing this option and clicking the Create link provided. This opens the New Address List dialog box shown in Figure 6-12.

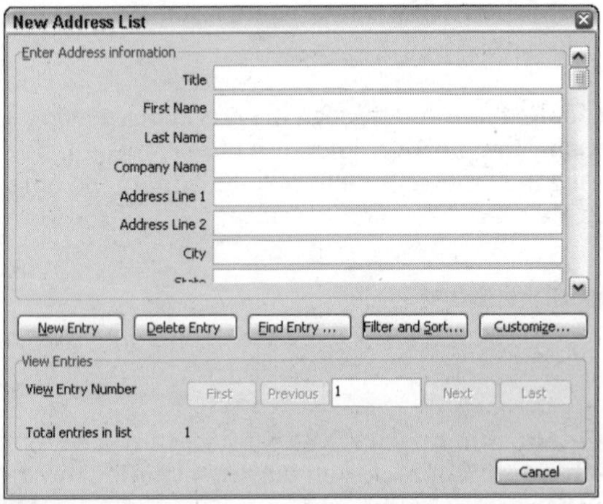

Figure 6-12: To create a new address list, enter information here.

The New Address List dialog box enables you to enter data in a number of fields that reflect the kind of information most often used in form letters. To create a new entry, click the New Entry button. If you make a mistake and want to delete an entry, click the Delete Entry button.

If you want to enter fields into your address list that aren't provided by default, click the Customize button. This opens a dialog box that enables you to add, delete, rename and re-order the fields in the New Address List dialog box. If, for example, your form letter refers to the recipient's spouse, you might want to create a new field labeled "Spouse's First Name."

Once you've created a list, or if you choose an existing list, you'll see a new link in the Mail Merge task panel, labeled Edit recipient list. Click this link to open the Mail Merge Recipients dialog box (see Figure 6-13), which provides additional options for fine-tuning your list. You can edit individual entries, uncheck the checkboxes to the left of the entries to keep entries from being used, or find a specific entry in a long list by clicking the Find button at the bottom.

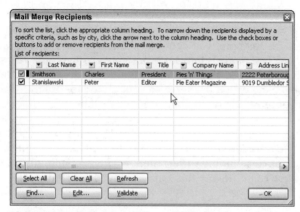

Figure 6-13: Edit your address list here.

To sort the members of your list alphabetically, click any of the column headings. To narrow the scope of recipients, click the downward pointing arrow next to any column heading and choose the Advanced option from the resulting menu. This opens the Filter and Sort dialog box shown in Figure 6-14.

Note   You can also access the Filter and Sort dialog box by clicking the Filter and Sort button in the New Address List dialog box.

Click the Filter Records tab to gain detailed control over which records are used in the mail merge. Choose the field you want to filter in the first column and then choose the type of comparison you want to make (equal, not equal, greater than, less than, greater than or equal, less than or equal, blank or not blank), and enter what you want to compare the field with.

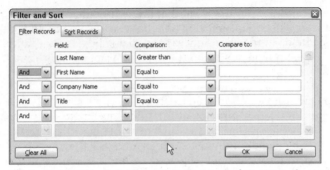

Figure 6-14: This dialog box gives you complete control over what data you use in your mail merge.

Tip

You can create extremely fine filters, up to six layers deep, by using all the blanks in the Filter Records tab. For instance, you could filter out everyone whose last name begins with W, whose first name is Edward, whose area code is 306, whose local phone exchange is 569, whose street address is between 2300 and 2400, and who lives in a city beginning with the letter R — if you wanted to. Use the small list boxes at the left to choose AND or OR to apply additional filters.

The other tab, Sort Records, enables you to sort your records by up to three fields. Enter the first field you want to sort the records by in the first blank, and whether you want to sort in ascending or descending order; then, in the remaining blanks, enter the fields you'd like to use to settle any ties among records sorted by the first field.

Once you've selected your data source, you can proceed to Step 4 of the Mail Merge process.

Step 4: Write your letter

Write your letter in the document space just as you normally would. When you come to a point in your letter where you need to enter recipient information to personalize it, you can add the necessary field.

The Mail Merge task pane offers an address block or a greeting line automatically (providing you with a number of formatting options when you select one of those options), or you can click More items to open the Insert Merge Field dialog box (see Figure 6-15), which includes all available fields.

If your database includes additional information that isn't available here (this is most likely to happen if you're using an existing database), choose Match Fields; this dialog box (see Figure 6-16) enables you to choose which fields, if any, in your database match additional options, such as Web Page URL or Spouse Middle Name, or to correct any mismatches between what Word thinks is in a particular column of information in your database and what really is there (which could arise if fields in Word and in the database have the same name but different purposes — for instance, if the database you're merging into your Word document uses "Title" for a field that contains the titles of books, instead of personal titles like Dr. and Mrs.).

Once your letter has been written, you can move on to the next step.

Figure 6-15: Use this list to choose which fields from your database you want to insert into your document.

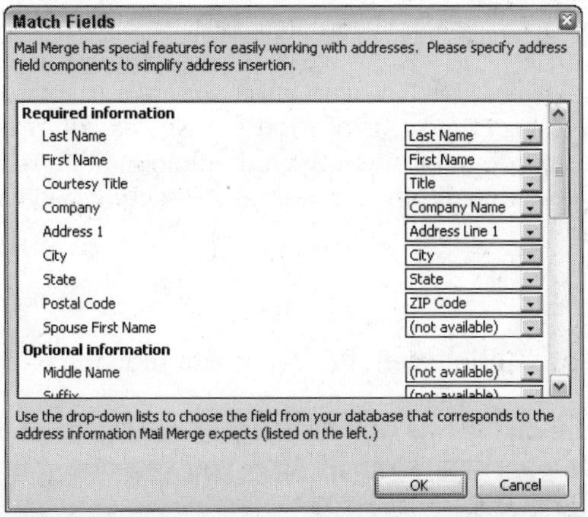

Figure 6-16: Use additional information from your databases by matching it with the correct name here.

Step 5: Preview your letters

Here's where you can verify that your form letters will look the way they're supposed to look with the personalized information added into them. In Figure 6-17, the merged information is highlighted; you can move from letter to letter using the buttons in the Preview your letters section of the task pane.

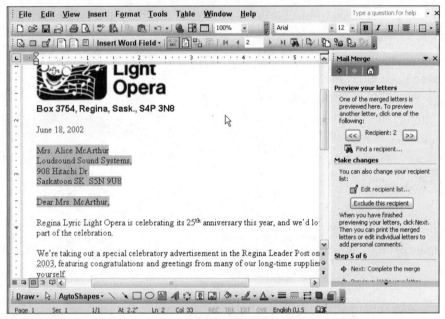

Figure 6-17: Here's what a form letter looks like when you preview it.

You can also change your recipient list on the basis of what you see as you preview your letters. If you simply want to exclude a recipient from the final mail merging, note that there's a button for that; if you need to edit your entire recipient list again, there's a link for that, too.

Step 6: Complete the merge

You're almost done! There are just two options left: Print and Edit individual letters.

If you choose Print, you'll see a small dialog box that asks if you want to print all the records, just the current one, or a particular range. After you've made your choice, you'll see the usual Print dialog box.

If you choose Edit individual letters, a nearly identical dialog box will again ask you if you want to merge all the records, just the current one, or a range of them. The records you choose to merge will be added to a new Word document that contains all of the resulting letters. You can then go through them one at a time and edit them as usual, to further personalize them.

The Mail Merge toolbar

If you look again at Figure 6-17, you'll see there's a new toolbar in view, beneath the Standard and Formatting toolbars. This is the Mail Merge toolbar, which contains a useful selection of tools to help you with your mail merge efforts. From left to right, they include the following:

✦ **Main document setup.** This is a quick way to set up a document for mail merge. Options include Letters, E-mail messages, Envelopes, Labels, and Directory. You can also turn a mail merge document back into a normal Word document (in other words, remove the mail merge information from it).

✦ **Open data source.** This opens a standard browsing window with which you can track down and open the data source you'd like to use in your mail merge document.

✦ **Mail Merge Recipients.** This opens the Mail Merge Recipients dialog box (refer to Figure 6-13).

✦ **Insert Address Block.** This inserts an address block like the one in the letter shown in Figure 6-17. (You first see a dialog box that enables you to specify exactly how you want the address block to look.)

✦ **Insert Greeting Line.** This inserts a greeting line like the one in the letter shown in Figure 6-17. Again, you first see a dialog box that enables you to specify how you want the greeting line to look.

✦ **Insert Merge Fields.** This opens the Insert Merge Field dialog box (refer to Figure 6-15).

✦ **Insert Word Field.** Use this button to insert other useful Word fields — for instance, the Merge Record number.

✦ **View Merged Data.** This enables you to preview your mail merge document with the data inserted.

✦ **Highlight Merge Fields.** Puts gray highlighting over the merge fields in your document, so you can see exactly where the data from your database has been inserted (this option is turned on in Figure 6-17). Remember, this shading doesn't print.

✦ **Match Fields.** This opens the Match Fields dialog box (refer to Figure 6-16).

✦ **Propagate Labels.** When you're using mail merge to create mailing labels, this command saves you time by copying the fields from one label to all the other labels in a mail merge document.

✦ **First Record, Previous Record, Go to Record, Next Record, Last Record.**
Use these controls to navigate through your merged document.

✦ **Find Entry.** This option enables you to search for a particular record by
keyword.

✦ **Check for Errors.** Click this button to check your merged document for errors
before you print it. You're given three options: You can simulate the merge
and get an error report in a new document, proceed with the merge and see
any errors as they occur, or simply proceed with the merge and get a report of
all the errors that occurred when it's over.

✦ **Merge to New Document, Merge to Printer, Merge to E-Mail, Merge to Fax.**
Use these buttons to choose the final output of the mail merge procedure.

Summary

In this chapter you learned ways to use dynamic, changeable data in Word documents, how to create forms, and how to carry out a mail merge. Major points
included the following:

✦ Fields are Word's way of letting you insert dynamic data — information that
changes from time to time — into your document.

✦ To insert a field, choose Insert ➪ Field, and then choose the type of field you
want from the list.

✦ Fields displaying ever-changing data have to be updated from time to time.
Use F9 to update a single field or range of fields.

✦ Fields can be used to carry out complex calculations that draw on information
contained elsewhere in your document.

✦ Use the Forms toolbar to create professional-looking forms that include text
fields, checkboxes, and even drop-down lists.

✦ The Mail Merge task pane takes you step by step through the process of creating individualized form letters or other merged documents.

✦ You can create the data for a mail merge yourself in Word or use other
databases, including those from Access and Excel — and even draw information from Outlook address books.

✦ Query options provide powerful filtering tools to help you merge only the
records you want.

✦   ✦   ✦

Outlines, Tables of Contents, and Indexes

Good organization is crucial to the success of any document. If the information presented isn't in some sort of logical order, it's much harder for the reader to understand. That not only undermines communication (the primary purpose of creating a document in the first place), it also undermines your credibility.

Fortunately, Word provides several organizational tools that can help you present your thoughts in crystal-clear fashion and make it easier for your readers to find the information they're looking for within your documents.

What Is an Outline?

In Word, an outline is a hierarchical listing of the headings within a document. This book, like most nonfiction books, began life as an outline, and that outline can still be traced in the various levels of headings that appear in each chapter. Major headings, like "What Is an Outline?" above, use the largest type; each subsequent level of heading uses slightly smaller type or other typographic devices to indicate subordination. All sub-subheadings relate in some way to the subheadings they're grouped under, which in turn relate in some way to the major heading under which they are grouped.

Word includes, as part of its Normal template, several levels of heading styles. By using these styles for your headings (Heading 1 for main headings, Heading 2 for subheadings, Heading 3 for sub-subheadings, and so forth) as you build your outline, you can create an organizational structure that's easy to modify and easy to move around in within Word.

Using Outline View

Word offers a special view, Outline view, to help you work with outlines. A typical outline in Outline view looks something like the one shown in Figure 7-1, which is an outline for a chapter of this book. You can turn on Outline view by choosing View ➪ Outline.

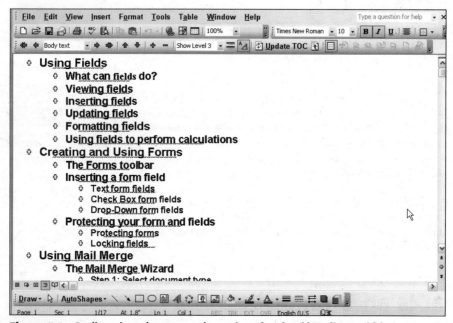

Figure 7-1: Outline view shows you the various levels of headings within your document.

In Outline view, Word automatically indents headings to show their relative importance to one another. In addition, it enables you to view only the level of headings that you want by using the Show Level drop-down list on the Outlining toolbar, which you can see in Figure 7-1 just above the document window. Clicking on this list enables you to view only those levels of the outline you want to see, from Level 1 all the way down to Level 9. You can also choose Show All Levels to see the entire outline, including paragraphs that don't use a heading style.

To the right of the Show Level drop-down list is the Show First Line Only button. Click this to see only the first line of all the paragraphs in your document (of all the styles you're viewing).

To the right of the Show First Line Only button is the Show/Hide Formatting button; click this to toggle formatting (e.g., different fonts, italics, underlined text) on and off.

Tip I recommend keeping formatting off while you're using Outline view to organize your document. Heading styles vary from template to template, which can be both distracting and confusing when you want to concentrate on organization instead of looks.

You'll examine the other buttons on the Outlining toolbar in the next section.

Creating and Modifying Outlines

All you have to do to create an outline is assign each level of the outline the appropriate heading style: Heading 1 for top-level heads, Heading 2 for subheads, and so on. You can write your outline first and then assign heading styles as appropriate, or you can assign heading styles as you work. It doesn't matter.

Rearranging your outline

Rearranging the order of your outline is also easy. If you're not already in Outline view, choose View ➪ Outline to get there. The buttons and drop-down list on the left end of the Outlining toolbar are controls for quickly and easily reorganizing your outline—and your thoughts. Place your cursor anywhere inside the outline element you want to rearrange, and then press the appropriate button or choose from the drop-down list the level you want to assign that element.

From left to right, these outlining controls are as follows:

✦ **Promote to Heading 1.** This makes the element a top-level heading.

✦ **Promote.** This moves the selected item one notch higher in the hierarchy by assigning it the next-highest outline level.

✦ **Outline level.** You can choose any of the nine available outline levels, or body text, from this drop-down list.

✦ **Demote.** This moves the selected item one notch lower in the hierarchy, assigning it the next-lowest outline level.

✦ **Demote to Body Text.** This assigns the Normal style to the selected item.

✦ **Move Up.** This moves the selected item above the item above it. The outline level doesn't change.

✦ **Move Down.** This moves the selected item below the item below it. Again, the outline level doesn't change.

Note Text associated with a selected item doesn't move; in other words, if you have normal text underneath text formatted as a heading and use Move Down on the heading, it will move underneath the normal text; the normal text doesn't move with it.

Using outline paragraph levels

Although the Heading 1, 2, 3, and so forth styles are assigned outline levels 1, 2, 3, etc., and can't be changed, you can apply the same outline levels to other paragraph styles. For example, you could choose to make Normal style correspond to outline level 1, just as Heading 1 style does. This capability to apply styles gives you enormous flexibility in designing your outline.

Word offers you nine outline levels. You can't change the outline levels assigned to various paragraph styles directly from Outline view, oddly enough; instead, you have to return to Normal or Print Layout view. Once you've done that, click on the paragraph to which you want to apply an outline level and then either choose Format ➪ Paragraph or right-click and choose Paragraph from the shortcut menu. Either method will open the Paragraph dialog box shown in Figure 7-2.

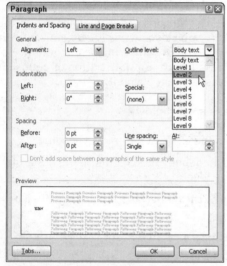

Figure 7-2: The Paragraph dialog box enables you to apply one of nine outline levels to your paragraphs.

Choose an outline level from the Outline Level drop-down list. To remove an existing outline level, choose Body Text.

Tip Because these effects can't be seen in Normal or Print Layout view, using outline paragraph levels enables you to "invisibly" outline a document. You could, for example, use levels simply to remind yourself which paragraphs are most important—in case you have to later shorten the document—without someone reading a printed copy ever being able to tell.

To view the results of your outline paragraph levels, switch to Outline view (see Figure 7-3). Level 1 paragraphs are flush with the left margin, Level 2 paragraphs are indented, and Level 3 paragraphs are indented still farther. Body text paragraphs are always indented one level further than the heading level they are within. Note that the paragraph outline levels are independent of the heading levels.

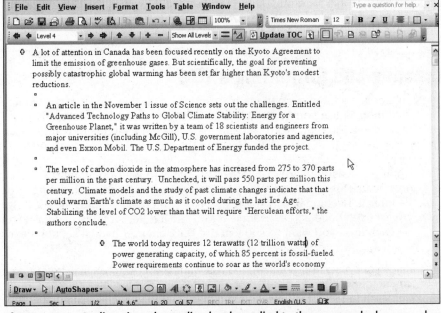

Figure 7-3: In Outline view, the outline levels applied to the paragraphs become clear.

Tip An outline not only keeps you organized, but it also makes it easier to move around in a lengthy document. By going to Outline view and collapsing a lengthy document to first-level heads alone, you can effectively shrink the document to a size much easier to work with—it might fit on one page instead of a hundred. Then you can simply click on the heading of the section you want to work on and expand it, make your changes, and then collapse that section again. This can save you a lot of scrolling.

Printing an outline

You can print an outline just as you would any other document. Go to Outline view, collapse or expand sections as you see fit, and then choose File ➪ Print or click the Print button on the Standard toolbar.

Building a Table of Contents

Another organizational tool Word offers is an automated method of creating a table of contents. A table of contents (TOC) is very similar to an outline in that it displays the information contained within a document in the form of a series of headings, usually arranged in a hierarchical format. In Word, however, the big difference between an outline and a table of contents is that the table of contents also lists the page in the document on which the information can be found.

Creating and formatting a TOC

You could create a table of contents by printing an outline, printing the whole document, and then figuring out on which page the various headings fall. Fortunately, you don't have to do that. Word will automatically build a table of contents for you, and let you format it as you see fit. Here are the steps to create a table of contents:

1. Apply a consistent series of paragraph styles to your document. The simplest ones to use are the same ones you use to create an outline: Heading 1, Heading 2, Heading 3, and so on. If you haven't used heading styles, however, you can still build a TOC as long as you use a different style in your document for each level you want to show in the TOC: chapter heads, section heads, and so forth.

2. Place your insertion point where you want the TOC to be inserted in your document, choose Insert ➪ Reference ➪ Index and Tables, and click the Table of Contents tab (see Figure 7-4).

3. The window at the left shows you what your TOC will look like in a printed document; the window at the right shows you what your TOC will look like in a Web document. In Print Preview, by default, page numbers are displayed and right-aligned, and a tab leader is already assigned. You can remove the page numbers and the right alignment, and remove or change the tab leader, as you see fit. (In the Web version, by default, your TOC entries are direct links to the appropriate pages, although you can change that by unchecking Use hyperlinks instead of page numbers.)

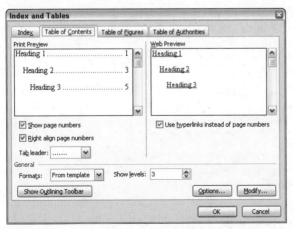

Figure 7-4: The Index and Tables dialog box includes controls for designing and formatting a table of contents for your document.

4. By default, your TOC is formatted in the way your current template calls for, which is relatively standard if you're using the Normal template. Word offers you a list of other formats from which to choose in the Formats drop-down list. Select each to see it previewed, and then choose the one you want. In addition, choose how many levels you want in your TOC. If you're using the From template option in the Formats drop-down list, you can click the Modify button to see all the available TOC styles in the current template, and alter any one of them by clicking on it, then clicking the Modify button.

5. Click Options to open the Table of Contents Options dialog box, which lists the currently available styles and shows you which ones Word is currently looking for to include in the TOC. By default, TOC level 1 is assigned to paragraphs with Heading 1 style, TOC level 2 to those with Heading 2, and so on. If you outlined your document in the usual way, these default options should work well for your table of contents. If you didn't, however, you can scroll through the list of styles to find the ones that you did apply to your headings, and indicate which level of the TOC you'd like items bearing those styles to appear as. Type the TOC level you'd like to assign to it in the space next to each style's name.

6. Click OK to return to the Index and Tables dialog box.

7. Click OK to insert the TOC into your document (see Figure 7-5).

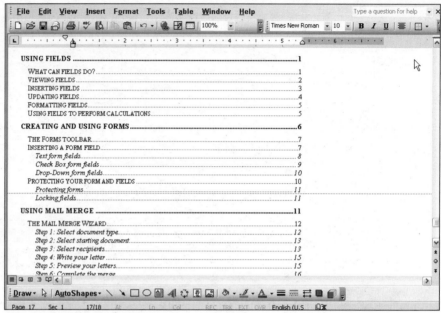

Figure 7-5: A newly inserted table of contents looks something like this. This example uses the Formal template.

Keeping your TOC current

The entries in the table of contents are built using a field code. This is helpful because as headings and page numbers change as a result of editing of the document, you can keep the TOC current simply by updating the field code. To do so, right-click on any entry in the TOC and choose Update Field from the shortcut menu. In the dialog box that appears, choose whether you want to update only the page numbers or both the page numbers and the TOC entries' names, and then click OK.

Cross-Reference   For more information on editing, formatting, and updating field codes, see Chapter 6.

Building a Table of Figures

A table of figures is a list of all the figures, equations, or illustrations in a document. Building one is very similar to building a table of contents: Word looks for a set of elements that all have the same style (the bullet style, for instance, or the style applied to figure captions), and places them in a table linked to the pages on which they appear. To create a table of figures (TOF), follow these steps:

1. Consistently apply a style to your figures or their captions.

2. Place your insertion point where you want the TOF to appear and choose Insert ➪ Reference ➪ Index and Tables, and then click the Table of Figures tab.

3. In the resulting dialog box, essentially identical to the TOC dialog box, Word shows you what your TOF will look like in print and in a Web document. For the print version, you can choose whether or not to display page numbers and whether you want them right-aligned with a tab leader, whether to include a label and number (e.g., Figure 3), and which items you want to include in the table: Captions (the default), Equations, Figures, or Tables. (By repeating this process and changing this option, you can create separate tables that list each type of item.)

4. Choose which format to apply to your table of figures.

5. Click Options to open the Table of Figures Options dialog box. Choose the style you want Word to look for when selecting the items to be included in your TOF.

6. Click OK to return to the Index and Tables dialog box.

7. Click OK to insert the TOF into your document.

Building a Table of Authorities

A table of authorities is used primarily in legal documents — it's a list of references made to other legal documents. Although the process is essentially the same as building a table of contents or a table of figures, marking the citations you want to add to the table is a little more complicated than simply assigning each the same style.

Marking citations

To mark citations, follow these steps:

1. Select the first full citation.

2. Choose Insert ➪ Reference ➪ Index and Tables, and then select the Table of Authorities tab.

3. Click Mark Citation. This opens the Mark Citation dialog box shown in Figure 7-6.

4. In the Selected Text box, edit the long citation until it looks the way you want it to appear in the table of authorities. (You can also format it using keyboard shortcuts such as Ctrl+B to bold it, Ctrl+I to italicize it, and so on.)

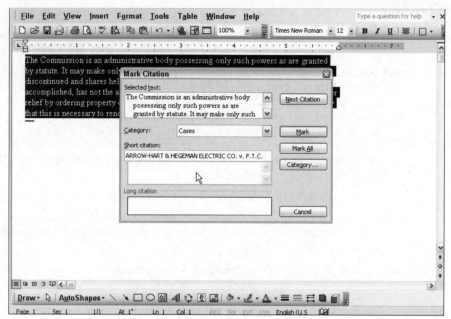

Figure 7-6: Use this dialog box to mark your citations before creating your table of authorities.

5. Select the category that applies to the citation from the Category drop-down list.

6. In the Short Citation text box, enter any short versions of the citation that appear in the document, so Word can search for them.

7. To mark a single citation, click Mark; to mark all the citations that match both the long and short versions you've just entered, click Mark All.

8. To move to the next marked citation in the document, click Next Citation. To mark another citation, return to the document, highlight it, and then repeat the preceding steps.

9. Once you've marked all your citations, click Close.

Inserting your TOA

You can insert a table of authorities (TOA) just as you would a table of contents or a table of figures. Place your insertion point where you want the TOA to appear. Then, as before, open the Index and Tables dialog box. From the Table of Authorities tab, perform the following steps:

1. Click the category of citation you want to include in your TOA, or click All to include them all.

2. Choose the format you want to use from the Formats list box.

3. If you want to replace any instance of five or more page references to the same citation with the text "passim" (Latin for "spread" or "scattered"), make sure the Use passim checkbox is checked.

4. If you want to keep the original formatting of long citations in the TOA, make sure Keep original formatting is checked.

5. Click OK.

Creating an Index

Personally, I can think of few things more annoying than a lengthy reference article or book without an index — especially these days, when people are accustomed to the search function built into so many Web sites. A good index isn't as handy as that, but it's as close as you can get in a printed document.

Creating an index by hand is a tedious and difficult task. Fortunately, Word can simplify the procedure for you somewhat (although it can't take it out of your hands altogether). Just as with building the various sorts of tables discussed earlier, Word does require you to first mark the words or phrases that are to be included in the index. You can do this using one word or phrase at a time, or you can use a concordance file (discussed in the section "Using a concordance file," later in this chapter) to semi-automate the process.

Marking words and phrases

Here are the steps to create an index by marking individual words and phrases:

1. Start at the very beginning (a very good place to start). Locate the first word or phrase you want to include in the index.

2. Highlight it, and then choose Insert ➪ Reference ➪ Index and Tables.

3. Click the Index tab and choose Mark Entry. This opens the Mark Index Entry dialog box (see Figure 7-7). The word or phrase you highlighted appears in the Main entry text box.

Tip   You can quickly get to the Mark Index Entry dialog box by pressing Alt+Shift+X.

4. If you want to add another word or phrase as a subentry under the main entry, type it into the Subentry text box.

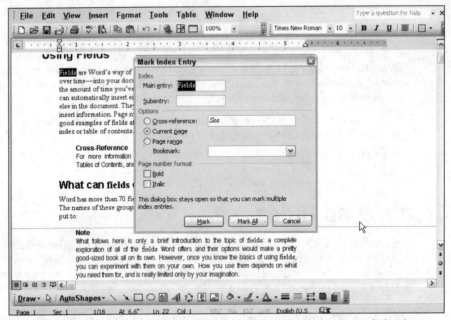

Figure 7-7: Build an index word by word using the Mark Index Entry dialog box.

5. Sometimes, instead of indicating a page number, you want to point readers to a different entry in the index. If that's the case, click the Cross-reference radio button and enter the appropriate text in the Cross-reference text box.

6. By default, Word inserts the page number of the highlighted word or phrase into the index. This is what the Current page option does.

7. If you'd prefer to have Word insert a range of pages instead of a single page number, click Page range. (You can do this only if you've already bookmarked the range; you select the range by choosing the correct bookmark from the Bookmark drop-down list.)

8. If you'd like page numbers to be in bold or italic, click the appropriate Page number format checkboxes.

9. Once you're satisfied with your choices, click Mark to mark the current selection as you've indicated, or click Mark All to mark every instance of the highlighted text within the document (but remember, this will mark every instance of the text — even instances you might not ordinarily index, such as uses of that text in excerpts from other sources).

10. Repeat this procedure with every word or phrase you want to add to the index.

Using a concordance file

The other method of creating an index, with the use of a concordance file, is particularly useful if many of the documents you create contain the same keywords or phrases. If you're already looking for a tool on any of the Word toolbars to help you create a concordance file, you can stop looking: It doesn't exist. A concordance file is simply a separate Word file set up as a two-column table.

Creating a concordance file

To create a concordance file, follow these steps:

1. Create a two-column table.

2. In the left-hand column, enter the text you want Word to search for and mark as an index entry.

3. In the right-hand column, type the text you want to appear in the index for that entry. You can create a subentry by typing the main entry followed by a colon, and then the text for the subentry.

4. Do the same for every other word or phrase for which you want Word to search and create an index entry.

5. When you're done, save the concordance file. (You can use any name you want.)

Marking index entries

Once you have a concordance file, you can use it to quickly mark index entries in any document. To do so, do the following:

1. Open the document you want to index.

2. Choose Insert ⇨ Reference ⇨ Index and Tables, and click the Index tab.

3. Choose AutoMark.

4. Word shows you the standard Open File dialog box; find the concordance file and then click Open. Word searches for the words and phrases you entered in the left-hand column and marks them as you indicated in the right-hand column.

Building your index

Once you've marked all the entries for your index, either one at a time or with a concordance file, you're ready to create your index:

1. Place your insertion point wherever you want the index to appear (typically at the end of the document, but it doesn't have to be).

2. Choose Insert ➪ Reference ➪ Index and Tables, and click the Index tab if it isn't already selected.

3. In the resulting dialog box, select a format for your index from the Format drop-down list. You can see what each format looks like in the Print Preview box.

4. Fine-tune the formatting with the other controls: You can right-align the page numbers and add a tab leader, change the number of columns used to display the index, and either indent subentries or simply run them straight on after the main entry.

5. Once you're satisfied with your formatting choices, click OK. Your index will be automatically inserted into your document in a new section of its own.

Keeping your index current

As with the three types of reference tables (table of contents, table of figures, and table of authorities), what you really end up with is a series of field codes, which you can update at any time to reflect the changing page numbers of the words and phrases you've marked as index entries. Just place the insertion point anywhere in the index and press F9, or right-click and choose Update Field from the shortcut menu.

Summary

Word's organizational tools make it easy for you to present your message in clear, unambiguous fashion and also make it easier for your reader to find specific information within your document.

✦ Outline View helps you organize your thoughts and then play around with that organization as you construct your document.

✦ Word can automatically create a table of contents, table of figures, or table of authorities for you based on the styles you apply to specific headings and other items.

✦ Word offers several built-in styles for tables of contents, authorities, and figures; you can also modify those styles as you see fit.

✦ Word can't quite build an index for you automatically, but it can shorten the procedure. It's still up to you to mark the text you want referenced in the index.

✦ A concordance file can make building an index easier; it's simply a two-column table with the left-hand column containing the words or phrases you want Word to mark for indexing in the finished document and the right-hand column containing the text that will refer to those words or phrases in the finished index.

✦ Tables of contents, tables of authorities, tables of figures, and indexes are all built on field codes and thus can be updated at any time by pressing F9.

✦   ✦   ✦

Styles and Templates

Styles and templates are one of the greatest timesavers Word has to offer—and one of the best ways to ensure that all your documents look their best and (just as important) have a look consistent with that of other, related documents.

Best of all, they're easy to use—as you'll see in this chapter.

What Are Styles?

A style is a set of preset formats for text—size, font, indent, and so on—that is given a name. You can apply a style to a paragraph of text, or to a few words, and all the formatting is done at once. For example, as I'm writing this book, I'm using a set of styles provided by the publisher. There's one style for the chapter title, another for major headings within the chapter, another for figure captions, another for Tips and Cross-References. Using the styles provided saves both me and my editors a lot of manual formatting.

Cross-
Reference
Styles are also used to format automatic tables of contents and outlines. See Chapter 7 for more information.

One of the major advantages of using styles is that when you make a change to a style (for example, you decide to change the font of your headings), all the paragraphs using that style also change, throughout your document. This saves you searching through your document and changing each paragraph individually (unless some of those paragraphs have had additional character formatting applied).

Types of styles

There are four types of styles: paragraph, character, table, and list:

✦ **Paragraph styles.** These styles, as the name implies, format an entire paragraph. Paragraph styles can include not just font type and size but any formatting that can be applied to paragraphs, including alignment, indents, space above and below, and justification. The style called "Normal" is the default paragraph style. This means that if you do not choose another style, all text is formatted with the Normal style.

Be aware that there is both a Normal style and a Normal template (covered later in this chapter) — it's easy to confuse the two. You can recognize a paragraph style when it's listed in the Styles and Formatting task pane (see Figure 8-1 in the next section of this chapter) by the paragraph symbol (¶) that appears beside it.

✦ **Character styles.** These styles are used to format words and phrases instead of whole paragraphs. Unlike paragraph styles, they do not deal with alignment, indents, spacing, and so forth. You could use a character style if you regularly need to highlight words in your document by making them, say, bold, italic, and red. The character style called Default Paragraph Font contains the same character formatting information as the Normal paragraph style. (You can use a paragraph style as a character style — it just ignores all the alignment and indent information.) Character styles can include only the formatting options that are available when you choose Format ⇨ Font, Format ⇨ Borders and Shading, or Tools ⇨ Language. Character styles are identified in the Styles and Formatting task pane by an underlined a̲.

✦ **Table styles.** Do you want all your tables to look the same throughout your document? A table style can include everything from text formatting to borders and shading to vertical and horizontal alignment within cells. You can create table styles that apply to the entire table or just to portions of it — just the header row, for instance, or the first column. Table styles are identified in the Styles and Formatting task pane by a grid icon.

✦ **List styles:** Once you've perfected the look of a list, make it a style and use it repeatedly. List styles enable you to choose whether to start the list with a bullet, number, or symbol, and set indenting and other formatting. As with tables, you can apply different styles to different parts of the list: level 1, level 2, level 3, and so on. List styles are identified in the Styles and Formatting task pane with a small icon of a list.

Saving style information

When you save any document, the styles used within it are also saved, so they're automatically available the next time you edit that document. However, if you want to use those styles in another document, you have to copy them from the first document to the second. If you find you need to use the same styles repeatedly in a multitude of documents, it's time to create a template.

What Are Templates?

A template is a special Word document with the filename extension .dot that is used to maintain a consistent look from document to document. Word comes with pre-fabricated templates for many common types of documents, including letters and faxes, memos, reports, newsletters, and Web pages.

In a template, all the unchanging items — the company logo and company name and address, for example, in the case of a letterhead — are inserted automatically. As a result, when you create a document using a template, all the fixed text and pictures are already in place, and you need only to enter your document-specific text.

Templates also contain styles, as well as macros and any changes that have been made to Word's default menus, keyboard shortcuts, and toolbar settings. Using the styles included with the template ensures that all documents created using that template will use the same fonts, sizes, alignment, and so forth. For example, in the Contemporary Report template (see Figure 8-1), styles are provided for the document title, chapter and part titles and subtitles, body text, and more.

In addition to the many templates you can use as is or modify, Word provides several wizards to help you automatically create faxes, letters, and other documents.

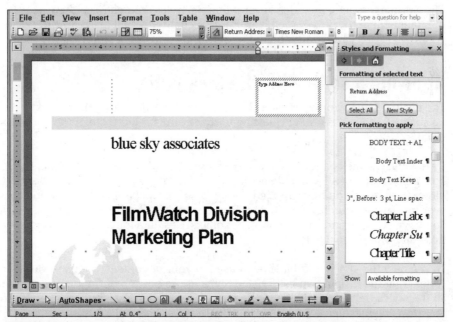

Figure 8-1: This document is based on the Contemporary Report template that comes with Word. Different styles (shown in the Styles and Formatting task pane on the right) are used to format the various sections of the report.

The Template That Wrote This Book (with a little help from the author)

Templates are very useful for long documents. This book is a good example: It was written using a special template created by the publisher for all the books in its Bible series.

The page formats and the styles for the headings, bullets, lists, and so on, which all stay the same from book to book, are stored in the template. This ensures that all the Bible books have the same "look," and also makes the formatting of each book a quick and simple task.

Note   Actually, all documents are based on templates — even the blank document Word opens automatically when you start the program. The default template is called Normal.dot; if you haven't chosen another template, that's the one you're working with. You can configure Word so that new documents are based on any template.

Applying Word's Built-in Styles

The Normal template includes several built-in styles. You can use them as they are or change them to suit yourself. Later in this chapter, you'll learn how to create your own styles and modify them, but in this section you'll simply apply them.

Applying a style with the task pane

The easiest way to apply a style is to open the Styles and Formatting task pane. To do so, click the Styles and Formatting button at the far-left edge of the Formatting toolbar.

By default, the task pane shows you the formatting of the selected text in the top box, and a menu of all available formatting. "Available formatting" includes any direct formatting you have applied — that is, formatting applied in addition to whatever formatting is dictated by the style of a particular section of text — any styles you have created, and three built-in heading styles. In a long, complex document, this can be an extensive list.

To see only the styles that have been used in your document, choose Available styles from the drop-down list labeled Show at the bottom of the task pane. To see all the styles that are available in the template you're using, choose All styles from the drop-down list.

Note Although this is called All styles, it doesn't necessarily show you all of the styles. Some may not be displayed. To precisely set which styles are displayed when you choose All styles, choose Custom from the Show drop-down list and check the styles you want to be visible from the Styles to be visible list.

To apply a style, simply select (in the manner indicated in the following list) the text to which you want to apply the style, and then click on the name of the style you want to use in the list in the task pane.

Select the text to be formatted as follows:

✦ If you want to apply a style to an entire paragraph, place the insertion point anywhere in the paragraph.

✦ If you want to apply a style to several consecutive paragraphs, highlight the paragraphs to be changed.

✦ If you want to apply a style to selected text only, highlight the text to be changed. It's best to apply formatting like this after you've applied a paragraph style; otherwise the paragraph style will override the formatting applied to just a section of the paragraph.

To change all the text of one style within a document to another style, follow these steps:

1. Select a small sample of the text whose style you wish to change. Its current formatting will be displayed in the top box in the task pane.

2. Click the Select All button to select all examples of text using that formatting throughout the document.

3. From the list of styles, click the style you wish to apply to the text.

Tip The alternative to using the task pane is to highlight the text to which you want to apply a style and choose the style you want from the Style list box on the Formatting toolbar (see Figure 8-2). This method has an advantage: If the list of styles is too long for you to see all of them, you can find a style quickly by clicking on the Style list box's drop-down arrow and typing the first letter of the style you are looking for. For example, press H if you are looking for Heading 1. The first style starting with H moves into view at the top of the list, where you can select it with a click. You can speed up the display of styles in this list somewhat by turning off the display of some of the formatting. In the Styles and Formatting task pane, choose Custom from the Show drop-down list; in the resulting dialog box, you can turn off some of the formatting by unchecking the boxes in the Other formatting area.

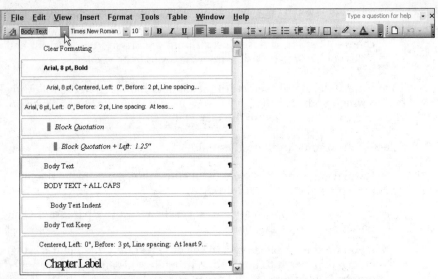

Figure 8-2: You can apply a style using the Style list box on the Formatting toolbar.

Applying a style with a keyboard shortcut

You can also apply styles with keyboard shortcuts; just select the paragraph(s) or text to which you want to apply the style as outlined above, and then press the appropriate key combination. Table 8-1 lists the keyboard shortcuts assigned by default to the Normal template. (You can assign your own keyboard shortcuts to styles; see the section "Creating styles," later in this chapter.)

Table 8-1 Built-in Styles		
Style Name	**Main Features**	**Shortcut Key**
Heading 1	Arial, 16 pt, bold	Ctrl+Alt+1
Heading 2	Arial, 14 pt, bold, italic	Ctrl+Alt+2
Heading 3	Arial, 13 pt, bold	Ctrl+Alt+3
Normal	Times New Roman, 10 pt	Ctrl+Shift+N

Alternative ways to apply styles

You can also apply styles in a couple of other ways. You can apply one style repeatedly to different paragraphs using the Repeat command; you can also copy a style from one section of text onto another section by using the Format Painter button.

Using the techniques described in Chapter 2, you can even build your own toolbar that contains buttons for all of your favorite styles.

Using Repeat

To apply the same style to a series of paragraphs, use the Repeat command, by following these steps:

1. Apply the style to the first paragraph you want to format.

2. Move your insertion point to the next paragraph you want to format.

3. Choose Edit ➪ Repeat Style, or press Ctrl+Y, or F4.

4. Move to the next paragraph you want to format and repeat Step 3.

5. Continue until you've applied the style to all the paragraphs you want.

Caution Although when you follow the procedure above you see the command Repeat Style, you're really using a command that repeats the last thing you did — whatever it was. So be careful not to do anything else between style applications, or pressing F4 or Ctrl+Y will repeat that action instead.

Using the Format Painter

To copy a style from one section of text to another, use the Format Painter. Follow these steps:

1. Highlight text that uses the style you want to apply to additional text.

2. Click the Format Painter button — it's marked with the icon of a paint brush — on the Standard toolbar to switch it on.

3. Use the Format Painter tool to highlight the text to which you want to apply the same style as the highlighted text. In effect you're "painting" the new text with the formatting you copied from the selected text.

Tip If you want to use the Format Painter to apply a particular style to several different sections of text, double-click it instead of just clicking it once. If you click it once, it turns itself off after you've used it once. If you double-click it, it stays on until you click the Format Painter button again (or click some other button).

Removing a style from text

If you apply a style to a paragraph by mistake, you can reapply the default Normal style by selecting the paragraph and pressing Ctrl+Shift+N (assuming that keyboard shortcut hasn't been reassigned to another style) or choosing Clear Formatting from the Style drop-down list or the Pick formatting to apply list in the Styles and Formatting task pane.

Similarly, if you have applied a character style and want to remove it, select the text and change it back to Default Paragraph Font by pressing Ctrl+Spacebar.

Determining which styles have been applied

You can determine which style has been applied to a paragraph by clicking on the paragraph and looking at the Style box on the Formatting toolbar or in the Formatting of selected text box at the top of the Styles and Formatting task pane.

If you're in Outline or Normal view, you can also have Word display style names down the left side of the screen (see Figure 8-3). If you frequently use styles and/or some of them look similar, this can be very helpful in identifying them.

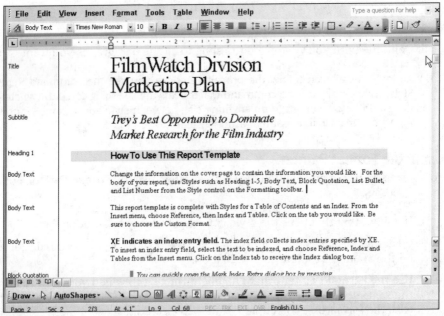

Figure 8-3: You can make Word display style names alongside the document text.

Displaying style names

To make Word display style names, follow these steps:

1. Make sure you are in Normal or Outline view.

2. Choose Tools ➪ Options, and go to the View tab.

3. In the Style area width text box in the Outline and Normal options section at the bottom of the View tab, specify a width for the area used to display style names (one inch is a convenient width but it doesn't really matter; you can adjust the width with your mouse later).

4. Click OK. The style names are now displayed down the left side of the document. You can adjust the width of the style names display area by dragging the onscreen divider left or right. To hide the display again, simply drag the divider all the way to the left.

Tip

If you use the Style area often, consider recording a macro that automatically adjusts it to a width you like; then you can simply run the macro (for the greatest convenience, put it on a toolbar as a button) whenever you want to see the Style area.

Cross-Reference

For detailed information on recording macros, see Chapter 49.

Using Reveal Formatting

Another way to get information about how text has been formatted is to place your insertion point within the text you want information about, and then open the Reveal Formatting task pane by choosing Format ⇨ Reveal Formatting or pressing Shift+F1 (see Figure 8-4). If you check the box labeled Distinguish style source at the bottom of the task pane, the style used for the text at the location of the insertion point will be revealed. As long as this task pane is open, you can view details of any other formatting by clicking elsewhere in the document.

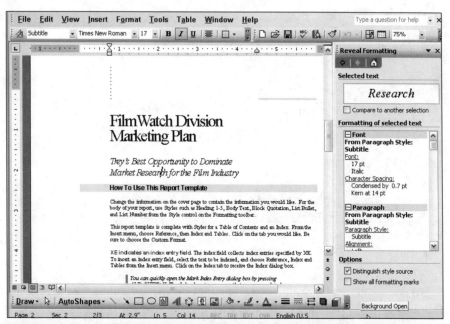

Figure 8-4: The Reveal Formatting task pane provides details about the formatting within your document — including applied styles.

Creating Styles

There are several ways to create a style. Here are two:

✦ Name a style and use dialog boxes to build the style by selecting the formatting features you want. This is the most complete method as it gives you access to some features that are not easy to see (such as rules for page breaks and special line spacing).

✦ Create the style using some existing text that you have already formatted the way you want. In effect, you give Word an example of the style, and Word takes it from there. This is a simpler method.

Creating a style using dialog boxes

To begin, click the Styles and Formatting button on the Formatting toolbar to open the Styles and Formatting task pane. Then click New Style within the task pane. This opens the New Style dialog box (see Figure 8-5). To continue, follow these steps:

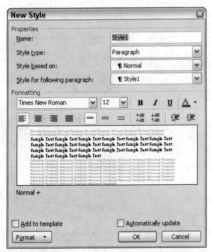

Figure 8-5: Use the New Style dialog box to create a new style.

1. Type a name in the Name box. Note that the style name is case-sensitive. This means that you could create a style named "Heading" and another one called "heading." The style name can be up to 253 characters. You cannot use the backslash (\), curly braces ({ }), or the semicolon (;), but you can use spaces.

2. Names appear in alphabetical order, so it's a good idea to name related styles in a similar way—for example: Head 1, Head 2, Head 3, rather than Major Head, Subhead, and Sub-Subhead. This makes styles easier to find because they are grouped together.

3. Choose a Style type. You can choose character, paragraph, list, or table. The basic formatting tools visible in the New Style dialog box vary depending on which type of style you're creating.

4. If you want to base your new style on an existing style, choose the style you want to base it on from the Style based on drop-down list. If you base your new style on an existing style, all the formatting of the existing style is used and you need only make changes in format where the two styles differ. This can be a big timesaver. For example, suppose you want all your top-level headings except for the first one to be indented by a quarter of an inch. You can use the existing Heading 1 style for your first top-level heading, then create a new style based on Heading 1 that includes the quarter-inch indent, which you can then use on all the subsequent top-level headings.

Tip   If the base style changes—for example, the font is changed to Times New Roman instead of Arial—all the styles based on it change, too. Suppose you want all headings in a document to use the same font, but you haven't decided yet which font that will be. Base all of your headings on the same style; then you only have to change the font of the base style to automatically change the font of all the headings in the document.

5. Many of the basic formatting tools have been made readily available in the New Style dialog box itself. Click the Format button at the bottom of the dialog box to gain access to all of the formatting dialog boxes, which are normally accessed by choosing Format from the menu bar. (Options that aren't applicable to the type of style you've chosen to create are grayed out.) The menu that opens when you click the Format button also includes the Shortcut key option, which leads to a dialog box where you can assign a keyboard shortcut to your style. The New Style dialog box includes a preview of what your paragraph looks like, and beneath it is a description of the various elements of the style. Other options in this dialog box include the following:

   • **Style for following paragraph.** This feature sets which style will be used in the paragraph following any paragraph that uses the style you're currently defining. For example, suppose you're defining your Heading 1 style. If you know that every time you use the Heading 1 style the next paragraph in the document should be in Normal style, choose Normal here. When you press Enter after typing Heading 1, the next text you type will automatically be set to Normal style.

   • **Add to template.** New and modified styles are automatically saved with the document, but not with the current template. To alter the current template to permanently include the new style, check this option.

- **Automatically update.** This has no effect when using the Normal template. If you are using any other template and change the format of a paragraph, the style is redefined and all the paragraphs using the same style are automatically changed. This can surprise you if you are not expecting it! You'll learn how to modify styles in the next section of this chapter.

Creating a style by using an example

To create a style by using an example, follow these steps:

1. Format a paragraph, section of text, list, or table with all the elements you want in your style. Use any of the Word formatting tools, such as font, borders, indents, and so on.

2. Click anywhere in the paragraph, section of text, list, or table.

3. Click the Styles and Formatting button on the Formatting toolbar to open the Styles and Formatting task pane.

4. Click the New Style button inside the task pane.

5. Type the name you want to give the new style in the Name text box in the Properties area.

6. Select any other properties you wish to add to the style, just as you did with a style created from scratch. The preview will show you what your new style will look like.

7. Click OK.

Modifying Styles

Just as there are several ways to create new styles, so there are several ways to modify existing ones. Two of these methods are using dialog boxes and using an example.

Modifying a style using dialog boxes

To modify a style using dialog boxes, follow these steps:

1. Click the Styles and Formatting button on the Formatting toolbar to open the Styles and Formatting task pane.

2. Select the style you wish to modify from the list and right-click on it.

3. From the shortcut menu (see Figure 8-6), choose Modify.

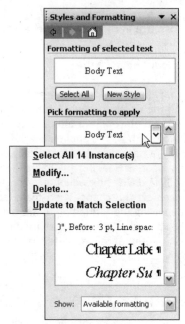

Figure 8-6: Right-clicking on the name of a style enables you to quickly modify or delete it.

4. The Modify Style dialog box appears; except for its title and the fact that you cannot change the Style type, it looks and works exactly like the New Style dialog box. Make any changes you wish, then click OK.

5. When you have finished, any text within the document that uses the style has changed to reflect the modification.

Modifying a style using an example

This is a quick and easy way to modify a style:

1. Click the Styles and Formatting button on the Formatting toolbar to open the Styles and Formatting task pane.

2. Select any paragraph, table, text, or list that uses the style you wish to modify by highlighting it or clicking somewhere within it.

3. Make whatever formatting changes you want.

4. Right-click on the name of the paragraph's original style in the Pick formatting to apply list in the task pane and choose Update to Match Selection from the shortcut menu.

5. All paragraphs using the same style should have changed.

Tip

If you wish, you can activate an option that allows you to update styles on the fly. Choose Tools ➪ AutoCorrect Options, and then click the AutoFormat As You Type tab. Check the box marked Define styles based on your formatting. Now if you add additional formatting to a section of text to which you've applied a style — say, you italicize something in the Heading 1 style — a new style is automatically added to your list of styles; in this case, it would appear as Heading 1 + Italics. If you then reapply the original style, a small Modify Style dialog box will open, giving you the option of updating the original style to reflect the changes (so that Heading 1 would add italics to its formatting) or reapplying the formatting of the style to the selection (which would remove the italics and return the text to the original Heading 1 style). You can also choose to automatically update the style in the future if you make any more changes to it.

Copying, deleting, and renaming a style

You can copy a style from one document or template to another using the Organizer (see Figure 8-7). To access the Organizer, choose Tools ➪ Templates and Add-Ins to open the Templates and Add-Ins dialog box, and then click the Organizer button within that box. When the Organizer dialog box opens, make sure the Styles tab is selected.

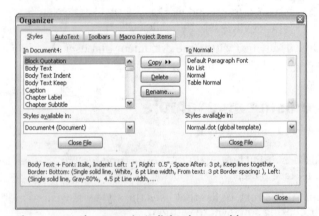

Figure 8-7: The Organizer dialog box enables you to copy styles (as well as other items) from one document or template to another.

This dialog box has two sides, listing the styles in two different files. If you open this dialog box while you have a document open, you'll see the style in use in your open document on one side and the styles in the Normal template on the other. However, you can open the file of your choice on either side. If one of them shows the incorrect document or template, click Close File under the incorrect one first, and then click Open File to bring up the Open dialog box. Make sure you have the correct setting in the Files of type list box. To open a document, choose Word Documents; to open a template, choose Document Templates.

✦ To copy a style using the Organizer, make sure the source file is on one side and the destination file is on the other. Highlight the style you want to copy by clicking on it and then click Copy. You should see the selected style appear in the destination file's Style list.

✦ To delete a style, click on the style name and then click Delete. (Note that built-in styles cannot be deleted.)

✦ To rename a style, click on the style name on either side of the dialog box and then click Rename. Type a new name for the style, click OK, and then click Close. (Note that built-in styles cannot be renamed.)

Using the Style Gallery

The Style Gallery is a tool to help you find styles, no matter which template they are in. It shows you an example of the style and tells you in which template it is saved. To use the Style Gallery, follow these steps:

1. Choose Format ⇨ Theme. Click the Style Gallery button at the bottom of the Theme dialog box to open the Style Gallery dialog box (see Figure 8-8).

2. Select the template you want to look at from the list on the left.

3. Click the Document radio button to see what your document would look like formatted with the styles in the selected template. (This assumes you've used Word's built-in styles in your current document; if you've used uniquely named styles you've created just for your current document, this won't have any effect.)

4. Click Example to see a sample document formatted with the template.

5. Click Style samples to see a document showing a sample of each style in the template.

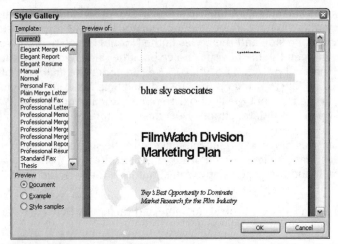

Figure 8-8: The Style Gallery dialog box can help you find the style you want from all those Word has to offer.

Once you have found a style you wish to use, you can copy it into your template using the Organizer.

Attaching a Template

As noted earlier, when you create a new document by clicking the New button on the Standard toolbar, you are creating a document based on the Normal (default) template.

However, if you create a new document using the menu instead of the toolbar, you can choose from a variety of other templates. Choose File ➪ New to open the New Document task pane, and then choose where you want to go to find templates. You can enter a keyword and search Microsoft.com for templates, go directly to the Templates home page at Microsoft.com, look for templates on your computer, or find templates on various Web sites.

Tip

If you've saved a lot of Word templates in a folder other than the default Templates folder, you might want to change where Office looks for templates by default on your computer. To do so, choose Tools ➪ Options and click on the File Locations tab. Highlight User templates in the File types column, then click Modify to browse to the folder you'd like to make the new default templates folder.

Because Office 2003 includes several Word templates, your first choice should probably be to click the On my computer link. This opens the Templates dialog box (see Figure 8-9). The templates available are grouped by type under various tabs.

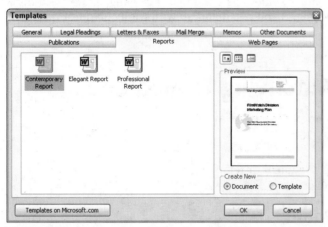

Figure 8-9: The Templates dialog box offers you a multitude of templates from which to choose.

Creating a new document with a template

To use a template, select the tab you require and then the template. When you create a document using a template other than Normal, it has no filename (it's just called Document in the title bar, like any other Word document you haven't saved yet); you can treat it just as you would a document created using the Normal template and name it whatever you wish.

Caution

When you use a template via the Templates dialog box, you're creating a new document based on that template. If you open a template using the normal File ⇨ Open command, you're opening the template document itself, and if you make changes and then save the file, you'll permanently alter the template. That's fine if that's what you want to do, but you need to be aware that the original template won't still be there waiting for you in the Templates dialog box; the next time you go that route, you'll find the altered template instead.

Attaching a template to an existing document

To attach a template to a document you have already created, choose Tools ⇨ Templates and Add-Ins. The dialog box shows the current template in use. Click Attach to select another template to use with the document. The styles from the attached template are added to the current document.

You can choose whether to automatically update the document with the styles in the saved template each time you open the document. You might want to do this if the template is a work in progress and you want to be certain that your document always reflects the latest version of it. On the other hand, you might want to decline this option if the template is something that might be changed unexpectedly without regard to your document; you could end up with wildly inappropriate styles without warning.

Creating and Modifying Templates

You can create a new template in two ways:

✦ From scratch

✦ From an existing document or template

Creating a template from scratch

To create a template from scratch, follow these steps:

1. Choose File ➪ New to open the New Document task pane.

2. Choose the On my computer link from the Other templates section of the task pane.

3. When the Templates dialog box opens, select the General tab, choose the Blank Document template, click the Template radio button in the Create New area, and click OK. The document name at the top of the window will be Template1 instead of Document1.

4. Create a document containing all the elements you would like to be part of your new template: text, pictures, styles, fields, forms, and so forth. You can also include macros, special toolbars or menus, AutoText, and shortcut key entries.

5. Save the document as usual. It will be automatically saved with the filename extension .dot in the Templates folder.

Tip

To add a new tab to those on the Templates dialog box, add a new folder under the Templates folder and add one or more templates to that folder. (By default, you'll find the templates folder in c:\Documents and Settings*username*\Application Data\Microsoft.) You can do this from the File ➪ Open dialog box or by way of My Computer or Windows Explorer. A new tab by that name, containing the templates you've stored in that folder, will automatically appear the next time you open the Templates dialog box. Note that the tab will not appear if your new folder doesn't contain any templates.

Creating a template from an existing document

If you have an existing document that you would like to use as a template—maybe you've created a document you've been using as your letterhead but you've only just learned about the Template feature—follow these instructions:

1. Open the document you want to use as a template.

2. Remove any document-specific text (e.g., the date or the address of a recipient).

3. Choose File ➪ Save As. The Save As dialog box appears.

4. Type a name for your template and then select Document Template in the Save as type list box. Word automatically switches you to your Templates folder.

5. Click Save.

Modifying templates

You can modify a template in much the same way you modify any other document. Follow the same procedures you use to create a template from scratch, but instead of opening a Blank Document as a template, open the template you want to modify. Make your changes, and then save it as usual.

To open a template and modify it, you have to use the File ➪ Open command and browse to the template in whatever folder it's located in. Using the Templates dialog box will open a document based on the chosen template, not the template itself. However, you can choose to open such a document as a template by clicking the Create New Template radio button, in which case you're effectively creating a copy of the original template, which you can then modify and save.

Note   You cannot save changes to a template when it is in use. If you created your current document by choosing a template, you cannot save it as a template using the same name. You have to give it a different name.

Modifying the Normal Template

For certain features, you need not use the method described above to modify the Normal template. If you wish to change the default font, for example, just choose Format ➪ Font, select the font type, size, and style you wish to use, and click the Default button. By making this small change, you are actually modifying the Normal template, and so you are prompted to verify that you really want to do that.

The same Default button appears in the Page Setup and Language dialog boxes. Choose File ➪ Page Setup to set the default paper size, printer bin, and margins, and many other options. Choose Tools ➪ Language ➪ Set Language to select the default language for spellchecking, the thesaurus, and grammar checking. (Some language dictionaries have to be purchased separately.)

To change any of the styles other than the Normal style in the Normal template, you need to open the template as instructed in the previous section.

Note   To locate Normal.dot, choose Tools ➪ Options and click the File Locations tab. Normal.dot is in the folder assigned to User templates; its location is specified in this tab. (On my system, it is in C:\Documents and Settings\(myusername)\Application Data\Microsoft\Templates.)

Summary

Styles and templates are both great timesavers and help ensure that your document looks its best — and follows the same formatting rules as related documents.

✦ Word provides paragraph, character, table, and list styles. You can use the preset ones or define your own.

✦ Templates are special Word documents that usually contain a collection of special styles but also include macros and changes made to Word's default toolbars and menus, as well as items such as text and pictures that are to appear on all documents based on that template.

✦ All documents are based on a template; if no other template is specified, then the document is based on Word's Normal template.

✦ You can apply styles from the Styles and Formatting task pane, from the Styles drop-down list in the Formatting toolbar, using keyboard shortcuts, or even with the Repeat command or the Format Painter.

✦ You can create styles from scratch and modify existing styles. You can even have Word update styles automatically as you add formatting to them during your regular Word editing.

✦ You can use the Organizer to copy and rename styles and to delete them from templates.

✦ The Style Gallery lets you preview how the preset styles in a template will affect the look of your current document (assuming it uses preset styles).

✦ You can create a new document from a template on your computer or on the Web, or attach a template to an existing document.

✦ You can create your own template simply by saving a Word document in template format; you can also modify existing templates as you would any other Word document.

✦ The Normal template can often be modified by clicking the Default button in related dialog boxes, such as the Format ⇨ Font dialog box, to name just one.

✦   ✦   ✦

Getting Graphical

Word is more than just a glorified typewriter. You can also use it to add pictures, drawings, graphs, and other graphics to your document, and to add sophisticated formatting touches such as bulleted lists, columns, and borders. While Word isn't a full-featured desktop publishing program like Microsoft Publisher, it can still create a sharp, professional-looking, eye-catching design for just about any type of document.

Using Bulleted and Numbered Lists

One of the most common types of formatting is a bulleted or numbered list. You can create such a list with a combination of indents, tabs, and typing, or you can enlist Word's help to eliminate most of these mundane tasks, so all you have to do is enter the information for each item. An example of each type of list is shown in Figure 9-1.

Using the Formatting toolbar

The tools to create a bulleted or numbered list are right on the Formatting toolbar. To create a numbered list, click the Numbering button; to create a bulleted list, click the Bullets button.

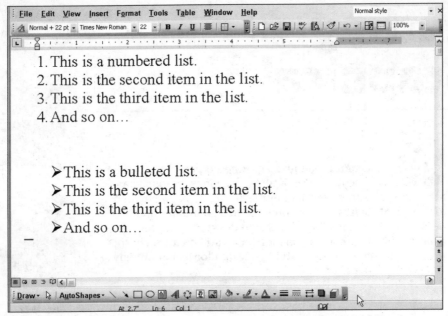

Figure 9-1: Word makes it easy to create numbered and bulleted lists like these.

Note   By default, Word assumes that you want a numbered list when you type a number as the first character of a paragraph, and assumes you want a bulleted list if you insert an asterisk as the first character of a paragraph; when you press Enter, it automatically inserts a number or bullet to start the next paragraph, and formats the paragraphs as items in a list. This behavior annoys some users; you can turn it off by choosing Tools ➪ AutoCorrect Options, and then choosing the AutoFormat As You Type tab and unchecking the Automatic bulleted lists and Automatic numbered lists boxes.

Cross-Reference   For more information on AutoCorrect options, see Chapter 3.

When you click either button, Word inserts either a number or a bullet. Whenever you press Enter at the end of a line, the next number or another bullet is inserted. When you've finished typing the list, press Enter, twice. After that, you can continue typing normally.

Formatting your lists

The lists in Figure 9-1 show possible formatting options for numbers and bullets, but you can format your numbered and bulleted lists any way you like. To do so, Choose Format ➪ Bullets and Numbering. This opens the Bullets and Numbering dialog box (see Figure 9-2).

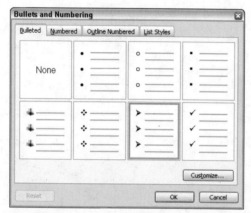

Figure 9-2: Choose the types of symbols and numerals you want to use in your bulleted and numbered lists in this dialog box.

Using the standard settings

The Bullets and Numbering dialog box has four tabs, three of which correspond to the three types of standard lists: Bulleted, Numbered, and Outline Numbered (which applies numbering to the various headings and subheadings of an outline). Each tab offers you a number of different formatting options for your lists; choose the one you want and click OK.

If you don't like any of the options Word provides, you can custom-design your list. You can either click Customize on any of the tabs or choose the List Styles tab.

Customizing bulleted lists

Choosing the Bulleted tab and then clicking the Customize button opens the Customize Bulleted List dialog box (see Figure 9-3). Here you can specify what you want to use as a bullet. You can choose from the six bullets shown at the top, or click Font to change the font from which those symbols are taken and apply other formatting options.

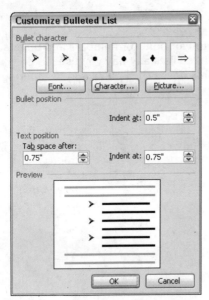

Figure 9-3: Word lets you choose any symbol you want to use as a bullet.

Cross-Reference   See Chapter 4 for more detailed information on the Font dialog box.

To use different symbols entirely, click Character. This opens the Symbol dialog box, from which you can choose any character from any font installed on your computer; this is particularly useful if you want to use something from a font that consists entirely of symbols or pictures, such as Wingdings.

Caution   If you use a symbol from a font you have on your computer and then share the document with someone who doesn't have that font installed, your recipient may see some other character, or just a placeholder, instead of the bullet you chose.

To use a picture for your bullet, click Picture. This opens a dialog box that displays the picture bullets that come with Office. These aren't part of any fonts; they're small graphics. Click Import to add additional picture bullets to this collection.

Use the Bullet position and Text position controls to adjust the indentation of bullets and text from the left margin. By changing these, you can get various effects, which are illustrated in the Preview area.

Customizing numbered lists

The Customize Numbered List dialog box is very similar to the Customize Bulleted List dialog box — it enables you to set indents and choose and format a special font for your numbers. You can also choose a number style (1, 2, 3 or i, ii, iii, or even A, B, C, which, of course, aren't actually numbers, but never mind . . .) and choose whether to start the list at 1 or some other number.

Customizing Outline Numbered Lists

The Customize Outline Numbered List dialog box is basically the same as the Customize Numbered List dialog box, except it lets you customize each of the nine possible levels of an outline. In addition, by clicking More, you can change which styles are associated with which outline numbers and what character appears between the number and the start of the outline text, among other things.

Tip

You can set the options for bulleted and numbered lists before you begin creating them; you can also change the formatting of a list after it's finished. Just place your insertion point anywhere inside the list, choose Format ➪ Bullets and Numbering, and customize it as described above. When you click OK, the new design is automatically applied to your list.

Using List Styles

You can see which list styles are available in your current document by clicking the List Styles tab in the Bullets and Numbering dialog box (see Figure 9-4). You can then create a new list style by clicking Add, or modify an existing style by selecting it and clicking Modify.

Cross-
Reference

For detailed information on creating and modifying styles, see Chapter 8.

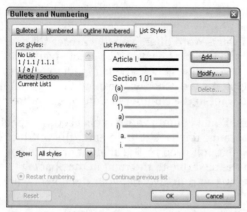

Figure 9-4: The List Styles tab of the Bullets and Numbering dialog box offers an easy way to preview, modify, and add list styles.

Using Columns

Arranging text in columns is a good way to break up an otherwise gray mass of print with a little white space. You can set columns before you begin entering text into a document, or you can apply columns to a document that's already underway or completed.

To set columns:

1. Choose Format ➪ Columns to open the Columns dialog box (see Figure 9-5).

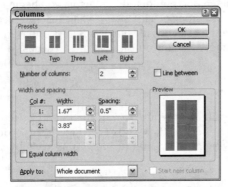

Figure 9-5: Setting your text in columns, using these controls, can make it more visually appealing.

2. Decide how many columns you want. Word offers you five preset column designs: One, Two, Three, Left, and Right. The latter two create pages with two columns of unequal width: If you choose Left, the left column is narrower than the right; if you choose Right, it's the other way around. If you want more columns, enter the number you want in the Number of Columns text box.

3. By default, the checkbox marked Equal column width is checked. To specify different widths for different columns, uncheck it; then enter the width of each column in the Width boxes above it, followed by the amount of space you want between that column and the next one to the right in the Spacing text boxes. The Preview area will show you roughly what your document will look like with those settings.

4. If you would like a dividing line between columns, check the Line between checkbox.

5. Finally, use the Apply to drop-down list to choose whether to put the whole document into columns or just use columns from the current location of your

insertion point onward. If you choose the latter, you also have the option to have the columns start immediately, even if they're in the middle of a page, or check the Start new column checkbox to jump to a new page to start the columns. If you're already using columns, checking this box forces your current column to end, and any text after the insertion point will go into the next column on the same page.

Tip

You can also choose to set a selected portion of text into columns. Just highlight the text you want in columns before beginning the procedures above; when you get to Step 5, the Apply to drop-down list will include the option of applying columns just to the selected text. If your document has more than one section, the Apply to drop-down list will include the option of applying columns just to the current section, the whole document, or just from your insertion point onward.

Cross-Reference

For more on formatting sections, see Chapter 4.

6. When you're satisfied with your selections, click OK (see Figure 9-6).

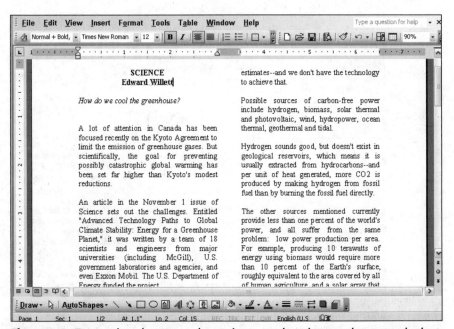

Figure 9-6: Text set in columns can be easier to read, and more pleasant to look at, than text that uses the full available width of the page. Note that you can see what the columns will look like only by using Print Layout view; Normal view shows only a single column.

Adding Borders and Shading

You can add borders not only to pictures but also to selected bits of text, from a single character or paragraph to an entire document.

Adding a simple border

To add a simple border to text (by a "simple" border I mean one that's a single solid line):

1. Highlight the text you want to place the border around (unless it's a single paragraph, in which case you only have to click somewhere within the paragraph).

2. Click the Outside Border button on the Formatting toolbar. By default, this adds a simple rectangular box around the selected text (see Figure 9-7). If you want something a little different, click the down arrow next to the Border button and select the kind of border you want from the menu. You can choose to draw a line only along one side, for example.

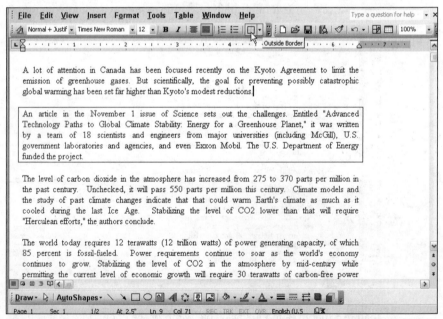

Figure 9-7: Adding a simple border around a paragraph takes a single mouse-click.

Adding borders to tables

Note that some of the Border options involve drawing inside borders on a grid. These borders are intended for use with tables. To add a border to a table, simply draw the table as usual, and then click the Border button and choose the kind of border you want. A typical choice would be All Borders, which outlines every cell and can make it easier for readers to see where rows and columns come together.

Cross-Reference   For more detailed information on formatting tables, see Chapter 5.

Fine-tuning your borders

For more complex borders, Word provides a dialog box, which you access by choosing Format ⇨ Borders and Shading (see Figure 9-8).

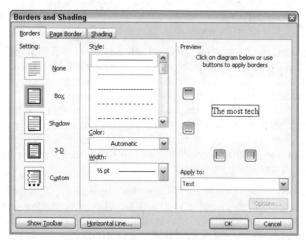

Figure 9-8: When you want a more sophisticated border than you can get with the Border button, bring up the Borders and Shading dialog box.

The Borders and Page Border tabs are virtually identical. (However, the Borders tab changes somewhat when you're applying borders to a table instead of to text.) Use the Borders property sheet to apply a border to a selected section of text or a table; use the Page Border property sheet to apply borders to entire pages. The controls that the two property sheets share include the following:

✦ **Setting.** This determines the type of border you're going to use. None, of course, means just what it says; so does Box. Shadow applies a drop shadow to the box; 3-D applies a preset effect that gives some borders the appearance of a picture frame. Custom applies to borders where you've removed one or more sides (more on that shortly) or otherwise altered the preset options. If you're applying a border to a table, All and Grid replace Shadow and 3-D; All applies the same border to all the cells in the table, while Grid applies your chosen border just to the outside of the table and outlines the cells with simple lines (which you can then format as you see fit).

✦ **Style.** From the scroll box, choose the kind of line you want to use to draw the border, from a simple straight line to dashed lines, dotted lines, combinations of thick and thin lines, and even wavy lines.

✦ **Color.** Pick a color, any color, for the lines of your border. (Obviously, this is of limited value if your document is going to be viewed only in printed format and printed only on a black-and-white printer.)

✦ **Width.** Select the width of line you want to use. How many and which widths are available depends on what kind of line you choose. Some lines come in many widths; some, like the double wavy line, come in only one.

✦ **Preview.** This not only shows you what your selected border will look like, it lets you remove the lines from one or more sides, either by clicking the buttons to the left of and below the Preview area, or by clicking directly on the sides of the border in the preview. In addition, you can change any line by choosing a different style, color, or width, and then clicking one of the buttons or on one of the lines. If you're working with a table, you have more controls; you can adjust both the outside edge of the table and the inner lines that surround the cells. You can even add diagonal lines with the buttons at the bottom left and right corners of the preview.

✦ **Apply to.** This tells Word where you want the border applied: to the whole paragraph, to selected text (if you highlighted any text before opening the dialog box), or, in the case of a table, to the whole table, to selected cells, or to the paragraph in which the table appears. Click the Options button to set how much space you want to leave between the text and the border (this button is active only if you're working with a paragraph border).

Note
One difference between the Page Border property sheet and the Borders property sheet is in the Apply to options. You can choose to apply page borders to the entire document, to just the current section, to just the first page of the current section, or to every page in the current section except the first page. (If the whole document is a single section, the latter two options can be used to apply borders to everything except the first page of the document or to the first page only.)

✦ **Art.** The Page Border tab adds this option to the mix; it enables you to add a decorative border to your pages like the one shown in Figure 9-9. Just choose the design you want from the drop-down list. Word automatically assigns a width to the border art, but you can increase or decrease it as you wish.

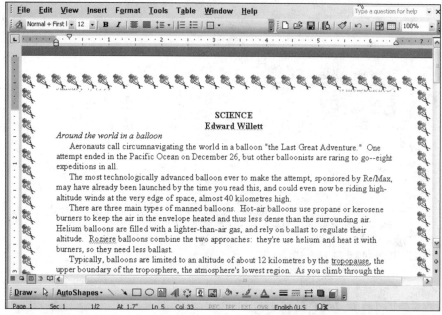

Figure 9-9: Word lets you add a decorative border to your pages.

Adding shading

In addition to, or instead of, using a border to set off a paragraph, table, section of text, or whole pages, you can use shading. Click on the Shading tab in the Borders and Shading dialog box (see Figure 9-10). Here's how it works:

1. Choose the color you want to use to shade the selected text or paragraph from the Fill palette, or click More Colors to access all the colors your computer and monitor are capable of displaying.

2. In the Patterns area, use the Style drop-down list to choose from various shades (given in percentages of the solid color) or a variety of patterns.

3. The Color drop-down list lets you choose a second color to use to draw the selected pattern over the Fill color.

4. The Preview area shows you what the fill looks like, and Apply To lets you apply the fill to just selected text or to an entire paragraph.

Tip

There's no provision for applying shading to an entire page, but you could do so by selecting all the text on the page before applying shading. If you have a table selected, you can apply shading to the whole table or just to the selected cell(s).

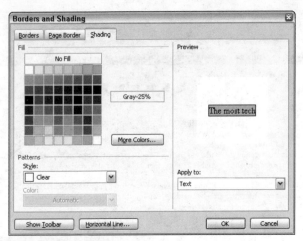

Figure 9-10: Highlight sections of text, or a paragraph, with colors and patterns.

Inserting Pictures

Word's very name makes it clear that its primary function is processing text, but that doesn't mean it can't handle pictures. In fact, it handles them quite well. You have three ways to insert pictures into a Word document:

✦ You can insert a picture file from your own computer or external media (a floppy, a CD, or some other data storage device).

✦ You can insert a picture from the Clip Gallery.

✦ You can import an image from a scanner or digital camera.

In addition, you can insert other specialized graphical elements such as AutoShapes, WordArt, a new drawing, or a chart.

Cross-Reference   This chapter provides basic instructions for inserting pictures into Word documents. For more information on working with AutoShapes and WordArt, see Chapter 43. For detailed information on working with graphics in all Office applications, see Chapters 43–45.

Inserting a picture file

To insert a picture file:

1. Place your insertion point where you want the picture to appear.

2. Choose Insert ⇨ Picture ⇨ From File. This brings up the Insert Picture dialog box, a standard dialog box for opening files that defaults to the My Pictures folder on your computer and to the Thumbnails view (see Figure 9-11).

Tip   You can change the folder in which Office looks for pictures by default by choosing Tools ⇨ Options and clicking on the File Locations tab. Highlight Clipart pictures under File types, and then click the Modify button to browse to the folder you'd like to look in by default.

3. Locate the picture file you want to insert. Double-click it or click Insert.

4. Word inserts the picture into your document.

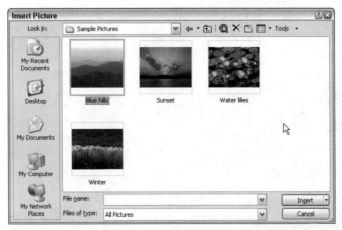

Figure 9-11: Word makes it easy to insert picture files into your documents.

Inserting clip art

Although the Open File dialog box enables you to easily identify files that are in a picture format supported by Word, finding the precise file you want can be difficult, especially if the files aren't clearly labeled. That's where the Clip Organizer becomes useful.

Cross-Reference For more information on using the Clip Organizer, see Chapter 43.

To insert clip art:

1. Place your insertion point where you want to insert the picture.

2. Choose Insert ➪ Picture ➪ Clip Art. This opens the Clip Art task pane.

3. In the Search for text box, type a keyword (or words) that describes the subject matter you want an illustration for; choose Search in to locate the collections of Clip Art you want to search; and specify the media type (which includes not only Clip Art but also Photographs, Movies, and Sounds). Figure 9-12 shows the results returned from searching for the word "balloon."

Figure 9-12: The Clip Organizer puts a well-organized collection of clip art at your fingertips.

4. Point at the picture you want to use and double-click it to insert it into your document (see Figure 9-13).

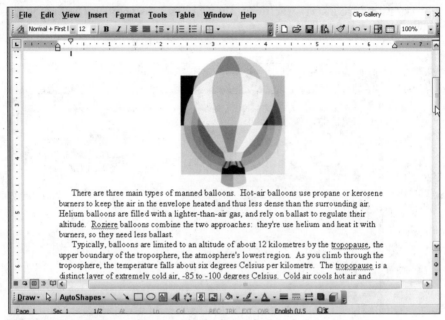

Figure 9-13: Here's my document with clip art inserted.

Inserting an image from a scanner or camera

To insert an image from a scanner or camera, choose Insert ➪ Picture ➪ From Scanner or Camera. Windows presents you with a list of all the scanners or cameras connected to your computer; choose the one you want to use and decide whether you want the picture's resolution to be Web-quality or print-quality. (Print-quality is of higher resolution than Web-quality.) Click Insert. To adjust the device's settings, click Custom Insert. To add the image to the Clip Organizer, select that checkbox.

Cross-Reference

Word's picture-editing tools are somewhat rudimentary. To get the most out of a scanned or digital-camera image, it's a good idea to first import it into a dedicated graphics or photo-editing program. Office 2003 comes with the new Microsoft Picture Library, which provides basic editing tools for pictures. For additional information on Picture Library, see Chapter 45.

Inserting AutoShapes

AutoShapes are shapes that Word can draw automatically. They include everything from boxes and ovals to arrows and starbursts. To insert an AutoShape:

1. Choose Insert ➪ Picture ➪ AutoShapes. This displays the AutoShapes toolbar (see Figure 9-14).

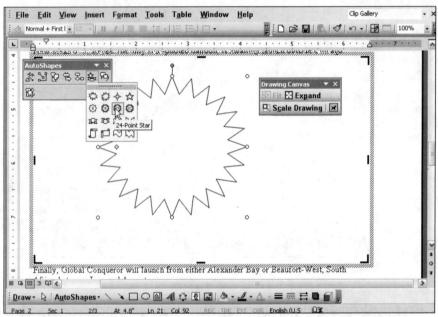

Figure 9-14: Here you can see the AutoShapes toolbar, one of its menus, and a 24-point starburst created by clicking on that menu. (The Drawing Canvas and Drawing Canvas toolbar are also visible; see the sidebar.) Note the diamond inside the shape; by clicking and dragging it, you can alter the starburst's appearance significantly.

2. Each button on the AutoShapes toolbar displays a different menu of shapes. Find the shape you want and click on it.

3. The Drawing Canvas opens (see sidebar). Your cursor changes to a crosshairs. Center the crosshairs where you want the center of the AutoShape to be and click. The AutoShape appears.

4. Most autoshapes can be adjusted. Those that are adjustable display one or more yellow diamonds. Click and drag these diamonds to adjust the AutoShape.

5. When you're satisfied with your shape, click anywhere outside it to return to normal text-editing mode.

Cross-Reference   For more information on AutoShapes, see Chapter 43.

The Drawing Canvas

The Drawing Canvas is essentially a graphic (a rectangle) into which you can insert other graphics. It opens immediately when you insert an organization chart, a new drawing, or an AutoShape.

The Drawing Canvas comes with its own toolbar (visible in Figure 9-14), which includes a handful of new tools. (To open this toolbar, right-click the Drawing Canvas and choose Show Drawing Canvas Toolbar from the shortcut menu.) The buttons enable you to shrink the Drawing Canvas to fit the drawing or to expand it to make room for more drawings. (You can expand drawings within the Drawing Canvas as usual without affecting the size of the canvas.) If you click and drag the handles on the sides of the canvas, you can adjust the size of the canvas without affecting the drawings it contains. If you click the Scale Picture button, however, the handles change, and you can then adjust the size of the canvas and the drawings on it at the same time. Finally, the Text Wrapping button enables you to control how text interacts with objects inside the Drawing Canvas.

Inserting WordArt

WordArt is a separate program that you can use in any of Office's applications to insert fancily formatted text. To insert WordArt in Word:

1. Choose Insert ⇨ Picture ⇨ WordArt. This opens the WordArt Gallery (see Figure 9-15).

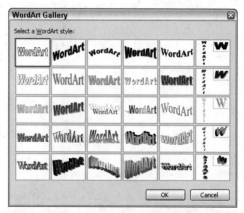

Figure 9-15: You can insert text in any of these colorful, eye-catching styles by using WordArt.

2. Choose the style of WordArt you want and double-click on it.

3. In the resulting dialog box, enter your text where it says Your Text Here; choose the font, size, and style (bold or italic) and click OK.

4. Your text (although it isn't really text anymore; it's now a picture), in the WordArt style you selected, will appear on the current page of your document. Drag it to where you want it, and edit it using the WordArt toolbar that appears at the same time.

5. When you're done, click anywhere outside the WordArt to deselect it and return to normal text-editing mode.

Cross-Reference   For more detailed information on using WordArt, see Chapter 43.

Inserting a drawing

In addition to AutoShapes, Word has other powerful drawing tools. To access all of them, choose Insert ➪ Picture ➪ New Drawing. Word opens the Drawing Canvas and, if it's not already open, the Drawing toolbar (see Figure 9-16).

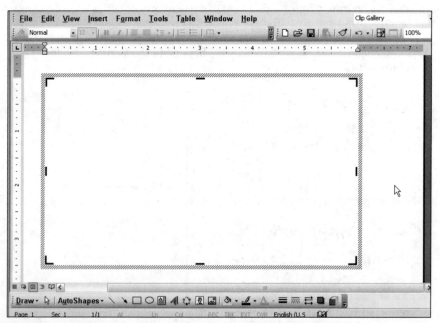

Figure 9-16: When you insert a new drawing in Word, Word first opens the Drawing Canvas, and then provides you with drawing tools in the Drawing toolbar (shown just below the document area in this image) to help you create a drawing.

Use the tools in the Drawing toolbar to create the image you want within the frame, and then click anywhere outside the frame to return to normal text-editing mode.

Cross-Reference For more detailed information on drawing, see Chapter 43.

Caution Just one thing to keep in mind as you add graphics to your Word file; every graphic increases the final size of the file and may also cause problems with stability, especially on less-powerful systems. It's better not to add pretty pictures just for the sake of adding them; add them only when they help your document communicate your ideas more effectively.

Summary

Word makes it easy for you to add any number of useful graphical elements to your documents, from fancily formatted bulleted and numbered lists to photographs, drawings, AutoShapes, WordArt, and more.

✦ You can create numbered and bulleted lists formatted any way you want with Word's Format ➪ Bullets and Numbering command.

✦ You can use List Styles to save formatting information for numbered and bulleted lists you use often.

✦ Arranging your text in columns is a good way to break up an otherwise intimidating mass of gray text.

✦ You can add borders to text, ranging from a simple black line to a border made up of repeating pictures.

✦ You can insert pictures either from files on your computer, from Office's Clip Organizer, or from a scanner or digital camera.

✦ The Drawing Canvas is a space in which you can place several graphics, which you can then move or resize as a unit.

✦ WordArt is a special program for creating fancily formatted text that is then inserted as a picture.

✦   ✦   ✦

Working with Others on Word Documents

As do the other Office applications (but to a greater extent), Word has many features that make it easier for teams of collaborators to create, review, and revise documents. Even if you're not part of such a team, you might find many of these features useful in helping you keep track of document changes.

Collaborating with Many Users on a Single Document

Word's two main tools for helping you collaborate with others are comments and the Track Changes feature. Both use the Reviewing toolbar (see Figure 10-1).

Figure 10-1: Activate the Reviewing toolbar for quick access to commands used in collaborating on documents.

The Reviewing toolbar opens automatically whenever you edit a comment, but you can activate it whenever you want by choosing View ➪ Toolbars. The toolbar's buttons provide one-click access to commands for viewing comments and changes, adding comments, tracking changes, and accepting or rejecting those changes.

Inserting comments

Someone who comments on a paper document usually returns it covered with red ink, pencil marks, sticky notes, and possibly coffee stains. Word's Comments feature replaces all of that (except for the coffee stains).

To insert a comment, place your insertion point in the word you want to comment on, or (if you're commenting on more than a single word) select the text you want to comment on, and then choose Insert ➪ Comment or click the Insert Comment button on the Reviewing toolbar.

How you enter your comment varies depending on what view you're in. If you're currently using Normal or Outline View, the Reviewing pane opens at the bottom of the window, and you type your comment into it (see Figure 10-2).

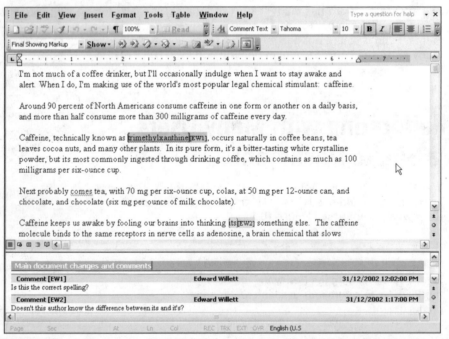

Figure 10-2: Type your comment into the Reviewing pane that Word opens at the bottom of the screen.

In the main text, Word indicates the comment by highlighting and placing brackets around the text to which the comment is attached. Once the Reviewing pane is closed (you can close it by clicking the Reviewing Pane button on the far-right side of the Reviewing toolbar), you can read the comment by simply pointing at the text the comment is attached to. The comment appears in a ScreenTip box, which also shows the reviewer's name (based on the information the reviewer supplied in the User Information tab of the Options dialog box) and the date and time when the comment was made (see Figure 10-3).

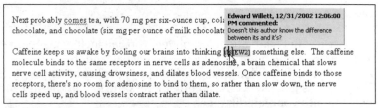

Figure 10-3: Here's a sample comment displayed as a ScreenTip over the text it refers to. It includes the commenter's name and the date and time the comment was made.

If you're in Print Layout, Web Layout, or Reading Layout View, comments are displayed by default in markup balloons, like the speech balloons of cartoons, down the right margin of the document (see Figure 10-4). A line is drawn from the Markup box to the text it refers to. When you insert a new comment, you type it directly into one of these boxes.

Cross-Reference You can change these indicators by choosing Show ⇨ Options from the Reviewing toolbar. See the section "Changing the way changes are displayed," later in this chapter.

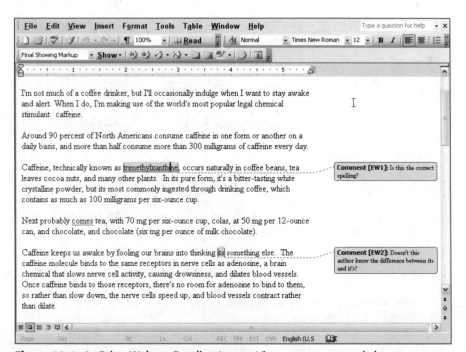

Figure 10-4: In Print, Web, or Reading Layout View, comments and changes appear in boxes down one side of the document for easier viewing.

Inserting voice comments

If your computer has a sound card and microphone, you can include a recorded comment. Place your insertion point or select text as usual, and then click the Insert Voice button on the Reviewing toolbar. This opens the Sound Recorder (see Figure 10-5), which works just like a tape recorder. Press the Record button and speak your comment into your microphone.

Caution   Inserting recorded comments can greatly increase the size of the final document, depending on the quality at which the sound files were recorded (the higher the quality, the larger the sound file).

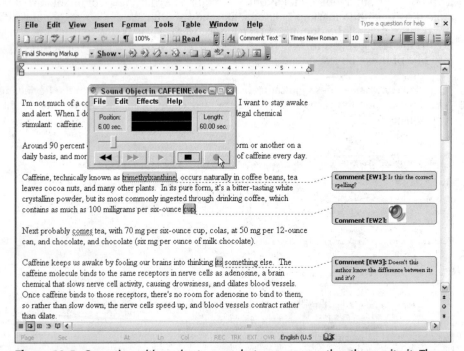

Figure 10-5: Sometimes it's easier to say what you mean rather than write it. The Insert Voice command lets you do just that.

The comment is inserted as a Sound Object, indicated by the icon of a loudspeaker inside the comment box or Reviewing pane. You or anyone else who also has sound capabilities can listen to the voice comment by double-clicking this icon.

Inserting handwritten comments

If your computer supports written input—maybe you have a Tablet PC, for example—you can add comments using handwriting. The comment is converted from handwriting to regular text and appears inside a comment balloon just like any other comment.

To add a handwritten comment, click the Add Handwritten Comment button on the Reviewing toolbar.

Finding and working with comments

You can move easily from comment to comment with the Browse Object tool, or by clicking the Previous Comment and Next Comment buttons on the Reviewing toolbar.

For more on the Browse Object tool, see Chapter 3.

Alternatively, open the Reviewing pane by clicking the Reviewing Pane button on the Reviewing toolbar. Once the pane is open, you can scroll through all the comments in the document.

You can view comments in the markup style you see in Print, Web, and Reading Layout Views and in the Reviewing pane at the same time; opening the Reviewing pane doesn't affect the view in the main window.

Sometimes you might want to view only the comments from one particular reviewer. To do so, choose Show ➪ Reviewers from the Reviewing toolbar, and then choose the Reviewer whose comments you want to review (or whose reviews you want to comment on) from the list provided.

You can edit comments in both the Reviewing pane and in the markup balloons. In the Reviewing pane you can change the formatting of comments just as you can any other bit of text in Word, either directly using the commands on the Formatting toolbar or by applying styles. (By default, Word applies the Comment Text paragraph style to comments.) In the markup balloons, you can change the formatting in a limited fashion, changing the font and making text italic, underlined, or bold, but not changing the size.

In the ScreenTip balloon, no formatting changes will be visible.

To delete a comment, right-click in the text it's attached to or in its Markup box and select Delete Comment from the shortcut menu, or left-click within the commented-upon text and click the Reject Change/Delete Comment button on the Reviewing toolbar.

Printing comments

Normally, comments don't print, but you can change that. Choose Document showing markup from the Print what drop-down list on the main Print dialog box. Comment marks and any other hidden text will then show up in the printed document, and the comments themselves will appear at the end of the document, beginning on a separate page.

Changing identifying information for comments

As you'll note in the preceding figures, the name and initials of the person who makes a comment appear in the Reviewing pane or Markup box. They're drawn from the User Information tab of the Tools ⇨ Options dialog box, so they can be changed by changing that information — and they should be if more than one person is using the same computer to comment on a document; otherwise it's impossible to tell which user made the comments.

Tip

It's not a good idea to put a new comment directly on top of an existing comment; it makes it more likely that subsequent reviewers may miss one of them. It's better to append new remarks to the ones that are already there. It's important, though, to use some sort of a delimiter to distinguish where one comment ends and the new one begins, and it's important to identify yourself as the person making the comment. One suggestion is to use **, followed by your initials, as the delimiter.

Tracking Changes in a Document

When you have more than one person making changes to a document, it becomes vital to everyone involved to have some way of telling which changes have been made, by whom, and when.

Word offers two main ways to identify the changes made to a document: You can track the changes as they're made, or you can compare the current document with another (perhaps earlier) version. Whichever method you use, the changes are marked in the document in the same way.

Tip

You can display tracked changes in a printed document the same way you can display comments, by choosing Document showing markup from the Print what drop-down list in the Print dialog box.

Tracking changes during editing

To track changes during editing, turn on Track Changes by choosing Tools ⇨ Track Changes ⇨ Highlight Changes or clicking the Track Changes button on the Reviewing toolbar. You can also double-click TRK on the Status Bar, or right-click it for additional options.

Word displays changes several ways. Text you've added to the document appears both underlined and a different color. Deleted text appears struck-through in Normal View. In Print, Web, or Reading Layout View, deleted text is indicated by the markup balloons (see Figure 10-6). In the text itself, added text appears underlined and in a different color.

Tip   You can customize all of these indicators by choosing Show ⇨ Options from the Reviewing toolbar. See the section "Changing the way changes are displayed," later in this chapter.

If you turn on the Reviewing pane, you'll see a list of all changes (also shown in Figure 10-6) and who made them. You can also determine who made a change and when by pointing at the change; that information is displayed in a ScreenTip box.

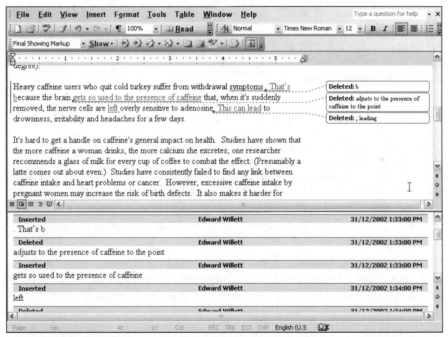

Figure 10-6: Changes to text are marked both in the text and (when in Print, Web, or Reading Layout View) in markup balloons down the right side of the document.

Changing the way changes are displayed

To change the defaults governing tracked changes, choose Tools ⇨ Options and click the Track Changes tab (see Figure 10-7), or choose Show ⇨ Options from the Reviewing toolbar.

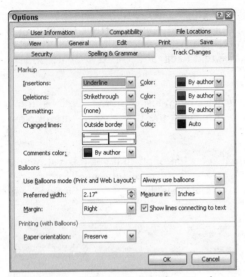

Figure 10-7: You can change the way changes are displayed using this dialog box.

Why would you want to change these defaults? Here are some possible reasons:

✦ **To minimize distracting colors.** Word gives each reviewer's changes a different color. Some people find that distracting. If you prefer, you can make Word display all changes in the same color, and rely on the Reviewing pane or the ScreenTip boxes to tell you who made the changes rather than trying to remember who's represented by which color.

✦ **To track formatting changes.** By default, formatting changes are simply accepted and not marked. To see them, select a color to display them in.

✦ **To change the location of the vertical line that indicates changed lines.** Word marks changed text with a vertical line along the left edge of the document. In Normal View, you're stuck with that line appearing along the left edge, but in Print, Web, and Reading Layout views, you can change the location of that vertical line to the right border or the outside border (the left margin of even-numbered pages and the right margin of odd-numbered pages if you've set up different odd and even pages in the Page Setup dialog box). You can also do away with the line altogether.

Hiding and displaying changes

A document that's been changed a lot can become very confusing to work with, what with all the markings Word adds onscreen. Fortunately, you can turn off the display of marked changes without stopping Word from tracking those changes. To do so, choose Show from the Reviewing toolbar, and simply uncheck the items you no longer want displayed: Comments, Ink Annotations (handwritten comments), Insertions, and Deletions and/or Formatting.

You can hide all changes at once by choosing View ➪ Markup. To show changes again, choose View ➪ Markup again.

Note   Even when changes and comments aren't visible in the text, you can see them in the Reviewing pane.

Accepting and rejecting changes

Eventually, if you're the one with the final say over a document, you're going to have to decide which of the many changes you're going to keep.

Use the Reviewing toolbar's Next and Previous buttons to move from change to change. If you want to keep the change, click the Accept Change button; if you want to reject the change, click the Reject Change button.

Caution   If a reviewer deletes something and you accept that change, the text marked as deleted disappears for good. Similarly, if a reviewer inserts something and you reject that change, the inserted text disappears. (In both cases, you can retrieve the text by clicking Undo.)

Click the downward-pointing arrows to the right of the Accept Change and Reject Change/Delete Comment buttons to see additional options: You can Accept or Reject All Changes in Document or Delete All Comments in Document.

Tip   To accept or reject all comments and changes from a single reviewer, choose Show ➪ Reviewers and make sure the reviewer in question is the only reviewer selected in the list provided. Then, click the downward-pointing arrows next to the Accept Change and Reject Change/Delete Comment buttons and chose Accept or Reject All Changes Shown or Delete All Comments Shown. Note that you won't get a "Do you really want to do this" question box; your decision takes effect immediately.

Comparing and merging two copies of a document

Sometimes reviewers will work on separate copies of a document. You can incorporate the comments and suggestions you have made in your copy of a document into someone else's copy, or vice versa, or create a new document to display the changes while leaving the original versions untouched.

Choose Tools ➪ Compare and Merge Documents, and find the document you want to merge with your document. Click Merge to merge your currently open document with the target document.

If you prefer to merge the target document with the document you currently have open, click the downward-pointing arrow to the right of the Merge button and choose Merge into current document from the menu. Now the changes and comments in the target document of the copy are added to your copy. (Text that exists in both versions is not duplicated.)

If you prefer to merge both the target document and the one you have open into a new document, choose Merge into new document.

Using Versions

Some documents go through multiple, major changes — and sometimes, those changes aren't for the better. Word can help you avoid the panic that comes with suddenly realizing, the day your document is due, that the 15 pages of material you deleted three weeks ago have suddenly become crucially important.

Word lets you store multiple versions of a document in a single file. You can keep track of who was responsible for each saved version, when that version was saved, and what that version contains.

Using the Versions function is much more efficient than simply storing each version as a separate file using the Save As command, because when you save multiple versions as a single file, Word stores only the differences among them, not a complete copy of each. Although that single file can grow quite large, it still takes up less space than multiple versions of the same file. As well, using the Versions function ensures that one or more versions of the document aren't overlooked, as they might be if they are separate files from other versions.

Tip   Word lets you insert a field anywhere you like in your document that shows the date and time that the document was last saved. Choose Insert ➪ Field, and select SaveDate in the Field Names list. The current date and time are automatically inserted whenever you save the document.

Saving versions

To save the document you're currently revising as a separate version, choose File ➪ Versions (see Figure 10-8). Click Save Now; this opens a secondary dialog box that includes a box into which you can enter identifying comments.

Another option in the Versions dialog box is a checkbox that tells Word to automatically save a version every time the document is closed. If many authors are working on a document, this ensures that everyone's version is properly recorded, even if individuals forget to use the Versions command.

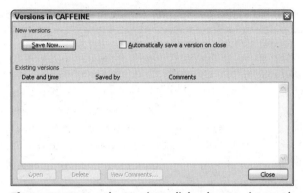

Figure 10-8: Use the Versions dialog box to view and manage versions stored together in a single file.

Working with earlier versions

If more than one version of a document exists, the Versions dialog box lists the other versions, who saved them, and any comments attached to them. (Click View Comments to see all of the comments text.)

You can work with an earlier version by double-clicking it. The current document and the selected version are displayed in separate windows, tiled horizontally. (Only one previous version can be open at any time.) You can edit the earlier version, but the changes you make won't appear in the current document. Instead, choose File ➪ Save As and save the edited version as a new document.

You can also delete any earlier version by selecting it in the Versions dialog box and clicking Delete.

Protecting Your Document

Just because you're sending out a document to a number of reviewers doesn't mean that you want all those reviewers to be able to see and comment on all the comments and changes made before they got hold of the document; nor does it mean that you want to allow them to change any content they want to, willy-nilly.

Word provides tools to help you ensure that only the information you want to distribute is distributed, and other tools to keep your document safe from unwarranted and unwanted changes.

To ensure that only pertinent information is distributed, make sure you use the Versions function described in the previous section. If the comments and changes made by every reviewer to date are saved in separate versions, you can choose any one of those versions from the list and save it separately as a new document. This prevents the recipient from seeing all the changes made by others.

To control the types of changes your reviewers can make, choose Tools ➪ Protect Document to open the Document Protection task pane (see Figure 10-9).

Figure 10-9: Restrict the changes reviewers can make to a document with the commands in the Document Protection task pane.

Word lets you set two types of restrictions: formatting and editing.

To set formatting restrictions, check the box marked Limit formatting to a selection of styles, and then click the Settings link. This opens the Formatting Restrictions dialog box shown in Figure 10-10.

All of the styles currently allowed (all of the styles available, usually) are checked to begin with. You can either leave all of these styles available, click the Recommended Minimum button to let Word choose which styles it feels absolutely should be allowed to remain, or uncheck all of the styles by clicking None, and then manually check only those styles you want to allow reviewers to use.

If you want AutoFormat to be able to do its thing no matter what restrictions you have put in place, check the Allow AutoFormat to override formatting restrictions checkbox at the bottom of the dialog box.

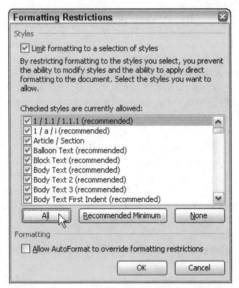

Figure 10-10: Here you can specify the only styles that may be used in your document.

Click OK to return to the Document Protection task pane. From there, you can set Editing restrictions by checking the checkbox titled Allow only this type of editing in the document, and then choosing the types of editing you will allow from the drop-down list provided:

✦ **No changes.** The reviewer can read the document, but that's it; no changes or comments are allowed.

✦ **Tracked changes.** This forces activation of the Track Changes function, so every change the reviewer makes is marked.

✦ **Comments.** This allows the reviewer to comment on the document, but not to change it.

✦ **Filling in forms.** This allows changes only within form fields.

If you choose No changes, a new section of the Document Protection task pane becomes available, called Exceptions (optional). Select portions of the document you want to allow all or some reviewers to freely edit, and then click the name of a user or group of users in the list provided, or click the More users link to open a dialog box in which you can enter the user names of those users who are exceptions to the No changes rule.

Once you're satisfied with the restrictions you've established, click the Yes, start enforcing protection button at the bottom of the Document Protection task pane.

Ensuring document security with digital signatures

A digital signature is an electronic, secure, encryption-based stamp of authenticity. Office allows you to digitally sign documents by attaching a digital certificate, a special file that is issued by certificate authorities (such as VeriSign, Inc., at www. verisign.com), or from your company's own internal security administrator or information technology (IT) department. Essentially, whoever issues your digital certificate verifies that you are who you say you are.

If you're sending a document to a series of reviewers sequentially, you might find it useful to ask each one to sign off on the document with a digital signature. When the file arrives at the next reviewer on the list with the digital signature intact, it verifies that the previous person to review the file was who he or she was supposed to be, and also that the file has not been altered since that person signed it. (Once the file is altered, the digital signature disappears.)

To digitally sign an Office file, first obtain a digital certificate. Then choose Tools ➪ Options and click the Security tab.

Click the Digital Signatures button, then, in the Digital Signature dialog box, click Add; this opens the Select Certificate dialog box, which lists all the digital certificates currently installed on your computer. Choose the one you want to use to sign the file, and then click OK to close the Select Certificate dialog box, and OK again to attach the certificate to the file.

To determine who last digitally signed a file, just choose Tools ➪ Options, click the Security tab, and click the Digital Signatures button.

Cross-Reference   For more on document security, see Chapter 46.

Using Master Documents

A master document is used to organize a set of related subdocuments; it's really a kind of "container" for the subdocuments. For example, if you were writing a book, you could create a master document (the book as a whole) that contains, say, 25 subdocuments (the chapters of the book).

In a network environment, master documents can be even more useful. A corporate annual report could be stored as a master document, made up of subdocuments such as reports from various departments and individuals. The person responsible for each report could work on a subdocument as needed; the editor of the overall report, or anyone else who needs to refer to it, can do so at any time by opening the master document, confident that it is as up-to-date as possible.

Creating master and subdocuments

To create a master document and subdocuments, follow these steps:

1. Create an outline of your master document. (For each section you want to turn into a subdocument, be sure to use the same heading style.)

2. Select the part of the document you want to break into subdocuments. (Make sure it begins with the heading style you've selected.)

3. On the Outline toolbar, click the Create Subdocument button.

   Word creates a new subdocument everywhere in the selection where the heading style that begins the selection appears. For example, if the selected area begins with Heading 1, a new subdocument will be inserted everywhere you used the Heading 1 style.

4. Save the outline.

   The outline becomes the master document; each subdocument is saved as a separate file with a name based on the text you used in its heading.

Converting documents to subdocuments

You can also turn an existing document into a subdocument of a master document. To do so, open the master document and place the insertion point where you want to insert the new subdocument. Click the Insert Subdocument button on the Outlining toolbar, and locate and select the file you want to insert.

Rearranging and editing subdocuments

You can quickly change the structure of a master document by adding, removing, combining, splitting, renaming, or rearranging its subdocuments. By default, the subdocuments are hidden when you open a master document, but you can use the Expand and Collapse Subdocuments buttons on the Outlining toolbar to see them in detail. When they're collapsed, each subdocument's name appears as a hyperlink; to open any subdocument, click its link (see Figure 10-11).

You can drag a subdocument heading to wherever you want to move it within your master document, and all its subsidiary text will go with it. To remove a subdocument and return its contents to the master document, place your insertion point inside its heading and click Remove Subdocument from the Outlining toolbar.

You can also combine or split subdocuments. To combine two or more, first move them next to each other by clicking and dragging the rectangular icon on the left side of the subdocument's heading window. Then select the subdocuments you want to merge by clicking the icon of the first subdocument and holding down Shift while you click the icon of the last subdocument. Then click the Merge Subdocument button on the Outlining toolbar.

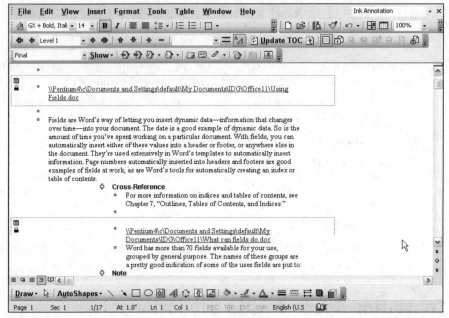

Figure 10-11: When collapsed, subdocuments show up in the master document as hyperlinks.

Note   When you save the master document, Word will save the merged subdocuments under the filename of the first subdocument; the additional subdocument's original versions remain saved under their old filenames, so you can always get them back!

To split a subdocument, click on the heading that begins it (or create a heading, if one doesn't exist; subdocuments must be constructed of outline levels, which in turn are built on heading styles) and then click the Split Subdocument button on the Outlining toolbar. When you save the master document, the new subdocument is assigned a name based on its heading.

Note   If someone in a networked environment is working on a subdocument, that subdocument is locked to everyone else in the workgroup. That means they can view it, but they can't modify it until whoever is working on it closes it.

Summary

Word has many features designed to make it easier for teams of people to work on the same document — features that can also benefit individuals who want to keep track of the changes they've made to a document.

✦ Word not only lets you insert comments, it keeps track of who inserted which comment and when.

✦ You can view comments in a variety of ways, from a ScreenTip you get when you hover your cursor over the text or in a comment attached to balloons down the right side of the page in Print Layout view.

✦ Word can track all changes to a document, from insertions and deletions to formatting changes, and indicate who made the change, and when.

✦ You can choose to accept or reject changes one at a time or all at once; you can also choose to accept or reject changes from a particular reviewer one at a time or all at once.

✦ Word lets you store multiple versions of a document as a single file, a more efficient option than storing every version of a document as a separate file.

✦ You can restrict the changes reviewers are able to make to a document by choosing Tools ⇨ Protect Document.

✦ Master documents are useful for organizing large documents with multiple sections, especially if different people are responsible for each section.

✦   ✦   ✦

Using XML in Word

If you've been using the World Wide Web for a while, you've probably heard about HTML (HyperText Markup Language) and know that it's the language used to create Web pages. It's called a "markup" language because it's written as a plain text file that has been "marked up" with codes — called *tags* — that Web browsers can interpret as instructions about how to display information.

Now you can use another, more powerful markup language: eXtensible Markup Language (XML), which holds the promise of enabling the free transfer of data between otherwise incompatible applications and platforms. Even though it's not really visible to the casual user, probably the most important improvement in Office 11 is the fact that you can now save most Office documents in XML format — meaning that they can be more readily shared with people who don't run Office.

What Is XML?

The best definition I've run across for XML is this: XML is a cross-platform, software- and hardware-independent tool for transmitting information.

It's easier to understand this if you compare XML to HTML. HTML was designed to display data, so it focuses on how data looks; XML was designed to describe data, so it focuses on what data is. Or, to put it another way, HTML is about displaying information, whereas XML is about describing information.

That being the case, XML is not a replacement for HTML. HTML tells a browser to do all sorts of things: set font sizes, create tables, create bulleted lists, insert horizontal rules. XML doesn't: what it does is structure and store information in such a way that it may be easily shared.

XML is able to do this because it has a big advantage over HTML: It's not limited to a set number of tags. Instead, every XML document defines its own tags, either internally or through association with an additional file called an *XML schema*.

A schema defines how the data stored in an XML document is organized. Among other things, it enables you to specify what kinds of data are acceptable. For example, you could use a good schema in association with an XML document template to ensure that all letters produced by a company's employees use the same date and address format, certain salutations and farewells, and so on. Using a schema ensures that you can create an endless series of XML documents that all store data the same way.

Figure 11-1 shows a bit of typical XML coding.

```
<reminder>
<to>Phyllis</to>
<from>George</from>
<title>Don't forget!</title>
<message>Don't forget to pay the water bill.</message>
</reminder>
```

Figure 11-1: XML is unprepossessing to look at, but powerful just the same.

What can XML be used for? Here are some examples:

✦ XML can separate data from HTML. When you put data into a Web page in HTML, the data is stored right inside the HTML code. XML enables you to store the data separately as XML files, while concentrating on using the HTML code to display that data. That means you can change the data that a Web page displays without having to worry about changing the HTML.

✦ XML can be used to exchange information. As already mentioned (and as is mentioned several times in this book), the biggest advantage XML brings to the table is that it can be read by many different types of applications. This means you can create documents in Office but share them with non-Office users (provided, of course, they have some way of viewing XML).

✦ XML can be used to store and organize data. Why would you want to use it? Because an XML database is readable by many different programs, whereas data stored in a straightforward Access database may not be.

Because the purpose of this book is to help you learn how to use Office, rather than teach you XML, I'm not going to go into much more detail about the language, except to point out later in this chapter how to use the tools Word provides for those who are conversant with XML.

Tip

For more information about XML, consult *XML All-in-One Desk Reference For Dummies* by Richard Wagner (Wiley, 2003).

Note

If you want to write your own XML or tinker with existing XML, you can use Word as an XML editor. There's nothing special about that capability: XML files are just text files, so you can edit them with Word as easily as you can with any other word processor or text editor, including the very simple Notepad that comes with Windows. If you do use Word in this way, though, don't save the resulting files as XML files; save them as plain text, and change the extension to .xml after they've been saved.

Saving a Word Document in XML Format

Because XML is now a native file format in Office, saving a Word document as XML is as easy as choosing File ➪ Save As, and then choosing XML Document from the Save as type drop-down list.

When you do so, though, two checkboxes you're not used to seeing in the Save As dialog box appear to the left of the Save button (see Figure 11-2).

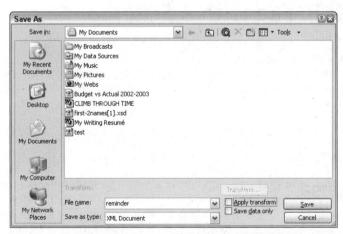

Figure 11-2: When you save a Word document in XML format, two new checkboxes appear in the Save As dialog box.

✦ Apply transform lets you use a file written in XSL (eXtensible Stylesheet Language) to transform XML into a desired output format — for example, HTML or a different dialect of XML. If you check this checkbox, the Transform button above it is activated. Clicking that opens a standard dialog box for opening a file. Locate the XSL file you want to use to transform the XML of the Word document you're saving, and click Open.

✦ If you check Save data only and click OK, you'll see a warning message telling you that "Saving the file through a transform or without WordML may result in the loss of document features." WordML is the XML schema (remember, a schema is what defines how an XML document is structured) that Word uses to include such important data as how the document should be formatted, where pictures and objects should be inserted, and other such advanced features. If you save data only, you're essentially just saving the text of the document; none of the special tags that WordML creates in the document to store formatting information survive. A transform, not surprisingly, similarly messes up WordML. The warning message box gives you an opportunity to change your mind by clicking Keep WordML.

If you keep both boxes unchecked, then the document is saved with WordML intact, and the next time you open it, it will act and look exactly like any other Word document.

Creating an XML File with a Schema

To create a new XML file associated with a particular schema, choose File ➪ New and click the XML document link in the New Document task pane. The XML Structure task pane immediately opens, informing you that, indeed, you can apply your own XML elements to a Word XML document, but that you must first select the schema; the task pane contains one link: Templates and Add-Ins.

Click the link to open the Templates and Add-ins dialog box, with the XML Schema tab selected (see Figure 11-3).

Adding a schema

Click the Add Schema button to open a standard browsing window for locating the schema you want to use. When you choose one, you'll be asked if you want to install the schema for all users on the current machine; choose yes or no, and the schema you've chosen appears in the Available XML schemas box of the XML Schema tab. Check it to associate it with your file.

Note   You can attach more than one schema to a document; elements from all of them will be available for your use in the document.

Figure 11-3: Use this dialog box to attach a schema to an XML file.

Before you click OK, you may want to click the XML Options button to call up the XML Options dialog box (see Figure 11-4). Here, you can set an option for saving your XML document (the same options that appear in the Save As dialog box when you choose Save As XML document) and options for validating schema (two of which also appear in the Templates and Add-ins dialog box) and for viewing XML.

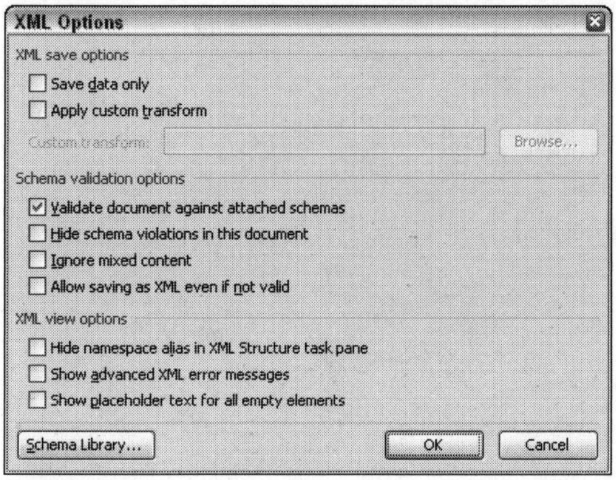

Figure 11-4: Set additional options for your XML file here.

Back in the Templates and Add-ins dialog box, you have two checkboxes at the bottom to consider:

✦ **Validate document against attached schema.** As noted earlier, one function that a schema can serve is to ensure that only valid data is entered into a particular XML document. Check this to have Word ensure that the data you enter doesn't violate the schema's rules.

✦ **Allow saving as XML even if not valid.** You might want to check this if your XML document is a work in progress that you don't have time to perfect in one sitting.

Caution   If you do check the Allow saving as XML even if not valid box, be sure to uncheck it before publishing an XML file online to avoid publishing one with schema violations.

The XML Structure task pane

Once you've made all your choices, click OK. A new task pane appears, called XML Structure. If you've started a fresh document using an existing schema, then all you'll see is a single element, called the *document element* or *root element*, the one that defines what kind of document this is, in the space labeled "Choose an element to apply to your current selection" (see Figure 11-5).

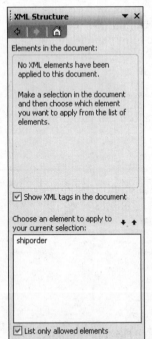

Figure 11-5: When you begin using a new schema, you have only one choice of tag, the one that defines the entire document.

Note The Templates and Add-ins dialog box also includes a button labeled Schema Library. Clicking it opens a dialog box that lets you add to the library any schema you have available; once a schema is added to the library, it appears in Available XML schemas in the Templates and Add-ins dialog box, ready to be checked and attached to the current document.

Click this element; an XML tag appears in the document space (assuming the Show XML tags in the document box is checked in the task pane, and why wouldn't it be?). Now you can begin building your document; sub-elements now appear in the Choose an element box. Each one you click will appear in the Elements in the document window at the top; if additional sub-elements are contained in that element, they'll appear below. By clicking above and below, you can move through the XML hierarchy of elements.

The elements, if the schema is well made, are self-explanatory, and tell you exactly what data should be placed inside them.

Figure 11-6 shows a document built from a schema designed for storing the information necessary to ship CDs. Word keeps track of where your cursor is in the document and displays only the elements available from that point of the document's structure.

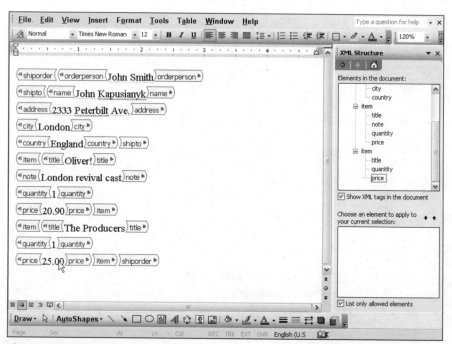

Figure 11-6: This XML document uses a schema for storing ordering information, with the XML tags displayed.

Applying a schema to an existing document

You can apply a schema to an existing document using basically the same procedure; choose Tools ➪ Templates and Add-ins, choose the XML Schema tab, apply the schema, and then insert the appropriate XML tags. Of course, the schema you're using should be designed for use with the type of document you've already created, or the tags won't make any sense!

Removing tags and changing attributes

To remove a tag, either double-click inside it — the whole tag is selected — and press Del, or right-click on the tag and choose Remove address tag from the shortcut menu. If you prefer not to use the XML Structure menu, you can also apply XML elements from the shortcut menu.

Some tags will have attributes — additional information — that isn't displayed in the main document. To set these attributes, right-click on a tag that has them and choose Attributes from the shortcut menu.

In the document shown in Figure 11-6, the root element, `shiporder`, has an attribute called `orderid` — the order number, in other words. In Figure 11-7, I've called up the Attributes dialog box to set that order number.

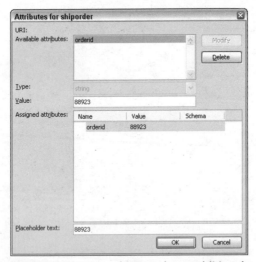

Figure 11-7: Some elements have additional attributes you can set.

Choose the attribute you want to set from the Available attributes list, and then click Add; the name of that attribute appears in the Assigned attributes text box. Now you can enter a value for that attribute in the Value text box. When you do, you'll see that the Add button has turned into a Modify button. Click it to set the attribute to the value you assigned. If the attribute supports more than one type of value, the Type drop-down list will be active.

Validating your document

If you enter a value that is not permitted by the schema, Word flags it for you with a shaded line down the left side of the document and the universal bar-across-a-circle sign for "that's not allowed" at the corresponding place in the XML Structure task pane. In Figure 11-8, I've generated this problem by entering a string of capital E's inside the quantity tag, which allows only numeric data.

You won't be able to save the file as an XML document until the problem is corrected (unless you've checked the Allow saving as XML even if not valid checkbox mentioned earlier). You can save the file as a Word document, but only Word will be able to read or process the XML.

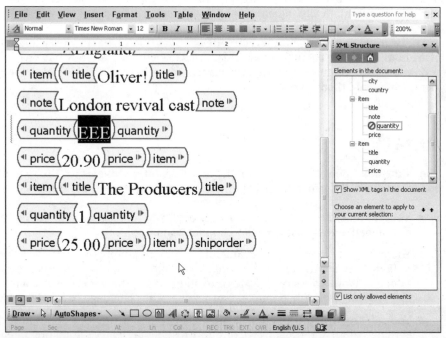

Figure 11-8: By default, Word checks your data against the document's schema and flags any data that isn't valid.

About Smart Documents

Smart Documents aren't something users will likely create for themselves, but they are something they're likely to run across — and I mention them here because they're based on XML.

Smart Documents are created by developers using XML schemas and a custom DLL. (DLL stands for Dynamic Link Library; DLLs are program modules that perform some specific function. You can't run them by themselves; instead, they're called into action by programs as needed.)

As you navigate through a Smart Document, it's able to detect the location of your cursor and display the most relevant information in the task pane. That might be some context-sensitive action you can perform, a word or two of help, suggested content, or links to data or related information.

Smart Documents can be distributed easily on a network, downloaded from the Internet, or sent via e-mail as templates. When you open the template, Office checks for the location of the *solution files,* the files necessary for the Smart Document's functioning. Assuming your security settings allow it, all the necessary files are downloaded and installed on your computer. Smart Documents can even update themselves automatically (again, assuming that security settings allow it).

In a networked environment, therefore, developers don't have to worry about how many computers are running a particular Smart Document; all they have to do is update the main document on the server, and any other installations of the document will update themselves.

Summary

One of the most powerful features of the new version of Office is its ability to save documents in XML format. In this chapter, you learned several advantages of XML:

✦ XML (eXtensible Markup Language) is designed to allow data to be freely exchanged across platforms and applications.

✦ You can save any Word file as an XML document simply by choosing Save As XML document. You can also choose to keep the formatting information contained in Word's version of XML or to simply save the data — or use a transform to transform the document into some other language or version of XML.

✦ You can create a new document from a schema (instructions about how data is to be stored and organized), or apply a schema to an existing document. Word displays the structure of the document and makes inserting XML elements a point-and-click operation.

✦ Word automatically compares the data you entered with the schema and flags any data that's invalid — and prevents you from saving the document in XML format until the problem is corrected.

✦ XML makes possible the development of Smart Documents that can provide context-sensitive help and information in programmable task panes in Word — and can even update themselves automatically.

✦　　✦　　✦

Using Excel

Worksheets and Workbooks

Workbooks, not worksheets, are the basic file in Excel—even if you're only using a single worksheet, it's still contained in a workbook. Workbooks, in essence, are the containers for worksheets. Think of workbooks as the ledger books that contain the pages on which you enter information. Worksheets are grids of cells arranged in rows and columns. When you first start Excel, or anytime you create a new workbook, you'll notice that you have three worksheets in your workbook. (It is possible to configure Excel to create new workbooks with a different number of worksheets, as you will discover later in this chapter.) Each worksheet is independent of the others, meaning that any changes you make in one worksheet are independent of changes made in the others.

Understanding Workbooks

Excel starts with a blank workbook titled "Book1" (see Figure 12-1). If you are starting a new project, simply use the blank default workbook and save it under a new name. (See the section on saving workbooks later in this chapter.)

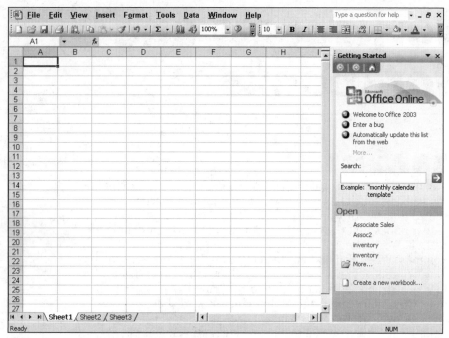

Figure 12-1: The default Excel workbook

Working with the Task Pane

Excel, like all Office applications, uses the concept of a task pane to help you work more productively. The task pane is the area that appears to the right of your worksheet, containing common tasks that you might want to accomplish. The task pane always has a title that describes what you see in it. For instance, the task pane shown in Figure 12-1 has the title Getting Started at the top, so it is often referred to as the Getting Started pane. Other task panes are similarly referred to by their titles. (The Getting Started pane is visible whenever you start Excel or whenever you click the Home icon at the top of any task pane.)

Task panes use many of the same controls that exist in other Excel windows. For instance, you can close a pane by clicking the Close icon in the upper-right corner of the pane. If you later want to display the pane, choose View ➪ Task Pane.

You should understand that the task pane is integral to working with Excel. In fact, even if you close the task pane, it can later appear automatically, because it is summoned by many Excel commands.

Opening new workbooks

There may be times when you want more than one workbook open at the same time. To open another new workbook, select File ➪ New from the menu. Excel displays the New Workbook pane at the right of your work area (see Figure 12-2).

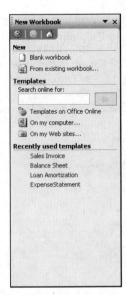

Figure 12-2: The New Workbook pane

To create a new workbook, click the Blank workbook link in the New Workbook pane.

The other choices in the New Workbook pane allow you to create new workbooks in different ways. For instance, you can click From Existing Workbook to pattern your new workbook after an existing one. You can also click any of the remaining three links (Templates Home Page, On My Computer, or On My Web Sites) to choose from different workbook templates. These templates are handy for pre-designed projects like invoices and expense reports. If one of the templates fits your needs, you can select it for your new workbook and have a head start on completing your work.

Opening existing workbooks

If the workbook you want to open is one you've recently had open, it will be listed in your File menu. Select File from the menu, and then look at the bottom of the drop-down menu options. Your most recently used files will be listed just above the Exit option. Click the name of the file you want to open.

Otherwise, you'll have to use the standard Open method. You can click the Open tool, click Open in the Home pane, or select File ⇨ Open from the menu. The Open dialog box (shown in Figure 12-3) allows you to choose from My Recent Documents, Desktop, My Computer, or My Network Places. The initial file listing is from the default file folder. Assuming you've done a standard installation of Office on drive `C:`, the default file folder is `C:\Documents and Settings\Your Name\My Documents`. (The `Your Name` portion of this file folder path is the username you use to log on to your computer.)

Figure 12-3: The Open dialog box

Select the file you want, and then click the Open button (or just double-click the desired file). If the file you want isn't in the default folder, use the standard Windows navigation methods to find the target folder or use the file-finding methods detailed later in this chapter.

Adding More Files to the List

The recently used files list has only four files in it by default, but you can set it to display up to nine files. To do this, follow these steps:

1. Select Tools ➪ Options from the menu.

2. Click the General tab.

3. Make sure that the Recently used file list checkbox has a checkmark in it.

4. Under entries, enter the number of files you want listed. You can either use the arrows to scroll through the numbers or type the number in directly.

5. Click the OK button, and the number of files remembered will be reset.

Working with Worksheets

When you first start Excel, or anytime you create a new workbook, you'll notice that you have three different worksheets in your workbook. Each worksheet is independent of the others, and you access them by clicking the tabs labeled "Sheet1," "Sheet2," and "Sheet3" at the bottom of the screen (see Figure 12-4) on the same level as your horizontal scrollbar. The tabs are called, appropriately enough, *sheet tabs*. You don't have to use all of the worksheets. You can add or delete worksheets at will. And if you'd rather start with more or less than three worksheets, you can easily change the default number.

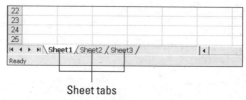

Sheet tabs

Figure 12-4: Excel's sheet tabs

Identifying rows and columns

Worksheets are grids of cells arranged in rows and columns. Each row (horizontal) has its own numerical designation, ranging from 1 to 65,536. Each column (vertical) has an alphabetical designation. The first 26 columns are A through Z. After that, they go from AA through AZ, BA through BZ, and so on, until you reach the final column, which is designated IV. It doesn't go all the way to IZ because Excel will allow only 256 total columns.

Cells are technically defined as the intersection of a row and column. Each cell in an Excel worksheet therefore has its own distinct designation based on the row and column that contain it, with the column noted first. For example, the cell at the intersection of column B and row 12 is designated as cell B12.

Cross-Reference   We'll be covering the methods of entering and manipulating data in the rest of the Excel chapters.

Moving around the grid

You can make any cell in the grid the "active" cell by clicking within it. Anything you type or paste goes into the active cell. In addition to the mouse method, you can use the keyboard to move around the grid. The arrow keys, Page Up, and so forth, change the active cell: If you press the down arrow key, the cell below the currently active one becomes the new active cell; if you press the right arrow key, the cell to the right becomes the new active cell, and so on. Table 12-1 details which keys and keyboard combinations achieve which results.

Changing the Cell Referencing System

Although the vast majority of people use the default cell reference style, you can use an alternative cell referencing system that uses a numerical designation for the columns. It's called R1C1 (an abbreviation for "Row 1, Column 1"), and the columns are numbered just like the rows, running from 1 through 256 instead of from A through IV. Using the R1C1 approach, the row is noted first and the column last. Thus, the cell at the intersection of Column 2 and Row 12 is called R12C2. To use this cell reference style, follow these steps:

1. Select Tools ⇨ Options from the menu.

2. Click the General tab in the Options dialog box.

3. Click the checkbox labeled "R1C1 reference style."

4. Click the OK button.

Whichever cell reference style you choose to use, the purpose and function of the cells doesn't change. You enter data into the cells, and then perform calculations on that data.

You can change the cell-referencing system anytime, and it should not be a problem with any of the existing cell references in your formulas. It is prudent, however, to decide upon a cell-referencing system prior to beginning work on your worksheet.

Table 12-1
Navigation Keys

Key	Action
Home	Moves to the first cell in the current row.
End	No effect unless followed by pressing one of the arrow keys (see below).
Page Down	Moves down one screen.
Page Up	Moves up one screen.
Down Arrow	Moves down one cell in the same column.
Left Arrow	Moves left one cell in the same row.
Right Arrow	Moves right one cell in the same row.
Up Arrow	Moves up one cell in the same column.
Ctrl+Down Arrow	Moves to the bottom cell in the current column if no cells in that column below the active cell have data in them. Otherwise, if starting from an empty cell or a cell that contains data but is above an empty cell, stops at the next cell with data in it. If starting from a cell with data in it, which is contiguous to other cells containing data, stops at the last contiguous cell that also contains data.
Ctrl+Left Arrow	Moves to the first cell in the current row (same as Home) if no cells in that row to the left of the active cell have data in them. Otherwise, if starting from an empty cell or a cell that contains data but is to the right of an empty cell, stops at the next cell with data in it. If starting from a cell with data in it, which is contiguous to other cells containing data, stops at the last contiguous cell that also contains data.
Ctrl+Right Arrow	Moves to the last cell in the current row if no cells in that row to the right of the active cell have data in them. Otherwise, if starting from an empty cell or a cell that contains data but is to the left of an empty cell, stops at the next cell with data in it. If starting from a cell with data in it, which is contiguous to other cells containing data, stops at the last contiguous cell that also contains data.
Ctrl+Up Arrow	Moves to the top cell in the current column if no cells in that column above the active cell have data in them. Otherwise, if starting from an empty cell or a cell that contains data but is below an empty cell, stops at the next cell with data in it. If starting from a cell with data in it, which is contiguous to other cells containing data, stops at the last contiguous cell that also contains data.
Ctrl+Home	Moves to cell A1.

Continued

Table 12-1 *(continued)*

Key	Action
Ctrl+End	Moves to the cell that represents the largest extent of your worksheet during this Excel session. Normally this is the intersection of the last row and column containing data. However, if you delete rows or columns, this navigation shortcut moves to the cell that represents where the largest extent was prior to the deletion.
End, Down Arrow	Does the same as Ctrl+Down Arrow.
End, Left Arrow	Does the same as Ctrl+Left Arrow.
End, Right Arrow	Does the same as Ctrl+Right Arrow.
End, Up Arrow	Does the same as Ctrl+Up Arrow.

Using the Go To command

To quickly navigate to a cell that is not readily visible because of the size of the worksheet, you can use the scrollbars or take the easy way and use the Go To command. To do so, follow these steps:

1. Select Edit ⇨ Go To from the menu, or press F5. This will bring up the Go To dialog box (see Figure 12-5).

Figure 12-5: The Go To dialog box

2. Under Reference, type the designation of the desired cell.

3. Click the OK button and the cursor will be placed in the desired cell.

Tip The Go To dialog box keeps a history of cells you've used it for. If you're using the same one over again, just double-click it in the Go To list (blank in Figure 12-5) instead of typing it again.

Adding and deleting worksheets

To add a worksheet, first click the sheet tab of the worksheet you want to put it before, and then choose Insert ⇨ Worksheet from the menu. You can add more than one worksheet at a time, too, but only as many as you currently have. Say you're starting with the default three worksheets. You can add two worksheets by clicking the first sheet tab, and then holding down the Shift key and clicking the second sheet tab. This selects both worksheets. Next, choose Insert ⇨ Worksheet from the menu just as you do for a single worksheet. Two worksheets will be inserted. If you had selected all three of the default worksheets, three worksheets would have been inserted. Because the number of worksheets to be added is determined by the number of worksheets you select, there is no way to create more than double the number of worksheets you have at a time.

To delete a worksheet, right-click its sheet tab, and then select Delete from the pop-up menu (see Figure 12-6). You will be asked to confirm or cancel the deletion. To confirm, click the OK button. To cancel, click the Cancel button. Deleting several worksheets is just as simple. Click the first one you want to delete, hold down the Shift key, and click the last one. All the ones in between will also be selected that way. Right-click any of the selected sheet tabs, and then follow the same procedure as for deleting one worksheet.

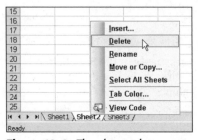

Figure 12-6: The sheet tab pop-up menu

The one drawback to this multiple deletion technique is that it's good for deleting contiguous worksheets only. If you need to delete multiple worksheets that are not side by side, use the same procedure, but hold down the Ctrl key while selecting the worksheets instead of the Shift key. The Ctrl key cannot be used to select a range of worksheets, however — only individual ones. You can use both approaches together if you need to. For example, if you have seven worksheets open and you need to get rid of the first three and the sixth one, you can use the Shift key approach to select the first three as a range of worksheets, and then use the Ctrl key approach to select the sixth worksheet individually.

Changing the default number of worksheets

To change the default number of worksheets, follow these steps:

1. Select Tools ➪ Options from the menu.

2. Click the General tab in the Options dialog box (see Figure 12-7).

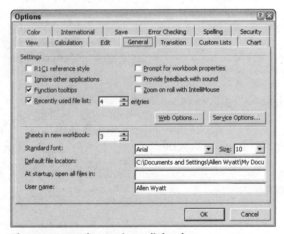

Figure 12-7: The Options dialog box

3. Choose the number of desired default worksheets in the Sheets in new workbook box. You can either enter the value directly or use the up and down arrows to increment or decrement the value.

4. Click the OK button to complete the procedure.

Moving and copying worksheets

Worksheets can be moved to another location, either within the same workbook or to another workbook. To move a worksheet within the same workbook, click the sheet tab and drag it to the desired position, and then release the mouse button. (As you are dragging, Excel displays a small triangle mark that indicates the location to which the workbook will be moved.) To copy the workbook, do the same thing, but press the Ctrl key before you drag the worksheet, and drop the worksheet before you release the Ctrl key.

To move a worksheet to another workbook you have open, follow these steps:

1. Right-click its sheet tab.

2. Select Move or Copy from the pop-up menu (refer to Figure 12-6). This brings up the Move or Copy dialog box (see Figure 12-8).

Figure 12-8: The Move or Copy dialog box

3. Pick the workbook from the To book drop-down list (if you select New Book from the list, you will create a new workbook containing only the selected worksheet).

4. Choose to place it before another worksheet or select Move to End.

5. To make a copy of the worksheet in the other workbook instead of moving the worksheet into it, click the Create a copy checkbox.

6. Click the OK button.

Caution   It's best not to move worksheets when other objects such as charts or other worksheets depend on the data within them.

If you prefer to not use the menus and the Move or Copy dialog box, there is another way you can move worksheets between workbooks: All you need to do is open both the source and target workbooks and display them both on the screen at the same time. (One way to do this is to choose Window ➪ Arrange and pick an arrangement style.) Then, simply click the worksheet you want to move and drag it to the position where you want it in the other workbook.

Renaming worksheets

All worksheets, when created, bear the name "Sheet#" with the "#" representing the number of the current worksheet. Although this does help to differentiate among the various worksheets in a workbook, it's not terribly informative. It may not matter if you're using a single worksheet for personal use such as balancing your checkbook, but if you're using multiple worksheets or if other people need to understand your worksheet arrangements, you'll probably want to give them more descriptive names like "January Sales" or "Midwest Shipments." To change a worksheet name, double-click the sheet tab. This will highlight the worksheet name, and you can type the new name over the default one. The size of the sheet tab will expand to fit the size of the worksheet title. You can use up to 31 characters in a worksheet name.

If you add lots of worksheets, or the titles on them are very large, you will end up with a situation where not all of the sheet tabs are visible at once. To view the ones that are out of sight, use the arrows in the lower-left corner of the screen (see Figure 12-9). They're styled like standard database controls. The one on the far left takes you to the first sheet tab, the one on the far right takes you to the last sheet tab, and the two in the middle advance the sheet tab view by one sheet tab left or right.

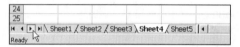

Figure 12-9: Sheet tab arrows

You can get more viewable area for the sheet tabs by clicking the dividing line between the sheet tabs and the horizontal scrollbar, and then dragging the divider to the right. This shortens the scrollbar, however.

Changing worksheet tab colors

When preparing your workbook, you might decide that you want different worksheet tabs to be different colors. Excel allows you to change the colors of individual sheet tabs, as desired. To change colors, follow these steps:

1. Right-click the sheet tab you want to change.

2. Select Tab Color from the pop-up menu (refer to Figure 12-6). This brings up the Format Tab Color dialog box (see Figure 12-10).

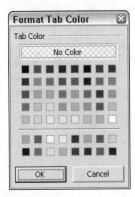

Figure 12-10: The Format Tab Color dialog box

3. From the range of available colors, select the one you want to use.

4. If you want to remove any color previously applied to a sheet tab, click on No Color.

5. Click OK.

Selecting and Using Ranges

Ranges are groups of cells. A range can be as little as two cells or as large as the entire worksheet. Ranges are used for many different purposes in Excel.

A range of cells is usually selected by clicking in the top-left cell and, while holding the mouse button down, dragging the pointer until it's in the lower-right cell of the desired range (see Figure 12-11). If you don't like dragging, you can also click in the top-left cell, move the pointer to the bottom-right cell of the range, hold down the Shift key, and click in the bottom-right cell.

Tip   Dragging from the upper-left cell is customary, but there is no actual requirement to do so. You can start in any corner of the range.

What if the range you want to select is larger than you can comfortably select using these methods? One way to select a large range of cells is to use the keyboard combinations detailed in Table 12-1, but hold down the Shift key while performing them. You can also select an entire row by clicking the row number to the left of the first cell in the row. Likewise, an entire column can be selected by clicking the column designation above the top cell in the column.

Tip   To select a very large range in a hurry, click the first cell in the range, and then select Edit ⇨ Go To from the menu. This will bring up the Go To dialog box. Under Reference, type in the cell designation of the opposite corner of the range. Hold down the Shift key and click the OK button.

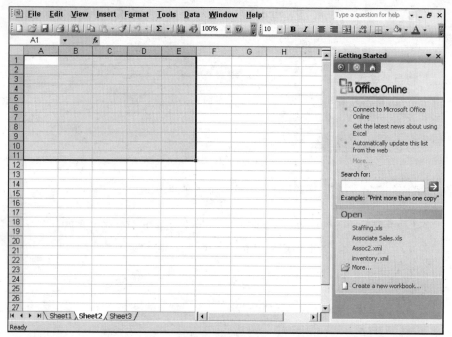

Figure 12-11: A selected range of cells, in this case A1 through E11

There's another aspect to ranges you'll want to keep in mind. Although a "range" is normally thought of as a series of contiguous cells, there's no real requirement that they be side by side. You can select a group of noncontiguous cells by holding down the Ctrl key while selecting them. For example, you can click in cell A1 and then, while holding the Ctrl key down, click in cell D5. The two cells are each selected and constitute a noncontiguous range.

Using Absolute and Relative References

Cells and ranges can be referred to by three approaches. The first two are essentially the same, but with one important difference. Using the normal cell-reference method, in which the top-left cell is called A1, a range that ran from that cell to D1 would be referred to as A1:D1. If it ran from A1 to H8, it would be referred to as A1:H8, and so on. You can designate an entire column or row by using it as both the start and end points of a range, as in A:A or 3:3.

Using absolute references

References to cells and ranges of cells are used quite frequently in formulas. (Formulas, along with worksheet functions, are discussed in depth in Chapter 15.) When you copy cells containing formulas to another location, Excel automatically adjusts any cell references in those formulas. Essentially, Excel changes the cell references to reflect the location into which you are copying the formula. For instance, assume that you have the formula "=B1+B2," and it is in cell B3. If you copy the contents of B3 and paste them into cell D3, the cell references are changed and the formula in D3 becomes "=D1+D2." This is done because Excel considers these normal cell references to be *relative references* — they are relative to the cell in which they occur.

Depending on your desires and worksheet planning, this might not be a good thing. For instance, you might want to copy the formula at cell B3 into another cell, and still have the formula point to the cells at B1 and B2. You do this by placing a symbol in front of the cell references to indicate that you want the reference to be *absolute* — to not change. The symbol you use is the dollar sign ($).

If you didn't want Excel to change the formula when you copy the cell contents, you would place the dollar sign in front of both the column and row references, as in "=$B$1+$B$2." You can also mix and match the position of the dollar signs as your needs change. For example, if you want only the row references to be absolute, but allow the column references to change as necessary, you can use "=B$1+B$2." Likewise, you could force the column references to be absolute but allow the row references to be relative if you use "=$B1+$B2."

Note   If you had copied the entire range of cells (B1 through B3) to a new location, the changes in the cell references would not have affected the total, because the data on which the formula acts would have moved as well. In that case, you wouldn't want to use the $ symbol, because that locks the formula in to using the original (and now empty) cells. For more information on using formulas, see Chapter 15, "Formulas and Functions."

Using names

The third method of referring to cells or ranges is to give them a descriptive name. Actually, all cells already have a name. It's just that calling a cell N372 is not really informative, other than giving its location in the grid. If you have a very small worksheet, it doesn't really matter much, but if you're doing anything large and complex, it can help a lot to refer to cells and ranges by such names as "Total" or "FebruaryCredits."

Naming a cell or range is about the easiest thing there is to do in Excel. Just click the cell (or select the range) you want to name, click in the Name box (see Figure 12-12), and then type the name you want to use. Press Enter to finalize it.

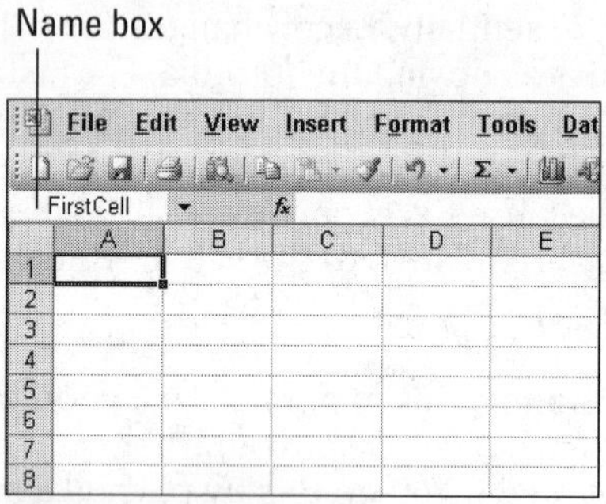

Name box

Figure 12-12: Excel's Name box

Caution When you use more than one word in a name, you can't use spaces. Use the underscore character (_) or a hyphen (-) instead. Names can be up to 255 characters, but ranges won't work right if you use more than 253 characters. Finally, if you use a named cell in a formula, it has the same effect as using the $ character — if you copy or move the cell containing the formula, the reference to the named cell will not change.

Saving and Closing a Workbook

To save a workbook, follow these steps:

1. Click the Save button in the toolbar. If this is the first time you've saved this workbook, you'll find yourself looking at the Save As dialog box (see Figure 12-13). If you've saved the workbook previously, it'll just save without any further effort on your part.

2. Using the Save in drop-down list, choose the folder in which you want to save the workbook.

3. Type a name for the workbook in the File name text box.

4. Click the Save button.

5. If you later want to save the same workbook under a different name, select File ➪ Save As from the menu and follow the same procedure as for a first-time save.

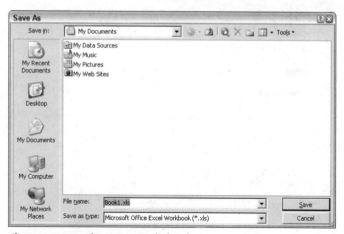

Figure 12-13: The Save As dialog box

6. If you want to save in some format other than Excel's native one, pick the format from the Save as type drop-down list before you click the Save button. Be aware that doing this will mean that the resultant file will have the limitations of the format it's saved in. (For instance, if the format you choose doesn't support different-colored worksheet tabs or some other Excel-centric feature, then if your workbook takes advantage of those features, those advantages will be lost once the save is complete in the foreign format.)

Make it a point to save your workbooks often. This habit provides "cheap insurance" in case your computer stops responding ("hangs") or the power goes out.

Setting backups

It's a really good idea to have Excel create automatic backups for you. That way, every time you save your workbook, the earlier version is saved as a backup file instead of being overwritten. To do this, in the Save As dialog box, select Tools ⇨ General Options. This will bring up the Save Options dialog box (see Figure 12-14). Click the Always create backup checkbox.

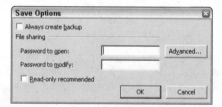

Figure 12-14: The Save Options dialog box

Caution   The backup files option is effective only for the file you set it on. You have to set the option on every single file you save, as there is no global backup option in Excel the way there is in Word.

Saving as a Web page

Some people like to share their Excel information with other people via the World Wide Web. To save an Excel file as a Web page, select File ➪ Save As Web Page from the menu. This brings up the Save As dialog box with Web options (see Figure 12-15).

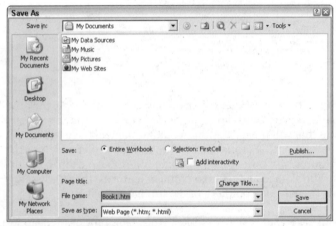

Figure 12-15: The Save As dialog box

There are a number of different things to consider when saving an Excel file as a Web page. The first is whether to save the entire workbook or a single worksheet (or portion of a worksheet, such as a range). You control this by using the Entire Workbook and Selection: Sheet radio buttons in the middle of the dialog box.

Notice the Add interactivity checkbox. This control allows you to specify whether people can interact with the Web page you are saving or publishing. If the checkbox is not selected, your data is saved as a static Web page, which is just fine for sharing information with other people. If you choose the checkbox, Excel includes features in the Web page that allow viewers to interact, in a limited way, with what is displayed.

Note   Even though the Add interactivity checkbox is selectable when publishing both the workbook or a selection, it doesn't seem to have any effect if you choose the option when publishing the entire workbook. This is essentially the same behavior as in Excel 2000 and Excel XP, although those versions grayed out the Add Interactivity control if you selected Entire Workbook, and Excel 2003 does not.

The title Excel uses for your Web page (that which is displayed in the title bar of the Web browser) will be the same as the name of the workbook. If you'd rather have a different title, click the Change button and type your new title into the resultant dialog box. This will not affect the workbook's filename but will change the title used for its Web page.

Instead of clicking the Save button, click the Publish button. This brings up the Publish as Web Page dialog box (see Figure 12-16).

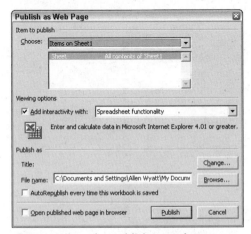

Figure 12-16: The Publish as Web Page dialog box

Caution   The interactivity of Web pages created with Excel is limited to users of Internet Explorer, version 4.01 and later.

By default, the entire selected worksheet is slated for publication. However, if you have cells selected when you choose Save as Web Page, the selection is the default. If you want to change this, make a different selection from the Choose drop-down list at the top of the dialog box. If you passed up the opportunity to choose interactivity, you can still add it here by clicking the Add interactivity with checkbox. There will be various options in the adjacent drop-down list box depending on what part of the sheet you're selecting to publish — for example, normal spreadsheet interactivity, PivotTable interactivity, or Chart interactivity.

You can change the title of the Web page here if you didn't already in the previous dialog box. To do so, click the Change button and enter the new title. Finally, click the Publish button.

Tip   Click the Open published web page in browser checkbox if you want to view the results of your save operation immediately in Internet Explorer.

Finding Workbooks

If you have lots of workbooks scattered around your system and you're not sure which one you need or where to find it, you can use the Open dialog box to track down the one that has the information you want in it.

Using any of the methods you learned earlier in the chapter (see "Opening existing workbooks"), display the Open dialog box. It should appear similar to what you see in Figure 12-17.

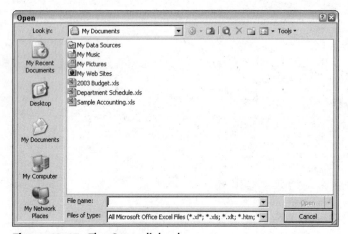

Figure 12-17: The Open dialog box

Select Tools ➪ Search. (The Tools menu is in the upper-right corner of the Open dialog box.) Excel displays the File Search dialog box, as shown in Figure 12-18.

With the File Search dialog box displayed, you are ready to search for the exact workbook you need. Follow these steps:

1. In the Search text box, enter the text you want to search for in your workbook. (You don't have to search for text; this just helps you narrow down the results of your search.)

2. Using the Search in drop-down list, indicate where you want to search.

3. Using the Results should be drop-down list, specify what types of Office documents should be searched. If you only want to search through Excel workbooks, make sure you clear all the checkboxes in the drop-down list except the one for Excel.

4. Click the Advanced tab (see Figure 12-19).

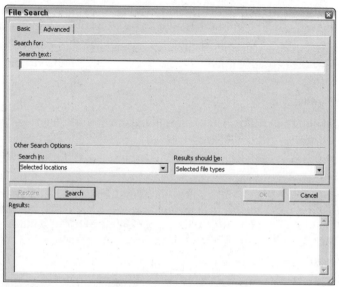

Figure 12-18: The Basic tab of the File Search dialog box

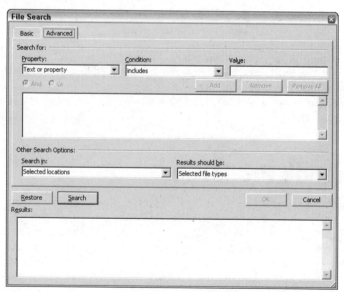

Figure 12-19: The Advanced tab of the File Search dialog box

5. In the Property drop-down list, select the item you're examining. This can be the filename, text contained within the file, or a variety of other options.

6. In the Condition drop-down list, pick which condition must be met; for instance, whether the property must include, begin with, or end with the value.

7. Enter the value under Value.

8. Once you've defined the criteria, click the Add button and the search criteria appear in the list of criteria.

9. If necessary, add more search criteria until you've narrowed the search sufficiently.

10. The two radio buttons labeled And and Or perform Boolean logic on your options. Clicking the And radio button means that the criterion you're adding must be met in addition to any other criteria; clicking the Or radio button means that either that value or others in the search can be met.

11. When you're ready to go, click the Find Now button.

For instance, say you're searching for a file that deals with a company named SEA. You know that the filenames of all the workbooks you've ever created for them start with "SEA," but they all have different endings. You could find all of them by selecting "File name" under Property, "begins with" under Condition, and typing "SEA" under Value.

Tip   If you're not finding the files you're looking for, expand the search by using the Look in feature at the bottom of the dialog box to choose different folders. The one way to make sure you're looking everywhere is to select the root folder and click the Search subfolders checkbox. That forces Find to look in every folder on the drive you're searching.

Setting Workbook Properties

You'll be doing yourself a favor if you set things up so that files are easy to find before you need to go looking for them. The best way to do this, other than by using intuitive filenames, is to use the workbook properties. These properties are a set of descriptive terms about the workbook. To set them, follow these steps:

1. Select File ⇨ Properties from the menu. This brings up the Properties dialog box (see Figure 12-20).

2. If it is not already selected, click the Summary tab. All the information on this form can be searched for with the File Search dialog box.

Figure 12-20: The Properties dialog box

3. Enter Title, Subject, and any other pertinent data. Keywords and Comments can be particularly useful in finding a file later.

4. When you're done, click the OK button to save the properties. When you save your workbook, the properties will be saved right along with it.

Summary

In this chapter, you learned how to work with workbooks and worksheets in Excel. Major points of the chapter included the following:

✦ Workbooks contain worksheets, just like ledger books contain pages.

✦ Worksheets are grids of cells arranged in rows and columns.

✦ You can change the active cell with the mouse, keyboard, or the Go To command.

✦ Worksheets can be added to or deleted from workbooks.

✦ Worksheets can be moved or copied.

✦ You can rename worksheets.

✦ Ranges are groups of cells, and there are a variety of methods for selecting ranges.

✦ Cells and ranges can be referred to by both absolute and relative references.

✦ Workbooks can be saved in other formats besides Excel.

✦ Worksheets can be saved as Web pages.

✦ You can use a variety of sophisticated search techniques to locate workbooks.

✦   ✦   ✦

Entering and Formatting Information

Although entering simple text and numbers is a piece of cake in Excel, there are some tricks that will make your life even easier. This chapter shows you how to use some of those tricks to enter and format information quickly and easily. You learn how to use Excel's fill series to easily extend a sequential series of labels, how to enter fractions so Excel doesn't think they're dates, and how to apply number formats. It also explains your different cell-editing options and how you can rearrange cells once they're in place or even add entire new rows and columns within worksheets.

Some simple planning, such as labeling rows and columns that contain data, will make your worksheets easier to use and understand. You can also add pop-up comments to cells if further explanation is needed. Furthermore, you can use font faces, sizes, styles, and colors as well as background colors and patterns to help create a look that will help viewers understand your data.

Excel has a large number of built-in formats for numbers, dates, and times, and you can create your own custom formats as well. If you don't want to work out all the details by hand, note that Excel's AutoFormat feature can instantly apply consistent looks to worksheets.

Entering Data

Anything you type or paste in an Excel worksheet goes into the active cell. Text, formulas, numbers, dates, and times are common examples of the kind of data Excel is designed to handle. Just click in the cell into which you want to enter data and you're ready to go. Type it, press the Tab or Enter key or just click another cell, and the data's entered.

Unless you're just whipping up a really simple quick 'n' dirty calculation for your own use, though, there's one thing you'll want to do first: label your data. At an absolute minimum, label the rows and columns of your worksheet. It's often useful to put in an overall title at the top of the worksheet as well, although the sheet tab can function in the same capacity. Data labels serve the same function for rows and columns as the names on sheet tabs do for worksheets. Without labels, all you'll have, no matter how carefully crafted your formulas and calculations are, is a meaningless jumble of data.

See the section entitled "Copying, Moving, and Merging Cells" later in this chapter for information about creating labels that span more than one row or column.

Creating data labels

There are two basic kinds of label arrangements. The first simply uses a single line of labels, either across the top of the worksheet to designate columns, or down the side of the worksheet to designate rows. Whether the line of labels runs horizontally or vertically, it usually begins in the first column (see Figure 13-1 for an example of the horizontal labeling scheme).

This type of data-labeling scheme is best used for delineating series of single values over time, by location, or by some other individual factor. One example is to show annual sales figures by office or individual. Another is to compare subscriptions by geographical region.

The other, more complex label arrangement uses both row and column labels. Because the first column of the worksheet is occupied by labels, as is the first row in the range of cells holding your data, the top-left cell in the range has no place in either labeling or containing data (see Figure 13-2). Although some people persist in trying to find some function for the first cell, apparently feeling there's something not quite right about leaving it blank, no one has ever managed to find a way to put an illuminating label in that cell with this type of label design. Inevitably, third parties viewing the worksheet try to fit any label in that cell into either the vertical or horizontal scheme of labels it's contiguous to, and there's no way to make it really clear to which one it belongs. Leave it blank.

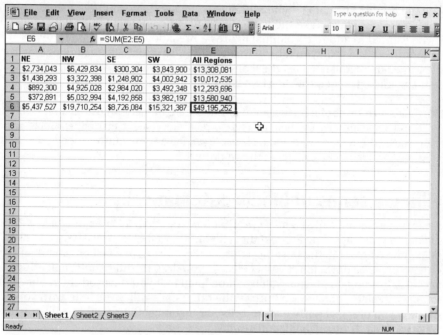

Figure 13-1: A horizontal line of labels ("NE," "NW," "SE," "SW," "All Regions")

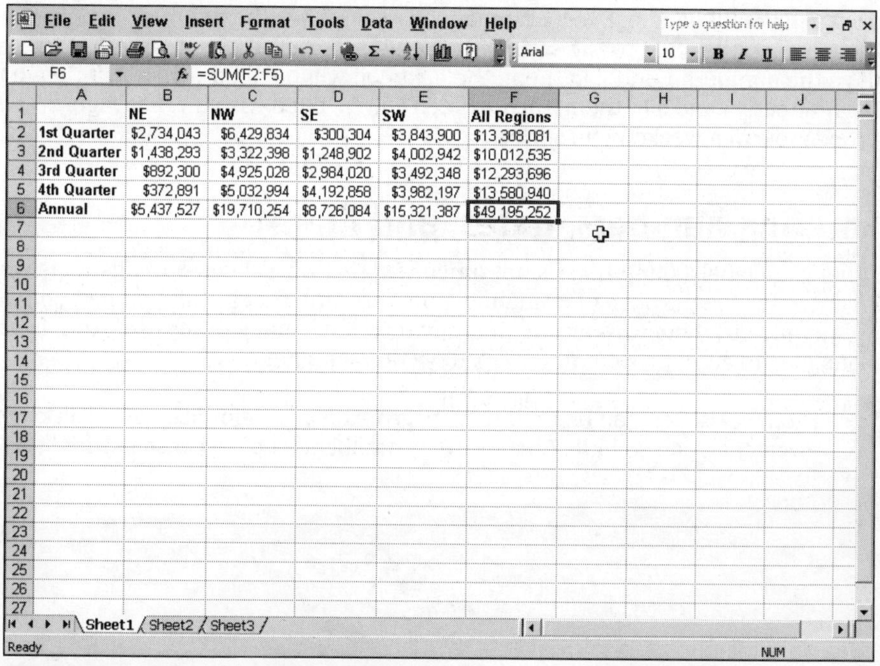

Figure 13-2: Column and row labels

Use the double-line data labeling scheme when you have multiple values to compare in various ways. Take the earlier example of comparing sales figures by office. If you wanted to add to the annual figures a breakdown of the data for each of the 12 months of the year, you'd have to have 13 rows of data instead of one. With a single value, an overall label for the worksheet will suffice, but with additional values in the worksheet, each row has to have its own label.

Note   Although most of the labels in worksheets are in the leftmost column or the top row or two under the title, there's no real requirement that either labels or data must be put in the traditional places. If you have some unusual needs, feel free to put your labels anywhere on the worksheet.

Filling a series of labels automatically

Excel has a feature called a *fill series* that lets you fill in a series of labels without having to type each one. For instance, if your first label is 1/1/03, you can click the fill handle (the dot in the bottom-right corner of the active cell or range) and drag it either across or down for several cells. As you drag the fill handle, a floating message will inform you of what value will be filled in if you released the mouse button. When you release the mouse button, the other cells will be filled in with subsequent dates. If you dragged for five more cells, for instance, they would be filled with 1/2/03, 1/3/03, 1/4/03, 1/5/03, and 1/6/03.

Excel recognizes many types of series, including numbers, times, dates, and days of the week. If you have two cells beginning the series and select them both before dragging the fill handle, Excel automatically calculates the differences between them and applies that to the series it generates. For example, if your first two cells have the numbers 1 and 2 in them, the next cell will be filled with a 3. If they have the numbers 3 and 5 in them, the next cell will be filled with a 7. See Figure 13-3 for an example of a weekday fill series.

Entering numbers, dates, and times

Other than labels, often there's not much text in a worksheet. Spreadsheets were invented for the purpose of crunching numbers, and that's still the most common use people put them to — although today they have many other uses, too, from managing inventory to keeping track of wedding invitations!

Cross-Reference   Excel worksheets can be used to manage text-based items like mailing lists, parts inventories, and so forth. Chapter 16 details the uses of spreadsheets for lists and databases.

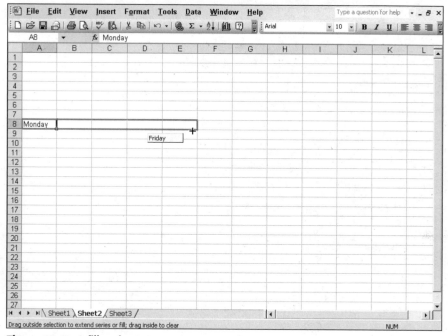

Figure 13-3: A fill series

Entering numbers

Entering numbers is every bit as simple as entering text, with a few caveats. Basically, just select a cell and enter the data. Excel does have limitations on numbers that you should be aware of, as illustrated in Figure 13-4. First, Excel's default cell format (called "General") will display only 11 characters. In the case of numbers, this means only 11 digits will be displayed. If you enter more than 11 digits, the number is displayed using scientific notation.

The second limitation is that, while Excel allows an unlimited number of digits to be entered, it restricts numbers to 15 significant digits. This means that anything beyond the 15-digit limit is converted to zeroes. (Note in Figure 13-4 that the Formula bar shows that everything after the fifteenth digit is zero.)

Caution   If you enter a number in a cell that is contained in a column with a fixed width, and that number is wider than the column width, it will not display. Instead, you will see a series of hash marks (#######) in place of the number. To solve this problem and enable the number to display properly, increase the column width so that it is at least as wide as the number. See the section entitled "Changing Column Widths and Row Heights" later in this chapter for details.

Formula bar

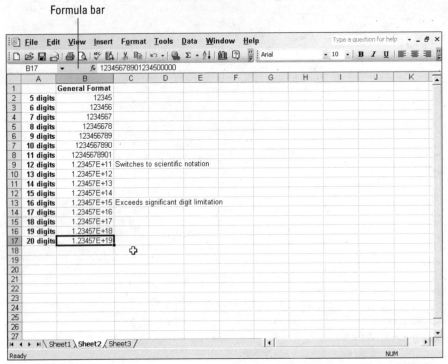

Figure 13-4: The number of digits you enter in a cell controls how that number is stored and displayed.

Values and What Excel Displays

When you enter information into a cell, Excel has to determine how to display that information. This determination process, called *parsing*, results in what you see on your screen after you move to another cell. In most cases, Excel applies the General format, unless you enter a date or time.

It is important to remember that Excel always differentiates between the contents of a cell and how those contents are displayed. The contents of a cell, or the cell's *value*, refers to the actual number or text within the cell. For instance, the value 1234 is a numeric value and can be contained within a cell. How a value is displayed depends on the formatting applied to the cell. For instance, with proper formatting applied, the value 1234 can be displayed as $1234 or $1,234 or 1,234 or 123400% or several other ways. The way the value is displayed, however, doesn't change the value that is stored in the cell—it is still 1234.

Dealing with Fractions

There's also a "gotcha!" if you work with fractions instead of decimal points. Although Excel will handle fractions properly if they're preceded by a whole number (such as 7 1/2), a fraction that stands alone (like 1/8) will be interpreted as a date (in this case, the 8th of January). To avoid this problem, you can either format the cell ahead of time to accept fractions (see the section "Using Number, Date, and Time Formats," later in this chapter) or you can just type a leading zero (e.g., 0 1/8).

Formatting the cell to accept fractions after the fact doesn't work, by the way—you have to think ahead. In the case of a fraction preceded by a whole number, Excel automatically formats the cell for fractions. Regardless of the formatting of the cell, the fraction will display in decimal format in the Formula bar.

Entering dates and times

Excel interprets dates and times as numbers, and you can use them just like any other number. You can subtract one date from another to see how many days apart they are, for example. To let Excel know that you're entering a date, use slashes or hyphens to separate the elements. For instance, 1-2 or 1/2 means that you're entering January 2 (see the sidebar "Dealing with Fractions"). If you just enter the month and day but don't specify the year, it defaults to the current year. You can use any combination of hyphens or slashes. To Excel, there's no difference between 1/2-03, 1-2/03, 1-2-03, or 1/2/03.

Whereas hyphens or slashes tell Excel that the number involved is a date, colons are the key to letting it know it's dealing with time. For instance, simply entering 3: in a cell is the same thing as entering 3:00:00 A.M. Excel always defaults to A.M. settings unless you specify P.M. or use military (twenty-four-hour) time. To do this, type a space and either a P or P.M. following the time (it doesn't matter if the letters are uppercase or lowercase), but you can't just type the hour and a colon; you have to follow it with at least one digit. For example, 3: P doesn't set a time, but 3:1 P or 3:01 P will. Watch out that you don't assume you're typing in the tens column if you just enter a single digit for the minutes, by the way—6:5 is the same as 6:05, not 6:50. As with the year situation, it's safest to type the whole number and not resort to the short version.

Editing Data

As you enter data or click a cell containing data, notice that the cell contents are displayed in the Formula bar, even if the contents are not a formula (refer to Figure 13-4). Any cell contents can be edited by clicking in the Formula bar and then typing the new data there, but you can also double-click the cell and edit the contents directly in the cell. If you'd rather use function keys, you can press the F2 key to switch the active cell to edit mode. Whichever method you use, the word Edit appears in the status bar on the lower left when you switch to edit mode.

Whether you're editing in the cell or in the Formula bar, whatever you enter in one appears in the other. If you're editing in the cell, the cursor is visible there, and the data in the Formula bar that is beyond the original insertion point of the changes drops down as though it were a subscript to show where the changes are being made. If you're editing in the Formula bar, both the subscript and the cursor display your current activity, but there is no indication in the cell, other than the changes themselves.

Cross-Reference   Chapter 15 deals with editing formulas.

Once you're in edit mode, the cell or Formula bar acts like a miniature text editor. You can use the arrow keys to move around, Home or End to jump to the beginning or end of the data, Insert to set for overtype or insert mode, Delete or Backspace to remove characters or selections, and so forth, just as though you were typing in a word processor.

Tip   The up and down arrow keys serve a special function in editing data. Pressing the down arrow key jumps the cursor to the end of the data. Pressing the up arrow key afterward returns you to the point you jumped from. If, however, the data takes up more than one line, the up and down arrow keys work normally, simply moving the cursor up or down one line. Oddly, if you press down while the cursor is on the last line, you will go to the end of the cell. Then, if you press up, the cursor is moved up one line, at the point directly above where you were before you pressed down.

Copying, Moving, and Merging Cells

There are a number of reasons why you might want to copy the information and formatting from one cell to another or to move a cell to another location entirely in the worksheet. The latter is the spreadsheet equivalent of a cut and paste operation in a word processor. Maybe you got partway through creating a worksheet and then decided to modify its look. Formatting changes in one cell can be copied to others, thus saving you an awful lot of work. Or you might realize that your worksheet design is flawed and you have to rearrange the cells. Whatever your reasons, Excel provides easy-to-use tools to accomplish the tasks.

Copying cells

To copy a cell to another location in the worksheet, follow these steps:

1. Click the cell you want to copy. This cell is referred to as the *source cell*.

2. Click the Copy button in the toolbar, press Ctrl+C, or right-click the cell and choose Copy from the shortcut menu. The border around the cell will change from a solid line to a moving dotted line.

3. Click the cell to which you want to copy so that it becomes the active cell. This cell is referred to as the *target cell*.

4. Click the Paste button (see Figure 13-5), press Ctrl+V, or right-click the cell and choose Paste from the shortcut menu. The data is pasted into the target cell, including any formatting (font styles and colors, background color, and so on) you previously applied to the source cell.

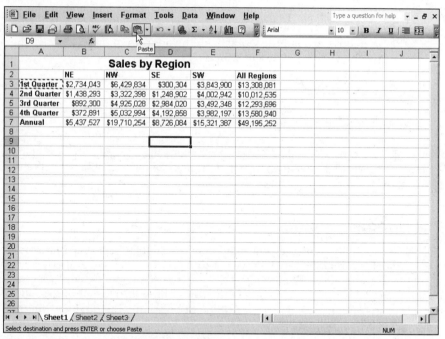

Figure 13-5: Copying a cell to a new location

The source cell remains selected, and you can paste into as many target cells as you want, either one at a time or en masse. If you want to paste the data into more than one cell in a contiguous range, the process is the same as for pasting into a single cell, except that you need to select the destination range, instead of one cell, before you paste.

Tip   You can copy a cell into multiple, noncontiguous cells as well as to a contiguous range of cells. To do so, hold down the Ctrl key while clicking the cells you want to paste into, and then click the Paste button in the toolbar. The results are pasted into all the selected cells regardless of their locations in the worksheet.

Moving cells

Moving a cell is even simpler, thanks to drag-and-drop.

1. Click anywhere on the border of the source cell (except for the fill handle in the bottom-right corner of the cell).

2. While holding down the mouse button, move the cell to the new location. As you move around the worksheet, the address of the cell under the pointer will be shown in a floating message.

3. Once you've got the cell where you want it, release the mouse button and the cell will move.

As with copy, all the original formatting comes along with the cell when you move it.

Tip   You can use the drag-and-drop technique to copy cells, too. Just hold the Ctrl key down while you're doing it and release it when you drop the cells into their new locations.

Merging cells

The capability to merge cells may seem unusual and useless, but it actually has a perfectly good function. If you want to create a data label that covers two or more rows or columns, cell merging is the way to go. Of course, you can just change the width of the column or height of the row containing a cell, but that affects the other cells in the same column or row. It might be stating the obvious, but only contiguous cells can be merged. Merging can be done horizontally, vertically, or both at once by selecting a range of cells. (See the section entitled "Entering Data" earlier in this chapter for more information on using data labels.)

Caution   If you merge cells and more than one of the selected cells contain data, you will receive a warning that only the data in the upper-left cell will remain after the merge. Never merge cells that already contain data you are unwilling to lose. Also, when you merge cells, any formulas that rely on the existence of those cells will be affected.

There are two methods for merging cells. One is really easy, but formats the text in a way you might not want. The other is more cumbersome, but gives you full control over text alignment. The cumbersome approach is as follows:

1. Select the range of cells you want to merge.

2. Right-click the selection.

3. From the pop-up menu, select Format Cells. This brings up the Format Cells dialog box.

4. Click the Alignment tab (see Figure 13-6).

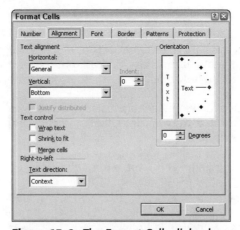

Figure 13-6: The Format Cells dialog box

5. Select the Merge cells checkbox.

6. Click the OK button.

To unmerge a merged cell, all you need to do is follow the same six steps, with the exception that you should clear the Merge cells checkbox in Step 5.

The easy way to merge cells is to select the range and then just click the Merge and Center button in the Formatting toolbar. This has the same effect as the menu approach, but forces you to accept center alignment. Fortunately, there's an easy workaround for this problem. While the merged cells are still selected, just click one of the other alignment buttons in the Formatting toolbar to change the alignment. If you want the merged cells left-aligned, click the Align Left button. If you want them right-aligned, well, you get the idea.

Note Merged cells lose their identity as separate cells in some ways, but not in others. The address of the merged cell as displayed in the name bar will be only the top-left cell of the merged range, yet you can use the Go To command to go to the merged cell by entering the name of any of the formerly individual cells.

Adding Comments to Cells

Comments are the Post-it pads of the Office world. They're notes you can attach to cells. To add a comment to a cell, follow these steps:

1. Right-click the cell.

2. Select Insert Comment from the pop-up menu. A yellow rectangle will appear next to the cell. Generally, it appears to the right of the selected cell, with the upper-left corner of the comment a little above the cell, but its exact location in relation to the cell depends on how much room there is on the upper right.

 Note Comments show up only within the worksheet proper, so if the cell you're commenting on is on the far right or top of the worksheet, the comment will appear on the left of or below the selected cell.

3. The comment already has your name at the top, although this can be deleted like any other text.

4. Type your comment.

5. Click anywhere outside the comment to complete it.

 Tip To change the name that appears at the top of a newly inserted comment, choose Tools ➪ Options from the menu to display the Options dialog box. At the bottom of the General tab, you can change the user name.

The cell now has a small red triangle in the upper-right corner. When you move the mouse pointer over cells that have this marking, the associated comments are displayed (see Figure 13-7). Moving the pointer elsewhere in the worksheet causes the comment to disappear from view again (although it remains attached to the cell, ready to be viewed again at any time).

 Caution While you type a comment, the text will scroll if you type more than will fit in the standard-size comment window, but the text beyond the bottom will not show when the comment is displayed. Make sure you resize the comment window so all the text shows at once before you complete the comment. If you need to resize it afterward, right-click the cell and select Edit Comment.

	A	B	C	D	E	F	G	H
1				Sales by Region				
2		NE	NW	SE	SW	All Regions		
3	1st Quarter	$2,734,043	$6,429,834	$300,304	$3,843,900	$13,308,081		
4	2nd Quarter	$1,438,293	$3,322,398	$1,248,902	$4,002,942	$10,012,535		
5	3rd Quarter	$892,300	$4,925,028	$2,984,020	$3,492,348	$12,293,696		
6	4th Quarter	$372,891	$5,032,994			$13,580,940		
7	Annual	$5,437,527	$19,7☐,254			$49,195,252		
8								
9								
10								
11								

Comment box text:
Allen Wyatt:
Represents a large
increase over last year's
totals. (Need to check
exact increase amount.)

Figure 13-7: A comment attached to a cell

Managing comments

If you right-click a cell that contains a comment, you'll find that you have three new options in the pop-up menu: Edit Comment, Delete Comment, and Show Comment. Selecting Edit Comment allows you to make changes in the text or to move or resize the comment window. Delete Comment, of course, removes the comment entirely. Show Comment changes the behavior of the comment so that it is constantly in view instead of showing only when the pointer is over the associated cell. This causes one more change in the pop-up menu: Show Comment changes to Hide Comment. Selecting the latter reverses the behavior of the comment window, causing it to appear only when you hover the pointer over the cell.

Tip   When a comment is displayed constantly with the Show Comment menu option, you can just click within the comment window to get full editing capability, including moving and resizing options.

Excel allows you to specify how comments should be displayed within a worksheet. If you choose Tools ➪ Options, Excel displays the Options dialog box. The View tab (see Figure 13-8) has a section labeled Comments. The three options in this section control the display of comments.

✦ **None** causes Excel to completely hide all comments, and you are left to stumble upon them as you happen to move the mouse pointer over a cell containing a comment.

✦ **Comment indicator only** is the default setting, and results in a small, red triangle at the upper-right corner of any cell containing a comment.

✦ **Comment & indicator** results in Excel displaying not only the red-triangle indicator but also all comments, even if the mouse pointer isn't hovering over a cell.

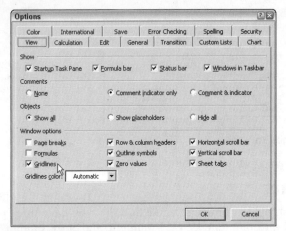

Figure 13-8: The View tab of the Options dialog box

Adding and Deleting Cells, Rows, and Columns

Inserting and deleting any part of a worksheet both follow pretty much the same procedure. You'll need to consider the effect the insertion will have on other cells, because they'll need to move aside in order to make room for the new cell. You have two options regarding where the other cells end up. In the case of an insertion, they can move either to the right or down; for deletion, they can move left or up. Pick the cell where you will make the change accordingly.

Adding cells

To insert a single cell, follow these steps:

1. Decide where you want to put the new cell.

2. Right-click the cell currently occupying that position. To insert a range of cells, select the range you want to insert, and then right-click anywhere within the range and follow the same process as for a single cell.

3. Select Insert from the pop-up menu.

4. This brings up the Insert dialog box (see Figure 13-9), which has four options on it. The first two, Shift cells right and Shift cells down, deal with individual cells or ranges of cells. The next two, Entire row and Entire column, insert a new row or column. If a new row is inserted, the row containing the selected cell moves down one to make room for the new row. If a new column is inserted, the column containing the selected cell moves right one to make room. Make your selection.

Figure 13-9: The Insert dialog box

5. Click the OK button.

You can't insert anything — row, cell, or column — that would cause any cell containing data to shift past the ends of the worksheet. Of course, this is a problem only if you have data in the cells at the extreme-right or bottom sides of the worksheet (column IV or row 65,536).

Deleting cells

You delete cells, rows, or columns in much the same manner as you insert them, and the Delete dialog box looks just like the Insert dialog box except for the title and a small matter of phrasing.

To delete cells, rows, or columns, follow these steps:

1. Right-click the cell or range of cells.

2. Select Delete from the pop-up menu.

3. The options in the Delete dialog box are to Shift cells left or Shift cells up. To delete an entire row or column, select Entire row or Entire column. Deleting an entire row moves the rows beneath it up one; deleting an entire column moves the columns to its right to the left. Make your selection.

4. Click the OK button to complete the deletion.

As with insertion, give thought beforehand to the effect that shifting cells in a particular direction will have on the cells around the deleted one(s).

Caution

When cells change their position because of the insertion or deletion of other cells around them, formulas that rely on their location are not affected because Excel automatically adjusts the formulas to reflect the new position. This is true even when absolute cell values are used in a formula. The new location simply becomes the new absolute cell value. However, if a cell containing data referred to by the formula is deleted, whether individually or as part of a row or column deletion, that's a different situation. In that case, the cell referred to by the formula is effectively wiped out and the formula will show a #REF error, which simply means that Excel cannot figure out what the formula should refer to. If this happens, use Undo to reverse the deletion.

Cross-Reference   See Chapter 12 for information on relative and absolute cell references.

Changing Column Widths and Row Heights

The width of columns and the height of rows are changeable by a variety of methods. Some of them take place automatically as you format data, others are managed with a mouse, and some utilize menu input.

Tip   Although columns will not expand on their own to accommodate the data you put into them, rows do change their height automatically to reflect the size of the fonts you use or the fact that you've applied word wrap. You can make a column expand to fit the material it contains by double-clicking the boundary to the right of its header. If you're more comfortable with menus, you can select the entire column and then choose Format ➪ Column ➪ AutoFit Selection. The same is true for rows, but you double-click the boundary underneath the row header. You can also use the menu selection Format ➪ Row ➪ AutoFit.

Changing column widths

To set a new column width, follow these steps:

1. Place your pointer on the dividing line between two column headings.

2. Click the primary mouse button. A floating message will give you the current width (see Figure 13-10).

3. Drag the boundary left or right. The size of the column to the left of the boundary will contract or expand accordingly, and the floating message will tell you what the column size you're selecting is as you move the boundary.

4. Release the mouse button to apply the new column width.

If you want to manually enter a specific number for column width, you can right-click the column header and select Column Width or you can select Format ➪ Column ➪ Width from the menu. This brings up a dialog box with only one function—to accept a new number. Do so, and then click the OK button.

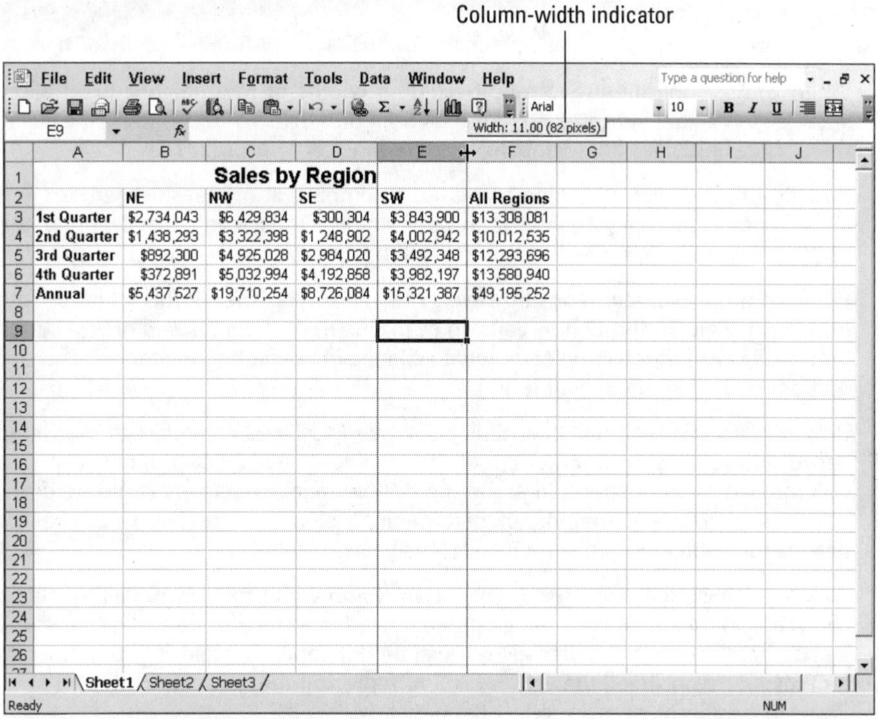

Column-width indicator

Figure 13-10: Resizing a column

Changing row heights

Row heights are handled in the same way as column widths, but you need to use the boundary between row headings instead and drag it either up or down to decrease or increase the row height. The row affected is the one above the boundary.

1. Place your pointer on the dividing line between two row headings.

2. Click the primary mouse button. A floating message will give you the current height.

3. Drag the boundary up or down. The size of the row above the boundary will contract or expand accordingly, and the floating message will tell you the row size as you move the boundary.

4. Release the mouse button to apply the new row height.

Values Used for Widths and Heights

When you use the menus to modify column widths or row heights, Excel allows you to specify a value that indicates the desired width or height. Understanding the significance of these values provides an interesting exercise in Excel historical trivia.

Row heights are specified using points—a common unit of measurement for fonts, where a single point is roughly equivalent to ¹⁄₂ of an inch. Thus, if you specify a row-height value of 36, you can rest assured that the row will be approximately one-half inch in height.

Columns are a different story, however. The values you specify for column width refer to how many digits (0 through 9) you can display in the column, based on the current default font for the worksheet. (You learn how to change the default font later in this chapter, in the section "Changing the default font.")

How did this come about? It is tradition. When Excel was created, the user interface was based on the DOS environment, and the leading spreadsheet program was Lotus 1-2-3. Column widths were specified according to how many characters could be displayed in a cell. This now-arcane method of determining column width has never been changed, despite many other improvements over the years.

What does this mean for you? If you set a column width to 10, you will be able to see 10 characters in the cell. If you change the font used in a cell or modify the font size, the number of characters you can actually see will be different. Likewise, if you modify the default font for your worksheet, the values used to represent the column widths are automatically changed, for all columns, to reflect the new font.

Manually setting a specific row height is handled similarly, but you right-click the row header and select Row Height or select Format ➪ Row ➪ Height from the menu to bring up the Row height dialog box. Type the new number, and then click the OK button to change the row height.

Resizing multiple rows and columns

To change the size of multiple rows at once, select the row headings of the ones you want to alter, and then click any of the boundaries in the selection and go ahead with the normal procedure as though you were doing a single row. All the rows in the selection are resized simultaneously. Resizing multiple columns simultaneously works the same way except, of course, you need to select the column headings and slide one of the column boundaries.

Hiding and Unhiding Columns, Rows, and Gridlines

Hiding a column or row doesn't affect anything but the visibility of cells. If you have a formula that refers to data in one of the cells in a hidden column or row, it will still work just fine. Hiding gridlines has no effect whatsoever except to improve the worksheet's appearance by removing the crosshatch of lines that defines the worksheet grid.

Hiding columns

To hide a column, right-click the column heading and select Hide from the pop-up menu. If you're more comfortable with menus, you can click any cell in the column and then select Format ➪ Column ➪ Hide. All the items in the column will disappear, from the column heading to the last cell.

Unhiding columns

How do you unhide a hidden column if you can't see it? Simple. Select the columns to either side of it, right-click one of their column headings, and select Unhide from the pop-up menu.

Tip

If you want to unhide column A, you obviously can't select columns on either side of it. Instead, press F5 to display the Go To dialog box. In the Reference box, enter A1, and then click OK. (Cell A1 is now selected, even though you cannot see it on the screen.) Now choose Format ➪ Column ➪ Unhide.

Hiding rows

Hiding rows works in exactly the same way except that you need to click the row headings involved instead of the column headings. If you're using the menu, you need to select Format ➪ Row ➪ Hide.

Hiding gridlines

To hide gridlines, follow these steps:

1. Select Tools ➪ Options from the menu. This brings up the Options dialog box (refer to Figure 13-8).
2. Click the View tab.

3. Uncheck the Gridlines checkbox.

4. Click the OK button.

To restore gridlines, reverse the operation, checking the Gridlines checkbox.

Using AutoFormat

If you'd rather not be bothered with making choices about font styles, borders, patterns, colors, and the like, Excel can do a pretty good job of handling all that for you. The feature is called AutoFormat, and it applies a set of predefined design options to a selected range of cells.

AutoFormat is flexible in that it allows you several options within the preset choices, but if it has a weakness, it's that it's restricted to a series of common uses in worksheet design.

Applying AutoFormat

To use AutoFormat, follow these steps:

1. Select the range of cells you want to apply it to (generally, your entire active worksheet area).

2. Select Format ➪ AutoFormat from the menu. This brings up the AutoFormat dialog box (see Figure 13-11), which shows samples of more than a dozen pre-designed formats for you to choose from.

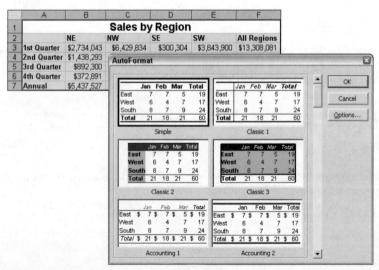

Figure 13-11: The AutoFormat dialog box

3. To pick one, click the sample image.

4. If you want to accept the design as is, click the OK button to implement it.

Figures 13-12 and 13-13 show two different formats applied to the same data. The first one is a simple and straightforward accounting format, whereas the second one is a much fancier three-dimensional approach.

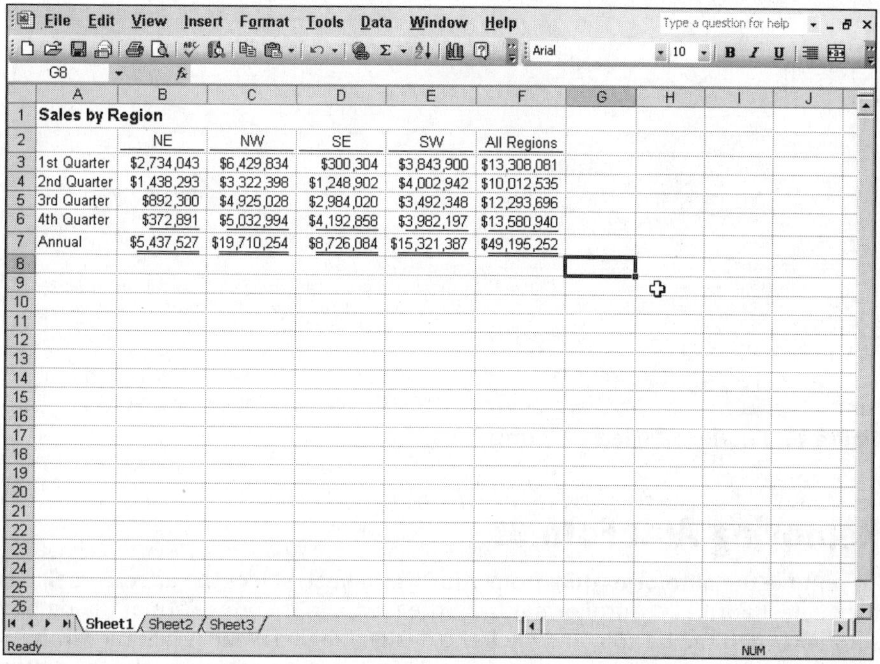

	A	B	C	D	E	F
1	Sales by Region					
2		NE	NW	SE	SW	All Regions
3	1st Quarter	$2,734,043	$6,429,834	$300,304	$3,843,900	$13,308,081
4	2nd Quarter	$1,438,293	$3,322,398	$1,248,902	$4,002,942	$10,012,535
5	3rd Quarter	$892,300	$4,925,028	$2,984,020	$3,492,348	$12,293,696
6	4th Quarter	$372,891	$5,032,994	$4,192,858	$3,982,197	$13,580,940
7	Annual	$5,437,527	$19,710,254	$8,726,084	$15,321,387	$49,195,252

Figure 13-12: The Accounting 4 format

Customizing AutoFormat

It's possible to use the basic AutoFormat but still apply some of the formatting yourself. You might, for instance, already have chosen colors, patterns, or fonts, but you want to use the border styles from the AutoFormat sample. In that case, before you click the OK button, click the Options button. This adds a series of checkboxes to the bottom of the AutoFormat dialog box, which allow you to customize the options that will be applied from the sample.

The new panel, labeled "Formats to apply," contains six options: Number, Font, Alignment, Border, Patterns, and Width/Height. Clicking the checkboxes to deselect them removes those options from AutoFormat; clicking them again to select them puts the options back in. The selected sample shows the results immediately so you can judge the effect.

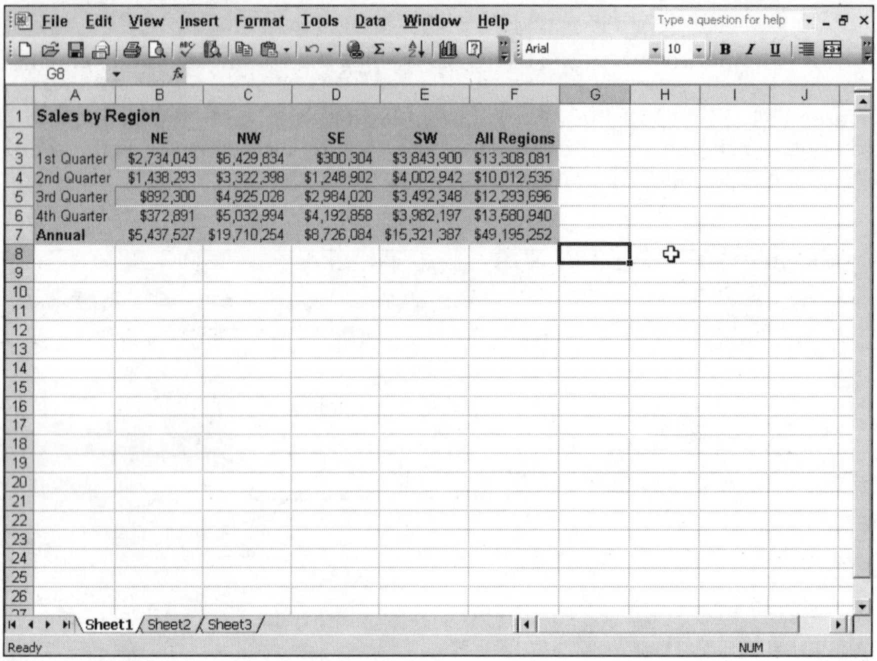

Figure 13-13: The 3D Effects 2 format

Removing AutoFormat

To remove the autoformatting from your worksheet, select the affected cells, and then select Format ⇨ AutoFormat from the menu. In the AutoFormat dialog box, scroll down to the bottom and click the design labeled None. Click the OK button to complete the removal of the formatting. This doesn't really bring the formatting back to the way it was before the first AutoFormat, however. None of your original formatting is retained (fonts, column widths, and so on)—the None style just applies default font, color, and so on.

Applying Fonts and Styles

Although you can present data perfectly well without fancy formatting of any kind, it's generally better to use it. Why? Two very good reasons. First, visual cues help to distinguish between the different parts of your worksheet and help people to understand what they mean at a glance. Second, the most attractive presentation is likely the one that will be most accepted.

Setting fonts for cells and ranges

You can apply fonts to entire cells, ranges of cells, and portions of the contents of cells. To set the font for an individual cell, click it, and then select the desired font from the drop-down font list in the Formatting toolbar (see Figure 13-14). To set the font for a range of cells, first select the range, and then select the font.

Note   The names of the fonts in the font list will vary from one system to another, depending on which fonts the user has installed.

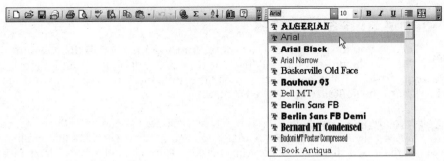

Figure 13-14: The Font list

The font can also be set for text within cells, right down to the single-character level. (This is true only for text, not for numeric values or formulas.) Double-click the cell to enter into edit mode; then, select the characters you want to apply the font change to. Select the desired font from the drop-down list in the Formatting toolbar.

Tip   If you want to apply one font to a cell but have some of the text within the cell be in a different font, you must set the font for the cell before you set the font of the characters. Otherwise, applying the font to the cell will override the individual character fonts within it.

Setting the size of fonts

To set the size of fonts, select the worksheet element you are going to apply the size change to, and then select the size from the drop-down Font Size list in the Formatting toolbar. As with font selection, you can apply the change to any worksheet element, whether it's an individual character within a cell, an entire cell, or a range of cells. The height of the row containing the affected worksheet element will adjust to accommodate the size of the font you choose, even if the size change is applied to only a single character within a single cell.

Tip   Instead of sizing a cell to fit its contents, you can resize the contents so they can be displayed within the cell's current width. To do this, right-click the cell you want to adjust and select Format Cells from the pop-up menu (alternatively, select Format ➪ Cells from the main menu). This brings up the Format Cells dialog box, from which you need to select the Alignment tab (refer to Figure 13-6).

Click the Shrink to Fit checkbox, and then click the OK button. It will take a few moments, but the text in the cell will be squeezed to fit within the cell. (See the following section for information on applying colors to fonts and other worksheet elements.)

Adding font attributes

Excel allows you to specify many attributes for the fonts used to display information. Three of the most commonly used attributes are **bold,** *italic,* and <u>underline</u>. To set fonts to bold, italic, or underline, click the Bold, Italic, or Underline buttons to the right of the Font Size list in the Formatting toolbar.

Note   If you choose to underline the contents of a cell, bear in mind that this might conflict visually with the bottom border if you're using one. For more information on borders, see the section "Applying Borders, Patterns, and Colors," later in this chapter.

If you want to select any of the lesser-used font attributes, or you just want complete control over the entire gamut of attributes, you need to use the Font tab of the Format Cells dialog box. (Choose Format ➪ Cells and click the Font tab.)

Changing the default font

The default font for Excel is Arial, a sans serif font also sometimes known as Swiss or Helvetica. Although Arial is good for headings, like most fonts that lack serifs (the fine details on the edges of characters), it lacks the kind of easy readability that makes for a good body font. The default size of the font is 10 points (a point is approximately ½ of an inch).

To set a new default font face or size, follow these steps:

1. Select Tools ➪ Options from the menu. This brings up the Options dialog box.

2. Click the General tab (see Figure 13-15).

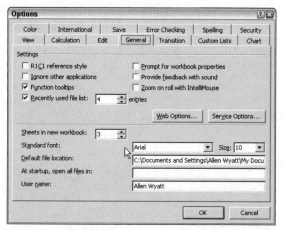

Figure 13-15: The General tab of the Options dialog box

3. Select the new font face from the drop-down list under Standard font.

4. If desired, select the new font size from the drop-down list under Size.

5. Click the OK button.

Aligning text horizontally

All text is, by default, left-aligned in the cell. Numbers, dates, and times are right-aligned. To change the alignment of cell contents, select the cell or cells you want to change, and then click one of the align buttons in the Formatting toolbar. The three main alignment buttons allow you to set left, center, or right alignment (see Figure 13-16).

In addition, there are two buttons for handling indented text: Decrease Indent and Increase Indent. Clicking Increase Indent adds a left indentation to the cell contents; each time you click the button, the contents are indented more. If you want the indentation to be less, click the Decrease Indent button. As with the Increase Indent button, each click applies the action again. Figure 13-17 shows an example of how indenting affects both text and numbers in cells. (Notice that the non-indented number, in cell C4, is right-aligned in the cell. This is the default alignment for numbers in Excel.)

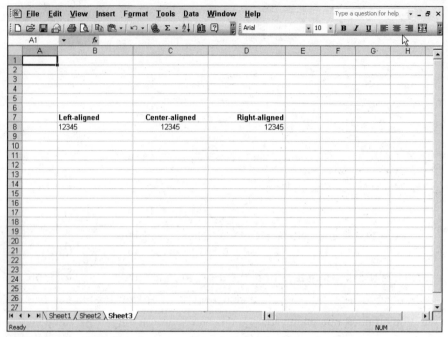

Figure 13-16: Left-aligned, center-aligned, and right-aligned cells

	A	B	C	D
1				
2				
3				
4		**Regular Text**	12345	
5		**1-click indent**	12345	
6		**2-click indent**	12345	
7		**3-click indent**	12345	
8				

Figure 13-17: Indented text within cells

To set more horizontal alignment options than the three basic ones and indentation, follow these steps:

1. Right-click the selected cell or range of cells.

2. Select Format Cells from the pop-up menu. This brings up the Format Cells dialog box.

3. Click the Alignment tab.

4. Under the Horizontal setting, you'll find several options: General, Left (Indent), Center, Right, Fill, Justify, and Center Across Selection. Make your selection.

5. Click the OK button.

The first four alignment options are ones that you're already familiar with—they simply duplicate the functions of the align buttons in the Formatting toolbar. The General setting is the default left-alignment. Left (Indent) is the same as indenting. Center and Right set center-alignment and right-alignment.

Fill alignment

Fill is an unusual function, not really having anything to do with alignment. What it does is repeat the cell contents as many times as will fit within the width of the column containing the cell. If the contents can't at least be doubled, nothing happens unless you expand the column width to the point where the additional characters will fit. Although this is not only useless but confusing if applied to normal text, it can be tremendously useful when you're using a cell as a buffer between other cells containing meaningful data. Simply place a single character such as an asterisk or slash in the cell, apply the Fill alignment to it, and you've got a divider cell that won't need any more attention no matter how much you change your worksheet, because the cell will fill with as many repeating characters as needed to adjust to the column width (see Figure 13-18).

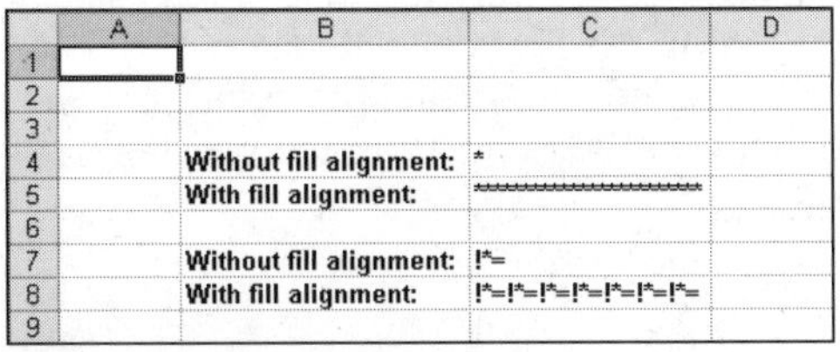

Figure 13-18: A fill-aligned cell

Horizontal justification

Justify performs the same action as it does in word processing, making the beginning of the first word on a line meet the left margin and the end of the last word on the line meet the right margin in multiline situations.

The effects in a worksheet cell, however, are not, generally speaking, worth the effort. Whereas justification in a word processor takes place over the width of an entire page, it takes place in Excel within the confines of a cell. Because few cells in any worksheet are wide enough to contain more than a few words on a line, justification tends to simply put wide gaps between two or three words, thus reducing the readability of the line (see Figure 13-19). Applying justification causes all the text in the cell to be displayed by increasing the row height to the degree necessary to show it all (if you haven't changed it from its default). You can click the Wrap Text checkbox on the Alignment tab to achieve the same effect without justifying the text.

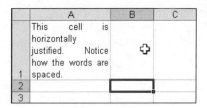

Figure 13-19: A horizontally justified cell

Centering text across a selection

The Center Across Selection option has an effect something like using the Merge and Center button. It takes several cells in a row and creates the appearance of one long cell with a single bit of centered text in the middle of it. Unlike merging cells, however, the cells involved do not lose their individual identity. In fact, you can still use them separately if you want to, and their separate contents will simply be centered in each cell. As with merging cells, its main utility is to create headings or titles that cover several columns.

To utilize Center Across Selection, type some text into one cell, and then select a range of cells using that cell as the starting point. Apply the Center Across Selection alignment to the range of cells and the text in the first cell will be centered across the entire range you have selected. The gridlines indicating the separate cells in the range will disappear, creating the illusion that the range is actually a single cell.

Aligning text vertically

The default vertical alignment is at the bottom of the cell. To set vertical alignment options, follow these steps:

1. Right-click the selected cell or range of cells.

2. Select Format Cells from the pop-up menu. This brings up the Format Cells dialog box.

3. Click the Alignment tab.

4. Under the Vertical setting, you'll find somewhat fewer options than for the horizontal alignments: Top, Center, Bottom, Justify, and Distribute. Figure 13-20 shows the effects of these alignment options. Make your selection.

5. Click the OK button.

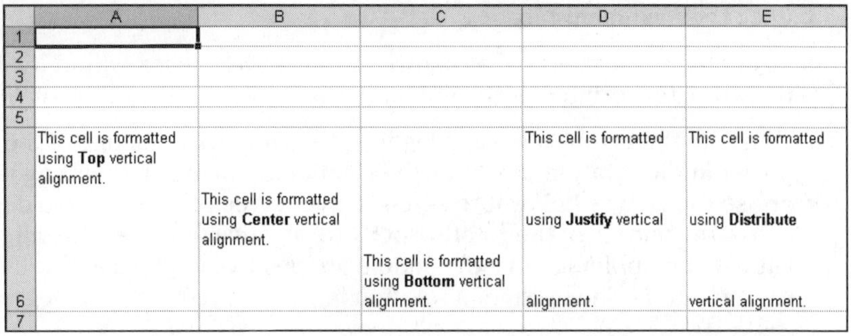

	A	B	C	D	E
1					
2					
3					
4					
5					
	This cell is formatted using **Top** vertical alignment.	This cell is formatted using **Center** vertical alignment.	This cell is formatted using **Bottom** vertical	This cell is formatted using **Justify** vertical	This cell is formatted using **Distribute**
6			alignment.	alignment.	vertical alignment.
7					

Figure 13-20: You can select different vertical alignment options in Excel.

The Justify setting works better in vertical alignment than it does in horizontal alignment, making the top and bottom lines of data line up with the top and bottom of the cell while evenly spacing all the lines. As with horizontal justification or word wrap, vertical justification expands the row height so that all the text in the cell is displayed at once (if you haven't changed the row height from its default).

In looking at Figure 13-20, you might not be able to discern the difference in how Justify and Distribute affect the contents of a cell. When there is quite a bit of information in a cell, the effect is not really noticeable. If there is only a small amount of text in a cell, however, you will see that Justify places the text at the top of the cell, whereas Distribute always attempts to evenly distribute the text throughout the available vertical space. Thus, if the cell contains only a single word that will fit on one line, Justify will place the text at the top of the cell and Distribute will place it in the center of the cell.

Rotating text

A common problem in worksheet layout and design is that the data in cells is not often as wide as the headings for the column containing the data cells. As a result, most of the cells in the worksheet are a lot of white space with a small bit of data. To solve this problem, Excel gives you two options — setting the text to vertical or rotating it.

Both are handled in the Orientation panel on the Alignment tab of the Format Cells dialog box (refer to Figure 13-6).

1. Right-click the selected cell or range of cells.
2. Select Format Cells from the pop-up menu. This brings up the Format Cells dialog box.

3. Click the Alignment tab.

4. To set the text to vertical as shown in Figure 13-21, click within the box with the word *Text* printed vertically (in the Orientation area of the dialog box).

5. To rotate the text as shown in Figure 13-21, you can click one of the degree points in the rotation box, drag the rotation pointer to the setting you want, or use the arrows below it to scroll to the degree of rotation you desire. Points below the middle of the rotation box are negative degrees and will result in left rotation; points above the middle are positive degrees and will result in right rotation. The maximum rotation in either direction is 90 degrees.

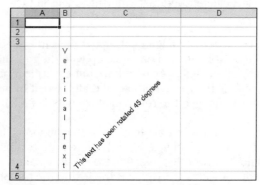

Figure 13-21: Excel provides two ways to rotate text

6. Click the OK button.

Applying Borders, Patterns, and Colors

You can dress up your Excel worksheet with all sorts of fancy options, either just for the sake of beauty or for the more practical reason that borders, patterns, and colors can help delineate the various areas of your worksheet and set off one piece or set of data from the rest.

Applying borders

A border is a line, either around an entire cell, on one or more sides of the cell, or even through the middle of a cell. Several basic border arrangements (left border, right border, top and bottom border, and so on) are available through the Formatting toolbar. Borders are best used when gridlines are not present. Otherwise, they tend to be hard to see, as every cell is already surrounded by a thin line.

To use borders, follow these steps:

1. Select the cell or range of cells you want to apply borders to.

2. Click the arrow to the right of the Borders button in the Formatting toolbar.

3. In the drop-down menu (see Figure 13-22), click the border style you want to apply.

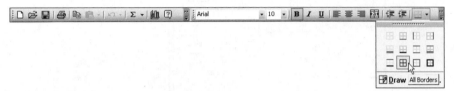

Figure 13-22: The Borders menu

If you are the artistic type, note that Excel provides a way for you to actually "draw" borders in your workbook. You do this using the Borders toolbar. To display the toolbar, choose View ➪ Toolbars ➪ Borders, or choose Draw Borders from the bottom of the Borders menu (Figure 13-22). When the Borders toolbar is displayed, the mouse pointer changes to a pencil, as shown in Figure 13-23.

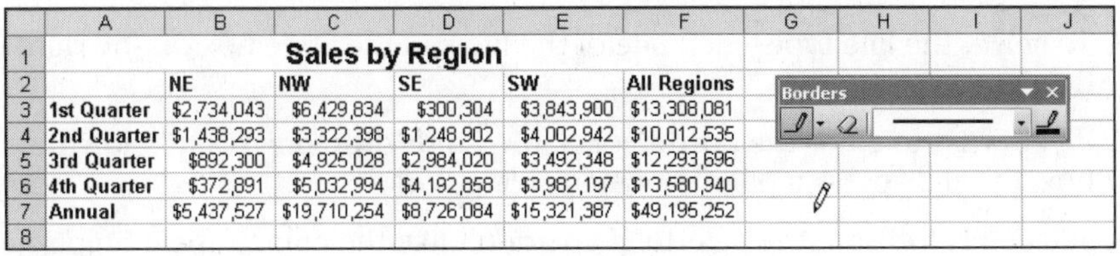

	A	B	C	D	E	F	G	H	I	J
1			**Sales by Region**							
2		NE	NW	SE	SW	All Regions				
3	1st Quarter	$2,734,043	$6,429,834	$300,304	$3,843,900	$13,308,081				
4	2nd Quarter	$1,438,293	$3,322,398	$1,248,902	$4,002,942	$10,012,535				
5	3rd Quarter	$892,300	$4,925,028	$2,984,020	$3,492,348	$12,293,696				
6	4th Quarter	$372,891	$5,032,994	$4,192,858	$3,982,197	$13,580,940				
7	Annual	$5,437,527	$19,710,254	$8,726,084	$15,321,387	$49,195,252				
8										

Figure 13-23: Use the Borders toolbar to draw borders

You can now click and draw borders on the cells in your workbook, as desired. If you want to change the line type or the color of the border, you can use the appropriate controls in the toolbar. You can even use the eraser tool to remove unwanted borders.

The most control over borders is attained through the Border tab of the Format Cells dialog box. Follow these steps:

1. Select the cell or range of cells you want to apply borders to.

2. Right-click the cell or within the range of cells.

3. From the pop-up menu, select Format Cells. This brings up the Format Cells dialog box.

4. Click the Border tab (see Figure 13-24).

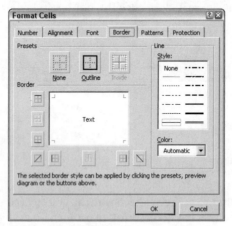

Figure 13-24: The Border tab of the Format Cells dialog box

5. Click the button that shows the type of border you want to apply.

6. To select the line type, click one of the lines in the Style box on the right of the Border tab.

7. If you want to color the border, click the Color drop-down list below the Style box. Excel displays a palette of available colors.

8. Select a color from the palette. If you don't like the color, repeat Steps 7 and 8 until you get one you like.

9. Click the OK button to finish.

Applying patterns

Patterns, properly used, can draw attention to different cells and help people to understand exactly what is most important. Improperly used, they can make your work impossible to read. A good rule of thumb is, when in doubt, use color instead.

Patterns are best applied to empty cells, rather than to cells with data in them. In this way, they can show that you meant to leave a particular cell blank, serving the same function as the phrase "This page intentionally left blank" in manuals.

To apply patterns, follow these steps:

1. Select the cell or cells you want to apply patterns to.

2. Right-click the cell or within the range of cells you've selected.

3. Select Format Cells from the pop-up menu. This brings up the Format Cells dialog box.

4. Click the Patterns tab (see Figure 13-25).

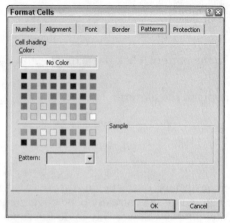

Figure 13-25: The Patterns tab of the Format Cells dialog box

5. You can select a background color for the cell at this time by clicking one of the color boxes in the palette. The Sample box shows the color you have chosen.

6. To access the patterns, click the arrow next to the word Pattern.

7. Click one of the patterns in the pop-up palette (see Figure 13-26). You will instantly be returned to the Patterns tab, where the pattern will be shown in the Sample box.

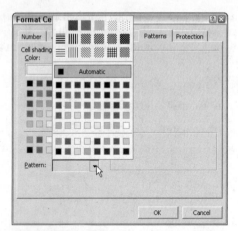

Figure 13-26: The Patterns pop-up palette

8. If you want to apply a color to the pattern, click the arrow next to the word Pattern again.

9. Click the color you want to apply to the pattern.

10. Click the OK button.

Applying colors

You can apply colors to either the background of the cell or the fonts within a cell, or both. One way to apply background colors has already been covered in the preceding section on patterns, but Excel offers a quicker way to do the same thing.

To apply background colors to cells, follow these steps:

1. Select the cell or range of cells you want to apply a background color to.

2. Click the arrow to the right of the Fill Color button in the Formatting toolbar.

3. In the pop-up palette (see Figure 13-27), click the color you want to use for the background.

Figure 13-27: The Fill Color palette

To apply colors to the fonts within the cell, the steps are absolutely identical, except that you click the arrow to the right of the Font Color button instead.

Using Number, Date, and Time Formats

Three commonly used styles specifically dedicated to numbers have their own buttons in the Formatting toolbar: currency, percent, and comma. Additionally, you can adjust the number of decimal points via the toolbar (see Figure 13-28). Numbers, dates, and times are, by default, right-aligned, and the styles work as follows:

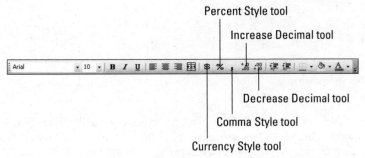

Figure 13-28: The three main number styles and the decimal buttons

✦ The currency style takes the number in the selected cell and converts it to the local currency as set on your system. In the case of U.S. dollars, it would convert the number "2000" so it reads "$2,000.00" by adding the dollar sign, commas at each thousand break, and a decimal point followed by two zeroes. The dollar sign might not, however, be right at the beginning of the number, because it rests at the leftmost side of the cell; how close it is to the actual number depends on the length of the number and the width of the cell.

✦ The percent style multiplies any number in the selected cell by 100 and appends a percent sign to it. A cell containing the number 3, for example, would be converted to read "300%." Because the percent sign resides at the far right border of the cell, it immediately follows the number.

✦ The comma style is identical to applying the currency style for American dollars, except that it does not attach a dollar sign.

✦ Adjusting the decimal point has two buttons: one for adding digits to the right of the decimal point and one for removing them. Each click on either button adds or removes one digit to the right of the decimal point.

Using the Style dialog box

All these styles are also accessible by selecting Format ⇨ Style from the menu. This brings up the Style dialog box (see Figure 13-29). Choose the style from the drop-down list under Style name, and then click the OK button to implement your choice.

Figure 13-29: The Style dialog box

> **Tip**   There are two variations on comma and currency styles in the Style dialog box. The comma(0) and currency(0) styles are identical to the comma and currency styles except that they do not add the two decimal points after the number. You can also select the Normal style to remove any of the other styles.

You can change any of the settings on the standard styles by clicking the Modify button, but it's better to just leave them alone and create your own if you need custom styles. Simply type the name of your new custom style into the Style name box, and then click the Add button. To alter the settings of your custom style, select it and click the Modify button. This brings up the standard Format Cells dialog box. Click the various tabs and make your custom formatting selections, and then click the OK button to return to the Style dialog box. Click the OK button in it to apply your new custom style to the current selection.

Other number formats

The number style buttons on the toolbar simply provide a shortcut to using standard number formats. The Percent Style button, for instance, causes the Percentage Number format to be applied. Oddly enough, the Currency Style button doesn't apply the Currency format but the Accounting format, as does the Comma Style button. You can access more detailed number formats in the Format Cells dialog box. To do this, follow these steps:

1. Select the cell (or range of cells) you want to apply the number format to.

2. Right-click the cell or within the range of cells.

3. From the pop-up menu, select Format Cells.

4. In the Format Cells dialog box, click the Number tab (see Figure 13-30).

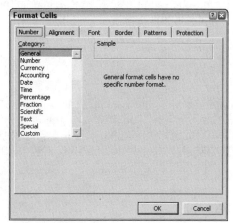

Figure 13-30: The Number tab of the Format Cells dialog box

5. Under Category, select the type of number format you want to apply (number, currency, accounting, fraction, and so on).

6. If the category presents options when selected, make your choices within them. Options might include such things as how many decimal places to show or what color to present negative numbers in.

7. Click the OK button.

Date and time formats

Excel interprets anything typed in normal date or time formats, such as 2/2/2004 or 6:54 P.M., as dates and times and automatically formats the cell they're typed into accordingly. However, you may want to manually change the formatting of a cell containing dates or times. To do so, follow these steps:

1. Select the cell (or range of cells) you want to apply the date or time format to.

2. Right-click the cell or within the range of cells.

3. From the pop-up menu, select Format Cells.

4. In the Format Cells dialog box, click the Number tab (see Figure 13-30).

5. Under Category, select either date or time.

6. Under Type, select the format you want the date or time to be displayed in.

7. Click the OK button.

Cross-Reference See the section entitled "Entering numbers, dates, and times" earlier in this chapter for more information on acceptable forms.

Custom Formats

In the rare event that the many built-in formats in Excel don't fit your needs, you can design and apply your own custom formats. The process itself is fairly simple, but the format codes are a bit disheartening at first glance. However, they follow a careful and logically designed pattern that, with a little practice, you will pick up quite easily.

Custom number formats

Number formats in Excel have four parts, divided by semicolons. The first part determines how positive numbers are displayed, the second part deals with negative numbers, the third with zeroes, and the fourth with text. You don't have to enter all the sections. For instance, if you're developing a number format in which you don't care about differences between the display of positive and negative numbers, all you have to do is enter the first section and that format will apply to all numbers.

Table 13-1 shows how the formatting codes are used in developing custom number formats.

Table 13-1 Custom Number Formats	
Formatting Code	*Meaning*
#	Placeholder for significant digits.
0	Placeholder for insignificant zeroes; adds zeroes if no number entered in that slot.
?	Placeholder for insignificant zeroes; adds spaces if no number entered in that slot.

Formatting Code	Meaning
,	Thousands separator if used in the main formatting code; divides number by 1,000 if placed to the right of the main formatting code.
.	Decimal point.
%	Percentage. Multiplies number by 100 and adds percentage sign after it.
/	Slash. Denotes fractions.
E+,E-	Shows numbers in scientific notation. Is not case-sensitive, so can also be e+ or e-. The codes to the right of it signify the number of digits in the exponent.
[color]	Brackets surround color designations. Color comes first in section, and must be one of the following: Black, Blue, Cyan, Green, Magenta, Red, White, or Yellow.
"text"	Displays the text within the quotation marks.
\	Backslash. Placed before a single character of text.
@	Displays text entered in the cell.
_	Underscore. Placed before a character, leaves a space the width of that character.
*	Asterisk. Like the Fill alignment option, fills the available space in the cell with the character following it.

Custom date and time formats

Date and time formats have only one section. They're quite a bit simpler than regular number formats, because dates have only days, months, and years to deal with and times have only hours, minutes, seconds, and fractions of seconds to consider. Table 13-2 shows how the formatting codes are used in developing custom date formats.

Table 13-2 Custom Date Formats	
Formatting Code	Meaning
d	Day numbering 1, 2, 3, . . ., 31
dd	Day numbering 01, 02, 03, . . ., 31
ddd	Day naming Sun, Mon, . . ., Sat.

Continued

Table 13-2 *(continued)*

Formatting Code	Meaning
dddd	Day naming Sunday, Monday, . . ., Saturday
m	Month numbering 1, 2, 3, . . ., 12
mm	Month numbering 01, 02, 03, . . ., 12
mmm	Month naming Jan, Feb, Mar, . . ., Dec.
mmmm	Month naming January, February, March, . . ., December
mmmmm	Month naming J, F, M, . . ., D
yy	Two-digit year
yyyy	Four-digit year

Times work in much the same manner as dates, in that they have only one section. Table 13-3 shows how the formatting codes are used in developing custom time formats.

Table 13-3
Custom Time Formats

Formatting Code	Meaning
h	Hour numbering 0, 1, 2, . . ., 23.
hh	Hour numbering 00, 01, 02, . . ., 23.
m	Minute numbering 0, 1, 2, . . ., 59.
mm	Minute numbering 00, 01, 02, . . ., 59.
s	Second numbering 0, 1, 2, . . ., 59.
ss	Second numbering 00, 01, 02, . . ., 59.
ss.00	Fractions of seconds.
AM/PM	Designates normal 12-hour clock. Can also be A/P.
[h]	Elapsed time in hours.
[mm]	Elapsed time in minutes.
[ss]	Elapsed time in seconds.

Note: Each time element is separated by a colon. Thus, to set time to show hours, minutes, and seconds, you might use hh:mm:ss. The two exceptions to the need for a colon are the AM/PM designation, which is separated by a space, as in h:mm AM/PM, and the fractional seconds, which are separated by a decimal point, as in h:mm:ss.00.

Caution   If you use m or mm to denote minutes but don't include any of the variants for hours or seconds, Excel will misinterpret your intent to mean months instead of minutes because months and minutes use the same codes.

Creating custom formats

To code the custom formats, follow these steps:

1. Select the cell (or range of cells) you want to apply the custom format to.

2. Right-click the cell or within the range of cells.

3. From the pop-up menu, select Format Cells.

4. In the Format Cells dialog box, click the Number tab (see Figure 13-30).

5. Under Category, select Custom.

6. Under Type, select the format closest in form to the new one you want to create.

7. Make the modifications to the format.

8. Click the OK button.

Now, when you want to apply the new custom format to any cell, just follow the normal procedure for applying formats, but select Custom under Category, and then your format under Type.

Tip   One cool way to "hide" the information within a cell is to apply a custom format consisting of nothing but three semicolons (;;;). Remember that custom formats consist of four parts, divided by semicolons. If you include just the semicolon dividers, you are telling Excel to display nothing if the value is positive, if it is negative, if it is zero, or if it is text.

Summary

In this chapter, you learned how to enter and format data in Excel. Major points of this chapter included the following:

✦ Anything you type or paste in an Excel worksheet goes into the active cell.

✦ Rows and columns containing data should be labeled.

✦ Excel's fill series lets you easily extend a sequential series of labels.

✦ Excel limits numbers to 15 significant digits.

✦ Fractions must be preceded by a whole number or Excel thinks they're dates.

✦ Double-clicking a cell causes it to enter edit mode.

✦ You can also edit cell contents in the Formula bar, even if the contents aren't a formula.

✦ Cells can be copied or moved to a new location, or they can be merged together to form one large cell.

✦ Comments can be added to cells.

✦ Individual cells and even whole rows and columns can be added or deleted.

✦ Row heights and column widths can be adjusted.

✦ Rows, columns, and gridlines can be hidden.

✦ Excel's AutoFormat feature instantly applies common formats to worksheets.

✦ Font faces, sizes, styles, and colors can be changed for any Excel element — from individual characters in cells to the entire worksheet.

✦ Cell contents can be aligned horizontally and vertically, and they can even be rotated.

✦ A variety of border options can be applied to cells.

✦ Cells can contain background colors and patterns.

✦ Excel has a large number of built-in formats for numbers, dates, and times, and you can create your own custom formats as well.

✦   ✦   ✦

Charts

Charts offer a way to represent complex data in an easy-to-understand visual format. With charts, patterns that might otherwise be hidden within a bewildering array of data are easily spotted. Excel's Chart Wizard lets you easily create a wide variety of chart types to handle various types of information. If the vast number of chart types and subtypes isn't enough for your particular situation, you can create and save your own custom chart formats for future use.

Creating Charts with Chart Wizard

Excel's Chart Wizard makes creating charts about as easy as it can possibly get. Just let it know what it is you want to chart, and then it's just a matter of making a few selections and your chart is on the page. To make a chart with Chart Wizard, follow these steps:

1. Select the range of data you want to make a chart from (see Figure 14-1). You might not want to select all the data that's available. In this case, we've chosen only the quarterly breakdowns by region, leaving out the totals.

2. Click the Chart Wizard button in the toolbar. This brings up the first Chart Wizard dialog box, Chart Type (see Figure 14-2).

3. Under Chart type, choose the kind of chart you want to create. The default choice is Column, but there are many others to pick from.

4. Under Chart sub-type, choose the specific variety of that chart type that you want to use. As you click each of the visual subtype representations, a description of the typical use of that subtype appears below it.

5. If you want to see what your data would look like, click the Press and Hold to View Sample button. The sample that's presented gives only an approximation of the appearance of the actual finished chart, as it's crammed into a very small area, but it should tell you what you need to know in a general sense.

	A	B	C	D	E	F	G	H
1			Sales by Region					
2		NE	NW	SE	SW	All Regions		
3	1st Quarter	$ 2,734,043	$ 6,429,834	$ 300,304	$ 3,843,900	$ 13,308,081		
4	2nd Quarter	$ 1,438,293	$ 3,322,398	$ 1,248,902	$ 4,002,942	$ 10,012,535		
5	3rd Quarter	$ 892,300	$ 4,925,028	$ 2,984,020	$ 3,492,348	$ 12,293,696		
6	4th Quarter	$ 372,891	$ 5,032,994	$ 4,192,858	$ 3,982,197	$ 13,580,940		
7	Annual	$ 5,437,527	$ 19,710,254	$ 8,726,084	$ 15,321,387	$ 49,195,252		
8								

Figure 14-1: Data selected for charting

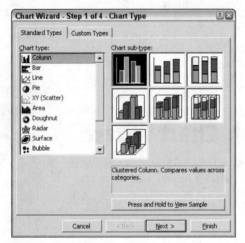

Figure 14-2: The Chart Type dialog box

6. If you want still more options of exotic chart types, click the Custom Types tab.

7. When you've made your selections about chart types, click the Next button. This brings up the second Chart Wizard dialog box, Chart Source Data (see Figure 14-3).

8. This shows a more accurate representation of how the finished chart will look. By default, the data series is taken from the rows of the selected range. If you want it taken from the columns instead, click the Columns radio button. You might want to try both to see which way your data is better presented. Just click each radio button in turn until you're satisfied with the presentation.

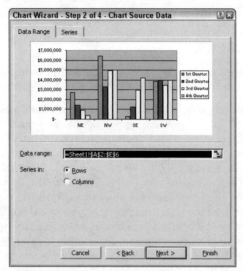

Figure 14-3: The Chart Source Data dialog box

9. If you want to view the range of cells that each row or column of data is taken from, click the Series tab.

10. Click the Next button to proceed. This brings up the third Chart Wizard dialog box, Chart Options (see Figure 14-4).

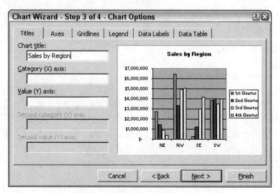

Figure 14-4: The Chart Options dialog box

11. Type a title for the chart in the Chart title edit box.

12. If you want any text below categories on the bottom part of the chart, type it into the Category (X) axis edit box.

13. If you want any text to the left of the values that range from the top to the bottom of the chart on the left side, type it into the Value (Y) axis edit box.

14. You can specify various options by clicking the other tabs, which will be covered in depth later in this chapter. Generally speaking, Excel does a very good job of interpreting the data you feed it and deciding which options to add for the most pleasing chart appearance, so it's not a good idea to mess with the other settings unless you have very specific requirements. They can all be altered after the chart is completed anyway (we will explore their uses for chart modification in a later section). Take the time to explore the various settings, however, because the sample chart display lets you see the effects of the different settings. Many of the options (such as data labels) merely clutter the chart to the point where it becomes useless as a conveyor of information. If you do want to add extras to the chart at this point, however, anything you put in can be removed after the chart is completed.

15. Click the Next button to proceed. This brings up the fourth and final Chart Wizard dialog box, Chart Location (see Figure 14-5).

Figure 14-5: The Chart Location dialog box

16. This is the simplest step of all. All you need to do is to decide whether you want the chart to be included in the worksheet it draws its data from or to be created as a separate chart sheet. Unless you have a very high-resolution system or a very small chart, it's usually best to make the chart on a separate sheet. If you try to put a large chart on the same worksheet as the original data, it's usually difficult to fit both so that they're readable. Click the appropriate radio button, and then click the Finish button.

17. The chart is created. If it is on a separate chart sheet, it looks like the one shown in Figure 14-6. If it's on the original worksheet, Excel places the chart right smack in the middle of the worksheet, as shown in Figure 14-7, and you have to move it manually as well as resize it so that all the data is shown. To move it, place the pointer anywhere within the table (so long as it isn't over a table element such as the title), hold down your mouse button, and drag it to its new location. To resize it, click any of the sizing handles around the edge and drag the handle in the direction you want to increase the size.

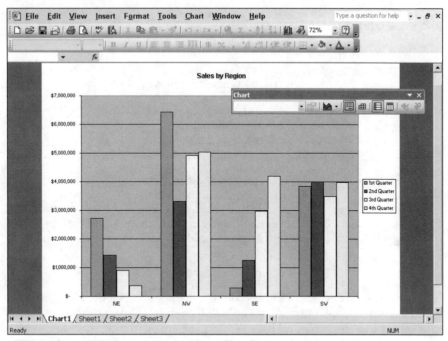

Figure 14-6: A chart as a separate chart sheet

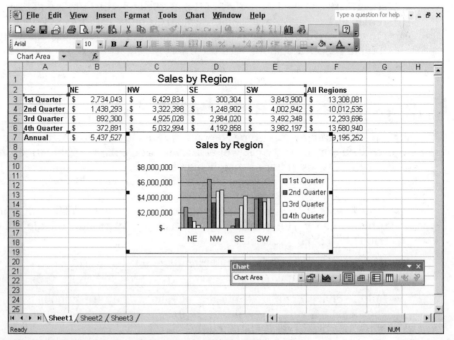

Figure 14-7: A chart on the original worksheet

Creating Charts from Noncontiguous Selections

You can create charts from noncontiguous selections. For instance, you might want to choose some, but not all, rows from a set of data. You do this by holding down the Ctrl key while making the selections. The selections are supposed to still make a rectangle when they're combined into the chart. In other words, you're theoretically able to do this only if you take the same number of cells from each row, but you don't actually have to do that. You can select three cells from one row, five from another, and so on, if you want to. The chart will simply fail to show anything you don't select, but everything you have selected will be in its proper place.

However, there is one thing you definitely do have to do if you're going to make a chart out of nonrectangular data and you want it to make sense—you have to start each data series in the same column. This is because the first cell in each data series will be the first thing on the chart. Unless all the data series start from the same base, there's no way to use the chart to make valid comparisons among them.

18. In both cases, the Chart toolbar will appear (I removed it from Figure 14-6 so that the full chart would be visible). You can leave the toolbar floating, or you can move it up into the main toolbar area with the other toolbars. Also, the Data menu will be replaced by a Chart menu. In the case of a chart that is placed as an object on the original worksheet, the Data and Chart menus will alternate, depending on whether you are working on the chart or the worksheet. When you click on part of the worksheet, the Data menu reappears, replacing the Chart menu, and the Chart toolbar disappears (even if you have moved it up into the main toolbar area). When you click the chart, the Chart toolbar reappears, along with the Chart menu, which replaces the Data menu.

Understanding Chart Types

There are 14 standard chart types in Excel, each with two to seven subtypes. There are also 20 custom chart types, which are variations on or combinations of the standard chart types, differing mainly in color and graphical appearance. The following alphabetical list describes each of the standard chart types:

✦ **Area charts** show the relative contribution of values over a period of time or other category. The greater the area taken up by a value, the more it contributes to the overall total.

✦ **Bar charts** are perhaps the most familiar chart type. They show values by the length of horizontal bars.

✦ **Bubble charts** compare three sets of values. They are much like XY (scatter) charts, with X and Y coordinates representing two of the values, but the size of the bubbles is determined by the third value.

✦ **Column charts** are a variant of the bar chart type. They show values by the height of vertical bars known as columns (having nothing to do with whether rows or columns from the worksheet grid are used as the source of the data series). Column charts are the default chart type in Excel.

✦ **Cone charts** are a variant of the bar or column chart type. The only difference is that they use cones instead of bars or columns.

✦ **Cylinder charts** are a variant of the bar or column chart type. The only difference is that they use cylinders instead of bars or columns.

✦ **Doughnut charts** are pretty much the same thing as pie charts, except that they aren't limited to a single data series. Instead of slices, each series is represented as a ring of the doughnut.

✦ **Line charts** have one Y value for every X value, like a mathematical function. A line chart is typically used to show changes over time.

✦ **Pie charts** are limited to a single data series (one row or column of data from the worksheet) and cannot display more complex series of data. The value of each element in the data series is assigned a slice of the pie, and all the slices add up to the total of the data series. However, they are visually appealing and simple to understand.

✦ **Pyramid charts** are a variant of the bar or column chart types. The only difference is that they use pyramids instead of bars or columns.

✦ **Radar charts** show data radiating outward from a central point. The center is zero, and category axes extend out from the center. Each series has a data point on each category axis, and the data points of a series are connected by a line. Series can be compared by the areas enclosed by their lines.

✦ **Stock charts** are used for plotting the values of stocks. Variants require three to five values in a given order: High-Low-Close, Open-High-Low-Close, Volume-High-Low-Close, or Volume-Open-High-Low-Close.

✦ **Surface charts** represent trends in values as a continuous curve across two dimensions.

✦ **XY (Scatter) charts** compare pairs of values, depicting them as sets of X and Y coordinates. One use of scatter charts might be to show the results of many trials in an experiment.

Modifying Charts

The Chart menu provides methods for modifying the data and structure of charts you've already created. The first four items on the Chart menu—Chart Type, Source Data, Chart Options, and Location—will be familiar to you if you've used the Chart Wizard. Those menu options bring up the exact same dialog boxes as you find in Chart Wizard.

The other three items are Add Data, Add Trendline, and 3-D View. 3-D View is more of a formatting issue and will be dealt with separately in the following section on formatting charts.

Changing chart types

You can select Chart ⇨ Chart Type from the menu and choose a new chart type by simply selecting one from the listings in the Chart Type dialog box. Click the OK button and the new chart type replaces the old one.

The Chart toolbar also has an option for selecting chart types. It includes 18 types, including all the standard types (except for stock charts) and a few of the more common subtypes. To access it, click the arrow to the right of the Chart Type button. The listed types are represented by icons (see Figure 14-8). Click any one of them and the old chart will be instantly changed to the new type.

If you want to try another type, repeat the process. To revert to the original chart type, just click the Undo button in the Standard toolbar.

Figure 14-8: The Chart Type icons on the Chart toolbar

Modifying and adding source data

If you want to change the source your data is drawn from in the worksheet, follow these steps:

1. Select Chart ⇨ Source Data from the menu. This brings up the Source Data dialog box (see Figure 14-9), which is the same as the one in Chart Wizard. Regardless of whether the chart is an embedded object in the source worksheet or a separate chart sheet, the dialog box will appear over the source worksheet.

2. To change the entire area from which the data is drawn, enter a new range in the Data Range box.

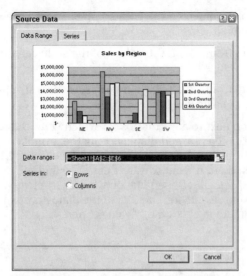

Figure 14-9: The Source Data dialog box

3. If you want to work with the source data for a smaller portion of the chart, click the Series tab (see Figure 14-10). Here you can choose to make changes to the range of data from which the portions of individual data series are drawn. Select the one you want to change from the Series list, or click the Add button to make a new data series.

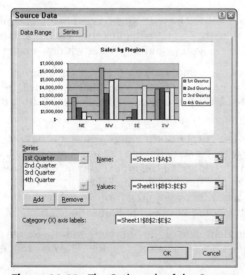

Figure 14-10: The Series tab of the Source Data dialog box

4. To change the range of data from which the name of the series is drawn, enter the new range in the Name box.

5. To change the range of data from which the values of the series are drawn, enter the new range in the Values box.

6. To change the range of data from which the categories are drawn, enter the new range in the Category (X) axis labels box.

7. You can click the grid button next to any edit box for which you need to specify a range. This collapses the dialog box and displays only the formula describing the data range from which the chart information is taken (see Figure 14-11). With the dialog box collapsed out of your way, it is easier to find the range you want in the source data and select it. Depending on what chart element you're changing the range of the source data for, the title of the dialog box will vary somewhat; it may read "Data Range," "Name," "Values," and so on.

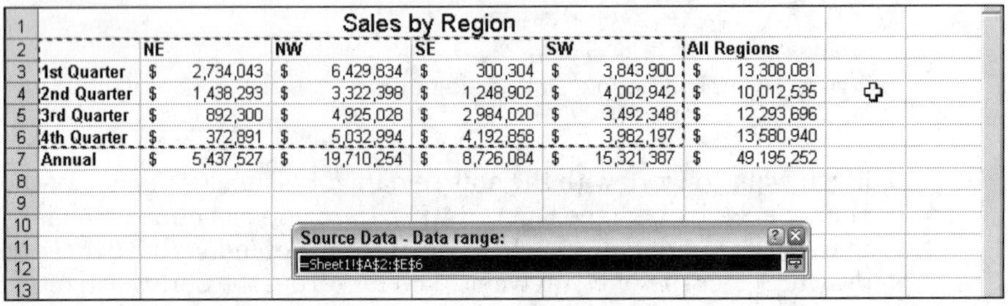

	Sales by Region					
	NE	NW	SE	SW	All Regions	
1st Quarter	$ 2,734,043	$ 6,429,834	$ 300,304	$ 3,843,900	$ 13,308,081	
2nd Quarter	$ 1,438,293	$ 3,322,398	$ 1,248,902	$ 4,002,942	$ 10,012,535	
3rd Quarter	$ 892,300	$ 4,925,028	$ 2,984,020	$ 3,492,348	$ 12,293,696	
4th Quarter	$ 372,891	$ 5,032,994	$ 4,192,858	$ 3,982,197	$ 13,580,940	
Annual	$ 5,437,527	$ 19,710,254	$ 8,726,084	$ 15,321,387	$ 49,195,252	

Source Data - Data range:
=Sheet1!$A$2:$E$6

Figure 14-11: The Source Data - Data Range dialog box

8. Initially, the dialog box floats above the worksheet, most likely obscuring part of the area you need to work with. To move it, click the title bar and drag the dialog box out of the way, just as you would any other window on your screen.

9. If you're adding a new data series, and you're working from a separate chart sheet, the Source Data Name or Source Data Values dialog box will be floating above the chart sheet, instead. Click the sheet tab of the worksheet the source data is located on.

10. Select the cell in the upper-left corner of the range you want to replace the original data source range with. Next, delineate the new data range by either pressing the mouse button and dragging the mouse till the entire new range is selected or by holding down the Shift key while clicking in the cell in the lower-right corner of the range. Either way, the formula depicting the new range will be displayed in the Source Data-Data Range dialog box.

11. Click the grid button on the right side of the Source Data-Data Range dialog box to return to the expanded Source Data dialog box. The new range will be listed.

12. Click the OK button to accept the changes.

You can also add a data series to the chart by using the Chart ⇨ Add Data menu option. The process is virtually identical to the previous one, except that you need to select the entire range including the labels and values, rather than selecting each one separately. It's up to you which approach you prefer.

Changing chart options

When you select Chart ⇨ Chart Options from the menu, you get the same Chart Options dialog box as you used with Chart Wizard. It has tabs for Titles, Axes, Gridlines, Legend, Data Labels, and Data Table.

Changing titles

The Titles tab (see Figure 14-12) lets you assign different titles to the chart and all its axes individually. If any of these currently has a title, it is shown in the appropriate edit box. Those elements without titles have blank edit boxes. Edit boxes for axes that do not apply to a particular chart are grayed out. To change an existing title, highlight the previous title and type over it; to add a title where there was none before, simply type the title into the appropriate edit box. Click in one of the other edit boxes to see the changes in the chart preview box on the right side of the dialog box.

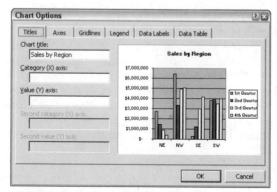

Figure 14-12: The Titles tab of the Chart Options dialog box

If you're going to change other chart elements, click the appropriate tab. If you're finished with your changes, click the OK button.

Changing axes

The Axes tab (see Figure 14-13) lets you choose whether to show each of the primary axes, as well as any secondary axes that you may have added (if the secondary axes don't exist, they won't show here).

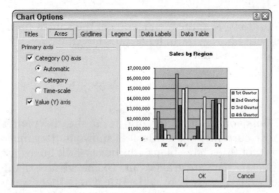

Figure 14-13: The Axes tab of the Chart Options dialog box

To remove the horizontal axis from your chart, deselect the Category (X) axis checkbox. To restore it, select that checkbox. The Category axis also gives you three radio buttons to choose from about how Excel interprets it. By default, the choice is Automatic. The other two are Category and Time-scale. When Excel finds the labels on your data range, it takes the labels that are normal text or numbers and assumes they are categories; if the labels are dates, Excel assumes a time-scale is needed, instead. Time-scales cannot be used with times, only dates — you have to have days, months, and/or years as labels to trigger time-scales on the X axis. It's best to leave this setting at Automatic and let Excel do its thing. If you try to force a time-scale on a series of labels that don't fit it, the results will be arbitrary and inaccurate.

To remove the vertical axis from your chart, deselect the Value (Y) axis checkbox. To restore it, select that checkbox. In the case of a 3-D chart, you have a Series (Y) axis and a Value (Z) axis instead.

If you're going to change other chart elements, click the appropriate tab. If you're finished with your changes, click the OK button.

Changing gridlines

The Gridlines tab (see Figure 14-14) lets you decide what kind of gridlines to show on both the Category (X) axis and the Value (Y) axis. In the case of a 3-D chart, you have a Category (X) axis, a Series (Y) axis, and a Value (Z) axis. The major gridlines show where larger values cross the chart, whereas the minor gridlines show where smaller values cross the chart. To put any gridline in, just put a check in its checkbox; to remove it, deselect its checkbox. (As a design consideration, the fewer the gridlines, the more readable the chart. Unless you really need the minor gridlines, it's usually best to leave them out.)

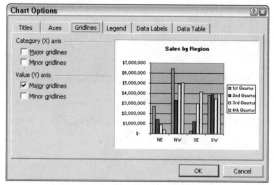

Figure 14-14: The Gridlines tab of the Chart Options dialog box

Caution

If you're going to use shortcut keys to put in the gridlines, bear in mind that on the X axis, they're labeled Major gridlines and Minor gridlines; on the Y axis, they're labeled Major gridlines and Minor gridlines.

If you're going to change other chart elements, click the appropriate tab. If you're finished with your changes, click the OK button.

Changing legends

The Legend tab (see Figure 14-15) has one checkbox and five radio buttons. The Show Legend checkbox has only one function — to include a legend on your chart. If it's checked, the radio buttons become active. They let you place the legend in different parts of your chart: Bottom, Corner, Top, Right, or Left. The Corner position means the upper-right corner. The Bottom, Right, and Left positions place the legend in the center position on one of the edges of the chart area. The Top position places the legend under the chart title.

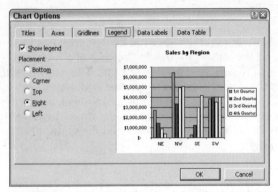

Figure 14-15: The Legend tab of the Chart Options dialog box

 Tip

You can also add or remove a legend by clicking the Legend button in the Chart toolbar.

If you're going to change other chart elements, click the appropriate tab. If you're finished with your changes, click the OK button.

Changing data labels

The Data Labels tab (see Figure 14-16) lets you assign labels to the data in the chart. Depending on the chart type, various options are active, whereas others are grayed out.

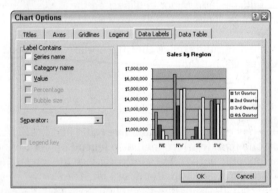

Figure 14-16: The Data Labels tab of the Chart Options dialog box

There are two other options at the bottom of the tab, both of them checkboxes: Legend key next to label and Show leader lines (not shown in figure). The first one puts a small colored box next to the data label keyed to the same color the corresponding data series has in the legend. The other one, which only shows up for pie charts, puts lines between the labels and the chart element they refer to (you need to move the labels away from the element before the leader lines show up).

If you're going to change other chart elements, click the appropriate tab. If you're finished with your changes, click the OK button.

Changing data tables

The Data Table tab (see Figure 14-17) has two checkboxes on it. Checking the first, Show data table, places a copy of the worksheet grid you used to create the chart underneath the chart. To remove the data table, deselect its checkbox. The other one, Show legend keys, puts a small colored box next to each data series in the data table keyed to the same color in the legend. The Show legend keys option is available only when you choose the Show data table option. To remove the legend keys feature, deselect its checkbox. (You can also add or remove data tables by clicking the Data Table button in the Chart toolbar.)

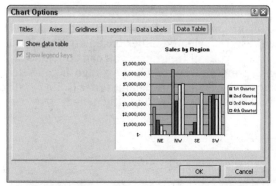

Figure 14-17: The Data Table tab of the Chart Options dialog box

Note   Not all chart types can show data tables; if the one you're using doesn't, the Data Table tab will not be available.

If you're going to change other chart elements, click the appropriate tab. If you're finished with your changes, click the OK button.

Relocating a chart

You can change an embedded chart into a separate chart sheet and vice versa by following these steps:

1. Select Chart ➪ Location from the menu. This brings up the same Chart Location dialog box you saw in the Chart Wizard.

2. To move an embedded object onto its own chart sheet, select the As New Sheet radio button. Type the name of the new chart sheet into the edit box or accept the one Excel suggests, and then click the OK button.

3. To change a chart from being on its own chart sheet to being an embedded object on another worksheet, select the As Object In radio button. Select the destination sheet from the drop-down list, and then click the OK button. The original chart sheet will be deleted if you move its chart to another worksheet, but you can re-create it by changing the chart back to being on its own chart sheet again.

Tip   You can embed a chart on another chart sheet as well as on a regular worksheet.

Adding trendlines

Selecting Chart ➪ Add Trendline brings up the Add Trendline dialog box (see Figure 14-18). The trendline is for the data series selected under Based on Series at the bottom of the Type tab. There are six types of trendlines you can add: Linear, Logarithmic, Polynomial, Power, Exponential, and Moving Average. If you select the Polynomial type, you can also specify its Order (the default order is 2). If you select the Moving Average type, you can also specify its Period (the default period is 2).

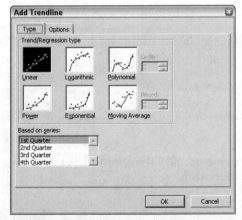

Figure 14-18: The Add Trendline dialog box with the Type tab showing

Note   Trendlines aren't available for all charts and won't work on most of the more exotic kinds like 3-D charts, doughnut charts, or radar charts. If your chart is one of these, the Add Trendline option on the Chart menu is grayed out. The chart types that you can add trendlines to are normal 2-D area, bar, bubble, column, line, stock, and XY (scatter) charts.

Under the Options tab (see Figure 14-19), you can set further options for your trendlines. Depending upon the trendline type you choose, some options may be grayed out. There are three sets of options:

✦ The first option on the Options tab lets you set the Trendline name. The Automatic default is composed of the type of trendline plus your data label for the affected data series. The Custom name can be anything you type into the edit box.

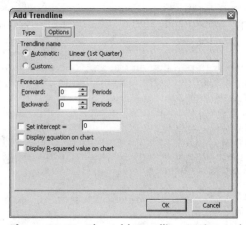

Figure 14-19: The Add Trendline Options tab

✦ The second option lets you set the Forward and Backward forecast periods.

✦ The final set of options includes Set intercept, Display equation on chart, and Display R-squared value on chart. These options deal with additional information that can be displayed in addition to the trendline. (You can play with these options to see which ones give you the exact chart appearance you want.)

Formatting Charts

Although all chart items can be formatted, the options vary from one element to the next. The only thing they all have in common is patterns, although textual elements also have fonts and alignment in common, as well as (sometimes) number formatting. There are two basic methods:

✦ **Using the pop-up menu.** You can format chart elements by right-clicking them and then selecting Format *chart element* from the pop-up menu. The actual name of the selected element will show on the menu in place of *chart element;* for instance, if you are formatting the chart title, the menu option will be Format Chart Title.

✦ **Using the Chart toolbar.** You can also format chart elements by clicking them to select them (or choosing them in the Chart Objects drop-down list in the Chart toolbar), and then clicking the Format *chart element* button in the Chart toolbar. As with the pop-up menu, the Format button's floating message will display the name of the selected element as you place the pointer upon it.

Tip   If you've lost your Chart toolbar, there could be a couple of reasons. If you're work-ing on a worksheet that has a chart as an embedded object, the Chart toolbar will disappear whenever you're working on any part of the worksheet other than the chart. To get it back, just click any part of the chart. In either an embedded object situation or with a separate chart sheet, if you've closed the Chart toolbar, you can get it back by right-clicking any toolbar and selecting Chart from the pop-up tool-bar menu.

The options in the pop-up menu vary depending on the type of chart element you've selected, but Clear is the only option in the pop-up menus that you won't find in either the Chart menu or the Chart toolbar. Clear has different results for dif-ferent chart elements. Generally speaking, it deletes the item from the chart. However, in the case of the plot area in 2-D charts or the floors and walls in 3-D charts, it merely makes them invisible. They are still present, as can be demon-strated by placing your pointer over the area where they were formerly visible; the floating message will still indicate their presence.

Whichever approach you take, pop-up menu or Format button on the Chart toolbar, a dialog box with tabs reflecting the formatting options appropriate to the particu-lar chart element will appear. Formatting options come in three basic classes: the same ones you're familiar with using in worksheets (such as formatting and color-ing fonts), the ones you're familiar with for setting chart element options (such as positioning the legend), and a few new ones that are obvious in their function (such as setting the spacing between columns).

Cross-
Reference   See the section entitled "Enhancing Charts" later in this chapter for more informa-tion on using the formatting options.

Handling 3-D Chart Views

One thing that is neither familiar from worksheets nor intuitive for those who haven't worked with 3-D programs is the handling of 3-D chart views. You can open the controls for 3-D charts in two ways. You can either select Chart ➪ 3-D View from the main menu or right-click most elements in a 3-D chart and select 3-D View from the pop-up menu. The option isn't available on the pop-up menu for all elements, even if they are part of a 3-D chart. For instance, you don't have 3-D view options for legends, axes, titles, and so on. Elements such as floors, walls, plot areas, and so forth, however, do have that option in their pop-up menus.

Using the 3-D View dialog box

Whichever menu you use, you'll get the 3-D View dialog box (see Figure 14-20). You can use four controls to alter the view: Elevation, Rotation, Perspective, and Height. All four can be adjusted by typing in specific values. Elevation values range from 90 to -90, Rotation from 0 to 360, Perspective from 0 to 100, and Height from 5 to 500. The first three can also be adjusted by clicking the arrow buttons near them.

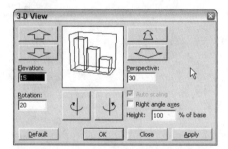

Figure 14-20: The 3-D View dialog box

There are also two checkboxes in the dialog box: Auto scaling and Right angle axes. Because perspective adjustments and right angle axes are mutually exclusive, you must clear the Right angle axes checkbox to make the Perspective controls appear. Auto scaling means that the fonts in the chart automatically adjust their size to accommodate changes you make in the chart. It's generally best to leave it checked.

When you've finished making your adjustments, click the OK button to apply your changes. If you want to return to the default 3-D settings, click the Default button.

Using the "Corners" method

There's an even better way to handle the view on 3-D charts; it's faster, more intuitive, and it's a lot more fun, too. Skip the menus, and move your pointer to a juncture of axes on the chart. When you get a floating message that says "Corners," you're in business. Click that point. Now, while still on that point, press your mouse button down and hold it. Move the mouse in any direction and the 3-D chart becomes a wireframe box that responds to your every move (see Figure 14-21).

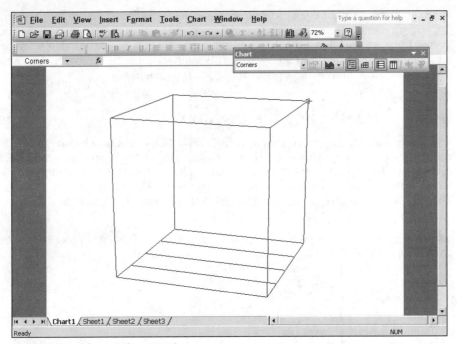

Figure 14-21: Interactive 3-D View

The floor of the chart is represented by the rectangle with lines across it, so you can tell which side is up. When you've got the box the way you want it, release the mouse button and you've got your reoriented 3-D chart. You can repeat this endlessly to make fine adjustments or experiment with different views of the chart.

Tip   If you totally botch the chart up to the point where you can't tell which side is which, just go into the standard 3-D View dialog box and click the Default button to fix it.

Enhancing Charts

The most basic approach to enhancing charts is to use the standard worksheet techniques of applying font styles, background colors, and so forth, to them. A chart title, for instance, can be changed to a larger font, italicized, and colored to make it stand out more than the usual, plain titles.

Background colors and patterns can also be applied to various chart elements with excellent effect. Figure 14-22 shows the earlier standard column chart with various effects applied. (If you see this chart in color — which you will if you follow the instructions that follow — you will be much more impressed than you are by seeing the black-and-white image printed in this book.)

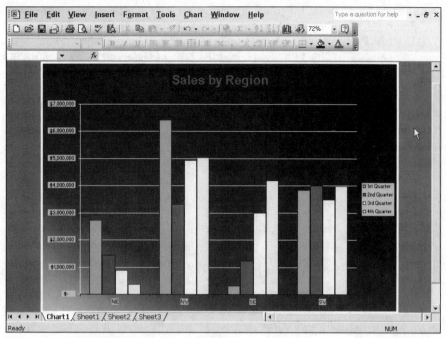

Figure 14-22: Enhanced Excel chart

This makeover was achieved by first giving the chart area a colored fill pattern. To do this, follow these steps:

1. Right-click the chart area, and then select Format Chart Area from the pop-up menu.

2. In the Format Chart Area dialog box (see Figure 14-23), click the Patterns tab.

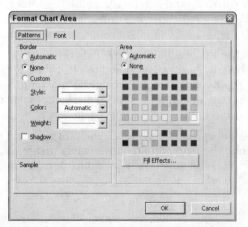

Figure 14-23: The Patterns tab of the Format Chart Area dialog box

3. Click the Fill Effects button. This brings up the Fill Effects dialog box (see Figure 14-24). There are four tabs in the Fill Effects dialog box: Gradient, Texture, Pattern, and Picture. The first three have pre-designed backgrounds you can add to chart elements, and the last one lets you use your own graphics files as background elements. This exercise uses a gradient.

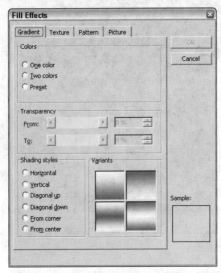

Figure 14-24: The Fill Effects dialog box with the Gradient tab showing

4. The basic gradient options are One color, Two colors, and Preset. If you choose to use one color, you can pick it from a drop-down list and your only other option is how dark it is. If you use two colors, you pick them both the same way, but you get no choice as to how dark they are. We chose Preset and chose Late Sunset from the drop-down list (see Figure 14-25). Under Shading styles, we picked Diagonal down and chose the upper-left example under Variants.

5. Click the OK button to finalize the gradient choice. This returns you to the Format Chart Area dialog box, where you also need to click the OK button. The results are a distinct improvement over the original chart, but several elements still need work. The chart title and the legend stick out like sore thumbs, and the background to the plot area is pretty dull.

6. To get rid of the plot area's background, right-click the plot area and select Clear from the pop-up menu. The background immediately disappears. However, the gridlines and axes are now nearly invisible, because they're black against a dark background.

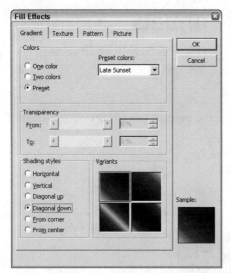

Figure 14-25: The Late Sunset gradient

7. You don't have to use the chart formatting options in this case. Because all we're looking for is a quick fix for a color problem, just click one of the gridlines so they're selected, and then click the Fill Color arrow in the Formatting toolbar and select white from the drop-down palette.

8. Next, select the category axis and click the Fill Color button (you don't have to go through the palette this time because the Fill Color button automatically uses the last color chosen from the palette).

9. Select the value axis and click the Fill Color button.

10. Select the legend, click the arrow to the right of the Fill Color button, and pick gold from the palette.

11. Select the chart title and select a font size of 24 from the drop-down list in the Formatting toolbar.

12. While the chart title is still selected, change the font color by clicking the arrow to the right of the Font Color button and picking red from the palette.

13. While the chart title is still selected, change its background to black by clicking the arrow to the right of the Fill Color button and picking black from the palette.

14. Save your workbook.

Saving Custom Chart Formats

Once you've developed a chart that you particularly like and want to use again, you can save it as a custom chart format. To do so, follow these steps:

1. Select the chart you want to use.

2. Select Chart ⇨ Chart Type from the menu. This brings up the Chart Type dialog box.

3. Click the Custom Types tab (see Figure 14-26).

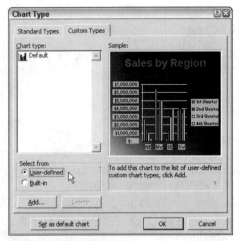

Figure 14-26: The Custom Types tab of the Chart Type dialog box

4. Click the User-defined radio button.

5. Click the Add button. This brings up the Add Custom Chart Type dialog box (see Figure 14-27).

6. Type a name for the chart under Name and a description of it under Description.

7. Click the OK button to return to the Chart Type dialog box.

8. If you want to use this as your basic chart from now on, click the Set as Default Chart button.

9. Click the OK button to finish.

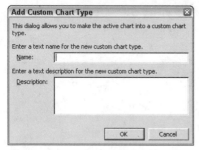

Figure 14-27: The Add Custom
Chart Type dialog box

Summary

In this chapter, you learned how to create, use, and modify charts in Excel.

✦ You create charts using Chart Wizard.

✦ Excel offers a variety of different chart types.

✦ Charts can be embedded as objects in a worksheet or they can be created as separate chart sheets. After creation, they can be changed from embedded objects to separate sheets and vice versa.

✦ You can change every aspect of a chart after it is created.

✦ The view of 3-D charts can be manipulated interactively.

✦ The appearance of charts can be enhanced by a variety of methods, some of which are specific to charts and some of which are standard worksheet approaches.

✦ You can save your own custom chart formats for future use.

✦   ✦   ✦

Formulas and Functions

You can put numeric or text values in any cell of an Excel worksheet, but the real power of Excel is unleashed when you create formulas. Although you can build either simple or complex formulas by hand using cell references, operators, and functions, Excel provides valuable shortcuts to formula creation. This chapter provides all the information you need to add formulas to your worksheets.

Excel also includes built-in, ready-to-use functions for everything from Boolean logic to financial calculations. Just as with formulas, Excel includes features and tools that allow you to easily add functions. This chapter also addresses the fastest way to get functions into your worksheets.

Working with Formulas

Formulas let you work on the data in your worksheet cells to produce mathematical and logical results. Without them, spreadsheets would be nothing more than nicely structured collections of raw data. With formulas, that data can be made to yield valuable information.

Formulas are constructed out of two basic elements: values and operators. Values can either be explicit (such as 345, 12, or -52) or they can be cell references (such as A2, E8, or F14). Cell references, as you learn later in this chapter, can even be named ranges. Cell references are used in formulas to tell Excel where to find the data to take action on.

Operators are instructions that tell the worksheet how to process the data. For example, you might use an addition operator or a multiplication operator on cells containing numbers. The operators you have at your disposal in Excel are detailed in Table 15-1.

Cross-Reference   Chapter 12, "Worksheets and Workbooks," discusses the basics of cell references.

| | Table 15-1 |
| | **Excel Operators** |

Operator	Purpose
-	Negation
%	Percentage
^	Exponentiation
*	Multiplication
/	Division
+	Addition
-	Subtraction
&	Concatenation (text addition)
=	Equality
<	Less than
>	Greater than
<=	Less than or equal to
>=	Greater than or equal to
<>	Inequality

Creating a formula

To create a formula, follow these steps:

1. All formulas you create begin with an equals sign (=). Select the cell into which you will be entering your formula and type an equals sign into it.

2. Type an explicit value or a cell reference. For instance, if you want to triple the value in cell A2, you enter the number 3 to start your formula. For your cell reference you can use individual cell references, ranges of cells, and names of cells or ranges, as appropriate for your needs.

3. Enter an operator and another value or cell reference. To continue with the example from the previous step, you would enter the multiplication operator (*) and a reference to cell A2 here. The formula now reads "=3*A2".

4. Repeat Step 3, adding operators and values or cell references, until you have completed your formula.

5. Press Enter to finish. The results of the formula will appear in the cell in which you entered it.

Note You can click the cells you want to include in your formula instead of having to type their references. Unfortunately, you still have to type the operators in between the cell references.

If you make an error in entering your formula, two things can happen. The most likely is that you will not get the results that you expected from the formula. This can be the result of not using the proper values or from using the wrong cell references, or even from using the wrong types of operators. You can correct such errors by examining your formula and making changes, as appropriate.

The second thing that can happen if you make an error is that you will see an error message. This often happens if you try to use an operator that is not listed in Table 15-1. For instance, the following formula would generate an error:

    =27;42

The reason this causes an error is that the semicolon (;) is not a valid operator. To correct these types of errors, dismiss any error messages you see and correct the formula so it is valid.

Understanding operator precedence

Operators aren't all treated the same by Excel. Some are processed before others. This is called *precedence*. The operators in Table 15-1 are listed in order of precedence. Some of them, though, have equal precedence. The multiplication and division operators (* and /, respectively), for instance, do, as do the addition and subtraction operators (+ and -). Also, the entire range of comparison operators (=, <, >, <=, >=, and <>) share precedence with one another. Other than that, the precedence runs in the order shown in the table.

For example, if you have the following formula, the multiplication will take place before the addition because multiplication has a higher precedence:

    =B3+B4*B5

If you want to change the order in which operations are processed, you can use parentheses to influence the outcome. Because anything within parentheses has a higher precedence than any operator, the same formula as before can be forced to perform the addition before the multiplication by placing the entire addition operation within parentheses:

    =(B3+B4)*B5

In the case of operators that have the same precedence, the decision about which operation to perform first depends on which one comes first in left-to-right positioning. In the following formula, division takes place before multiplication because the division operator comes first:

```
=B3/B4*B5
```

Displaying and editing formulas

The cell containing a formula normally displays not the formula itself but the results of the formula; formulas are displayed in the Formula bar anytime you click a cell containing a formula (see Figure 15-1). You can make a cell temporarily display the formula instead of its result by double-clicking the cell or by selecting the cell and pressing F2. (These actions inform Excel that you want to edit the cell contents, as discussed in Chapter 13. When editing the contents of a cell, you have access to any formula within the cell.)

To make all the cells in a worksheet display their formulas as their normal behavior, select Tools ➪ Options from the menu, and then click the View tab. On the View tab, select the checkbox labeled Formulas and click the OK button.

The Difference Between Negation and Subtraction

You probably noticed in Table 15-1 that the negation symbol and the subtraction symbol are identical (-). Although they can be made to perform identical functions, there is a distinction between them. The negation operator changes the sign of a number (positive numbers become negative and vice versa), whereas the subtraction operator subtracts the referenced value from the preceding value. Because the negation operator has a higher precedence, this can be a tricky problem if you have a situation in which you need to use both. In the following formula (assuming that both cells have positive numbers in them), the first value is turned to a negative and the second is subtracted from it; the effect is the same as adding two negative numbers:

```
=-B3-B4
```

If the value in the cell B3 were 5 and the value in the cell B4 were 3, you'd end up with a result of -8, because the value in B3 (5) is negated (changed to -5) and then the value in B4 (3) is subtracted from it. If, however, you wanted to find the negative value of the subtraction instead, you'd have to use parentheses to force the operations to take place in the desired order, as in the following example, which would yield a result of -2 by producing the negative value of the operation 5-3:

```
=-(B3-B4)
```

AVERAGE	▾	✗ ✓	*fx* =B3+B4+B5+B6						
	A	B	C	D	E	F	G	H
1			Sales by Region					
2		NE	NW	SE	SW	All Regions		
3	1st Quarter	$ 2,734,043	$ 6,429,834	$ 300,304	$ 3,843,900	$ 13,308,081		
4	2nd Quarter	$ 1,438,293	$ 3,322,398	$ 1,248,902	$ 4,002,942	$ 10,012,535		
5	3rd Quarter	$ 892,300	$ 4,925,028	$ 2,984,020	$ 3,492,348	$ 12,293,696		
6	4th Quarter	$ 372,891	$ 5,032,994	$ 4,192,858	$ 3,982,197	$ 13,580,940		
7	Annual	=B3+B4+B5+B6						
8								

Figure 15-1: The Formula bar displays the formula.

Caution

If you exercise the option to display all formulas in the cells all the time, you won't have a good-looking worksheet, because the cells have to expand to the size of the formulas in order to show them. At the very least, you'll have to reverse the option when you're ready to present your results, and that might mean last-minute design corrections or unpleasant surprises, because you won't have seen the final appearance of the worksheet or the results of the calculations beforehand.

Whatever approach you take to displaying formulas, they can be edited either in the cell or in the Formula bar. To edit in the Formula bar, simply click within it. If the cursor doesn't land exactly where you wanted it to, move the cursor into the position where you want to edit, and add or delete to your heart's content. You can continue to put in operators by typing, and cell references either by typing or pointing with the mouse.

Tip

To replace a cell reference in the Formula bar with another one, highlight the cell reference you want to replace, and then click the cell you want to replace it with.

To edit a formula in the cell, you have to first double-click the cell — even if the formula is already displayed within it — or select the cell and press F2. Setting the formula display option in the View tab does not change the editing behavior of cells, only the visibility of the formulas they contain.

Copying and Moving Formulas

You can use the standard menu or toolbar techniques to move or copy a cell containing formulas or functions. Excel also lets you use drag and drop to accomplish both procedures.

There's an important difference between the two methods other than the obvious one that when you copy a cell, the original one remains where it was, but when you move it, the original one isn't there anymore. When you move a cell, none of the cell references in a formula are affected in any way at all; they come along fully intact. When you copy it, however, that's not true. The cell references change to reflect the new position of the cell. For instance, if you move a cell two columns to the right and three rows down, all the cell references in the formula contained within it will shift by the same amount.

Caution   When you copy or move a cell or range of cells, you replace any data in the destination cells. When moving, you are warned that you're about to replace the previous contents.

The only way around this is to use absolute cell references within the formula.
However, there are times when you won't want to do this, because you do want the
references to change. It's fine for the cell references to be locked in absolutely if
you're moving only the cell containing the formula. If you're moving the cells it
refers to as well, as when you reposition an entire range of data and formulas, you'll
want the cell references in the formula to change along with the placement of the
cells it refers to.

**Cross-
Reference**   You can find complete details on relative and absolute addressing in Chapter 12.

Copying via the toolbar or menu

You copy formulas and functions via the menu or toolbar in the following manner:

1. Select the cell or range of cells you want to copy.

2. Click the Copy button on the toolbar. Alternatively, select Edit ⇨ Copy from
   the menu or right-click the copy source and select Copy from the resultant
   pop-up menu.

3. Click in the cell you want to paste the cell into (if you're copying a range of
   cells, click in the cell in the upper-left corner of the range you want to paste
   the range into).

4. Click the Paste button on the toolbar. Alternatively, select Edit ⇨ Paste from
   the menu or right-click the paste destination and select Paste from the resultant pop-up menu.

Moving is done in the exact same way, with the exception that you use the Cut button instead of the Copy button for the toolbar method. The menu differences are
that you select Edit ⇨ Cut from the main menu or right-click the selection and select
Cut from the pop-up menu.

Using the Paste Special command

You can use the Paste Special command on either the regular or the pop-up menu
to control which attributes of the copied or cut cell are pasted into the new location. Of particular interest with respect to formulas and functions is the Values
option on the Paste Special dialog box (see Figure 15-2). Selecting that radio button
means that only the results of the formula, not the formula itself, are pasted into
the destination cell. The result, once pasted in this manner, is permanently fixed
and will not change in this cell even if it changes in the original one.

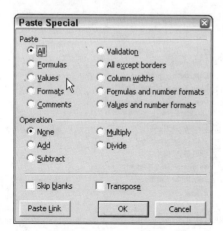

Figure 15-2: The Paste Special dialog box

You can also use Paste Special to paste only the formula itself, leaving behind any cell formatting options from the original cell, by selecting the Formulas radio button.

Tip The Paste Special dialog box is an invaluable tool when you want to customize how you paste data in Excel. Take some time to experiment and explore what each option in the dialog box does. You will find the time well spent when you have a special copying need at a later date.

Once you have specified how you want Excel to perform the pasting, click the OK button to complete the Paste Special operation.

Using the drag-and-drop method

Excel's native method for copying and moving cells is easier than the standard Windows method of cut and paste—do it by dragging and dropping. To move a formula, just select the cell or cells you want to move, click the border of the cell (anywhere except for the fill handle), drag it to the position you want to place it in, and release the mouse button. To copy it, do the same thing, but hold down the Ctrl key while you release the mouse button, and then release the Ctrl key (if you release the Ctrl key before you release the mouse button, you'll move, not copy, the cell).

Modifying how you copy

If you don't want to mess with the menu or toolbar, you can still manage to modify exactly how Excel performs a paste operation. After selecting the source cell or cells, right-click the dark cell border and drag it to the cell you want to put it into. When you release the right mouse button, you'll get a pop-up menu that lists a number of options (see Figure 15-3).

B7	▼	fx =B3+B4+B5+B6						
	A	B	C	D	E	F	G	H
1				Sales by Region				
2		NE		NW		SE	SW	All Regions
3	1st Quarter	$ 2,734,043	$	6,429,834	$	300,3	Move Here	1
4	2nd Quarter	$ 1,438,293	$	3,322,398	$	1,248,9	Copy Here	5
5	3rd Quarter	$ 892,300	$	4,925,028	$	2,984,0	Copy Here as Values Only	6
6	4th Quarter	$ 372,891	$	5,032,994	$	4,192,8	Copy Here as Formats Only	0
7	Annual	$ 5,437,527					Link Here	
8							Create Hyperlink Here	
9								
10							Shift Down and Copy	
11							Shift Right and Copy	
12								
13							Shift Down and Move	
14							Shift Right and Move	
15								
16							Cancel	
17								
18								
19								
20								

Figure 15-3: Copy as values only.

You can pick any of the options presented. Most of the options are self-explanatory; some of them provide a quick way to perform the tasks for which you normally use the Paste Special dialog box.

Using Range Names in Formulas

Although the standard cell reference method is a functional way to manage formulas, it goes all the way back to the earliest spreadsheets, and hasn't really improved since the dawn of time, relatively speaking. Compared with the other advances in Excel, it's pretty much a Stone Age method.

When you use cell references, you're forced to convert your natural thought processes into something the program can comprehend. It's far better to make the program do that kind of conversion while you're able to just move along and get your job done. The most natural way to think of formulas is to assign names to the cells and ranges of cells with which you'll be working.

 Cross-Reference   The process by which you assign names to ranges is discussed in detail in Chapter 12. This section focuses on how to actually use those range names in formulas.

For example, do you think of sales forecasts as B1+B2+B3 and so forth, or do you naturally think of them in terms of First Quarter, Second Quarter, Third Quarter, and Fourth Quarter? Is a finance charge calculated as H7*H8, or is it the average daily balance times the monthly percentage rate?

Fortunately, Excel accommodates natural human methods of expressing our thoughts and can take care of translating those into cell references without our having to specifically direct it to do so. The only real stumbling block is that Excel can't handle spaces between words, but you can just leave them out or use underscores instead. Examples are `AverageDailyBalance` or `Average_Daily_Balance`. You could also just abbreviate it `ADB`, of course. One other thing to keep in mind is that, although you can use numbers in cell or range names, you can't start the name with a number. Thus, `Quarter1` is fine, but `1stQuarter`" won't work.

If you're dealing with a simple one-line formula, naming the individual cells is a good solution. If you've got something more complex, though, that approach can quickly become tedious. Although you can name each and every cell in an entire worksheet and painstakingly state their formulas in words, there's a much easier way to do it—name an entire range of cells and let Excel sort them out.

Say you have a worksheet like the one shown in Figure 15-4, which shows commission income by week for four salespeople. You can select the range of cells from B2 to B5 and name it `Week1`, and then do the same for C2 to C5, naming it `Week2`, and so on. In the F column, then, all you have to do is enter the formula `=Week1+Week2+Week3+Week4` and Excel will understand that you mean to add the cells from this row that fall in those ranges. Because of this, you can use the same formula in each row.

Tip   You could do the same thing by naming a range in the rows and adding them in columns as well. An even easier approach, if your worksheet layout allows for it, is to name the entire row or column instead of a smaller range of cells within the row or column.

	A	B	C	D	E	F	G	H	I	J	K	
	F2	▼	ƒx =Week1+Week2+Week3+Week4									
1		Week 1	Week 2	Week 3	Week 4	Total						
2	Dan	$283.97	$397.42	$341.07	$201.73	$1,224.19						
3	Martha	$157.23	$102.98	$232.15	$301.11	$793.47						
4	Millie	$794.12	$652.38	$805.41	$973.24	$3,225.15						
5	Peter	$1,032.12	$783.12	$842.95	$918.18	$3,576.37						
6	Total	$2,267.44	$1,935.90	$2,221.58	$2,394.26	$8,819.18						
7												

Figure 15-4: Name ranges used for formulas (see the Formula bar)

Using Arrays in Formulas

Closely related to ranges are *arrays*. Arrays are sets of values, and the values can either be entered into cells on your worksheet or directly input into a formula as constants. When the values are entered into cells, the cells holding them are said to constitute an *array range*.

Array formulas are used to perform multiple calculations and then return either a single result or multiple results. For instance, let's say that you have five values in the range A3:E3 and that you want to multiply those values by the range H3:H7. Further, you want to place the results starting at cell C9. You could use an array formula to find the results in this manner:

1. Select the cells in the range C9:G13. This is where the results of multiplying each number in one range by each number in the other range will be placed.

2. Type the formula =A3:E3*H3:H7.

3. Press Ctrl+Shift+Enter.

That's it. The key is in step 3; pressing Ctrl+Shift+Enter informs Excel that you are entering an array formula. The result is that you can now see the result of multiplying each number in one range by each other number in the other range. In addition, the contents of the cells selected in step 1 now contain the array formula, enclosed within braces (see Figure 15-5). The braces indicate that the formula is an array formula.

	A	B	C	D	E	F	G	H	I	J	K	L
C9			fx	{=A3:E3*H3:H7}								
1												
2												
3	1	2	3	4	5			6				
4								7				
5								8				
6								9				
7								10				
8												
9			6	12	18	24	30					
10			7	14	21	28	35					
11			8	16	24	32	40					
12			9	18	27	36	45					
13			10	20	30	40	50					
14												

Figure 15-5: Excel automatically encloses array formulas in braces.

Array formulas are often used in advanced computations, or in special needs computations, and Excel handles them very well. Array formulas are also required for some types of functions that depend on arrays.

Note   If you enter an array formula that results in multiple computations being placed in multiple cells (as in the example provided here), you must select all the cells involved in the array formula if you want to later delete the formula. For instance, if you wanted to delete the array formula in this section's example, you could not do so by simply selecting cell C9 and pressing Delete. Instead, you must select the entire array range, C9:G13, and then press Delete.

Understanding Functions

Functions are an intrinsic part of Excel. They allow you to perform a wide range of complex computations, anywhere from calculating a simple average to determining double-declining balance amortization.

Excel, when installed, provides more than 230 worksheet functions. The number of functions available on your system can be even higher, because you can add functions through the use of special add-ins.

Obviously, covering each and every function available in Excel could consume an entire book in itself. A more productive approach is to examine ways that you can quickly locate and add functions to your worksheet. Fortunately, Excel makes this easy to do. With a little practice, you will understand how to locate the exact function you need and how to use it to gain your desired result.

Functions are entered into a cell in the same way you enter a formula — you precede the function name with an equals sign. The only time you don't need to include the equals sign is if you are using the function within a larger formula. The following is an example of how you would use a function; in this case, the absolute value of whatever is in cell F3:

```
=ABS(F3)
```

Notice the use of the equals sign, followed by the function name, and then an argument within parentheses. The arguments (some functions require more then one, in which case they are separated by commas) are not limited to single cells references, but can be more complex:

```
=ABS(F3+F4-F5)
```

Similarly, you can use functions in other formulas:

```
=(F3+15)*ABS(H5)
```

As you start to work with the more than 230 worksheet functions available to you, you will find that they are generally easy to use and very flexible. Indeed, functions greatly expand what you are able to do with Excel.

Inserting Functions

Excel's Insert Function feature saves you a great deal of effort when it comes to putting functions into your worksheets. It puts a large library of functions — mathematical, financial, logical, and others — right at hand for your convenience. To use it, follow these steps:

1. Select the cell you want to put the formula's result into.

2. Click the Insert Function button, which is positioned just to the left of the Formula bar, or choose Insert ➪ Function. Excel displays the Insert Function dialog box (see Figure 15-6).

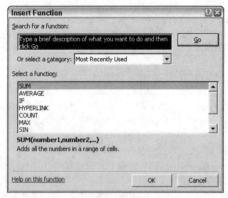

Figure 15-6: The Insert Function dialog box

3. Excel provides two ways to narrow down the number of functions from which you can choose. The first method involves searching for a function by entering a plain-English description of what you want the function to do, and then clicking Go. The second method requires you to use the category drop-down list to select the category of function you want. There are several categories of functions, such as Statistical, Database, Date & Time, and so on. There are also two special categories: Most Recently Used and All. The Most Recently Used category keeps track of the functions you've been using lately so, if you're repeatedly using the same ones, you don't have to go hunting for them. The All category is every function in all the categories.

4. When you search for a function or choose a function category, the list of functions at the bottom of the dialog box changes to reflect the appropriate options. Scroll down if necessary until you reach the name of the function you want to employ, and then click it. A description of both the structure and usage of the selected function appears at the bottom of the Insert Function dialog box.

5. Click the OK button to proceed. This brings up the Function Arguments dialog box (see Figure 15-7). Based on the cell you selected before you started to insert a function, along with the function you selected, Excel automatically tries to guess which range of cells you intend to apply the function to. You can adjust the range or change it entirely to suit your desires if Excel guesses wrong. The result of the formula, if applied to the specified range, is shown at the bottom of the dialog box.

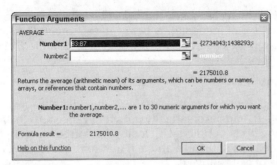

Figure 15-7: The Function Arguments dialog box

6. Excel tentatively enters the function formula into the selected cell and displays it in the Formula bar. Any changes you make in the range at this stage, however, are automatically reflected in both places, and you can abort the function formula entirely by clicking the Cancel button or pressing the Esc key. The formula result at the bottom of the dialog box changes along with any modifications you make.

If the dialog box is obscuring a part of the worksheet that you want to see, you can of course drag it out of the way.

7. If you want to keep the automatically selected range (if any), no extra action is required. If you want to change the range, simply select a new one with your mouse on the worksheet. Continue to select cells or ranges for each value as needed for the particular function you're using.

8. When you are satisfied with the values, click the OK button and the function formula is finalized. The result will show up in the selected cell.

Using AutoSum

Practically everyone who uses Excel wants to total rows and columns. That makes SUM the one function used more often than any other. Microsoft has made it even easier to use by putting an AutoSum button on the Standard toolbar, symbolized by the Greek letter sigma (Σ). To use it, follow these steps:

1. Select the cell where you want the sum to show up. For best results, this should be right after the end of the cells containing the numbers you want summed. In the case of a row, this is the first blank cell on the right side; in the case of a column, it is the first blank cell on the bottom end. You can't use AutoSum to put a total at the left of a row or at the top of a column even if you wanted to put one in such a nonstandard location. If you'd rather have a gap between the data and the total, though, you can select a cell that's farther

away. For instance, if you selected a cell that was two cells below the range you were summing instead of immediately below it, the total is the same. That's because, although the cell in between would also be added, blank cells are considered to hold zeroes.

2. Click the AutoSum button.

3. Excel assumes that you want to add the numbers immediately above the selected cell or to its left, and automatically puts that range into the function formula. The range of cells is outlined with a moving dotted line (see Figure 15-8). If the selected cell has data both above it and to the left, Excel defaults to choosing the range of cells above it.

	A	B	C	D	E	F	G	H
1			Sales by Region					
2		NE	NW	SE	SW	All Regions		
3	1st Quarter	$ 2,734,043	$ 6,429,834	$ 300,304	$ 3,843,900	=SUM(B3:E3)		
4	2nd Quarter	$ 1,438,293	$ 3,322,398	$ 1,248,902	$ 4,002,942	SUM(number1, [number2], ...)		
5	3rd Quarter	$ 892,300	$ 4,925,028	$ 2,984,020	$ 3,492,348			
6	4th Quarter	$ 372,891	$ 5,032,994	$ 4,192,858	$ 3,982,197			
7	Annual	$ 5,437,527	$ 19,710,254	$ 8,726,084	$ 15,321,387			
8								

Figure 15-8: AutoSum in action

4. You can change the range if it isn't what you wanted. Just click in the beginning cell of the range you really want and drag until you reach the ending cell.

5. Press Enter to finalize the AutoSum.

Tip   If you want to specify the range the AutoSum will act on beforehand, select it and click the AutoSum button. The total will be put into the blank cell either immediately to the right of selected data in a row or into the one immediately beneath selected data in a column. If you select only part of a possible range of data and there is no blank cell right after your selection, the results will be put into the first blank cell after the entire possible range in the same row or column as your selected data.

Using Other Automatic Functions

Although it might be the most common of all functions, SUM is not the only one that can be used automatically in your worksheets. You can insert several other common functions — AVERAGE, MAXIMUM, MINIMUM, and COUNT — just as easily as SUM.

To automatically add these common functions to the current cell, simply click the arrow at the right side of the AutoSum tool. Excel displays a drop-down menu, as shown in Figure 15-9.

Figure 15-9: Automatically inserting functions

When you choose one of the options in the drop-down menu, that function is the one that is inserted. All the same techniques you used with AutoSum can be used with the other automatic functions.

Note   If you click the More Functions option, the Insert Functions dialog box is displayed, as described earlier in this chapter.

The following sections describe the purpose behind each of the automatic functions available from the menu, with the exception of SUM, which was described in the preceding section.

How averages work

Averages are the arithmetic mean of a set of numbers contained within cells. For instance, if you have three cells containing the values 7, 14, and 3, their average is 8. Averages require at least two values to generate meaningful results, as the average of any single number is itself. Averages are calculated in Excel by applying the AVERAGE function to a range of cells as follows:

    =AVERAGE(F3:F8)

You can also apply it to sets of numbers in which the numbers are contained in non-contiguous cells, in which case the proper form is

    =AVERAGE(F3,G2,H9)

Determining the maximum and minimum values

The MAX function returns the value of the highest number in a set of cells. For example, if you had the values 229, 573, 842, and 132 in a range of cells and sought the maximum value, you'd get a result of 842. The MAX function can come in very handy if you want to do something like applying a minimum penalty to an account. (This is very common in business.) For instance, let's say you have a calculated penalty in cell B7, and you want to choose either it or $50, whichever is higher. All you need to do is apply the MAX formula as follows:

```
=MAX(B7,50)
```

The MIN function performs the opposite role, seeking the minimum value and returning the value of the lowest number in a set of cells. If you had a worksheet that detailed the highlights of 14 different construction bids you received, you could use the MIN function to return the lowest bid amount, as follows:

```
=MIN(B32:O32)
```

Counting numeric values

The COUNT function is used to determine the number of numeric values within a range or list of cells. For instance, consider the following instance of the COUNT function:

```
=COUNT(E7:E22)
```

If the range E7:E22 contains three blank cells, four cells that have text in them, and the rest contain numbers, COUNT will return the value 9. Why? Because nine cells have numbers in them, and the rest do not. COUNT also considers zero to be a numeric value, so if a formula returns a zero or if a cell contains the value 0, that cell is included in the value returned by COUNT.

Using Links

The data in your worksheets doesn't have to come from within them. You can establish a link between different data sources in Office programs through linking and embedding (any other Windows programs that support linking and embedding will also work), and any change to the data in the original file is reflected in your worksheet. To link to data in another program, follow this procedure:

1. Create and save the source file (database, document, and so on).

2. Select the item you want to put into your worksheet.

3. Copy the item (data, text, and so on). If you're using the main menu, select Edit ➪ Copy. You can also simply click the Copy button on the toolbar or right-click the selection and then select Copy from the pop-up menu.

4. Open your worksheet.

5. Select the cell where you want to create the link.

6. Using the main menu, select Edit ⇨ Paste Special. Alternatively, right-click and select Paste Special from the pop-up menu.

7. In the Paste Special dialog box (see Figure 15-10), select the type of object you are going to be linking to.

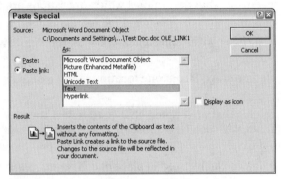

Figure 15-10: The Paste Special dialog box

8. Select the Paste link radio button, and then click the OK button to complete the link.

Caution   In the Paste Special dialog box, the Paste radio button is selected by default. If you don't click the Paste link radio button, it'll look as though you made the link correctly because the selected data will indeed show up in your worksheet. However, it will be a static paste, rather than an active link, and the data will fail to update in your worksheet when you change it in the original data source.

You might remember from earlier in the chapter that the Paste Special dialog box is handy for controlling what is pasted from one cell to another in a worksheet. You might also have noted that the Paste Special dialog box shown in Figure 15-10 looks nothing like the Paste Special dialog box shown earlier in the chapter (Figure 15-2). The reason for this is that when you choose the Paste Special function, Excel recognizes what type of information you have on the clipboard. Based on that recognition, Excel modifies the options available in the Paste Special dialog box. Excel will only offer you options that make sense for the data or objects you are attempting to paste.

Summary

In this chapter, you learned how to create formulas and utilize functions in Excel.

✦ Formulas always begin with an equals sign (=).

✦ Formulas are constructed using values, cell references, and operators, which tell Excel how to process the data to calculate a desired result.

✦ Operators have a precedence that determines which operations are performed first.

✦ Formulas can be edited either within the cell that contains them or within the Formula bar.

✦ Formulas can be copied or moved from one location in the worksheet to another.

✦ Cell references in formulas that are copied change to reflect the new position unless absolute references are used. Formulas that are moved retain their original cell references.

✦ Cell names and range names can be used in place of cell references in formulas.

✦ Arrays are sets of values; array formulas perform multiple calculations on arrays.

✦ Excel provides more than 230 worksheet functions that you can use to perform specialized or complex calculations.

✦ The Insert Function tool provides a valuable and easy shortcut to using functions in your worksheet.

✦ The most commonly used functions are SUM, AVERAGE, MAX (maximum), MIN (minimum), and COUNT.

✦ The AutoSum button provides an easy way to automatically use the most common worksheet functions.

✦   ✦   ✦

Lists and Databases

Dictionaries are databases. Encyclopedias are databases. So are phone books, almanacs, tide tables, and the like. Most of these static databases are organized in some sort of simple ascending alphabetical or chronological sequence. Computerized databases, though, are capable of much greater flexibility. The order in which items exist in an Excel database is not important, as various operations (such as sorting and filtering by a number of factors) can be performed on the data.

Note Although Excel is a great tool to use for simple databases, you should be aware that Microsoft Office includes an application that is specialized for databases. If your database needs are large or complex, or if your database needs to be accessed by many people at once, you should use Access. For more information about Access, refer to Part VI, "Using Access."

Understanding Lists and Databases

Databases are organized collections of information. In that sense, practically every source of data you've ever used has been a database.

Defining lists

Lists and databases are the same thing in Excel. Although Microsoft defines a list in Excel as "a series of worksheet rows that contain related data," that's a pretty good thumbnail description of a basic database, and many worksheets that people create fit that definition.

Records and fields

Although you're used to thinking in terms of rows and columns in Excel worksheets, the proper database parlance is to call the rows "records" and the columns "fields." Thus, every database record (a row of cells) is composed of the data in each cell in that row (the individual field entries).

Whereas a row (or "record") can contain many types of data, the data that goes into a particular column (or "field") is always the same kind. For instance, you might have a database that consists of annual mean temperatures for a range of years. The first column would be the year, the second the mean temperature for a city, the third the temperature for another city, and so on. In order for the database to make sense, in each row the year would always have to be entered in the first column. If you entered it in the third column, it would be impossible for you to properly utilize the information because the database would be looking for a temperature and find the year instead.

In the list shown in Figure 16-1, the database consists of a series of records, as described previously.

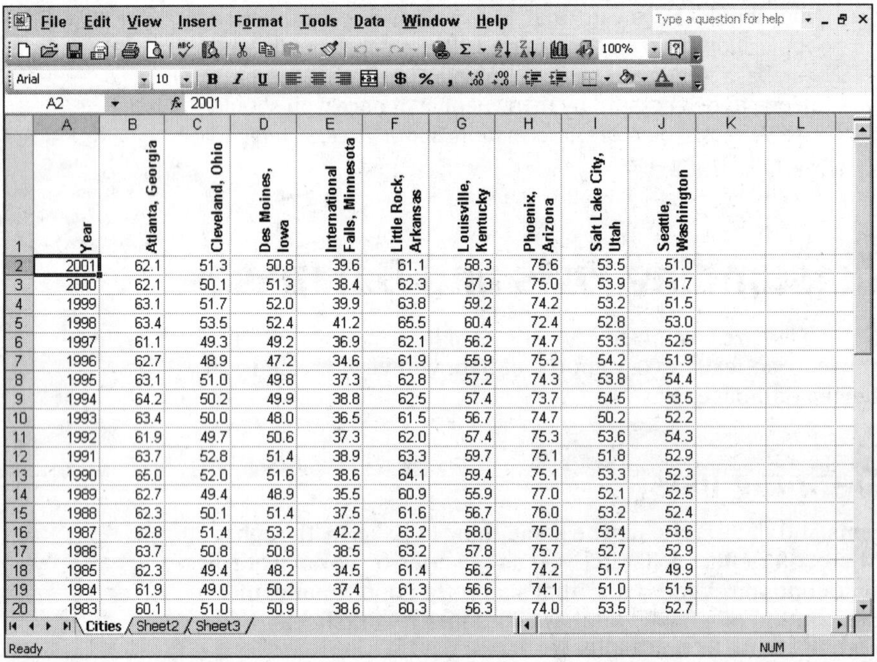

Year	Atlanta, Georgia	Cleveland, Ohio	Des Moines, Iowa	International Falls, Minnesota	Little Rock, Arkansas	Louisville, Kentucky	Phoenix, Arizona	Salt Lake City, Utah	Seattle, Washington
2001	62.1	51.3	50.8	39.6	61.1	58.3	75.6	53.5	51.0
2000	62.1	50.1	51.3	38.4	62.3	57.3	75.0	53.9	51.7
1999	63.1	51.7	52.0	39.9	63.8	59.2	74.2	53.2	51.5
1998	63.4	53.5	52.4	41.2	65.5	60.4	72.4	52.8	53.0
1997	61.1	49.3	49.2	36.9	62.1	56.2	74.7	53.3	52.5
1996	62.7	48.9	47.2	34.6	61.9	55.9	75.2	54.2	51.9
1995	63.1	51.0	49.8	37.3	62.8	57.2	74.3	53.8	54.4
1994	64.2	50.2	49.9	38.8	62.5	57.4	73.7	54.5	53.5
1993	63.4	50.0	48.0	36.5	61.5	56.7	74.7	50.2	52.2
1992	61.9	49.7	50.6	37.3	62.0	57.4	75.3	53.6	54.3
1991	63.7	52.8	51.4	38.9	63.3	59.7	75.1	51.8	52.9
1990	65.0	52.0	51.6	38.6	64.1	59.4	75.1	53.3	52.3
1989	62.7	49.4	48.9	35.5	60.9	55.9	77.0	52.1	52.5
1988	62.3	50.1	51.4	37.5	61.6	56.7	76.0	53.2	52.4
1987	62.8	51.4	53.2	42.2	63.2	58.0	75.0	53.4	53.6
1986	63.7	50.8	50.8	38.5	63.2	57.8	75.7	52.7	52.9
1985	62.3	49.4	48.2	34.5	61.4	56.2	74.2	51.7	49.9
1984	61.9	49.0	50.2	37.4	61.3	56.6	74.1	51.0	51.5
1983	60.1	51.0	50.9	38.6	60.3	56.3	74.0	53.5	52.7

Figure 16-1: A weather database

Working with Databases

The first row of a database has to contain the labels for the fields. Microsoft advises you to format these cells as text before you type any of the labels, but there doesn't seem to be any real need for this action. Generally speaking, a column label that isn't text is pretty rare, and the General format, which is the default when you type text, seems to work just fine with all the database operations.

Note Formatting the cells as text after the fact works without a hitch, so there's even less reason to do it beforehand. The only possible exception would be if you were using some sort of unusual label (like a date) for your fields.

Formatting labels

Microsoft suggests that you use some sort of formatting that differs from the formatting of the records as an aid to Excel in determining which parts of the worksheet contain records and which contain labels. Experimentation, however, demonstrates that this is unnecessary. As long as the labels are in the first row of the database, Excel knows they're labels. Because most people format the labels so that they stand out from the data anyway, such as by using bold or italic styles or color, this is an easy suggestion to accommodate, however; and there's no real reason to not do it.

There are compelling reasons, though, to actually do the formatting of the labels last instead of first. The various fields in your database are likely to have different formatting. For instance, one field may be Currency-formatted, whereas another is Date-formatted, and so on. Because you probably don't know in advance how many records you'll be putting into the database, the only way to format all the cells in the column that you might end up using is to format the whole column at once. And, because the first cell in any column contains the field label, that's a problem, because you'll be formatting the field label at the same time as all the other cells in the column.

So go ahead and type the labels first, so you can see exactly what formatting needs to be applied to which column, but don't bother with formatting that first row until you're done with all the field formatting for each column.

Creating a database

Here's the database creation process, step by step:

1. Type the field labels in the first row.

2. For any field that requires formatting (such as currency or date), right-click the column head to select the entire column.

3. From the pop-up menu, select Format Cells (see Figure 16-2).

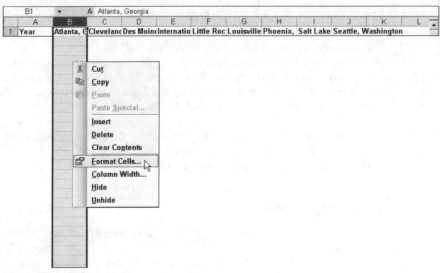

Figure 16-2: Formatting an entire column

4. From the Number tab of the Format Cells dialog box, select the desired format under Category. On the other tabs, make any other formatting selections you want (such as font style and color), and then click the OK button to complete the formatting of the column.

5. Repeat Steps 2 through 4 as many times as necessary until all the columns requiring formatting are done.

6. Right-click the row heading for the labels.

7. From the pop-up menu, select Format Cells.

8. From the Number tab of the Format Cells dialog box, select either Text or General format under Category. On the other tabs, make any other formatting selections you want (such as font style and color), and then click the OK button to complete the formatting of the field labels.

9. Type the record data starting on the second row, entering one field of data in each column (see Figure 16-3).

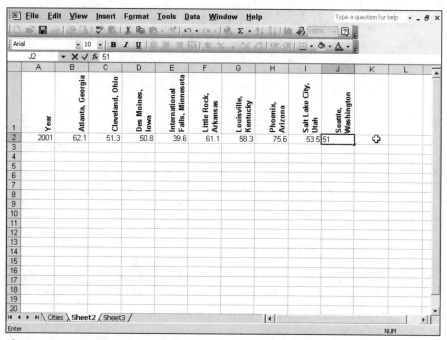

Figure 16-3: Entering the records

10. Repeat Step 9 as needed until all the records have been entered into the database.

Caution

You should have only a single database on a worksheet. Even though it's physically possible to have more than one, you run a risk of confusing Excel when it comes to manipulating the data. Because you can have multiple worksheets in a workbook, this requirement doesn't pose any kind of practical problem.

Entering and Editing Records

Fortunately, you don't have to manually type in the rows and columns for the database. You can use a data-entry form instead, which greatly simplifies the whole process and helps to prevent data-entry errors as well.

Unfortunately, Excel has some wonderfully useful techniques for database entry that aren't supported in the data-entry form approach, but can be used only with the type-it-in-the-cell approach. Which method you end up using for data entry will depend entirely on your particular needs and desires.

Using the data-entry form

Once you've established your basic database, you can use the data-entry form to delete or edit data in any field of any record. You can also use it to input entirely new records. You can use the data-entry form with an existing database, or you can use it with a new one, even before you put in a single record.

If you're going to use the data-entry form with a new database that doesn't have any records in it yet, you have to at least have the labels in place. Beyond that, you should also have formatted the columns and the label row as detailed in the preceding section, but that's not a requirement for using the data-entry form. Having at least the labels in place is required because without some indication that you're working on a database, the data-entry form won't work. If you're using it with an existing database, that problem doesn't exist, because Excel can tell what you're doing.

To use the data-entry form, follow these steps:

1. Select any cell within the database. This cell can be within a record or within the field labels on the top row, just as long as it's not outside the database.

2. Select Data ➪ Form from the main menu.

3. This brings up the data-entry form, as shown in Figure 16-4. The form is named for the worksheet it comes from. In this case, it's named "Cities."

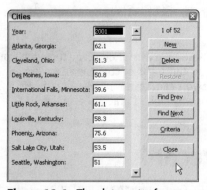

Figure 16-4: The data-entry form

4. The form has edit boxes for each of the fields in your database. The fields that run from left to right in the worksheet run from top to bottom in the data-entry box, and Excel has automatically assigned keyboard shortcuts to the field names. In the data-entry box in Figure 16-4, for instance, Alt+A will take you to the Atlanta, Georgia, field, Alt+S will take you to the Des Moines, Iowa,

field, and so on. Most of the time, though, it's easier to just use the Tab key to move from field to field. By default, the first record is the one that is displayed (regardless of which cell in the database you selected) and its first field is always selected to start with. The current record number and the total number of records is shown in the upper-right corner; the "1 of 52" in the example means that the first record is shown and there are 52 in the database as a whole.

5. To edit the current record, simply tab to the field you want to change, and then enter the new data. If you change your mind about the new data and want to revert to the original data, just click the Restore button or press the Esc key. You can also revert to the original data by clicking the Find Prev or Find Next button. That will move you to either the previous or next record without implementing the changes. However, you cannot move to a previous record if the current record is the first one; nor can you move to the next record if the current record is the last one.

Caution

Pressing the Esc key when no changes have been made will close the data-entry form.

6. When you're finished, press Enter and the new data will replace the old in your database. The next record in the database will now be displayed. You can also implement the changes by clicking the Close button. This, however, will also close the data-entry form, so do this only if you're finished.

Tip

You can walk through the entire database by repeatedly pressing Enter without entering any new data.

7. To permanently remove the current record, click the Delete key. When you do this, you will receive a pop-up warning message asking you to confirm that you really mean to delete the record (see Figure 16-5).

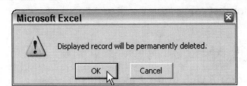

Figure 16-5: Record-deletion warning message

Caution

When you delete a record from the database with the data-entry form's Delete button, the warning message isn't kidding about its being permanently gone. You can't even use the toolbar's Undo button to reverse the action the way you can with any of the other data-entry form actions.

8. To enter a new record, click the New button. The record number information displayed in the upper-right corner will change to read "New Record." All the fields will go blank and you can enter the new data. Clicking the Close button will close the data-entry form and add the new record to the end of the database on the worksheet. Pressing Enter will add the new record and clear the fields so that you can enter another new record.

9. When you are finished with the data-entry form, click the Close button.

Using keyboard entry

Plain old keyboard entry, just the same as entering any other worksheet cell data, seems a bit unglamorous and tedious compared with using the data-entry form, but there are some real advantages to it.

With keyboard data entry, it's true that you surrender the automation of the data-entry form approach, but you gain a great deal of control over the data-entry process. You can control the type of data entered into any cell, you can set upper and lower limits on that data, and you can display messages about the cell. The messages come in two flavors. One is a general one that is displayed anytime anyone selects that cell. The other is an error message that is displayed only when data entered into a cell falls outside the acceptable range established for that field.

All three options — setting data validation parameters, defining error messages, and defining cell entry messages — can be done in a single process. However, for the sake of clarity, they are each set out separately in the following segments.

Caution

The same problem you faced when formatting the columns exists with the row of field labels. When you've finished applying the data validation options to all the columns in your database, you have to face the fact that you've applied them to each cell in the field labels in the process. Although it's probable that this won't cause any particular problem, it could interfere if you want to change the text of the labels at some point. It's best to select the row head for the field label row and clear all the data validation for that row as the last step.

Data validation parameters

To set values and parameters for data validation, follow these steps:

1. Select the column heading for the field you want to apply the data validation to.

2. Select Data ➪ Validation from the main menu.

3. The Data Validation dialog box (see Figure 16-6) has three tabs: Settings, Input Message, and Error Alert. If it is not already selected, click the Settings tab.

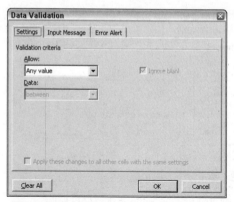

Figure 16-6: The Settings tab of the Data Validation dialog box

4. Choose from one of the values under Allow (for a description of these values, see Table 16-1).

Table 16-1
Value Settings for Data Validation

Allowed Value	Meaning
Any Value	No restrictions.
Whole Number	Restricted to numbers without decimals.
Decimal	Restricted to numbers, but allows decimals.
List	Restricted to a preset list of options.
Date	Restricted to calendar data.
Time	Restricted to clock data.
Text Length	Restricted to specified length.
Custom	Restricted to custom formula.

5. Choose from one of the options under Data (described in Table 16-2). (The Data field is disabled for some of the Allow options.)

Table 16-2 Options for Data Validation Values	
Option	**Meaning**
Between	The value must fall between minimum and maximum values.
Not between	The value must not be between the specified values.
Equal to	The value must be the same as the specified value.
Not equal to	The value must not be the specified value.
Greater than	The value must be more than the specified value.
Less than	The value must be less than the specified value.
Greater than or equal to	The value must be the same as or more than the specified value.
Less than or equal to	The value must be the same as or less than the specified value.

6. The parameters displayed depend on the options chosen under Allow and Data. Enter the parameters for the restrictions. In many cases, these are simply minimum and/or maximum values, such as the lowest and highest numbers or the earliest and latest dates allowed.

7. Click the OK button to finish.

Caution

The Clear All button on the bottom of the Data Validation dialog box doesn't just clear the entries on the currently selected tab. It clears all the entries on all three tabs. Don't use it unless you mean to do that. If you click Clear All by mistake, clicking Cancel will restore the cleared values if they were previously entered and accepted.

List, text length, and custom values

Three of the value options listed in Table 16-1 require further explanation. The List option draws from a predefined list of values. You can type them in directly under Source (separated by commas), or you can specify a range of cells in that space that contain the list of acceptable entries. Text length, despite the name, does not require that it be applied to text. You can also specify the length of a number with it. (In other words, you can specify the number of digits in a number.) The Custom setting limits the entry to anything that fits a formula you've designed. As with the List parameters, you can either type it in directly (under Formula), or specify a cell reference that contains the formula.

Error messages

Any time you set validation parameters (anything other than All Values), an error message will be generated if inappropriate values are entered. The default error message has a title of simply "Microsoft Excel" and is so general as to be virtually meaningless — "The value you entered is not valid. A user has restricted values that can be entered into this cell." To change this, follow these steps:

1. Select the column heading for the field you want to create an error message for.

2. Select Data ⇨ Validation from the main menu.

3. Click the Error Alert tab (see Figure 16-7).

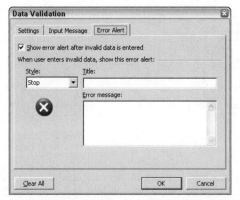

Figure 16-7: The Error Alert tab of the Data Validation dialog box

4. Under the Style drop-down list, you can choose from three kinds of error alerts: Stop, Warning, and Information. Stop is the default, and presents a red circle with a white X in the middle of it when an error occurs. Warning shows a yellow triangle with a black exclamation point in the middle, and Information shows a dialog balloon with a blue "i" in the middle. Each of the three gives you the option to enter the title and text of the error message, or both. If you do not specify one of them, it will remain at the default setting. The three differ as follows:

   • The Stop error message presents Retry and Cancel buttons (see Figure 16-8). The effect of both is identical, with only a small technical difference. The Retry button highlights the erroneous entry, meaning that anything you type will replace it. The Cancel button deletes the erroneous entry, also leaving you free to type a new one.

Figure 16-8: The Stop error message

• The Warning error message presents three options: Yes, No, and Cancel buttons (see Figure 16-9). Clicking the Yes button enters the erroneous value even though it's supposed to be excluded. Clicking the No button is identical to clicking the Retry button for the Stop error message — it highlights the erroneous entry so you can type a new one. The Cancel button, once again, simply deletes the erroneous entry and leaves the cell selected, so you can type a new entry if you want to or move on.

Figure 16-9: The Warning error message

• The Information error message presents only OK and Cancel buttons (see Figure 16-10). Clicking the OK button enters the erroneous value, whereas clicking the Cancel button deletes the erroneous entry and leaves the cell selected.

Figure 16-10: The Information error message

5. Click the OK button to complete the process.

Cell input messages

Cell input messages are not an integral part of the data-validation process but a fairly frivolous add-on. These messages are displayed whenever a cell containing them is selected. Although they can be used to say things like, "Enter such and such a value in this cell," the purpose of the cell should already be obvious from the field label. If it isn't, give some serious thought to rewriting your field labels.

In actual practice, cell input messages have limited utility and tend mainly to simply obscure part of the database from view. If you must use them, use them sparingly, or you will find that they make the database totally unworkable. However, in some cases they can serve to help idiot-proof your worksheets, as in the example in Figure 16-11.

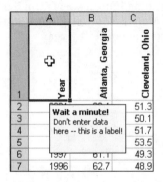

Figure 16-11: A cell input message

To create a cell input message, follow these steps:

1. Select either the column heading for the field or the individual cell you want to apply the data validation to.

2. Select Data ⇨ Validation from the main menu.

3. Click the Input Message tab.

4. Enter the title and text of the error message. If you do not specify the text, no message will appear, even if you do specify a title. If you do specify a title, the title will show in the first line of the message in bold print.

5. Click the OK button to complete the process.

Sorting and Filtering Data

The main reason why the order in which you enter the records in your database doesn't ultimately matter is that you can sort and filter them after they're entered. Sorting simply changes the order in which the records are displayed, whereas filtering creates a display of only those records that fit criteria you have specified.

Sorting data

The easiest way to sort is to simply select any cell in the column you want to sort by and then click either the Sort Ascending or Sort Descending buttons on the Standard toolbar. The Sort Ascending button sorts from A to Z (it's the one with A on top and Z on the bottom). Technically speaking, it sorts from zero to Z, but that wouldn't make as good an icon. The Sort Descending button sorts from Z to A (okay, Z to zero), and it's the one with Z on top and A on the bottom. Figure 16-12 shows an expanded weather database sorted in ascending order by year.

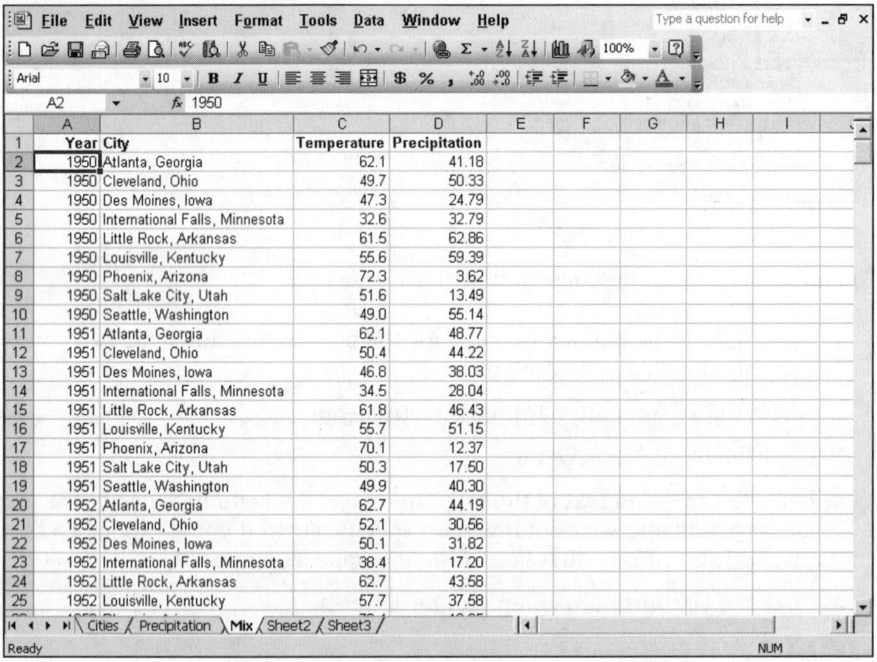

Year	City	Temperature	Precipitation
1950	Atlanta, Georgia	62.1	41.18
1950	Cleveland, Ohio	49.7	50.33
1950	Des Moines, Iowa	47.3	24.79
1950	International Falls, Minnesota	32.6	32.79
1950	Little Rock, Arkansas	61.5	62.86
1950	Louisville, Kentucky	55.6	59.39
1950	Phoenix, Arizona	72.3	3.62
1950	Salt Lake City, Utah	51.6	13.49
1950	Seattle, Washington	49.0	55.14
1951	Atlanta, Georgia	62.1	48.77
1951	Cleveland, Ohio	50.4	44.22
1951	Des Moines, Iowa	46.8	38.03
1951	International Falls, Minnesota	34.5	28.04
1951	Little Rock, Arkansas	61.8	46.43
1951	Louisville, Kentucky	55.7	51.15
1951	Phoenix, Arizona	70.1	12.37
1951	Salt Lake City, Utah	50.3	17.50
1951	Seattle, Washington	49.9	40.30
1952	Atlanta, Georgia	62.7	44.19
1952	Cleveland, Ohio	52.1	30.56
1952	Des Moines, Iowa	50.1	31.82
1952	International Falls, Minnesota	38.4	17.20
1952	Little Rock, Arkansas	62.7	43.58
1952	Louisville, Kentucky	57.7	37.58

Figure 16-12: Database entries sorted by year

The drawback to this method, as with so many things that are simple to use, is that it lacks real power. Often, you'll find that you need to sort by more than one column. For instance, you might need to sort a customer database by both state and product ordered so that you can determine which products are selling best in which states. Or you might want to sort the weather database by year and temperature.

To sort by multiple columns, follow these steps:

1. Select any cell in the database.

2. Select Data ⇨ Sort from the menu. If you failed to select a cell in the database, Excel will tell you it can't find it. In that case, go back to Step 1.

3. In the Sort dialog box, the default is to sort by the field of the active cell in ascending order (see Figure 16-13). You can click the drop-down list to pick any field in the database, and you can select either ascending or descending order for that field by clicking the appropriate radio button to the right of the field selection.

Figure 16-13: The Sort dialog box

4. You can choose to sort by a second field by selecting a field in the topmost Then By area of the dialog box. There is also a third area for a sort field, identical to the second, which works the same way. Selecting fields in these areas increases the complexity of the sorting operation. The database will first be sorted by the top field, and then by the middle field, and finally by the lower field. It is not necessary to use all three panels; you can perform a sort on just two fields if you want to.

5. To perform the sort, click the OK button. Figure 16-14 shows the weather database sorted by year and temperature (both in ascending order).

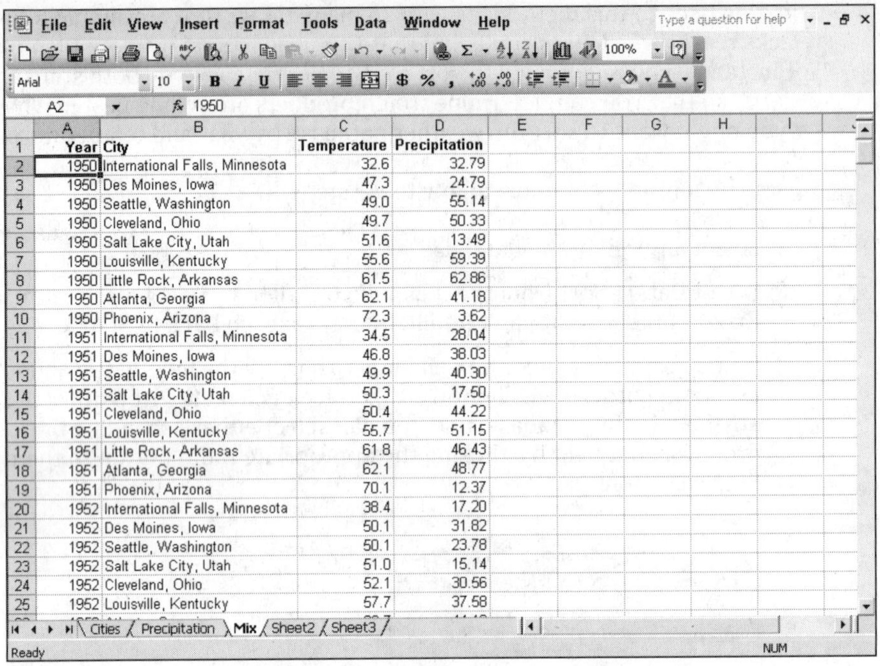

Figure 16-14: Weather database sorted by year and temperature

Filtering data

Filtering your data is much more powerful than simply sorting it. Instead of being limited to three columns as you are for a sort, you can filter on any or all columns in your database. Filtering removes from view any record that doesn't match your criteria (but not from the database or worksheet). When you're done, you can restore all the records to view.

To filter your data, follow these steps:

1. Select any cell in the database.

2. Select Data ➪ Filter ➪ AutoFilter from the menu.

3. AutoFilter creates a set of drop-down menus for every field in your database, and places an arrow at the end of each field name. Clicking these arrows shows the menu options. Figure 16-15 shows the drop-down menu for the Temperature field.

	A	B	C	D	E
1	Ye ▾	City ▾	Temperatu ▾	Precipitatic ▾	
2	1950	International Falls, Minnesota	(All)	32.79	
3	1950	Des Moines, Iowa	(Top 10…)	24.79	
4	1950	Seattle, Washington	(Custom…)	55.14	
5	1950	Cleveland, Ohio	32.6	50.33	
6	1950	Salt Lake City, Utah	33.6	13.49	
7	1950	Louisville, Kentucky	34.5	59.39	
8	1950	Little Rock, Arkansas	34.6	62.86	
9	1950	Atlanta, Georgia	34.7	41.18	
10	1950	Phoenix, Arizona	34.8	3.62	
11	1951	International Falls, Minnesota	35.0	28.04	
12	1951	Des Moines, Iowa	35.3	38.03	
13	1951	Seattle, Washington	35.5	40.30	
14	1951	Salt Lake City, Utah	35.6	17.50	
15	1951	Cleveland, Ohio	35.8	44.22	
16	1951	Louisville, Kentucky	36.2	51.15	
17	1951	Little Rock, Arkansas	36.4	46.43	
			36.5		
			36.6		
			36.7		
			36.9		
			61.6		

Figure 16-15: AutoFilter in action

4. In addition to listing every value for that field in the database, the menu has options for All (the default), Top 10, and Custom. To filter for only those records that show a specific value, click that value (for example, you could choose to show only those records in which the temperature is 56.0 degrees by clicking the number 56.0).

5. Selecting the Top 10 option from the drop-down menu brings up the Top 10 AutoFilter dialog box (see Figure 16-16). The default value, as the name implies, is to show the top 10 items in the list. However, you can select either top or bottom, the number 10 can be changed to any value from 1 to 500, and you can select percent instead of items. Thus, you might choose to show the top 80 percent, or the bottom five items. Although there is nothing to prevent you from selecting a percentage over 100, the result is the same as selecting 100.

Figure 16-16: The Top 10 AutoFilter dialog box

6. Selecting the Custom option from the drop-down menu brings up the Custom AutoFilter dialog box (see Figure 16-17). The field name is already entered, and the default is to show rows where the selected field equals a particular value (the blank box on the right side holds a drop-down list of all the values in that field). You can change the comparison operator by selecting a new one from the drop-down list where the word "equals" shows by default. The options cover just about everything you could imagine filtering by, as shown in the following list:

- Equals
- Does not equal
- Is greater than
- Is greater than or equal to
- Is less than
- Is less than or equal to
- Begins with
- Does not begin with
- Ends with
- Does not end with
- Contains
- Does not contain

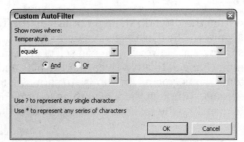

Figure 16-17: The Custom AutoFilter dialog box

7. Once you choose the comparison operator, you can either select a value from the drop-down list on the right or type in a value of your own. You can either click the OK button to implement the filtering at this point, or you can specify one further criterion for filtering.

8. When you add a second criterion for filtering, you have the option of using either a logical And or logical Or. With And, both criteria must be true; with Or, either criterion can be true. Click either the And or the Or radio button to select it.

9. Select the comparison operator and value the same way you did for the first criterion, and then click the OK button to implement the filtering operation.

To restore the view so that all the rows are visible, either select All from the drop-down menus of each field used as a selection field for the filtering, or select Data ⇨ Filter ⇨ Show All from the menu. To turn off AutoFilter, select Data ⇨ Filter ⇨ AutoFilter from the menu.

Subtotaling data

Excel's subtotal feature is accessed via the Data menu, and is used with a sorted list. It's not useful for every single type of database you can create, but only for those in which values can be kept track of for specific, repeated factors. Figure 16-18, for example, shows a database of authors, which includes the titles and prices of some of their books.

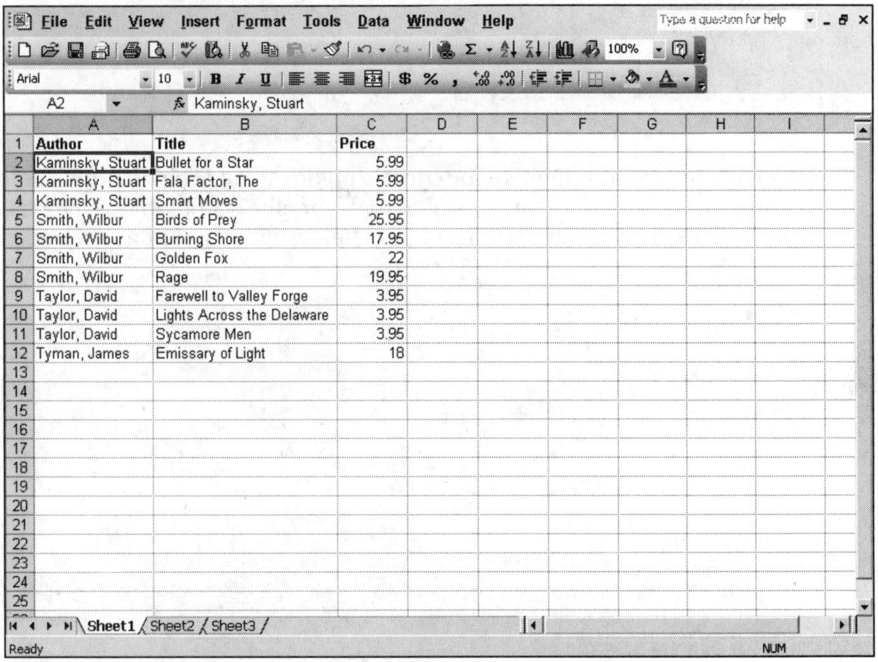

Figure 16-18: Author database before subtotaling

To subtotal the prices of the books by author, follow these steps:

1. Sort the database by the field you want to subtotal. In this case, that would be the Author field.

2. Select any cell within the database.

3. Select Data ⇨ Subtotals from the menu.

4. In the Subtotal dialog box, click the drop-down list labeled At each change in and select the field that you want to subtotal (see Figure 16-19).

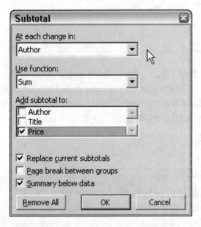

Figure 16-19: The Subtotal dialog box

5. Select a function from the Use function drop-down list. The functions listed in the drop-down list are the names of actual worksheet functions, some of which you learned about in Chapter 15. The available functions are as follows:

- Sum
- Count
- Average
- Max
- Min
- Product
- Count Nums
- StdDev
- StdDevp
- Var
- Varp

6. Select the fields for which you want to show subtotals in the Add subtotal to area.

7. Click the OK button to add the subtotals. The results are shown in Figure 16-20.

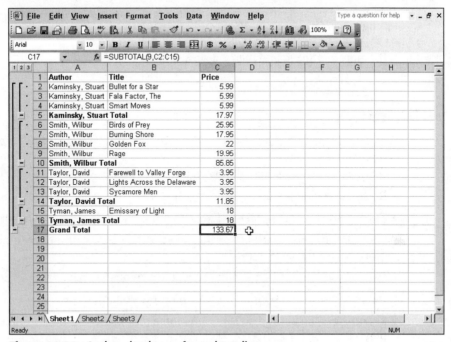

Figure 16-20: Author database after subtotaling

You can shrink the database so that only the subtotals show by clicking the minus signs to the left of the records.

To remove the subtotals, you can either click the Undo button immediately after adding the subtotals or select Data ⇨ Subtotals from the menu, and then click the Remove All button.

Using Excel Data in a Mail Merge

To use Excel data in a mail merge in Microsoft Word, follow these steps:

1. Select the data you want to use.

2. Click the Copy button on the toolbar or select Edit ⇨ Copy from the menu.

3. Switch to Word or open it if it isn't open.

4. If necessary, click the New Document button to create a blank document.

5. Click the Paste button on the toolbar or select Edit ⇨ Paste from the menu.

6. Save the new document. The Excel data is now in Word format and ready for use with mail merge.

Alternatively, you can just save your workbook and open it as the data source while performing the mail merge in Word.

For more information on mail merge, see Chapter 6.

Summary

In this chapter, you learned how to create and manipulate databases in Excel.

✦ Databases are composed of records.

✦ Records are composed of fields.

✦ The first row of a database in Excel contains the field labels.

✦ Records can be entered either through the data-entry form or by typing directly into the cells.

✦ Data validation can be used to prevent erroneous entries.

✦ Data can be sorted by individual or multiple columns.

✦ Records can be filtered so that only those that meet certain criteria are displayed.

✦ Databases can be subtotaled.

✦ Excel databases can be used in Word mail merges.

✦   ✦   ✦

Templates, Forms, and Graphics

Templates — pre-designed worksheets with the basic elements already in place — can vastly simplify your tasks. In addition to Excel's built-in templates, you can also create your own to use repeatedly.

Forms are a specialized type of template used to duplicate the functions of regular paper forms such as order forms, invoices, and so forth. Some of the built-in templates that come with Excel are forms. Forms can contain controls that add automation, such as checkboxes and buttons, and you can use macros written in Visual Basic to extend the functionality of the controls.

You can spice up your worksheets and forms with graphics, either imported or created with Excel's graphics tools, such as WordArt.

Using Excel's Templates

Excel comes with a few ready-to-use templates, such as an expense report, sales invoice, and time card. To use one of the built-in templates in Excel, start just as if you were going to create a new workbook:

1. Select File ⇨ New from the menu. Excel displays the New Workbook task pane. (You can't use the Ctrl+N keyboard shortcut, nor can you use the New button on the toolbar, as both of these approaches simply create a new workbook based on the default Workbook template and don't give you the options of the task pane approach.)

2. In the task pane, you can see several ways to open new workbooks. Near the bottom of the pane is the On My Computer link; click this link. Excel displays the Templates dialog box.

3. In the Templates dialog box, click the Spreadsheet Solutions tab (see Figure 17-1).

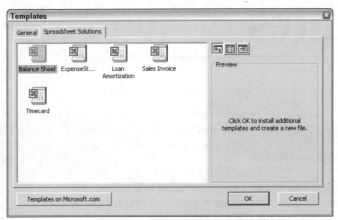

Figure 17-1: The Spreadsheet Solutions tab of the Templates dialog box

4. Click on the icon for the template you want to load. If available, a preview of the template's appearance will show on the right-hand side of the dialog box.

5. Click the OK button to load the template.

6. If the template contains macros, you may receive a warning about the possibility of macro viruses. If the template you're using is from an untrustworthy source, it's probably wise to click the Disable Macros button. Presumably, Microsoft's built-in Excel macros are virus-free, however. If you want to be able to use the template's macros, click the Enable Macros button.

> **Note**   You can turn off the macro warning message by selecting Tools ➪ Macro ➪ Security from the menu. Once in the Security dialog box, click the Low radio button to disable macro checking. You should do this only if you're absolutely certain that there is no possibility of any macro virus ever being found in any Excel documents or templates you ever load. It's a very good idea, in any case, to have anti-virus software installed on your system and to use it regularly.

7. Excel uses the template as the basis of a new workbook, as shown in Figure 17-2.

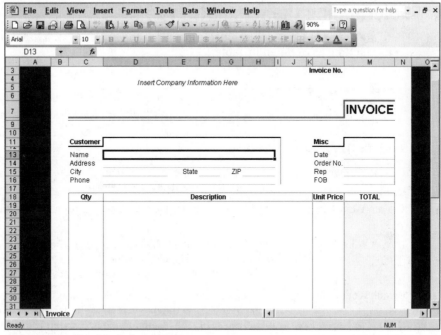

Figure 17-2: The loaded template

8. Make your document-specific changes.

9. Save the worksheet under a new name (Excel will automatically save it as a workbook instead of as a template so you don't overwrite the original).

If you want to save the revised workbook as a new template instead of as a finished workbook, follow the instructions for saving a custom template in the following section. Make sure you use a name other than that of the original template on which you based your custom one, unless you want to overwrite and erase the original one.

Creating a Template

In addition to using the built-in templates that come with Excel, you can create your own. When should you create a template? It is probably wise to do so whenever you find yourself facing a repetitive task that will repeatedly use the same setup.

In most cases, you won't want to include actual data in a template, but you'll want headings, labels, formatting, and the like to be consistent across workbooks based on the same template, so you'll need to create those elements and apply those attributes. A good rule of thumb is to remember to create all the elements that will always be needed, and none of those that won't always be.

Determining the template type

There are different ways you can use templates, and each of them has a slightly different function, as outlined in Table 17-1.

Table 17-1 Template Options	
Template Type	**Function**
Custom Workbook	The workbook is available for loading via the File ⇨ New menu approach by choosing its tab and name.
Custom Worksheet	The worksheet is available for insertion from the sheet tab pop-up menu.
Default Workbook	The workbook is the default one created whenever you use the New button. You can also use the File ⇨ New menu approach and choose Workbook from the General tab.
Default Worksheet	The worksheet is the default for all the worksheets on a new workbook. It's also the one that is inserted into a workbook when you select the Insert ⇨ Worksheet menu command.

Saving a workbook as a template

To save a workbook as a template, follow these steps:

1. Select File ⇨ Save As from the menu.

2. In the Save as Type drop-down list, select Template. This will automatically switch you to the Templates folder. (The location of the Templates folder can vary, depending on what version of Windows you are using and how your copy of Office was installed.)

3. You can either accept this folder or save the template somewhere else, such as in a subfolder under Templates.

4. Type a name for your template. If you are saving the template as the default workbook, you have to use the filename book.xlt (but you only have to type "book"—the file extension will be added automatically). If you are saving the template as the default worksheet, you have to use the filename sheet.xlt (again, you don't have to type the extension). For a custom workbook or worksheet that isn't the default one, you can type any filename you desire.

Make sure you double-check the name you provide for your template. If you use the same name as an existing template, you will overwrite that template with what you are saving. If this is what you want to do, there is no problem. If not, you will want to pick a different template name or make sure you rename the existing template.

5. Click the OK button to complete saving the template.

When you save a workbook as a template, you can't just type the .xlt file extension. Although it is possible to do that, and it will be saved under that name, it won't be saved as a template. It'll just be saved as a regular workbook with an irregular file extension. In order to save it as a template, you have to select the Templates option in the Save as Type drop-down list.

Creating your own template tab

If you save your templates in the default Templates folder, they will appear on the General tab of the Templates dialog box. If you want to, though, you can create your own tab in the Templates dialog box by creating a subfolder under the proper Templates folder. The tab will have the name you assigned to the subfolder. Any templates you save into that subfolder will be shown on that tab and can be loaded just like the built-in templates (see Figure 17-3).

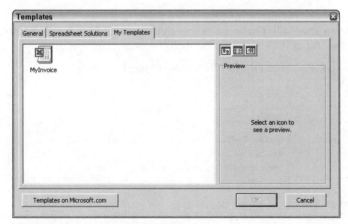

Figure 17-3: A custom template tab

If you want to create your own template tab, finding the proper location in which to create your folder can be tricky. For instance, on a Windows XP system, the proper

place to create the folder is C:\Documents and Settings*User Name*\
Application Data\Microsoft\Templates. In this example path, you would
substitute the user's name, such as Jane Doe, in place of "User Name."

This may sound straightforward enough, but you may not be able to locate this
folder on your system. The reason is that, by default, Windows XP does not display
hidden folders — and it just so happens that Application Data is a hidden folder.
Therefore, in order to create your own template tab, you must first instruct
Windows (not Excel) to display hidden files and folders. You do that by displaying
any folder you like on your system, and then choosing Tools ➪ Folder Options and
clicking on the View tab. One of the options in the dialog box is entitled Show
Hidden Files and Folders; make sure this option is selected, and then click OK.

Note   The instructions provided here to display hidden files and folders will work on
Windows XP. If you are using a different version of Windows, your instructions may
vary from those described here.

Inserting custom worksheet templates

You can't just insert a custom worksheet template into a workbook through the
usual methods, because the File ➪ New and File ➪ Open commands open only workbooks. Also, using the Insert ➪ Worksheet menu approach will insert only the
default worksheet. To insert a custom worksheet that is not the default worksheet,
follow these steps:

1. Right-click on the sheet tab of the worksheet you want to insert your custom
   worksheet to the left of.

2. From the pop-up menu (see Figure 17-4), select Insert.

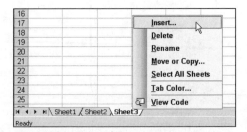

Figure 17-4: The sheet tab pop-up menu

3. This brings up the Insert dialog box, which is very similar to the Templates
   dialog box shown in Figure 17-1. Click the tab that contains the custom worksheet you want to add, and then select the desired template.

4. Click the OK button. The custom worksheet will be inserted.

5. If you want to reposition the custom worksheet, click on its sheet tab and drag it into the desired position.

Tip

If you want to open a new workbook that contains nothing but a custom worksheet template, use the File ➪ Open menu command and select the custom worksheet as if it were a regular workbook. Instead of the default workbook, this will open one that has only a single worksheet in it, and that worksheet will be the custom worksheet template that you just selected.

Creating Forms

Another use of custom templates is to create forms. Forms are a specialized type of template used to duplicate the functions of regular paper forms such as order forms, invoices, and so forth. Some of the built-in templates that come with Excel are forms of this sort.

Unlike normal worksheets and templates, forms often disregard the traditional grid look and opt for larger areas for data entry, as one of their advantages is that they can serve a dual purpose. They can be used for keyboard entry or they can be printed and filled out by hand. For this reason, many forms hide the cell grid entirely and opt for borders to set off key areas from one another.

Other than design considerations, forms are created pretty much like any other template. You make the basic outline, including all those elements that will remain unchanged from one form to the other, such as your company name and logo, and leave blank all those areas, such as customer name and address, that will vary from one usage of the form to the next.

Form controls

You can also add automation to your forms by using buttons and drop-down lists. You can key the buttons to macros written in Visual Basic to expand the functionality of the form as far as your programming ability can take you.

To access the form controls, you'll need to display the Forms toolbar. To do this, choose View ➪ Toolbars and select Forms from the toolbar list. This will give you access to the Forms toolbar. Initially, it's free-floating, as shown in Figure 17-5. You can drag it into the normal toolbar area and drop it there if you wish, or you can leave it free-floating and move it as necessary during your design activities. The decision whether to permanently dock the Forms toolbar or just shut it down when you're not using it depends entirely on how often you plan on using it.

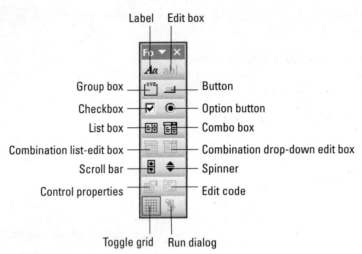

Figure 17-5: The Forms toolbar

The controls on the Forms toolbar can greatly enhance your forms. Some of them, of course, are more useful than others, and they're not all available for the new version of Excel. Table 17-2 describes the forms controls.

Table 17-2	
Forms Controls	

Control	Function
Label	Used to place text on a form.
Edit box	No longer available in Excel. Provided for backward compatibility with Excel 5.0 dialog sheets.
Group box	Used to outline a group of controls.
Button	Used to trigger an associated macro.
Checkbox	Used to select an option.
Option button	Similar to a checkbox, but each option button in a group is mutually exclusive.
List box	Presents a list of options.
Combo box	A drop-down list box; the options are not visible until you click on the box.
Combination list-edit box	No longer available in Excel. Provided for backward compatibility with Excel 5.0 dialog sheets.

Control	Function
Combination drop down-edit box	No longer available in Excel. Provided for backward compatibility with Excel 5.0 dialog sheets.
Scroll bar	Used to scroll through a series of values; displays a moving bar to indicate where in the list of values the current value lies.
Spinner	Similar to a scroll bar, but without the moving bar.
Control properties	Brings up the Format Control dialog box for changing control properties. Same as right-clicking on the control and selecting Format Control from the pop-up menu.
Edit code	Brings up Visual Basic for programming linked macros.
Toggle grid	Turns the visibility of all cell gridlines in the worksheet on and off.
Run dialog	No longer available in Excel. Provided for backward compatibility with Excel 5.0 dialog sheets.

Using a control on a worksheet

To use a control on a worksheet, follow these steps:

1. Click on the desired control in the Forms toolbar.

2. Click on the place on the worksheet where you want to put the control.

3. The control appears on the worksheet as shown in Figure 17-6. Note that controls are not contained within a cell on the worksheet but lie on top of the cells.

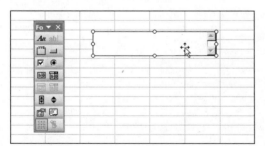

Figure 17-6: A list box control

4. Reposition and resize the control so that it is at the size and placement you desire. You reposition controls by dragging them to a new position. You resize controls by clicking and dragging one of the eight handles that appear around the perimeter of a selected control.

Tip   You can reposition a form control with fine-tuning by using the arrow keys to move it one pixel at a time.

5. On some controls that contain text, you can change the text to suit yourself, including setting different fonts, font sizes, and font colors.

6. Right-click on the control and select Format Control from the pop-up menu. Alternatively, click the Control Properties button on the Forms toolbar.

7. In the Format Control dialog box (see Figure 17-7), click the Control tab and change the settings you want to customize the actions of the control. These vary somewhat depending on the nature of the particular control (not all controls have a Control tab). For the list box control in this example, the settings include the following:

   • The Input range is where you specify the cells containing the values you want displayed in the list box.

   • The critical setting is the Cell link. This determines where the current value is displayed. You can either type a value directly into the edit box or select a cell by clicking on it in the worksheet itself.

   • Selection type controls what can be selected by the user in the list box: Single (one item), Multi (multiple items), or Extend (a range of items).

   • 3D shading, if selected, changes the "depth" with which the list box is displayed.

   • If you want, click the worksheet icon to the right of the edit box to collapse the dialog box out of the way while you're selecting cells in the worksheet.

8. Click the OK button to complete the process.

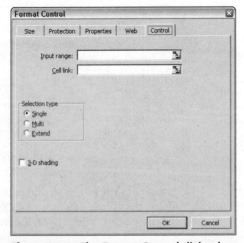

Figure 17-7: The Format Control dialog box

Using macros with form controls

Although macros can be used with all form controls, the Button control is specifically designed for working with them and has no other use but to trigger a macro. To use a Button control, follow these steps:

1. Click the Button control on the Forms toolbar.

2. Click on the place in the worksheet where you want to put the button.

3. The Button control appears on the worksheet, but is immediately obscured by the Assign Macro dialog box (see Figure 17-8).

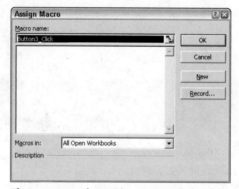

Figure 17-8: The Assign Macro dialog box

4. The Macro name setting is based on the default name of the button. Change the name if you wish by simply typing in a new one.

5. If you want to apply an existing macro to the button, select it from the list of macro names and click the OK button.

6. If you want to program a macro, click the New button, which will launch Visual Basic, as shown in Figure 17-9.

7. If you want to record a macro, click the Record button. This brings up the Record Macro dialog box shown in Figure 17-10.

8. You can assign a keyboard shortcut for the macro (so that it runs whenever you hold down the Ctrl key and select the shortcut key) by entering the key as a Shortcut key. If the shortcut key you choose for your macro is a capital letter, the keyboard shortcut will automatically be changed to Ctrl+Shift+Key.

9. Click the OK button. The Stop Recording toolbar will appear.

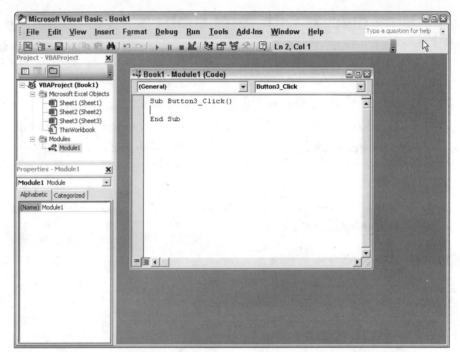

Figure 17-9: Programming a macro in Visual Basic

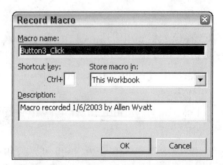

Figure 17-10: The Record Macro dialog box

10. Perform the actions you want recorded in the macro (such as keystrokes and mouse clicks), and then click the Stop button on the Stop Recording toolbar.

11. Save the workbook. From now on, clicking the button will automatically perform the actions you recorded.

Cross-Reference For more information on macros, see Chapter 49.

Protecting Worksheets and Workbooks

One of the biggest frustrations with worksheets is that once your hard work in creating them is done, it's easy for someone else — or even you — to change them by accident. All it takes is a few wrong keystrokes or someone who doesn't understand what he or she is doing and your work is trashed.

Fortunately, you can protect your work from unwanted changes. There are three levels of protection. All elements on a worksheet, such as cells and form controls, are set to protected status by default. This has no effect, however, unless the next level of protection — worksheet protection — is invoked. The third level of protection is the workbook level, which prevents anyone from doing such things as adding or deleting the worksheets that make up the workbook.

Unprotecting cells and other elements

Because worksheet elements have protection turned on by default, setting worksheet protection means not only that no one can mess with things like button text, but that no changes at all can take place in any cell. Any attempt to alter the contents of a protected cell results in an error message. Because it's likely that, at least some of the time, you'll want some values to change (in a form, for instance), you'll need to remove protection from the cells you want people to be able to change. You can't do that after the worksheet is protected, so make sure you determine ahead of time which elements you do and don't want to protect.

To remove protection from a cell or other element, follow these steps:

1. Right-click on the cell or other element.
2. Select Format Cells (or Format Control, Format Picture, etc.) from the resultant pop-up menu.
3. Click the Protection tab (see Figure 17-11).
4. Uncheck the Locked checkbox.
5. Uncheck any other protection options you don't want protected (such as Lock text, Hidden, etc.). These will vary from one element to the next.
6. Click the OK button to complete the task.
7. Repeat these steps for each element you want to unprotect.

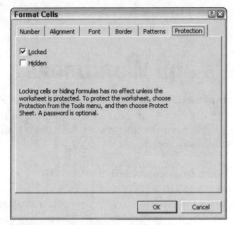

Figure 17-11: The Protection tab

Selectively protecting cells

Excel also enables you to protect ranges of cells so that only specific users can modify those cells. This is handy when you know that a group of different people will be using a workbook, and you want only particular people to be able to modify particular cells. To take advantage of this feature, follow these steps:

1. Select the range of cells you want to limit to certain users for editing.

2. Choose Tools ➪ Protection ➪ Allow Users to Edit Ranges. Excel displays the Allow Users to Edit Ranges dialog box (see Figure 17-12).

Figure 17-12: The Allow Users to Edit Ranges dialog box

3. Click the New button. Excel displays the New Range dialog box (see Figure 17-13).

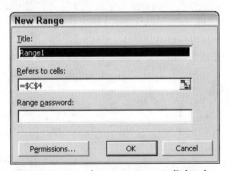

Figure 17-13: The New Range dialog box

4. In the Title box, enter the name you want to use for this protected range.

5. The Refers to cells box should contain the range you want protected. This should, by default, be set to the range you selected in Step 1. If you want to choose another range instead, feel free to do so.

6. In the Range password text box, enter a unique password that will apply specifically to this range.

7. Click OK to define the range. You are asked to re-enter the password you assigned in Step 6.

8. Define additional ranges for protection, as desired.

9. Click OK.

Tip   When you start defining different protected ranges and coming up with unique passwords for each range, managing the passwords can get cumbersome very quickly. Before closing the Allow Users to Edit Ranges dialog box (see Step 9), consider clicking the Paste Permissions Information Into a New Workbook checkbox. Doing so causes Excel to save all your range protection information — including passwords — in a new workbook. You can then use that workbook as a "key" for later understanding how you protected this workbook.

Protecting worksheets

The cell protection level cannot take effect with an unprotected worksheet. To protect the worksheet, follow these steps:

1. Select Tools ⇨ Protection ⇨ Protect Sheet from the menu.

2. In the Protect Sheet dialog box (see Figure 17-14), you can specify exactly what you want able to be done in a protected worksheet.

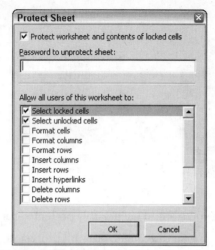

Figure 17-14: The Protect Sheet
dialog box

3. You can also type in a password, although this is optional. Do this only if it's absolutely necessary. If you assign a password to the worksheet, it cannot be unprotected again without that password. If you forget it, you're out of luck. Period.

4. Click the OK button to complete the process.

5. If you entered a password, you'll be asked to confirm it by typing it in again. Do so, and then click the OK button to finish.

With the worksheet protected, users (yourself included) will not be able to modify cells or objects that you have protected. In reality, you won't be able to do anything that you didn't explicitly permit in Step 2 (refer to Figure 17-14). If you try to modify a protected cell or object, Excel displays a warning message indicating that you cannot change what you are trying to change (see Figure 17-15).

Figure 17-15: Excel informs you if a cell cannot be changed.

If the cell that the user is trying to change is part of a range of cells that you defined as available for limited editing (see the previous section), then a different type of dialog box appears, as shown in Figure 17-16. In this case, the user is prompted for a password. If the user provides the proper password, he or she can modify the cell. If the proper password is not provided, then the user cannot make any changes to the cell.

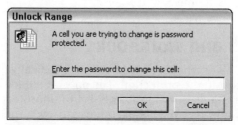

Figure 17-16: Trying to change a protected cell range results in the user's being prompted for a password.

Protecting workbooks

Workbook protection has nothing to do with the protection of cells or other worksheet elements. Rather, it relates to the overall structure and content of the workbook as a whole. For instance, if someone tries to rename a worksheet in a protected workbook, he or she won't be able to.

To protect a workbook, follow these steps:

1. Select Tools ➪ Protection ➪ Protect Workbook from the menu.

2. The Protect Workbook dialog box (see Figure 17-17) enables you to select or deselect protection for Structure or Windows.

Figure 17-17: The Protect Workbook dialog box

3. You can also type in a password, although this is optional. Do this only if it's absolutely necessary. If you assign a password to the worksheet, it cannot be unprotected again without that password. Again, if you forget it, you're out of luck. Period.

4. Click the OK button to complete the process.

5. If you entered a password, you'll be asked to confirm it by typing it in again. Do so, and then click the OK button to finish.

Unprotecting worksheets and workbooks

To remove the protection from either a worksheet or workbook, you basically make the same menu selections you made to add the protection. The only difference is that the phrasing of the menu options changes from Protect Sheet to Unprotect Sheet and from Protect Workbook to Unprotect Workbook; otherwise, even the shortcut keys remain the same.

Caution

If you have password-protected the workbook or worksheet, you'll be asked to enter the password before the unprotection can take place. As mentioned earlier, you have to enter the right password or you can never unprotect the workbook or worksheet. Bear in mind that passwords are case-sensitive — "PASSWORD" is not the same thing as "password" or "PassWord."

Adding Graphics to Excel Worksheets

Although worksheets are usually used to hold text, dates, times, and numbers, they can also be dressed up with graphics. While an overuse of graphics can rapidly detract from the appearance and functionality of the best-designed worksheets, sometimes a judicious use of graphical elements can vastly improve the look and understandability of your work.

Adding a corporate logo to a form, for instance, is a common graphical need in Excel. You might also want to use the built-in drawing tools to add callouts that emphasize or clarify the different parts of your worksheet.

There are several different ways to add graphics to your worksheets, but they are divided into two categories: importing images and using drawing tools.

Importing images

There are two basic methods for importing images. One is via the standard menu; the other is via the Drawing toolbar, which is brought up by clicking the Drawing button on the Standard toolbar. Figure 17-18 shows both methods of importing images.

File Formats Supported

There are a huge number of ways in which graphics can be formatted in a disk file. Fortunately, Excel supports a wide range of file formats for graphics. This means that chances are very good that Excel can understand what to do with the type of graphic file you want to add to your worksheet. You can import all of the following graphic file formats:

✦ Compressed Macintosh PICT (.pcz)

✦ Compressed Windows Enhanced Metafile (emz)

✦ Compressed Windows Metafile (wmz)

✦ Computer Graphics Metafile (cgm)

✦ CorelDraw (cdr)

✦ Encapsulated PostScript (eps)

✦ FPX (fpx)

✦ Graphics Interchange Format (gif, gfa)

✦ Joint Photographic Experts Group (jpeg, jpg, jfif, jpe)

✦ Kodak Photo CD (pcd)

✦ Macintosh PICT (pct, pict)

✦ PC Paintbrush (pcx)

✦ Picture It! (mix)

✦ Portable Network Graphics (png)

✦ Tag Image File Format (tif, tiff)

✦ Windows Bitmap (bmp, dib, rle, bmz)

✦ Windows Enhanced Metafile (emf)

✦ Windows Metafile (wmf)

✦ WordPerfect Graphics (wpg)

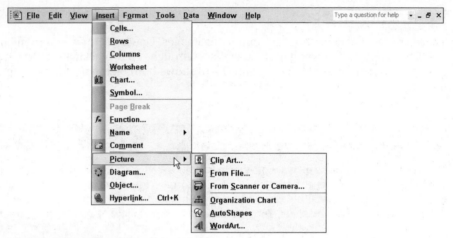

Figure 17-18: Image-importing options

Importing from the Clip Gallery

To import clip art from Microsoft's Clip Gallery, follow these steps:

1. Select Insert ➪ Picture ➪ Clip Art from the menu, or click Insert Clip Art on the Drawing toolbar.

2. Excel displays the Clip Art task pane at the right side of your worksheet area (see Figure 17-19).

3. In the Search For text box, enter a word or two that describes the type of clip art you want to see.

4. Use the Search In and Results Should Be drop-down lists to limit the graphics returned in your search.

5. Click Go. The images that meet your criteria are displayed in the task pane. As you place your pointer on each one, a floating message will inform you about the keywords associated with the image, the size of the image, and the fact that it's in Windows Metafile (.WMF) format. In addition, a drop-down arrow appears at the right side of the image.

6. Click the drop-down arrow for the image you want to insert. A number of options are provided.

7. Choose Insert from the drop-down menu (see Figure 17-20) in order to import the image into Excel.

8. Close the Clip Art task pane.

Figure 17-19: The Clip Art task pane

Figure 17-20: The Clip Art drop-down menu

Note   If you see a small globe icon in the lower-left corner of any clip-art images (in the task pane), this indicates that the image is available at the Microsoft Web site. If you select the image, you can still insert it in your worksheet (if you are connected to the Internet), and the globe icon will not be evident in what you inserted.

Importing from other storage media

To import images from your hard drive or other storage medium, follow these steps:

1. Select Insert ➪ Picture ➪ From File from the menu, or click Insert Picture on the Drawing toolbar.

2. Using the Insert Picture dialog box (see Figure 17-21), navigate to the folder containing the image you want to import.

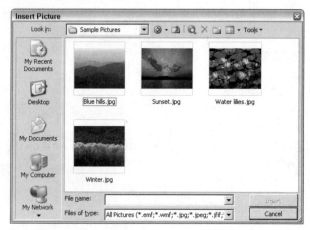

Figure 17-21: Inserting a picture

3. Select the image you want to insert.

4. Click the Insert button.

Importing from digitizing devices

To import images from a digitizing device, such as a digital camera or a scanner, follow these steps:

1. Select Insert ➪ Picture ➪ From Scanner or Camera from the menu.

2. In the dialog box, select the device you intend to use (if you have only one, it will be the only one in the list and there is no need to make a selection).

3. Select the image quality. Choose Web Quality for smaller file sizes and Print Quality for highest resolution (don't use Print Quality for applications that will be viewed only onscreen — even very expensive monitors won't show any significant improvement in the image as a result).

4. Click the Insert button to run the scanner or camera, and the image will be digitized and imported into Excel. If you want to use the standard controls for your device instead of letting Excel run it automatically, click the Custom Insert button instead.

Adding AutoShapes

Excel provides a rich assortment of drawing tools called AutoShapes with which you can add graphical elements to your worksheets. AutoShapes are available via either the menu or the Drawing toolbar. They're a collection of pre-designed, adjustable shapes — ranging from simple lines to complex shapes.

Accessing AutoShapes from the AutoShapes menu

To access AutoShapes from the menu, select Insert ⇨ Picture ⇨ AutoShapes. To get to them from the Drawing toolbar, simply click on the word "AutoShapes." The menu selection method creates a floating toolbar, whereas the Drawing toolbar selection method displays a menu. Figure 17-22 shows both the floating toolbar (on the upper right) and the menu versions (on the lower left). The menu version shows the AutoShapes available with the Basic Shapes selection.

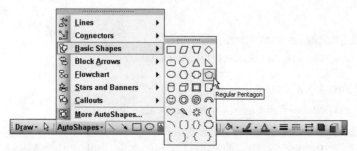

Figure 17-22: The AutoShapes toolbar and menu

Both versions present the same options:

✦ Lines

✦ Connectors

✦ Basic Shapes

✦ Block Arrows

✦ Flowchart

✦ Stars and Banners

✦ Callouts

✦ More AutoShapes

The menu options run from top to bottom, while the same toolbar options run from left to right.

Accessing AutoShapes from the Drawing toolbar

The Drawing toolbar (see Figure 17-23), in addition to providing access to the AutoShapes menu, also has four of the most commonly used AutoShapes right on it: Line, Arrow, Rectangle, and Oval.

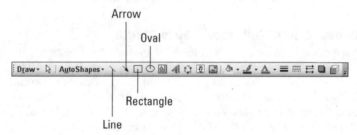

Figure 17-23: The Drawing toolbar

Placing an AutoShape in a worksheet

To place an AutoShape in your worksheet, follow these steps:

1. Select the desired AutoShape.

2. Click on your worksheet and hold down the mouse button.

3. To accept the default size, simply release the mouse button. To resize the shape, move the pointer before releasing the mouse button. In the case of lines, you need to drag the mouse from one point to another in this manner in order for them to appear. To maintain the original ratio of the shape, hold down the Shift key while resizing the shape.

Note The text box is an odd object. It can either act as a stand-alone like other graphical objects or be used in tandem with AutoShapes. When used by itself, it simply creates an area on the worksheet where you can type text. However, if you select an existing object and then click the Text Box button, you can add text directly to the object itself.

Modifying AutoShape objects

Once an AutoShape object is in place, it can be selected and modified very easily with the tools on the Drawing toolbar. Here's how they work:

Note If the selected type of AutoShape doesn't support the particular option, it will be grayed out. For instance, the rectangle shape doesn't support the arrow styles, so none of them are available if you click the Arrow Style button while a rectangle shape is selected.

✦ The fill color and font color buttons on the Drawing toolbar are exactly like the ones on the Formatting toolbar, and you can, in fact, use the ones on either toolbar for the exact same effect.

✦ The Drawing toolbar, however, also has a Line Color button. It works exactly like the other two color buttons, but clicking it establishes the color of the shape's outline.

✦ The Line Style, Dash Style, and Arrow Style buttons bring up menus from which you can choose line thickness, dashed and dotted lines, and several types of arrows, respectively (see Figure 17-24 for an example of the types of dashed and dotted lines available).

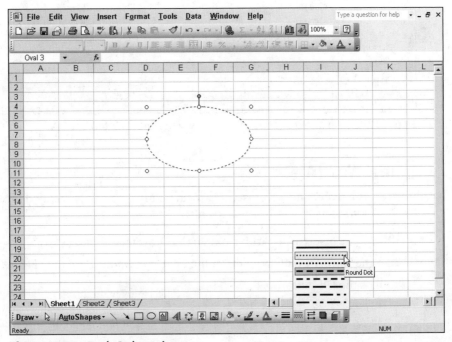

Figure 17-24: Dash Style options

✦ The shadow and 3D options each, in their own way, give an appearance of depth to an object. The two options are mutually exclusive. An object can have either a shadow or a 3D effect, but not both.

Figure 17-25 shows an arrow object with various modifications from the Drawing toolbar applied to it.

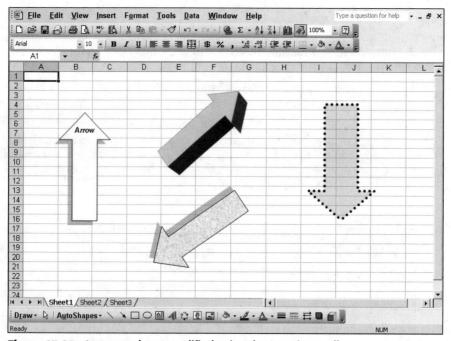

Figure 17-25: An arrow shape modified using the Drawing toolbar

Using WordArt

WordArt is a technique for presenting plain text in a colorful and vivid format. To insert WordArt images, follow these steps:

1. Click the Insert WordArt button on the Drawing toolbar.

2. In the WordArt Gallery, click on the style you want to use (see Figure 17-26).

3. Click the OK button.

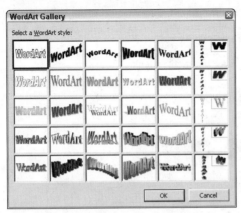

Figure 17-26: The WordArt Gallery

4. This brings up the Edit WordArt Text dialog box, as shown in Figure 17-27. Type your text in the Text area of the dialog box. You can specify the font face, font size, and whether it's going to be bold or italic via the options at the top of the dialog box.

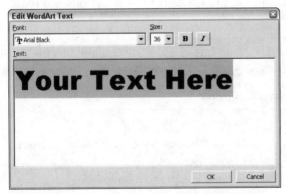

Figure 17-27: The Edit WordArt Text dialog box

5. Click the OK button.

6. The WordArt now appears on the worksheet, along with its own toolbar (see Figure 17-28).

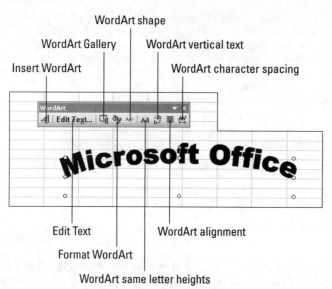

Figure 17-28: The WordArt toolbar

Table 17-3 shows the functions of the WordArt toolbar buttons, left to right.

Table 17-3	
WordArt Toolbar Buttons	

Button	Function
Insert WordArt	Inserts a new WordArt object.
Edit Text	Changes the text in the current WordArt object.
WordArt gallery	Modifies the current WordArt object with the same options as you originally had when creating it.
Format WordArt	WordArt presents options for choosing colors, fill effects, precise size, protection, etc.
WordArt shape	Gives you several options regarding the basic shape of the WordArt object.
WordArt same letter heights	Makes all letters the same height.
WordArt vertical text	Makes the text run vertically.
WordArt alignment	Alters the alignment of the WordArt object.
WordArt character spacing	Adjusts the spacing of the letters in the object.

Summary

In this chapter, you learned how to create and utilize templates, forms, and graphics in Excel, and how to protect worksheets and workbooks. Key points of the chapter included the following:

✦ Excel comes with built-in templates and forms you can use.

✦ These templates require the use of add-in utilities.

✦ You can create your own templates for both worksheets and workbooks.

✦ Forms can contain controls such as spinners and buttons, which add automation.

✦ Controls can be keyed to macros written in Visual Basic.

✦ Cells are automatically protected by default, but that protection doesn't take effect until the worksheet is protected.

✦ Workbooks can also be protected.

✦ Graphics can be added to worksheets, either by importing existing files or by direct creation with Excel's graphics tools.

✦　✦　✦

PivotTable and PivotChart Reports

If you've read about sorting, filtering, and subtotaling data in Chapter 16, "Lists and Databases," you probably think those capabilities are pretty impressive, and I'm inclined to agree with you. PivotTables, though, take data tables to new heights. They allow you to interactively alter the structure of tables so that you or others can view the information they contain from multiple perspectives.

PivotChart reports are a combination of a regular PivotTable approach and the look of a regular chart. Like PivotTables, you can dynamically alter the data, yet the presentation is in a chart format instead of a table format.

Working with PivotTable Reports

A PivotTable report is a new, interactive table created from an existing, static table. Although the PivotTable can be placed on the same worksheet as the original table from which it gets its data, it is generally better to put it on its own worksheet in the same workbook.

One of the great advantages of using PivotTables, other than the increased ease with which you can manipulate and study your data, is that no matter what you do in the PivotTable, the structure and format of your original data remain safe, secure, and unchanged.

Creating PivotTables

The process of creating PivotTables is automated in Excel through the services of the PivotTable Wizard. A PivotTable is usually based on a standard Excel database list, although you can use outside data sources as well, or combine multiple Excel database lists into a single PivotTable report. Like the database lists you used in Chapter 16, the ones you use for PivotTables need to have field names in the first row so the PivotTable Wizard knows how to group the data in the columns.

PivotTables aren't very useful for simple data sources. The more complex the original data, the more you'll find PivotTables to your liking. A good rule of thumb is that you need at least four fields, at least one of which should have multiple types in it. Figure 18-1 shows an example of minimum useful source data for a PivotTable.

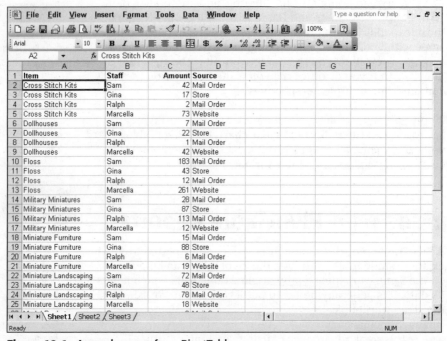

Figure 18-1: A good source for a PivotTable

To turn this data source into a PivotTable, follow these steps:

   1. Click any cell in the data source.

Caution   If you've applied automatic subtotals to your data, remove them before you start to create a PivotTable. PivotTables apply their own subtotals and grand totals.

2. Select Data ⇨ PivotTable and PivotChart Report from the menu.

3. In the PivotTable Wizard (see Figure 18-2), the data source is already selected because you had clicked one of its cells. You can also select either an External data source or Multiple consolidation ranges (using identically structured Excel databases to create one PivotTable).

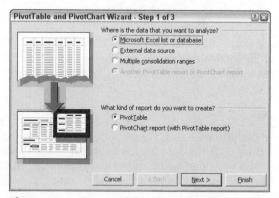

Figure 18-2: Step 1 of the PivotTable Wizard

4. Choose whether to create just a PivotTable or both a PivotTable and PivotChart. If you don't create a PivotChart at this point, you can do it later from your PivotTable.

5. Click the Next button.

6. If you're using a single data source, the next step is simply to confirm that Excel has selected the proper range for the data source (see Figure 18-3). If it hasn't, you can correct it. Click the grid icon to collapse the dialog box out of your way.

Figure 18-3: Step 2 of the PivotTable Wizard for single data sources

7. Click the Next button and move to Step 12 of this list (Steps 8 through 11 are for multiple data sources only).

8. If you're using multiple data sources, things get a little bit more complex. First, you'll need to tell the wizard whether to automatically create a page field or whether you'll do it yourself later (see Figure 18-4).

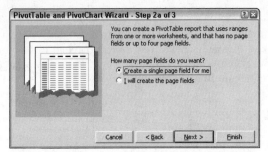

Figure 18-4: Step 2a of the PivotTable Wizard
for multiple data sources

9. Click the Next button.

10. In Step 2b for multiple data sources (see Figure 18-5), specify the range for
each data source and then click the Add button to add it to the listing. You
can remove any range you've added by selecting it and pressing the Delete
button. The Browse button is used to open other workbooks you want to
draw data sources from.

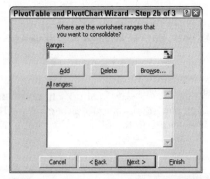

Figure 18-5: Step 2b of the PivotTable
Wizard for multiple data sources

11. Click the Next button.

12. In the final dialog box of the PivotTable Wizard (see Figure 18-6), you need to
select whether to place the PivotTable on a new worksheet or an existing
worksheet. The default is for a new one.

Figure 18-6: Step 3 of the PivotTable Wizard

13. You can simply click the Finish button at this point, but you'll make it easier on yourself if you first click the Layout button. If you finish the PivotTable without configuring its layout, you can still change the layout at any time, but the wizard's layout dialog box is much more intuitive and easier to use. The Options button lets you set various options for the PivotTable, but that dialog box is accessible at any time after you create the PivotTable, and you'll deal with it later.

14. The PivotTable and PivotChart Wizard - Layout dialog box (see Figure 18-7) graphically illustrates the way PivotTables work. The fields from the database source are represented by buttons on the right side. Simply drag the buttons to the positions you want them to occupy in the PivotTable.

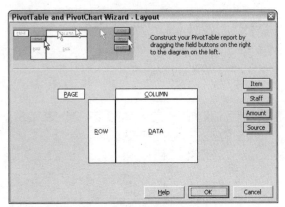

Figure 18-7: The PivotTable and PivotChart
Wizard - Layout dialog box

15. This example uses the fields Item, Staff, Amount, and Source. The example begins by looking at the number of each item sold by each staff member, so you drag the Item button into the ROW area, the Staff button into the COLUMN area, and the Amount button into the DATA area. You also want to be able to see how these relationships are affected by the source of the orders, so you drag the Source button into the PAGE field area. Figure 18-8 shows how the PivotTable and PivotChart Wizard - Layout dialog box looks when all the fields are in place.

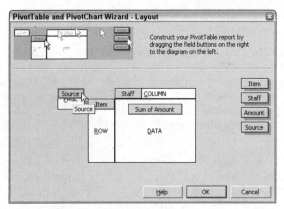

Figure 18-8: The finished layout

16. Click the OK button to return to the PivotTable Wizard.

17. Click the Finish button.

18. The PivotTable is created, as shown in Figure 18-9.

	A	B	C	D	E	F	G	H	I	J	K
1	Source	(All)									
2											
3	Sum of Amount	Staff									
4	Item	Gina	Marcella	Ralph	Sam	Grand Total					
5	Cross Stitch Kits	17	73	2	42	134					
6	Dollhouses	22	42	1	7	72					
7	Floss	43	261	12	183	499					
8	Military Miniatures	87	12	113	28	240					
9	Miniature Furniture	88	19	6	15	128					
10	Miniature Landscaping	48	18	78	72	216					
11	Model Rockets	48	1	29	6	84					
12	Model Trains	19	4	71	12	106					
13	Paint	37	26	97	15	175					
14	Rugmaking Kits	23	48	2	2	75					
15	Winter Village Miniatures	147	111	17	78	353					
16	Yarn	11	287	3	128	429					
17	Grand Total	590	902	431	588	2511					
18											

Figure 18-9: The PivotTable on a new worksheet

Note When you click the Finish button in the PivotTable Wizard, you might see the PivotTable toolbar and the PivotTable Field List dialog box on the screen, in addition to the finished PivotTable. For the sake of clarity, these can be dismissed, as has been done in Figure 18-9.

Understanding the PivotTable toolbar

If you are satisfied with the work done by the PivotTable Wizard, there is no need to be concerned about the PivotTable toolbar. If you want to manipulate, edit, or format your PivotTable, you will find the PivotTable toolbar (Figure 18-10) quite helpful.

Tip If the PivotTable toolbar is not visible on your screen, you can display it by choosing View ➪ Toolbars ➪ PivotTable.

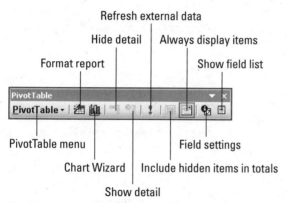

Figure 18-10: The PivotTable toolbar

The various tools on the PivotTable toolbar allow you to control all aspects of your PivotTable. The toolbar tools are shown in Table 18-1.

Table 18-1 PivotTable Toolbar Tools	
Tool Name	**Purpose**
PivotTable Menu	A series of menu commands that take different actions on your PivotTable. Some menu items duplicate menu options available in the regular Excel menus.
Format Report	Displays the AutoFormat dialog box for your PivotTable.
Chart Wizard	Creates a PivotChart from the current PivotTable.

Continued

Table 18-1 *(continued)*	
Tool Name	**Purpose**
Hide Detail	Suppresses detail information in the PivotTable.
Show Detail	Displays any detail information previously hidden.
Refresh External Data	Updates the PivotTable based on the underlying data source.
Include Hidden Items in Totals	If you have hidden detail, you may still want the subtotals and totals to reflect that detail, as if it were displayed.
Always Display Items	Allows you to specify that certain PivotTable items should always be displayed.
Field Settings	Displays the PivotTable Field dialog box for the selected field. Allows you complete control over how Excel displays field information.
Show Field List	Displays the PivotTable Field List dialog box.

Modifying PivotTables

There are three basic ways to modify PivotTables: Use the built-in data limitation features; rearrange the fields; or alter the data in the original data source and then refresh the PivotTable based on those changes.

Rearranging the fields

Each of the fields in the PivotTable's page, column, and row areas has a drop-down list featuring all the items in that field. Figure 18-11 shows the drop-down list for the Source field.

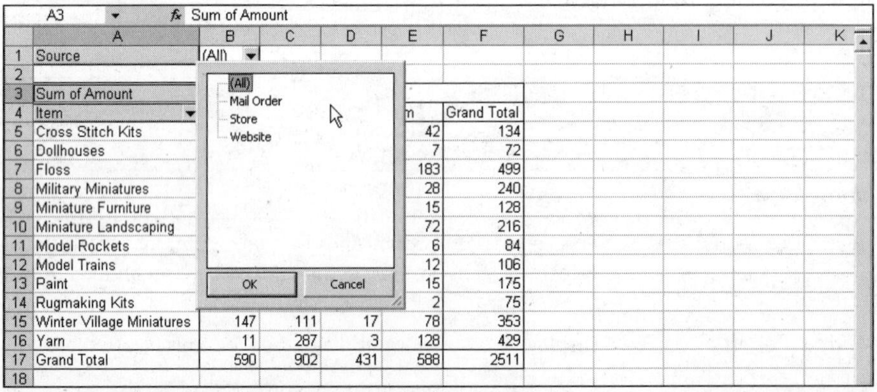

Figure 18-11: A drop-down page field list

To limit the page display in the PivotTable to a subset of the possible sources, simply select one of the fields other than All and click the OK button. The entire PivotTable will adjust to show only that page of data.

The Source field used in this example is placed in the page field area of the PivotTable, and your only options in that case are to choose one of the fields, or to choose all of them at once. The row and column field areas, however, allow you to choose multiple subsets simultaneously. Figure 18-12 shows the drop-down list for the row field area, which in this PivotTable holds the Item field from the original data source.

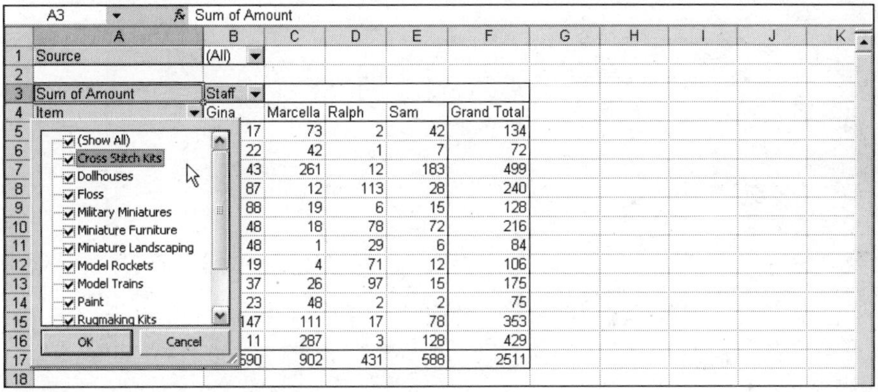

Figure 18-12: A drop-down row field list

Removing listed items

To remove any of the items in the listing from the display, all you have to do is uncheck the item and click the OK button. The PivotTable will be redrawn without that item. You can select or deselect as many items as you want to, as long as at least one item remains selected. To restore the display, simply revisit the drop-down list and recheck the deselected items, and then click the OK button again.

Restructuring the PivotTable

To restructure the PivotTable, start by choosing the PivotTable Wizard option from the PivotTable Menu on the PivotTable toolbar, or by choosing the PivotTable and PivotChart Report option from the Data menu. Either way, Excel again displays Step 3 of the PivotTable Wizard (refer to Figure 18-6). You can then click the Layout button and repeat the layout process you followed when originally creating the PivotTable.

Another way to restructure the PivotTable is to simply click a field label in the PivotTable and drag it to a new position. When you drop the field, the PivotTable will automatically readjust to fit the new layout.

Caution   If you drag a field off the PivotTable, it will be completely removed from the PivotTable. If you did not intend to do this, you can correct it by going back into the Layout dialog box and restoring the field there or simply drag the name of the field from the PivotTable toolbar back into the PivotTable.

A third way to restructure is to use the PivotTable field list, which is accessed by clicking on the PivotTable Field List option on the PivotTable toolbar (see Figure 18-13).

A3	▼	ƒₓ	Sum of Amount				
	A	B	C	D	E		
1	Source	(All)	▼				
2							
3	Sum of Amount	Staff	▼				
4	Item ▼	Gina	Marcella	Ralph	Sam	Grand Total	
5	Cross Stitch Kits	17	73	2	42	134	
6	Dollhouses	22	42	1	7	72	
7	Floss	43	261	12	183	499	
8	Military Miniatures	87	12	113	28	240	
9	Miniature Furniture	88	19	6	15	128	
10	Miniature Landscaping	48	18	78	72	216	
11	Model Rockets	48	1	29	6	84	
12	Model Trains	19	4	71	12	106	
13	Paint	37	26	97	15	175	
14	Rugmaking Kits	23	48	2	2	75	
15	Winter Village Miniatures	147	111	17	78	353	
16	Yarn	11	287	3	128	429	
17	Grand Total	590	902	431	588	2511	
18							
19							
20							
21							
22							

PivotTable — PivotTable ▾

PivotTable Field List ▾ ✕
Drag items to the PivotTable report
☐ Item
☐ Staff
☐ Amount
☐ Source

Add To   Row Area ▼

Figure 18-13: The PivotTable field list

You can drag fields from the field list, as desired, and drop them into the different areas of the PivotTable. You can also select a field and use the area drop-down list, at the bottom of the PivotTable Field List dialog box, to assign fields to different areas of the PivotTable.

To make a PivotTable change to reflect changes in the original data source, just click the Refresh External Data button on the PivotTable toolbar.

Formatting PivotTables

PivotTables are automatically formatted as they're created, and the basic formatting, such as column width and table size, alters dynamically as you choose various options while using the PivotTable. You can also apply all the standard formatting methods to PivotTables that you can to any worksheet. You can, for instance, change the font color, size, and style. But PivotTables offer a special version of the AutoFormat approach that can save you lots of time and trouble.

To use AutoFormat with PivotTables, follow these steps:

1. Click anywhere within the PivotTable.

2. Either click the Format Report button on the PivotTable toolbar or select Format ➪ AutoFormat from the menu. This brings up the AutoFormat dialog box (see Figure 18-14), which shows samples of pre-designed formats for you to choose from. These samples are different from the standard AutoFormats designed for use with normal worksheets.

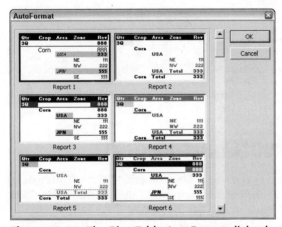

Figure 18-14: The PivotTable AutoFormat dialog box

3. To pick one, click the sample image.

4. Click the OK button to complete the process. Figure 18-15 shows the same PivotTable with a new AutoFormat applied to it.

Caution

Unlike the normal usage of AutoFormat, you can't just return to the original settings by returning to the AutoFormat dialog box and clicking the design labeled None. If you do this, you'll discover that you've removed the formatting that was applied automatically when you created the PivotTable. If you want to remove an AutoFormat that you just applied, use the Undo button instead.

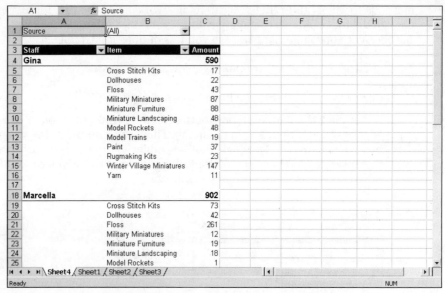

Figure 18-15: The PivotTable with a new AutoFormat applied

Working with PivotChart Reports

PivotCharts can be created at the same time you create a PivotTable or afterward from an existing PivotTable. You can have a PivotTable without a PivotChart, but the reverse is not true. PivotCharts draw their data from PivotTables, and if you try to create one without an existing PivotTable, Excel will create the PivotTable for you.

Using PivotChart reports

If you didn't create a PivotChart during the PivotTable creation process, all you have to do to create one is to click anywhere within your PivotChart, and then click the Chart Wizard button (either on the Standard toolbar or on the PivotTable toolbar). A PivotChart based on the PivotTable will instantly be generated and will appear on its own chart sheet, as shown in Figure 18-16.

Note   The appearance of your chart is dependent upon the way you have fields placed in your PivotChart. Because the AutoFormat tool (described in the previous section) can automatically move fields from area to area in a PivotTable, this can affect the appearance of your PivotChart.

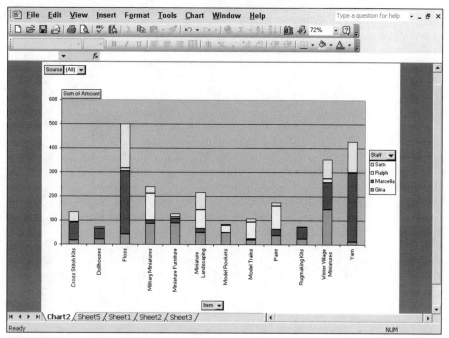

Figure 18-16: A PivotChart

You'll recognize the similarities between the PivotChart and the PivotTable it's based on. Not only do both show the same data, but the PivotChart has moveable field buttons with drop-down lists just as a PivotTable does.

When a PivotChart is active, the PivotTable toolbar shows a PivotChart menu instead of a PivotTable menu, and the items on it are specifically geared toward charts. The standard Chart toolbar also appears when you create a PivotChart. PivotCharts, for all their increased capabilities, are still Excel charts, and you can use the Chart toolbar just as you can with a normal chart. You can select chart elements, change chart type, and so on, as you can with any chart. The By Row and By Column buttons, however, are grayed out.

Altering PivotCharts

To alter the layout of a PivotChart, you can simply drag the field buttons from place to place on the chart (from category axis to legend, for example). Figure 18-17 shows the effect of moving the Source field button from the page field area to the category axis. The category axis is the equivalent of the row area on the PivotTable, and the column fields in the PivotTable are the equivalent of the series fields in the PivotChart.

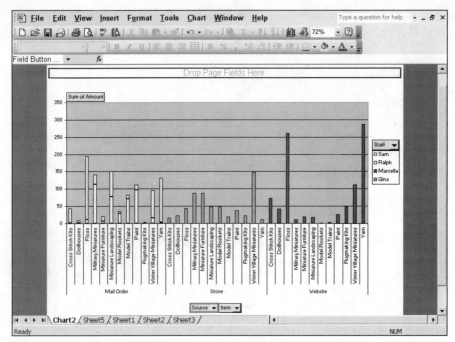

Figure 18-17: The same PivotChart with a repositioned field button

Another way to alter the layout of a PivotChart is to just change the PivotTable. PivotTables and PivotCharts exist in a totally synchronous relationship—whatever you do to one, you automatically do to the other at the same time. If you check the PivotTable that's the source for your PivotChart after you alter the layout of the PivotChart, you'll see that it has changed, and if you change a PivotTable that's associated with a PivotChart, you'll see that the PivotChart has changed, too.

Caution   Changing the layout of a PivotChart removes some of the formatting, so if you're planning on formatting the chart, don't bother with it until you're satisfied with the layout.

Summary

In this chapter, you learned how to create and use PivotTables and PivotCharts.

✦ PivotTables and PivotCharts enable you to interactively restructure the presentation of data.

✦ PivotTables are created with the PivotTable Wizard.

✦ PivotCharts can be created along with PivotTables or from existing PivotTables.

✦ Both PivotTables and PivotCharts can be modified by placing the field buttons in different positions.

✦ Field buttons have drop-down lists that contain the items in that field. By choosing which items are active, you can alter the display of the PivotTable or chart.

✦ PivotTables are automatically formatted during creation. The formatting can be altered by standard worksheet means or by using the AutoFormat option. AutoFormats for PivotTables are different from the ones applied to normal worksheets.

✦ PivotTables and PivotCharts are synchronized so that any change made to a PivotTable changes the associated PivotChart and vice versa.

✦   ✦   ✦

Using Excel to Analyze Data

This chapter covers the many ways in which you can analyze data in Excel. Data tables are useful when you have a tightly limited series of fixed variables to test. Goal Seek enables you to rapidly and easily test for the results of changing a single variable. Solver, an add-in, performs the same actions as Goal Seek but offers far more flexibility and power. Circular references — which Excel normally treats as errors — can be used with the Iteration option, enabling them to be processed. The Circular Reference toolbar also enables you to trace the operation of circular references so they can be corrected, if necessary.

Creating and Using Data Tables

Of all the ways you can use Excel to analyze data, data tables have to be the clunkiest, ugliest approach. They're complex to set up and are of limited utility, and the constraints on their construction prevent you from creating anything remotely presentable. However, you can skip some of the official rules and still manage to come up with some fairly useful output within those limitations.

Dealing with a fixed series of variables

Data tables are of value only when you have a fixed series of variables to deal with. Suppose, for instance, that you're considering how many people to assign to a particular project. Obviously, you can't use values like 4.29 women or 17.36 men in the real world. Because you're limited to dealing with whole numbers and you doubtless have some idea of the number of staff that it's remotely possible to assign to the project, you can set up a data table to test the cost of your various options.

Solving a sample problem

Suppose you have to assign somewhere between three and nine junior engineers to a project. You know the pay rate is $42.00 per hour for that rank and the project is due in two weeks. We'll leave aside the complex question of how many it'll take to actually accomplish the task for now and just look at the single variable of how much money it will take to keep a certain numbers of engineers employed on the project for its duration.

To solve this problem with a data table, follow these steps:

1. Place the data on which the formula works in a column. In Figure 19-1, this is done in cells B1 through B3.

	A	B	C	D	E	F	G	H	I	J	K
					E2 ▾ *fx* =B1*B2*B3						
1	# Staff	3			Total Cost						
2	Hourly Pay	$42.00		# Staff	$10,080.00						
3	# Hours	80		4							
4				5							
5				6							
6				7							
7				8							
8				9							
9											

Figure 19-1: Data table layout

2. Enter a formula to calculate the results. Our formula multiplies the number of staff members times their hourly pay times the number of hours for the project (B1*B2*B3). The formula must go into a cell at least two cells to the right of the data column. In this example, it is three cells over (to E2) so that there is a gap between the data and the table, but this is not necessary. In fact, the formula can be placed anywhere on the spreadsheet as long as there is an empty column to the left of it to hold variables.

3. Type the variable values in the column to the left of the formula, starting one cell down from the formula. In this case, that's D3 through D8. Because we're testing for the different costs associated with between 3 and 9 staff members, and B1 already holds the value 3, we type in only the values 4 through 9.

4. Now we're ready to create the actual data table. Select the rectangular area that includes the formula and the variables. In this example, it's D2:E8 (see Figure 19-2).

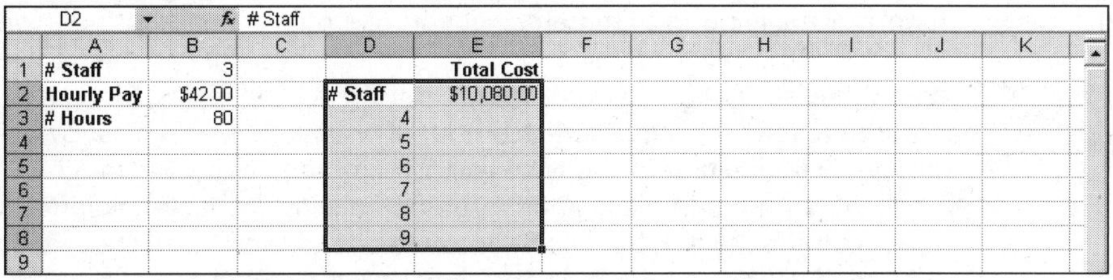

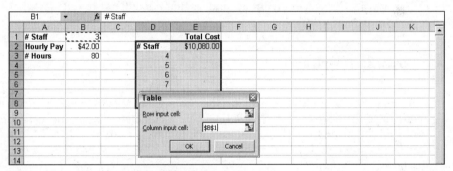

Figure 19-2: The data table selection area

5. Select Data ➪ Table from the menu.

6. In the Table dialog box (see Figure 19-3), click Column input cell. If the data and table were in rows instead of in columns, you'd click Row input cell.

Figure 19-3: The data table dialog box

7. Click on the cell that holds the initial value for which you're testing variables. In this case, that's B1.

8. Click the OK button.

9. The data table applies the formula to each variable and puts the outcome next to them, as shown in Figure 19-4.

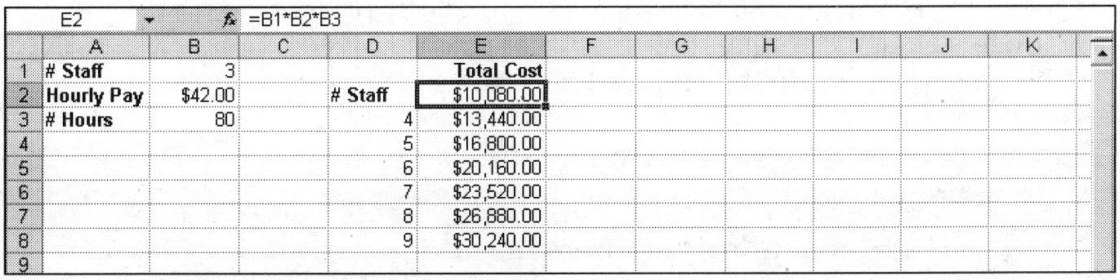

Figure 19-4: The completed data table

Tip   There is actually no requirement that you use only a single formula with a data table. You can place as many as you want to side by side, and they will all use the same variables. You could, for instance, put the formula B1*B2 in cell F2, and the amount of money required for each hour of operation would be shown in cells F2 through F8 in addition to the total cost already shown in E2 through E8. You can put all the formulas in place at once, before making the table, or you can add formulas after the initial table has been created, and then reselect the table area to accommodate the new formula and remake the data table.

Using Goal Seek

Goal Seek is a much faster way to calculate variables. It's limited to finding a single answer to a single problem, but it requires no special setup, and you don't have to jockey your worksheet layout around so that it's difficult to tell just what's what as you do with data tables.

How it works

Figure 19-5 shows a familiar situation with a couple of new twists. Once again, we're trying to figure out how to manage the project, but this time we're on a tight budget and need to show a profit. The figure in E2 is calculated by multiplying the number of staff times their hourly pay times the number of hours (=B2 * C2 * D2). The figure in F2 is calculated by subtracting this amount from the budget (=A2 - E2).

	F2	▾	fx =A2-E2							
	A	B	C	D	E	F	G	H	I	J
1	Total Budget	# Staff	Hourly Pay	# Hours	Total Costs	Profit				
2	$10,000.00	6	$42.00	80	$20,160.00	-$10,160.00				
3										

Figure 19-5: Profit/loss calculation

Solving a sample problem

We're sure we need six people to complete the project, so now we're going to use Goal Seek to determine how much the pay rate needs to be cut in order to bring it in on budget. To do this, follow these steps:

1. Click on the cell whose value you want to change. In this case, it's F2, the profit margin.

2. Select Tools ⇨ Goal Seek from the menu.

3. The Goal Seek dialog box will appear (see Figure 19-6). The Set cell value is already filled in because you had selected it before invoking Goal Seek. If you had not done so, or if you had clicked on the wrong cell, you would need to click on the desired cell at this point.

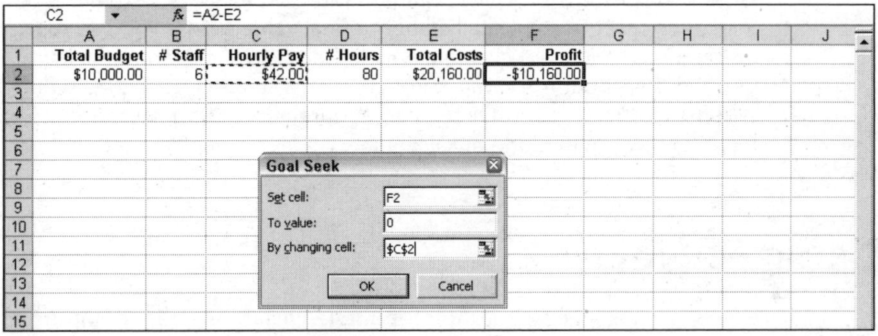

Figure 19-6: The Goal Seek dialog box

4. In the To value text box, set the value you're solving for. Because we just want to break even, the value in this example is zero.

5. To set By changing cell, click on the cell that holds the value you want Goal Seek to adjust to achieve the value you specified for the profit. In this case, we want to adjust the hourly pay rate to the point where the project doesn't operate at a loss, so we select C2.

6. Click the OK button.

7. Goal Seek will now perform a series of calculations, trying out various possibilities, and rapidly find an answer. Figure 19-7 shows the Goal Seek Status dialog box after the problem has been solved. Note that the value in C2 has been changed so that the formula in F2 solves to zero.

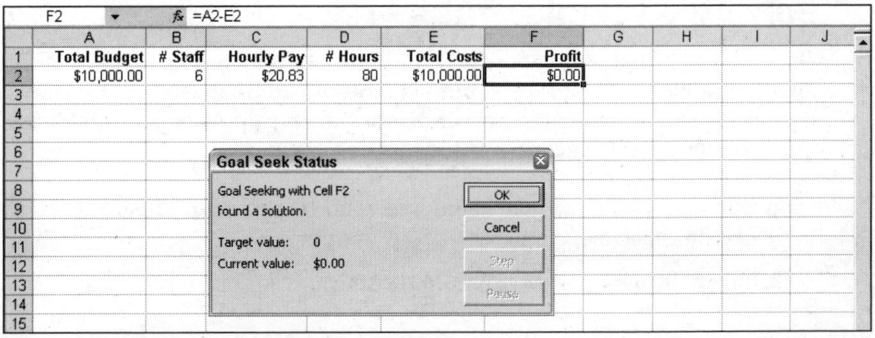

Figure 19-7: The Goal Seek Status dialog box

8. To accept the new values, click the OK button. To reject them and return the values to the original ones that were there before you ran Goal Seek, click the Cancel button.

Note   The Step and Pause buttons aren't of much use unless you're calculating a very large value using a very slow computer, or you are very fast with a mouse. Goal Seek is so fast that it'll usually find the final value before you can react. If you are quick enough, you can click the Pause button to freeze the calculation, and then use the Step button to walk through the calculation as it tries different values. When you click Pause, it becomes a Continue button, which you can click to resume the normal mode of calculation.

Using Solver

Where Goal Seek is a great solution for single variables, more complex situations call for the power of Solver. Solver is an add-in, so you won't find it on your Tools menu unless you've already installed it.

Installing the Solver add-in

To install Solver, follow these steps:

1. Select Tools ⇨ Add-Ins from the menu.

2. In the Add-Ins dialog box, click the checkbox next to Solver Add-In so that it's checked.

3. Click the OK button.

4. You may see a dialog box asking if you want to install the add-in. Click the Yes button to install it.

Solving a sample problem

Once Solver is installed, you can find it on the Tools menu. Solver works in a very similar manner to Goal Seek's, but it's kind of like Goal Seek on steroids. You'll find the process quite familiar but appreciate the extra power. To apply it to the same situation we used Goal Seek for, follow these steps:

1. Click on the cell whose value you want to solve for. This is called the *target cell*. In this case, it's F2, the profit margin.

2. Select Tools ⇨ Solver from the menu.

3. The Solver Parameters dialog box will appear (see Figure 19-8). The Set Target Cell value is already filled in because you had selected it before invoking Solver. If you had not done so, or if you had clicked on the wrong cell, you would need to click on the desired cell at this point.

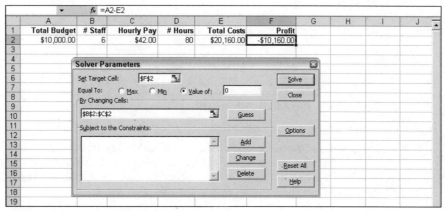

Figure 19-8: The Solver Parameters dialog box

4. Under Equal To, you have a choice of Max, Min, and Value of. The first two, of course, are for setting a maximum or minimum value. The third is for setting a specific value that must be met, no higher and no lower. In this example, we want to just break even, so the Equal To value is set to zero.

5. To set By Changing Cells, you can type in or select a range of cells. To select a series of noncontiguous cells, either type them in, separated by commas, or select them on the worksheet while holding down the Ctrl key. Alternatively, you can click the Guess button and Solver will do its best to figure out which cells you're willing to change to achieve your desired results in the target cell. In this case, we're willing to adjust either the hourly pay rate or the number of staff so the project doesn't operate at a loss. Therefore, we select B2:C2.

6. So far, the process has pretty much duplicated the steps we took when using Goal Seek, but here's where they diverge. Under Subject to the Constraints, you can set limits on what Solver will do to achieve the goals. Click the Add button to put in the first constraint.

7. In the Add Constraint dialog box (see Figure 19-9), specify the cell you want to constrain changes to in the Cell Reference box, and then select a constraint operator from the drop-down list in the middle. In this case, we're simply specifying that the value in B2 has to be an integer, so we're done with the process.

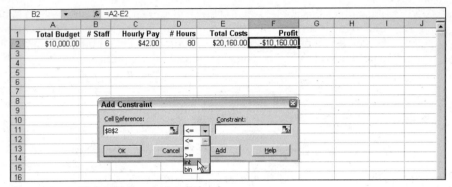

Figure 19-9: The Add Constraint dialog box

8. If you were adding just one constraint, you'd click the OK button at this point to input the constraint to Solver. Because we're adding more, click the Add button. This has the same effect as the OK button, but leaves the dialog box open and with the values cleared for the next entry.

9. Still setting constraints on B2, we need to keep it between 3 and 9 staff members. Specify B2 again in the Cell Reference text box, and then select the >= (greater than or equal to) constraint operator from the drop-down list in the middle. This time, we have to add the value we want after the operator, so we'll type a 3 in the Constraint text box.

10. Click the Add button.

11. For the last constraint on B2, specify B2 in the Cell Reference box and select the <= (less than or equal to) constraint operator from the drop-down list in the middle. Type a 9 in the Constraint text box.

12. Click the Add button.

13. Specify C2 in the Cell Reference text box, and then select the >= (greater than or equal to) constraint operator from the drop-down list in the middle. No engineer will settle for less than $10 per hour, so we'll type a 10 in the Constraint text box.

14. Click the OK button.

15. The constraints are all shown in the Solver Parameters dialog box (see Figure 19-10).

16. You can click the Options button if you want to set additional specific options, such as the amount of time you're willing to spend on the calculation.

17. To find the answer to the problem, click the Solve button.

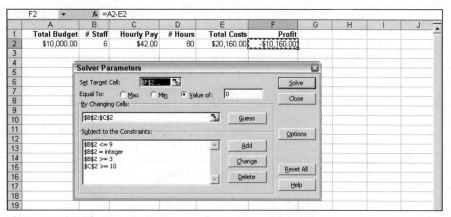

Figure 19-10: The constraints are in place.

18. Solver will now run through a series of calculations, trying out various possibilities, and rapidly find an answer. Figure 19-11 shows the Solver Results dialog box after the problem has been solved. Note that the values in B2 and C2 have both been changed within their constraints so that the formula in F2 solves to zero.

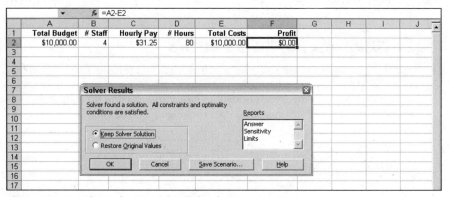

Figure 19-11: The Solver Results dialog box

19. You can choose any or all of three reports on the Solver action by clicking the words Answer, Sensitivity, or Limits under Reports on the right-hand side of the dialog box.

20. To accept the new values and create the reports, make sure the Keep Solver Solution radio button is selected, and then click the OK button. To reject them and return the values to the original ones before you ran Solver, click the Cancel button (the reports won't be created in this case). You can also select the Restore Original Values radio button and click the OK button to reject the new values, but that's extra work for nothing, unless you want to create the reports without actually changing the values.

Tip You can use the Save Scenario button to keep this solution and others on hand for later review. Click that button, and then provide a name for the scenario. You can recall it by selecting Tools ➪ Scenarios from the menu and then clicking the Show button in the Scenario Manager dialog box.

Circular References and Iteration

Normally, formulas require a fairly simple approach in which the solution is derived from the values in different cells. If the solution were to be derived from the cell containing the formula or another cell dependent on that cell, you'd have a circular reference. A circular reference may never be able to be solved at all because the result will keep changing itself. Some specialized formulas, however, require circular references. Fractal images, for instance, are generated by repeated iterations of the same formulas. Fortunately, Excel is capable of handling both situations.

Circular references as errors

For this example, create a worksheet in which you put the formula =C2 in cell A2, the value 500 in B2, and the formula =A2+B2 in cell C2. Excel is set by default to treat circular references as an error condition. Normally, setting up a situation in which a formula refers to itself will result in the warning message seen in Figure 19-12.

	C2	▼	*fx*	=A2+B2						
	A	B	C	D	E	F	G	H	I	J
1	Investment	Return	New Investment							
2	0	500	=A2+B2							
3										

Microsoft Excel

⚠ Microsoft Excel cannot calculate a formula. Cell references in the formula refer to the formula's result, creating a circular reference. Try one of the following:

• If you accidentally created the circular reference, click OK. This will display the Circular Reference toolbar and help for using it to correct your formula.
• For more information about circular references and how to work with them, click Help.
• To continue leaving the formula as it is, click Cancel.

[OK]　[Cancel]　[Help]

Figure 19-12: Circular reference warning

Using circular references

If you find yourself in one of those rare situations requiring circular references, click the Cancel button. To get Excel to let you use circular references, you have to tell it you want to. To do so, follow these steps:

1. Select Tools ⇨ Options from the menu.

2. In the Options dialog box (see Figure 19-13), click the Calculation tab.

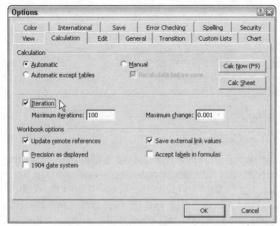

Figure 19-13: The Calculation tab of the Options dialog box

3. Click the Iteration checkbox.

4. The Maximum iterations setting tells Excel how many times to repeat the formula. Type whatever value you need.

5. The Maximum change setting is a limit on uselessly minimal iterations. Excel will halt the repetition of the formula regardless of the Maximum iterations setting if the values resulting from the last iteration have changed by less than the amount specified in Maximum change. Type in the value you need.

6. Click the OK button. Excel will now permit you to use circular references. Figure 19-14 shows the completed circular formula after 100 iterations.

	A	B	C	D	E	F	G	H	I	J
1	Investment	Return	New Investment							
2	49500	500	50000							
3										
4										

Figure 19-14: The completed circular formula

Using the Circular Reference toolbar

If you're in a normal situation and the circular reference is an error, just click the OK button when you see the warning message. The Circular Reference toolbar will appear, as shown in Figure 19-15, and arrows on the affected cells will show which cells are involved in the circular reference.

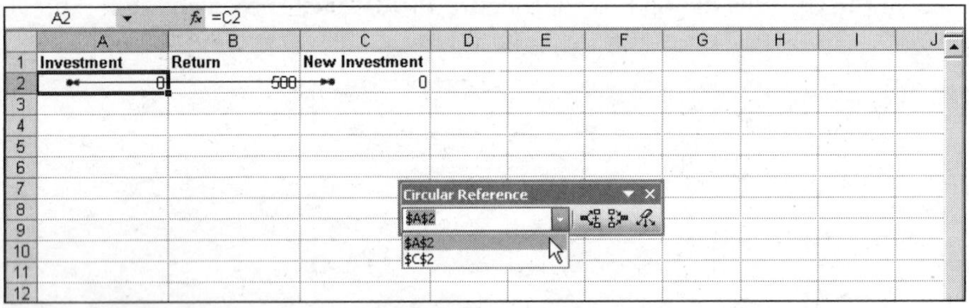

Figure 19-15: The Circular Reference toolbar

If the problem is not readily apparent, click the Navigate Circular Reference button to view a list of all the affected cells. Clicking on any reference in that list selects that cell. Use the Remove All Arrows button to clear the arrows, and then click the Trace Dependents button to see what cells are affected by this cell. Click the Remove All Arrows button again and then click the Trace Precedents button to see which cells affect this one. Once you have traced out the route of the circular reference (which isn't always as easy as in this example), you can take action to solve the problem at its source by modifying the formula to remove the circular references.

Summary

In this chapter, you learned how to analyze data in Excel using data tables, Goal Seek, and the Solver add-in, as well as how to avoid or utilize circular references.

✦ Data tables are useful only in circumstances in which you have a tightly limited series of fixed variables to test.

✦ Data table formulas must be set up in a specific location in relation to the variables to be tested. If the original data on which the formula is based is in a column, the variables must also be in a column; if it is in a row, then the variables must be in a row.

✦ Goal Seek enables you to rapidly and easily test for the results of changing a single variable regardless of the structure of the worksheet you're using it on. Just specify the value you're seeking and the variable you're willing to change to achieve it, and Goal Seek finds the best answer automatically.

✦ Solver is an add-in that performs the same actions as Goal Seek but offers far more flexibility and power. You can use it to alter multiple variables in the search for a particular result, and those variables can be constrained to remain within certain limitations you specify.

✦ Circular references occur when a formula is dependent upon itself, either directly or indirectly, for its answer.

✦ Although Excel normally treats circular references as an error, you can use the Iteration option to allow them to be processed.

✦ The Circular Reference toolbar provides you with the capability to trace the operation of a circular reference so that you can correct it.

✦   ✦   ✦

Using XML in Excel

One of the quickly developing areas of Excel is its support for the XML language. Excel first supported XML in Excel 2002, and its support has greatly increased in Excel 2003. This means that you can now do more with XML than ever before and that it is easier to perform XML-related tasks.

This chapter introduces you to both XML and the ways that Excel provides XML support. You primarily learn how to load and save data in two XML formats, but you also learn a bit about the promise XML holds for the future.

Note Discussions about XML can quickly get very technical. That is not the purpose of this chapter. This chapter focuses on how to use the XML features of Excel; it is user-oriented. If you are looking for XML information that is developer- or programmer-oriented, you should refer to a book written specifically for that audience. (Trust me; entire books can be and have been written about XML.)

What Is XML?

XML is an abbreviation for eXtensible Markup Language. Like other markup languages (such as HTML, HyperText Markup Language; and SGML, Standard Generalized Markup Language), XML provides a way to "mark up" information so it can be understood in a structured manner by a wide variety of programs. Excel understands information that has been marked up with XML, which means that it can read the XML tags and interpret them so that information can be used in the way defined by those tags.

If you are familiar with HTML, you know that the language can be used to define how a Web browser displays information. In other words, HTML defines, for the most part, the format of information. XML, on the other hand, defines the content itself; it does not define how that information should be formatted or displayed. For instance, XML can be used to define content — such as City, PartNumber, PhoneNumber, and Temperature. Once defined, the characteristics of data identified by the definition are well understood by a program like Excel. For instance, XML is used to define the characteristics of a PartNumber and then used to identify data that should be treated as a PartNumber. Excel reads the XML tags, understands the definition, and therefore knows how to store and display content subsequently defined as a PartNumber.

Looking at an XML file

An XML file is nothing but a plain text file, interspersed with tags that are used to define data elements. The tags follow the same pattern as is used in HTML files: an opening tag surrounded by angle braces (as in <abc>), and a closing tag that is the same, with the exception of a leading slash (as in </abc>). Because an XML file is a plain text file, you can easily open and edit it with a text editor like Notepad.

One thing that sets XML apart from other markup languages is that it is *extensible*. This means it is not static but can evolve to meet the needs of different people or organizations. Whereas a language such as HTML has a set number of tags that do a well-defined number of tasks, XML provides a limited number of tags and provides the means to define your own tags for your own special purposes.

For instance, consider the following data record, defined using XML:

```xml
<?xml version="1.0" ?>
<inventory-items>
    <item>
        <PartNumber>GN1039-24</PartNumber>
        <quantity>215</quantity>
        <unit>Spool</unit>
        <bin>NW-02-1</bin>
        <dates>
            <purchased>April 16, 2002</purchased>
            <stored>April 20, 2002</stored>
            <rotated>September 20, 2002</rotated>
            <expire>November 29, 2005</expire>
            <destroy>November 30, 2005</destroy>
        </dates>
        <prices>
            <purchase>5.7</purchase>
            <wholesale1>6.33</wholesale1>
            <wholesale2>7.58</wholesale2>
            <wholesale3>9.18</wholesale3>
            <retail>11</retail>
            <salvage>5.76</salvage>
        </prices>
    </item>
</inventory-items>
```

Notice the use of tags throughout the file. In this example, each pair of tags defines a component of an inventory record. For instance, the retail price of the item is defined by the `<retail>` and `</retail>` tag pair. The tags used in an XML file can vary, depending on the specific needs of the data contained in the file. Excel can read data formatted in this manner and display it.

How Excel uses XML

Excel considers XML to be one of its native formats. This means that Excel can read XML-encoded data and convert it into the standard Excel format. In the next section you learn how to identify and load XML files.

Caution Excel can read only *well-formed* XML files. This means that there must be no coding errors in the file being read. If there are coding errors and you attempt to load the file, Excel displays a warning message and will not load the data in the file. If this occurs, you have no choice but to get a corrected copy of the XML file or to use a text editor to open the file and correct any formatting problems.

When you choose to save a file in an XML format, Excel can produce two types of XML files:

✦ **Generic XML format.** This XML format is nothing but a plain-vanilla XML representation of data in a range. The resulting XML file contains definitions of data but not definitions of how that data should be formatted or displayed.

✦ **XML spreadsheet format.** This XML format relies heavily on the extensibility feature of XML. The file is a plain text file, but the XML tags were developed by Microsoft specifically for use with Excel. The special tags define attributes of cells, rows, columns, styles, worksheets, and the workbook as a whole. In other words, this type of file is an XML representation of everything necessary to completely reconstruct an Excel workbook.

Using XML Data Sources in Excel

If you have a file that contains XML-encoded data, you don't need to do anything special in order to use the file in Excel. This is because Excel knows how to read XML files. When you display the Open dialog box by any of the normal means, XML files show in the file listing, provided the Files of type drop-down list is set either to All Files, All Microsoft Excel Files, or XML Files. As shown in Figure 20-1, you can distinguish XML files from other Excel files by the unique icon that appears to the left of the filename.

When you choose to open an XML file, there are several ways that Excel can handle the file. If the XML file has an associated XSL (XML style sheet) file, Excel loads the style sheet so it knows how to display the data in the XML file. If there is no XSL file, Excel asks how you want to treat the data being loaded (see Figure 20-2).

XML file

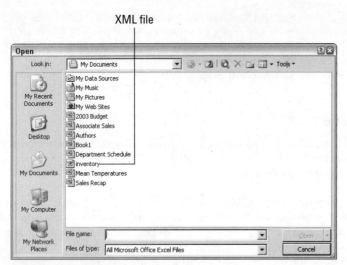

Figure 20-1: XML files appear in a regular file list in the Open dialog box.

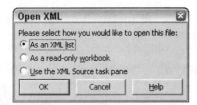

Figure 20-2: Excel provides several options for opening XML files.

Note   If you are loading an XML spreadsheet, as opposed to generic XML data, the file contains enough information that Excel knows how to load it without having to ask what you want to do. Later in this chapter you learn how to save your Excel data as an XML spreadsheet.

In most instances, you will want to load an XML file as an XML list. When you do, the data is displayed in the normal Excel manner. Several of Excel's tools are automatically active, as well. For instance, AutoFilter is turned on automatically, as is the XML toolbar. In addition, the XML list boundary is shown as a blue line outline around the data.

Figure 20-3 shows an example of an XML list created from an XML file. The data in the file follows the same inventory format described earlier in this chapter. Each of the XML tags from the file is translated into a column label. If you refer to the example XML code earlier in the chapter, you will notice tags such as `<PartNumber>`, `<quantity>`, `<unit>`, and so on. Each of these is treated as a column label.

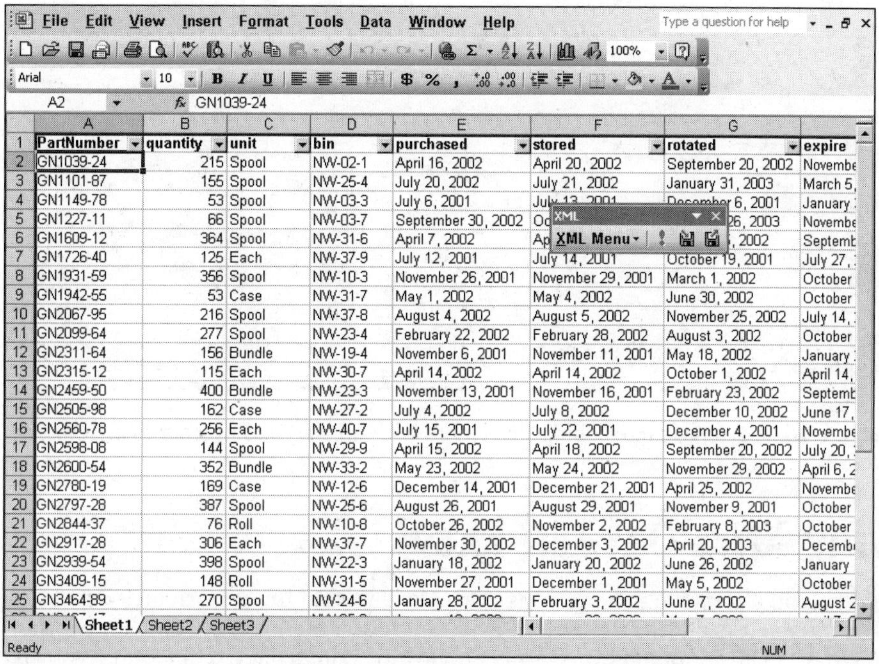

Figure 20-3: An example XML list created by loading an XML file

After an XML file is loaded, you can work with it the same way that you do other workbooks. There is one difference, however, if you loaded generic XML data into a worksheet. In this case Excel surrounds the XML list with a blue line. This line is used to mark the boundaries of the XML list. This information is essential within Excel in order to keep track of where the top-level XML structure begins and ends. Essentially, the blue boundary indicates which information is considered a portion of the XML list.

To add more information to the XML list, simply select any cell within the list. The blue boundary expands, enveloping one more row. In addition, a large blue asterisk appears in the first cell of the last row (see Figure 20-4). This marker indicates where you can start entering data if you want it included in the XML list. When you later select a cell somewhere outside the blue boundary, the asterisk disappears and the blue boundary contracts so that it surrounds only the actual data in the list.

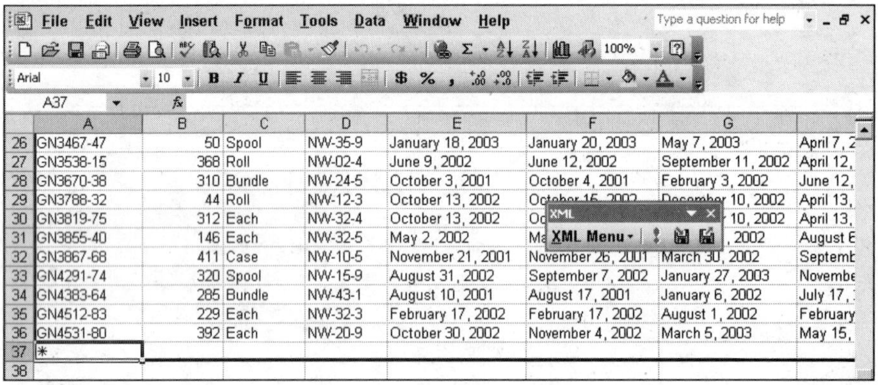

Figure 20-4: A large asterisk indicates where you can start adding data to an XML list.

Saving XML Data in Excel

When you save a file in Excel, it is normally saved in the proprietary Excel format. For the most part, this file format is understood only by Excel and some other Microsoft Office applications. You can, however, instruct Excel to save your data in one of the two XML formats it understands: generic XML or as an XML spreadsheet.

The following two sections describe how to use each format for saving your data.

Exporting data in generic XML format

You can save your Excel data in a generic XML format. This format is great if you are preparing data that will be used by a program other than Excel. For instance, you might have a specialized analysis program that utilizes XML. Excel can create a generic XML file that could be used as input for the other program.

To export information in a generic XML format, follow these steps:

1. From the menu, select Data ➪ XML ➪ XML Source. Excel displays the XML Structure pane on the right side of the window (see Figure 20-5).

Figure 20-5: The XML Structure pane

In the XML Structure pane, you can refine the relationship of the worksheet data to XML tags. These tags are contained within an XML schema file, which does nothing but define the layout of an XML file.

Note When you first load an XML list, if there is no schema file associated with the file, Excel creates one based on the structure of the XML list itself. For help with understanding schema files, refer to a comprehensive XML book, such as *XML Bible, Second Edition*, by Elliotte Rusty Harold (Wiley, 2001).

2. If you want to change to a different schema map, click the XML Maps button at the bottom of the pane to display the maps associated with the list, and then click Add. Excel displays a standard Open dialog box that you can use to locate the schema file you want associated with the data.

3. Locate the desired schema file, and then click Open. Excel displays the schema's layout in the XML Source pane, as shown in Figure 20-6.

Figure 20-6: An XML schema file is loaded in the XML Source pane.

4. Drag one of the XML nodes from the structure "tree" and drop it on the appropriate heading in your data list. In the example shown in Figure 20-6, you can drag the Associate node and drop it on the Associate heading in cell A1.

5. Repeat Step 4 for each node you want to map to your data.

6. From the main menu, select Data ➪ XML ➪ Export. Excel displays the Export XML dialog box, which is really just a standard Save dialog box.

7. In the Name box, enter the name you want for your XML file.

8. Click Export. Your data is saved in a generic XML file.

Saving an XML spreadsheet

Saving an XML spreadsheet is a very simple process. All you need to do is create your workbook as you normally would, and then follow these steps:

1. From the main menu, choose File ➪ Save As. Excel displays the Save As dialog box.

2. Using the Save as type drop-down list, choose XML Spreadsheet.

3. In the Name box, provide a name for your file.

4. Click Save.

Caution

When you save a workbook as an XML spreadsheet, a few workbook elements are not saved in the format. You cannot, at this time, save charts, OLE objects, images, drawing objects, groups/outlines, or VBA projects in an XML spreadsheet. If your workbook contains any of these items, you might want to save a regular Excel workbook in addition to an XML spreadsheet.

When you save your data in the XML spreadsheet format, Excel saves it as an XML file that contains all the information necessary to re-create your workbook. Because it is an XML file, you can open it using Notepad or any other text editor. Figure 20-7 shows an example of an XML spreadsheet file, opened in Notepad.

Figure 20-7: An Excel XML spreadsheet file, opened in Notepad

Excel and Smart Documents

Office 2003 includes a feature referred to as *Smart Documents*. If you want to get a handle on what Smart Documents are, think of them as templates on steroids. Smart Documents, entirely coded in XML, allow both Excel and Word to be configured entirely according to a developer's needs. In other words, Smart Documents allow developers to design document-centered applications using Excel and Word.

From an Excel user's perspective, there isn't much to know about using a Smart Document. All you do is open the Smart Document workbook — according to the instructions provided by the developer — and then work within the environment created by the Smart Document. That environment can include special forms, customized task panes, and different user controls.

As you work with and navigate through a Smart Document, the document itself can detect the location of your cursor (which cell you have selected at the moment) and display the most relevant information in the task pane. That might include context-sensitive help, context-appropriate actions you can take, suggested content, or links to other data or related information.

When you are done using the Smart Document, you simply exit the program according to the developer's instructions.

Notice that the developer dictates much of how a Smart Document is used. An entire book could no doubt be written about how to develop Smart Documents. Creating your own Smart Documents is beyond the scope of this book, as it involves heavy-duty XML coding and using custom DLLs. (A DLL is a dynamic link library module — a program that is called into action as necessary to accomplish specific tasks in the Smart Document.)

Summary

In this chapter, you were introduced to the eXtensible Markup Language, or XML, and how Excel supports it. You learned how to load and save data in the two major XML formats supported by Excel, and you learned how Smart Documents are closely tied to XML.

✦ XML is used to define the structure and content of data.

✦ Excel allows you to load generic XML data and XML spreadsheets.

✦ XML data, after it's loaded into Excel, can be manipulated in much the same manner as regular Excel data.

✦ You can use the XML Structure pane to map the relationship between an XML schema file and the data in a worksheet.

✦ Excel data can be exported to a generic XML file, or it can be saved in a special XML spreadsheet format.

✦ XML files can be loaded and viewed with a regular text-editing program, such as Notepad.

✦ Smart Documents provide a way for developers to create context-sensitive documents using XML.

✦ ✦ ✦

Using Outlook

Outlook Overview

Outlook is designed to help you manage information and enhance productivity, whether you're working alone in a home office or as part of a large workgroup. It can help you keep track of your e-mail messages, appointments, meetings, tasks, and contacts, and work with others to assign tasks, schedule meetings and appointments, and monitor meeting attendance and task completion.

Outlook works best with Microsoft's Exchange Server, but even if your organization doesn't run Exchange, Outlook has information-management tools galore that you may still find useful.

Note Even if you've never used Office, you may be familiar with Outlook Express, the basic message-management software that's built into Windows. Although it handles e-mail in much the same way Outlook does, Outlook Express is a very different product; among other differences, it lacks Outlook's powerful productivity tools.

Working with Outlook Folders

Outlook organizes its content into folders, which you can see in Figure 21-1. You call up this Folder List by clicking the Folder List icon at the bottom of the Navigation Pane, the leftmost pane in the figure. (Exactly what folders you'll see depends on your own installation; for instance, if you're working with Exchange Server, you may not see Personal Folders as you do in Figure 21-1).

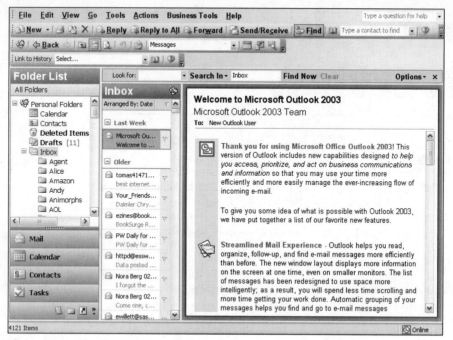

Figure 21-1: The Outlook window, showing the Folder List at the top left

You can access the contents of a specific folder by clicking on it. By default, the Inbox folder is open; the pane at right displays the currently selected message: a welcome message that Outlook opens when you run it for the first time.

Although you can add folders of your own at any time, Outlook's default Personal Folders include the following:

✦ **Calendar.** As initially configured, this folder displays the current day, divided into hours, and a small monthly calendar for access to other events.

✦ **Contacts.** This is where you store names, addresses, and other information about the people who are important to you for one reason or another. Whenever you use Outlook, you have ready access to the data stored here.

✦ **Deleted Items.** Anything you delete from another folder goes here, so nothing you delete accidentally is gone forever — at least, not until you empty the Deleted Items folder.

✦ **Drafts.** This is the folder in which you can save drafts of messages, so you can review and polish them up later before sending them. It's also useful for saving unfinished messages for later completion.

✦ **Inbox, Outbox,** and **Sent Items.** These folders list e-mail messages you've received, written, and already sent, respectively.

✦ **Journal.** This folder records your activities; it can track everything from how often you send e-mail to a particular contact to which documents you open with other Office applications, and when. You have to activate it first, though; when you click on it, Outlook asks you if you really want to turn it on and points out that the Activities tab on any contact item is the best way to track e-mail. If you want to activate the Journal anyway, click Yes.

✦ **Junk E-mail.** This is the folder to which Outlook routes messages it believes may be junk e-mail, based on settings you provide.

✦ **Notes.** Here's where you can jot down random thoughts. Outlook lets you post the notes you create here into their own windows — sort of like paper sticky notes, but electronic.

✦ **Tasks.** This folder displays tasks you or someone else has defined for you. You can prioritize the tasks and double-click on them to read and modify details.

✦ **Search Folders.** These are new in Office 2003. They contain the results of searches you have conducted in your Personal Folders; but in addition to that, they contain the search parameters. Therefore, you can save a search you conduct frequently (by default, you have search folders for messages marked for Follow Up, for Large Messages, and for Unread Mail). Rather than having to re-create the search parameters each time you need to look for a particular type of item, you can simply click on the appropriate Search Folder.

Search Folders are covered in detail in Chapter 22.

The Outlook folders do *not* correspond to folders on your hard disk, and their contents are not individual files. Instead, Outlook stores all of your information in your Exchange mailbox, or in one gigantic mailbox file specified in the properties for your Personal Folders information service.

Creating new folders

To create a new custom folder within your Personal Folders, choose File ➪ Folder ➪ New Folder. In the Create New Folder dialog box, select the folder hierarchy level at which the new folder should be placed using the folder list at the bottom of the dialog box in the area labeled Select where to place the folder. Use the Folder contains drop-down list to specify the type of Outlook folder you want: Calendar Items, Contact Items, Journal Items, Mail and Post Items, Note Items, or Task Items. Name the folder, and then click OK. The folder is added to your Folder List.

Using the Navigation Pane

The Folder List is really one pane of the Navigation Pane, which corresponds to what used to be called the Outlook Bar in previous versions of Office. You can adjust the size of the visible pane by clicking and dragging the thin bar with the little dots on it at the bottom of the pane. If you drag it up to shrink the pane, you'll see more large buttons on the Navigation Pane. If you drag it down, more of the buttons disappear, replaced instead by small icons at the very bottom of the Navigation Pane (see Figure 21-2).

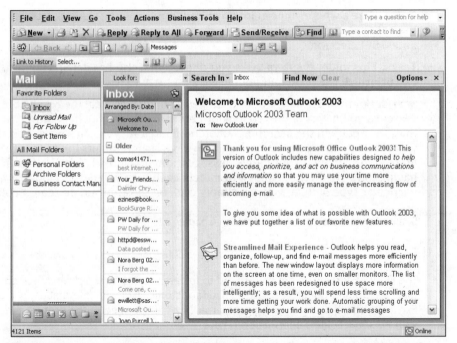

Figure 21-2: You can make the Navigation Pane as tall as you want, reducing the bar's buttons (at the lower left) to small icons.

Whether the Navigation Pane's buttons are displayed full-size or as small icons, they work the same way: Just click to activate one of Outlook's various views (more on those in a minute).

You can customize the Navigation Pane in a small way by right-clicking any button on it and choosing Navigation Pane Options. This opens the dialog box shown in Figure 21-3. Are there certain Outlook functions you think you'll never use? You can remove any button from the display by unchecking it in this list, and reposition any button by selecting it, and then clicking Move Up or Move Down. Clicking Reset returns the Navigation Pane to its default configuration.

Figure 21-3: Use this dialog box to customize the Navigation Pane's appearance.

Working with and Customizing Views

Whenever you click one of the buttons in the Navigation Pane or open a folder from the complete Folder List, Outlook displays the information you asked for in one of many possible views.

You're not limited to the default views Outlook offers you; you can change to another view, modify an existing view, or create your own view.

For example, Figure 21-4 shows the Day view, the default view you get when you open the Calendar folder from the Folder List or click the Calendar button in the Navigation Pane.

Within each view, there may be a number of subviews; to change the subviews in Calendar, for instance, click on one of the other options in the Calendar toolbar: Work Week, Week, or Month. Figure 21-5 shows you the Month view, for comparison purposes.

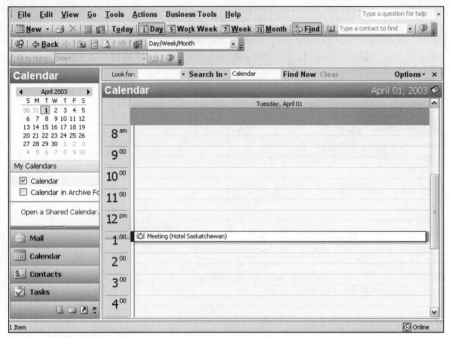

Figure 21-4: This is the default Day view in Outlook's Calendar.

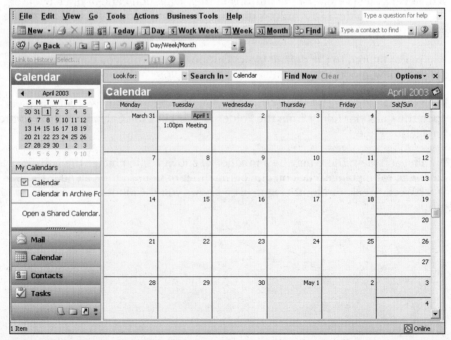

Figure 21-5: This, by way of comparison, is the Month view.

Switching views

Like Calendar, each view offers several additional options. To switch between the available views, choose View ➪ Arrange By ➪ Current View and select the view you want from the submenu.

Tip   If you find yourself frequently changing views, choose View ➪ Arrange By ➪ Show Views in Navigation Pane. This creates a Current View list in the Navigation Pane. Click the radio button for whichever view you want. As well, the Advanced Toolbar includes a drop-down list with all of the Current View options listed.

Customizing views

Outlook lets you alter existing views or create new ones from scratch.

To customize the current view, choose View ➪ Arrange By ➪ Current View ➪ Customize Current View to display the dialog box shown in Figure 21-6.

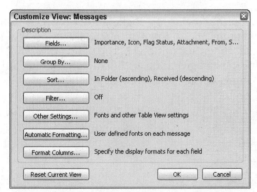

Figure 21-6: Use Outlook's Customize View dialog box to modify views.

This dialog box offers numerous options, detailed in the following sections.

Fields

Click the Fields button to open the Show Fields dialog box shown in Figure 21-7. Choose a field you want to include in the view from the list at left (use the Select available fields from drop-down list to choose the source of the fields displayed), and add it to the view by clicking the Add button. You can remove a field from the view by highlighting it in the right-hand box and clicking the Remove button. You can rearrange fields in the view by highlighting them in the right-hand box and using the Move Up and Move Down buttons. If you have a field that will display information on more than one line, you can set the maximum number of lines that will be displayed from the Maximum number of lines in Multi-line mode drop-down list.

Figure 21-7: Add, delete, and rearrange fields in a particular view using this dialog box.

Group By

You can place related items together within a view by clicking the Group By button. This opens the dialog box shown in Figure 21-8. If the Automatically group according to arrangement button is checked, the other options in the dialog box will be grayed out because Outlook is taking care of grouping automatically. Uncheck that box, however, and you can arrange items within your view as you like.

Figure 21-8: Group related items visually with these tools.

Choose what criteria you want to group items by from the Group items by drop-down list, and specify whether they should be grouped in ascending or descending order. Each unique value in the field you've chosen in the Group items by list becomes a main heading in the view, with all the items that match that value grouped beneath it. An example of how this works in your Contacts folder is shown in Figure 21-9, where contacts are grouped by first name.

Figure 21-9: Grouping divides the information in your view into smaller groups that are easier to work with.

You can choose the source of the fields you use for groupings from the Select available fields from drop-down list. You can also choose how to display groups: All expanded, All collapsed, or All last viewed. When groups are collapsed together, they work like the tree-type folder list in Windows Explorer — you can display or hide the individual items under each heading by clicking the +/− icon to the left of the group's name.

Tip   An easier way to create the most commonly used groups is to right-click on a column head in the current view and choose Group by This Field from the shortcut menu. Alternatively, choose Group By Box, which causes Outlook to add an empty area just above the items, into which you can drag column headings and arrange them into groups and subgroups. Subgroups allow you to fine-tune your grouping; for example, within a Last Name group you could group by, say, Business Name, to keep all the Smiths who work for Arctic Air Conditioning separate from the Smiths who work for Havana Heating.

Sort

This button opens a dialog box very similar to the Group By dialog box, enabling you to sort items in a view by any field you choose, in either ascending or descending order. You can carry out a multilevel sort — for example, sorting by Last Name, then by First Name, and then by Address.

Tip   A quicker way to sort a field in an Outlook view is to right-click the column heading for that field and choose Sort Ascending or Sort Descending. Quicker still, click the column heading for the field to sort it in ascending order, and click it again to reverse the sort order.

Filter

You can filter a view to limit the information displayed to items matching specific criteria. Click Filter to open the dialog box shown in Figure 21-10. The options available here depend on which folder you're working with, but generally speaking, you can filter a view based on the text present in one or more fields, or by people associated with the item (for example, those who have been invited to a meeting).

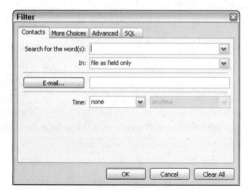

Figure 21-10: Use the Filter dialog box to limit displayed information to only items of particular interest in an Outlook view.

You can use additional filtering options based on the categories into which you can place Outlook items (more on that in the "Assigning items to categories" section later in this chapter). Switch to the More Choices tab and choose Categories to select from those available. This tab also has other useful miscellaneous filtering options.

The Advanced tab offers even more filtering options, enabling you to build incredibly complex filters using conditions for the contents of every field Outlook has. For example, you could create a filter that showed you only messages of high importance, for which a receipt was requested, that were sent by a particular contact on a specific day. Select the field you want to use for filtering from the sub-menu that opens when you click the Field button, and then choose the appropriate conditions from those provided in the Condition drop-down list, and enter or select the appropriate value.

The SQL tab enables you to build complex queries against data in your Outlook folder.

Other Settings, Automatic Formatting, Format Columns

These three buttons enable you to alter the appearance of the current view. The Other Settings button enables you to set the fonts used in columns and rows, the style of line used for grids and group headings, the look of AutoPreview (and whether or not to use it), where the Reading pane should be located (or if it should be turned off), and more.

Use automatic formatting to specify the formatting for specific items, such as unread messages, and create automatic formatting rules for other items that you want drawn to your attention.

Finally, the Format Columns button enables you to determine the appearance of various fields for which options are available and set the width and alignment for the columns that display those fields (in views that use columns, obviously).

Resetting the current view

If you make changes to the current view that, on second thought, you'd rather not keep, click Reset Current View to undo them *en masse*.

Note   View types vary in how many customization options they offer, but you always have *some* options.

Using the Field Chooser

Another tool for customizing a view is the Field Chooser, which you open by right-clicking on a field name in the current view and choosing Field Chooser from the shortcut menu (see Figure 21-11).

The Field Chooser offers you a collection of buttons representing fields (you can choose which fields are offered by using the drop-down list at the top of the Field Chooser). To add a field to the view, just drag its button from the Field Chooser to the desired location along the column heading area, much as you do when customizing a toolbar.

Figure 21-11: The Field Chooser makes adding fields to a view a simple click-and-drag operation.

Creating views from scratch

To create a new view from scratch, choose View ➪ Arrange By ➪ Current View ➪ Define Views. This opens the Custom View Organizer (see Figure 21-12).

Figure 21-12: Outlook enables you to easily create and organize your own custom views.

This dialog box shows you all of the views for the current folder, and lets you copy any view, modify any view (clicking Modify opens the Customize View dialog box we've just explored), or create one from scratch.

If you click New, the Create a New View dialog box opens; you simply name your new view, choose the type of view it should be (Table, Timeline, Card, Day/Week/ Month, or Icon) and specify whether it can be used within the current folder, visible to everyone who has access to the folder on your computer or network; within the current folder, visible only to yourself, as the creator of the folder; or in all folders of the type currently open.

Click OK, and the Customize View dialog box opens.

Once you've created a new view, it becomes available just like the others, through the View ⇨ Arrange By ⇨ Current View menu, the Current View list in the Navigation Pane (if you've activated that option), or the Current View list on the Advanced toolbar.

Assigning items to categories

Categories are keywords that can help you organize the information you store in Outlook. You can use them to help you find, sort, filter, or group items in all your folders.

Categories are useful for making it easier to find things in folders that may hold (in the case of, for example, my Inbox) thousands of items. For example, you could assign various contacts to the Personal or Business categories rather than create separate folders for them. Then you could use the Filter option described earlier to create views that show only one or the other.

To assign an item to a category, just right-click the item and choose Categories from its shortcut menu. In the resulting dialog box, check the categories to which you want to assign the item. You can add and delete Outlook categories using the Master Category list, which you can access by clicking the Master Category List button in the Categories dialog box.

Using Outlook Today

The Outlook Today "page" is a simple but effective summary view of your daily activities. It lists the appointments and tasks you've scheduled, displays an inventory of your mail folders, and lets you look up names in your Contacts folder quickly.

To open it, click on Shortcuts in the Navigation Pane (by default, it's one of the small icons at the bottom) to open the Shortcuts folder, then click Outlook Today (see Figure 21-13).

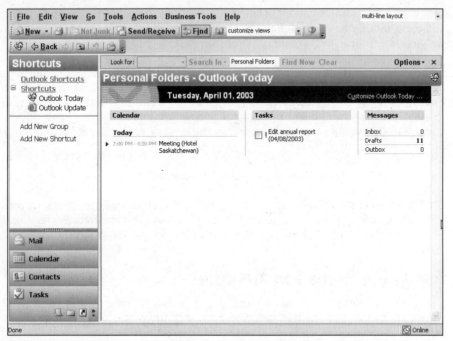

Figure 21-13: With Outlook Today, you can see at a glance the challenges that face you today.

Outlook Today is relatively self-explanatory, but keep in mind a few points:

✦ Outlook Today works like a Web browser, so you have to click items listed on it only once to view them (but don't worry, if you double-click by accident, the items will still open). Clicking a calendar or task item displays the item's details in a separate window. Clicking a heading such as Calendar or Tasks displays the corresponding folder.

✦ You can control Outlook Today's behavior by clicking Customize Outlook Today. The resulting page has a box you can check to ensure that Outlook Today is the first thing you see whenever you start the program, if that's what you want. Other options govern what you see in each of the three main headings (Messages, Calendar, and Tasks) and Outlook Today's style—that is, its overall look.

Configuring and Using Multiple Mail Accounts

Many people keep multiple e-mail accounts, perhaps one at work or school, another at a local ISP, and others at various Internet domains or with free e-mail providers. With Outlook, you can set up, manage, and access all of them. You can use them individually or all at once.

Adding e-mail accounts

To add a new e-mail account to Outlook, follow these steps:

1. Make sure you have the following information available for any account you want to enter:

   - Your e-mail address — that is, yourname@yourprovider.net

   - Your logon ID. This will typically be the "yourname" part of yourname@yourprovider.net

   - Your password

   - Name and type of the incoming mail server.

   - Name and type of the outgoing mail server.

2. Select Tools ➪ E-mail Accounts from the menu to open the E-mail Accounts Wizard.

3. Choose the Add a new e-mail account radio button, then click Next.

4. Choose which type of server your new account will be working with: Microsoft Exchange (common in corporate environments), POP3 or IMAP (both commonly used by Internet Service Providers), HTTP (for Web-based e-mail services such as Hotmail), or Additional Server Types.

Note   If you're setting up additional e-mail accounts in Outlook at work, you should probably check with your system administrator to make sure he or she doesn't mind the extra traffic it will generate on the company's servers.

5. Enter your user information, logon information, and server information. Outlook asks for your name, your e-mail address, your user name, your password, and the name of your server(s) (see Figure 21-14). If you have to log on using Secure Password Authentication, check that box (your e-mail service provider will tell you if you need that checked or not).

Note   If you wish, you can check the Remember password checkbox so you don't have to enter it every time you want to check your e-mail. While this is a convenience, it also makes it possible for anyone who has access to your computer to check your e-mail too, so consider carefully the environment in which you're working.

6. Click More Settings to give this mail account a name and provide other user information (an organization name and a reply e-mail address), and choose the connection you want to use to access this account. You also have the option here to leave a copy of your messages on the server; choosing this provides you with a backup of your messages, but it also may fill up your mailbox, resulting in additional messages to you bouncing.

7. Click Next, then click Finish in the final congratulatory screen, and you're done!

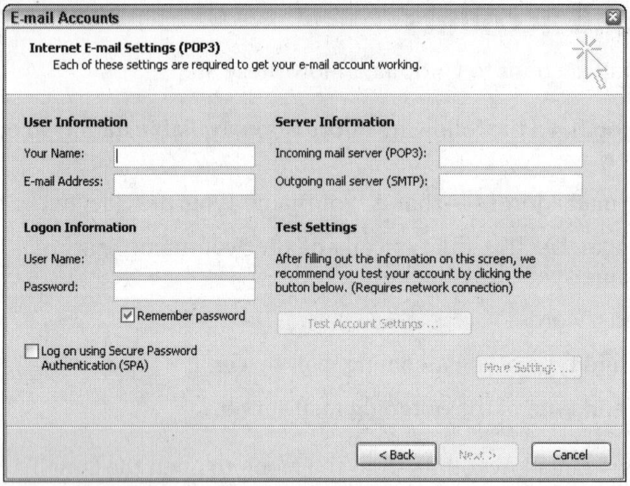

Figure 21-14: Outlook asks for all the necessary information to contact your e-mail provider.

Modifying e-mail accounts

Once Outlook has been configured to work with an e-mail account, you can modify it at any time by choosing Tools ➪ E-mail Accounts and this time clicking the View or change existing e-mail accounts radio button. When you click Next this time, the dialog box shown in Figure 21-15 opens. Click on the account you want to change and click Change, to reopen it for editing.

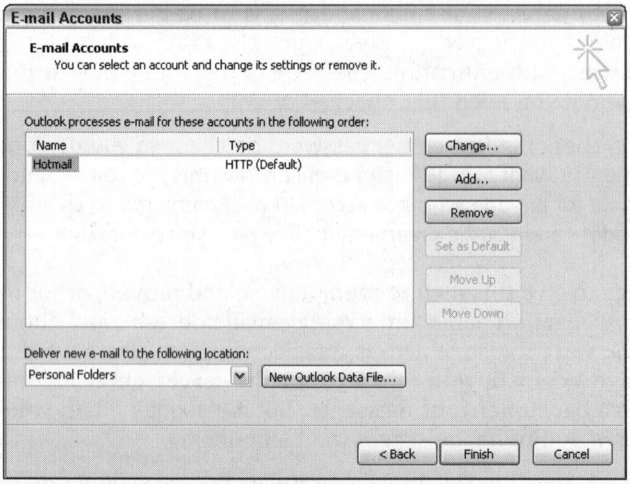

Figure 21-15: Choose the e-mail account you wish to modify from this list.

You can also use this window to specify the folders to which you want to send new e-mail — Personal Folders or Archive Folders, or an Exchange Mailbox if you have an Exchange service.

Tip   Be sure to click the New Outlook Data File button. By default, Outlook saves data in the same format used by Outlook 97 through Outlook 2002 (the version in Office XP). However, you can choose to save data in a brand-new format that provides an improved size limit and better supports multilingual Unicode data, but isn't compatible with the last four versions of Outlook. If you won't be sharing your personal file folders with anyone, this is your better bet.

Reading Messages

Obviously, to read your messages, you first must receive them. Click the Send/Receive button on the toolbar. This will automatically contact every account and pick up any mail from it after it sends all queued messages (there is no option in Outlook to just receive messages without sending). If you want to retrieve the messages from just one account of several, click Tools ➪ Send/Receive in the menu, and then select the account you want from the submenu.

Received messages show up in your Inbox (see Figure 21-16). By default, you will see a list of messages, grouped by the day they arrived. If you'd prefer to be able to preview the messages at a glance, you can choose View ➪ AutoPreview, which displays the message in the Inbox list (I've turned this feature on in Figure 21-16), and/or activate the Reading pane (which I've also done) by choosing View ➪ Reading Pane and either Right or Bottom, depending on where you'd like to see it.

The Reading pane, as you can see, offers you a handsome little view of the message.

You can also double-click on any message to open it.

Addressing and Sending Messages

The simplest way to prepare a message is to reply to one you've received. If you're viewing a message and click the Reply button, an e-mail message will appear, ready to go, and pre-addressed to the person who sent you the original message.

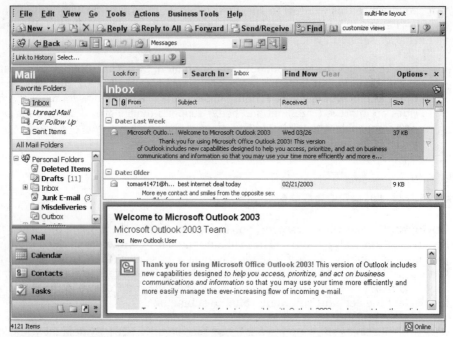

Figure 21-16: This is my Inbox with AutoPreview and the Reading Pane turned on.

Creating a new message from scratch

To create a new message from scratch, address it, and send it, follow these steps:

1. If you're in Mail view, click New; alternatively, click the downward-pointing arrow next to the New button in the Standard toolbar and choose Mail Message from the menu; or use the keyboard combination Ctrl+N.

2. Outlook opens a blank message window (see Figure 21-17); enter the e-mail address of the recipient in the To field.

3. If you desire to send a copy of the message to another person besides the recipient, enter his or her address in the Cc field ("cc" is short for carbon copy, a throwback term to the days of typewriters).

4. If you have contacts in your Contacts folder, you can enter the e-mail addresses from it, instead of typing them in. To do so, click either the To button or the Cc button.

Cross-Reference   For more information on entering contacts in the Contacts folder, see Chapter 24.

5. In the Select Names dialog box (see Figure 21-18), select the name(s) of the recipient(s) to whom you want to send the message; then click the To button.

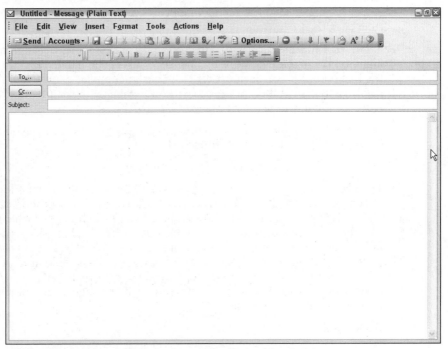

Figure 21-17: Type and format your message in this window.

Figure 21-18: Rather than type addresses and possibly make a typo, you can select message recipients from your Contacts folder.

6. Select the name(s) of the recipient(s) you want to Cc on the message, and then click the Cc button.

7. If you want to send a copy to a person or several persons but not have their names show in the header of the message, select the names, and then click the Bcc button ("bcc" is short for blind carbon copy; it allows you to send a message to many different people without revealing to recipients who else received the message).

8. Click the OK button to return to the blank message. The names you have entered are shown in the appropriate fields.

9. Enter a topic for the message in the Subject box.

10. Type your message in the main window. You can choose a format for it by choosing Format ➪ Plain Text, Format ➪ HTML, or Format ➪ Rich Text. If you choose HTML, your message is essentially a mini–Web page — which means you can use basic formatting, including different fonts, font sizes, colors, bold, italic, and underlining options, left, center and right alignment, indents, bulleted lists, and more. Many of those options are available in Rich Text, as well. Plain Text is the safest bet, though, since your recipient may not have his or her e-mail program configured to read HTML messages, and much of your formatting will thus be lost.

11. Click Send.

You're not locked into using Outlook to create a new e-mail message. Choose Actions ➪ New Mail Message Using to open a submenu of other items, including the following:

✦ **More Stationery.** Outlook provides numerous background images you can use to dress up your e-mail if you're using HTML format; choose the one you want from the list provided (a preview window shows you what it will look like).

✦ **Microsoft Word (Plain Text).** This option enables you to compose a Plain Text e-mail message directly in Word instead of in Outlook.

Tip

You can use Microsoft Word as your default e-mail editor if you like; it offers many more formatting options than Outlook for HTML and RTF messages. To activate it, choose Tools ➪ Options, select the Mail Format tab, and check the Use Microsoft Word to edit e-mail messages checkbox. It's possible, depending on any previous settings Outlook may have found when the new version was installed, that Word is already set as your default e-mail editor, in which case you can make Outlook the default editor by unchecking this box.

✦ **Microsoft Office.** You can compose an e-mail message that's an Access Data Page, an Excel Worksheet or a Word Document directly from Outlook by choosing one of those options from this submenu.

✦ **Plain Text.** You can't do much formatting with plain text, but the recipient can be certain that unsavory code isn't lurking within the pretty graphics, either. For straightforward communication of words, plain text can't be beat. Unless you've removed it as your default e-mail editor, Word will open just the same, but the formatting options will be limited.

✦ **Rich Text Format.** This form of text allows more formatting than plain text, but not as much as HTML. Its formatting instructions can be understood by many different programs running on many different platforms.

✦ **HTML (no stationery).** Just what it says; this is the default format for Outlook messages.

Spellchecking messages

To spellcheck a message, choose Tools ➪ Spelling or press F7.

Saving Messages

Messages are automatically saved by Outlook within its own system of items — the Outlook equivalent of files. That's why, for instance, when you start Outlook, your Inbox contains the same messages that it contained when you last used it. It's not only incoming messages that are affected — messages you send are saved, too, in the Sent Items folder by default. In addition to incoming and outgoing messages, ones you are working on but haven't sent are automatically saved in Outlook's Drafts folder. This is a nice feature, especially if you're carefully wording an important message over a period of time, because the worst that can happen to you is you'll lose your last few minutes of work. Beyond this, older items in folders can be automatically moved into archive folders (which are separate from the default storage folders) after a specified period of time.

Cross-Reference
For more on archive folders, see Chapter 22.

Tip
You can deliberately save a message that you're working on to the Drafts folder at any time without waiting for the automatic save to take place. Just select File ➪ Save from the menu, press Ctrl+S, or click the Save icon on the toolbar.

To save a message in a non-Outlook folder, select File ➪ Save As from the menu. Navigate to the folder in which you want to save the file and choose from the Save as type drop-down list what format you want to save the message in: HTML, Text Only, Outlook Template (so you can create future messages based on that message), or Outlook Message Format (which means you'll have to open it in Outlook to read it). The filename defaults to the message subject.

Printing Messages

To print a message to the default printer, simply select the message and click the Print button. To print multiple files, select them and click the Print button. You select a range of contiguous messages by clicking on the first message in the range, holding down the Shift key, and then clicking on the last message in the range. To select noncontiguous messages, hold down the Ctrl key while clicking on each one. When multiple messages are printed in this manner, several messages are printed on each page.

You can gain more control over the printing process by selecting File ⇨ Print from the menu instead of using the Print button on the toolbar. You can also use the Ctrl+P keyboard shortcut instead.

Selecting File ⇨ Print or pressing Ctrl+P brings up the Print dialog box (see Figure 21-19). In addition to the usual options such as choosing a printer or setting the number of copies, this dialog box has special features dedicated to Outlook. Here's how they work:

✦ The Print Style panel has two built-in styles. The default is Memo Style, which is used for printing messages as text.

   The Print Options panel offers you two options for this style. Selecting the top checkbox in this panel, Start each item on a new page, will cause each message to be printed on a new page. The second one, Print attached files, should be used only with attached files that are printable — text or other files Office recognizes, such as Word documents. It's inadvisable to select this option if the attached file is a program, for instance.

✦ The other print style, Table Style, is used to print not a specific message but a list of messages in the current folder. When you select this style, the Print Options panel changes to a Print Range panel. It also has two options. Unlike the previous panel, these options are mutually exclusive, so they use radio buttons instead of checkboxes. The first one, All rows, will cause a list of all the messages in the currently open folder to print. The second one, Only selected rows, means that only those items you have selected will print.

Using Page Setup

For more control over how either Memo Style or Table Style will print, take a moment before choosing File ⇨ Print to choose File ⇨ Page Setup. This gives you the option to set up either style or to define print styles for future printing jobs, which enables you to create custom print styles.

Both dialog boxes look essentially the same (see Figure 21-20).

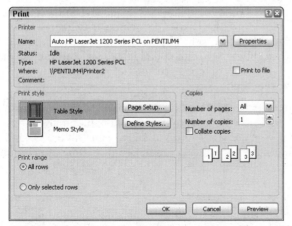

Figure 21-19: The Print dialog box provides the tools you need to transfer Outlook items to paper.

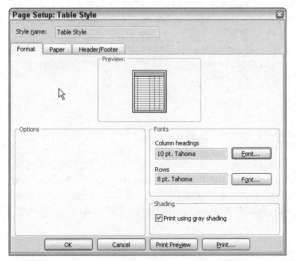

Figure 21-20: Use the Page Setup dialog box to specify how your messages should look when printed.

Modifying existing styles

The Page Setup dialog box has three tabs:

✦ The Format tab shows you a preview of the style you're working on and lets you set fonts and font sizes for the most important elements of the style: Title and Fields for Memo Style; Columns and Rows for Table Style. You can also choose to add gray shading to the style, or to remove it.

✦ The Paper tab lets you choose the type of paper (e.g., legal, letter, A4) you want to print on and, if necessary, the particular printer tray from which the paper should be drawn. You can also set margins here and either portrait or landscape orientation. In addition, you can specify the size you want to print at, anything from the full page to ⅛ of a page to special sizes designed to fit into specific types of pocket calendars.

✦ The Header/Footer tab lets you add (what else?) a header and/or footer. You can enter the text for the left, center, and right side of each and choose the font size, style, and color. You can also automatically insert all or any of the following: page number, number of pages, date of printing, time of printing, and user name.

A handy Print Preview button lets you see exactly how your items will look on paper, and a Print button calls up the Print dialog box.

Creating a new style

You may want to leave Outlook's default styles alone and create your own. To do so, choose File ➪ Page Setup ➪ Define Print Styles in the Define Print Styles dialog box, you can choose either Table Style or Memo Style, then choose Copy. This will open the Page Setup dialog box, but now you're working on a copy of the original style. Design the style as you'd like, give it a new name, and click OK. Your new style will now be available for use with future print jobs; it will even show up in the list of Print styles in the Print dialog box.

Deleting Messages

At first glance, deleting a message seems a simple enough task. Just select it (or them), and then press the Del key. Outlook, however, has a built-in system to protect you from accidentally deleting important messages: When you delete a message, it's transferred into the Deleted Items folder, analogous to the Recycle Bin on the Windows desktop.

Recovering deleted messages

To recover a message from the Deleted Items folder, click either the Folder List button on the Navigation Pane or the Mail button; either will reveal the Deleted Items folder. Click on the Deleted Items folder to show its contents, select any message you want to recover, and simply drag it to the Inbox (or any other folder in which you want to store it).

Cross-Reference   For more information on how the Deleted Items folder works, see the section "Archiving Messages" in Chapter 22.

Permanently deleting messages

To permanently delete individual messages from the Deleted Items folder, just select them and press the Del key. You'll be prompted to confirm that you really want to permanently remove them. Click Yes to confirm.

To permanently delete all the messages in the Deleted Items folder, right-click on it and choose Empty "Deleted Items" Folder from the shortcut menu, or choose Tools ⇨ Empty Deleted Items Folder.

Automatically deleting when exiting Outlook

To clear out the Deleted Items folder every time you exit Outlook:

1. Select Tools ⇨ Options from the menu.
2. In the Options dialog box, click the Other tab.
3. Check the checkbox labeled Empty the Deleted Items folder upon exiting.
4. Click the OK button.

Summary

In this chapter, you learned how to navigate from view to view in Outlook and how to customize those views, and the Navigation Pane, to better suit your purposes. You learned how to use Outlook for managing multiple e-mail accounts, and how to read, create, address, and send messages, as well as how to save, print, and delete them. Highlights from this chapter include the following:

✦ Outlook provides you with numerous folders for organizing your information, and enables you to create all the special folders you want.

✦ Outlook's views are numerous, flexible, and completely customizable.

✦ Outlook Today is a handy one-page look at what tasks await you on the current day.

✦ Outlook can manage one or more e-mail accounts and provides a handy wizard for setting them up and editing their properties afterward.

✦ The Send/Receive button transmits and picks up messages in a single operation.

✦ You can enter recipient information using Outlook's Contacts folder.

✦ Messages can be printed individually or en masse, and you can print a list of messages.

✦ Deleted messages are moved to the Deleted Items folder.

✦   ✦   ✦

Advanced Message Management

Outlook's message-management tools go far beyond merely sending and receiving messages, as described in Chapter 21. You can sort and group messages, have Outlook filter them as they arrive, and more. You can send attachments, add a digital signature, and send a business card. You can archive old messages, import messages saved in other locations or on other computers, or export messages to another program. We'll look at all these functions and more in this chapter on advanced message management.

Organizing Messages with Search Folders

Outlook 2003 features a brand-new, very powerful feature for finding and organizing messages: Search Folders.

Essentially, a Search Folder is a folder in which you save not only the results of a search but also the parameters for that search. As more messages arrive that meet those parameters, they're added to the Search Folder automatically; you don't need to conduct your search again.

Search Folders are displayed with your other Personal Folders when you click either Folder List or Mail on the Navigation Pane. By default, Outlook includes three Search Folders: For Follow Up, which shows items flagged for follow-up; Large Messages (by default, messages more than 100 KB in size are considered Large); and Unread Mail. Figure 22-1 shows the three default Search Folders.

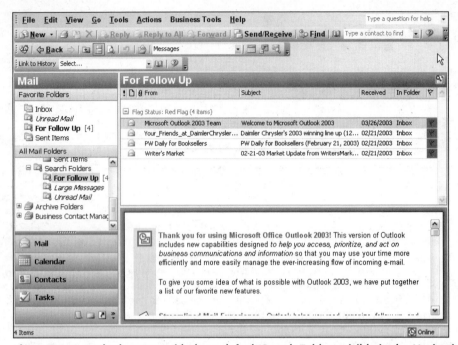

Figure 22-1: Outlook comes with three default Search Folders, visible in the Navigation Pane. This figure shows four flagged messages in the For Follow Up folder.

Note   Search Folders differ from ordinary folders in that the messages they contain are still located in their original folders; the Search Folders simply point you to them (they're shortcuts, in other words).

Creating a new Search Folder

To create a new Search Folder, either choose New ➪ Search Folder (remember that you have to click the downward-pointing arrow to the right of the New button to open the New menu; otherwise, Outlook simply creates a new item appropriate to whichever view you're in), choose File ➪ New ➪ Search Folder, or right-click on an existing Search Folder and choose New Search Folder from the shortcut menu.

You'll see the New Search Folder dialog box, shown in Figure 22-2, with a number of preset Search Folders available for your use, divided into four groups: Reading Mail, Mail from People and Lists, Organizing Mail, and Custom.

Figure 22-2: Outlook provides you with several preset Search Folders, ready to be activated, in addition to the three that are activated by default.

Some of these Search Folders can be used only as is — that is, they can't be changed; if you choose them, you're merely activating a Search Folder that Outlook has already set up for you. Other Search Folders include options for you to set in the Customize search folder area of the dialog box.

For example, if you select the Mail from specific people Search Folder, as shown in Figure 22-2, you have the option to either type in the names or select from your contact list or Outlook address books the names of the people whose messages you want to appear in the Search Folder. The Old mail Search Folder lets you define old mail as anything older than one day, up to 99 months.

You can also choose where you want to search for mail: Personal Folders, Archive Folders, or other folders you may have set up.

If you want to create a unique Search Folder of your own, one that differs from anything Outlook provides, choose Create a custom Search Folder from the Custom group of the Select a search folder list.

Then, click the Choose button to open the Custom Search Folder dialog box. Type a name for your Search Folder, and then click Criteria. This opens the Search Folder Criteria dialog box, shown in Figure 22-3. (This is essentially the same dialog box you'll see when you conduct an Advanced Find, discussed in the section "Finding the message you want," later in this chapter.)

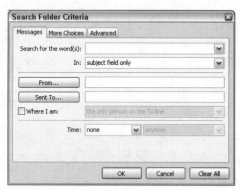

Figure 22-3: Set the criteria for a custom Search Folder here.

You can specify numerous criteria under the three tabs in this dialog box. You can enter keywords to search for, and specify whether to look for those words only in the subject field, in both the subject field and message body, or in frequently used text fields. You can specify addresses whence messages were sent or addresses to which they were sent; the time the message was sent; and the categories to which the message belongs. You can also specify that you are interested only in messages that are read or unread, that have attachments or that don't have attachments, whose importance is high, normal, or low, or that fall within a specific size range, or, in fact, that match specific conditions for any field that Outlook includes.

When you've set the criteria you need, click OK. This returns you to the Custom Search Folder dialog box, where you have to click the Browse button to specify the folders in which the Search Folder should look for matching messages.

Finally, click OK again, and your new Search Folder will appear with the others in the Folders list.

Customizing a Search Folder

To customize an existing Search Folder, right-click on it and choose Customize this Search Folder from the shortcut menu. This works the same way as creating a Custom folder; you'll see a dialog box into which you can type a new name for the Search Folder, if you wish; you can also specify which mail folders you want searched. Then click the Criteria button to open the Search Folder Criteria dialog box (Figure 22-3). You can change any of the existing criteria in the Search Folder as described in the preceding section.

Caution If you customize an existing Search Folder without changing its name, you'll lose the criteria Outlook has already put into it. If you'd prefer not to risk messing up your default Search Folders, use the New Search Folder command instead.

Quick-flagging Messages

Another new feature in Outlook 2003 for organizing your messages is called *quick-flagging*. Quick-flagging enables you to mark messages with different-colored flags — rather like sticking different-colored pins into a list of messages on a bulletin board — which you can then use to identify messages that need following up in some fashion.

To flag a message with the default-colored flag, simply click the light-colored box with the dim outline of a flag in it at the right end of the message in the message list (see Figure 22-4). By default, flagging a message marks it for follow-up — which means it automatically shows up in the For Follow Up Search Folder, shown back in Figure 22-1.

Figure 22-4: Four messages in my inbox are flagged; note that the For Follow Up Search Folder therefore now has four messages in it.

To change the color of a flag, right-click on the flag and choose the color you want from the shortcut menu. This same menu has a Set Default Flag command that enables you to choose the color you want to use by default; there's also a Clear Flag command for unflagging a message and an Add Reminder command that enables you to specify what kind of follow-up is needed: Call, Do not Forward, Follow up (the default), For Your Information, Forward, No Response Necessary, Read, Reply, Reply to All, and Review. In Figure 22-4, I've used the Add Reminder command to tell myself to follow up by midnight on Friday, March 26, 2004; you can see the reminder in the gray part of the AutoPreview display in the bottom pane, known as the Information Bar.

Creating Mail-Filtering Rules

The Rules Wizard can be your most useful tool in Outlook. With it, you can set up a series of rules that will automatically process your e-mail. The rules are applied in a particular sequence, and you can change that sequence at will.

You can create rules to handle incoming e-mail or outgoing e-mail. For instance, you can have all messages from a particular person or address sent to a particular folder, which is very useful if you subscribe to multiple mailing lists. To utilize Outlook's mail-filtering rules, follow these steps:

1. Choose Tools ➪ Rules and Alerts.

Note   If you're using an HTTP mail account (that is, a Web-based e-mail account like Hotmail), you'll receive a message when you choose this command telling you that e-mail rules can't be used to filter that account's messages.

2. You'll see the Rules and Alerts dialog box, which is empty the first time you open it. Click the New Rule button to start the Rules Wizard.

3. The first step in creating a rule is to choose between creating a rule from a template (see Figure 22-5) or creating a blank rule. The Rules Wizard includes several templates for rules. You can choose the template that comes closest to what you want to do (e.g., Move messages with specific words in the subject to a folder, or Move messages from someone to a folder), and then edit it. However, because the templates are created with the same steps that are offered to you if you choose the Start from a blank rule radio button at the top of the dialog box, that's what we'll do in these step-by-step instructions.

4. When you select Start from a blank rule, the first step is to select when messages should be checked; the options are Check messages when they arrive or Check messages after sending.

5. Begin designing the criteria upon which Outlook will take the action you select (see Figure 22-6) — for example, messages from particular people or a specific distribution list, flagged messages, messages with specific words in the body of the message, etc. When you select one of these conditions, it is

added to the description of the rule in the lower part of the dialog box. Note that people or distribution list is underlined, like a hyperlink; clicking this option opens an address list, enabling you to specify the people whose messages you want to catch with your filter.

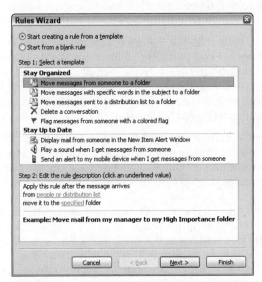

Figure 22-5: Outlook's Rules Wizard provides templates for several commonly used rules.

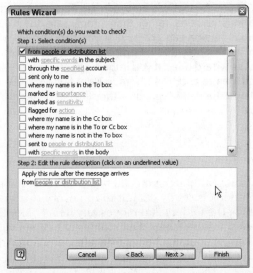

Figure 22-6: Outlook offers numerous criteria for filtering messages.

6. Once you have specified the messages upon which Outlook should act, specify the action it should take. Again, there are many basic options: move it to a specified folder, assign it to a category, forward it to a particular person, and so on. You edit the details of these general actions to make them more specific, browsing for the folder to which you want the message moved (you can also create a brand-new folder, if you prefer), adding the e-mail address of the person to whom you want it forwarded, and so on.

7. Specify any exceptions to your rule. For instance, suppose you belong to the Raising Unusual Pets listserver and you want to filter out the thousands of messages you receive that don't pertain to your own pet interest of raising salamanders. You can create a rule that sends all messages from that listserver to the Deleted Items folder unless (here's where you'd put in the exception) the body of the text contains the word "salamanders."

8. Finally, you name the rule, and then choose whether to turn on the rule and/or run it now on all the messages already in your inbox. If you have more than one active non-HTTP e-mail account, you can also choose to apply the rule to all accounts; otherwise, it applies only to the current account.

Once the rule is turned on, you don't have to worry about it again unless you want to fine-tune it, in which case you can simply choose Tools ➪ Rules and Alerts again. You'll find your new rule in the initial Rules and Alerts dialog box, complete with description. You can click Change Rule to alter it, Copy to create a copy of it in any folder you wish, Delete to get rid of it, Run Rules Now to run the rule on messages already received, or Options to either export your rule to a previous version of Outlook or import rules from a previous version.

Tip   Rules created in Outlook 2003 are not compatible as is with rules created in previous versions of Outlook, so use the Options button in the Rules and Alerts dialog box to export rules to previous versions, rather than simply save the rules into a file folder where the previous version can access it. If you export rules, you have the option to save them as Outlook 2000 Compatible Rules Wizard rules or Outlook 98 Compatible Rules Wizard rules. If you import rules from a previous version of Outlook, it's a good idea to click the Upgrade Now button in the Options dialog box to upgrade them to the newer version — they'll work better.

Archiving Messages

Archiving takes place automatically, although you can take control of the process. The AutoArchive function in Outlook is set by default to run every two weeks. At that time, it scans the contents of the folders and moves any items older than a set amount of time into Outlook's archive folder. Each folder can be set with a different archiving age, and you can, of course, change how often the AutoArchive function runs. You can also have AutoArchive automatically delete items — either permanently, or by moving them to the Deleted Items folder (so you can review them before they are permanently deleted).

Setting the frequency

To set the frequency of archiving:

1. Choose Tools ➪ Options.

2. Click the Other tab in the Options dialog box.

3. Click the AutoArchive button.

4. In the AutoArchive dialog box, set the number of days between archiving. You can either type the number or use the scrolling arrows.

5. Click the OK button to return to the Options dialog box.

6. In the Options dialog box, click the OK button to complete the process.

Setting the AutoArchive delay

To set a folder's AutoArchive delay:

1. Click the Folder List button on the Navigation Pane.

2. Right-click the name of a folder in the list.

3. Select Properties from the shortcut menu.

4. In the folder's Properties dialog box, click the AutoArchive tab (see Figure 22-7).

Figure 22-7: You can specify the AutoArchive settings for individual folders in the folder's Properties dialog box.

5. Set the maximum age of messages in months, weeks, or days. Messages older than this age will be AutoArchived. If you don't want the folder to be archived at all, clear the radio button.

Note   AutoArchive operates off the date an item was last modified, not when it was received. If you move an item from one folder to another or change the flag or the read status, then the item has been modified; the date of that change will be used to determine if the item should be AutoArchived or not.

6. If you want to set a folder other than the default archive folder as the destination for archived items, click the Browse button and pick one (or create a new one).

7. Alternatively, you can select the lower radio button to prevent archiving and have old items deleted instead.

8. Click the OK button to complete the action.

Exporting and Importing Messages

When I travel, I take my laptop computer with me and check my e-mail messages as usual while I'm away. Because I don't want my mailbox to exceed its quota, I download the messages from the server when I retrieve them — which means they exist only on my laptop and can't be downloaded again onto my desktop system when I get home.

Note   Outlook downloads messages from your server by default. If you want to leave a copy of messages on the server, you can set that option. Choose Tools ⇨ E-mail Accounts. Check the View or change existing e-mail accounts radio button and click Next. In the E-mail Accounts dialog box, select the e-mail account you want to edit, then click Change; in the resulting dialog box, click the More Settings button; in the Internet E-mail Settings dialog box, click the Advanced tab. Check the Leave a copy of messages on the server checkbox in the Delivery area of the dialog box. You can also choose to remove messages from the server after the number of days you specify, and/or to remove messages from the server when you delete them from the Deleted Items folder.

That leaves me with the problem of transferring the messages I've downloaded into my laptop onto my desktop system, as that's where I want them for easy referral once I'm done traveling. That's where Outlook's Import and Export command comes in. I export the messages I've downloaded into a file that I can then import into my desktop system.

Exporting messages

To export messages to a file:

1. Choose File ➪ Import and Export, and, if you have the Business Contact Manager installed, Outlook. This opens the Import and Export Wizard dialog box shown in Figure 22-8.

Figure 22-8: The first step to exporting messages is to open this dialog box.

2. Choose Export to a file from the list of options, and click Next.

3. From the Create a file of type list, choose Personal Folder File (.pst). This is the format in which Outlook saves the information in your Personal Folders. (Although the folders in Outlook look like they're the same kind of folders you see when you browse Windows, they're not; they can't be opened outside Outlook.)

4. In the next screen, choose the folder to export from. If you choose Inbox and check the Include subfolders box, you'll export all the mail saved in the usual places. (Click Filter if you'd like to limit what you export by keyword, date, or other criteria.)

5. Finally, select the location to which you'd like to save the .pst file you're about to create. By default, it's named backup.pst, but you can change that, too. If you're exporting it over the top of a previous .pst file of the same name, it appends itself to it rather than erasing it; you can specify either Replace duplicates with items exported, Allow duplicate items to be created, or Do not export duplicate items.

6. Click Finish. This opens a new dialog box, which enables you to assign a password to the .pst file (so not just anyone can open it) and to encrypt it, if you so choose.

7. Click OK, and you've successfully exported your messages to a file.

Importing messages

To import messages from a .pst file into Outlook:

1. Choose File ⇨ Import and Export ⇨ Standard (if you have Business Contact Manager installed; otherwise, it's just File ⇨ Import and Export).

2. Choose Import from another program or file, and click Next.

3. Choose Personal Folder File (.pst) from the Select file type to import from list. Click Next.

4. Browse to the location of the .pst file you want to import (you have the same options about duplicates to choose from), and click Next.

5. Select the folder within the .pst file you want to import from, and choose whether to import items from it into the current folder or into another of your existing folders (which, again, you can browse through).

6. Click Finish. Outlook imports the messages.

Sending Business Cards

Digital business cards, or vCards, are the electronic equivalent of the cardboard that clutters up Rolodexes all over the world. They've become the industry standard for the electronic exchange of contact information; many other programs besides Office (such as Palm Desktop) are able to open and display them. These files are imported into address books such as Outlook's Contacts Folder. You can send the information entered into any of your Outlook Contacts as a vCard. Open the Contacts folder, highlight the contact, and choose Actions ⇨ Forward as vCard. This will create a new e-mail message with the vCard (.vcf file) attached to it, as shown in Figure 22-9. (The Subject is automatically entered as the name of the contact.)

All you need to do is address the message and click the Send button.

Tip   You can also save a contact as a vCard. This is useful in case you want to include it with a signature on your e-mail (see the following section). To do so, double-click on a contact to open it and select Export to vCard file from the File menu. Outlook will let you select a folder and a name for the file. The default folder is Signatures, and the default filename is the name of the contact. Click the Save button to finish.

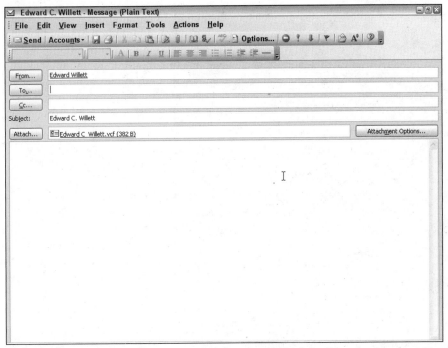

Figure 22-9: Sending a vCard is the digital equivalent of slipping a business card into an envelope.

Using Signatures and Receipts

A signature, or sig, is not necessarily just your name; it's simply a bit of text that's added automatically at the end of e-mail messages you send. Of course, there's nothing to prevent you from using your name alone as the sig on your messages, but most people also add quotations, statements of company policy, Web addresses, and so on.

Creating a signature

To create a signature for your messages, follow these steps:

1. Select Tools ➪ Options from the menu.

2. In the Options dialog box, click the Mail Format tab (see Figure 22-10). If you already had some signatures created, you could select which one you wanted to use as your default signature from the drop-down list at the bottom of the tab.

3. Click the Signatures button.

4. The Create Signature dialog box is blank at first, as no sigs have been added yet. Click the New button.

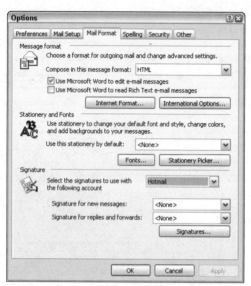

Figure 22-10: The Mail Format tab of the Options dialog box (Tools ➪ Options) lets you attach a signature to your e-mails.

5. In the Create New Signature dialog box, type a name for your new sig. By default, the second option is to start with a blank signature. If you had other sigs to choose from, you could also click the second radio button, which is Use this existing signature as a template. You would then pick one from the drop-down list. The third radio button, Use this file as a template, allows you to browse your computer for any text file you'd like to base your sig on — perhaps a special quotation you've already stored somewhere.

6. Click the Next button.

7. Type your signature text into the text area at the top of the Edit Signature dialog box (see Figure 22-11). The Font and Paragraph buttons enable you to choose fonts and alignment (assuming you're using HTML or RTF — formatting options aren't available for plain text; and, of course, any fancy formatting you add will be wasted unless your recipients are also capable of viewing e-mail formatted in HTML or RTF). The Clear button erases the text area, and the Advanced Edit button invokes the appropriate editor application for the type of message the sig will be used with (e.g., Rich Text, Word; HTML, FrontPage; plain text, Notepad).

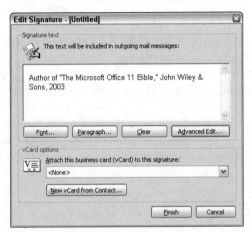

Figure 22-11: Write and format your signature file here.

8. If you want to attach an existing vCard file as part of the sig (see the preceding section), select it from the drop-down list; you can also click the New vCard from Contact button to create a new vCard based on any item in your Contacts folder (again, see the preceding section).

9. Click the Finish button to complete signature creation.

10. Back in the Create Signature dialog box, the sig is now listed and the Edit and Remove buttons are active.

11. Click the OK button to return to the Options dialog box.

12. In the Options dialog box, click the OK button to finish the process.

When you send a message, if you have selected a default sig in the Mail Format tab, it will automatically be included (in fact, it will automatically appear in your e-mail editor whenever you start a new e-mail). Otherwise, or if you want to use another sig in addition to the default, you'll have to pick one. To do so, choose Insert ➪ Signature, and choose the signature you want from the list; choose More to open the Create Signature dialog box again.

Setting up message receipts

Making sure your e-mail has arrived is much like sending snail mail with a Return Receipt Requested form. To set things up so that you get confirmation, follow these steps:

1. Select Tools ➪ Options from the menu.

2. If it is not already selected, click the Preferences tab.

3. Click the E-mail Options button.

4. In the E-mail Options dialog box, click the Tracking Options button.

5. In the Tracking Options dialog box, click the two checkboxes labeled Read receipt and Delivery receipt (a delivery receipt tells you the message has made it to its destination computer; a read receipt tells you the recipient has actually looked at it).

6. If you don't want other people to receive such receipts from you, click the radio button labeled Never send a response. (Your other options are Always send a response and Ask me before sending a response, which is probably the best option.)

7. Click the OK button to return to the E-mail Options dialog box.

8. In the E-mail Options dialog box, click the OK button to return to the Options dialog box.

9. In the Options dialog box, click the OK button to complete the operation.

Note   Bear in mind that not all e-mail programs support sending receipts, and that someone else may use the Never send a response option.

The instructions above will ask for receipts for all the messages you send. You can also set receipt options for an individual message by clicking the Options button on the Standard toolbar of the Outlook e-mail editor and then checking Request a delivery receipt for this message and/or Request a read receipt for this message in the Voting and Tracking options area.

Attaching Files to Messages

Attaching files to messages is a great way to send word processing documents, pictures, music and video clips, and even programs to other people. In fact, you can attach just about any file on your computer to an e-mail message and send it to someone else — although they'll have to have the right program to open it, of course.

Note   Keep in mind that to protect themselves against viruses, many organizations prevent executable programs from being delivered to their computers — the e-mail might get through, but the attachment won't. Check with your recipient before trying to send such an attachment. Also keep in mind that sending a large file unexpectedly is considered rude; again, clear it with your recipient first.

Attaching a file is easy. With a message open, click the Insert File button (it looks like a paper clip) or choose Insert ➪ File. Alternatively, drag and drop the attachment file from a file-management window (My Computer, Windows Explorer, or a file-management view in Outlook) into the body of the message.

Tip   You can also send most Office documents as an e-mail message attachment from within the applications you use to create them. For example, from within Word, choose File ➪ Send To ➪ Mail Recipient (as Attachment).

To send an Outlook item of any type (such as an existing message or a contact or a task or a note) choose Insert ➪ Item. This lets you browse through your Outlook folders. The recipient just drags the item from the message onto the icon for the Outlook folder where it belongs. (Of course, an Outlook item will be useful only to a recipient who is also running Outlook.)

Originally designed to transmit only ordinary text, e-mail systems must take special measures to send files. Files attached to or inserted into an e-mail message must be encoded in ordinary text characters for the trip and then decoded and converted back into files on the recipient's computer. Outlook and other e-mail programs handle the encoding and decoding process automatically and transparently. Your only concern is ensuring that the mail programs at both the sending and receiving ends use the same encoding formats.

Two encoding formats are in widespread use: UUENCODE and MIME. (Another, BIN-HEX, is used for Macintosh files.) They enable you to send e-mail messages containing embedded objects and files inserted at specific points in the message, not just attached at the end.

MIME, Outlook's default, is generally preferable and is the only option Outlook offers if you're sending HTML-formatted messages. However, if your recipient's software understands only the UUENCODE format, you must set up Outlook accordingly.

To use UUENCODE format, open the Options dialog box (Tools ➪ Options), click on the Mail Format tab, and then click the Internet Format button. Check the box labeled Encode attachments in UUENCODE format when sending a plain text message. Outlook will still send attachments with HTML messages in MIME format, but it will send any attachments to plain-text messages in UUENCODE.

Even when both the sending and receiving programs are using the same encoding format, attached or inserted files still won't get through unless both sides use the same character sets for the encoding/decoding process. This is most likely to be a problem when you are communicating internationally. Clicking the International Options button next to the Internet Format button on the Message Format tab opens a dialog box that enables you to change the character sets for default and individual messages to one appropriate to the language you're using.

Finding the Message You Want

If you have several messages in a folder (as of this writing, I have 3,496 messages in my inbox, for example), finding the specific one you're interested in can be quite a chore. For example, you may have several on one subject, from one person, delivered on the same date, and so on. Outlook's Find feature makes it easy to find what you're looking for. (It's very similar to the Search Folders option described earlier, but it doesn't automatically route items matching the search criteria to a special folder.) To use it, follow these steps:

1. Click the Find button on the Standard toolbar to activate the Find bar; it appears across the top of the folder viewing pane.

2. Enter the text you want to search for in the Look for text box (see Figure 22-12).

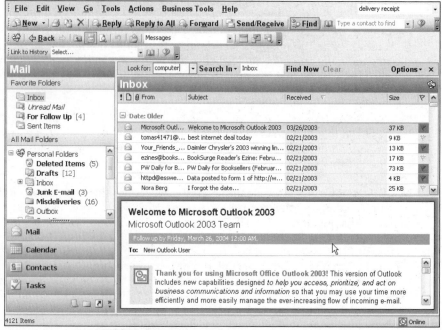

Figure 22-12: Outlook's Find tools are ready and waiting for you above your list of messages. In this example, I've entered the search term "computer."

3. Click Search In to choose where you want to search: the current folder, All Mail Folders, Mail I Received or Mail I Sent; or select Choose Folders and specify which folders you want to search.

4. If you want to search more than just the subject headings, click Options and make sure Search All Text in Each Message is selected. (This takes longer, as you'd expect.)

5. Click the Find Now button.

6. The Find feature will search through all your messages in the specified folder or folders and filter out any that don't meet the search criteria. When the search is complete, the word "Clear" will no longer be grayed out next to the Find Now button.

7. If you'd like to save that search as a Search Folder, you can now choose Save Search as Search Folder from the Options menu.

Note For more on Search Folders, see the section "Organizing Messages with Search Folders" earlier in this chapter).

8. Click Clear to reset the Find box to its initial state and unhide the messages the search hid.

For more detailed searches, choose Options ⇨ Advanced Find. This opens the Advanced Find dialog box shown in Figure 22-13, which is very similar to the Search Folder Criteria dialog box (again, see the section "Organizing Messages with Search Folders" earlier in this chapter).

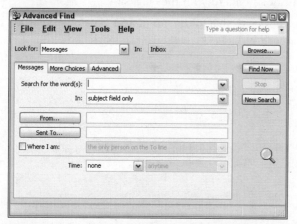

Figure 22-13: Advanced Find provides complete control over searches. If you can't find something using this dialog box, it probably doesn't exist.

Summary

There's more to e-mail management than just reading messages, and Outlook enables you to take full advantage of every possibility:

✦ Create Search Folders that remain permanently active, showing you whenever messages meeting your search criteria have arrived and making them readily accessible.

✦ Flag messages for follow-up in a variety of colors, and add reminders to those messages about what kind of follow-up is required.

✦ Set up automatic rules that route messages to folders, delete them, flag them, or perform other actions as required.

✦ Modify how Outlook archives old messages.

✦ Export messages to files for use by other computers, and import them from files, too.

✦ Create vCards — virtual business cards — and send them via e-mail.

✦ Automatically add a personal note called a signature to the end of each e-mail message you send.

✦ Set options so that you receive confirmation when your messages are received or read.

✦ Attach files or Outlook items to your messages.

✦ Locate particular messages in a folder, no matter how overcrowded that folder is.

✦   ✦   ✦

Outlook Security

Viruses. Trojans. Proliferating junk e-mail. Identity theft. Scams. It seems as though every day brings word of another threat to legitimate users of the Internet — and a lot of those threats seem centered on e-mail.

For that reason, Outlook 2003 contains more security features than ever before. This chapter examines what it can do to make your e-mail communication more secure and provides some basic tips that apply no matter what communications software you may use.

Dealing with Junk E-mail

A recent survey conducted by Symantec revealed that 37 percent of respondents receive more than 100 unsolicited junk e-mails (commonly known as *spam*) each week at home and at work, with 63 percent receiving more than 50.

A majority of respondents — 69 percent — either agreed or strongly agreed with the statement that "spam is harmful to e-mail users," and another 77 percent were concerned or very concerned about their children reading spam inappropriate for minors. In addition, more than half of the respondents also indicated that they spend more than 10 minutes each day reading spam — and that the volume of spam they're receiving is on the rise.

You can find numerous third-party solutions for dealing with spam, but right out of the box, Outlook 2003 offers its own junk e-mail filter, which evaluates whether an unread message should be treated as junk e-mail based on several factors, including the content (it looks for certain key words often found in junk e-mail).

Using Outlook's junk e-mail filter

Outlook's junk e-mail filter is on by default, but you can turn it off or adjust its settings. Choose Actions ➪ Junk E-mail ➪ Junk E-mail Options to open the dialog box shown in Figure 23-1.

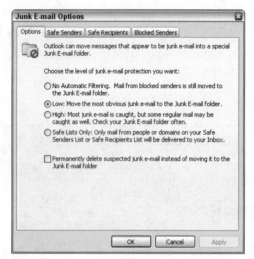

Figure 23-1: Adjust the level of automatic junk e-mail protection provided by Outlook with this dialog box.

By default, the junk e-mail filter is set to Low, which catches the most obvious junk e-mail and sends it to the Junk E-Mail folder (one of your created-by-default mail folders).

The other three choices are:

✦ **No Automatic Filtering.** This turns off the junk e-mail filter.

✦ **High.** This will catch most junk e-mail, but it may also misidentify some legitimate e-mail as junk e-mail. If you choose this option, double-check the mail moved to your Junk E-mail folder often to make sure non–junk e-mail hasn't been sent there by mistake.

✦ **Safe Lists Only.** If you choose this option, the only e-mail you'll receive will be that which comes from people or domains in one of your trusted lists (more on that in the next section, "Using the Junk E-mail Filter Lists").

At the bottom of the dialog box is a checkbox that allows you to permanently delete junk e-mail instead of just moving it to the Junk E-Mail folder. As far as I'm concerned, checking this could never be a good idea; it's too easy for non–junk e-mail to be misidentified as junk e-mail.

Using the Junk E-Mail Filter Lists

Another way Outlook determines what is and what isn't junk e-mail is via filter lists. There are three, each of which can be accessed from its own tab in the Junk E-Mail Options dialog box: Safe Senders, Safe Recipients, and Blocked Senders.

Figure 23-2 shows the Safe Senders tab; the Safe Recipients and Blocked Senders tabs are identical except for the checkbox at the bottom, which they don't have.

Figure 23-2: By adding e-mail addresses or domains to your junk e-mail filter lists, you tell Outlook which messages it should accept and which it should treat as junk.

Here's how the three filter lists differ:

✦ The **Safe Senders** list helps you fine-tune the automatic junk e-mail filter. If an e-mail from someone whose messages you want to receive is incorrectly identified as junk e-mail, you can add that sender to this list. You don't just have to add individual e-mail addresses, either; you can add entire domain names. To do so, click Add and type the e-mail address or domain name you want to add to this list. You can also import a list of addresses saved as a text file by click-ing the Import from file button, or export your list as a text file by clicking the Export to file button. To have your junk e-mail filter trust all e-mail from peo-ple in your Contacts folder, check the box at the bottom of the dialog box.

✦ The **Safe Recipients** list is where you add the addresses or domain names of mailing lists or distribution lists to which you subscribe. E-mail sent to any of these addresses (which, of course, are then forwarded to you) will never be treated as junk e-mail, no matter what the content. Again, you can import the list from a file or export it.

✦ The **Blocked Senders** list is the place to put addresses or domain names from which you receive only junk e-mail. Messages from the addresses or domain names on this list are always treated as junk e-mail, even if their content isn't identified as such by the filter. You can also import and/or export this list.

Tip   Another way to add addresses or domain names to any of these filter lists is to right-click on a message and choose Junk E-mail from the shortcut menu; you can then choose Add Sender to Blocked Senders list, Add Sender to Safe Senders list, or Add to Safe Recipients list. You can also access the Junk E-Mail Options dialog box from this shortcut menu.

Specific e-mail addresses in the lists take precedence over domain names, which means that you can block an entire domain name (by adding it to the Blocked Senders list) but still receive messages from specific addresses within that domain by adding those addresses to the Safe Senders list.

If you find a message in your Junk E-Mail Folder that shouldn't have been moved there, right-click on it and choose Junk E-Mail ⇨ Mark as Not Junk from the shortcut menu. This will move the message back to your Inbox; you'll also be prompted in a dialog box to check "Always trust e-mail from (the message sender)" if you want to add the sender to your Safe Senders list, and check the e-mail address to which the message was sent in a list marked "Always trust e-mail sent to the following addresses" if you want to add that address to your Safe Recipients list.

Turning Off Web Beacons

Junk mail senders obviously prefer to send their messages to active e-mail addresses rather than to those that are inactive or defunct. One way they determine whether the e-mail addresses they've just spammed are active is with a *Web beacon*. These are HTML messages that include links to external content — pictures, maybe, or sounds. If you open or preview one of these messages, that content is downloaded, which tells the sender that your e-mail address is valid and active. This can move you from a one-time mailing list to a send-'em-all-the-spam-we-got mailing list.

Outlook now lets you prevent this from happening. The prevention mechanism is active by default, but if you want to adjust the settings, here's how:

1. Choose Tools ⇨ Options.

2. Click the Security tab.

3. Click the Change Automatic Download Settings button in the Download Pictures section of the dialog box. This opens the Automatic Picture Download Settings dialog box shown in Figure 23-3.

Figure 23-3: Use these settings to turn off Web beacons.

4. By default, all the options in this dialog box are active. The first, Don't download pictures or other content automatically in HTML e-mail, prevents Web beacons from operating; however, choosing this option can mess up some legitimate HTML e-mail by preventing graphics from displaying; so the second and third options, which allow downloads from e-mail addresses in your Safe Senders and Safe Recipients lists and Web sites in the Trusted Zone, are also selected by default. (Look for more on security zones in the "Secure content" section later in this chapter.) If you want to block all HTML content (the safest option of all), deselect all these options.

5. Finally, by default, Outlook warns you before it downloads blocked content when you're editing, forwarding, or replying to e-mail. You can still choose to download it if you wish. You'd want to turn this off only if for some reason it's interfering too much with your most common e-mail tasks.

Outlook's Security Settings

Turning off Web beacons is only one of the security functions Outlook provides. You've already seen some of the others in passing; they're on the Security tab of the Options (Tools ⇨ Options) dialog box you had to open to get to the External Content Settings dialog box in Figure 23-3.

Figure 23-4 shows the Options dialog box with the Security tab selected. The Security tab is divided into four sections: Encrypted e-mail, Security zones, Download Pictures, and Digital IDs (Certificates). We've already looked at Download Pictures; now let's look at the others.

Figure 23-4: Select Tools ➪ Options to access the Security tab, where you'll find most of Outlook's security functions.

Encrypted e-mail

There are four checkboxes in the first section of the Security tab:

✦ **Encrypt contents and attachments for outgoing messages.** Encryption prevents anyone except those who have the key from reading the contents of messages or viewing attachments. There's more on encryption later in this chapter. By default, you choose encryption on a message-by-message basis; choose this, and all outgoing messages are encrypted.

✦ **Add digital signature to outgoing messages.** (Look for more on Digital IDs when we get to the bottom of this dialog box.) Again, by default, attaching digital signatures is done on a message-by-message basis; this option attaches your digital signature to all outgoing messages.

Note

A digital signature in this context is not the same as the sig file you can set up to automatically append text to an e-mail message.

✦ **Send clear text signed message when sending signed messages.** This ensures that if you send a digitally signed message to someone whose e-mail software doesn't support digital signatures, he or she will still be able to read your message.

✦ **Request S/MIME receipt for all S/MIME signed messages.** This automatically requests a receipt from anyone to whom you send an encrypted and signed message, so you know it was received. (S/MIME is the encryption protocol used by default by Outlook.) You'd still want to use the standard "Request a read receipt for this message" in the Message Options dialog box (choose Options from the Standard Toolbar when composing a new message) to be notified when the message was actually read.

You can use the Settings button in the Encrypted e-mail section of the Security tab to alter the default Outlook security settings by choosing a different Secure Message Format and specifying which digital certificates you want to use as your signing certificate and your encryption certificate.

Security zones

Security zones were described in the section "Turning Off Web Beacons"; by default, material that comes from one of your security zones is exempt from the blocking of downloadable content.

Caution When you change security zones in Outlook, you also change security zones in all other applications, including Internet Explorer.

Click the Zone Settings button to set up your security zones. This opens the Security dialog box shown in Figure 23-5.

Figure 23-5: Security zones help prevent unwanted or dangerous content from being transferred to your computer.

There are four security zones: Restricted sites, which contains Web sites that could potentially damage your computer or data; Trusted sites, which contains Web sites that you trust not to damage your computer or data; Local intranet, which contains Web sites that are on your organization's local network; and Internet, which contains all sites you haven't placed in the other three security zones.

To add a site to any zone, select the zone you want to add the site to, and then click the Sites button. This opens a dialog box into which you can type the URL of any site you want to add to that zone.

At the bottom of the Security dialog box are two buttons, Custom Level and Default Level. Of course, by default, the level of security in any security zone is set to the Default Level. To change the level of security, you can either use the slider at the left (if you change the default level of security you'll see a warning message, though) or you can click Custom Level to open the dialog box shown in Figure 23-6 and take even greater control of security settings.

Note   If you don't see the slider, it means you or a program you've installed has changed the level of security. Click the Default Level button to return the zone to its default settings and reactivate the slider.

Figure 23-6: Take complete control of security settings here.

Don't worry if you change your mind about changing the security level of a zone; you can always return to the default level by clicking the Default Level button in the Security dialog box.

Digital IDs (certificates)

A *digital certificate* is an electronic, encryption-based, secure stamp of authenticity. Outlook enables you to digitally sign documents by attaching a digital certificate. Digital certificates are special files issued by certificate authorities (such as VeriSign, Inc., at www.verisign.com) or from your company's own internal security administrator or information technology department. Essentially, whoever issues you your digital certificate vouches to whoever is interested that you are who you say you are.

Click Import/Export to import an existing Digital ID from a file to your computer, or to export your Digital ID to a file.

If you don't yet have a Digital ID, click Get a Digital ID. This takes you to a page on Microsoft's Office Web site, where you can find out how to get one. It also provides links to various certificate authorities.

Why Can't I Open That?

Sometimes you'll receive e-mail messages that display the paperclip icon of an attachment in the Attachment column of your list of e-mails, but no matter how hard you try, you can't access that attachment.

This isn't a bug in Outlook; it's a feature designed to protect you from possibly hazardous files.

Attachments to e-mail messages are one of the favorite ways to spread viruses, worms, and Trojans (see the sidebar "What Are Viruses, Worms, and Trojan Horses?" for an explanation of these). When you open the attachment, the virus, worm, or Trojan activates and spreads to your system, and possibly your entire network. It may even mail copies of itself to many or all of the contacts in your Contacts folder or Inbox.

To prevent this, Outlook checks the file type of each attachment that arrives (or that you send) against a list of the types of files most likely to carry such unwanted cargo. If the attachment is a file type containing code that can run without warning—such as .bat., .exe, .vbs, and .js files—then Outlook blocks them and, although it shows you with the paperclip that such an attachment exists, you're unable to either see or access it.

If you send an attached file of this type (see Table 23-1 for a list), Outlook will display a warning that other Outlook users may not be able to access it.

What Are Viruses, Worms, and Trojan Horses?

In the physical world, viruses are tiny bits of genetic material that infect living cells, turning them into virus factories that create many copies of the original virus; worms are primitive, cylindrical life forms that live in a variety of environments, including the insides of some animals; and the Trojan Horse, according to Homer, was a giant wooden horse that concealed invading Greek soldiers.

In the computer world, all three terms have different—but related—meanings. All three have something else in common: They're all bad news for your computer.

Although macro viruses are the most common type of virus, and the only type that infects Office documents (which is why I discuss them in detail in this section of the chapter), they're not the only type of virus. Technically, a *computer virus* is any program designed to copy itself, usually without the user's knowledge. Just as a real-life virus makes copies of itself by infecting a living cell and turning it into a virus factory, so a computer virus program replicates by attaching itself to a program or file on your PC. When you run the infected program or open the file, you also unwittingly activate the virus. The virus may lurk in your computer's memory, infecting every program you run and every disk you access. The virus may destroy files, take up disk space, make your computer display strange characters, or seemingly do nothing at all. More viruses probably fall into the "annoying" category than the "destructive" category, but that's no reason not to take precautions.

Worms can be just as destructive as viruses (just as a tapeworm can cause you as much grief as a flu virus) but in a different way. Worms, like viruses, can replicate themselves, but instead of spreading from file to file, as viruses do, they spread from computer to computer. Typically, they'll mail copies of themselves, usually attached to a seemingly harmless message, to every address they can find in your Outlook address book. When someone opens the attachment to the e-mail, the worm runs itself just once, then starts looking for more connections to other machines it can exploit.

Trojan Horses are well named. When such a program arrives at your computer looking like something highly desirable, it is really hiding a nasty surprise in its belly. While the part of the program you see may apparently be doing exactly what you expect it to, a hidden part of the program could be destroying files or stealing your passwords and e-mailing them to someone else—usually not someone you'd be inclined to share them with. Although a Trojan Horse isn't a virus or worm, viruses and worms can be delivered via Trojan Horses.

To avoid viruses, worms, and Trojan Horses, never open attachments sent to you by people you don't know, or even people you do know who didn't warn you the attachment was coming, without double-checking with the person who sent it to make sure it's harmless. In addition, scan all incoming files with good third-party anti-viral software (see the section "E-mail Safety Tips," later in this chapter).

Microsoft suggests that if you must send one of these types of files to an Outlook user, you either post it to a secure server on the Internet or your network and then provide a link to the person so he or she can download it, or you package the files (for instance, as a .zip file), which Outlook will permit your recipient to open.

Table 23-1
File Types Blocked by Outlook

File Extension	File Type
.ade	Microsoft Access project extension
.adp	Microsoft Access project
.app	FoxPro-generated application
.bas	Microsoft Visual Basic class module
.bat	Batch file
.chm	Compiled HTML Help file
.cmd	Microsoft Windows NT Command Script
.com	Microsoft MS-DOS program
.cpl	Control Panel extension
.crt	Security certificate
.csh	Unix shell script
.exe	Program
.fxp	FoxPro file
.hlp	Help file
.hta	HTML program
.inf	Setup Information
.ins	Internet Naming Service
.isp	Internet Communication settings
.js	JScript file
.jse	Jscript Encoded Script file
.ksh	Unix shell script
.lnk	Shortcut
.mda	Microsoft Access add-in program
.mdb	Microsoft Access program
.mde	Microsoft Access MDE database
.mdt	Microsoft Access add-in data
.mdw	Microsoft Access workgroup information
.mdz	Microsoft Access wizard program
.msc	Microsoft Common Console Document

Continued

File Extension	File Type
	Table 23-1 *(continued)*
.msi	Microsoft Windows Installer package
.msp	Windows Installer patch
.mst	Visual Test source files
.ops	FoxPro file
.pcd	Photo CD image or Microsoft Visual Test compiled script
.pif	Shortcut to MS-DOS program
.prf	Outlook profile information
.prg	FoxPro program source file
.reg	Registration entries
.scf	Microsoft Windows Explorer command
.scr	Screen saver
.sct	Windows Script Component
.shb	Shortcut into a document
.shs	Shell Scrap Object
.url	Internet shortcut
.vb	VBScript file
.vbe	VBScript Encoded Script file
.vbs	VBScript file
.wsc	Windows Script Component
.wsf	Windows Script file
.wsh	Windows Script Host Settings file
.xsl	XML file that can contain script

Digital Signatures and Encryption

You've already encountered digital certificates in the Security tab of the Options dialog box (Tools ➪ Options). Exactly how they're used varies depending on the environment in which you're using them.

To send and receive encrypted messages over the Internet, your recipient has to have a copy of your digital certificate, and you have to have a copy of his or hers. You can send yours to your recipient by attaching your digital certificate (which has the .cer extension) as a file to a message, or you can even have it delivered to your recipient on external media, such as a CD or floppy disk. However, the easiest way for you to exchange digital certificates is for you and your correspondent to send each other digitally signed messages.

To digitally sign a message, simply click the Digitally Sign button on the message editor's Standard toolbar; in Word, it's at the far right. You have two options: Sign This Message and Encrypt This Message.

When your recipient receives the digitally signed message and adds your e-mail name to Contacts (by right-clicking on your address and choosing Add to Contacts), he or she also adds your digital certificate. Once you've done the same with the digitally signed message he or she sends you, you can encrypt and decrypt messages sent to and from each other.

Permissions

New in Outlook 2003 is the ability to restrict what a recipient can do with the e-mail you send. This is done through the Information Rights Management feature that is part of Office 2003 Professional Edition.

For more on Information Rights Management in Office, see Chapter 46.

To restrict access to an e-mail message, click the Permission button on the Standard toolbar (it's a red circle with a dash inside it). By default, this toggles the message from Unrestricted Access to Do Not Forward. If Do Not Forward is selected, the recipient can read the message but can't forward, print, or copy it.

If permission is set to Do Not Forward, your recipient must either be using Outlook 2003 or download a special program available for free from Microsoft.com in order to read it.

The InfoBar at the top of the message informs you when permission is set to Do Not Forward (see Figure 23-7).

System administrators can create custom Permission policies; if any such policies exist on your network, they'll appear as a submenu when you click the Permission button, so you can choose the one you want.

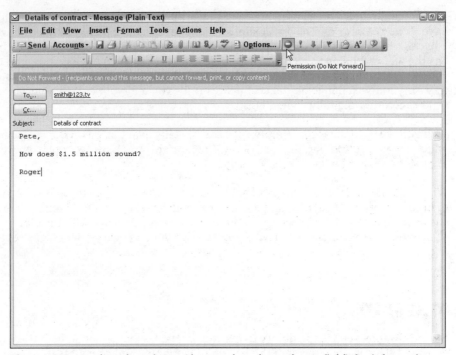

Figure 23-7: Look at the InfoBar (the gray bar above the To field) for information about the restricted Permission setting. (The mouse pointer is pointing at the Permission button.)

E-mail Safety Tips

Finally, here are some safety tips everyone ought to know (but too many people don't):

✦ **Be wary of e-mail from people you don't know.** That e-mail from a strange address could just be spam, but it could contain something more dangerous, especially if it has an attachment. Don't go by the subject line; spammers often put "Re:" there to fool you into thinking you're getting a response to a message you sent. Another common tactic is to use a subject line like "Here's the information you requested."

✦ **Be wary of e-mails from people you *do* know.** A number of e-mail worms in circulation actually take over their victim's contact list and send themselves out to everyone in it, often hiding themselves in a document file taken at random from the victim's hard drive. If a message looks odd, or you weren't expecting it, contact the sender and ask them if they sent it. You could be doing them a favor by alerting them to the presence of a worm on their system.

✦ **Don't trust Outlook to block all dangerous attachments.** Someone could have sent you a virus concealed in a file type that Outlook will permit. Some of the worst viruses are so-called macro viruses, which embed themselves in Word or Excel documents as macros.

✦ **Install security updates on your system.** If you're working with Office in a corporate networked environment, your IT people will probably take care of this, but if you're the one in charge of Office, or it's on your home system, then you should make sure you keep up with the latest security updates and download and install them as they become available. There are sometimes several security patches a month; check for them often. Most of the damage done to systems by malicious programs could have been prevented if this advice were followed.

✦ **Scan incoming e-mail for viruses.** Outlook blocks certain risky attachments, but it doesn't confirm whether or not they contain viruses. For that you need anti-virus software. The two most popular are Norton AntiVirus from Symantec (`www.symantec.com`) and McAfee VirusScan (`www.mcafee.com`). These and other anti-virus programs can scan not only your system to make sure you're not already infected but also incoming and outgoing e-mail to make sure you're neither receiving nor inadvertently sending viruses, worms, and Trojan Horses. In addition, always make sure your virus definitions are current; new viruses are released daily.

✦ **Don't respond to spam under any circumstances.** When you respond to unsolicited junk mail asking to be removed from the sender's mailing list, it's quite likely that all you will accomplish is to confirm to the spammer that your e-mail address is valid and active.

✦ **Keep your e-mail address private wherever possible.** This prevents spammers from getting hold of it. Many people maintain a second e-mail address, often with a free Web e-mail service, for public use (registering for Web sites, online shopping, posting to Usenet newsgroups, etc.) and share their primary e-mail address only with people with whom they really want to communicate.

✦ **Never click on links provided by people you don't know, or visit URLs they recommend.** They may direct you to Web sites that contain code with the potential to wreak havoc on your system.

Summary

Learning to use Outlook's built-in security features can make your online communication both safer and more pleasant. With Outlook, you can do the following:

✦ Filter out some junk e-mail and assign specific senders to a list of junk e-mail senders

✦ Prevent the downloading of graphics and other items in HTML e-mails that tell senders of junk e-mail that your address is valid and active

✦ Set up security zones that determine what content can be trusted and what content should be restricted

✦ Avoid some of the risk of attachments that might carry dangerous code, because Outlook won't let you access them

✦ Obtain and use a digital certificate to digitally sign and encrypt e-mail, for greater security

✦   ✦   ✦

Creating and Maintaining a Contact List

Although Outlook is best known for its e-mail–management tools, it should come as no surprise that it also excels at managing lists of contacts. After all, what's the point of being able to make and manage messages if you have no one to send them to?

This chapter covers using Outlook's contact database, beginning with using the built-in forms to enter contact data. You can also use the All Fields tab to enter more detailed data not covered in the General and Details tabs of the contact form.

As I pointed out in Chapter 21, Outlook has several built-in views (and the capability of creating custom views) for everything, and contacts are no exception. You can edit contact data either in the views or via the data-entry forms.

Contacts can be grouped the same way as messages can, and contacts can be associated with other contacts as well as items in other Outlook folders.

Note	Users of either Office Small Business Edition or Office Professional Edition have an additional Outlook-based product called Business Contact Manager designed specifically for sales professionals and small-business owners. I won't cover it in detail, since it isn't something that will be much used by the majority of Office users, but I do provide a quick overview of it in the section "Introduction to Business Contact Manager" at the end of this chapter, so those who are interested in it can begin exploring its capabilities.

Adding a Contact

To open the Contacts folder, just click the Contacts button in the Navigation pane; or double-click it in the Folder List.

For more information on the Navigation Pane, see Chapter 21.

To add a new contact, click the New button on the toolbar while you're in the Contacts folder, or choose File ➪ New ➪ Contact at any time.

You can actually create a new contact without ever clicking a button or opening a menu: Just double-click a blank area anywhere in the pane displaying your contacts. (The first time you open Outlook, of course, this area is completely blank except for a note saying "Double-click here to create a new Contact.")

What can get complex is gathering all the information that Outlook can hold. Of course, there's no requirement that you fill in all the blanks — it's just that Outlook can cover anything you come up with. If all you've got is basic data such as name, phone number, and e-mail address, just use that. On the other hand, if you want a place to keep track of things like nicknames, birthdays, and anniversaries, and even to store digital certificates, you've got it.

To add a contact, follow these steps:

1. Click the New button or choose File ➪ New ➪ Contact.

2. In the new contact form's General tab (see Figure 24-1), enter the contact's full name in normal format, such as "John Albert Smith." The name will automatically be entered in the format "Smith, John Albert" under File as when you tab out of the Full Name box.

Outlook is smart enough to realize that sometimes a middle name belongs with the given name, and sometimes it belongs with the surname. In other words, while it automatically files John Albert Smith as "Smith, John Albert," it would automatically file Manfred von Richtofen as "von Richtofen, Manfred."

If you would prefer to have the name filed as "John Smith" instead of "Smith, John," choose that option from the File as drop-down menu.

3. If you want to enter more detailed name information, click the Full Name button. This will bring up a dialog box with such options as title, suffix (Jr., Sr., and so on), and middle name. Enter the data and click the OK button to return to the new contact form. Although this information does not appear in separate fields on the main form, it is included in separate field entries in the database.

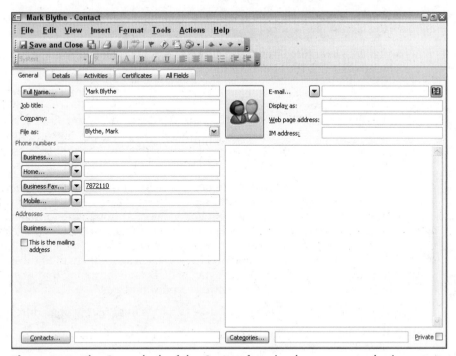

Figure 24-1: The General tab of the Contact form is where you enter basic contact information.

4. Fill out the Job title and Company fields. When you enter a company name, three more options appear in the drop-down list under File As to file by company name, to file by the contact's name with the company name in parentheses after it, or to file by company name with the contact's name in parentheses after it.

Tip   The best way to choose a File As format is by however you usually think of the contact. If you think, "I need to call Joe Brown at ABC Corp.," then file the contact by name, with the company name in parentheses: Brown, Joe (ABC Corp.). If you think, "I need to call our ABC rep, Joe Brown," then file the contact by company name, with the contact name in parentheses: ABC Corp. (Brown, Joe).

5. The Address field is set by default to the business address, but three addresses can actually be entered—business, home, and other. Select which one you want to enter by clicking the downward-pointing arrow. You can enter all three if you want. Clicking the Business button brings up a Check Address dialog box in which Outlook has already parsed the information you entered into its component parts, such as street address and ZIP code. You can also specify the Country/Region, which you can select from a drop-down list

(Outlook does a very good job of determining the country from most addresses). After doing so, click the OK button.

6. If you have entered multiple addresses, display the one you want snail mail to go to and click the checkbox labeled This is the mailing address.

7. Enter the contact's telephone numbers. You can use any format you like — 234-555-4321 or even just 2345554321 — and Outlook will redisplay it in the format (234) 555-4321 once you click on another field. Although the form lists only four numbers, several more are accessible via the arrow buttons, just as with the Address field. (If you just enter a seven-digit number, Outlook assumes it is in your area code and adds that to the front of the number automatically.)

8. Enter the contact's e-mail addresses, either by typing it in or (probably the easiest way to ensure you don't make an error) by copying it and pasting it from an e-mail message you sent or received. Although the form lists only one e-mail address, two more are accessible via the arrow button, just as with the Address field. The Display as option lets you choose what you want displayed in the To field when you compose a new message — instead of the e-mail address, it can be the contact's name, nickname (anything that works as a mnemonic for you), or anything else you want to use.

9. Enter the contact's Web page address and Instant Messaging address, if any.

10. If desired, click the button with the little cartoon people on it to include a photo with the contact.

Once you've entered the information, you can click Save and Close, or click one of the other tabs to continue providing information about this contact.

Tip   Quite often when you're entering contacts you want to enter several, one after the other. Click the Save and New button (just to the right of the Save and Close button) to save the current contact and immediately open an empty Contact form, ready for you to enter the details of your next contact.

Here's what you'll find under the other tabs in the New Contact dialog box:

✦ Under the Details tab (see Figure 24-2), you can enter a variety of additional data, such as the contact's nickname, spouse's name, the directory server and e-mail alias the contact uses for Online NetMeetings, and so forth. The Birthday and Anniversary fields have a calendar available via a click on the downward-pointing arrow. By default, the current date is shown, but other months are available by using the left- and right-pointing arrows to scroll through the year. Once you're in the right month, click the date.

Tip   If you want to enter the year, too, you can type it in directly. Outlook's perpetual calendar will even tell you what day of the week that was — which makes it a pretty good way to find out what day of the week you or anyone else was born on!

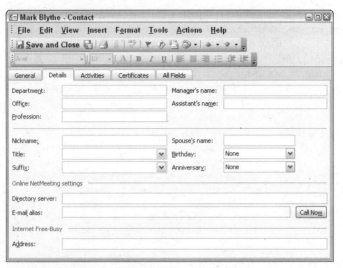

Figure 24-2: Enter additional information about a contact using the Details tab.

✦ The Activities tab doesn't take any entries from you. It simply lists all Outlook items with which the contact is associated,. For example, it lists e-mail messages you've sent to this contact. It also lists any Outlook items you've linked the contact to using the Actions ➪ Link command.

Cross-Reference
For an explanation of how to associate contacts and other Outlook items, see the section "Associating Contacts with Other Outlook Items," later in this chapter.

Tip
The Activities tab's greatest use, as far as I'm concerned, is in helping you find messages you sent or received from a contact that have since been dispersed to any number of folders within your Inbox.

✦ If you have a digital certificate for this person and want to use it in secure e-mail messages, click the Certificates tab. Click the Import button, find the certificate, and open it to add it to the list.

Note
A digital certificate is a piece of security software that acts as an identification card to computers that can read it, proving that the person who possesses it is who he or she says he or she is.)

Cross-Reference
For more on using digital certificates to send secure e-mails, see Chapter 23.

✦ To view or change specific fields, click the All Fields tab (see Figure 24-3). The Select from drop-down list enables you to choose various types of fields to display, such as phone number, address, and so on. (The most all-inclusive of these options is All Contact fields.) Enter data under the Value column next to the field name. Press Enter or click anywhere else on the form and the information is accepted in the field (the contact must still be saved to keep the change, though). In addition to entering new information here, you can also edit existing data. All changes you make here are instantly reflected in the appropriate fields on the other tabs.

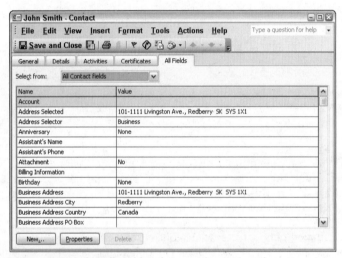

Figure 24-3: The All Fields tab is an alternative place to enter data for your contacts.

Outlook even lets you add new fields so you can provide additional information about a contact: for instance, Pet Name or Shoe Size. To add a new field:

1. With the All Fields tab selected, click the New button.

2. In the New Field dialog box, type a name for the field.

3. Select a Type for the data (text, number, date/time, and so forth) from the drop-down list.

4. Select a format (this varies depending on the data type) from the second drop-down list.

5. Click the OK button to complete creation of the new field.

6. Enter the data for the new field under the Value column. Unless you enter data, this field is visible only by selecting User-defined fields in this folder under Select from. If there is an entry under this field, it can also be viewed by selecting User-defined fields in this item.

To complete the entry of contact information using any of the tabs, click the Save and Close button on the toolbar or use the Ctrl+S keyboard combination.

Note You can also add a contact in any of the default Contact folder views except the address card views by clicking in the first row under the column headers and then entering the data for the new contact. However, this is a comparatively awkward approach because you must scroll or tab to fill in the fields for the new contact.

Tip You don't have to return to your mail folders to send an e-mail using a contact; just right-click on the contact and choose New Message to Contact from the shortcut menu to open a new e-mail message form with the contact's e-mail address already in the To field. You can also choose from the shortcut menu New Appointment with Contact, New Meeting Request to Contact, New Task for Contact, and New Journal Entry for Contact.

Importing Contacts

Sometimes you might want to import into your Contacts folder addresses that are stored in some other format: as a vCard file, for instance, Netscape Mail, or even an Excel spreadsheet or other database.

To do so, choose File ➪ Import and Export. (If you have Business Contact Manager, you'll need to also choose Standard from the Import and Export submenu.). This opens the Import and Export Wizard (see Figure 24-4).

Figure 24-4: Use this wizard to import addresses stored in another format.

First you're asked to choose which of several actions to perform. To import a database file, for instance, choose Import from another program or file. When you click Next, you're asked to choose the specific type of file you want to import, and then to locate the specific file. You're given the option of replacing any duplicates that turn up in the imported data with the imported data, allowing duplicates to be created, or not importing duplicate items. Finally, you're asked to select a destination Outlook folder for the contacts you're importing; by default, naturally, it's the Contacts folder, although you can put them in a different Outlook folder, or even create a new one for them, if you wish.

When you click OK, you'll see the Import a File dialog box, which shows you the action you're about to perform so you can double-check it; once you start importing, the action can't be canceled, and it will tie up your computer for a few minutes (how many depends on the size of the file).

Contact data will import most easily if the data in the outside file is labeled in a way that that matches up with fields in Outlook. However, if it doesn't, and if you don't want to go into the outside file and use whatever program created it to relabel the data it contains, you can click Map Custom Fields in the Import a File dialog box. This opens another dialog box that presents you with the values from the outside file on the left and the available Outlook Contact fields on the right. You can drag a value from the left to the appropriate field on the right. Then, when you return to the Import a File and click OK, Outlook will know where the data in each field of the outside file should go in the new contacts it creates.

If you don't either relabel the data in the original file or take the time to map custom fields, you're likely to get an error message and importing will abort.

In my experience, importing and exporting can be kind of hit and miss, with the resulting data sometimes requiring a lot of cleaning up; still, it's generally faster than typing all that information yourself, contact by contact.

Opening and Editing a Contact

You can edit contact fields directly in the Address Cards, Detailed Address Cards, or Phone List views (see the following section on viewing contact lists). However, not all fields are visible in these situations, and the easiest way to edit contact data is by using the same form you used to add the contact to begin with. To do so, follow these steps:

1. Double-click the contact's listing.

2. Select the tab containing the data you want to edit. If neither the General nor Details tab has the fields you want to edit listed, select the All Fields tab.

3. Edit the data.

4. To save the listing, click the Save and Close button. To exit without saving, just close the Contact dialog box. Outlook will ask you if you want to save changes; click No if you're sure you want to discard it.

Viewing Your Contacts

By default, Outlook offers you seven Contacts views; you can easily switch among them by clicking the radio buttons in the Current View area of the Navigation Pane.

Table 24-1 shows these seven views and their contents. The By Category, By Company, By Location, and By Follow-Up Flag views are grouped by those parameters (see the following section on grouping contacts).

Table 24-1	
Contacts Views	
View	**Contents**
Address Cards	Name, follow-up flag, address, phone numbers, e-mail addresses
Detailed Address Cards	The full listing from the General tab except for the picture field
Phone List	Flag status, icon, attachment, name, company, file as, phone numbers, journal, categories
By Category	Flag status, icon, attachment, name, company, file as, categories, phone numbers
By Company	Flag status, icon, attachment, name, job title, company, file as, department, phone numbers, categories
By Location	Flag status, icon, attachment, name, company, file as, state, country/region, phone numbers, categories
By Follow-Up Flag	Flag status, icon, attachment, name, company, file as, phone numbers, categories

Cross-Reference   Remember, you can also create your own views if you don't like any of the available ones. For detailed information on customizing and creating views, see Chapter 21.

Creating Groups

Although there is no Group By Box command for contacts in the Address Card views, you will find that you can use it in every other view. In fact, the By Category, By Company, By Location, and By Follow-up Flag views are grouped by those parameters (see the preceding section on viewing contact lists). Groups are great for helping you keep track of contacts who all have a common trait, whether it's last names that begin with the same letter or a favorite color.

For more information on grouping items in Outlook, see Chapter 22.

In this method of grouping, you activate the Group By box above the listings by right-clicking any field header and choosing Group By Box from the shortcut menu. Drag the field header into the Group By box, and the listings automatically group themselves accordingly. Up to four fields can be stacked in this manner, with each group being subordinate to the one before it. The order of the fields, and therefore the stacking of subgroups, can be changed by dragging the field headers into new positions in the Group By box; or you can select Group By This Field.

The second method of grouping is to right-click the blank record at the top of the window (the one containing the field labeled "Click here to add a new contact") and select Group By from the pop-up menu. In the Group By dialog box, shown in Figure 24-5, you choose fields from drop-down lists.

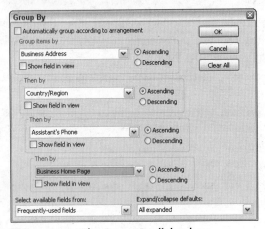

Figure 24-5: The Group By dialog box

Once again, up to four fields can be stacked. When you're finished choosing the fields, click the OK button to implement the grouping.

Creating Distribution Lists

You can create another kind of group: a distribution list. A distribution list is a list of contacts that are saved under a single name in your Contacts folder, so you can send messages (or tasks, or appointments, or other Outlook items) to all of them at once without having to select each contact individually each time.

To create a distribution list, follow these steps:

1. Choose File ➪ New ➪ Distribution List. This opens a simple dialog box (see Figure 24-6) where you can enter a name for your list.

2. Click the Select Members button if you want to select a contact to add to the distribution list from your existing contacts, click Add New if you want to type the name and e-mail address of a new addition to the distribution list, and click Remove to remove the currently highlighted list member from the list.

3. Click Update Now to add new members to the list while keeping the dialog box open; click Save and Close to save the new distribution list and close the dialog box.

Figure 24-6: Use this dialog box to create a new e-mail distribution list.

Associating Contacts with Other Outlook Items

It's often useful to know not only who's who, but who's associated with whom or responsible for what. Outlook takes this need into account and provides a simple method for associating contacts with different items in the various folders. You can associate a contact with other contacts, with tasks, with journal entries, and so forth. To link a contact with an item, follow these steps:

1. Select the contact you want to associate with an item.

2. Select Actions ⇨ Link ⇨ Items.

3. In the Link Items to Contact dialog box (see Figure 24-7), select the folder in the top panel that contains the item you want to associate.

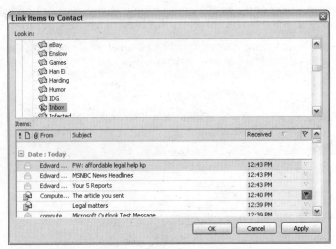

Figure 24-7: The Link Items to Contact dialog box lets you link contacts to messages, notes, or any other Outlook item.

4. In the bottom panel, select the item or items you want to associate with the contact. To select a contiguous range of items, click the first item in the range, hold down the Shift key, and click the last item in the range. To select a non-contiguous group of items, hold down the Ctrl key while clicking each item.

5. Click the OK button.

The associated items will now appear on the Activities tab in the form for the contact. You can remove an association at any time by highlighting it on the Activities tab and then choosing File ⇨ Delete (or simply pressing Delete).

Mail-merging Outlook Contacts with Word

It's only natural that you would, from time to time, want to use your Outlook Contacts listings with Word in a mail-merged document. Thanks to the integration of Office applications, you can do so easily. To use your contacts in a Word mail merge, follow these steps:

1. Open the Contacts folder.

2. Select those contacts you want to use in the mail merge. To select noncontiguous contacts, hold down the Ctrl key while clicking their listings.

3. Select Tools ➪ Mail Merge from the menu.

4. The Mail Merge Contacts dialog box will appear (see Figure 24-8). Choose which contacts you want included in the mail merge by clicking the appropriate radio button under Contacts.

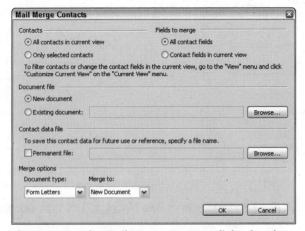

Figure 24-8: The Mail Merge Contacts dialog box lets you set up your contacts for merging into a Word document.

5. Choose whether you want all fields included in the mail merge or only the fields in the current view by clicking the appropriate radio button under Fields to merge.

6. Choose whether to create a new document or to use an existing document by clicking the appropriate radio button. If you decide to use an existing document, you can click Browse to open a standard file open dialog box from which you can navigate to the mail merge document you want to use. When you locate it, select it and click the OK button to return to the Mail Merge Contacts dialog box.

7. To save the group of contacts you've chosen for this mail merge for future use or reference, specify a filename where indicated.

8. Choose the appropriate Merge options: Document type (form letters, mailing labels, envelopes, or catalog) and Merge to (new document, printer, or e-mail).

9. Click the OK button to proceed.

10. Next, either the existing document will be opened or the new one will be created, with the Mail Merge toolbar open. If the former, printing will begin; if the latter, click the Insert Merge Field button to open a list of available fields and insert them into your Word document as desired (see Figure 24-9).

Figure 24-9: The Insert Merge Field dialog box in Word lets you insert Outlook contact fields into your Mail Merge document.

Introduction to Business Contact Manager

Business Contact Manager is essentially an extended version of the regular Contact manager. It adds fields of use primarily to small-business owners and sales representatives, allowing them to keep track of the companies and individuals they do business with so that they can maximize sales and track sales opportunities (along with such things as how far along prospective sales are, their revenue potential, and how close they are to closing). You can keep track of activities related to the contact and run useful reports that can summarize information about your business contacts and opportunities — for instance, which contacts you've neglected by not calling for six months or a year.

Business Contact Manager has its own folder in Contacts and several views, chosen from radio buttons in the Navigation Pane. The Business Contact dialog box looks a little different from the regular Contact dialog box but collects much of the same information, plus some of the additional sales-related information I mentioned, such as State (Active or Inactive), Status (Current or Overdue), and Rating (from bad to great).The Contact history area at the bottom of the General tab shows you information about recent activity related to the contact, from e-mails to scheduled meetings (see Figure 24-10).

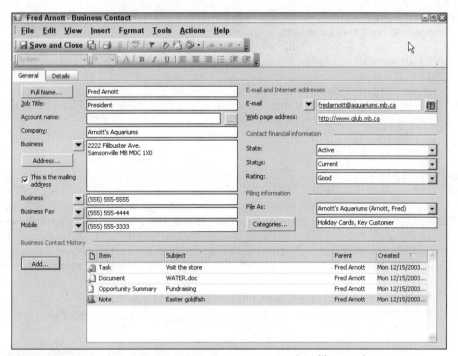

Figure 24-10: Business Contact Manager contacts are just like regular contacts; the only differences are in the information Outlook asks for in addition to name, street address, phone number, and e-mail address.

The Details tab lets you add, as you might expect, more details, such as the source of the sales lead, the preferred method of contact (e-mail, fax, phone, letter, Instant Messenger, face-to-face, etc.).

Once you've entered contacts into Business Contact Manager, you can perform a number of actions. Select a contact or range of contacts, and then choose Actions ⇨ New Opportunity for Contact, New Phone Log for Contact, or New Business Note for Contact. Each option opens a new dialog box where you can enter the necessary information (or, in the case of a Phone Log, click Start Timer as you begin a call in order to maintain an accurate record of how much time you've spent on the phone with a particular contact).

Several views of your information are available under Business Tools on the menu bar, including Accounts, Business Contacts, Opportunities, Product List, and Business Services (which opens an Internet browser and links you to Microsoft bCentral).

To run a report—and Outlook offers more than 20 of them, organized into four categories: Business Contacts, Accounts, Opportunities, and Other—choose Business Tools ➪ Reports and choose the category and then the specific report you want to run.

Business Contact Manager promises to be a useful tool for many sales representatives and small-business owners—provided they have Office 2003 Small Business Edition or Office 2003 Professional Edition.

Summary

In this chapter, you learned how to add contacts to Outlook, which kinds of information a Contacts listing can contain, and how to edit the contents. You also learned about the different views of Contacts listings that are available in Outlook, how to group different contacts by various fields, how to link contacts to other items in Outlook's folders, and how to use Outlook's contacts in Word mail merges:

✦ Outlook's built-in forms make entering contact data simple.

✦ The All Fields tab enables you to enter data not covered in the General and Details tabs of the Contact form.

✦ Contact data can be edited either in the views or via the data entry forms.

✦ Outlook has several built-in views—ways of looking at the contact information—and you can create custom views as well.

✦ Contact listings can be grouped, just as messages can.

✦ Contacts can be associated with other contacts, as well as items, in other Outlook folders.

✦ Contacts can be easily exported to Word for use in mail merges.

✦   ✦   ✦

Managing Your Time with Calendar

Beyond the message- and contact-related capabilities of Outlook is another job the application is really good at: helping you manage your time (and, if you're in a position to do so, other people's time, too!).

This chapter helps you get a grip on Outlook's Calendar feature, beginning with the Outlook Today view, which gives you a quick handle on your day by showing you the appointments and tasks you need to deal with and how much e-mail is in your Inbox, Outbox, and Drafts folders.

This chapter also explores how you can assign tasks to yourself or to other people (alas, other people can assign you tasks as well!); how Calendar is used to schedule appointments, keep track of events, and invite other people to meetings; and how you can import scheduling data into Calendar from other scheduling programs, and send information from Calendar to others.

The Outlook Today View

Outlook Today (see Figure 25-1), as mentioned in Chapter 21, is designed to give you a quick handle on what's facing you right now. You open it by clicking the Shortcuts button in the Navigation Pane and then clicking the Outlook Today shortcut. Outlook Today lists calendar events for the next several days, shows you how much e-mail is in your Inbox, Outbox, and Drafts folders, and provides a list of pending tasks. The checkboxes next to the tasks are there so you can signify that you've finished them. When you check one, the task is grayed out; it won't be there in Outlook Today the next day. You can go to the Calendar, Messages, or Tasks folders by clicking on their names.

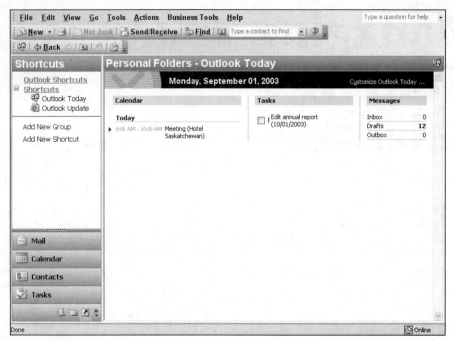

Figure 25-1: The Outlook Today view shows you at a glance what you've got on the go.

Outlook Today's settings aren't graven in stone. As you've probably come to expect in Office in general and Outlook in particular, you can customize it to suit yourself. You can set it up so that it's the default opening screen in Outlook, add other e-mail folders, change the number of days shown in the calendar, and control how the Tasks list is presented.

To customize Outlook Today, follow these steps:

1. In Outlook Today, click the Customize Outlook Today link (shown at the upper-right in Figure 25-1). This brings up the Outlook Today options page (see Figure 25-2).

2. To make Outlook Today your default startup screen in Outlook, click the checkbox labeled When starting, go directly to Outlook Today.

3. To add folders to or remove them from the Message list in Outlook Today, click the Choose Folders button. In the resulting dialog box, check a folder to include it in the Message list or uncheck it to remove it from the list. By default, Outlook already has the three most likely candidates included — Drafts, Inbox, and Outbox. Depending on your personal needs, however, you may want to remove one or more of these or even add the Sent Items folder or the Deleted Items folder. If you don't want any folders in your Message list, click the Clear All button. Click OK to return to the options page.

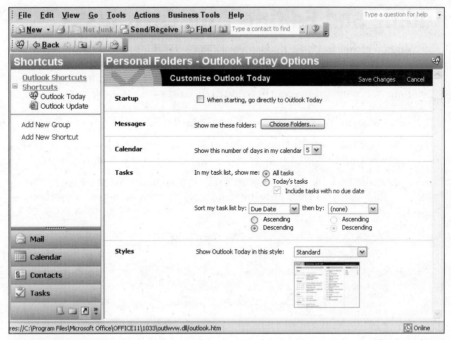

Figure 25-2: The Outlook Today options screen lets you customize Outlook Today as you see fit.

4. To set how many days of calendar events are shown, choose a number from 1 to 7 from the list box labeled Show this number of days in my calendar.

5. The Tasks list has the most options. Under the In my task list, show me category, the default is All tasks. If you want to see only one day's tasks, click the Today's tasks radio button instead. Check the Include tasks with no due date checkbox if you don't want some of your tasks to slip by unnoticed.

6. Next, you can choose how the Tasks list is sorted. The default is by due date. However, you can instead choose to sort by importance, creation time, or start date. You can add a second layer of sorting by specifying another field. The possible fields are the same for both. The default sort order is descending (e.g., A–Z). If you'd prefer to change this, select the Ascending radio buttons.

7. From the Show Outlook Today in this style list box, select the layout you want for Outlook Today. A small preview area below the list box helps you choose.

8. Click the Save Changes button.

Adding and Editing Your Own Tasks

You can either assign a task to yourself or send a request to someone else to take on a task (of course, they can send you such a request as well). (In theory, the person to whom you send a task request can refuse it, but in most companies, the chain of command makes this moot!) To add a task, follow these steps:

1. Click the Tasks button in the Navigation Pane to open the Tasks folder.

2. Click the New button. (In Outlook, you can also create a new Task, no matter what folder you are in, by selecting New ➪ Task from the menu.)

3. In the task form (see Figure 25-3), type a name for the task in the Subject field, just as if you were entering a subject line for an e-mail message.

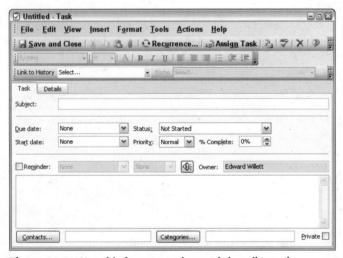

Figure 25-3: Use this form to assign and describe tasks.

4. Select a Due Date and Start Date (if you wish — they're optional) by clicking on the downward-pointing arrows next to those boxes and selecting dates from the pop-up calendars.

5. Select a status for the task from the drop-down list. The options are Not Started, In Progress, Completed, Waiting on someone else, and Deferred.

6. Select a priority for the task from the drop-down list. The options are Low, Normal, and High.

7. Select a % Complete from the drop-down list. The options are 0%, 25%, 50%, 75%, and 100%. You can also type any number into the % Complete text box.

Note Few people actually use this field, but it can be valuable if you want the person who assigned the task to you to be able to check on its status without having to phone or e-mail you directly.

8. If desired, check the Reminder checkbox and select a date and time from a pop-up calendar and a list of half-hour increments for the day, respectively.

9. If desired, click the Speaker icon next to the time box to select a sound that will be played at the reminder time. This brings up a dialog box in which you can click a Browse button to select a sound file.

10. You can use the buttons on the bottom of the task form to associate contacts or categories with this task; these are people or information that can help you carry out the task.

Note Associating a contact is *not* the same as assigning a task; the contacts you associate are not notified in any way, unlike the person to whom you assign the task.

11. Select the Private checkbox if you don't want other people with access to this folder to be able to view this task.

12. Click the Save and Close button on the toolbar.

To edit an existing task, click on it in Outlook Today view or in any other view that displays tasks. This opens the task form, which you can then alter as you desire. Once you've made your changes, click Save and Close.

Assigning a Task to Someone Else

If you followed the procedure just described, you've created a task that you own. This may be exactly what you want, if you're planning your own time, but if you're in the fortunate position of being able to plan someone else's time, too, then you'll want to assign the task to someone else.

To do that, create a new task as described previously and then click the Assign Task button on the toolbar. This causes some changes to the task form, as shown in Figure 25-4.

The Assign Task button has vanished, and the task blank now has a To field just like an e-mail message. In addition, the notation at the top indicates that it is currently an unsent e-mail message. Click the To button to select a recipient, and then click the Send button. The recipient receives the task in an e-mail and can either accept it or reject it; if it's accepted, it's automatically added to the recipient's task list.

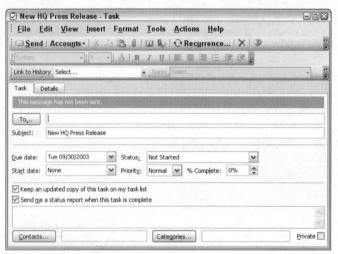

Figure 25-4: The task assignment form is where you assign tasks to someone other than yourself.

By default, Keep an updated copy of this task on my task list and Send me a status report when this task is complete are checked. The former option ensures that you don't forget about a task you've assigned, by keeping it in your task list, while the latter notifies you when the task has been marked complete by the recipient.

Note   The Details tab is used for recording such information as the amount of time spent on completing the task, the mileage accumulated in the process, and so forth.

Using Calendar

If you've ever said to someone something like "Yeah, Tuesday at 4:30 will be fine," only to realize later that you already have something scheduled for that time slot, you're going to love Calendar. Calendar enables you to manage your time more efficiently, scheduling appointments and events with ease.

First, some definitions. In Outlook parlance:

✦ An *appointment* is time blocked off on your calendar for a specific purpose over a limited period of time.

✦ A *meeting* is an appointment to which you invite other people. During that time, you normally can't be doing anything else, and your calendar will show that you are busy and unavailable (unless you specify otherwise), preventing your being scheduled into two places at once.

✦ An *event* is something that takes place over a period of at least 24 hours, and it doesn't necessarily mean that you're unavailable during it. For example, a three-day-long seminar is an event, but you may have free periods during those days when you'll be available for appointments.

Figure 25-5 shows the basic Calendar screen, with an appointment scheduled for 8 a.m. Although this is a one-day view, you can also select weekly or monthly calendar views. There are actually two categories of the weekly view — you can choose either a Work Week or just a Week. The Work Week, of course, is for Monday through Friday. You select each of these views by clicking the appropriate button on the toolbar.

Cross-
Reference

All of these Calendar views can be modified; see Chapter 21 for details.

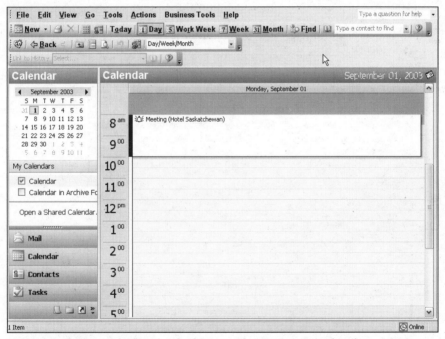

Figure 25-5: The Outlook Calendar lets you plan your time in detail.

Tip

You can use the small calendar display at the top of the Navigation Pane to move around among the months, scrolling back and forth via the left- and right-pointing arrows. To see the appointments scheduled for a particular date, click the date. To return to the current day, click the Today button on the toolbar.

Creating and Managing Appointments and Events

You can add a new appointment to a particular date and time by double-clicking the time slot in the appointment book while viewing that day. Alternatively, you can just click the New button while you're in Calendar view. The only difference between the two approaches is that the first one brings up the appointment form with the correct date and time already inserted.

 Tip   You can type a brief note to yourself into any time slot just by clicking on it; you don't have to create a full-fledged appointment.

Once you're in the appointment form, follow these steps:

1. Type a subject for the appointment into the first field of the Appointment tab (see Figure 25-6).

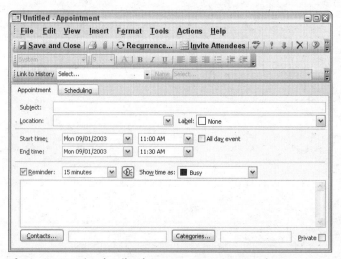

Figure 25-6: List details about your appointment here.

2. Enter the location of the meeting in the second field.

3. A selection of color labels is available for various types of appointments (e.g., Birthday, Personal, Phone Call, etc.) to help you keep them straight; choose these from the Label drop-down list.

4. If this is an event, check the All day event checkbox.

5. Set the start time and end time for the appointment. If it's an event instead of an appointment, only the starting day and ending day will be available. Otherwise, you need to set both the date and time of the appointment.

6. If you want to be reminded about the appointment ahead of time, make sure the Reminder checkbox is checked and specify how far in advance you wish to be reminded. Click the Speaker icon to select a sound file to be played at that time.

7. Under Show time as, choose Free, Tentative, Busy, or Out of Office. (Each of these has its own color-coded label as well.)

8. Add any comments in the text area.

9. If desired, specify which contacts are associated with this appointment by clicking the Contacts button at the bottom of the screen and selecting them from your Contacts listings.

10. If desired, assign categories to the appointment by clicking the Categories button.

11. If you want the appointment to be private, enable the Private checkbox.

12. Click the Save and Close button on the toolbar.

If you are dealing with other people also using Outlook on your network, you can invite others to a meeting, appointment, or event by clicking the Scheduling tab (see Figure 25-7).

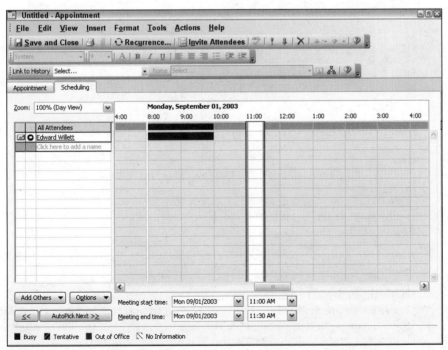

Figure 25-7: Invite others to your meeting, appointment, or event with the Scheduling tab.

To invite others to the meeting, appointment, or event, follow these steps:

1. Click the Add Others button or type their e-mail addresses or aliases using the field labeled Click here to add a name.

2. Choose the location from which you want to add others to the appointment — your address book or a public folder (one that's available on the network). In the Select Attendees and Resources dialog box (see Figure 25-8), select a contact and click the Required button if that person's presence is necessary (notice that you're already listed as required, as it's your appointment!). Click the Optional button if someone's presence is desired but not necessary. Click the Resources button if the person is providing necessary information for the meeting.

Tip   Many people use Resources not to enter the name of a person but to note required physical resources like a conference room, projector, or other piece of equipment that may have to be reserved. You can type directly into any of these fields.

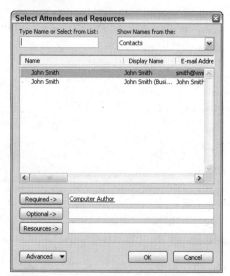

Figure 25-8: The Select Attendees and Resources dialog box

3. Click the OK button to return to the Scheduling tab.

4. Click AutoPick Next to automatically find the next time when the people you've listed are available. Use the << button to find the previous time slot when all the people are available. The box to the right of the list of attendees gives you a graphical representation of people's availability.

Note Make sure the time you originally specified isn't available before using AutoPick. The bar at the top of the scheduling chart shows you the cumulative availability of the entire group.

5. Click the Appointment tab.

6. Because others from your Contacts listings are being invited, the appointment blank now has a To field with their names filled in.

7. If this is an online meeting, click the checkbox that now appears labeled This is an online meeting using, and choose the online meeting software you'll be using from the drop-down list (Microsoft NetMeeting, Windows Media Services, or Microsoft Exchange Conferencing are your options). Depending on which software you're using, you'll see different blanks for additional information (such as Directory Server for NetMeeting or Event Address for Windows Media Services) below.

8. Click the Send button to issue the appointment notification.

Importing Appointments and Events

If you have scheduling data such as appointments in another program, Outlook can convert it to its own format. You can import calendar data in either the iCalendar format (designed to enable people using not just different scheduling programs but even different types of computers — iCalendar works with Macintosh systems, too — to exchange calendar information) or vCalendar format (designed for the exchange of calendar data among people using different scheduling applications but not different types of computers), or from other scheduling programs such as Lotus Organizer or Schedule+. To do so, follow these steps:

1. While in Calendar view, select File ⇨ Import and Export from the menu.

2. In the Import and Export Wizard, select the action you wish to take.

3. Click the Next button.

4. If you chose to import an iCalendar or vCalendar file, you will be taken to a standard file Open dialog box. Select the desired file and click the Open button (or double-click the file).

5. If you chose to import from another program or file, you'll see the Import a File dialog box. Select the file type and options you want.

6. Click the Next button.

7. Click the Browse button to select the file. You will be taken to a standard file Open dialog box. Select the desired file and click the Open button.

8. Select the duplicate handling option you desire. Your options are to allow duplicate items to overwrite current ones, to allow duplicates to coexist, or to not import duplicates.

9. Click the Next button.

10. Make sure that Calendar is selected as the destination folder.

11. Click the Next button.

12. The final screen of the Import and Export Wizard shows the file you're importing; click Finish to end the importing process.

Sending Calendar Information to Other Users

Other users on your network can view your calendar data (at least the data you haven't marked as private), but you may want to send information to others who are not on your network. In that case, you can simply e-mail them the appointment. If they're using Outlook, you can just attach the appointment, but if they're not, you'll need to convert it to iCalendar format. Fortunately, Outlook takes care of that little detail for you, and it's simply a matter of making an alternate menu selection. To send calendar data to others, follow these steps:

1. If you are looking at the appointment listing on the main Calendar screen, click on the appointment you want to send. If you're looking at the appointment form itself, the appointment is already selected and you don't need to do anything special.

2. Select Actions ➪ Forward (to send to another Outlook user) or Actions ➪ Forward as iCalendar.

3. An e-mail message will be created (see Figure 25-9) with the calendar data included as a file attachment, which appears in the Attach field. If it's in Outlook format, it will just list the name of the appointment. If it's in iCalendar format,.ics will be appended to the name.

4. Click the To button to select additional recipients from your Contacts listings, or type an e-mail address if they're not among your contacts (or they're people you e-mail so often that you can just start typing in their names and Outlook autocompletes them for you). If desired, do the same with the Cc field.

5. Type a message in the text area.

6. Click the Send button.

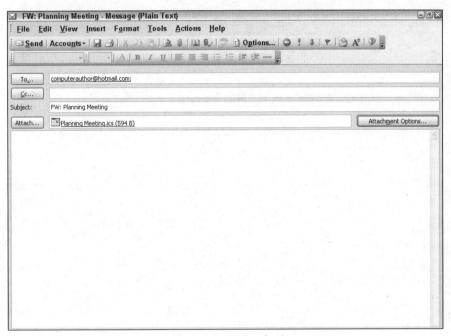

Figure 25-9: Forwarding calendar data in iCalendar format

Summary

Outlook can look after your time as well as your messages. Its numerous features enable you to easily take control of many day-to-day tasks, including the following:

✦ Outlook Today gives you a quick handle on your day by showing you the appointments and tasks you need to deal with and how much e-mail you have to deal with — all in one place.

✦ You can customize Outlook Today in various ways and designate it as your default opening screen in Outlook.

✦ Tasks can be set up for yourself or for assignment to other people, and other people can assign you tasks as well.

✦ Calendar can be used to schedule appointments, keep track of events, and invite other people to meetings.

✦ You can import scheduling data into Calendar from other scheduling programs.

✦ You can send information from Calendar to other Outlook users and to users of scheduling programs that accept the iCalendar format.

✦   ✦   ✦

Using PowerPoint

Beginning a Presentation

PowerPoint is probably the most popular example of what's known as *presentation software*. It could just as easily be called communications software (if that wouldn't get it confused with Outlook), because the goal of a presentation is the effective communication of ideas. PowerPoint lets you present your ideas clearly and concisely, augmented by pictures, sound, and even video. This chapter describes some of the basic tools PowerPoint provides for the construction of a presentation and suggests some things to keep in mind as you begin; in later chapters in this part of the book, you'll learn to work with the various elements of a presentation in more detail.

Note   Throughout the next few chapters, keep in mind PowerPoint terminology. A PowerPoint document is referred to as a *presentation*. A PowerPoint *slide show* is the display of a presentation's slides one by one, unencumbered by the toolbars, menus, etc., used to create them.

Planning Great Presentations

Before you barrel full-throttle into the creation of your presentation, take a little time to plan. Here are some things to consider:

✦ **Your message.** Remember that your goal is to communicate. Mentally summarize the core of your message and carefully muster the facts you intend to use to support that message. Give some thought to exactly what text, images, and sounds will most effectively communicate your message.

✦ **Your audience.** The most effective presentation is one tailored to the people who are receiving it. If you're giving a technical presentation to a group of engineers, your presentation will probably look a lot different from one you might present on the same topic to a group of salespeople in the first morning session of a convention that featured an open-bar reception the night before.

✦ **Your medium.** PowerPoint presentations are not necessarily presented on a computer; your PowerPoint slides may have been converted into overhead-projector transparencies or even a printed handout, which will make you feel pretty silly if you included music and animated transition effects with every slide. Even computer presentations can vary; a presentation displayed on a giant projection screen can obviously contain a lot more detailed information than one presented on the screen of your laptop computer.

✦ **The venue.** If you're presenting to a large audience in a large room, you should generally use larger text and images (which will limit how much you can fit onto each slide). If the room is going to be very dark, slides with light-colored backgrounds can help lighten it and provide additional ambient lighting to enable your audience to see you.

The virtues of simplicity

PowerPoint enables you to create slides with complex backgrounds, exciting graphics, background sound, animation, and even video clips. However, that doesn't mean you necessarily should use all of these! Too much clutter of this sort and your message may get lost in the confusion.

Make sure your key points are presented clearly, forcefully, and simply, and your presentation will be a success, even if you never did find a good place to insert that fabulous video clip of a dog catching a Frisbee.

Once you've thought carefully about what you want to accomplish with your presentation, you're ready to plunge into PowerPoint itself.

Working with the PowerPoint User Interface

The first thing to familiarize yourself with is the way that PowerPoint displays information. PowerPoint's View menu offers three ways to see your presentation while you edit it, plus a Slide Show view to display the slides alone:

✦ **Normal.** Divided into three resizable panes, Normal view is your main presentation editing tool. The largest pane displays a single slide and enables you to edit the slide's contents. Although all panes can be resized by clicking and dragging their borders, the narrow-by-default pane on the left shows you either a scrolling list of all your slides and their text in outline form, or thumbnail images of your slides in order, top to bottom, depending on which tab is selected: Outline or Slides. The pane at the bottom lets you type in your speaker's notes using a simple word processor.

You can edit as well as browse slide text in the outline pane—see the section "Using Outlines to Plan and Organize," later in this chapter for more details.

✦ **Slide Sorter.** This displays thumbnail miniatures of all the slides in the presentation. You can assign transition effects with the Slide Sorter toolbar (described in Chapter 30)—if you do, corresponding icons and notations appear below slides with the effects.

✦ **Notes Page.** This displays an editable print preview of your speaker's notes. PowerPoint creates a separate page of notes for each slide, with a copy of the slide as well as the note text. You can move the slide and text box around on the page, and you can add more text boxes and graphics, but you can't change the slide content in this view.

✦ **Slide Show.** The Slide Show view is crucial for testing and giving presentations, but you can't edit slides while you're showing them.

For more information on both Slide Sorter view and slide shows, see Chapter 31.

Note the three little buttons at the bottom left of the PowerPoint window (shown in Figure 26-1, just to the left of the horizontal scrollbar). Clicking these buttons gives you an alternative way to switch between Normal view and Slide Sorter view or begin a slide show from the current slide, although you don't get a button for the Notes Page.

Zooming in PowerPoint

PowerPoint lets you change the magnification at which you view your slides. Even when the entire slide fits into the window, you may want to zoom in further to see your slide in greater detail. Choose View ➪ Zoom to set the percentage of full-size at which you want to view the slide. The default setting, Fit, tells PowerPoint to adjust the zoom setting automatically to make the current slide fit the slide pane, no matter what size it is (it varies depending on which other panes are open, what size window you're running PowerPoint in, even the size and resolution of your monitor).

You can work in close at a high magnification and still keep track of what the slide looks like as a whole by selecting the Slides tab of the left viewing pane. The miniature version of the slide visible there will change as you change details in the main pane.

Choosing a Slide Layout

Whenever you choose File ➪ New in PowerPoint, or click the New button on the Standard toolbar, PowerPoint opens the New Presentation task pane, which offers you four ways to begin a presentation: Blank presentation, From design template, From AutoContent wizard, and From existing presentation (see Figure 26-1). We'll look at starting a Blank presentation in this chapter; the other options are covered in later chapters.

For more information on PowerPoint design templates and the AutoContent Wizard, see Chapter 28.

Using Slide Layout

Once you've clicked the Blank presentation link in the New Presentation task pane, PowerPoint opens the Slide Layout task pane (Figure 26-2), which offers you a number of slide layouts you can apply, divided into Text Layouts, Content Layouts, Text and Content Layouts, and Other Layouts. All of these are pre-designed slides whose placeholder contents you can replace with your own (except, obviously, for the Blank Slide Layout, the first one in the Content Layouts section, which is the slide to choose if you want to create a slide entirely from scratch).

The word "Content" in PowerPoint's Slide Layout task pane refers to anything that's not text: tables, charts, clip art, pictures, diagrams, organization charts, or media clips.

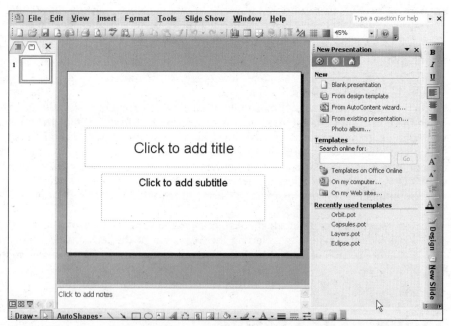

Figure 26-1: PowerPoint offers you several ways to begin a new presentation.

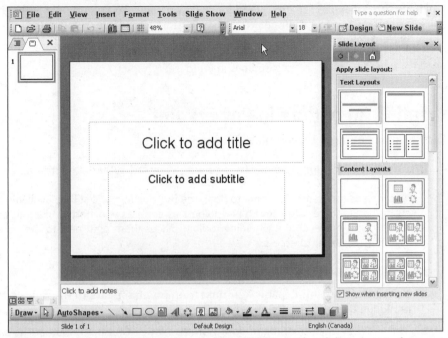

Figure 26-2: Choose the layout for your first slide from the Slide Layout task pane.

The task pane shows you thumbnail-sized previews of each slide layout to help you make your selection. Hovering your cursor over one of these previews generates a ScreenTip that gives you the layout's title and describes exactly what it's designed for — for example, Title Slide; Title, 2 Content and Text; Title, Media Clip and Text; and so on.

Click the slide layout you want to use; the slide in the main workspace immediately changes to that layout.

Once you've chosen a slide layout for your first slide, you're on your way. Enter text, graphics, charts, and tables as you see fit; apply backgrounds, slide transitions, animation, and more, and you'll soon have a presentation you can be proud of. You'll learn how to work with all of these elements in subsequent chapters.

Using Outlines to Plan and Organize

PowerPoint's ability to turn an outline into a slide presentation makes it a powerful tool you can use to quickly create presentations that clearly communicate your ideas, because you can see those ideas, and their organization, as you work. You can swiftly reorganize a presentation by moving elements of the outline (and hence the slides that go with them).

You have three ways to create an Outline in PowerPoint. You can type it in, begin with an outline from AutoContent Wizard, or import an outline from another program, such as Microsoft Word.

For information on creating outlines in Word, see Chapter 7.

Creating an outline in PowerPoint

To type in an outline in PowerPoint:

1. Turn on the Outlining toolbar by selecting View ➪ Toolbars ➪ Outlining.

If you don't turn on the Outlining toolbar, the buttons in it will still be available to you in the Standard and Formatting toolbars as soon as you start working in the outline pane; however, the Outlining toolbar places them right next to the pane, making them easier to access.

2. Select the Outline tab in the leftmost pane of Normal view.

3. Click inside the outline pane. Your insertion point appears to the right of the small icon of a slide in the upper-left corner.

4. Type the first main heading of your outline. Notice that it appears at the same time in Slide view (see Figure 26-3).

5. Press Enter. This creates a new slide; type the second main heading of your outline.

6. Continue adding main headings until the top level of your outline is complete.

Adding subheads

To add subheads, type the text for the subheads underneath the main head, pressing Enter after each subhead. Don't worry about the fact that this creates a lot of new slides.

Once the subheads are typed, select them, and then click the Demote button on the Outlining toolbar. This turns them into subheads on the same slide as the main head above them (see Figure 26-4). You could select one or more and click Demote again to create sub-subheads; you can also turn a subhead back into a slide title (creating a new slide in the process) by selecting it and clicking the Promote button on the Outlining toolbar.

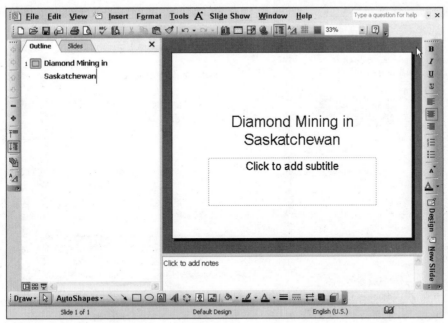

Figure 26-3: The first main heading of your outline also appears as the heading of the first slide in Slide view. Note the Outlining toolbar, visible to the left of the outline pane.

Importing an outline

To import an outline created in another program, such as Microsoft Word, first make sure the outline you want to import uses heading styles. PowerPoint looks for these styles when deciding which parts of the outline are main heads and which are subheads or body text. To import an outline:

1. Choose File ➪ Open.

2. In the Files of Type box in the Open dialog box, choose All Outlines.

3. Select the outline you want to import and click Open. The imported outline appears in the outline pane in PowerPoint; each major heading appears as an individual slide title, and each subheading appears as bulleted text on the slide (see Figure 26-5).

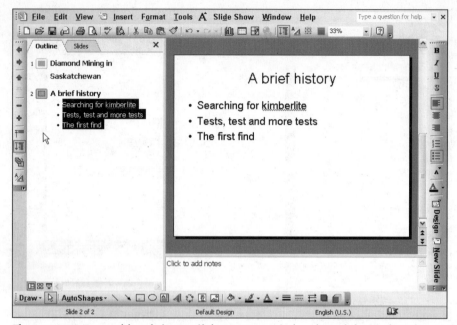

Figure 26-4: Type subheads just as if they were main heads and then select them and click Demote to create slides like this.

Tip

You can turn a Word outline (or any other Word document) into a PowerPoint presentation very easily. Open the document in Word and choose File ⇨ Send To ⇨ Microsoft PowerPoint. Each paragraph using the Heading 1 style becomes the title of a new slide, each paragraph using the Heading 2 style becomes the first level of text, and so on. Anything that uses the Normal style will not transfer to PowerPoint.

Cross-Reference

For more information on using styles in Word, see Chapter 8.

Reorganizing an outline

You can also easily reorganize your presentation using the Outline tools.

Rearranging slides

In the presentation shown in Figure 26-6, a slide entitled "West Store" appears after "East Store." To move the "West Store" slide in front of "East Store," click on the "West Store" slide icon and drag it above the "East Store" slide icon. A horizontal line appears within the outline to show you exactly where you're about to move the slide.

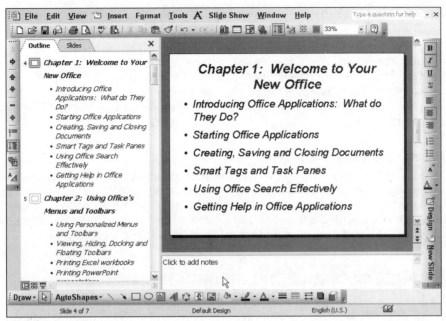

Figure 26-5: Here's what a portion of the outline for this book looks like when imported into PowerPoint.

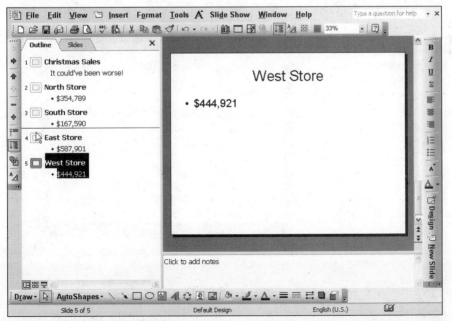

Figure 26-6: You can move slides and text around with ease in PowerPoint's outline pane by highlighting and dragging.

Rearranging text

To rearrange items that are close to one another, you can also use the Move Up and Move Down arrows on the Outlining toolbar. Clicking these arrows moves selected text up or down one line in the outline. If, for example, in Figure 26-6, I were to click on West Store and then click Move Down, the West Store heading would move under its own sales figures. That would demote it and remove its slide; instead, both the West Store sales figure and its heading would become subheads of Slide 4, East Store.

Hiding subheads and text

To get a better idea of the "big picture" of your presentation's organization structure, you sometimes need to hide subheads and body text in the outline. Use the Collapse and Expand buttons to hide everything except the slide titles for the selected text; use the Collapse All and Expand All buttons to hide everything except the slide titles in the entire outline (see Figure 26-7).

Formatting text within an outline

By default, your outline appears in a simple, sans serif screen font. However, by clicking the Show Formatting button at the bottom of the Outlining toolbar, you can see how the slide titles and body text of your slides are formatted (see Figure 26-8).

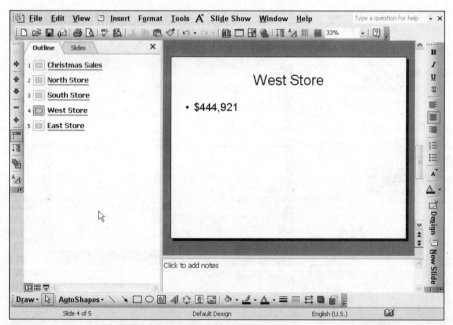

Figure 26-7: Collapse All hides everything in your outline but the slide titles, which makes it much easier to see the overall organization of your presentation and move slides around within it.

Whether Show Formatting is on or off, you can format text in Outline view just as you would on the slide itself, choosing the font, size, and style.

Note Even with Show Formatting on, changes to the font color show up only in the Slide pane, not in the outline pane, where text is always black.

Cross-Reference For more information on working with text in PowerPoint, see Chapter 27.

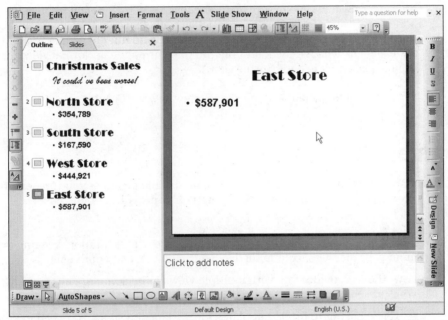

Figure 26-8: The Show Formatting command makes it easy to see how text is formatted throughout your presentation.

Navigating Through a Presentation

You have several ways to move from slide to slide in a presentation in Normal view. You can also use Slide Sorter view to easily find your way around. Here are your options:

✦ One way to navigate in Normal view is to use the outline pane. Find the title of the slide you want to see and click anywhere within the title or any of the sub-heads that appear on that slide. The slide will automatically appear in the Slide View pane.

✦ You can also use the scrollbars to the right of the Slide View pane. Scrolling down will take you to each slide in turn; they're arranged in one long vertical column. You can also click the Next Slide and Previous Slide buttons at the bottom of the scrollbar to jump quickly, one slide at a time, up and down in the presentation.

Tip   If you're a keyboard fan, note that Page Up and Page Down will move you through the slides one by one. Home will take you to the first slide in the presentation, and End will take you to the last one.

✦ Slide Sorter view shows you thumbnail versions of all your slides at once (or as many as will fit on one screen). To access Slide Sorter view, choose View ⇨ Slide Sorter. Slide Sorter view is particularly useful when you're fine-tuning your slide show, because it enables you to set a number of properties for each slide and easily move them around. (To open any slide in Normal view, just double-click on it in Slide Sorter view.)

Cross-Reference   For detailed information on using Slide Sorter view, see Chapter 31.

Summary

This chapter provided some tips to keep in mind while planning your presentation and introduced some of the basic tools PowerPoint provides. Points covered included:

✦ Before you begin, think long and hard about your presentation, keeping in mind your message, your audience, your medium, and your venue.

✦ PowerPoint provides you with multiple views to help you organize and design your presentation.

✦ Use Slide Layout to insert templates for the kinds of slides you need in your presentation, then just fill in the placeholders.

✦ Outlines are a powerful tool for quickly building a presentation that sets out your ideas clearly and logically. You can easily rearrange slides using Outline view; promote points to main heads (creating new slides) or demote main heads to subheads (combining slides) and even format text.

✦ PowerPoint offers several different ways to navigate through your presentation; choose the one that works best for you.

✦   ✦   ✦

Entering and Formatting Text

Many people think of presentations in terms of their visual impact, and certainly that's important, but at the heart of most presentations is text. Remember that the goal of a presentation is to communicate, and our most basic communication tools are words. Fortunately, PowerPoint makes it easy to enter words, edit words, and (not to leave visual impact entirely out of the picture) make them look great in the bargain!

Entering and Editing Text

As described in Chapter 26, one way to enter text in PowerPoint is in the outline pane of Normal view. You can also enter text in the slide pane by choosing a slide layout that includes text or drawing a text box in an existing slide. Once text is entered, you can edit it just as you would in Word. If you're editing in the slide pane, clicking on any text and then clicking escape will select the entire text box; if you're editing in the outline pane, just place your insertion point where you want to make changes.

Entering text in the outline pane

As described in Chapter 26, text you type into the outline is automatically added to the slides in the presentation. By high-lighting text and clicking the Demote button on the Outlining toolbar, you can create subheadings in the outline. These will appear on the slide as bulleted lists underneath the slide titles.

Cross-Reference   For more information on creating presentations using out-lines, see Chapter 26.

Entering text in the slide pane

As already mentioned, you have two ways to enter text in the slide pane: Choose a slide layout that includes text, or draw a text box in an existing slide.

Using Slide Layout

To enter text using Slide Layout:

1. Open the Slide Layout task pane. It opens automatically when you choose File ⇨ New and select Blank presentation from the New Presentation task pane; it also opens when you insert a new slide into a presentation by clicking the New Slide button on the menu bar. You can open it at any time by choosing Format ⇨ Slide Layout or by right-clicking on an existing slide and choosing Slide Layout from the shortcut menu.

2. Choose a slide layout that includes text and click on it. This creates a new slide with placeholders where the text is to appear (see Figure 27-1).

3. Click anywhere inside one of these placeholders. The instruction to "Click to add (title, subtitle, text, etc.)" disappears and is replaced with a regular PowerPoint text box into which you can type your text (see Figure 27-2).

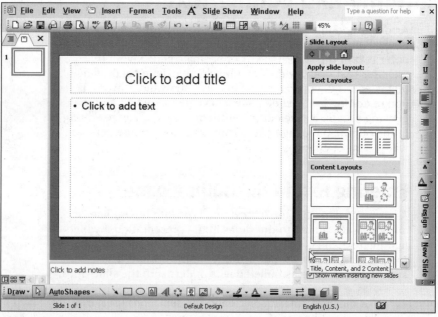

Figure 27-1: Slide Layout inserts placeholders where your text will appear.

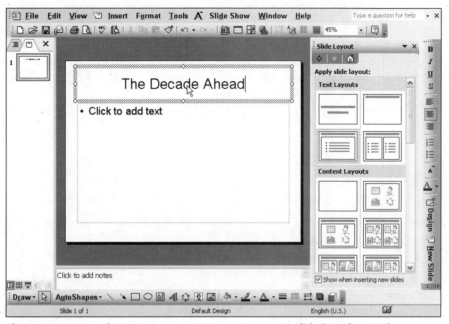

Figure 27-2: Type the text you want to appear on your slide into the text boxes created by Slide Layout.

4. When you're done entering text, click anywhere outside the text box to deselect it.

Drawing a text box

Follow these steps to add text to any slide, whether you're building it from scratch or you created it with Slide Layout:

1. Choose Insert ➪ Text Box. Your mouse pointer changes to what looks (to me, anyway) like a tiny stick drawing of a sword: a long vertical line with a short horizontal line crossing it near the base.

2. Place the pointer wherever you want the insertion point of your new text box to appear, and click once. A small text box will appear (see Figure 27-3).

3. Type your text.

4. Again, when you're done typing your text, click anywhere outside the text box to deselect it.

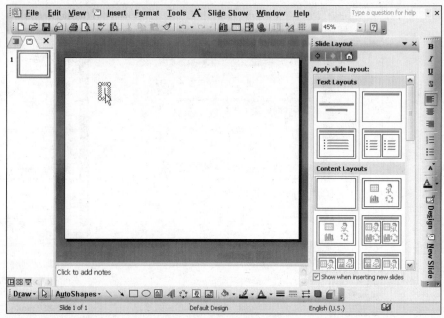

Figure 27-3: When you first create a text box, it's not very prepossessing!

Note   You can draw a text box larger than the one shown in Figure 27-3 by clicking, holding, and dragging your mouse pointer after choosing Insert ⇨ Text Box. This can help you visualize where your text will appear, but it's not necessary; the text box will automatically expand to accommodate any text you type into it.

Editing text

Once text is entered, you can edit it just as you would in Word. If you're editing in the slide pane, clicking on any text will automatically select the text box that contains it and place your cursor where you clicked; if you're editing in the outline pane, just place your insertion point where you want to make changes. You can perform any of the following:

✦ **Insert new text.** Place your insertion point where you want to add new text, and then type it in. The existing text will move out of the way.

✦ **Delete one character at a time.** Place your insertion point to the left of the first character you want to delete and press Delete. Each time you press Delete, another character to the right of the insertion point will be deleted. (To delete one character at a time to the left of the insertion point, press Backspace instead.)

✦ **Delete several words at once.** Highlight the text you want to delete and press Delete.

✦ **Cut text.** This removes text from its current location but saves a copy to the clipboard. Highlight the text you want to cut, and then choose Edit Í Cut or press Ctrl+X.

✦ **Copy text to the clipboard.** Highlight the text you want to copy, and then choose Edit Í Copy or press Ctrl+C.

✦ **Paste text from the clipboard into a new location.** Place your insertion point where you want the text to appear or create a new text box for it, and then choose Edit Í Paste or press Ctrl+V. The text, complete with formatting, will appear.

✦ **Replace existing text.** Highlight the text you want to replace and either type or paste in the new text. The existing text is automatically deleted.

Tip   Double-clicking inside a word selects the entire word; triple-clicking selects an entire paragraph (which, in PowerPoint, is typically the same as selecting an entire bulleted item). Clicking inside a textbox and then pressing Ctrl+A will select all the text in the textbox. You can also click and drag, of course, to highlight however much text you want.

Tip   If you want to move text from slide to slide, it's generally best to work in the outline pane, where you can see the contents of several slides at once and easily cut and paste (or drag and drop) among them. If, however, you're concerned about how the text looks on a particular slide (where a line of text breaks, for instance), you'll probably want to work in the slide pane.

Importing Text from Other Applications

Sometimes the text you want in your presentation already exists elsewhere on your computer. You have several ways to import this text.

Copying and pasting

Probably the easiest way to place this text into your PowerPoint presentation is to open the file in its originating program, copy it to the clipboard, and then open your PowerPoint presentation and simply paste the text wherever it's supposed to appear. Of course, you'll probably then have to reformat it to suit the presentation.

Importing directly to PowerPoint

If you prefer, you can import a word processing file directly into PowerPoint. To do so:

1. Choose Insert ⇨ Object.

2. In the Insert Object dialog box, select the Create from file radio button (see Figure 27-4).

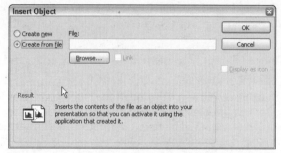

Figure 27-4: Insert existing text into your PowerPoint presentation using the Insert Object dialog box.

3. Use the Browse button to locate and select the file you want to insert.

4. Click OK.

The file appears on the current slide (see Figure 27-5).

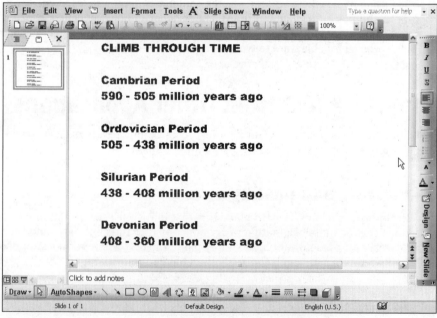

Figure 27-5: This PowerPoint text started life as a Word document.

Editing imported text

You can't edit imported text as you would text you typed into a regular PowerPoint text box. If you single-click on it, you get handles, which you can use to change its size or shape, and you can drag it around on the slide, but you can't change the contents. That's because it's really an embedded object. Because it's still in its original file format, you have to access the controls of the application in which it was created in order to edit it.

To do so, double-click on it. This opens a miniature window of the program in which it was created (in this case, Word). Now you can edit it using Word's controls. When you're done, click anywhere outside the object.

Cross-Reference   For detailed information about working with linked and embedded objects, see Chapter 42.

Formatting Text

You can format text in either the slide pane or the outline pane, although if you want to format text in the outline pane, it's a good idea to click Show Formatting on the Outlining toolbar (the bottom-most button). With Show Formatting selected, the text in the outline pane appears as it will on the finished slide, except it will always appear in black regardless of any other color you've assigned it.

To format text, of course, you must first highlight it, as in any other application. Then click the appropriate formatting button on the Formatting toolbar (which you can see running down the right side of the PowerPoint window in Figure 27-5 but which is undocked in Figure 27-6 so you can see the buttons on it more easily). The following sections cover each formatting option.

Figure 27-6: PowerPoint's Formatting toolbar contains all the commands you need to give the text on your slides the appearance you choose.

Tip   If you don't see some of the buttons shown in Figure 27-6 on your Formatting toolbar while it's docked in its usual position at the right of the PowerPoint window, click the Toolbar Options button (the downward-pointing arrow) at the bottom of the toolbar to see the rest. If you still don't see all the buttons, choose Add or Remove Buttons ➪ Formatting. I've added every button available to the toolbar shown in Figure 27-6.

Font and size

Two menus and two buttons on the Formatting toolbar determine the font and size used for your text:

✦ **Font.** Use this list box to choose the typeface you want to apply to your text. The names of the fonts are shown in the fonts themselves to make this selection easier.

✦ **Font Size.** Choose an appropriate size from this list box. Sizes are given in points, which are 1/72 of an inch. In other words, 72-point text is one inch high; 36-point text is half an inch high, and so on. You can apply a size that doesn't appear in the list by typing it directly into the Font Size list box.

Font sizes apply to printed copy; the size of type displayed on a screen may vary quite a bit, depending on the monitor being used.

✦ **Increase Font Size.** This button increases the size of selected text to the next largest size in the Font Size list box.

✦ **Decrease Font Size.** This button decreases the size of selected text to the next smallest size in the Font Size list box.

Style

Four buttons change the style of the text:

✦ **Bold.** This button makes text bold.

✦ **Italic.** This button italicizes text.

✦ **Underline.** This button underlines text.

✦ **Text Shadow.** This button adds a shadow slightly below and to the right of the text (see Figure 27-7). It makes it look as if the text is floating slightly above the surface of the slide. The shadow color is automatically determined by the slide background color.

Alignment

PowerPoint also provides three alignment buttons; unlike Word, it doesn't provide a button for justifying text (you have to use the Format menu for that — more on that in the section "The Format menu," later in this chapter), probably because PowerPoint slides generally contain too little text for justification to very often be either useful or effective.

✦ **Align Left.** This button aligns text flush against the left side of the text box.

✦ **Center**. This button centers text within the text box.

✦ **Align Right.** This button aligns text flush against the right side of the text box.

Text in PowerPoint is aligned relative to the text box that contains it, not to the outside edges of the slide on which it appears, which means your text can be centered within its text box but be off-center on the slide, if the text box itself is off-center.

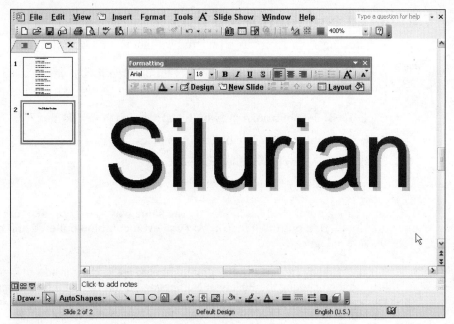

Figure 27-7: In addition to Bold, Italic, and Underline, PowerPoint adds a Shadow button to the mix, which adds a shadow to the text, as shown here.

Promoting and demoting heads

Many slides are in point form, with a slide title followed by several subheads, typically bulleted. The easiest way to edit these kinds of slides and adjust the size of text is in the outline pane.

Cross-Reference For more information on editing slides in the outline pane, see Chapter 26.

However, the slide pane has two commands that you may choose to use instead:

✦ **Decrease Indent.** This button moves text closer to the left side of the text box and changes its formatting to that of the next higher level of PowerPoint's hierarchy of subheads (generally, it gets bigger, and the bullet changes shape). If the text is already a first-level subhead, this button is not available.

✦ **Increase Indent.** This button moves text farther to the right and demotes it to the next lower level of the PowerPoint subhead hierarchy (generally, it gets smaller and the bullet changes shape). If it is a slide title, it gets demoted to a bulleted subhead.

Bulleted and numbered lists

Use the following steps to create a bulleted list inside a PowerPoint text box.

Note Some slide layouts include placeholders for bulleted lists. If you're using one of those, bullets will appear automatically and you can ignore Step 1 below.

1. Click the Bullets button. A gray bullet appears in your text box.

2. Type the first list item. The bullet turns black.

3. Press Enter. A new gray bullet appears.

4. Continue until the list is complete.

You can create a numbered list in exactly the same way — except, of course, you click the Numbering button in Step 1. You can even combine bulleted and numbered lists (see Figure 27-8).

Tip If you've already created a bulleted or numbered list, clicking inside an item in the list and then clicking the Bullets or Numbering button has the effect of removing the bullet or numbering from the item you clicked on. You can also turn a bulleted list into a numbered list, or vice versa, by selecting the whole list and clicking either the Numbering or Bullets button.

Spacing

You can automatically increase or decrease the spacing between paragraphs (which PowerPoint, just like Word, defines as any text you enter prior to pressing Enter; on most PowerPoint slides, paragraph spacing effectively means the spacing between bulleted subheads) a little bit at a time by highlighting the paragraphs (or just clicking inside one of them if there are only two) and then clicking Increase Paragraph Spacing or Decrease Paragraph Spacing.

Note By default, these commands are among those not on the toolbar. They can be added by clicking Toolbar Options at the bottom of the normally docked Formatting toolbar and then selecting Add or Remove Buttons. Be careful when using them. It's generally better to use the line spacing button to increase or decrease the spacing *between* the paragraphs, as opposed to using the Increase or Decrease Paragraph Spacing buttons, which increase the spacing of the paragraph itself. This is especially true if your bulleted text spans more than one line on each bullet point.

In addition, you will probably never want to go below .75 line spacing, as anything lower tends to cut off the ascenders and descenders of your text.

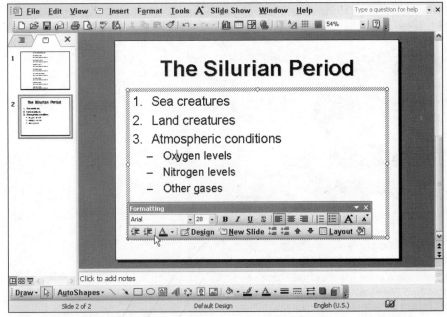

Figure 27-8: Bulleted and numbered lists are easy to create and combine in PowerPoint to help you present your ideas more clearly.

Color

You can change the color of any text by highlighting it and then clicking the Font Color button. This applies the color currently shown on the button to the high-lighted text. Clicking the down arrow next to the button opens a small graphical menu showing standard colors and recently used colors. Clicking More Colors from that menu opens palettes from which you can choose any color your computer can display to apply to your text (see Figure 27-9).

Other buttons on the toolbar

The Formatting toolbar also includes buttons labeled Design, New Slide, Layout, and Background. Design opens the Slide Design task pane. New Slide inserts a new slide and opens the Slide Layout task pane, Move Up and Move Down can be used to move items in a list up or down one spot at a time, and Layout opens the Slide Layout task pane without creating a new slide. Background enables you to select a background fill for the slide.

Cross-Reference For more information on using design templates and backgrounds, see Chapters 28 and 29.

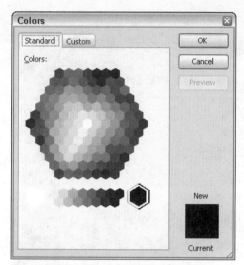

Figure 27-9: Use the Colors dialog box to choose a color for your text — from a standard palette of colors like this one, or a custom palette that makes available all the colors your computer can display.

The Format menu

Some additional formatting options for text are available by choosing the Format menu. If the Formatting toolbar buttons don't give you enough control over the way your text looks, the options on the Format menu may.

✦ **Font.** The Font dialog box (see Figure 27-10) puts all the controls for Font, Style, Size, Effects, and Color in one location. It also adds a new effect, Emboss, which makes letters look as if they protrude slightly from the surface of the slide and lets you superscript or subscript text and even fine-tune the degree to which your superscript or subscript is offset. Click Preview to see what the selections you make look like applied to the selected text, without closing the dialog box. You can add the Emboss and Superscript and Subscript (and many other) icons to your toolbar by going to Tools ⇨ Customize and looking in the Format category.

✦ **Bullets and Numbering.** The Bullets and Numbering dialog box (see Figure 27-11) lets you fine-tune the look of bulleted and numbered lists. You can select from the bullets offered or use different characters (by clicking Customize) or picture bullets (by clicking Picture) and set their size relative to the text and their color. Click the Numbered tab to choose from several types of numerals for numbered lists and set the size, color, and starting number.

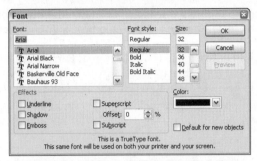

Figure 27-10: The Font dialog box includes many commands you can find on the Formatting toolbar, plus a couple of extra ones, such as the controls for subscripts and superscripts that let you set the exact location of their baselines relative to surrounding text.

✦ **Alignment.** Choose Alignment to apply left and right alignment to text or to center it. From this menu, you can also justify text, an option which, as I noted earlier, is not available from the Formatting toolbar unless you customize it using Tools ➪ Customize.

✦ **Line Spacing.** Specify the spacing between lines and before and after paragraphs using this dialog box (see Figure 27-12). You can choose to measure line spacing in either lines (single, double, and so on) or points. This give you much finer control over spacing than you get from the Paragraph Spacing buttons on the Formatting toolbar.

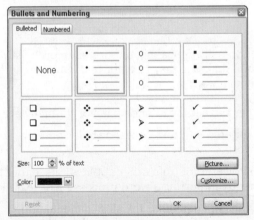

Figure 27-11: Fine-tune bulleted and numbered lists in this dialog box.

✦ **Change Case.** Case refers to the way words are capitalized. PowerPoint offers you several options in the little Change Case dialog box: sentence case (First letter of first word capitalized), lowercase (no letters capitalized), uppercase (ALL LETTERS CAPITALIZED), title case (First Letter Of Each Word Capitalized), and toggle case (reverses all letters from the way they were initially typed: cAPITAL lETTERS bECOME lOWERCASE lETTERS aND vICE vERSA).

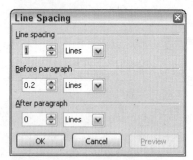

Figure 27-12: Specify line and paragraph spacing with these controls.

✦ **Replace Fonts.** This powerful tool lets you change all instances of a particular font within your presentation to a different font. Just select the font you want to change in the top list box and the font you want to change it to in the bottom list box, and then click Replace.

Summary

Good presentations have to be visually appealing, but first and foremost they have to contain good text. PowerPoint makes it easy to enter text, edit it to perfection, and then format it just the way you want it.

✦ You can enter text in either the outline or slide pane of Normal view.

✦ In the slide pane, text is entered into text boxes; once it's entered, you can edit it just as you do in Word.

✦ You can import text into PowerPoint from other applications, either by copying and pasting or by directly importing a word processing or text file.

✦ You can format text in either the outline or the slide pane.

✦ The Format toolbar provides buttons for the most commonly used formatting commands; the Format menu provides additional commands.

✦   ✦   ✦

Using Templates and Wizards

Not everyone has the knack, the knowledge, or (especially) the time to design a presentation entirely from scratch. Sometimes you just want to enter your information and let PowerPoint do all the work of making it look great. PowerPoint is more than equal to the task, with a number of tools to get your presentation up and running as quickly as possible.

Using the AutoContent Wizard

The AutoContent Wizard gets you going quickly by providing you with both a design and suggested content for a variety of common presentation types.

Whenever you choose File ➪ New, you'll see From AutoContent wizard as one of the options in the New Presentation task pane (see Figure 28-1). Just click it to start the wizard.

From the introductory screen, click Next to open the first of three screens in which you provide AutoContent Wizard with the information it needs to help you. The three screens are as follows:

✦ **Presentation type.** Click All (see Figure 28-2) to see all the presentation types the AutoContent Wizard can help you create (everything from Recommending a Strategy to a Group Home Page to a Project Post-Mortem), or click General, Corporate, Projects, or Sales/Marketing to see just the presentations in those areas. Choose the presentation type you want and click Next.

Tip   You can add your own templates to the AutoContent Wizard in any of the categories by clicking the Add button; you can remove any template you don't want in the AutoContent Wizard by highlighting it and clicking Remove.

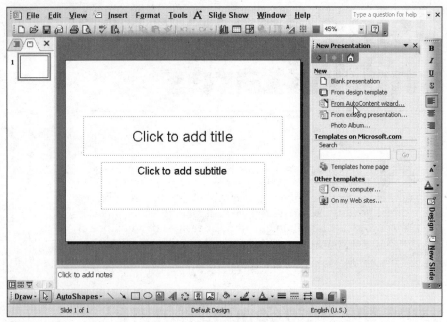

Figure 28-1: The AutoContent Wizard is ready to help you every time you open PowerPoint or start a new PowerPoint presentation: Just click.

Figure 28-2: What sort of presentation would you like to create? The AutoContent Wizard can help you with the most common types.

✦ **Presentation style.** Presentations can be designed to be displayed on a computer screen, on the Web, as black-and-white overheads, as color overheads, or as 35mm slides. Choose the type of output you're planning to use, and then click Next. (You can always make changes to the type of output later on if your plans change.)

✦ **Presentation options.** In the third and final screen, you enter a title for your presentation and any text you'd like to appear as a footer on each slide. You can also specify whether you want the date the slide was last updated and the slide number to appear in the footer.

Once you've made all these choices, click Finish. The AutoContent Wizard creates a presentation of the type you've specified with slides that are typical of that kind of presentation (see Figure 28-3). Each slide contains suggestions as to what sort of content should appear there. You can use or ignore those suggestions as you wish. At this point, the presentation is entirely yours to edit — but you're already way ahead of where you would be if you'd started from scratch.

Figure 28-3: The AutoContent Wizard adds suggested content to all the slides in the presentations it creates to help you with the process of creating your own presentation.

Using the Slide Layout Task Pane

As noted in Chapter 27, whenever you start a new presentation or insert a new slide, the Slide Layout task pane provides you with a number of slide layouts from which to choose (see Figure 28-4). When you choose one, the new slide that appears has placeholders in it, into which you can insert your own content.

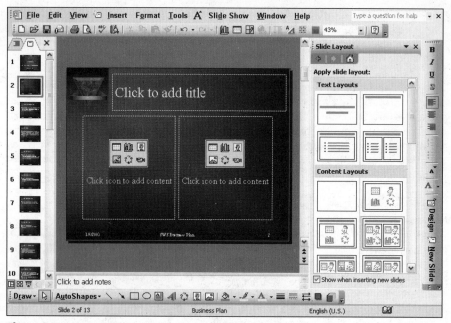

Figure 28-4: PowerPoint provides you with a wide selection of pre-designed slide layouts, into which you can insert your own content.

Exploring the available layouts

The available slide layouts are divided into four categories:

✦ **Text Layouts** contain only text. Options include a title slide, a blank slide with a title across the top, and slides that contain bulleted lists.

✦ **Content Layouts** contain almost everything but text. When you choose a content layout, you'll see one or more little boxes on the slide, each of which contains six options: Insert Table, Insert Chart, Insert Clip Art, Insert Picture, Insert Diagram or Organization Chart, and Insert Media Clip. Click the button within the Content box that represents the type of content you want to insert. Content Layouts arrange this content in a variety of ways on the slide. Some slides include titles.

✦ **Text and Content Layouts** combine titles, bulleted lists, and content.

✦ **Other Layouts** are a hodgepodge of layouts that contain specific types of content — for instance, a bulleted list and clip art, or a chart and a bulleted list, or a title and a chart, or a title and a diagram or organization chart.

Changing an existing slide

These slide layouts are good for more than just inserting new slides; you can also use them to change the layout of existing slides. To do so, bring up the slide you want to change in Normal view, and then choose Format ⇨ Slide Layout (or right-click and choose Slide Layout from the shortcut menu). This opens the Slide Layout task pane; click on the new layout you want to apply to the existing slide and it is automatically applied.

Figure 28-5 shows a slide created using the Title and Text layout from the Text Layouts section of the Slide Layout task pane, while Figure 28-6 shows the same slide with the Title, Text, and Content layout from the Text and Content Layouts section of the Slide Layout task pane applied (note the empty Content box waiting for the appropriate content to be added).

You can experiment with as many different slide layouts as you like without losing any of the text you've already entered.

If you choose a slide layout that doesn't contain space for text you've already entered, PowerPoint will simply drop a text box containing your text over the top of what's in the slide layout (see Figure 28-7), and you'll have to do some juggling to make it all fit.

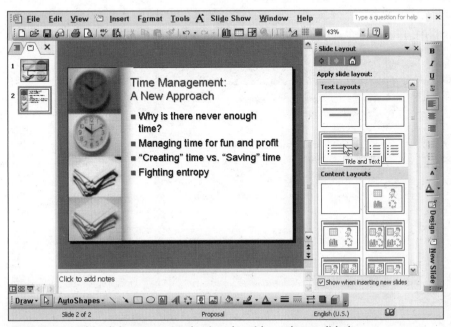

Figure 28-5: This slide was created using the Title and Text slide layout.

Figure 28-6: This is the same slide shown in Figure 28-5, with the Title, Content, and Text layout applied.

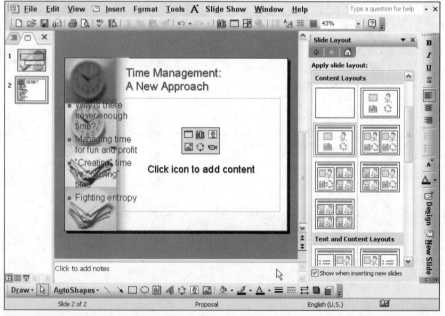

Figure 28-7: If you choose a slide layout that doesn't have a placeholder for text you've already entered, you'll end up with the text from your slide in a text box overlaying the slide's placeholders.

Using Masters

According to the Bible, no man can serve two masters, but in PowerPoint, three masters can serve you: Slide Master, Handout Master, and Notes Master can all help you maintain a consistent style throughout your presentation.

Slide Master

On the Slide Master, you can set text characteristics such as font, size, and color, plus a background color or graphic and special effects such as shadowing and bullet style, which will then be applied by default to all the slides in that presentation.

Using the Slide Master also means that if you want to make a global change—for example, to the style of all the slide titles in a presentation—you don't have to change each title on each slide: You can simply make the change on the Slide Master, and all the slide titles that use that Master will change appearance automatically.

You can also use the Slide Master to make anything you like appear on every slide in the presentation. A typical example would be the company logo. Rather than insert it as a separate picture on each slide, just insert it once on the Slide Master and it will appear on each slide automatically.

You can create more than one Slide Master in the same presentation, so you can base, for example, your introductory slides on one Slide Master, the core of your presentation on a second, and the conclusion on a third.

Opening the Slide Master

To open the Slide Master, choose View ➪ Master ➪ Slide Master (see Figure 28-8).

Formatting the Slide Master

To format the Slide Master, follow these steps:

1. Click once inside the text box containing the type of text you want to format.

2. Highlight the type of text you want to format (for example, Second level).

3. Format the text just as you would within an ordinary text box, using PowerPoint's regular formatting tools. You can change the font, style, and alignment, and add borders and a background color to the text boxes.

 Cross-Reference For more on formatting text in PowerPoint, see Chapter 27.

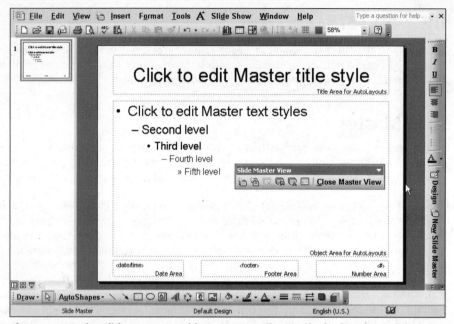

Figure 28-8: The Slide Master enables you to easily specify the layout of elements that appear on many slides — a great saving of time and effort.

4. Add any content you would like to appear on every slide: that is, a text box, a picture, a diagram, a chart, a table — even a movie or a sound. You can also change the Slide Master's background, either by choosing Format ⇨ Background or by right-clicking on the background and choosing Background from the shortcut menu.

5. To add text that will appear on every slide, insert a new text box by choosing Insert ⇨ Text Box, and then type the text you want to appear.

Note

Typing within the text placeholders that appear automatically when you view Slide Master does not produce text that appears on every slide. You use the Slide Master placeholders only to edit text styles.

6. When you're finished making changes to the Slide Master, click Close Master View on the Slide Master View toolbar.

Cross-Reference

For more information about working with graphics in PowerPoint, see Chapter 30.

Tip By default, PowerPoint automatically deletes a Slide Master when all the slides that follow it are deleted, or when another design template is applied to all the slides that follow it. The Preserve Master button on the Slide Master View toolbar prevents a Slide Master from being automatically deleted by PowerPoint in those circumstances. To ensure that your Slide Master remains available to you the next time you open the presentation you're working on, click this button.

Adding a Title Master

The Title Master is a special form of the Slide Master that applies only to the slides in your presentation that use the Title slide layout. Use it when you want your Title slides to have a different format from the other slides in your presentation.

To add a Title Master, click the Insert New Title Master button on the Slide Master View toolbar. PowerPoint creates a standard Title Master that you can then format as you like, just as you formatted the Slide Master.

Note Each Title Master is paired with the Slide Master from which it was created. These pairs are called *slide-title master pairs,* and they're displayed together in the slide pane in Normal view; use the scrollbar to move from one to the other or click on the corresponding thumbnails in the outline pane.

Tip You can apply the various design possibilities displayed by the Slide Design task pane, discussed later in this chapter, to a Slide Master as well as to individual slides.

Handout Master

The Handout Master works just like the Slide Master, except it lets you format handouts instead of slides.

Handouts can help your audience follow your presentation more easily. The handouts can include images of slides (which may be helpful if some audience members can't easily see the computer or projection screen on which you're showing your presentation, if they want to take notes, or if they want to be able to study the presentation in detail later) plus any additional information you want to supply.

To create handouts, follow these steps:

1. Call up the Handout Master by choosing View ⇨ Master ⇨ Handout Master (see Figure 28-9).

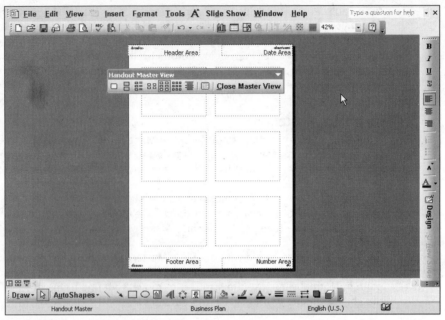

Figure 28-9: The Handout Master enables you to customize handouts just as the Slide Master enables you to customize slides.

2. When you print handouts, you can choose among several different layouts in the Print dialog box. To help you design your Handout Master, PowerPoint lets you preview the various layout options using the Handout Master View toolbar. The boxes in the main body of the Handout Master represent images of slides. Possible print layouts include one slide per page, two slides per page, three slides per page with room for text alongside each one, four slides per page, six slides per page, nine slides per page, or no slides per page — just the outline.

Cross-Reference   Printing is covered in more detail in Chapter 31.

3. Make any other changes you want to the handouts — adding text that will appear on every handout, graphics, a background, and so forth.

4. When you're satisfied with the appearance of your Handout Master, click Close Master View on the Handout Master View toolbar.

5. To print Handouts, choose File ➪ Print, and then choose Handouts from the Print what list box in the Print dialog box (see Figure 28-10). Choose the layout you want to use in the Handouts section of the dialog box and whether you want slides to be arranged so they read horizontally from left to right (so that in a four-slide arrangement, slide 1 would be in the upper-left corner,

slide 2 to the right of it, slide 3 under slide 1, and slide 4 to the right of slide 3) or vertically (slide 1 in the upper-left corner, slide 2 beneath it, slide 3 to the right of slide 1, slide 4 beneath slide 3). When you've made your selections, click OK to print.

Caution   The handout page does not automatically indicate how the slides are arranged, so consider adding a text box to the Handout Master that explains how the slides are to be read.

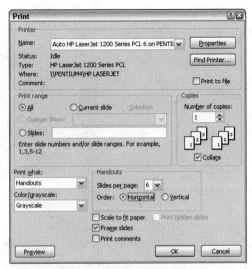

Figure 28-10: Select the layout you want to use for printing your handout in the Print dialog box.

Tip   The slide placeholders in the Handout Masters cannot be resized. If you need additional formatting capabilities for your handouts, use File ➪ Send To Microsoft Word.

Notes Master

Notes are even more useful than handouts. In fact, they can be used as handouts, especially if you want to provide additional information about individual slides. They're also useful for creating speaking notes for the presenter.

Notes pages consist of an image of an individual slide with a text area underneath. You can enter notes in Normal view in the Notes pane directly under the Slide View pane.

The Notes Master works much like the other masters we've looked at: It lets you set default formats for the text you enter into notes, relocate or change the size of the slide image that appears on each notes page, and add any other graphics, fills, or backgrounds you might want.

To customize the Notes Master, follow these steps:

1. Open the Notes Master by choosing View ⇨ Master ⇨ Notes Master (see Figure 28-11).

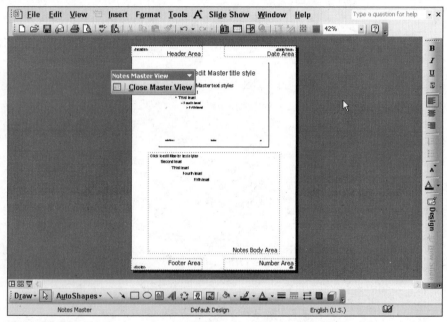

Figure 28-11: Customize your notes pages by changing the Notes Master.

2. At the top of the Notes Master is a small representation of the Slide Master. The only changes you can make to it here are to its size and position (you can change its size by clicking on it and tugging on its handles, and move it by clicking on it and then dragging it).

3. Format the text in the Notes box the way you want text to be formatted on all your notes pages. As with the Slide Master, you can format text differently depending on its level in the hierarchy — that is, whether it is a title, a subtitle, a sub-bullet, and so on.

4. Add any graphics you want to appear on all notes pages, along with any borders, fills, or backgrounds you want on all pages.

5. When you're satisfied, click Close Master View on the Notes Master View toolbar.

6. Print your notes pages by choosing File ⇨ Print and then selecting Notes Pages from the Print what drop-down list in the Print dialog box.

Using Design Templates

Design templates are preformatted master slides that PowerPoint provides to make it possible for anyone to create a good-looking presentation even if they don't know the first thing about design. The AutoContent Wizard uses these templates, but you can also access them directly.

Accessing the design templates

When you choose File ⇨ New, From Design Template is one of the options that appear in the New section of the New Presentation task pane.

Note Simply clicking the New button on the toolbar doesn't open the New Presentation task pane; for that you have to use the File ⇨ New command. Clicking New opens a blank title slide and the Slide Layout task pane.

Clicking on the From design template link opens the Slide Design task pane (see Figure 28-12), which is divided into three sections under the blanket heading Apply a design template: Used in This Presentation (this is a new presentation, so the only thing used in it is a very basic black-on-white design); Recently Used, which shows any templates you may have applied recently (and which doesn't appear if you haven't yet applied any templates); and Available for Use, which shows you most of what's available — but not all. If you scroll to the bottom, you may see another "template" labeled "Design Templates on Microsoft.com." Clicking this will prompt Office to look for additional templates on the Microsoft.com Web site, so you need an active Internet connection if you choose this option.

Tip You can also open the Slide Design task pane by clicking the Design button on the Formatting toolbar, docked by default to the right side of the PowerPoint window.

If you point at any of these designs, its name, indicative of its appearance (more or less), will pop up in a ScreenTip.

Tip Having trouble seeing what these designs really look like? Point at any one of them and you'll see a downward-pointing arrow. Click on that, and then click the option Show Large Previews, and you'll get a much better look at the various designs in the task pane.

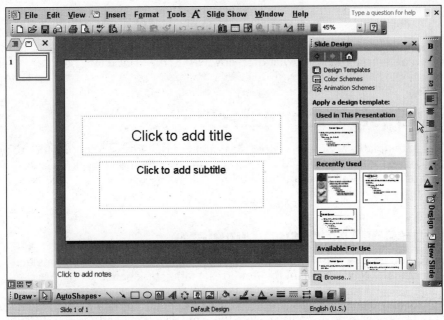

Figure 28-12: PowerPoint's design templates, available from the Slide Design task pane, can help you create a good-looking presentation without having to design every aspect of it yourself.

Choosing a slide layout

When you've found a template you'd like to work with, click on it, and the title slide that PowerPoint creates automatically whenever you start a new presentation will suddenly be transformed to match the design you chose (see Figure 28-13). All subsequent slides will use that same design unless you choose to change it.

Modifying and applying the design templates

Whenever you use a design template, what you've really done is attach a Slide Master to your presentation—which means you can modify the design template by modifying the Slide Master, as described earlier in this chapter.

You can apply any of the design templates in the Slide Design task pane by clicking on it. By default, the template is applied to all slides in the presentation; to apply a template to a single slide, point at the design, click on the downward-pointing arrow, and choose Apply to Selected Slides from the shortcut menu. Of course, if you select more than one slide in the Thumbnails task pane, the design template will be applied only to those you've selected.

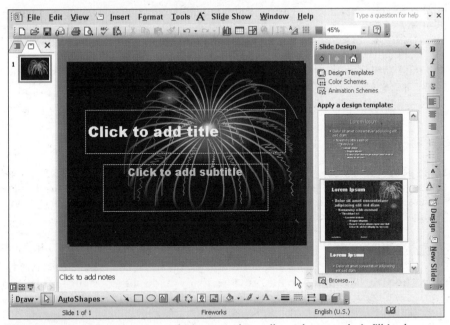

Figure 28-13: When you use a design template, all you have to do is fill in the blanks; your background and color scheme are already taken care of. (Compare this with Figure 28-12 and you'll note that I've turned on the Show Large Previews option in the task pane in this figure.)

Creating and Saving Your Own Templates

Any time you make changes to any of the masters, you're essentially creating your own template. If you create a design you really like, you'll probably want to save it as a template so you can use it in future presentations. (Of course, you'll also want to save it as a presentation so you can make immediate use of it.)

To save your current presentation as a design template, follow these steps:

1. Choose File ⇨ Save As.

2. In the Save as type list box, select Design Template.

3. Type a name for your new template in the File name field.

4. Click Save.

The template, which includes all of the masters you've formatted plus all of the slides currently in the presentation, is automatically saved in the default file folder for templates. The next time you start a presentation using a design template, or choose Format ➪ Slide Design, you can apply the template you've saved by clicking the Browse link at the bottom of the Slide Design task pane. This will open the template folder, where you should find the template you created and saved.

As noted earlier, you can also add your template to the AutoContent Wizard for easy access.

Summary

Some people really enjoy creating PowerPoint presentations from scratch, but others just want to get the job done as quickly as possible while still producing a professional-looking, aesthetically pleasing final product. PowerPoint's Design Templates and ready-made slide layouts make that possible.

✦ The AutoContent Wizard does the hard work of designing a presentation to meet your needs by asking you a few simple questions.

✦ The Slide Layout task pane provides ready-made slide designs for just about every need; all you have to do is replace the placeholders with your own content.

✦ The Slide Layout task pane can also be used to instantly redesign a slide with a single click of your mouse.

✦ Use the Slide Master to place repeating elements on all the slides in your presentation — anything from a background image to a logo to text.

✦ The Handout Master lets you determine how printed handouts made from your presentation will look.

✦ The Notes Master lets you lay out pages that include both images of your slides and any additional text you want.

✦ Design templates can also be used directly, without going through the AutoContent Wizard, to create a good-looking presentation.

✦ Any presentation you're particularly happy with can be saved as a design template, so it can form the basis of future presentations.

✦   ✦   ✦

Creating Charts and Tables

Charts and tables created in PowerPoint bring your data to life in a presentation, making it more interesting and easier to understand, replacing lists of numbers with visual representations (in the case of charts) or organizing it so that relationships among various data are more readily apparent (in the case of tables).

Exploring Chart Types

Before creating a chart, you must decide which type to use. The following list describes the basic types of charts you can create in PowerPoint, except for organization charts, which are covered in the section "Creating an Organization Chart or Diagram," later in this chapter.

- ✦ **Column charts** usually show data over time. They can be 2-D or 3-D, and the bars can be stacked or shown as a split over 100 percent. Figure 29-1 shows a column chart with the same figures charted in 2-D and 3-D.

> **Note** The small boxes to the right of the charts in Figure 29-1 are called *legends* or *keys*. These can also be placed inside the area of the chart. They help the user interpret the information in the chart. The legends in Figure 29-1 identify the colors of each of the sets of columns, although of course you can't see the colors in this book.

- ✦ **Bar charts** are horizontal column charts (or column charts are vertical bar charts — it depends on how you look at it!). They can be useful when you have many bars of one data series (a "data series" is a set of related data points; in Figure 29-1, for instance, East, West, and North are the data series). Like column charts, they can be 2-D or 3-D.

- ✦ **Line charts** show trends more clearly, as each data point is joined. A steep line indicates a big rate of change. They can be 2-D or 3-D.

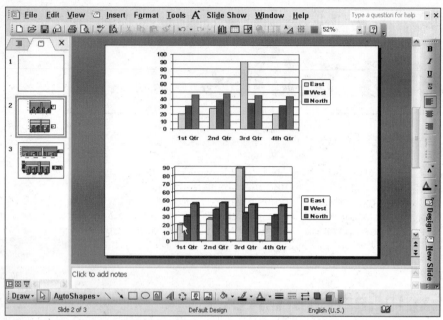

Figure 29-1: A column chart in both 2-D and 3-D

✦ **Pie charts** show how each item contributes to the whole. Often, the data is shown as percentages, to illustrate the contribution of each slice of the pie. They can be 2-D or 3-D.

✦ **XY (Scatter) charts** are used to plot pairs of values.

✦ **Area charts** are line charts with the area below the line filled. When the series are stacked, it shows how each series contributes to the total.

✦ **Doughnut charts** are pie charts with a hole in the center.

✦ **Radar charts** show each series charted from a central point, and with its own axis.

✦ **Surface charts** are 3-D charts that show ranges of figures color-coded according to value.

✦ **Bubble charts** compare three sets of values: Two are charted against the vertical and horizontal axes; the third is represented by the size of the bubble.

✦ **Stock charts** are specifically designed to show prices on the stock market. Up to five values can be shown — volume, opening price, closing price, high price, and low price.

✦ **Cylinder, Cone, and Pyramid charts** are variations of 3-D column charts that use cylinders, cones, and pyramids instead of rectangular columns.

How PowerPoint Names Its Axes

Most charts, such as column charts, have two axes. You probably learned them in school as the x and y axes, but PowerPoint prefers to use the terms *category axis* and the *value axis*, because although the x axis is usually the category axis and the y axis is usually the value axis, they can be reversed. Sometimes, in 3-D charts, there is a third axis, known as the *series axis*; in that instance, what you'd usually think of as the y axis becomes the series axis, while the z axis becomes the value axis—and the obvious opportunities for confusion there are why it's probably best to forget about x, y, and z axes in PowerPoint charts and just remember category, value, and series axes. Here's how they work:

✦ The category axis is often used to show time, such as month, quarter, or year.

✦ The value axis often shows volume, such as dollars, kilograms, or quantity.

✦ The series axis often shows separate sets of data, such as the data for different products or regions. If there is no third axis, the series are often shown by using different-colored columns next to one another.

Maybe an example will make this clearer: A 3-D chart showing how many copies of a particular book were sold each month for a year by 12 bookstores in different cities would use all three axes: The category axis would include 12 categories, one for each month; the value axis would show the number of books sold; and the series axis would show which bookstore sold them.

Creating and Editing Charts

When you create a new slide using Slide Layout, you can add a chart to any slide that contains a content placeholder (just click the Insert Chart icon inside the placeholder). Some slide layouts also contain placeholders just for charts.

You can also add a chart to any slide by choosing Insert ➪ Chart or clicking the Insert Chart tool on the Standard toolbar.

A chart in PowerPoint is really an object, which in Office parlance means that it is really being created by a separate subprogram (WordArt is another example of this kind of object). That's why when you first insert a chart, and whenever you're editing it, you'll see a special toolbar, a different menu (with new menu items such as Data and Chart), and the datasheet window. Figure 29-2 shows all of these.

Note It is very easy to click in the wrong place and move from the chart subprogram back to PowerPoint. To get back to the chart subprogram from PowerPoint, double-click the chart area on the slide.

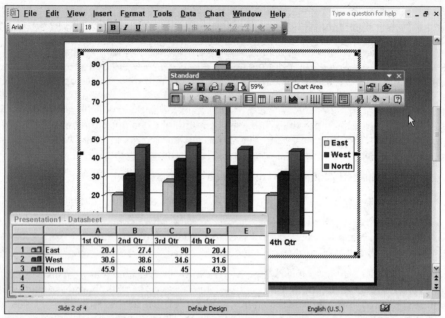

Figure 29-2: This is what you see when you insert a chart (with the exception that I've undocked the Standard toolbar so you can see it better). Note that the menu and toolbars are different from what you usually see in PowerPoint.

To complete your chart:

1. Make sure the chart is open for editing (double-click on it if it isn't), and then choose Chart ➪ Chart Type and select the type of chart you want (see Figure 29-3). (Alternatively, click on the Chart Type tool in the Standard toolbar; this opens a small shortcut menu with icons representing each of the major chart types.)

2. Enter your own data in the datasheet window to replace the sample data, using the sample data as a template. The chart changes to show your own data as soon you enter it. Here's how it works:

   • Type category labels in the top row. Type series labels in the leftmost column. To enter additional series or categories, simply type the data in the next available row or column. To delete a category or series, click on the column or row label (the letter D or number 3, for example) to highlight the column or row, and then press Delete.

   • Move around the datasheet window using the mouse or the arrow or tab keys. If the columns are too narrow, find the Column-width tool on the boundary between the column header and the next column header to the right and drag to make the column wider. Alternatively, right-click on the column header and choose Column Width. In the resulting dialog box, you can enter a specific width, choose to use the standard width, or click Best Fit to fit the datasheet's columns and rows to your data.

- When your data is in dollars, you can type the dollar sign in front of any of the numbers. PowerPoint will insert the dollar sign on the value axis automatically. For other currencies, or other types of numbers, highlight the data and choose Format ⇨ Number. Select from the extensive category lists the way you want numbers displayed.

- If you do not want to show all the data on the chart, you can exclude a row or a column. Select the row/column by clicking on the header and choose Data ⇨ Exclude Row/Col.

- If the datasheet window is hidden and you need to see it, choose View ⇨ Datasheet or use the View Datasheet tool on the Standard toolbar to redisplay it.

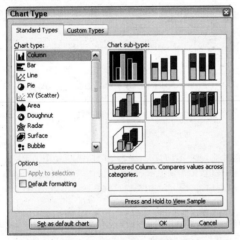

Figure 29-3: Use the Chart Type dialog box to decide what your chart will look like.

Tip   You don't have to retype your data into the datasheet if it already exists — for example, in an Excel worksheet. Instead, import it by choosing Edit ⇨ Import File or clicking the Import File tool on the Standard toolbar.

3. Make changes to your chart using the Chart ⇨ Chart Options dialog box (see Figure 29-4). Six tabs are available:

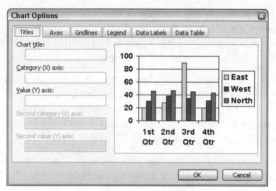

Figure 29-4: Use the Chart Options dialog box to change the look of your charts.

- **Titles.** Add a title to the chart or to any of the axes: category, series, or value. A title is often required in order for the value axis to show what unit of measure your chart is using — for example, dollars, kilograms, or thousands.

- **Axes.** Show or hide the axes and select the type of category axis — whether category or timescale.

- **Gridlines.** Show or hide major and minor gridlines on any axis.

Tip   Avoid the use of gridlines if possible — they clutter the chart.

- **Legend.** Show or hide the legend (the key) and determine its placement. Later, you can drag the legend inside your chart. Careful positioning of the legend enables you to make the chart itself as large and easy-to-read as possible.

- **Data Labels.** Show the data value against each point, or the label, or the percentage, if applicable.

- **Data Table.** A data table shows all the data in a table underneath the chart. Use this tab to show or hide it. A data table makes a chart look very cluttered and is hard to read in a presentation but provides valuable detail for some purposes.

4. When you are finished with your chart, click anywhere on your slide outside the chart object to return to PowerPoint. Your chart appears on your slide. You can now move it or resize it using the white handles.

Tip

It's usually better to resize the chart by dragging the herringboned edges of the chart "window" while the chart is open, as sometimes charts can become distorted when resized from PowerPoint itself. You can prevent the chart's text from distorting if you do resize it in PowerPoint, however. Whenever you are formatting an axis or the legend, one of the tabs in the Format dialog box is Font. Choose that tab, and then uncheck the Auto scale box. For more information on formatting the parts of your chart, see the section "Formatting Charts" later in this chapter.

Editing charts

You can change various elements of your chart at any stage — the data, the chart type, or many aspects of the chart's appearance.

Changing data

To change the data, you need to return to the datasheet. Double-click on the chart in PowerPoint. If the datasheet doesn't appear (which it won't if you hid it the last time you had the chart open), choose View ➪ Datasheet. Any changes you make to the datasheet will immediately be reflected in the chart. Click anywhere outside the chart to return to PowerPoint.

Changing chart types

To change chart types — from a bar chart to a line chart, for example — choose Chart ➪ Chart Type or use the Chart Type tool on the Standard toolbar. If you use the menu, choose the new chart type in the Chart Type dialog box and click OK.

Tip

If a chart doesn't look right, the first thing to check is the datasheet. You may have the wrong type of data for the type of chart you've chosen. For example, an XY chart has pairs of values, not categories.

Swapping data series

If you have typed the categories and the series the wrong way, or if you decide to swap the way the data is shown, choose Data ➪ Series in Rows or Data ➪ Series in Columns. Alternatively, you can choose the tools By Row or By Column from the Standard toolbar. Figure 29-5 shows the difference.

Controlling 3-D views

If you have chosen a 3-D chart, such as a column chart or a pie chart, you can control the elevation, rotation, and perspective of the chart and the angle of the axes. Choose Chart ➪ 3-D View (see Figure 29-6). You can either type in figures (in degrees) for Elevation and Rotation, or use the buttons provided to elevate or rotate the chart as you see fit.

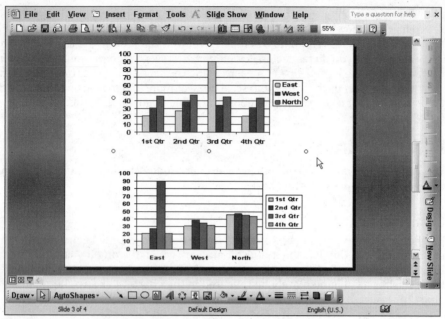

Figure 29-5: Data series can be shown in either columns or rows. In the top example, they're shown by row; in the bottom, by column. Both charts convey the same information but enable you to make different comparisons.

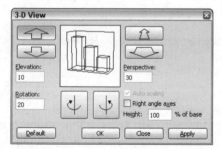

Figure 29-6: Adjust the 3-D appearance of charts with the 3-D View controls.

If the Right angle axes checkbox is unchecked, you get two additional buttons (shown in Figure 29-6 — they're the ones with the distorted arrows on them above the Perspective box) that enable you to increase or reduce perspective; and if Auto scaling is unchecked, you can also define the height of the chart as a percentage of the size of the base. (This is especially useful for 3-D pie charts that are too "thick.") If Right angle axes is checked, perspective is set (to keep all axes as right angles), but you can select Autoscaling, which automatically adjusts the contents of the chart to fit as the 3-D effect is applied.

Click Apply to see your chart change. Click OK when you have finished.

Formatting Charts

You can format many individual parts of your chart. The trick is to select the item you want changed and then find the appropriate dialog box. As you move your mouse over the chart, ScreenTips appear, showing you what will be selected if you click: plot area, walls, a series, the legend, etc.

Tip You can quickly check the value of a chart element, such as a column or bar, by pointing at it. The ScreenTip will tell you what the chart element represents and the value assigned to it.

Right-click on any element to open a shortcut menu offering you a number of options (which vary from element to element). The top item will read Format [name of the chart element you're selecting] — for example, Format Plot Area, or Format Data Series. Alternatively, you can click on the item you want to change and choose Format ➪ Selected.

The dialog box that appears depends on the object selected.

Tip If you're having trouble selecting the chart element you want, you can select it by using the Chart Objects drop-down list on the Standard toolbar (see Figure 29-7).

Figure 29-7: You can use this Chart Objects drop-down list on the Standard toolbar to more easily select the part of the chart you want to format.

Formatting data series

Be careful to check whether you have selected Format Data Series or Format Data Point. If you click a second time on a bar or a line on your chart, the individual item, rather than the whole series, will be selected. If you have selected a data point instead of a data series, click somewhere else on the chart to deselect it and then click just once on the series. Details of the dialog boxes vary depending on which chart type is selected.

Figure 29-8 shows the Format Data Series dialog box for a 2-D bar chart. (A 3-D column chart has a Shape tab instead of Axis and Y Error Bars tabs.) This dialog box has five tabs.

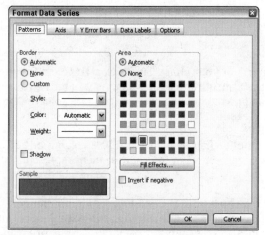

Figure 29-8: You have numerous options when it comes to formatting a selected data series.

✦ **Patterns.** Change the outline of the bars under the Border section, and the fill color and patterns of the bars under the Area section. For some interesting effects, click the Fill Effects button. You now have a choice of Gradient, Texture, Pattern, or Picture to fill the bars. You could choose, for example, a photo of piles of cash to fill the bars in a series representing sales over time.

✦ **Axis.** Here you can choose which axis you wish to plot the data against. This is used when you want two different units of measure on the same chart — for example, dollars and percentages. Use one axis for dollars and the other for percentages.

✦ **Y Error Bars.** These indicate the margin of error present in data points in your chart. (If you don't know what they are, you probably don't need to use them.)

✦ **Data Labels.** These show the value of each bar for this series. Here you can choose what each label contains. (The placement and size of the labels are controlled by selecting an individual label — or the entire series data labels — and choosing Format ⇨ Selected Data Labels.)

✦ **Options.** This tab controls the look of the series: You can set the overlap (if any) of series and the width of the gap (if any) between categories.

Note Remember that the preceding tabs are those present in the Format Data Series dialog box for a 2-D bar chart. Other types of charts will have other tabs with different or additional commands. This example list of options gives you an idea of the kinds of details you can exercise control over as you format your charts.

Format plot or chart area

Select either the Plot Area or the Chart Area and choose Format ⇨ Selected Area to select a border, a font for any text that appears in the area, and a background.

Format legend

Select the legend and choose Format ⇨ Selected Legend. The tabs for this are Patterns, Font, and Placement. Under Placement, indicate where the legend should be placed.

Tip You can also drag a legend to place it where you want. This is often better than using the placement option described here, as dragging the legend into place gives you more control over the resizing of your chart to allow for the legend. By clicking and dragging its handles, you can also resize (or vary the shape of) the legend so that it fits better.

Format category axis

Select the Category Axis and choose Format ⇨ Selected Axis. The tabs for this are Patterns, Scale, Font, Number, and Alignment. The Scale tab enables you to choose the number of categories to show between tick marks and to show the categories in reverse order. The Scale tab also enables you to move the value axis, if you don't want it on the left. The Number tab is for number formatting, and the Alignment tab enables you to put the axis labels at an angle, which is useful if they are overlapping. In the right-hand side of the Patterns tab, you can set where your axis labels will appear and whether or not you'll have tick marks.

Format value axis

Select the Value Axis and choose Format ⇨ Selected Axis. The tabs for this are also Patterns, Scale, Font, Number, and Alignment. The Scale tab, the only one that isn't self-explanatory, enables you to choose the minimum and maximum values for the axis, as well as the major and minor units. It also enables you to specify where the category (x) axis crosses the value axis.

Note   This brief discussion has only touched on some of the numerous formatting options available to you as you build a chart in PowerPoint. Explore and experiment with them yourself to discover what you can do.

Add a trendline

A *trendline* is a line through your data, not necessarily linking the points but showing the trend of the data. This feature is available only on some 2-D charts. Select a series, right-click to call up the shortcut menu, and select Add Trendline. Choose the method you want to use to calculate the trend, and any other options (see Figure 29-9).

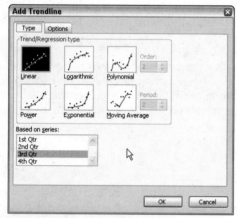

Figure 29-9: Trendlines can be inserted for a selected series on some 2-D charts.

Mixed chart types

You can mix some kinds of charts. For example, you can combine a column chart and a line chart, or a column chart and an area chart. To do so:

1. Create a 2-D column chart using all the data.

2. Select the series you want to show as a line or area chart.

3. Select Chart ➪ Chart Type and choose a line or area chart. Make sure that Apply to Selection is turned on.

4. Click OK. The selected series changes to a line or area chart (see Figure 29-10). The other series continue to be displayed as columns.

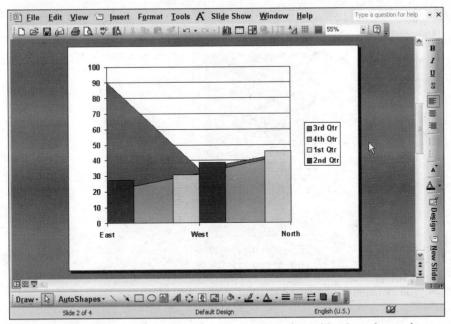

Figure 29-10: This graph displays the information as a combination of area chart and column chart.

Saving custom charts

Office provides you with numerous pre-designed chart formats to draw from as you create your own, and once you have designed your own, you may want to save it to use again.

The Chart ➪ Chart Type dialog box has two tabs: Standard Types and Custom Types. To view the pre-designed charts, select Custom Types and make sure the radio button Built-in is selected (see Figure 29-11). Try clicking each of the chart types to see how your data will look. If you want to use one, click OK.

To save your own design:

1. Create your chart.

2. Choose Chart ➪ Chart Type.

3. Select the Custom Types tab and then click the User-defined radio button in the Select from area.

4. Click the Add button and enter a name and description for your chart. It will be added to the list of Custom Types.

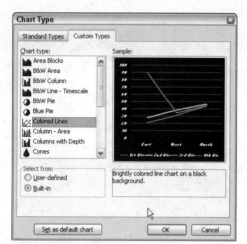

Figure 29-11: Just as PowerPoint provides design templates for your presentations, so it also provides pre-designed chart formats you can apply to your own charts.

To apply your custom-designed chart format to your data, choose the chart type either before or after entering your data. Choose Chart ⇨ Chart Type. Select the Custom Types tab, select User-defined, and select your design.

Tip   A user-defined custom chart is a machine-specific setting. Creating one on your computer doesn't make it available to someone opening the presentation on a different computer.

Creating an Organization Chart or Diagram

In addition to its charting feature, PowerPoint has a feature that enables you to add an organization chart or one of five different types of diagrams to your presentation: a cycle diagram, a radial diagram, a pyramid diagram, a Venn diagram, or a target diagram.

To insert an organization chart or diagram into your presentation, you can use any of the slide layouts that include content. Click the Insert Diagram or Organization Chart icon in the content placeholder or choose the slide layout called Title and Diagram or Organization Chart from the Other Layouts section of the Slide Layout task pane. (Alternatively, you can insert a diagram into any slide by choosing Insert ⇨ Diagram.) Whichever option you choose, the Diagram Gallery opens (see Figure 29-12).

Click on the type of diagram you want to insert, and then click OK.

Figure 29-12: The Diagram Gallery offers easy insertion of a variety of useful diagrams.

Inserting an Organization Chart

Anyone who has ever had to draw organization charts, either by hand or computer, will appreciate this feature. You simply add boxes where you want them and type in the information. The formatting and sizing is done for you automatically. Figure 29-13 shows an example of a simple organization chart.

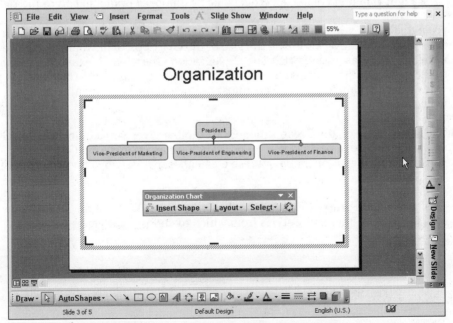

Figure 29-13: Organization charts like this are easy to produce.

When you insert an organization chart, it begins life much like the one shown in Figure 29-13; you can type whatever text you want into any of the boxes. A special Organization Chart toolbar opens, too.

To build on this basic chart, click on the box to which you want to add related boxes and click on the downward-pointing arrow on the right end of the Insert Shape button on the Organization Chart toolbar. You have three options:

✦ **Subordinate.** This inserts a box directly below your selected box and connects the two with a vertical line.

✦ **Coworker.** This inserts a box at the same hierarchical level as your selected box.

✦ **Assistant.** This inserts a box below your selected box and slightly to the side, connected to your selected box by a right-angle line.

You can adjust the layout of the chart in a number of ways. Click on a manager box — that is, one that has subordinate boxes attached to it — and choose one of four layouts:

✦ **Standard** is the layout shown in Figure 29-13, with each new level of the hierarchy on the same level, and new levels directly below.

✦ **Both Hanging** creates a vertical chart, with the manager box at the top and subordinate boxes branching off of a vertical line in both directions below.

✦ **Left Hanging** creates a vertical chart with boxes branching off to the left.

✦ **Right Hanging** creates a vertical chart with boxes branching off to the right.

From this menu, you can also choose Fit Organization Chart to Contents, which does just what it says, shrinking the size of the chart box to fit whatever you've put into it as tightly as possible; Expand Organization Chart, which expands the chart to the maximum size allowed by the slide; and Scale Organization Chart, which provides you with handles so you can adjust the size of the chart manually, as you would a graphic.

The Select menu on the Organization Chart toolbar gives you a quick way to select all the elements of a particular level or branch, all assistants, or all connecting lines. You can then format any of these elements separately by choosing Format ➪ AutoShape.

Finally, the AutoFormat button opens the Organization Chart Style Gallery, which offers you many interesting styles from which to choose (see Figure 29-14).

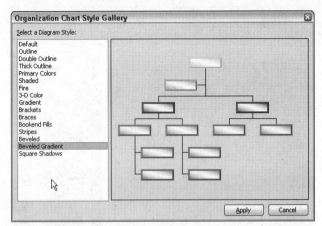

Figure 29-14: The Organization Chart Style Gallery offers numerous options.

Tip   You can manually adjust the overall appearance of your organization chart by selecting it (make sure you've selected the whole chart, not an individual element of it) and choosing Format ➪ Organization Chart. This opens a dialog box that lets you set colors, lines, size, and positioning.

Tip   If you're having trouble with things moving where you don't want them while you're working in the Organization Chart applet, turn off AutoLayout by choosing Layout ➪ AutoLayout from the Organization Chart toolbar.

Inserting a diagram

Although the five types of diagram you can insert are quite different from one another, the Diagram toolbar that opens when you insert one is the same.

Each diagram consists of several shapes and accompanying text. For example, in Figure 29-15, I've inserted a cycle diagram, which consists of shapes that form a circle and text placeholders. Simply click on the text placeholders to activate them, and then type in your text.

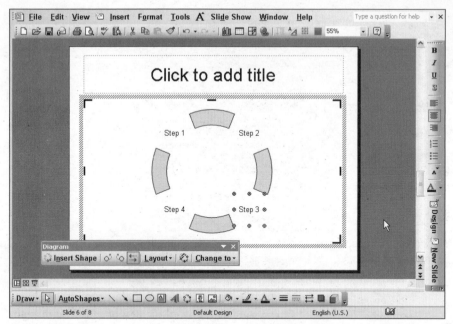

Figure 29-15: No matter what kind of diagram you insert, the controls for it are basically the same.

The toolbar then provides you with the following tools:

✦ **Insert Shape** inserts another of whatever shape makes up the diagram: another of the curved shapes shown in Figure 29-15, another level in the pyramid diagram, another circle in the Venn diagram, etc. It also inserts another accompanying text placeholder.

✦ **Move Shape Backward** and **Move Shape Forward** move shapes one step up or down in the diagram (or one step farther around the cycle, etc.).

✦ **Layout** offers Fit Diagram to Contents, Expand Diagram, and Scale Diagram, which work just the same as they do for an organization chart.

✦ **AutoFormat** opens the Diagram Style Gallery, which offers several different appearance options.

✦ **Change to** lets you change one diagram into another, just by choosing the type you want from the list. This is a great way to experiment with different methods of presenting the same information.

Again, as with the organization chart, you can manually format any element of your diagram by clicking on it and choosing Format ➪ AutoShape, or you can adjust the overall look of the diagram by clicking on it outside of one of its elements and choosing Format ➪ Diagram.

Tip   You can also change the shapes of the diagrams by clicking on the existing shape(s), going to the Drawing toolbar, selecting Draw ⇨ Change AutoShape, and selecting the AutoShape you prefer. This is especially handy for tasks such as changing a cycle diagram to one with arrows.

Creating and Editing Tables

Tables are very useful for displaying numbers or text in an organized, easily understood fashion. Creating tables in PowerPoint is very similar to creating tables in Word. Unfortunately, PowerPoint tables don't allow you to do calculations or sorting. If you need this functionality and want to use Word tables or Excel worksheets, however, you can import these items into PowerPoint.

Cross-Reference   For detailed information on creating tables in Word, see Chapter 5.

Both the Insert Table tool and the Tables and Borders tool are available. However, they are more limited — for example, you cannot do calculations or sorting. (If you need those capabilities, you can create tables in Word or Excel and import them into PowerPoint — a procedure covered in the section "Inserting Excel Worksheets and Word Tables," later in this chapter.) Figure 29-16 shows a table in PowerPoint and the Tables and Borders toolbar.

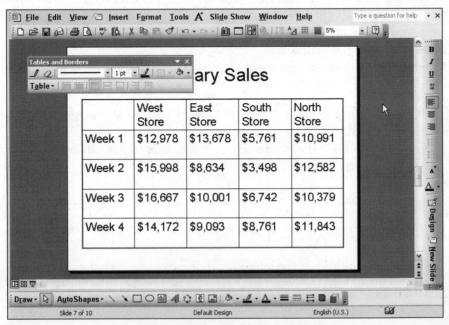

Figure 29-16: Here's a typical PowerPoint table.

Creating a table

Select a slide layout that includes content or a table, and then click the Table icon in the content placeholder or click on the table placeholder. Alternatively, choose Insert ➪ Table or the Insert Table tool from the Standard toolbar. This will place a table in the center of your slide.

In either case, you're first asked in a small dialog box how many rows and columns you require. Once you've decided how many rows and columns you want, the table appears on your slide with the cursor flashing in the first cell, ready for you to enter information. To move from cell to cell, use the Tab or arrow keys. When you have finished entering information, click anywhere on the slide outside the table to deselect it.

If you draw your table using the Tables and Borders tool from the Standard toolbar, you can design a table and decide where to place the cells by dragging. Use the Draw Table tool from the Tables and Borders toolbar to draw any size table with cell locations of your choice.

Cross-Reference   See Chapter 5 for detailed information on the Table tool and the Draw Table tool on the Tables and Borders toolbar.

Editing a table

You have several ways to rearrange your table and enhance the text. The following sections describe these options.

Inserting rows/columns

If you misjudge the initial size of your table or overlook some pertinent data, you may need to add new rows or columns to your table. Here's how:

✦ To add a new row at the bottom of the table, press Tab when you are in the last cell of the table.

✦ To insert a row in the middle of your table, click on any cell in the row that will be below the new row. Right-click to display the shortcut menu. Choose Insert Rows.

✦ To add a column at the end of your table, select the last column. To do this, place the mouse over the border at the top of the last column of your table. The cursor changes into a black down arrow. Click to select the column and right-click to display the shortcut menu. Select Insert Columns.

✦ To insert a column in the middle of your table, select a column, right-click, and choose Insert Columns from the shortcut menu. The column is inserted to the left of the selected column.

Tip For more control over the side on which columns or rows will be inserted, use the Table toolbar; choose Table, and a drop-down menu will appear with a number of options.

Note The enlarged table may not fit on your slide. Drag the white handles on the edge of your table to make it smaller. Otherwise, make the columns or rows smaller to fit. (See the following section.)

Changing column widths and row heights

To change column width or row height, move the mouse over the border between two columns or rows. The cursor changes shape to a Column Width tool. Drag this tool to change the width of the column or the height of the row. If you change the size of the overall table using the white handles, the column widths and row heights will change proportionately.

Tip Double-clicking while the cursor is changed to the Column Width tool will resize the column to fit any existing text.

Formatting

The text in the table can be formatted in the same way as in Word and Excel. Use the Formatting toolbar or the Format menu for features such as font, size, and alignment. Use Format ➪ Colors and Lines to change borders, fills, and text alignment for selected cells. The Format ➪ Table menu command is used to format the entire table at once.

You can change a complete row or column by selecting it. To select a column, either drag the mouse over the cells in the column, or click with the black down arrow pointer that appears when you place your cursor at the top of the column. Select a row by dragging the mouse over the cells in the row.

Tip If you want to use tabs in a column — for example, to line up numbers — you may have found that when you press Tab, you move to the next cell. To overcome this, press Ctrl+Tab instead of Tab. You can position your tabs as you do in Word. To see the ruler, choose View ➪ Ruler.

Cross-Reference See Chapter 4 for more information about setting up tabs.

Inserting Excel Worksheets and Word Tables

Word tables and Excel worksheets have more power than PowerPoint tables. Create your tables in Word or Excel and you can import them into PowerPoint using one of several methods described in the following sections. Each method has its advantages and disadvantages. You *can* simply copy and paste, but the formatting may be lost.

Inserting an Excel worksheet

There are two ways to import an Excel worksheet into your PowerPoint presentation: You can choose the Insert ➪ Object menu command or use the Edit ➪ Copy command (in Excel), followed by the Edit ➪ Paste Special command (in PowerPoint). Both methods can be used to link a table in PowerPoint to the data in Excel.

Cross-
Reference

For more detailed information about linking and embedding objects, see Chapter 42.

The Insert Object method

Here's how to insert an Excel worksheet using the Insert ➪ Object command:

1. Create your table in Excel and save the file. You can exit from Excel if you like.

2. In PowerPoint, select the slide onto which you want to put the table.

3. Choose Insert ➪ Object (see Figure 29-17).

4. Select Create from file and then browse to find the Excel file.

5. Select Link if you want the table in your presentation to be automatically updated if the original file is changed.

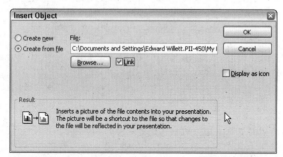

Figure 29-17: Choose both Create from file and Link to insert your Excel worksheet as a table and keep it current with the original file.

6. The table is inserted onto your current slide in the center. You can move and resize it as you like.

Caution

The text may become distorted if you change the proportions of the table as you resize it.

7. You can go straight to Excel to make changes by double-clicking on the table in PowerPoint. Any changes are made both in Excel and PowerPoint; however, if you change the table in PowerPoint, be sure to save the changes in Excel when prompted to do so (which will happen when you close the Excel window); otherwise, the changes will be lost.

8. You can also make edits in the original Excel file; you will be prompted to update links the next time you open the PowerPoint file.

The Copy and Paste Special method

To insert an Excel worksheet into your PowerPoint presentation using the Copy and Paste Special commands:

1. Create your table in Excel and save it.

2. Select the range you wish to import into PowerPoint.

3. Copy it to the clipboard using Edit ⇨ Copy, clicking the Copy button on the toolbar, or pressing Ctrl+C.

4. Switch to PowerPoint and select the slide onto which you want to put the table.

5. Choose Edit ⇨ Paste Special (see Figure 29-18). You can choose from several different formats. Read the Result box to learn how the various methods differ. One of the best methods is Paste Link and Microsoft Excel Worksheet Object; not only will your table look good, it will be linked to the original file. Any changes made to the Excel worksheet will be reflected in your PowerPoint table.

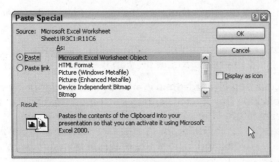

Figure 29-18: Choose Paste Special and Paste link instead of Paste to maintain a link with your original file.

6. Move or resize the table to fit on your slide. Make sure that the text is not distorted when you change the size.

7. You can go straight to Excel to make changes by double-clicking on the table in PowerPoint. Any changes you make in Excel are made in PowerPoint. (Again, be sure to save the changes in Excel before returning to PowerPoint.)

Adding a Word table

The methods used for inserting an Excel worksheet into PowerPoint work equally well for Word tables. Either choose Insert ➪ Object or use Copy and Paste Special.

Note, however, that if you choose Insert ➪ Object ➪ Microsoft Word Document and the Word document you choose to insert consists of more than just a table, the entire document will be inserted into your presentation, so this option works best if the document consists entirely of a single table. Selecting the table you want to insert into your presentation in Word, choosing Copy and then going to PowerPoint and using Edit ➪ Paste Special ➪ Microsoft Word Document Object will insert only the selected table, not any other text that may be in the document.

Summary

Charts and tables are two powerful tools for organizing your data in a fashion that makes it easier for the viewers of your presentation to understand the relationships among the facts you've collected. Highlights of this chapter included:

✦ PowerPoint provides a plethora of chart types, both familiar and esoteric, in both 2-D and 3-D.

✦ You can insert a chart either by creating a slide that uses a Slide Layout containing either a Content or a Chart placeholder, or by choosing Insert ➪ Chart (or simply by clicking the Insert Chart button on the toolbar).

✦ Use the datasheet to enter the data that creates your chart or to alter that data later.

✦ Every element of a chart, from the fonts used in the labels in the legend to the thickness of the lines and the background fill, can be tweaked and formatted.

✦ The Diagram Gallery, chosen either from a content placeholder or by choosing Insert ➪ Diagram or clicking the Insert Diagram button on the toolbar, makes it easy to create an organization chart, cycle diagram, radial diagram, pyramid diagram, Venn diagram, or target diagram. A special Diagram toolbar provides all the tools you need to tweak and format the diagram once it's been created.

✦ You can create a table in a PowerPoint presentation and edit it just as you would in Word.

✦ If you already have your data in tabular format in an Excel worksheet or Word table, you can insert it directly into PowerPoint with either the Insert ➪ Object command or by using Edit ➪ Copy in Excel or Word and Edit ➪ Paste Special in PowerPoint.

✦   ✦   ✦

Adding Graphics and Special Effects

Multimedia (pictures, animation, video, and sound) can bring your presentation to life. You can create slide transitions to bring your slide onscreen with a variety of special effects. You can also work with actions, which enable you to put buttons on slides to show them in a random fashion, rather than in a linear sequence, or to run other programs, macros, sounds, or video clips.

Note All computers can show transition effects. However, for high-quality sound, you need a good sound card, and for good video, you need a high-quality video card. Check the Windows Control Panel to see what multimedia and sound capabilities you have.

Adding Pictures and Multimedia

Most of the pictures you use in PowerPoint will be bitmap images. (See the sidebar "Bitmap versus Vector Graphics" for more information.) The term *multimedia* covers pictures, video, and sound in any combination.

Office provides many pictures for your use in all your applications. You can also create your own images using PowerPoint or a graphics program, or import images from a digital camera, scanner, or other sources. You can edit your images to a certain extent within PowerPoint, but you usually have far more editing power in a graphics program.

Cross-Reference Office 2003 comes with a new program called Microsoft Picture Library that you can use to edit photographs; it's discussed in detail in Chapter 45.

Bitmap versus Vector Graphics

Be aware of the difference between a bitmap and a vector graphic image. Scanned pictures, digital camera images, and photographs are all bitmap images. All of the paint-type graphics programs also produce bitmaps.

A bitmap image is made up of dots. Bitmap images can be saved in a variety of formats, each with its own filename extension. Some common ones you may see are .pcx, .gif, .bmp, .jpg, .png, and .tif. There are many more. If you enlarge bitmaps, you may find that the straight lines develop jagged edges as each dot is enlarged. Another thing to be aware of is the size of the file. Bitmap files tend to be large.

Some graphics programs, especially CAD and graphic design programs such as Corel Draw and Illustrator, produce vector graphic images. Vector graphics are created with a series of mathematical statements that specify lines (.wmf and .emf are both vector file formats). The advantage of these files is that you can make the pictures any size and they always retain their high quality — no jagged edges. If you use the Drawing toolbar — to draw AutoShapes in Word, for example — you are drawing vector graphics.

Adding images

Adding an image to a slide can enhance it significantly. You could add a picture that amuses — a cartoon character, for example — or a picture of the item or items being discussed. You may also want to put your company logo onto your slide or many slides.

Caution

Be careful to use images that are appropriate for the presentation: Cartoons, for example, are suitable only under certain circumstances! Also be careful not to use images you don't have permission to use. Images, like words, are protected by copyright.

You can import an image using the following methods:

✦ Choose Insert ⇨ Picture ⇨ Clip Art. This opens the Clip Art task pane, which enables you to search by keyword for images contained in Office's Clip Organizer. The task pane shows you thumbnails (miniatures) of your pictures so you can easily find the right image. (The Clip Organizer also includes photographs, movies, and sounds.)

✦ Use Insert ⇨ Picture ⇨ From File to browse your computer's various drives to find the image you want. If you find yourself doing this often, though, you might want to move the images you're using regularly into the Clip Organizer. The Clip Art task pane includes a link labeled Organize clips that lets you do this.

Note

This may take a long time if you've got a lot of clips on your computer, and you have to be prepared to tell the Organizer where to look for the clips and how to organize them, so don't undertake it unless you've got a good-sized chunk of time.

✦ Acquire an image from a scanner or digital camera. (Be aware that this may create extremely large PowerPoint files if the images were scanned or photographed at extremely high resolutions.)

✦ Create your own illustrations using one of the various tools PowerPoint provides for the purpose, including AutoShapes and the Drawing toolbar. (Be aware that these illustrations are part of your presentation, and can't be saved as individual graphics files for use in other applications, although you can copy and paste them into other applications if you wish.)

✦ Use the Photo Album feature if you have numerous images to insert. It's available from Insert ➪ Picture ➪ New Photo Album.

Cross-Reference Many of these options apply to all Office applications and are dealt with in detail in Chapter 43.

Adding an image from the Clip Organizer

To add an image from the Clip Organizer to your slide, follow these steps:

1. Make sure you are in Normal view. If you want to use buttons, rather than the menu, ensure that the Drawing toolbar is showing. If not, select it from the View ➪ Toolbars menu.

2. Click the Insert Clip Art tool on the Drawing toolbar, or choose Insert ➪ Picture ➪ Clip Art. The Clip Art task pane appears (see Figure 30-1).

Figure 30-1: Use the Clip Art task pane to search the Clip Organizer for images you may want to use.

3. Enter a keyword that describes the kind of image you're looking for; in Figure 30-1, I've entered "balloon."

4. Clip Art is organized into collections. Choose which collections you want to search and specify which media types you're interested in. In this case, we're inserting an image, so we could limit the search by unchecking Movies and Sounds in the Results should be field.

5. Click Go. The Clip Art task pane displays thumbnails of any images it finds that match your keyword.

6. When you place your mouse over a thumbnail of a picture, the Clip Organizer gives you information about its name, file type, and size, and the keywords associated with it, as shown in Figure 30-2.

7. To insert the picture, double-click it.

Figure 30-2: The Insert Clip Art task pane provides you with detailed information about each clip in a ScreenTip.

You have other options besides simply inserting the clip. If you click on the downward-pointing arrow that appears when you point at one of the thumbnails, you'll open a shortcut menu that offers you several other options. For instance, you can copy it to the Office clipboard, delete it from the Clip Organizer, copy it to another collection, edit its keywords, or find similar clips.

You can get more detailed information about any clip, and get a better look at it, by choosing Preview/Properties. This opens the dialog box shown in Figure 30-3, where you can see all kinds of details and edit the clip's keywords.

Figure 30-3: The Preview/Properties dialog box provides detailed information about any picture you may want to insert.

Cross-Reference

When you have a picture on the slide and you select it (you can tell when a picture is selected because it has white handles around it), the Picture toolbar is automatically displayed. It contains some very useful features, described in detail in Chapter 43.

You can use the Drawing toolbar to create your own illustrations and diagrams, and to edit your clip art. It, too, is described in detail in Chapter 43.

Inserting a picture from a file

To insert an existing picture from your computer without going through Clip Organizer, choose Insert ➪ Picture ➪ From File. This brings up an Insert Picture dialog box that provides thumbnail images so you can preview the available pictures. Select the picture you want to insert and click Insert. Or, simply double-click the picture you want.

Inserting a Photo Album

Brand new in the 2003 version of PowerPoint is the Photo Album feature, which allows you to include multiple pictures in a presentation more easily.

To insert a photo album, choose Insert ➪ Picture ➪ New Photo Album. This opens the dialog box shown in Figure 30-4 (although when you first open it, most of it is grayed out, because no pictures have been added to the album yet).

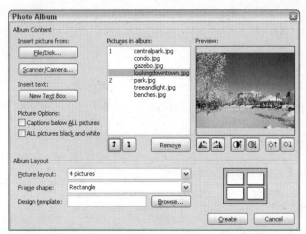

Figure 30-4: The New Photo Album command makes it easy to insert multiple pictures into your presentation at once, without having to manually arrange them on your slides.

The first step is to add pictures to your album; you can select them from files on your computer by clicking the File/Disk button, or you can add them from a scanner or digital camera by clicking the Scanner/Camera button. The pictures you add are listed in the Pictures in album box in the order in which they'll appear in your presentation. You can change the order of a picture by highlighting it and then clicking one of the two buttons underneath the list of pictures with up and down arrows on them; you can remove any picture you've added to the list by highlighting it and clicking Remove.

You also have a few basic editing controls available for each picture; you can rotate it left or right, increase or decrease contrast, or increase or decrease brightness using the controls under the Preview area.

Notice in Figure 30-4 that there are numbers down the left side of the Pictures in album list. These tell you which slide your pictures are on; in this case, the first four pictures will appear on Slide 1 and the next three on Slide 2.

To add a text box the same size as your pictures to any slide, highlight one of the pictures in the Pictures and album list on the slide where you want to the text box to appear, and click New Text Box. The words "Text Box" appear in the list of pictures, and you can reposition it just as you did pictures. Once you create the slide, that text box, the same size as the pictures, will be waiting for you to add text.

You can also automatically create smaller text boxes into which you can type captions by checking the Captions below ALL pictures box. If you want all pictures to be black and white (perhaps because you're creating a printed presentation rather than one to be shown on a computer), check the ALL pictures black and white box.

In the Album Layout area at the bottom of the Photo Album dialog box, you can choose a layout for your pictures from the Picture layout drop-down list: 1 picture, 2 pictures, 4 pictures, 1 picture with title, 2 pictures with title, 4 pictures with title. You can also choose the shape of the pictures from the Frame shape drop-down list: Rounded Rectangle, Beveled, Oval, Corner Tabs, Square Tabs, and Plaque Tabs are your choices. (The little thumbnail to the right of the drop-down list gives you a good idea of what each of these choices looks like.)

Finally, if you want to apply a Design template to your Photo Album slides, you can do so by clicking the Browse button.

When you're happy with your choices, click Create. PowerPoint automatically creates a title slide that reads "Photo Album by (Your Name)," along with however many slides it takes to accommodate all the photos in your photo album. Figure 30-5 shows a photo album slide using the 4 pictures with title layout and the Plaque Tabs frame shape. The next step would be to click the Click to add title placeholder and title the slide.

Once you've created your photo album slides, you can add additional formatting such as background art, slide transitions, and more.

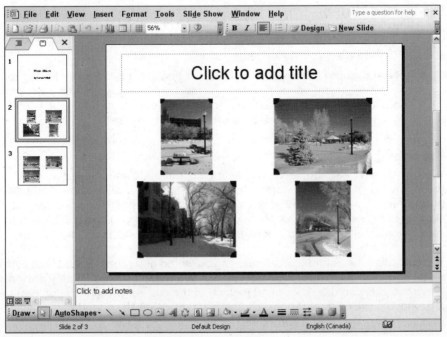

Figure 30-5: Here's a typical Photo Album slide.

Working with sound

Adding sound to your presentation can draw the attention of the audience or add humor. I wouldn't use too many sounds, though; they'll lose their impact and may become irritating. Whether or not sound is appropriate depends on the type of presentation you are giving. Moreover, sound files — unless they're very simple ones — can take up a lot of disk space.

Inserting sounds

PowerPoint provides you with some sample sound files. You can usually find more in the Windows\Media folder and you can use any others you may have on your computer. PowerPoint also offers automatic links to help you download new sound files from the Internet. There are four methods for inserting sound:

✦ **From the Clip Organizer.** Inserting a sound from the Clip Organizer is exactly like inserting Clip Art: Choose Insert ⇨ Movies and Sounds ⇨ Sound from Clip Organizer to open the Organizer, and then enter a keyword and choose Sounds (you can be more specific about what kinds of sounds, if you wish) in the Results should be field.

✦ **From a file.** Choose Insert ⇨ Movies and Sounds ⇨ Sound from File, and then browse for the sound file you want to insert.

✦ **From a CD.** Choose Insert ⇨ Movies and Sounds ⇨ Play CD Audio Track, and you'll be given the option to specify which track or tracks on the current CD you want to play, or even what specific section of the CD, specified by the time code, you want to play. You can also choose to loop the track indefinitely. Of course, you must have the CD you want to play from in the drive for this to work during your presentation.

✦ **Record a sound.** Choose Insert ⇨ Movies and Sounds ⇨ Record Sound to bring up a small control panel. (For this to work, obviously, you must have a microphone hooked up to your computer, and a sound card.) Name the sound you're about to record, and then press the Record button.

The Sound icon

When you insert a sound, an icon appears on your slide and you are prompted with the following: "How do you want the sound to start in the slide show?" You have two options: Automatically and When Clicked. If you choose the first, the sound will start as soon as the slide appears in the presentation; if you choose the second, the sound won't start until you click on the Sound icon that appears on the slide.

You can move the Sound icon around as you would any other picture. You can also resize it, but be aware that it doesn't have much detail and will quickly grow pixilated. You can also drag the sound icon off of the edge of the slide if you don't want it to show in your presentation. Of course, if you've set the sound to play when the icon is clicked, this isn't a good thing to do!

Note You can achieve more control over the way a sound is played if you use the custom animation effects, covered in the section "Using Animation Schemes," later in this chapter.

Working with movies

Adding a video clip adds life to your presentation. You might like to use one on the first or the last slide, or insert one that runs repeatedly during a coffee break until you return to continue the presentation.

Tip Some people use PowerPoint to create training modules instead of presentations, or to create continuously running demonstrations or sales presentations that run on computers at trade shows or in stores. For such purposes, video is an excellent way of drawing attention or explaining a product. Just be aware that full-motion video files take up a tremendous amount of disk space, even though they may not increase the file size of the actual PowerPoint file by much.

Inserting video

PowerPoint provides you with some simple animated clips in the Clip Organizer, which you access, as you've probably figured out, by choosing Insert ➪ Movies and Sound ➪ Movies from Clip Organizer. Your other option is — you guessed it — Insert ➪ Movies and Sound ➪ Movie from File, which enables you to browse your computer for any movie files (in .asf, .avi, .mpg, or .wmv formats) you may already have stored on it.

Tip To see an animated clip from the Clip Organizer in action, click on the downward-pointing arrow that appears when you point at a clip, or right-click the clip itself, and choose Preview/Properties from the shortcut menu. The animation plays in the Preview window in the Preview/Properties dialog box. Note that animated .gifs are not considered movies or video; you can insert them just as you would a non-animated .gif file, by using the Insert ➪ Picture ➪ From File or Insert ➪ Picture ➪ From Clip Organizer commands.

When you insert a video clip, the first frame of the video appears on your slide; you can then can move and resize the video frame just as you would any other object, although if you enlarge it, you'll find that the resolution diminishes.

Note You can achieve more control over the way a video clip is played if you use the custom animation effects, which are covered in the "Using Animation Schemes" section later in this chapter.

Tip If you find you cannot play a particular sound or video in PowerPoint, try Windows Media Player. Choose Insert ➪ Object and select Create from File. Browse to find and open the file. It is placed on your slide as an object and is run using the Windows Media Player.

Using Slide Transitions

Slide transitions are special effects that make the change from one slide to the next in your presentation more interesting. You may be tempted to use a different transition after each slide, but this can confuse the audience. A better option is to use the same transition for all the slides in one logical section — for example, the introduction. When you change to another section, change to another kind of transition. This is a subtle way of telling the audience that you have changed to a new subject.

Selecting the slides

The first step in applying transitions, obviously, is to select the slides you want to use for the transitions. You can do this either in Normal view or in Slide Sorter view. In Normal view, click the Slides tab in the leftmost view pane to see the slide thumbnails.

✦ To apply a slide transition to an individual slide, click to select the slide (a border appears around it).

✦ To apply a transition effect to a group of slides, click on the first slide and then hold down the Shift key and click on the last slide in the group. (This is typical Windows behavior for selecting a group of contiguous items.)

✦ To apply slide transitions to various slides that aren't necessarily contiguous, click on them one by one while holding down Ctrl.

Adding transitions

When you have selected the slides to which you want to apply a transition, click on the Slide Transition tool or choose Slide Show ➪ Slide Transition. The Slide Transition task pane appears (see Figure 30-6). To create a transition, use the following steps:

1. Choose the transition effect you want from the Apply to selected slides list. When you make a selection, it's previewed for you on the selected slides — assuming the Auto Preview checkbox at the bottom of the task pane is selected, which it is by default. (If you're in Normal view, you can see the transition effect better than you can in Slide Sorter view because the Normal view of the currently selected slide is much larger.)

2. To control the speed of the transition, choose Slow, Medium, or Fast from the Speed drop-down list in the Modify transition area of the task pane.

3. You can choose to play a sound when the slide is shown. Choose the sound you want from the Sound drop-down list, or choose Other Sound to browse for a sound stored elsewhere on your computer. By default, the sound is played only once, but if you check the Loop until next sound checkbox, you can cause it to play repeatedly, stopping only when the next sound is played, usually when you advance to the next slide. Only .wav files can be attached to transitions.

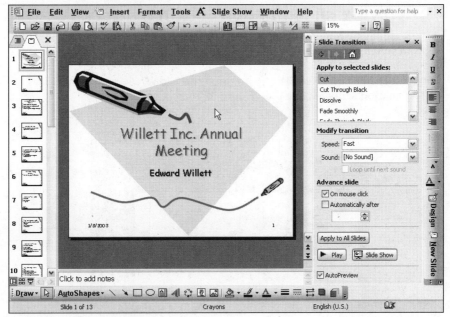

Figure 30-6: Fine-tune the transition from slide to slide using the Slide Transition task pane.

Note   If the next slide transition doesn't include a sound and you've chosen to loop the sound from the previous transition, you have to add the sound called Stop Previous Sound to your transition to end the loop.

4. When giving a presentation, you normally want to advance from one slide to the next by clicking the mouse. If you are creating a presentation you want to run on its own, however, you can move from one slide to the next automatically. In the Advance Slide section of the task pane, select Automatically after and enter the length of time the slide must be on the screen before the next slide appears.

5. Now choose Apply to Master or Apply to All Slides.

You can preview your transitions in the current view by clicking Play, or click Slide Show to view the effects as they'll appear when you run your slide show.

Using Animation Schemes

Animation schemes take you one step beyond slide transitions, offering even more effects. You can make lines of text fade in one by one, for instance, or flash, or zoom out toward the viewer and then back into place. Animation schemes turn your slides into little bits of Hollywood, right on your desktop.

Applying an animation scheme

To apply an animation scheme, first select the slides to which you want to apply the scheme, just as you did to apply a slide transition.

Choose Format ➪ Slide Design to open the Slide Design task pane, and click the Animation schemes link (see Figure 30-7).

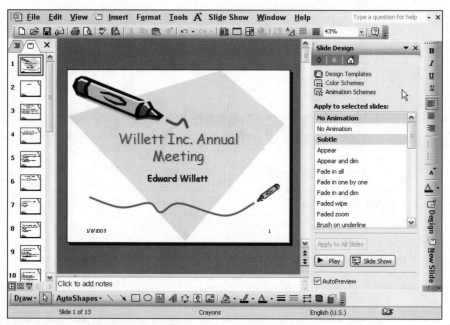

Figure 30-7: Apply animation schemes from the Slide Design task pane.

The schemes are grouped as Recently Used (if there are any recently used schemes; if not, this section won't appear), No Animation, Subtle, Moderate, and Exciting. Click the one you want to apply to the selected slides. You can also apply the animation scheme to the Master—in which case it will be used by all slides based on the Master—or simply apply it to all slides in the presentation.

Again, you can preview the animation effect by clicking Play, or view it in the context of your slide show by clicking Slide Show.

Applying custom animations

If you want more options for animation, switch to Normal view and choose Slide Show ⇨ Custom Animation. This opens the Custom Animation task pane shown in Figure 30-8.

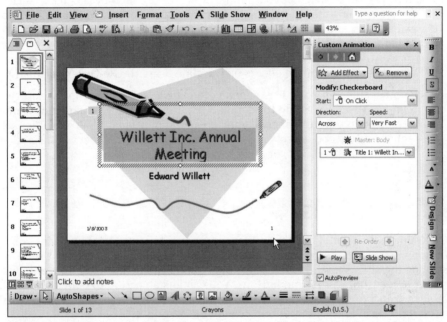

Figure 30-8: The Custom Animation task pane provides tools that can make your slides come alive.

Here's how it works:

1. Select the element of the slide to be animated — for example, a bulleted list or an object such as a picture. In Figure 30-8, I've chosen the slide's main title.

2. Click Add Effect. This opens a small shortcut menu with four categories of effects: Entrance, Emphasis, Exit, and Motion Paths. Each has dozens of options from which to choose. When you choose one, it's added to the list of animations on the slide.

Tip Have some fun with the Motion Paths option. One of its sub-options is Draw Custom Path. You can draw a line, a curve, a freeform shape, or a scribble that the selected object will then follow!

3. Now modify the animation. You can choose to have it run when you click on it, at the same time as the previous animation effect you entered (if there's more than one on this slide), or after the previous animation effect. You can also modify its size (or other salient features — this varies from animation to animation) and speed.

> **Note**   You can find additional options for modifying these effects by clicking on them in the list, opening the shortcut menu by clicking on the downward-pointing arrow that appears, and choosing Effect Options. Among other options, you can attach a sound to the animation here.

4. Change the order of the effects on the slide using the Re-Order buttons.

5. If you decide you don't like an animation effect, select it in the list and click Remove. (Don't be afraid to remove animation effects. The audience is more interested in the substance of your presentation than in how cool it looks; in fact, too many cool effects are likely to annoy those members of the audience looking for substance over style.)

Creating Actions

On a slide, actions are links that initiate some event. PowerPoint provides some buttons that represent commonly used actions — advancing to the next slide or starting the slide show, for example — but actions can be initiated from any object on the screen, not just Action buttons. You can link an action to text, an object, a table, a graph, or an image, and decide whether the action is to be taken when the cursor moves over the item or only when you click on it.

You can use actions to link to a specific slide, another PowerPoint presentation, a Word document, an Excel spreadsheet, a macro, a site on the Internet or intranet, or to run another program (although if your computer is a bit on the slow side be careful of this one; it could take a long time to get that program running, bringing your presentation to a halt and letting your audience's attention wander).

Actions are useful if you are using PowerPoint to create a rolling demonstration or onscreen training course. You could insert Action buttons that enable the person viewing the slide show to choose which section to cover next. In a training course, clicking on the right answer could take users to the next question, whereas clicking on the wrong answer could take users back to the beginning of the section they are covering.

Action buttons

The standard Action buttons provided with PowerPoint are Custom, Home, Help, Information, Back or Previous, Forward or Next, Beginning, End, Return, Document, Sound, and Movie.

Tip Although each of these buttons has a descriptive name, you can use them for any function. You can decide what action they initiate.

To add an Action button to your slide, follow these steps:

1. Make sure you are in Normal view.

2. Choose Slide Show ➪ Action buttons or click the AutoShapes tool on the Drawing toolbar and choose Action buttons. A set of Action buttons is displayed.

3. Click the Action button of your choice.

4. Click the slide on which you would like to place the button. The Action Settings dialog box appears (see Figure 30-9).

Figure 30-9: Use the Action Settings dialog box to create a variety of useful actions.

5. Decide whether you want the action to be taken when you click the button or when the cursor moves over it. Click the relevant tab: Mouse Click or Mouse Over.

Tip It is far safer to take an action by clicking, as it is easy to move your mouse over a button by mistake!

6. Select what is to happen when you click the Action button:

- **Hyperlink to.** This enables you to go to a specific slide in the current slide show — for example, to the first or last; to go to another slide show, run it, and return to the same place or run it and continue; to go to an Internet address; or to go to any other file. (Unless you have a fast Internet connection, be wary of connecting to an Internet site during a presentation.)

- **Run program.** Click Browse to locate the program.

- **Run macro.** If you have recorded macros for use in the presentation, you can choose the one you'd like the Action button to activate from the list provided. If no macros have been recorded, this option isn't available.

- **Object action.** This is not available for Action buttons; it's used to assign actions (Edit or Open) to inserted options such as Excel worksheets or Paint images.

7. You can also have a sound play when you click an Action button, by selecting Play Sound. Select the sound you want to be played from the drop-down list.

8. If you select Highlight Click, then when you click the button in the slide show, the button is highlighted for a moment to indicate that it has been clicked. This is available for certain objects only.

9. To test your Action button, click OK on the dialog box and run the slide show. Click the Action button to ensure that it is working correctly.

Creating a sample action

You may want to have a button that restarts the slide show by returning to the first slide. To place such a button on a slide, follow these steps:

1. Go to the slide on which you want to put the Action button and make sure you are in Normal view.

2. Click AutoShapes on the toolbar and select Action Buttons.

3. Select an Action button and then click on your slide to place it where you would like it. The Action Settings dialog box will appear.

4. Select the Hyperlink to radio button, and then choose First Slide from the drop-down list.

5. Click Play Sound and select a sound from the drop-down list.

6. Click OK to close the dialog box.

7. Test the Action button by clicking the Slide Show View tool. You should see your Action button on the screen. Click it. You should see the Action button change color, hear the sound you selected, and be taken to the first slide in your presentation.

Action settings

If you choose not to use one of the built-in Action buttons, you can use other objects to link to actions. You could use some text, a video clip, a sound, an AutoShape, a macro button, and so forth. To do so, select the object, and then choose Slide Show ➪ Action Settings. The resulting dialog box is the same as the one for Action buttons (refer to Figure 30-9).

Summary

PowerPoint offers you many ways to add visual life to your presentations:

✦ Adding an image to a slide is worth a thousand words. Choose images appropriate to the tone of your presentation using the Clip Organizer.

✦ To add several photos at once to your presentation, use the new Photo Album feature.

✦ Adding sound or video is very effective at drawing attention but uses a lot of disk space.

✦ Adding slide transitions makes the changeover from one slide to the next more interesting, but it's best to use the same transition for several slides, rather than a different transition for each slide.

✦ Preset animations let you bring elements of your slide onto the screen from different directions and with different effects, including sound.

✦ You can customize the way objects come onto the screen by choosing the sequence and timing, and also what sounds accompany them.

✦ Finally, you can create actions. These are useful for rolling demonstrations or onscreen training courses. By clicking on a specific item, for example, you can go to a particular slide, run another program, or run a macro.

✦   ✦   ✦

Finalizing Your Slide Show

O nce your presentation is ready to go, PowerPoint can
do much more for you than just display one slide after
another. You can print supporting materials to distribute to
the audience and record a narration to accompany the show.
You can package the entire presentation on a CD so you can
show it on another machine — even one without PowerPoint
installed. In a corporate environment, you can give your presentation over a network, using the Online Collaboration feature to get everyone together to confer. You can even deliver
your presentation over an intranet or the Internet.

Creating a Slide Show

The Slide Show feature is built into PowerPoint. You do not
need to do anything special to create a slide show — just create the slides and save the presentation. Slide Sorter view is
used to see all the slides in sequence.

Rearranging the slide show

Click the Slide Sorter View tool, which is at the bottom of your
window at the left, or choose View ➪ Slide Sorter. This displays
several slides at once and opens the Slide Sorter toolbar (see
Figure 31-1).

In this view, you can drag the slides from one position to
another to change the sequence in which they will appear.
(Note that you'll have to save the presentation again in order
to preserve these changes.) Use the Zoom tool on the Standard
toolbar to see more or fewer slides on the screen. To delete a
slide, click on it and press Delete, or right-click on it and
choose Delete Slide from the shortcut menu.

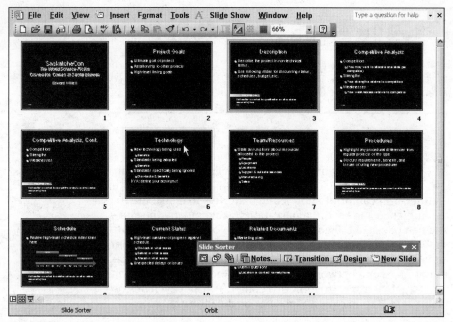

Figure 31-1: You can most easily change the order of the slides in your presentation in Slide Sorter view. Here, the Slide Sorter toolbar has been undocked and moved to the lower-right corner of the window so you can see it better.

Caution   PowerPoint doesn't ask you if you are sure before it deletes a slide, so make sure you really do want to delete the one you've selected. If you make a mistake, click the Undo toolbar button or press Ctrl+Z to get it back immediately.

If you want to move around the slide show in a different sequence, you can branch from one section to another, or even go to another program, by assigning actions.

Cross-Reference   For more information about actions, see Chapter 30.

Hiding slides

Because of time constraints or for other reasons, you may want certain slides not to appear in your presentation, without wanting to delete them.

You can hide them instead. Select a slide and click the Hide Slide button on the Slide Sorter toolbar to hide it, or right-click on the slide and choose Hide Slide from the shortcut menu. To unhide the slide, select it and click the same button again. You can recognize hidden slides in Slide Sorter view because the slide number has a gray diagonal line through it.

Tip If you are running a slide show and want to show a hidden slide, right-click and choose Go to Slide, and then click on the number of the slide you want to show. Slide numbers of hidden slides appear in parentheses. Alternatively, if you already know the number of the hidden slide, you can simply type it and press Enter.

Adding comments

You can add comments to slides in Normal view. Much like the paper sticky notes without which modern offices would grind to a halt, they are easy to insert and just as easy to remove.

Cross-Reference PowerPoint's comments feature is similar to that in Word. For more information about Word's comments feature, see Chapter 10.

Comments are intended for the use of those reviewing the presentation before it is finalized. If you route the presentation to several people, they can each add their comments, and review other people's comments. Each comment starts with the author's name. In addition, each person can choose to run the slide show with or without comments showing.

Here's how it works:

1. Make sure you are in Normal view. Then, choose Insert ➪ Comment. A window into which you can type your comment appears (it's even the same color as a yellow sticky note), along with the Reviewing toolbar (see Figure 31-2).

Tip Once the Reviewing toolbar is active, you can insert a comment by clicking the Insert Comment button on the toolbar.

2. Type the comment and then click outside the comment area.
3. You can move from comment to comment by clicking Next Item or Previous Item on the Reviewing toolbar.
4. Each comment that you insert creates a little marker that appears on the slide (see Figure 31-3). You can move these markers wherever you want — even right off the slide. Pointing at a marker reveals the comment it represents. To edit a comment, click on the marker that represents it, and then click Edit Comment on the toolbar. Note that the text attributes (color, size, font) cannot be changed.

Note These markers appear in Normal view only; they're hidden if you run a slide show that contains slides with comments.

5. Click Insert Comment on the toolbar to add a new comment; click Edit Comment to edit the comment.

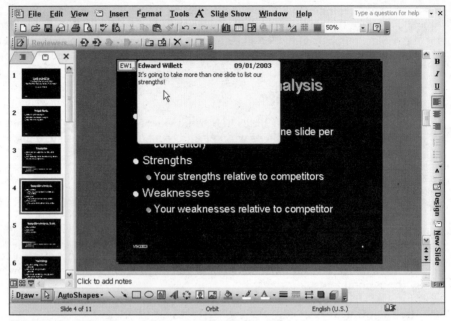

Figure 31-2: Comments are comparable to paper sticky notes on your page. You can move them anywhere. Notice the Reviewing toolbar beneath the Standard toolbar.

6. Click the Markup button on the toolbar (it's the leftmost button) to show or hide comments.

7. Comments can be printed. Choose File ⇨ Print, and make sure the Include comment pages box at the bottom of the Print dialog box is checked. (The only time it's not available is when you're printing an outline.)

Note   The Reviewing toolbar offers other useful options if several people suggest changes to a presentation. Use the Reviewers button to view changes made by all or just certain reviewers, and use the Apply and Unapply buttons to either accept their changes (incorporating them into the presentation) or reject them. A special Revisions task pane makes this easier, offering you a view of the changes made by the reviewer in either List or Gallery form. You can send a presentation via e-mail to other people for comments by choosing File ⇨ Send To ⇨ Mail Recipient (for Review). This instantly creates an e-mail message, using your default e-mail client, with the subject containing the text "Please review 'name of presentation,'" and the presentation attached.

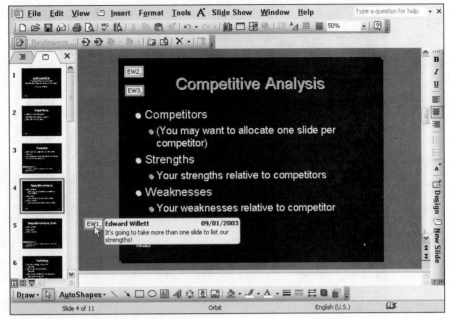

Figure 31-3: This slide has three comments on it, indicated by markers. I've moved one marker right off the slide and pointed at it to reveal its contents.

Adding speaker notes

Speaker notes are printed notes that the presenter uses as a guide while speaking. Whenever you turn around to look at your slides while giving a presentation, you run the risk of losing the attention of the audience. Speaker notes help you avoid this problem, because an image of the slide is printed on the top of the note and the points you want to make are printed at the bottom. (It's sort of like having eyes on the back of your head.) Here are some guidelines:

✦ Speaker notes can be typed into the Notes pane that normally appears beneath the slide in Normal view. You can make this part of the screen larger by dragging the gray bar upward.

✦ Another method is to choose View ➪ Notes Page. This shows the speaker notes as a full page, with an image of the slide at the top and a text box containing the notes at the bottom (see Figure 31-4). Click the Zoom tool to make them readable. You can format your notes as you would any other text.

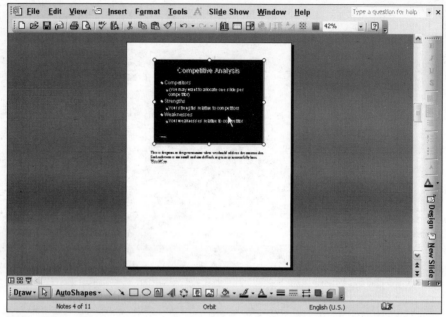

Figure 31-4: The Notes Page view shows you what your speaker notes will look like when printed; you can also enter and format your notes here.

✦ You can also add speaker notes while running the slide show. In the slide navigation shortcuts on the lower-left corner of the slide, click on the one farthest to the right and choose Screen ➪ Speaker Notes. Type your notes in the box provided, and then click Close.

✦ To print speaker notes, choose File ➪ Print. Select Notes Pages from the Print what drop-down list.

Handouts

Handouts are pages with several slides printed on them. They are intended to be handed out to the audience as a reminder of what was covered in the presentation. However, you may also find them useful for reviewing your presentation ahead of time, especially if you have to be away from your computer. You can fit up to nine slides on one letter-sized page.

To print handouts, choose File ➪ Print. Under Print what, select Handouts. Then decide how many slides per page you want to print and in what order. Click Preview to see how your handout will look (see Figure 31-5).

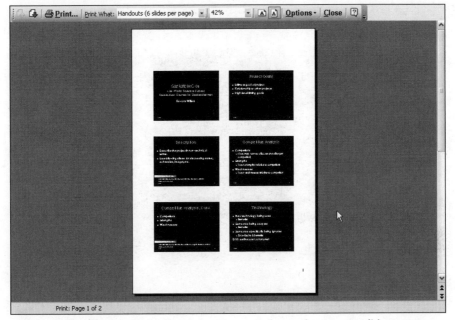

Figure 31-5: When you print handouts, you can choose how many slides per page to print.

Summary slides

A summary slide puts the titles of selected slides on one slide. This is useful for producing an introductory slide that indicates to the audience what subjects you'll be covering, or a closing slide to reinforce your main points. Select the slides you want to summarize in Slide Sorter view by holding down the Ctrl key and clicking on each slide in turn. Click the Summary Slide button on the Slide Sorter toolbar to insert a new slide with the title Summary Slide. The titles of each of the selected slides are listed as bulleted items (see Figure 31-6).

Note

If you have selected more than one slide and the Summary Slide tool is not available, it is probably because one or more of your slides do not have a title placeholder. If you need to include a slide with no title placeholder in the summary slide, you can type its information in manually, or you can change to a slide layout that has a title placeholder. Type in the appropriate text and simply drag the title placeholder off the edge of the slide if you don't want it to show in the presentation.

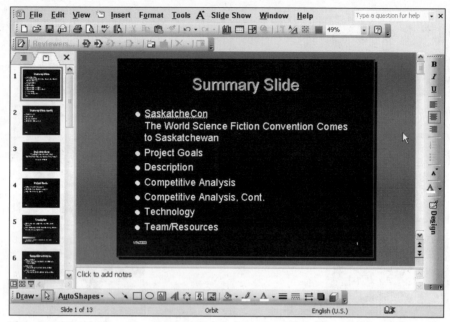

Figure 31-6: When you create a summary slide, the titles of the slides you chose in Slide Sorter view are listed as bulleted items.

Playing the Slide Show

The quickest way to play your slide show is to press F5. Alternative methods are as follows:

✦ Choose View ➪ Slide Show.

✦ Choose Slide Show ➪ View Show.

✦ Click the Slide Show (from the current slide) button at the bottom left of your screen.

Tip   If PowerPoint is not running, you can right-click on the filename in My Computer or Windows Explorer and choose Show to view your slide show.

Moving between slides

To go to the first slide, press Home. To go to the last slide, press End. To end the slide show before it is finished, press Esc. To see a list of the controls you can use in a presentation, press F1 during the slide show.

Table 31-1 shows the mouse and keyboard actions for moving between slides or points on a slide.

Table 31-1 Moving Between Slides	
To the Next Slide/Point	*To the Previous Slide/Point*
Enter	Backspace
Right arrow	Left arrow
Down arrow	Up arrow
N	P
PgDn	PgUp
Space	Right-click (you must first turn off "Popup menu on right mouse click")
Mouse click	

Writing on slides (annotations)

During a slide show, you may want to write on the slide or circle an important item. To do this, click on the middle of the three navigation shortcuts on the lower-left corner of the slide while running the slide. Select from three pointer options: Ballpoint Pen (which makes a thin line), Felt Tip Pen (which makes a thicker line), and Highlighter (which puts a transparent wash of color over selected items on the slide).

Drag the mouse on the screen to draw (see Figure 31-7). You can hold down the Shift key while drawing to keep your lines straight. The following list covers some additional features:

✦ To choose a different pen color, click the shortcut again and choose Ink Color from the shortcut menu. (If right-clicking doesn't work, go to Tools ➪ Options, click on the View tab, and make sure the Popup menu on right mouse click checkbox is checked, as it should be by default.)

✦ The annotations will stay in place until you exit the presentation by pressing Esc. At that point, you'll be offered an option to keep or discard the annotations.

✦ You can't right-click to get to the Pointer Options menu when you have a pen or highlighter selected instead of an arrow. Instead, click the second control from the left in the lower-left corner of your slide. You can also press Ctrl+A to change the pointer back into an arrow and then right-click and choose Pointer Options from the shortcut menu.

✦ To erase all your annotations, choose Erase All Ink on Slide from the Pointer Options menu. To selectively erase your annotations, choose Eraser to turn your pointer into an eraser.

✦ To continue with the slide show, click the shortcut and choose Pointer Options ➪ Arrow Options ➪ Automatic. When you choose Automatic, the pointer automatically disappears if it is not used for 15 seconds.

Tip　When you are giving a presentation, it is handy to be able to display a plain black screen or a plain white screen, to ensure you have the full attention of the audience. To do this, press B for a black screen or W for a white screen. Press any key to continue with the slide show.

Setting up the slide show

In a presentation, the default is to move from slide to slide manually — by pressing a key, for example. However, you can also create self-running presentations for use at trade shows or kiosks. In the slide transitions, you can set the amount of time each slide must stay on the screen before automatically moving to the next slide. Choose Slide Show ➪ Set Up Show to see the options available (see Figure 31-8).

Figure 31-7: On this slide, I've circled SaskatcheCon with the ballpoint pen and Saskatchewan with the felt-tip pen, and highlighted Edward Willett.

Figure 31-8: Use the Set Up Show dialog box to change the options for your slide show.

You have three show types from which to choose:

> ✦ **Presented by a speaker (full screen).** This is the normal option for a presentation. Slides are moved manually from one to the next.
>
> ✦ **Browsed by an individual (window).** This presents the show in a special browser, a version of Internet Explorer (see Figure 31-9).
>
> ✦ **Browsed at a kiosk (full screen).** This prevents the slide show from being modified in any way by the audience, although the viewer can advance through slides at his or her own pace if you've provided navigation buttons. The slide show automatically restarts after five minutes of inactivity and repeats itself when finished.

In the Set Up Show dialog box, you can also do the following:

> ✦ Select the pen color for annotating slides. (This option is active only if Presented by a speaker (full screen) is selected.)
>
> ✦ Decide to run the show without narration or animation.
>
> ✦ Select the range of slides to be shown, or a custom slide show. (See the section "Custom slide shows" later in this chapter.)
>
> ✦ Choose to run the slide show automatically or manually.
>
> ✦ Make use of multiple monitors (if your computer supports this option): one to show the slide show and another to show the special Presenter View, which includes details on what bullet or slide is coming next, enables presenters to see their speaker notes, and lets them jump directly to any slide.

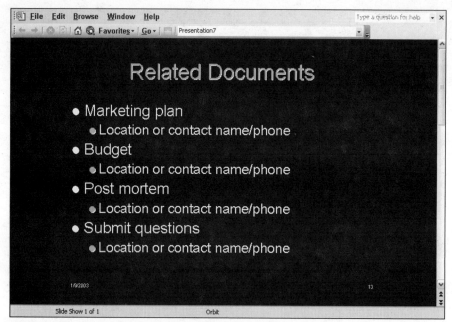

Figure 31-9: When you choose Browsed by an individual (window), the screen displays the slide show in a modified version of Internet Explorer. The toolbar is similar to Explorer's, but the menus are specific to slide shows.

✦ Make use of any graphics acceleration features your video card may have.

✦ Set the resolution at which your show should run: 640×480 for greater speed but lower resolution, or 800×600 for higher resolution but slower transitions between slides.

Setting slide timings

To set the timings for an automatic, self-running slide show, go to Slide Sorter view and select the slides for which you want to set a certain timing. Click the Slide Transition tool on the Slide Sorter toolbar or choose Slide Show ⇨ Slide Transition. This opens the Slide Transition task pane.

Check the Automatically after checkbox in the Advance slide section of the task pane and enter the number of seconds the slide must be displayed.

Note Uncheck the On mouse click checkbox if you don't want the slide to advance when the mouse is clicked. If you leave both options turned on, PowerPoint will advance to the next slide either when you click the mouse or when the time is up, whichever comes first.

Rehearsing slide timings

Rather than set the timing for each slide in the Slide Transition task pane, you can do it on-the-fly, while watching your slide show, by using the Rehearse Timings command. This enables you to vary the timing according to what feels right, rather than just guessing as you have to do in the Slide Transition task pane.

In Slide Sorter view, choose Slide Show ➪ Rehearse Timings or click the Rehearse Timings button. The slide show starts, with the Rehearsal toolbar visible in the upper-left corner of the screen.

The timer starts to run. Whenever you're ready to advance to the next slide, click the Next button on the toolbar. The timer resets. Continue this procedure until you reach the end of the slide show, at which time a dialog box informs you "The total time for the slide show was *xx* seconds. Do you want to keep the new slide timings to use when you view the slide show?" Choose Yes, and the next time you run the slide show automatically, each slide will display for the preset length of time.

Note   If you want to use timings for your show, make sure the Using timings, if present radio button is selected in the Advance slides section of the Set Up Show dialog box (Slide Show ➪ Set Up Show).

Custom slide shows

Once you have created a slide show and presented it, you'll often find you have to repeat the show to another audience, but with some changes. Perhaps you want to hide certain slides, or change the sequence. Create a custom show for this.

Choose Slide Show ➪ Custom Shows. In the resulting dialog box, click New. In the Define Custom Show dialog box (see Figure 31-10), type a name for the custom show, click on the slides you wish to use, and click Add to add them to the list. (To transfer several slides at once to the custom show, hold down the Ctrl key and click on the slides you want, and then click Add.)

To change the sequence of the slides in the custom show, select a slide or slides in the Custom Show list, and then use the up and down arrows.

Click OK when you're done. You can view the show by clicking the Show button in the Custom Shows dialog box.

To set up the custom show, choose Slide Show ➪ Set Up Show. In the Show slides area, click the Custom Show radio button and select your custom slide show from the drop-down list.

To switch back to the full slide show, choose Slide Show ➪ Set Up Show and change the setting under Show slides to All.

Figure 31-10: Select the slides you want to use in a custom show, and rearrange their order.

Using Recorded Narration

You can record narrations to accompany a self-running slide show. Narrations are also useful to store the verbal part of your presentation so that you can put the entire presentation on the Web, to make the presentation available to someone who was not able to attend, or to simply store your presentation along with the speech. You can also use the feature to store comments made during a presentation.

You'll need a microphone and sound card to record narration, and anyone who wants to hear it must also have a sound card and speakers installed on his or her computer. The quality of the speech will vary from system to system. You can record your narration at various levels of quality; just remember that the higher the quality, the more disk space the resulting file will require.

Tip   An alternative to recording sound is to use speaker notes to type the accompanying speech. Doing so uses far less space and avoids potential hardware conflicts and sound-quality issues.

You can record the narration before or during the presentation, and you can record the narration for the entire show or for individual slides. The narration will take precedence over all other sounds attached to a slide, so only the narration will be played unless the other attached sounds are in a different format (e.g., a MIDI file instead of a .wav file) or your sound card supports the playing of two .wav files at once; not all of them do. When you record a narration, a Sound icon appears on each slide (in views other than Slide Show view).

When you play the slide show, you can choose to run it with or without the narration. Choose Slide Show ➪ Set Up Show and select Show without narration if you don't want the narration to play.

Tip One way to minimize the amount of disk space your narration takes up is to change the default .wav file created by the recorder into a more compressed format, such as .mp3. A number of software packages let you do this.

Recording a narration

To record a narration, choose Slide Show ➪ Record Narration. The Record Narration dialog box appears (see Figure 31-11). Here's how it works:

✦ Notice the figures regarding disk use and maximum record time. You probably don't want to fill your hard drive with a sound file!

✦ Choose Set Microphone Level to ensure that the volume is satisfactory.

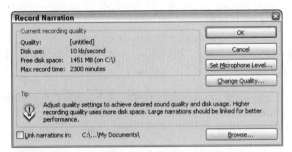

Figure 31-11: The Record Narration dialog box gives you an idea of how much space you will use on your disk. Choose Change Quality to change how much space is needed — the higher the quality, the more space you'll need.

✦ Choose Change Quality and find an appropriate combination of Format and Attributes. Choose the best quality you can use with the disk space you have available. You can save a new combination of Format and Attributes under another name.

Note Quality levels are given in the format "11,025 kHz, 8 bit, Mono," followed by a notation such as "10 kb/sec." This tells you the sampling rate, how the data is stored, whether it's monaural or stereo, and how quickly recording at this rate will eat up disk space. The higher the numbers, the higher the recording quality. The top quality offered, "48,000 kHz, 16 Bit, Stereo," will fill up your disk at the rate of 187 KB/sec — but with a good microphone, you'll get near-CD-quality sound.

✦ If you are recording a large narration, choose Link narrations in and select an appropriate folder. The default folder for linked narrations is the same folder as your presentation. When you link narrations, the narrations are stored in a separate file. If you don't link narrations, the audio is stored within the presentation file.

✦ Click OK and your slide show will start. Record away! To stop recording, press Esc.

Note

When you record narration, PowerPoint also takes note of the timings you use to move from slide to slide. When you stop recording, PowerPoint asks if you want to save your timings as well. This makes recording a presentation intended to run on its own very easy and ensures that the slides and the narration will be in sync.

Re-recording narrations

To re-record narrations — perhaps to correct errors or add new information — select the slide and choose Slide Show ➪ Record Narration and click OK. Record your new narration and press Esc to stop.

Caution

Be careful which slide you stop on. Advance to the slide *after* the one on which you want to stop. For example, if you want to stop on slide 8, then go to slide 9 to stop — otherwise, the new recording will not be saved to slide 8.

Packaging Your Presentation for a CD

Many people create their presentations on one computer but want to run the slide show on another computer.

Provided you have a CD burner available to you, you can use the Package for CD command to put your presentation (and any others you may need) onto a CD that can be played on any other computer, even if it doesn't have PowerPoint installed. You do this from within PowerPoint.

Follow these steps:

1. Choose File ➪ Package for CD. The Package for CD dialog box shown in Figure 31-12 appears.

2. Name the CD.

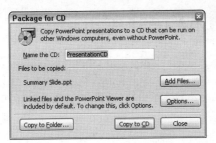

Figure 31-12: Packaging your presentation onto a CD for use on another computer is easily accomplished via this dialog box.

3. By default, all linked files are copied to the CD (for example, Excel spreadsheets you've inserted, sound files, etc.), as is the PowerPoint Viewer, which enables computers that don't have PowerPoint installed to play PowerPoint presentations. To change these options, click the Options button. In the dialog box that appears (see Figure 31-13), you also have the option to include any embedded TrueType fonts (something you should choose if you've used fonts that may not be available on the other computer). You can also assign passwords to your files to protect them against unauthorized viewing or modification. Click OK when you've set the options to your satisfaction.

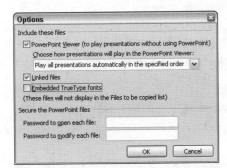

Figure 31-13: Use the Options dialog box to specify how you want your presentation saved to CD.

4. If you simply want to copy the currently active presentation to the CD, click the Copy to CD button.

5. To copy additional presentations to the CD, click Add Files and browse for the presentations you want to add.

Options for Saving Your Presentation

Normally, you save your PowerPoint presentation as a (what else?) PowerPoint presentation. However, PowerPoint offers several other ways to save presentations for various specialized purposes. The one you'll probably use most often is the one that's included right on the File menu, Save as Web Page, but you should also be aware of others.

Putting your presentation on the Web

There are two ways to put PowerPoint presentations on the Web. One is to save files as Web pages; the other is to "publish" them on the Web. If you publish your presentation on the Web, you will be the only person able to edit it. You can make a subset of the slides available and you can choose the browser for which your presentation will be formatted. Some features are available only on the latest browsers. It is important to know which browser and what version of the browser your audience is going to use. If you choose a new version of the browser and your audience has only an older version, it will not display correctly.

If you want to create a Web presentation that other people can edit, save your presentation to the Web as directed in the following section.

Saving a presentation as a Web page

You can save a presentation in Web format on your computer. Use the following method:

1. Open the presentation you want to save in Web format.

2. Choose File ⇨ Save as Web Page. A variation of the Save As dialog box appears (see Figure 31-14).

> **Note**   Pay attention to the title of the Web page. It is the name people see in their browser's title bar when they access the Web presentation, and it appears in their history list (and Favorites list if they save it as such). Therefore, it's important to give it a descriptive title. To change the title, click the Change Title button and enter the new title.

3. The name and other details are already filled in. Choose a location to save it in. Click Save.

4. You can now view the presentation in a regular Internet browser (see Figure 31-15), using the tools along the bottom to navigate and display or hide the outline and notes panes; or you (or anyone else) can click Slide Show and view the presentation as a full-screen slide show.

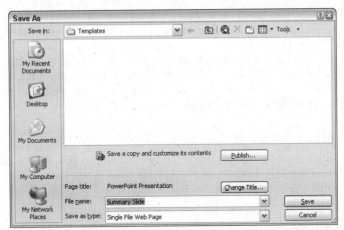

Figure 31-14: When you choose Save as Web Page, this is the dialog box that opens.

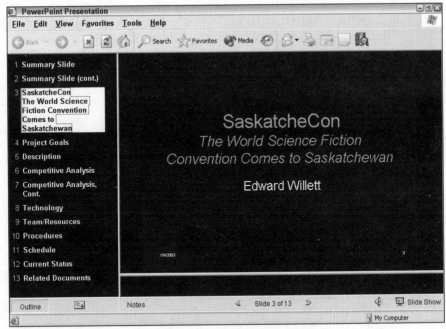

Figure 31-15: Here's how a presentation looks in a browser.

Note   By default, PowerPoint saves presentations as a single-file Web page, which contains all your graphics and other elements within a single file. If you prefer, you can choose Web Page from the Save as type list, instead of Single File Web Page. This saves all the graphics, sounds, etc., as separate files inside a file folder. This enables you to modify elements of the presentation simply by replacing those files with different ones of the same name. (Using the same name is essential.) However, to the viewer, both types of Web pages look the same.

Publishing a presentation on the Web

When you publish a presentation on the Web, as opposed to simply saving it as a Web page, you have special features available that make it run like a slide show. You can move from slide to slide, see the notes pages, and see the outline expanded or collapsed.

To publish a presentation:

1. Open the presentation you want to publish.

2. Choose File ➪ Save as Web Page.

3. Click the Publish button. You have the option to publish the complete presentation, just a select range of slides, or a custom show; you also have the option to display speaker notes. Figure 31-16 shows the various options available in this dialog box.

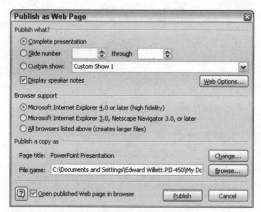

Figure 31-16: Use the Publish as Web Page dialog box to set additional options for how your Web page will appear.

4. If you know that everyone in your audience uses Internet Explorer 4.0 or later, choose that option. If not, choose either of the next two options.

5. Click the Web Options button to customize your presentation setup further. Numerous commands are available here, including the capability to customize the colors of your slide navigation controls, include slide animations, and more.

6. The Publish command also publishes a copy of the presentation to your computer; click the Change button to change the name it's saved under; click the Browse button to select the location to save it to.

7. If you check the Open published Web page in browser checkbox, as soon as the Web page has been created, you will be taken to your default browser to see the results.

8. Click Publish.

Other file formats for saving presentations

PowerPoint lets you save presentations in several other formats. These are just a few:

✦ **Windows Metafile (.wmf).** This saves slides as graphics, as do TIFF Tag Image File Format, Device Independent Bitmap, and Enhanced Windows Metafile. You'll be asked if you want to export just the current slide as a graphics file, or every slide in the presentation.

✦ **GIF Graphics Interchange Format (.gif), JPEG File Interchange Format (.jpg), and PNG Portable Network Graphic Format (.png).** These save slides as graphics readily viewable by Web browsers.

✦ **Outline/RTF (.rtf).** This saves the presentation outline as an outline, preserving most text formatting. It doesn't save any graphics.

✦ **Design Template (.pot).** This saves the presentation as a template, which can then be used as a guide for the creation of other presentations.

✦ **PowerPoint Show (.pps).** Presentations saved in this format always open automatically as a slide show.

✦ **Web Page (.htm).** This saves presentations in a form readable by a Web browser.

✦ **PowerPoint 97-2003 & 95 Presentation (.ppt).** This is necessary only if your recipient has PPT 95, as this setting saves in a format compatible with this version. PPT 97, 2000, and 2002 (XP) can all read PPT 2003 formats, so there is no need to "backsave" with this setting for use with those versions. In fact, it is recommended that you do not do this.

Printing

You may often want or need to print the slides in black and white, and not in the colors used for the presentation. (In fact, you may have no choice, if only a black-and-white printer is available to you.) You can preview how your slides and handouts will look in black and white by clicking the Color/Grayscale button. If you do want to print slides in color for proofing purposes, you will save a lot of time and resources by printing handouts instead of full-page slides.

You can print slides, outlines, speaker notes, and audience handouts. You can print them in color, grayscale, or pure black and white. Table 31-2 shows how objects print in grayscale or pure black and white.

Table 31-2 Grayscale Versus Pure Black and White		
Object	*Grayscale*	*Pure Black and White*
Text	Black	Black
Text shadows	Hidden	Hidden
Embossing	Hidden	Hidden
Fills	Grayscale	White
Frame	Black	Black
Pattern fills	Grayscale	White
Lines	Black	Black
Object shadows	Grayscale	Black
Bitmaps	Grayscale	Grayscale
Slide backgrounds	White	White
Charts	Grayscale	Grayscale

Printing slides

To print your slides, choose File ➪ Print. Figure 31-17 shows the Print dialog box.

You can select the range of slides to be printed. Make sure that you have chosen Slides in the Print what list box. Indicate whether you want the slides to be scaled to fit paper rather than staying scaled as they are on the screen, whether you want to print a frame around the slides, whether you want to print hidden slides, and whether comments and any ink markup should be included.

Figure 31-17: The Print dialog box contains some special options for PowerPoint. The Print what list box is especially important.

Click Preview to see exactly what your slides will look like when printed. Preview will even take into account whether your printer is capable of printing color or not; if it is and you choose to print in color, the Print Preview will be in color. If your printer can print only black and white, even if you choose to print in color, the Print Preview shows you what the result will be in black and white.

Figure 31-18 shows a slide in Print Preview. The Print Preview toolbar provides straightforward options: You can move to the next item; click Print to send the job to your printer; view slides, notes pages, or outline view; zoom in and out; change the orientation of the page (for handouts, notes pages, and Outline view only); and, using the Options button, access many of the commands you've already seen on the Print dialog box. Click Close to exit Print Preview and return to the Print dialog box.

Note   You can access Print Preview from PowerPoint at any time by choosing File ➪ Print Preview.

Printing speaker notes

To print speaker notes, choose File ➪ Print and select Notes Pages under the Print what list box. You have the same options as for printing slides. Prior to printing, you can insert a header and footer by choosing View ➪ Header and Footer and selecting the Notes and Handouts tab.

Figure 31-18: Print Preview lets you see exactly what your presentation will look like when printed.

Printing handouts

To print handouts, choose File ➪ Print and select Handouts under the Print what list box. You have the same options as for printing slides, plus you can choose how many slides to print on one page and the order in which they appear on the page — horizontal or vertical. Prior to printing, you can insert a header and footer by choosing View ➪ Header and Footer and selecting the Notes and Handouts tab.

Printing an outline

Outlines print as they are displayed in the outline pane of Normal view. Whichever levels are showing will print — you can print all the text in your outline or just the slide titles. You can also show or hide formatting.

Printing files in Word

Choosing File ➪ Send to ➪ Microsoft Office Word takes you to the dialog box shown in Figure 31-19. You can send notes pages and outlines to Word and touch up the formatting there. (Word provides a greater selection of formatting tools for text.) Select Paste Link if you want to keep the copy in Word up to date with the information in the PowerPoint presentation.

Figure 31-19: Use this dialog box to format slides, notes pages, and your outline when you send them to Microsoft Word.

When you click OK, Word loads and the slides and notes pages are inserted into a table. Outlines are created using Outline Styles.

Broadcasting over the Internet or an Intranet

If you want to share your presentation with people in different locations, you can broadcast it over the Internet or your corporate intranet. You can include live video and audio. You use either Outlook or another e-mail program to schedule the broadcast. Each person in the audience needs a Web browser in order to see the presentation; they'll also benefit from a broadband connection, although it's not absolutely necessary.

The presentation can be recorded and saved on the Web so that it can be replayed at any stage. If you want to broadcast the presentation to more than 10 people, you need to have Internet Explorer 4.0 or later, and a Windows Media Server. If you're in a corporate environment, consult your system administrator if you need more information about your system and setup.

When you go through the setup to broadcast a presentation, you are asked to provide information for a Lobby Page. This is the page that is displayed before the presentation begins and is used to show a countdown to the presentation and any last-minute messages from the presenter.

Setting up a presentation broadcast

To set up a presentation broadcast:

1. Choose Slide Show ➪ Online Broadcast ➪ Settings (see Figure 31-20) to set up the format for your broadcast. You select audio and video options (None, Audio only, or Video and audio), the Slide show mode (Resizable Screen or Full Screen), whether to display speaker notes, and where to save the broadcast files. Under the Advanced tab, you can set up a remote Windows Media Encoder, enter a URL for an audience chat room so your audience can provide feedback on your presentation, and choose which Windows Media Server you want (which enables you to have more than 10 viewers, if you have one available). Click OK when you are satisfied with your settings.

2. Select Slide Show ➪ Online Broadcast ➪ Schedule a Live Broadcast. In the resulting dialog box (see Figure 31-21), type a description of the broadcast and contact information.

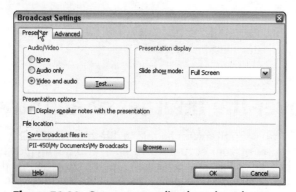

Figure 31-20: Set up your online broadcast here.

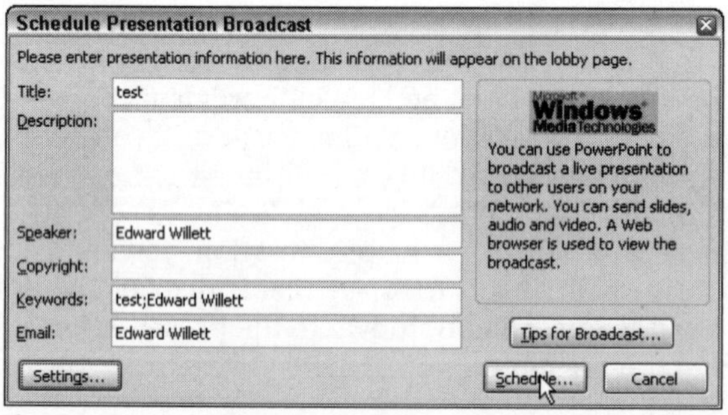

Figure 31-21: Enter information about your broadcast here.

3. Click Schedule and you are taken either to Outlook or to your default e-mail client.

> • If you use Outlook, a meeting request form will appear; use it to set up an online meeting. The link to the broadcast is already set up.

Cross-Reference

See Chapter 25 for more information on scheduling meetings.

> • If you use another e-mail client, use the new e-mail message form that appears to send an e-mail message announcing the broadcast. The URL of the broadcast will be embedded in your e-mail message.

Starting a presentation broadcast

You should start the broadcast as close to the scheduled start time as possible. Follow these steps:

1. Open the presentation you want to broadcast.

2. Choose Slide Show ⇨ Online Broadcast ⇨ Start Live Broadcast now.

Viewing a presentation broadcast

It is a good idea to join the broadcast a few minutes before it starts. When the Lobby Page is opened, it displays a countdown to the start of the broadcast. If there is a delay in starting the broadcast, the host can send a message that displays on the Lobby Page. If you want to continue working, you can minimize the Lobby Page.

✦ If you are an Outlook user, you will be reminded shortly before the broadcast. Click the Join Broadcast button.

✦ If you are using another e-mail client, click the URL on the e-mail message that invited you to the broadcast.

Summary

PowerPoint provides you with many powerful tools for finalizing and fine-tuning your slide show and sharing it with others:

✦ You can change the sequence of the slides and hide slides and delete slides in the Slide Sorter view.

✦ You can print notes pages and handouts as aids to your presentation and automatically create summary slides.

✦ Reviewers can add comments to your presentation; you can run the slide show with or without comments.

✦ While the slide show is playing, you can temporarily annotate slides.

✦ You can run a slide show by advancing the slides automatically, at intervals you specify, or manually.

✦ You can set up custom slide shows that display some or all of the slides in your presentation in a different order.

✦ You can record a narration to accompany the show so that you can give a presentation even if you can't physically be there to accompany it.

✦ The Package for CD command makes it easy to burn your presentation onto a CD for use in a different computer.

✦ You can broadcast your presentation over the Internet or an intranet.

✦   ✦   ✦

Fine-Tuning Your Presentation

In This Chapter

Practice makes perfect

Troubleshooting your slide show

Essential tips for powerful presentations

Creating your presentation is only half the battle: Now, you or someone else has to deliver it. While you may have created a stand-alone presentation for use on a Web site or in a kiosk somewhere, most PowerPoint presentations are given live, with the slides serving to more fully illustrate and emphasize the points made by the presenter.

Considering that polls indicate that the fear of public speaking ranks higher than the fear of death in many people, a brief chapter offering some tips for making the presentation go as smoothly as possible might be welcome.

Practice Makes Perfect

Entertainers know the value of rehearsing. Professional athletes practice daily. Politicians run over speeches umpteen times before finally delivering them.

Why then are so many presenters unwilling to rehearse?

There is no substitute for repeatedly rehearsing your presentation, and any accompanying speech. Here are some suggestions for making that rehearsal as effective as possible:

+ **Be conscious of your body language and the message it communicates.** If you look nervous in front of the audience—because you're fidgeting with a pen, shifting your weight from one foot to the other, constantly running your fingers through your hair, biting your nails, etc.—then the audience will be tense, too. It's really a sympathetic reaction on their part as they imagine themselves in your place. Therefore, when you're rehearsing, practice looking relaxed, even if you don't feel relaxed. In addition, don't go to the other extreme and freeze stiffly, or clasp your hands rigidly behind your back. The key is to use natural hand and body motions — as though you're delivering the speech not to a roomful of strangers, but to people you know and feel comfortable with.

✦ **Consider using props.** A pointer, of either the wooden or laser variety, can help draw attention to important points on the screen and, unlike the built-in annotation tool in PowerPoint, doesn't tie you to the computer keyboard.

✦ **Move around the room.** If you're free to move around the room, do so. You'll hold your audience's attention better than if you're stuck to a lectern. A wireless microphone is therefore preferable to one on a stand. You can still use the lectern to hold notes, props, or perhaps even the computer keyboard if you have to advance the slides manually, but don't use it as a barrier between yourself and your audience.

✦ **Learn your presentation so well that you don't need to rely on notes.** This doesn't mean you have to memorize your presentation word for word; in fact, you probably shouldn't, because rote memorization usually sounds like rote memorization and is only one step away from propping yourself behind the lectern and reading a script word for word. The goal is to learn your material so well that an occasional glance at notes, or better yet at the current PowerPoint slide, is enough to jog your memory, and to learn your material so well that you can present it extemporaneously, speaking in a natural, unstilted fashion.

✦ **Eliminate verbal placeholders.** Placeholders in PowerPoint are objects that simply hold open a place for the actual object you want to insert there. Similarly, verbal placeholders are sounds or words, or fragments of words, that hold open a place for what you really want to say. Everybody uses these in normal conversation — sounds and phrases such as "um," "uh," "you know," "like." However, this is one part of normal conversation you don't want in your presentation. Again, rehearsal is the key. When you know your material well, you don't need to make meaningless sounds while you gather your thoughts for the next point you want to make.

Note   This doesn't mean you should talk nonstop without a pause. It's fine to pause every now and then to gather your thoughts and perhaps glance at your notes; those pauses give the audience members time to gather their thoughts and shift their weight in their chairs. Just don't fill the pause with an "um" or "er," which will make you sound either nervous or uncertain. Silence is fine, in small helpings.

✦ **Practice in front of an audience.** Theater companies frequently invite a small number of people to dress rehearsal, and then hold "previews" before they officially open a play. The presence of an audience changes everything; line deliveries change because of the feedback the audience provides; laughter may result in pauses that were never needed in rehearsal; schtick that had the director rolling on the floor may fall flat as a steamrolled pancake in front of an actual audience. Similarly, that turn of a phrase you think is perfection personified may elicit nothing but a politely puzzled frown from someone who isn't you. Making your presentation in front of an actual person instead of the mirror may reveal to you that you're not communicating the ideas you want to communicate—or, at least, not communicating them as well as you need to if your presentation is to be successful. (On the plus side, though, if you're really good, you might even find you have to pause for laughter, too!)

Troubleshooting Your Slide Show

Rehearsing your role in the presentation is all very well, but it will result in a top-notch presentation only if the heart of that presentation, the PowerPoint slide show, goes off without a hitch.

Here are some pitfalls to avoid. Most of them can be avoided with a little extra planning before giving the presentation—or even a little extra thought during the design process.

✦ **Equipment problems.** The best way to avoid these is to show up early for your presentation and ensure that everything works. Turn everything on, double-check the connections, and start the presentation. If sound is involved, make sure it plays when it's supposed to and can be heard. In addition, never rely on your laptop's battery, no matter how fully charged you think it is; if there's an outlet nearby, use it. (Make sure the cord isn't in a place where it can be tripped over; tape it down if you have to.) Don't leave Standby Power Management turned on in your laptop; it can take forever for a laptop to come back to life from standby, and sometimes you'll even have to reboot it.

✦ **Cropped slides.** Make sure the projector's resolution (if a projector is involved) matches your computer's. Be cautious about putting anything too close to the edge of a slide: If the screen is a little too small (or too close to the projector), your audience could miss information.

✦ **Hard-to-read slides.** Slides that look just fine on the computer screen may look awful under presentation conditions. To avoid the most common problems, make sure your text is large (almost never smaller than 24-point); avoid both dark fonts on dark backgrounds and light fonts on light backgrounds; avoid dark backgrounds in a poorly lit room and light backgrounds in a well-lit room; and use animations sparingly (they distract the audience and clutter up the slide; use them only when they help you make a specific point).

Tip

If you're not sure what the lighting conditions will be in the room where you'll be presenting, make two versions of your presentation: one with dark backgrounds and one with light backgrounds. That way, you'll be prepared no matter what the ambient lighting is like.

✦ **Overcrowded slides.** "TMI" is more than a catchphrase you use when some-one provides "too much information" about his or her personal life; it can also be a problem with PowerPoint slides. Too much information on a PowerPoint slide results in a cluttered slide that's hard to read. Generally, any slide that you have to show for more than five minutes while you talk about it probably has too much information on it and should be broken down into additional slides. One or two minutes per slide is a better goal to aim for.

✦ **Inconsistent appearance.** This can be a problem in a presentation prepared by more than one person. Maybe someone decided halfway through to use a different font than anyone else, or a different background color. Look for these problems and correct them before you give the presentation; aim for a consis-tent look to all your slides. That means not only the same fonts, colors, and backgrounds but also the same style of illustrations: A presentation illustrated with a photo on one page, a cartoon on the next, and a scrawled doodle scanned in from the back of a napkin on the next is generally one that needed a little more work before it saw the light of day.

✦ **Poor-quality graphics.** Images, like animations, should be used sparingly and only when they help communicate the points you're trying to make. If you do have a good use for an image, make sure it is of a high-enough resolution to both look good and be recognizable. You don't want the audience straining their eyes to try to figure out what that blob in the corner of the slide is when you're trying to convince them to invest in your company.

✦ **Complete failure.** Even if you test all your equipment ahead of time, some-thing could still go catastrophically wrong when it comes time to launch your presentation. Therefore, you should always have a low-tech backup plan and the equipment necessary to carry out that plan if needed: If you've created a set of overheads just in case the computer setup didn't work, for instance, then make sure you also request the presence of an overhead projector. For the ultimate backup plan, use PowerPoint's handout-printing capability to prepare a paper version of the presentation.

Ten Top PowerPoint Tips

Finally, here are answers to ten of the most common questions people ask about PowerPoint. If your question isn't answered here (or elsewhere in this book), you might try http://support.microsoft.com, which includes lists of frequently asked questions, the searchable Microsoft Knowledge Base, links to newsgroups, a variety of customer service options, and a ton of other helpful information.

1. How do I change an entire presentation's format?

The Master Slides hold the formats for all the slides in your presentation. Any changes made to these affect all the slides based on them. There are three masters: Slide, Handouts and Notes. To change the Slide Master, choose View ➪ Master ➪ Slide Master (see Figure 32-1).

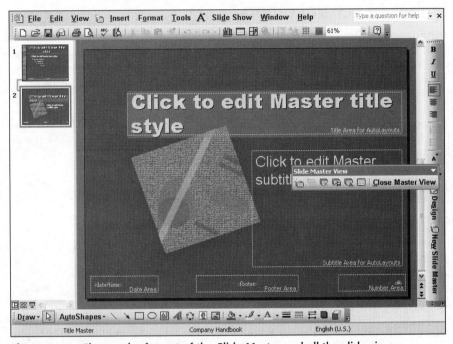

Figure 32-1: Change the format of the Slide Master and all the slides in a presentation will change.

There are two different Slide Masters: one for title slides (shown in Figure 32-1) and one for other slides. Click where the Masters say click (i.e., where it says "Click to edit Master title style") and edit the contents of each of the placeholders as you see fit. You can also change the background image for the Master, and thus for all slides; and even insert a picture onto a Master that will then appear on all slides.

When you have made your changes, click Close Master View on the Master toolbar.

Masters are covered in detail in Chapter 28.

2. How can I copy one object's format to several others?

The Format Painter tool can quickly copy formatting from one object to another. Select the object whose formatting you want to copy. Click the Format Painter button on the Standard toolbar, and your mouse pointer changes to look like the Format Painter icon on the button. Click on the object to which you want to apply the formatting.

To copy the formatting to several objects at once, double-click the Format Painter tool and then click on each object in turn. When you have finished, click the Format Painter tool again.

3. Where on the Web can I find additional clip art, textures, sounds, and video?

On the Web, Microsoft provides additional items for you to use in your presentations. When you choose Insert ⇨ Picture ⇨ ClipArt or Insert ⇨ Movies and Sounds ⇨ Movie from Clip Organizer or Sound from Clip Organizer, the Clip Art task pane that opens includes a link labeled Clip art on Office Online (see Figure 32-2). If you're connected to the Internet, clicking this will take you to Microsoft's Clip Art and Media Home, part of the Office site maintained by Microsoft. You can search for and select what you want to download from here. It will automatically be placed in your Clip Organizer.

For more information on using the Clip Organizer in PowerPoint, see Chapter 30. For more information on the Clip Organizer in general, see Chapter 43.

4. How can I set the defaults for drawing objects?

Suppose you decide that you want all drawing objects to have a certain thickness of border and color or fill. Draw one object with those features. Choose Format ⇨ AutoShape (see Figure 32-3) and format the shape as you see fit, and then check the Default for new objects checkbox before clicking OK. This sets the default for the active presentation.

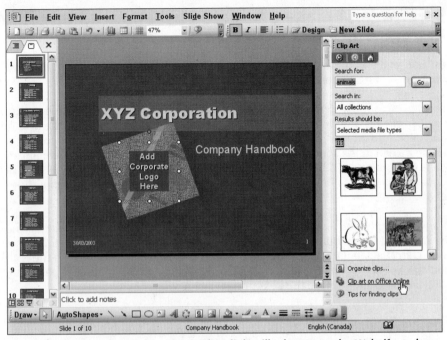

Figure 32-2: The Clip art on Office Online link will take you to the Web, if you have access, where you can pick up additional clip art, movies, and sounds.

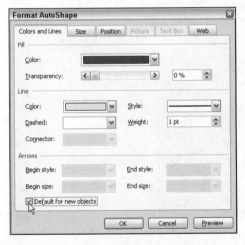

Figure 32-3: The Default for new objects checkbox on the Format AutoShape dialog box sets the default for your presentation.

Cross-Reference

Office's drawing tools are described in detail in Chapter 43.

5. How can I make a bulleted list show up one item at a time during my presentation?

An effective way to present a bulleted list is to show one bullet at a time during your presentation. How can you do that in PowerPoint?

Create your slide with the bulleted list. Then choose Slide Show ➪ Custom Animation to open the Custom Animation task pane (see Figure 32-4). Highlight the first bullet, and click Add Effect. Choose Entrance, and pick the entrance effect you want from those provided. As soon as you choose an effect, it is previewed in the main slide pane (assuming AutoPreview is checked at the bottom of the task pane, as it is by default), so you can immediately see what it will look like when used in a slide show.

For each point, you also need to specify how the animation should begin; typically, if you're building a bulleted list point by point, you want to click to bring in each point, so the default option, On Click, works fine. You can also have all the entrances happen simultaneously, or set a specific amount of time to pass after the previous entrance before the next one occurs.

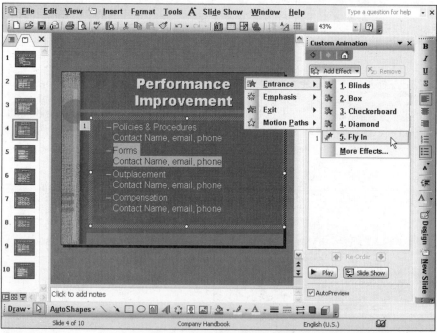

Figure 32-4: Use the Custom Animation task pane to create a build effect on a bulleted list.

Cross-Reference For more detailed information on custom animations, see Chapter 30.

6. What are comments and how do they work?

Comments are small text boxes that you can attach to slides, much as you would use paper sticky reminder notes on a paper document. You can pass the presentation to other people to run on their computer so that they can add their own comments. Use the File ➪ Send to ➪ Mail Recipient (for Review) menu command if you like. When you give the presentation, you can hide the comments.

To add comments, choose Insert ➪ Comment. The Reviewing toolbar automatically appears. The registered user name appears at the beginning of the comment, as shown in Figure 32-5. Type your comment and then click the slide.

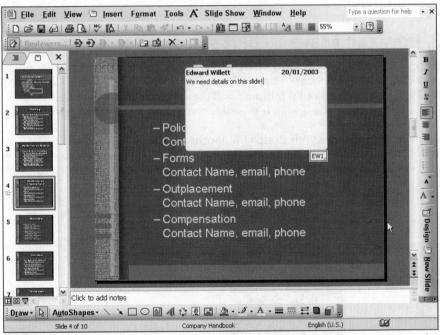

Figure 32-5: A comment is like a paper sticky note. The user's name automatically appears at the beginning of the comment.

You can hide comments (or reveal them, if they're already hidden) while you're working on a presentation by clicking the Markup button on the Reviewing toolbar or choosing View ➪ Markup.

Cross-Reference   For more information on inserting comments, see Chapter 31.

7. What is a summary slide?

After you have created a series of slides, you can automatically create a single slide that summarizes the slides you select by including the title of each slide. Go to Slide Sorter view, hold down the Ctrl key, and click on each slide you want to include in the summary.

Click the Summary Slide button on the Slide Sorter toolbar. The summary slide is inserted before the first selected slide, with the title of each selected slide appearing as a bullet.

Cross-Reference   For more information on summary slides, see Chapter 31.

8. How can I save a chart's design for future use?

You can save the design of any chart you create. To save the design, first create your chart and then choose Chart ⇨ Chart Type. Select the Custom Types tab and click the User-defined radio button. Click the Add button, name your design, and type a description. The design is added to the list of user-defined chart types.

When you want to use your design for another graph, select Chart ⇨ Chart Type. Select the Custom Types tab and the User-defined radio button. You should see your design on the list (see Figure 32-6). Select it and it will be applied to your graph.

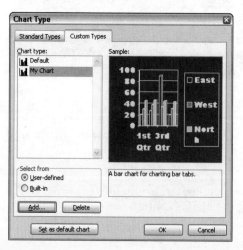

Figure 32-6: If you save a custom-made chart design on the Custom Types tab of the Chart Type dialog box, you can use it repeatedly.

Cross-Reference Charts are covered in detail in Chapter 29.

9. How do I change one AutoShape into a different one?

If you have added an AutoShape and you decide you'd rather it be a different shape, you can change it. You may have been using the flowchart shapes and want to change from one shape to another. Select the shape you want to change and click the Draw Menu tool on the Drawing toolbar. Select Change AutoShape and select the new shape you want. You can also change the proportion of the shape by dragging the yellow diamond handles.

Cross-Reference AutoShapes are covered in more detail in Chapter 43.

10. How can I copy a complete presentation for use on another computer?

PowerPoint Viewer is a program supplied with PowerPoint (or you can get it from the Web at www.microsoft.com) that lets you run a slide show on a computer that does not have PowerPoint loaded. (The license allows you to copy this program freely.) To copy your presentation for use on another computer, choose File ➪ Package for CD. In the dialog box, click Options, and make sure that the PowerPoint Viewer option is checked under Include these files.

Click Copy to CD in the Package for CD dialog box, and all the necessary files will be burned onto a CD to enable another computer to display your presentation (assuming, of course, that you have access to a CD burner and the other computer has a CD-ROM drive).

Cross-Reference For a more detailed discussion of transporting presentations, see Chapter 31.

Summary

In this chapter, you learned some tips for delivering a successful PowerPoint presentation and the answers to ten commonly asked questions. Highlights included the following:

✦ Rehearsal is key to delivering your part of a PowerPoint presentation.

✦ Even if you're nervous, do your best to appear as if you're at ease.

✦ Know your material cold, so you don't have to either memorize it or read it.

✦ Avoid embarrassment by checking and double-checking the equipment before you begin a presentation — and have a backup plan, such as overhead transparencies, ready just in case.

✦ Design your presentation with legibility in mind — and if you're not sure what the lighting conditions will be in the room where you'll be showing your slide show, consider making two versions: one for use in good lighting, one for use in poor.

✦ PowerPoint offers numerous tools for formatting slides, entire presentations, or just selected points, including the Slide Masters (for entire presentations) and the Format Painter (for selected points).

✦ Additional clip art is readily downloadable from Microsoft's Web site.

✦ Animation can be used effectively to bring in points one at a time, but in general, animation should be used sparingly to avoid distracting the audience rather than communicating with it.

✦ The Package for CD command puts all the files necessary to show your presentation on another computer — even one without PowerPoint! — onto a CD (provided, of course, you have access to a CD burner).

✦   ✦   ✦

Using Access

Fundamentals of Access

◆ ◆ ◆ ◆

In This Chapter

Using Access to manage data

The elements of an Access database

How to plan a database

◆ ◆ ◆ ◆

Access is a full-featured relational database management system. Before you can learn how to use Access, you need to learn a few fundamentals of databases in general, and Access in particular. This chapter starts on the ground floor of databases, where you learn the terminology that you need to survive in "Accessland."

If you are already familiar (and comfortable) with working with databases, chances are good that you can skip over this chapter and jump right to Chapter 34, "Creating a Database," where you learn how to create databases and fill them with data.

Basic Database Concepts

Perhaps the simplest definition of a database is that it is an organized collection of information. It doesn't really matter what the information is; it could be just about anything. The following are all examples of databases:

+ Names and contact information for all the homeowners in your neighborhood

+ All the movie information from your collection of DVDs

+ Account information for all the companies to which you owe money

+ The repair history for your 1965 Ford Mustang

+ Information about the photographs in your photo albums

The list could go on and on. The bottom line is that if the information can be organized in some coherent fashion, it qualifies as a database. If your database is small (for example, your list of credit cards), you can probably manage the information manually. In such instances, you might use a traditional management method such as a card file or a simple list on a piece of paper.

As the database becomes larger, your management task becomes more difficult. For those tasks, you need specialized computer software. Access is an example of a classification of software known as *database management software.* In other words, Access helps you to create and efficiently manage the content of a database — any database. Access provides the structure, tools, and features necessary to help you make sense of your collection of information.

In Access, a database consists of more than just raw information. In addition to data (organized into tables), Access databases can also contain related queries, forms, reports, and programming instructions. It is helpful to understand what is meant by each of these items.

Access tables

A table, in Access, is the organized representation of your data. Tables contain related information, and there can be more than one table in any given database. Access provides tools to not just organize information in a single table but also to maintain relationships between multiple tables in a database.

For example, you might have a database that contains information about your DVD movie collection. One table could contain all the movie titles, and another could contain the names of all the actors and actresses. Still another table contains information about the ratings used by the movies. All three tables contain related information, so they belong to the same database.

Tables are made up of *fields* and *records.* Fields represent a single piece of information, such as a movie title or a purchase date. Records are individual collections of fields. For instance, name, address, and phone number are individual fields, but taken together, these fields represent a record of an individual.

In the database world, the terms *record* and *row* are often used synonymously. Similarly, the terms *field* and *column* are used synonymously. This is because the information in a table can be expressed as a series of columns and rows, much like an Excel worksheet. The columns represent fields, and the rows represent individual records, as shown in Figure 33-1.

Fields

Title	Pub Date	Last Update	Synopsis	Article N	K1	K2	K3	K4	K5	K6
Finding Related Words	7/29/2002	7/29/2002	How to locate a	904	290					
Selecting an Entire Paragraph	7/29/2002	7/29/2002	Different ways y	905	196					
Selecting a Word	7/29/2002	7/29/2002	Using the mous	906	196	198				
Understanding Sections	7/29/2002	7/29/2002	What is a sectio	907	221					
Creating Sideheads	7/29/2002	7/29/2002	How to stick a s	908	286					
Animated Menus	7/29/2002	7/29/2002	Want to liven up	909	232					
Understanding Grayscale Images	7/29/2002	7/29/2002	Exactly what do	910	181					
Selecting Drawing Objects	7/29/2002	7/29/2002	How to select o	911	181					
Duplicating Drawing Objects	7/29/2002	7/29/2002	How to make co	912	215					
Moving Drawing Objects	7/29/2002	7/29/2002	Put your drawin	913	181					
Fast Spelling Corrections	8/19/2002	8/19/2002	How to easily c	914	275					
Selecting Individual Cells in a Table	8/19/2002	8/19/2002	Methods for sel	915	186					
Headings On Your Printout	8/19/2002	8/19/2002	Making sure tha	916	207	183				
Quickly Moving Your Table	8/19/2002	8/19/2002	How to make sh	917	210					
Resizing Your Table	8/19/2002	8/19/2002	A quick way to	918	212					
Doubling Your Money	8/19/2002	8/19/2002	Make your print	919	235					
Making Use of Extra Labels	8/19/2002	8/19/2002	How to use the	920	235					
Saving Money on Printing Labels	8/19/2002	8/19/2002	Don't use your e	921	235					
Printing an Outline	8/19/2002	8/19/2002	Printing an outli	922	202	183				
Printing a Short Selection	8/19/2002	8/19/2002	How to print jus	923	183					
Nifty Zooming	8/19/2002	8/19/2002	Using the mous	924	200	198				
*				0						

Record: ◄◄ ◄ 899 ► ►◄ ►* of 919

Records

Figure 33-1: Data tables are composed of columns and rows.

Later in this chapter you learn how to plan for a database, which involves determining which fields you want in a table. You then put that information to use in Chapter 34, where you create an actual database.

Access queries

Some databases contain many tables, or contain tables that have quite a few fields and records in them. When you work with large databases, there are times you want to work with only a subset of the information contained in the database. For example, if you have a database of customer contacts, you might want to see only those customers who lived in Colorado, or only those customers who purchased more than $1,000 of your products. In such instances, Access allows you to create *queries* to view just the information you want.

In Access, a query defines the database information you want to view. This query definition is stored in Access as part of the database, so that you can use it over and over again. Essentially, it limits or filters the information in a database. Access allows you to get as complex or as specific as you desire in your queries.

Because queries allow you to work with just a subset of your database, they are very helpful. They not only allow you to see just the information you need, but they also help protect the information you don't need from being changed accidentally.

Cross-Reference
You learn detailed information about how to use queries in Chapter 36.

Access forms

A database exists to store information. After you determine the information your database will contain, you need to enter the data. Later, you might want to examine, add to, or change that data. Access provides several ways you can enter information in a database. One of the most powerful methods is through the use of forms.

In Access, forms are custom display screens that allow you to view, enter, and edit information. Access allows you to design forms so they display exactly the information you want, and in the way you want to see it. Besides displaying information, forms can also include buttons, text boxes, labels, and other objects that can be programmed to perform specific tasks. Figure 33-2 shows an example of an Access form.

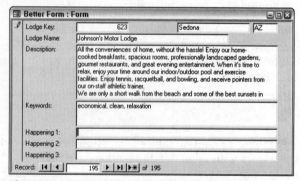

Figure 33-2: Access forms are used to enter and edit data.

Forms are saved in Access as a part of your database. You can have as many forms in your database as you desire.

Cross-Reference
You can find detailed information about how to design and use forms in Chapter 35.

Access reports

When you are working with a data table in Access, you can choose to print the data in the table. This is a handy feature, but it isn't very practical in the real world. Raw data — arranged in a table format — is generally unappealing except to the geekiest of users. Because of this, Access allows you to create defined reports that are generated based upon information contained in your database.

Essentially, an Access report is a template that defines how data should be displayed. Reports can be generated either to the screen or to another output device, such as a printer. Reports include static information (headers, labels, lines, or other elements), as well as dynamic information pulled from a table or from the results of a query. Reports can perform simple data manipulation, such as sorting or filtering data, or even perform elemental calculations. Figure 33-3 shows an example Access report.

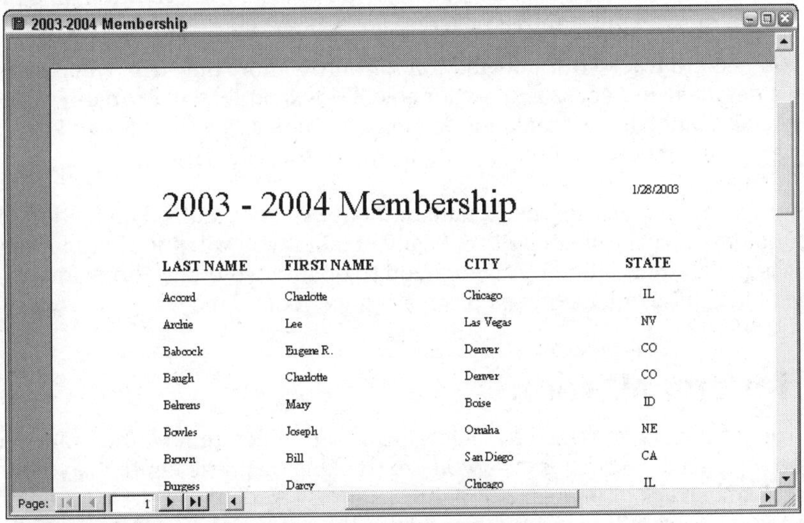

Figure 33-3: An Access report, printed to the screen

The key thing to remember is that the reporting feature of Access is extremely versatile — you are given a blank "canvas" on which to create your report, and then how your report eventually appears is limited only by your imagination.

Reports are saved as a part of your Access database. You can define as many reports as you desire, which is a great feature when you want to create custom output for different needs.

Cross-Reference   You can find detailed information about how to design and use reports in Chapter 37.

Planning a Database

Before you start to develop a database, you need to plan it. The first step in effective planning is to realize that not every collection of information is well suited to being maintained with database management software such as Access. Two particular areas come immediately to mind:

✦ If the amount of data to be maintained is small and will remain small, using Access is probably overkill. For example, you generally don't use Access to keep track of the fertilizing schedule for your backyard garden. Although you can do it, no real advantage is gained by using Access for such a simple task. For simple tasks, you can keep track of the necessary information on a piece of paper, or even put it into a program such as Excel.

✦ If you need to track your information for only a short time, the value of creating a database in Access is questionable. For example, you probably won't use an Access database to track phone messages unless you wanted to keep them for a very long period of time, perhaps for historical analysis.

Earlier in this chapter, you learned that a database is an organized collection of information. If you keep this definition firmly in mind, you will find that planning a database is not all that difficult. All you need to do are two things: Look for obvious ways the data can be organized and always reduce redundancy.

Look for organization

The nature of the data you need to maintain will often dictate how that information should be organized. For instance, if you are tracking business contacts, you probably want to keep track of names, companies, addresses, e-mail addresses, and several phone numbers. In this case, the nature of the data — contact information — dictates the organization of that data.

As you are considering the data you need to manage, jot down your initial organization thoughts on a piece of paper. As you continue to consider your data, additional organizational categories might present themselves.

Tip   In database design, there is a direct correlation between organization and fields. As you determine what you are tracking, these items become the basis for the individual fields in the tables of your database.

Reduce redundancy

It is easy for related information in a database to quickly become redundant. For instance, if you are developing a database of customers of your company, you might decide that your table organization should include the following:

✦ Name

✦ Company

✦ Address 1

✦ Address 2

✦ City

✦ State

✦ ZIP Code

✦ Office Phone

✦ Home Phone

✦ Mobile Phone

✦ E-mail

This seems simple enough, and you can quickly (within minutes) set up an Access table with fields that correspond to this organization. A couple of more minutes, and you can even have data entered.

One of the first things you will notice, however, is that you start to see redundancies in your data. For instance, you might have many customers who live in the same city. Over time, as information is entered for each customer record by different people in your department, you notice discrepancies in the way the city names appear. One person might enter a city as "Los Angeles," another as "Las Angeles," and still another as "LA."

In this case, the city name has become redundant, and this redundancy offers the possibility for inconsistent data (such as the spelling differences). A more efficient approach in Access is to move redundant data to a different table. For instance, you might develop another table that uses the following organization:

✦ ZIP Code

✦ City

✦ State

Now, you can go back to your original customer table and get rid of the City and State fields. Once you know the ZIP Code for your customer, Access can find the corresponding city and state in the other table. This is done by using the Access tools, which help establish a relationship between your customer table and your ZIP Code table. By splitting up the data in this way, you have less redundancy because the city and state are not repeated in every record. The result is more consistent data — less chance for errors.

Note   Designing efficient databases is a complex topic — it has even been the subject of entire university-level courses. If you are interested in learning more about the topic, you should investigate the many books available on the subject and find one that is most applicable to the type of work for which you use Access.

Summary

If your database needs have progressed beyond what you can comfortably manage on a pad of sticky notes, on a legal pad, or on a handheld computer, you need a database management system, such as Access. In this chapter, you have learned the fundamentals of Access and how those fundamentals apply to using the program. Specifically, you have learned that:

✦ Access is a powerful database management system.

✦ Access databases are composed of tables and other objects, such as queries, forms, and reports.

✦ Data tables are similar to Excel worksheets. They are composed of fields (columns) and records (rows).

✦ Queries allow you to work with subsets of a larger database.

✦ Forms are used to conveniently enter or edit data in a database.

✦ Reports are used to display or print database information.

✦ Access databases can contain multiple tables, queries, forms, and reports.

✦ When planning an Access database, you should look for ways to naturally organize your data and reduce redundancy.

✦   ✦   ✦

Creating a Database

T his chapter covers how to create a new database and
work with the primary component of any database — its
tables. Access database tables, as you learned in Chapter 33,
are similar in many ways to Excel worksheets. The first task in
creating a database is to create one or more tables to hold the
database's data. Access provides three primary ways to create tables, but you can also import data from other database
programs (you can export to other database formats, also).
Access can link to databases created in other database programs as well. Once you have a database either created or
linked to, you can change its look, sort and index the data,
and print it.

Creating a New Database

When you first start Access, you are presented with a normal
Office-type screen: menu at the top, data area at the left, and a
Task pane at the right. By default, the data area is empty,
awaiting your command to either load an existing database or
to create a new one.

There are several commands you can use to create a new
Access database:

   ✦ Click the Blank Database link on the Home pane.
   ✦ Choose File ➪ New.
   ✦ Press Ctrl+N.
   ✦ Click the New button on the toolbar.

It is interesting that out of these four methods, the final three
have the same result — all they do is display the New File
pane at the right of the screen. If you then click the Blank

Database link on the New File pane, you get to the same dialog box (shown in Figure 34-1) that you get when you simply click the Blank Database link from the Home pane.

Figure 34-1: Creating a new database

The File New Database dialog box is where you specify a name for the database you are creating. Access supplies a default name for the database, such as db1, db2, and so on, but it is best to give your database a more descriptive name. You can then click Create, and Access displays the screen shown in Figure 34-2.

Figure 34-2: The Database window

At the left-hand side of the screen, you can see the different objects your database can contain: Tables, Queries, Forms, Reports, and so on. (You learned about many of these objects in Chapter 33, "Fundamentals of Access.") If you click one of the objects, the right-hand side of the screen shows the objects in the database that are of that type. The first step in creating a new database is to define the tables that will be contained in it, so the Tables object category should be selected.

The Database window presents three ways you can create new tables for your database:

✦ Create Table in Design View

✦ Create Table by Using Wizard

✦ Create Table by Entering Data

Each of these methods is examined in the following sections.

Designing a new table

The most common method of creating a new table is to use Design view. In this view, you can examine the different fields in the table, along with their characteristics. To create the table, double-click Create Table in Design View option in the Database window. You will see the Design view for the new table appear, as shown in Figure 34-3.

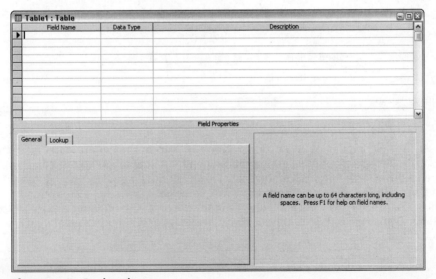

Figure 34-3: Design view

Design view features three columns at the top of the screen (Field Name, Data Type, and Description), two tabs at the lower left, and a help area at the lower right. To design your table, provide field names in the Field Name column, and then choose a data type in the Data Type column. Optionally, you can include comments about each field in the Description column.

In Chapter 33 you learned that fields in Access represent individual pieces of data. In order to store the information in a table correctly, Access needs to know something about that information. For this reason, you must assign a data type to each field in your table. The different data types available are shown in Table 34-1.

<table>
<tr><td colspan="2" align="center">Table 34-1
Data Types</td></tr>
<tr><td>*Data Type*</td><td>*Description*</td></tr>
<tr><td>Text</td><td>Used to put a maximum of 255 characters into a field. "Text" doesn't just mean letters in this case but can also include numbers, punctuation, and any other characters.</td></tr>
<tr><td>Memo</td><td>Used to put larger text entries into a field, up to 65,536 characters.</td></tr>
<tr><td>Number</td><td>Used for numerical fields.</td></tr>
<tr><td>Date/Time</td><td>Used for date and time fields. Can run from the year 100 to 9999.</td></tr>
<tr><td>Currency</td><td>Used for monetary fields.</td></tr>
<tr><td>AutoNumber</td><td>Used to automatically assign a unique value to a record.</td></tr>
<tr><td>Yes/No</td><td>Used for binary (true/false) fields.</td></tr>
<tr><td>OLE Object</td><td>Used to link or embed objects in a field.</td></tr>
<tr><td>Hyperlink</td><td>Used to establish the URL to a resource either on the Internet or locally.</td></tr>
<tr><td>Lookup Wizard</td><td>Used to create a list of possible options in a field.</td></tr>
</table>

When you select a data type, several options appear on the General tab (see Figure 34-4). The available options vary depending upon the data type you select. For instance, the Currency and Number data types ask how many decimal places you want, but the Text data type does not. Also, some data types have an option in which you can specify a Format, whereas others don't. You have several formatting options available for the Number or Date/Time data types, but none for Text.

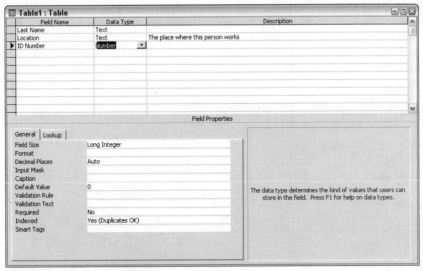

Figure 34-4: The General tab

Note

Although you aren't required to make any formatting choices, you might want to consider some of the more important options. Caption, for instance, can help you avoid a common problem with Access databases. Access automatically uses the field name on reports. However, if you insert a caption, it will appear instead of the field name. If you have a very long field name, using a shorter caption can vastly improve the appearance of your database output.

Required fields

One of the options available for each data type is the Required option. This option, which can be Yes or No, indicates whether the user, when entering data, must enter something in this particular field. You should give serious thought to which fields should have required data entry. Not all of them are critical in most databases, but some are. In a customer list database, for instance, you should certainly require information for name, address, and ZIP code, although a fax number might be included.

Assigning a primary key

In database terminology, a *key* is a field by which a record can be easily retrieved. Access strongly encourages (but does not require) you to designate a primary key for each table in your database. The primary key is usually used to tie records in different tables together. Thus, if you are only going to have a single table in your database, you won't need to specify a primary key. However, if you're going to create a multiple-table database, you'll have to have one.

The primary key should be some absolutely unique item, such as a driver's license number or company ID number. (These also make good primary keys because it is unlikely they will change.) To make a particular field the primary key, click the Primary Key button on the toolbar or right-click the field name and select Primary Key from the pop-up menu (see Figure 34-5).

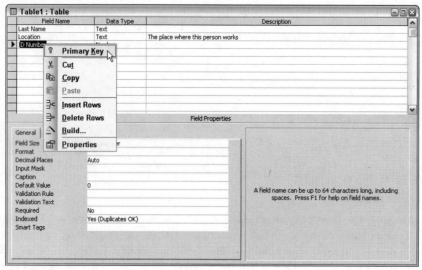

Figure 34-5: Setting the primary key

Saving your table

To save your table, click the Save button on the toolbar. You'll then see a dialog box asking for the table name. Either accept the default one or supply your own, and then click the OK button.

After your table is saved, it appears in the right-hand side of the Database window whenever you have the Tables object category selected in the left-hand side.

Creating a table with a wizard

Another way to create a new table in a database is through the use of a wizard. If you double-click the Create table by using wizard option in the Database window (refer to Figure 34-2), you will then see the Table Wizard, shown in Figure 34-6.

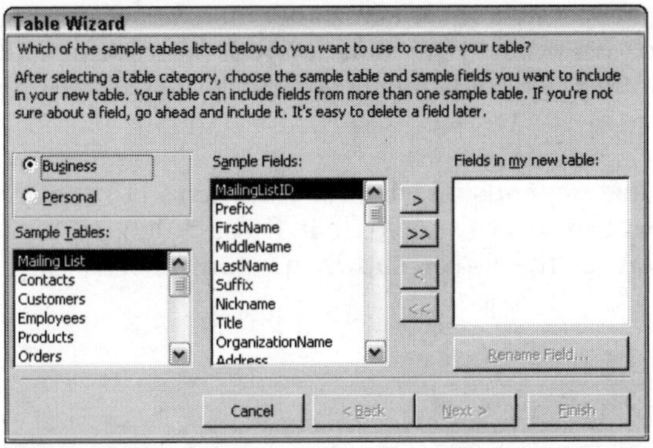

Figure 34-6: The Table Wizard

Using the controls in the wizard, you should specify whether you intend this table to contain Business or Personal data. Depending on your choice, the options available in the Sample Tables list will change. Likewise, when you select one of the sample tables, the options available in the Sample Fields list will change.

To select a field, just click the field you want and then click the right-pointing arrow that appears to the right of the field list. The field is then moved to the Fields in My New Table list. Once the field is in that list, you can rename it (by clicking the Rename Field button) or you can remove it from the list by clicking the left-pointing arrow between the field lists.

When you are satisfied with the fields selected, just click Next, and you see the next step in the wizard, shown in Figure 34-7.

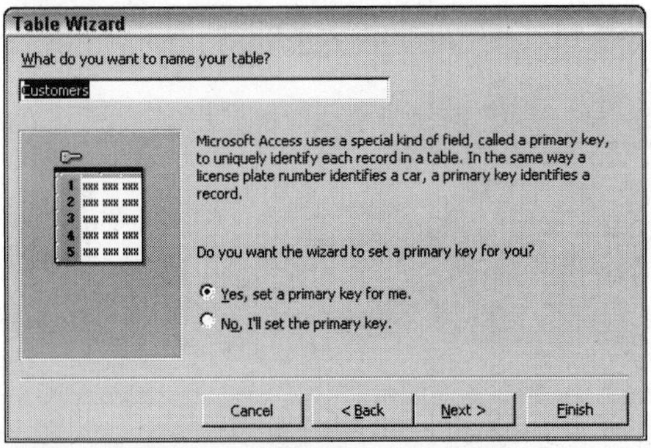

Figure 34-7: Picking a table name

In this step of the wizard, you can specify a table name and you can indicate whether you want Access to create a primary key field for you. (You learned about primary keys earlier in this chapter.) Generally it is best to pick the primary key yourself.

What happens when you click Next depends on whether you wanted to specify a primary key or you specified that the wizard should do it. If you indicated that you want to pick the primary key, you see the screen shown in Figure 34-8.

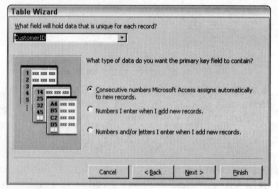

Figure 34-8: Picking a primary key

At the top of the screen you can use the drop-down list to specify which field you want used as the primary key. Then you can use the three radio buttons to indicate the type of data you want in the primary key field. When you are done, click Next and you see the final step of the Table Wizard, shown in Figure 34-9.

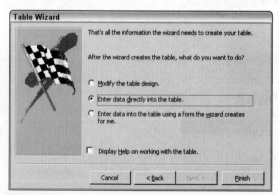

Figure 34-9: The final screen of the Table Wizard

With the wizard finished, Access needs to know what you want to do next. The default is to start entering data directly into the table. You can pick either of the other options available, depending on your preferences. When you click Finish, the wizard ends.

Tip   I generally choose Modify the Table Design. This ends the wizard and displays the table in Design view, as discussed earlier in this chapter. This gives me an opportunity to see exactly what the wizard has done, before I start entering data.

After the Table Wizard creates your table, it appears in the right-hand side of the Database window whenever you have the Tables object category selected in the left-hand side.

Creating a table by entering data

The third way to create a new table is by simply entering data. If you double-click the Create table by entering data option in the Database window (refer to Figure 34-2), your new table is opened in Datasheet view, as shown in Figure 34-10.

Field1	Field2	Field3	Field4	Field5	Field6	Field7	Fielc

Table1 : Table

Record: 14 ◀   1 ▶ ▶I ▶* of 21

Figure 34-10: Datasheet view for your table

You will become intimately familiar with Access's Datasheet view, as you use it quite a bit when entering and editing data. If you need information on how to enter data in the datasheet, refer to the discussion later in this chapter.

While you are entering data in your new table, you might want to rename some of your fields. The easiest way to do this is to right-click the field name, at the top of the column, and choose Rename Column from the resulting menu. You can also, if desired, double-click the field name in order to change it.

When you are through entering information in the table, just close it by clicking the Close button in the upper-right corner. You are asked if you want to save your information. Assuming you do, click Yes and provide a name for the table you just created.

Creating a Table by Importing or Linking

In Access, you can use databases that were created outside of Access. The two ways to do this are called importing and linking. When you import an external database, you're using it as the basis for a new Access database, and the records in it are converted to Access format. When you link to an external database, the original database is used instead of creating a new one in Access. You can make changes in the linked database from within Access without affecting its format. File formats that can be imported or linked in Access include the following:

- ✦ dBASE databases
- ✦ HTML tables and lists
- ✦ Lotus 1-2-3 spreadsheets
- ✦ Microsoft Excel worksheets
- ✦ Microsoft Access databases
- ✦ Microsoft Access projects
- ✦ Microsoft Exchange
- ✦ Microsoft FoxPro databases
- ✦ ODBC databases
- ✦ Paradox databases
- ✦ SQL tables
- ✦ Text files (both CSV and fixed-width)

To import or link to databases, follow these steps:

1. From the menu, choose File ➪ Get External Data.
2. In the submenu, choose either Import or Link Tables.

3. You'll see nearly identical file-choosing dialog boxes in either case. The only difference between them is that the file open button is labeled Link in one case and Import in the other. Navigate to the folder containing the database you want, and then select it and click the Link or Import button.

4. Different import wizards will be activated depending upon what type of database you are importing. Figure 34-11 shows a screen from the Import Spreadsheet Wizard. The wizards allow you to specify which fields you do and don't want imported, and to change the field name and sometimes the data type. Take whatever actions you desire on each screen, clicking the Next button each time you're ready to move on.

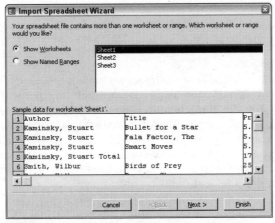

Figure 34-11: The Import Spreadsheet Wizard

5. When you've reached the last screen of the import wizard, click the Finish button to complete the task. The database will be imported (or linked, depending on which command you choose).

Adding and Editing Data

It's easy to add a new record to a database in Access. The last line in any Access table is always a blank record, waiting to be filled in. You edit data in a table by viewing the table in Datasheet view, not in Design view. If you're not already in it, you get to Datasheet view by clicking the View button on the toolbar, or by choosing View ➪ Datasheet View. Figure 34-12 shows the Datasheet view for an example table.

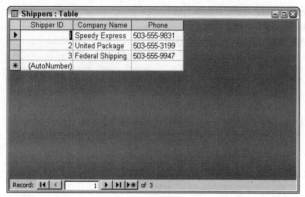

Figure 34-12: You'll always find a blank record at the bottom of any table.

Note that the blank record is marked by an asterisk on the left-hand side, whereas the currently selected record is indicated by a rightward pointing arrow. The instant you place the cursor in the blank record, the asterisk is replaced by that right arrow. When you begin typing in the blank record, a pencil appears on the left, indicating that you're working on that record, and a new blank record instantly appears beneath the one you're working on. To continue entering data, press your Tab key to move between fields. When you've filled in the final field, the Tab key will take you to the first field in the next blank record.

To edit currently existing data, as opposed to entering new data, place the cursor where you want to make changes and use your normal editing techniques. For example, if you want to insert some text, just start typing. If you want to delete the character before the cursor, press the Backspace key. If you want to replace the entire contents of the field, highlight it and then type over it.

Cross-Reference

You can also use data entry forms to add or edit the data in a table. See Chapter 35 for more information on this topic.

Changing the Appearance of a Table

The appearance of a table is amenable to all sorts of changes. Just as in Excel, you can vary the row heights and column widths in the datasheet grid. You can also alter the appearance of the grid itself, changing line characteristics as well as foreground and background colors. The fonts can be altered to suit your needs. You can move fields around, hide and unhide them, and freeze and unfreeze them. Although these options are all available via the Format menu, it's often easier to perform them with the mouse right in the table.

Setting row heights

To change row heights, place the mouse pointer on the bottom line of any row header. When the pointer changes to a vertical double arrow with a bar across it, hold the mouse button down and move the pointer up to decrease row size; move it down to increase it. When the rows are the desired height, release the mouse button. Note that you can't resize just one row; every row in Access is the same size. If you want precise control over the exact size, you can choose Format ➪ Row Height from the menu (or right-click the record selector and select Row Height from the pop-up menu), and then type in the height in the Row Height dialog box. That dialog box also has a checkbox labeled Standard Height. Selecting this checkbox will return the row height to the default setting.

Setting column widths

To change column widths, place the mouse pointer on the right border of any column header. When the pointer changes to a horizontal double arrow with a bar across it, hold the mouse button down and move the pointer left to decrease column width; move it right to increase it. When the column is the desired width, release the mouse button. Unlike rows, each column can have a different width.

If you want precise control over the exact column width, you can choose Format ➪ Column Width from the menu (or right-click the column header and select Column Width from the pop-up menu), and then type in the desired width in the Column Width dialog box. That dialog box also has a checkbox labeled Standard Width. Selecting this checkbox will return the column width to the default setting. In this case, it's not as useful as with rows, as the width of contents varies greatly across columns. However, there's also a Best Fit button that will analyze the column contents and compute a proper width for it.

Customizing datasheet properties

To change the entire datasheet at once, you can right-click the title bar and select Datasheet from the pop-up menu (or choose Format ➪ Datasheet from the main menu). This brings up the Datasheet Formatting dialog box, as shown in Figure 34-13. Here's how to use it:

✦ **Cell Effect** has three radio buttons: Flat, Raised, and Sunken. The flat version is the default. This places the cells of the table on the same level as the gridlines. The raised version means that the cells are raised above the gridlines, making the lines appear to be engraved between the cells. The sunken version does the opposite, making the lines appear to be higher than the cells.

✦ **Gridlines Shown** has two checkboxes that let you have the vertical or horizontal gridlines either visible (checked) or invisible (unchecked). These settings affect only the flat cell effect; in either the raised or sunken effects, the gridlines are present regardless of this setting.

✦ **Background Color and Gridline Color** are the drop-down lists. The available colors are Black, Maroon, Green, Olive, Dark Blue, Violet, Teal, Gray, Silver, Red, Bright Green, Yellow, Blue, Fuchsia, Aqua, and White.

✦ **The Sample panel** lets you see the effects of your choices before you commit them to the actual table. Changes in color, gridlines, and so on show up here right away.

✦ **Border and Line Styles** are two complementary drop-down lists. The one on the left is where you choose which lines you want to affect. The one on the right is where you pick what the line you selected in the drop-down list on the left will look like. The options available for the lines are Transparent Border, Solid, Dashes, Short Dashes, Dots, Sparse Dots, Dash-Dot, Dash-Dot-Dot, and Double Solid.

✦ **Direction** controls whether the fields in the datasheet are shown left to right or right to left. You shouldn't need to change this setting unless you are working with a language that has a different directional orientation than English.

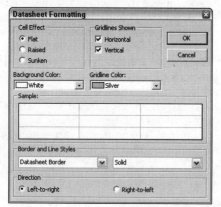

Figure 34-13: The Datasheet Formatting dialog box

When you're happy with your design choices, click the OK button to put them onto the table.

Customizing fonts

To change the datasheet's fonts, right-click the title bar and select Font from the pop-up menu (or choose Format ⇨ Font from the main menu). This brings up the Font dialog box, as shown in Figure 34-14.

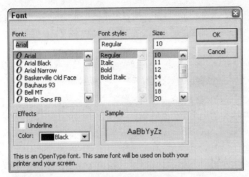

Figure 34-14: The Font dialog box

This is the standard font options dialog box you see in any Office application, except that it has only two Effects options, Underline and Color. Select the font face, the style, and the size. To choose a different color for the fonts, select one from the drop-down list labeled Color. The Sample panel shows the effects of each option. When you've made your selections, click the OK button. The font setting affects the entire table. Although the row height will automatically increase or decrease to accommodate changes in font size, the column width will not.

Moving fields

You can rearrange the fields (columns) in a table by dragging and dropping them. Click a column header so the entire column is selected. Click it again, but this time hold the mouse button down. Drag the column to the new position (indicated by a dark vertical bar) and drop it there.

If you want to move several adjacent columns at once, click the first one and, while holding the mouse button down, move it until all the desired columns are selected. Release the mouse button, click again on any of the column headers in the selection, and then drag and drop just the same way you would with a single column.

Hiding and unhiding columns

Sometimes, possibly for display purposes, you might not want some fields to show in the datasheet, but you don't want to delete the data they contain. In that case, you'll find the Hide Columns command pretty handy. To use it, right-click a column header and select Hide Columns from the pop-up menu. The column will immediately disappear from view. How do you get it back when there's no column to right-click anymore? Select Format ➪ Unhide Columns from the main menu. This displays the Unhide Columns dialog box (see Figure 34-15).

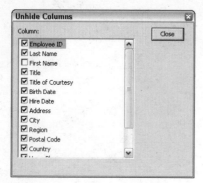

Figure 34-15: The Unhide Columns
dialog box

This dialog box has a listing of all the fields on it. The currently hidden ones show
an unchecked checkbox. Simply check the checkbox and click the Close button to
make the column visible again.

Tip   You can also hide columns by selecting Format ➪ Hide Columns from the main
menu. To unhide them, select Format ➪ Unhide Columns from the main menu.
This brings up the Unhide Columns dialog box, and you can uncheck the checkboxes of every field you want hidden.

Freezing and unfreezing columns

Freezing columns — making them stay put and still visible when you scroll the
table's datasheet — is a little bit tricky. You can select any column or range of
columns to freeze, but you can't unfreeze particular columns; you have to unfreeze
all of them. To freeze a column, right-click a column header and select Freeze
Columns from the pop-up menu (or choose Format ➪ Freeze Columns from the main
menu). The column will move to the left-hand side of the table. When you scroll the
table, that column will remain on the left-hand side, unmoving. To freeze multiple
contiguous columns, select them all first, and then freeze them. To freeze multiple
noncontiguous columns, select them one at a time and freeze them individually.

When you want to unfreeze them, you'll find that there's no unfreeze command on
the right-click pop-up menu, so you need to choose Format ➪ Unfreeze All Columns
from the main menu.

Sorting Data

When you want to sort your data in an Access table, the simplest way is to click anywhere in the column you want to sort the records by, and then click either the Sort Ascending button or the Sort Descending button on the toolbar. The records in the table will all be sorted based on the chosen field.

You can sort by one or more fields at once. Access gives the top priority in a sort operation to the leftmost field. The secondary priority is given to the field that's second from the left, and so on. You can take advantage of this default sort priority by rearranging your fields prior to sorting. (See "Moving fields" in the preceding section for details on how to accomplish this.)

Say you want to sort a database by location and then by last name. Move the location field to the leftmost position, and then move the Last Name field to the second position from the left. Select both columns, and then click one of the sort buttons on the toolbar (in this case, let's make it Sort Ascending). The records will be rearranged so that those people who work at the location with the lowest alphabetical rank will be listed first. For example, the staff at the Arizona location would come before the staff at the Washington location. Within each of these locations, the staff's last names would be listed in ascending alphabetical order without regard to the names at the other location.

Cross-Reference

If you find the need to repeatedly view your table sorted in different ways, you should create a query that includes the sort order desired. You can learn more about queries in Chapter 36.

Adding an Index

Indexing a table based on the contents of a field helps Access search and sort databases faster. You can set up an index on a single field or on multiple fields. Indexing is most useful in fields with several different entries, such as a Telephone Number field. In fields that have many duplicates, such as the State field for a mailing list of local customers, indexing will do nothing to speed up sorts if you create an index based on that single field. In cases such as this, you can increase the value of your index by indexing on multiple fields.

Using a single field

To create an index on a single field, follow these steps:

1. Make sure the table is in Design view. If you're in Datasheet view, you can change to Design view either by clicking the View button on the toolbar or by choosing View ➪ Design View.

2. Click the field by which you want to index.

3. In the General tab, look at the Indexed property. If it doesn't say No, there's already an index on this field. Otherwise, select either the Yes (Duplicates OK) or Yes (No Duplicates) option. Allowing duplicates is the normal procedure wherever two or more entries in one field could reasonably be expected to have identical values. For instance, you should allow duplicates in a Last Name field or a ZIP Code field, as these aren't things that are necessarily unique to only one record. The field for a Social Security number or an employee ID number, on the other hand, should not allow duplicates.

Using multiple fields

To create an index that uses multiple fields, follow these steps:

1. Make sure the table is in Design view. If you're in Datasheet view, you can change to Design view either by clicking the View button on the toolbar or by choosing View ➪ Design View.

2. Click the Indexes button on the toolbar.

3. In the Indexes dialog box (see Figure 34-16), you'll find the current indexes for the table. To add a new one, click in a blank under Index Name and type the name of your new index.

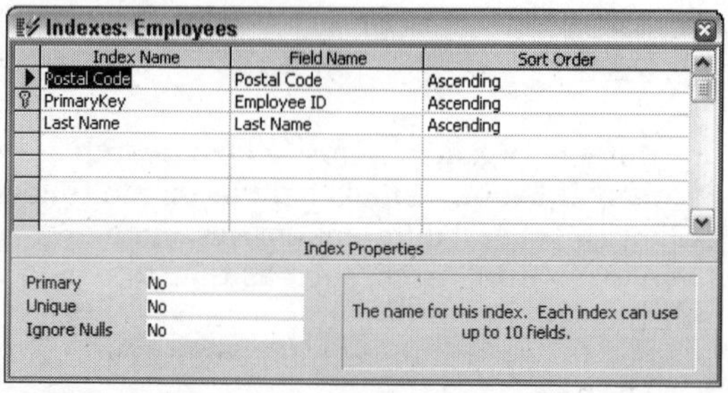

Index Name	Field Name	Sort Order
Postal Code	Postal Code	Ascending
PrimaryKey	Employee ID	Ascending
Last Name	Last Name	Ascending

Index Properties

Primary	No	
Unique	No	The name for this index. Each index can use up to 10 fields.
Ignore Nulls	No	

Figure 34-16: The Indexes dialog box

4. Tab to the adjacent Field Name cell.

5. A downward pointing arrow will appear in that cell. Click it and you'll be presented with a list of all the fields in the table. Select the one you want to index by.

6. The default sort order is Ascending. If you want to change this, click the Sort Order cell and then click the downward arrow and select Descending from the drop-down list.

7. Tab twice to get to the next blank Field Name cell (do not fill in the Index name cell for this row). Repeat Steps 5 and 6 for as many fields as you want to add to your multiple index.

Printing a Table

You need to be in Datasheet view to print a table. There are two ways to do it: one via the Print button on the toolbar, the other via the menu commands. If you just click the Print button, that's all there is to it, and the entire table is printed right away. To give yourself more options, try the menu approach:

1. Choose File ➪ Print from the menu or use the Ctrl+P keyboard combination.

2. In the Print dialog box, select the number of copies you want printed.

3. If desired, click the Selected Record(s) radio button to print only the records you've highlighted.

4. Click the Properties button if you want to change properties specific to your printer, including the page orientation.

5. Click the Setup button to change page margins.

6. Click the OK button to print.

The printout on your printer will be the same as the view on your screen, so you might want to take advantage of rearranging fields, hiding columns, and so on, before you do your printing.

 You can get more professional-looking printed results from your database by creating reports. You can learn how to create and use reports in Chapter 37.

Exporting Table Data

Just as you can import other database programs' output into Access, you can use Access to save a file in those programs' formats. File formats that can be exported from Access include the following:

✦ dBASE databases

✦ HTML tables and lists

✦ IDC/HTX tables and lists

✦ Lotus 1-2-3 spreadsheets

✦ Microsoft Access databases

✦ Microsoft Access projects

✦ Microsoft Excel worksheets

✦ Microsoft FoxPro databases

✦ ODBC databases

✦ Paradox databases

✦ SQL tables

✦ Text files (both CSV and fixed-width)

To export an Access database, follow these steps:

1. Select the database object you want to export from the Database window.

2. Select File ⇨ Export from the menu.

3. In the Export To dialog box (see Figure 34-17), select the format you want to save the database in from the drop-down list under Save as type.

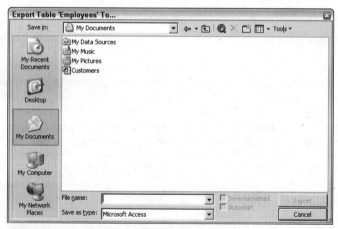

Figure 34-17: The Export To dialog box

4. Enter a filename for the database.

5. Click the Save or Save All button.

Summary

In this chapter, you learned how to create new database tables from scratch, via the Table Wizard, as well as by entering information directly into a table. You also learned how to import and export different database formats, how to add and edit data, and how to alter the appearance of a table's datasheet.

✦ Access tables are much like Excel worksheets, when viewed in Datasheet view.

✦ Database tables are laid out in rows and columns. The rows contain records, and the columns contain fields.

✦ The last line in any Access table is always a blank record so you can enter new records easily.

✦ The Table Wizard can walk you through the process of creating a new database table.

✦ Access can import from or link to databases created in other database programs and can export files in those formats as well.

✦ You can adjust the appearance of a table's datasheet.

✦ Tables can be sorted, indexed, and printed.

✦ ✦ ✦

Working with Forms

This chapter deals with Access forms, which were introduced in Chapter 33, "Fundamentals of Access." Access
has a few ways of assisting you in your form design. The simplest, AutoForm, lets you pick from three layouts. The Form
Wizard gives you greater control (allowing you to use multiple
tables in a single form, for one thing) but requires more effort
and input on your part. The third way is via a collection of different wizards called *control wizards,* which provide a great
deal of assistance when adding new controls to a form.

You have full freedom to alter the content and look of a form
after you create it.

Using AutoForm

AutoForm is a special tool that takes all the drudgery out of
creating forms. Just tell it what table or query you want to use
as the basis for the form and AutoForm does the rest of the
work for you.

The basic method

The basic AutoForm feature creates a simple left-aligned, one-
column form. To use it, follow these steps:

1. In the Database window, click either the Tables or
   Queries button at the left side of the window.

2. Select a table or query on which you want to base
   your form.

3. Click the New Object: AutoForm button on the toolbar.
   Alternatively, you can achieve the same effect by choosing Insert ⇨ AutoForm from the menu.

The advanced method

A more sophisticated approach to AutoForm offers much better options and is almost as easy:

1. In the Database window, click the Forms button at the left side of the window.

2. In the Database window, click the New button, at the top of the window.

3. In the New Form dialog box (see Figure 35-1), select one of the AutoForm options.

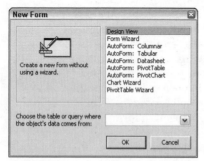

Figure 35-1: The New Form dialog box

4. Select a table or query from the drop-down list at the bottom of the dialog box.

5. Click the OK button to complete the task.

Choosing a layout

There are three types of layouts in AutoForm — columnar, tabular, and datasheet. Figures 35-2 and 35-3 illustrate the differences among these three approaches.

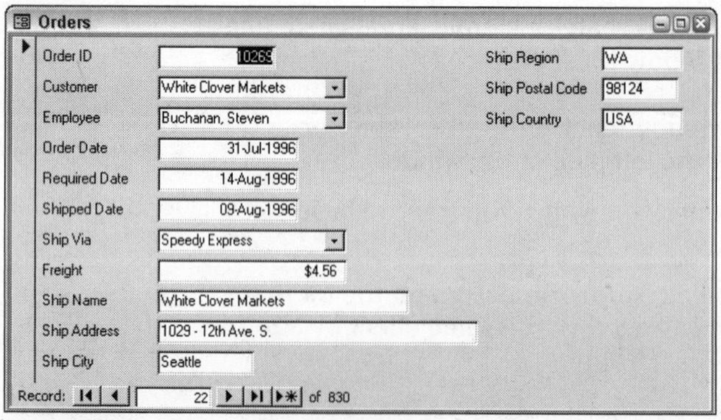

Figure 35-2: A columnar form

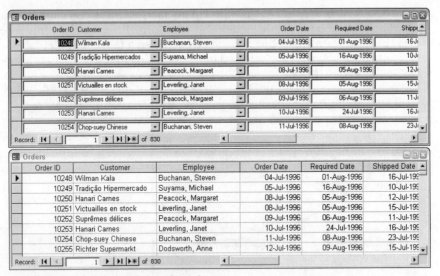

Figure 35-3: Tabular and datasheet forms

If you look back at the New Form dialog box (Figure 35-1), you will also notice that AutoForm can create PivotTable and PivotChart forms, if desired. These types of forms are very helpful for viewing certain types of data, but they are not that great for entering or editing data.

Cross-Reference The PivotTable and PivotChart forms in Access function identically to PivotTables and PivotCharts in Excel. For more information, see Chapter 18.

Using the Form Wizard

If you're willing to trade the ease of using AutoForm in order to get more control over the outcome of your form's design but don't want to work up a form from scratch, Form Wizard is just the ticket. In just a few more steps than with AutoForm, you can create a form that contains only those fields you specify, in the layout you want, with the background of your choice. To use Form Wizard, follow these steps:

1. In the Database window, click the Forms button at the left side of the window.

2. Double-click Create Form By Using Wizard. Alternatively, click the New button at the top of the Database window and, in the New Form dialog box (see Figure 35-1), select Form Wizard.

3. If you opted for the New Form dialog box approach, you can select the table you want to base the form on from the drop-down list in the New Form dialog box (although you don't have to at this stage), and then click the OK button.

4. The first screen of Form Wizard (see Figure 35-4) is where you choose which fields from which tables are included in your form. If you came to this screen via the New Form dialog box and already selected a table in it, that table will already be showing as the selected one here. Otherwise, the first table alphabetically will be the one that's showing. Either way, you can choose any table or query by selecting it from the drop-down list. When it's selected, its fields will appear under the Available Fields listing on the bottom-left side.

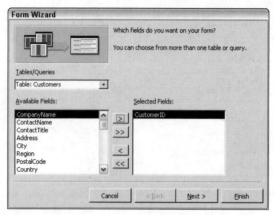

Figure 35-4: Choosing tables and fields in Form Wizard

5. Next, you need to tell Form Wizard which fields to put on the form from those that are available. To move every field from the Available Fields listing to the Selected Fields listing, click the >> button. To move one particular field, select it and click the > button.

   When at least one field is in the Selected Fields listing, the < and << buttons become active. They work just like the > and >> buttons, but in reverse, moving fields out of the Selected Fields listing back into the Available Fields listing.

6. If you want multiple tables to appear on your form, you have to select them one at a time, as the act of selecting a table replaces any fields in the Available Fields listing with the fields from the selected table. Fields already added to the Selected Fields listing are unaffected by selecting a new table.

7. If you change your mind and don't want a particular table to be included on the form, that's no problem. Although there is no button specifically designed to remove a table from the form once it's been chosen, all you have to do to accomplish this is to move any field from that table out of the Selected Fields area. If you're not completely certain which fields belong to which tables, just clear them all out with the << button and start from scratch.

8. When you're satisfied with your field selections, click the Next button.

9. If you're using a single table on your form, jump to Step 12. If you've chosen more than one table, you'll have to make a couple of selections (see Figure 35-5). The first selection is which table will be the main one. Select the main table from the listing on the upper-left side. The display area on the right side will show the basic structure of the form.

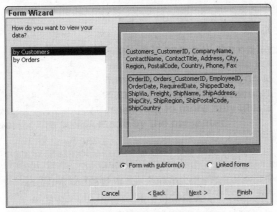

Figure 35-5: Form Wizard's multiple table options

10. Generally speaking, you have two options about the way the tables are put together — a form with subform(s) or linked forms. However, if you've selected two tables and the one you chose for the main table on the form includes all the fields found in the other table (for instance, if you chose Orders and Customers, all the customer data is also a part of the orders table), your only option is Single form. If you find yourself in this situation, try reversing which one is the main table. In this example, if you make Customers the main table, Orders is a proper subtable for it.

11. When you're satisfied with the form structure, click the Next button to proceed. If you chose Linked forms, jump to Step 14.

12. The next screen (see Figure 35-6) is where you choose the layout for your form. Depending on whether you're using multiple tables, your layout options will be different. A single table has layout options of Columnar, Tabular, Datasheet, Justified, PivotTable, or PivotChart. A multiple-table form does not include the options for Columnar or Justified layouts. Click the radio button for the layout you want to use. The display area on the left side of the dialog box shows how each will look.

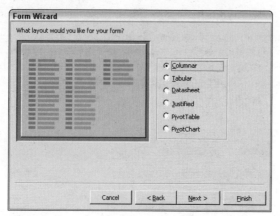

Figure 35-6: Form Wizard's form layout options

13. When you have selected the layout you want, click the Next button.

14. The next screen (see Figure 35-7) is where you choose the style of the form. Click the various style names and observe the display area on the left side of the dialog box to see what they look like.

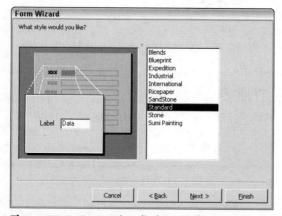

Figure 35-7: Form Wizard's form style options

15. When you have selected the style you want, click the Next button.

16. The final screen of Form Wizard (see Figure 35-8) lets you assign a title to the form (or you can just accept the wizard's suggested title) and choose whether to open the form for data entry or in Design view.

17. When you're ready to complete your form, click the Finish button.

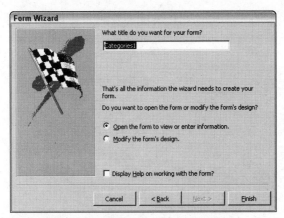

Figure 35-8: Form Wizard's final screen

Designing a Form

If you want to take a total hands-on approach, you can skip all the assistance that Access has to offer and just create forms yourself on a blank canvas.

The easy way

The easiest way to get to the blank canvas stage is to use the following steps:

1. In the Database window, click the Forms button at the left side of the window.

2. In the Database window, click the New button at the top of the window and, in the New Form dialog box (Figure 35-1), select Design view.

3. Select the table you want to base the form on from the drop-down list and click the OK button.

The hard way

Another approach, which is more difficult, is covered here only for the sake of completeness:

1. In the Database window, click the Forms button at the left side of the window.

2. Double-click Create Form in Design View, at the right side of the Database window.

3. In the blank form (see Figure 35-9), right-click the black square in the upper-left corner of the Form window and select Properties from the pop-up menu.

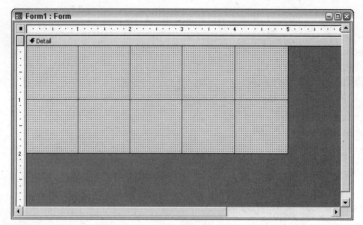

Figure 35-9: A blank form in Design view

4. In the Form properties dialog box, click the Data tab (see Figure 35-10) and select the table you want to base the form on from the drop-down list next to Record Source.

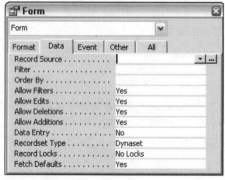

Figure 35-10: The Data tab of the Properties dialog box for the form

5. Close the properties dialog box by clicking the X in the upper-right corner.

Note   Whichever method you use to get to the blank canvas stage, you now need to add controls to the blank form. This process is covered in "Adding Controls to a Form," later in this chapter.

Modifying a Form

Regardless of which technique you use to create a form, you're not stuck with the results. Anything in a form can be modified. You can change the size and placement of form elements (even the size of the form itself), and you can add and delete elements as well. To change anything in a form (see the following list), the form has to first be in Design view. To get there if you are in Form view, click the View button on the toolbar or choose View ➪ Design View from the menu.

✦ **Increasing and decreasing height.** Once in Design view, you can place the pointer over the bottom of the form, where it will turn into a vertical arrow split by a bar. If you hold down the mouse button and move the mouse down, you will increase the height of the form. Holding down the mouse button and moving the mouse up will decrease the height of the form.

✦ **Shrinking and expanding horizontally.** If you place the pointer over the right side of the form, it will turn into a horizontal arrow split by a bar. Holding down the mouse button at this point allows you to shrink the form horizontally by moving the mouse to the left, or expand the form horizontally by moving the mouse to the right.

✦ **Moving the controls.** You can move the various elements (controls) on the form as well. Simply place the pointer over a control, press the mouse button down and, while holding it, move the control to the desired location (the pointer will change to a hand while you do this).

✦ **Deleting controls.** To delete a control, click it once and then press the Delete key.

Note   Controls can be sized as well, just like the form itself. Because this technique is an integral part of adding controls, however, it is covered in the following section.

Adding Controls to a Form

The elements that make up a form are called *controls*. The most common control in a form is the text box, which, when linked to a data source in a table or query, displays the data from the source field on the form. Changes made in the text box on the form are reflected in the field data in the table. The form shown in Figure 35-11 is largely composed of text boxes and their associated labels.

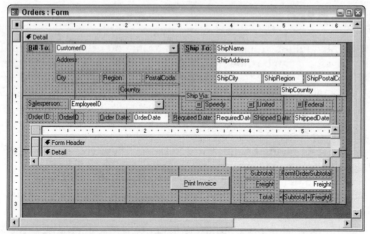

Figure 35-11: A form composed mostly of text boxes

Discovering the Toolbox

The Toolbox (shown at the right side of Figure 35-11) is the primary way in which you add controls to a form. Table 35-1 shows the Toolbox buttons and how they're used. (You can see the name of a Toolbox tool by hovering the mouse pointer over a button for a short time. You should see a ToolTip appear that matches the names shown in Table 35-1.)

Table 35-1
Toolbox Buttons

Button	Purpose
Select Objects	Switches back to the normal mouse pointer.
Control Wizards	Some controls (such as the list box) have wizards that can help you make selections regarding their properties. This toggle switch, when pressed, causes those wizards to be activated when the control is dropped onto the form.
Label	Adds a label to a form. These labels are unbound controls, not associated with any data.
Text Box	Adds an unbound text box and its associated label to a form.
Option Group	Groups together radio buttons, checkboxes, and so on.

Button	Purpose
Toggle Button	Adds a toggle button to a form. Toggle buttons indicate yes/no options.
Option Button	Adds an option button (which everyone but Microsoft calls radio buttons) to the form. Option buttons are used to indicate mutually exclusive options.
Check Box	Adds a checkbox to a form. Checkboxes are used to indicate options that are not mutually exclusive.
Combo Box	Adds a combo box to a form. Combo boxes are a combination of text boxes and drop-down list boxes.
List Box	Adds a list box to a form. List boxes present a list of predetermined options.
Command Button	Adds a command button to the form. Command buttons are used to initiate actions like printing records and opening other forms.
Image	Adds an image (GIF, JPG, PCD, and so on) to the form.
Unbound Object Frame	Frame used for objects not stored in tables.
Bound Object Frame	Frame used for objects stored in tables.
Page Break	Creates a page break for multipage forms.
Tab Control	Creates multiple pages in a form, which are accessible via tabs.
Subform/Subreport	Adds subforms to a form or subreports to a report.
Line	Adds an unbound line to the form for design purposes.
Rectangle	Adds an unbound rectangle to the form for design purposes.
More Controls	Allows access to more controls, such as ActiveX objects.

Working with text boxes

Text boxes created with the Form Wizard or AutoForm are invariably bound to data in the associated table or query. Text boxes can also be unbound—that is, not linked to data—and they can contain formulas much like a worksheet cell in Excel, in which case they are said to be calculated controls.

Changing and Deleting Text Box Labels

Access always hangs a label on a text box, and, in my opinion, it's always too far away from it. It's also always on the left, while you might want it above the text box. In fact, you might not want a label at all. Fortunately, you don't have to accept the default placement.

✦ If you don't want the label, just select it and press the Delete key; the text box will remain. (If you select and delete the text box, though, the label will be deleted along with it.)

✦ If you want to move the label in relation to the text box, select the text box and move the pointer to the upper-left corner of either the text box or its label. When the pointer changes to a pointing finger, press the mouse button and drag the text box or the label until they're just where you want them.

✦ You also don't have to accept the label text that Access provides. To change it, select the label, and then click within it and you're in normal editing mode for the label text.

Using the field list

There are two ways to place text boxes onto a form. The first, which creates bound controls, is via the field list. You display the field list by choosing View ➪ Field List.

To add a text box that is bound to a field in the list, select the field and then drag it onto the form. You can add several fields at a time. To add a contiguous range of fields, select the first one. Then, while holding down the Shift key, select the last one. All the fields in between the two will be selected. Next, click within the selection and drag it onto the form. To add a noncontiguous range of fields, select the first one. Then, while holding down the Ctrl key, select the next one. Continue in this manner until you have selected all the fields you want to add. Next, click any selected field and drag it onto the form; all the others will come along.

Using the Toolbox

The second way to add text boxes to a form is to use the Toolbox. This method adds unbound text boxes. Click the Text Box button in the Toolbox, and then click the form at the point where you want to place the text box. The text box and a label will be created at that point.

Note

The other controls are added in the same way as unbound text boxes. Just click the button in the Toolbox, move the pointer to where you want to drop the control, and click the form at that point.

Using control wizards

The option group, combo box, list box, and subform/subreport controls all give you assistance in the form of control wizards that walk you through each step of getting the control up and running. The option group control wizard is typical of the kind of process you'll be using with control wizards:

1. Make sure the Control Wizards button in the Toolbox is pressed.

2. Click the Option Group button in the Toolbox.

3. Click the form where you want the option group to be placed.

4. After a few moments, the Option Group wizard will appear (see Figure 35-12). Type the label for the first option. As you type, a pencil will appear to the left of the line you're typing on and another line will open up underneath, ready for the next label.

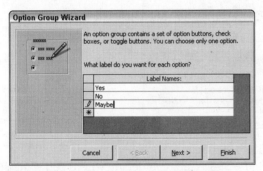

Figure 35-12: The Option Group wizard's opening screen

5. Press the Tab key to get to the next line. Continue to type labels on each succeeding line until you have entered all the options you desire.

6. When you have entered all the labels, click the Next button.

7. The next screen (see Figure 35-13) asks you to decide whether there will be a default choice and, if so, which one it will be. If you decide to have a default choice, select it from the drop-down list.

8. Click the Next button.

9. The next screen (see Figure 35-14) lets you set values for each option. To accept the default values, click the Next button.

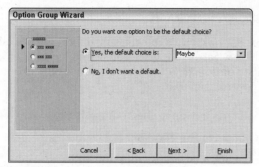

Figure 35-13: Setting a default choice

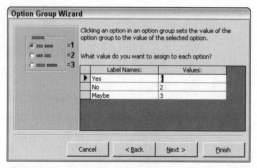

Figure 35-14: Setting the values

10. The next screen (see Figure 35-15) lets you decide where you want the values stored. The default option is to save the values for later use. Optionally, you can decide to store the value in a particular field in the table. If this is your choice, select the field from the drop-down list.

11. Click the Next button.

12. Next, you get to choose what kind of display the option group will show: option buttons (radio buttons), checkboxes, or toggle buttons (see Figure 35-16). You also need to decide what kind of style (etched, flat, raised, and so on) the option group will show. The display area on the left side of the dialog box shows the effect of each option.

13. When you're happy with your group display options, click the Next button.

14. The final screen of the Option Group wizard (see Figure 35-17) lets you pick a caption for the option group. Type it into the edit box or accept the one that the wizard suggests.

15. When you're done with the caption, click the Finish button to complete the procedure.

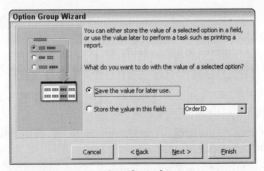

Figure 35-15: Storing the values

Figure 35-16: Choosing display options

Figure 35-17: The final screen of the Option Group wizard

Summary

In this chapter, you learned how to create forms with AutoForm, with the Form Wizard, and from scratch. You also learned how to modify forms and how to add controls.

✦ AutoForm lets you pick from three different layouts.

✦ Form Wizard gives you greater control but requires more effort and input on your part.

✦ You can use multiple tables with the Form Wizard.

✦ You can create a blank form, which you need to populate manually.

✦ No matter which technique you use, any part of a form can be modified after the fact in Design view.

✦ The Toolbox provides a great variety of controls that can be added to forms.

✦ Most forms are comprised of text boxes and their associated labels.

✦ The control wizards provide a great deal of assistance when adding new controls to a form.

✦   ✦   ✦

Using Queries

It's Access's ability to retrieve valuable and meaningful
information from your data that makes it truly valuable.
You ask Access questions about your data by using queries —
a set of parameters that you create and apply to the data.
Based on your query, Access returns a subset of your
database. Querying an Access database is similar to using filtering on an Excel worksheet, but much more powerful.

How Queries Work

There are three basic query types:

+ **Select.** The most commonly used type of query is the
  select query, which selects and displays records based
  on criteria you create.

+ **Action.** This is not a single type of query but describes a
  category of query. Action queries are used to simultaneously alter several records in one operation. The action
  can take four forms: delete, append, update, and make-
  table. A delete action deletes several records at once,
  append is used to add many records from one database
  to another one, update is used to simultaneously change
  the value of a group of records, and make-table creates a
  new table based on the criteria specified.

+ **Crosstab.** The crosstab query is used to compare summarized values by two factors (for instance, sums of
  sales by salesperson for each product).

Queries return a subset of the data in your database. The data
returned from a query is shown in a datasheet. Even though
the presentation of the data (in the datasheet) might look like
what you see when you view a datasheet for a table, there is
one important difference — the datasheet returned by a query
represents dynamic results, not an actual table. Figure 36-1
shows the results of a select query.

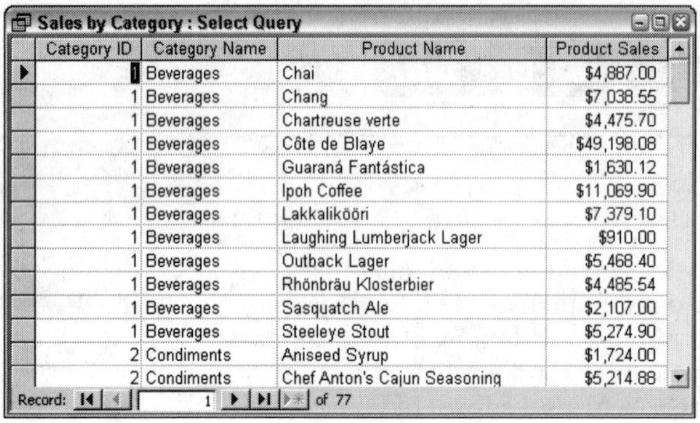

Sales by Category : Select Query

Category ID	Category Name	Product Name	Product Sales
1	Beverages	Chai	$4,887.00
1	Beverages	Chang	$7,038.55
1	Beverages	Chartreuse verte	$4,475.70
1	Beverages	Côte de Blaye	$49,198.08
1	Beverages	Guaraná Fantástica	$1,630.12
1	Beverages	Ipoh Coffee	$11,069.90
1	Beverages	Lakkalikööri	$7,379.10
1	Beverages	Laughing Lumberjack Lager	$910.00
1	Beverages	Outback Lager	$5,468.40
1	Beverages	Rhönbräu Klosterbier	$4,485.54
1	Beverages	Sasquatch Ale	$2,107.00
1	Beverages	Steeleye Stout	$5,274.90
2	Condiments	Aniseed Syrup	$1,724.00
2	Condiments	Chef Anton's Cajun Seasoning	$5,214.88

Record: 1 of 77

Figure 36-1: Results from a select query

Creating and Editing Queries

Although the Query Wizards are very easy to use and will suffice for most of your querying needs, bear in mind that they cover only a handful of possible queries. If you want to realize the full power of database queries, you'll have to design your own.

Designing your own query

Fortunately, designing your own queries is a very easy process:

1. In the Database Window under Objects, click Queries.
2. Double-click Create Query in Design View.
3. The Show Table dialog box will overlay the Design view at first (see Figure 36-2). Click the tables or queries you want used as the basis of your new query, and then click the Add button (you can also just double-click the table or query to add it).
4. When you're done, click the Close button. The table is added to the query window (see Figure 36-3). If you want to bring back the Show Table dialog box later, you can click the Show Table button on the toolbar or select View ➪ Show Table from the menu.
5. Whenever you create a new query, Access assumes you want a select query. If you want one of the other types instead, click the Query Type button on the toolbar and select the desired type from the drop-down list.

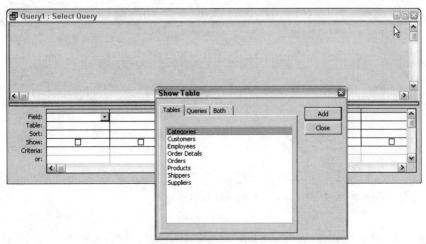

Figure 36-2: The Show Table dialog box

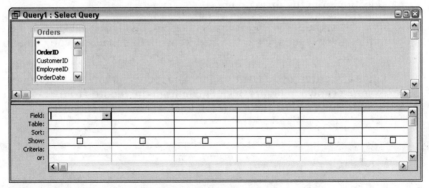

Figure 36-3: The table added to the query window

6. To put a field from the table into the query, either select it from the table listing and drag it into the Field box or just double-click it to add it to the next available Field box. Alternatively, you can click in the Field box and a drop-down list of all the available fields will become available (see Figure 36-4). The asterisk represents all the fields combined. Adding it is the same as adding all the fields individually.

Tip   Although using the asterisk is handy, it is not the most efficient way to run a query. If you will be using only a subset of your fields, or if your query will return quite a few records, then specify the individual fields to be included, rather than using the asterisk.

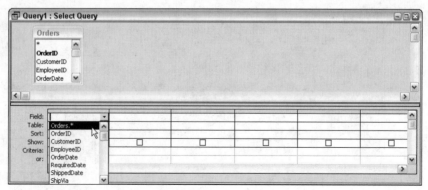

Figure 36-4: The drop-down field list

7. Once you've entered a field in the Field box, the Table box is automatically filled in for you. If desired, you can choose a sort order — ascending, descending, or not sorted (the default) — by clicking in the Sort box and making a selection from the drop-down list.

8. By default, the Show checkbox is checked. If you don't want this field to show in the query results, clear the checkbox. In this manner, you can apply criteria to a field without having to display it in the query results.

9. Enter any criteria you want to filter the records by in the Criteria box. In the example shown in Figure 36-5, I'm limiting the records to those that have "Sweden" in the `ShipCountry` field.

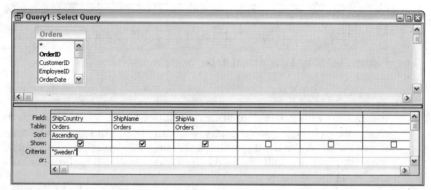

Figure 36-5: Entering criteria

10. Add more criteria in the Or box. You can have a total of nine criteria per field. (See the section "Using query criteria," later in this chapter, for more information on setting up your criteria.)

11. Make sure to include all other fields that you want to appear in the query results. Any fields not listed in a Field box will not appear.

12. Click the Run button on the toolbar to implement the query. Figure 36-6 shows the query results.

Query1 : Select Query		
Ship Country	Ship Name	Ship Via
Sweden	Berglunds snabbköp	Speedy Express
Sweden	Berglunds snabbköp	United Package
Sweden	Berglunds snabbköp	Speedy Express
Sweden	Berglunds snabbköp	United Package
Sweden	Berglunds snabbköp	United Package
Sweden	Folk och få HB	United Package
Sweden	Folk och få HB	Speedy Express
Sweden	Folk och få HB	Federal Shipping
Sweden	Folk och få HB	Speedy Express
Sweden	Berglunds snabbköp	Federal Shipping
Sweden	Berglunds snabbköp	Federal Shipping
Sweden	Folk och få HB	United Package
Sweden	Berglunds snabbköp	Federal Shipping
Sweden	Folk och få HB	Federal Shipping

Record: 1 of 37

Figure 36-6: The query results

Note   Although query results are temporary, the datasheet used to display the results has all the properties of a normal datasheet. You can resize the rows and columns, move columns, enter and edit data, sort by fields, and so on, just as though it were a normal datasheet.

Editing a query

To edit the query itself, click the View button on the toolbar or select View ➪ Design View from the menu to return to the Design view. Once there, you have the same capabilities you had when originally designing it. You can add more tables, add to or change the criteria used in the query, or remove fields and tables from it (if you want to add a new table, don't forget to click the Show Table button on the toolbar).

To remove a field from the Field box, simply highlight it and delete it, by pressing either the Delete key or the Backspace key. Once you click anywhere else in the query window, that field will be removed from the query. To remove a table, click the table and press the Delete key.

Using query criteria

The most important aspect of designing a query is the use of criteria. If you simply specify a particular possible value as the criteria — as in the use of "Sweden" in the preceding example — you'll get all the records that have that particular value.

However, the possibilities inherent in the criteria values are much greater than such a simple match. For starters, you can use the `Like` keyword and the wildcard character (*) in your criteria. Here's how it works:

✦ The following, if entered in the criteria for `ShipCountry`, would return any country that started with "sw," such as Sweden or Switzerland.

```
Like "Sw*"
```

✦ You can also specify that a term should end with a particular set of characters. The following would return countries such as Iceland, Ireland, Switzerland, and England.

```
Like "*land"
```

✦ Or you can combine the two approaches and look for those terms that both begin and end with particular characters. The following example would return both Spain and Sweden:

```
Like "S*n"
```

✦ You can even specify countries that contain certain letters:

```
Like "*tze*"
```

✦ And if that's not enough, you can specify that you want a range of letters by using brackets and the wildcard. The following example will return every country that starts with s, t, or u:

```
Like "[S-U]*"
```

✦ In addition to the wildcard, you can also use the placeholder character (?) in your criteria. For example, you could use the following to get England, Ireland, and Iceland:

```
Like "???land"
```

✦ You can also use Boolean operators in your criteria. For instance, you could specify that you don't want any orders shipped to Sweden, and you'd get back every order that was shipped anywhere else:

```
Not "Sweden"
```

✦ You can use the And and Or operators as well:

```
"Sweden" And "England"
"Sweden" Or "England"
```

✦ When it comes to dates, you need to use hash marks (#) instead of quotation marks to set them off. Thus, you'd look for January 1, 2007, as follows:

```
#1/1/07#
```

✦ You use the Boolean operators (And, Or, and Not) just the same way as you would with a text field, but there's a special operator called Between And that you'll want to use to specify a range of dates:

```
Between #1/1/07# And #2/1/07#
```

✦ In addition to these approaches, you can use plain old numerical symbols as well. For instance, if you wanted to find all orders whose shipping charges were less than $100.00, you could put the following in as the criterion for the Freight field:

```
<100
```

The comparison operators you can use are shown in Table 36-1.

Table 36-1
Comparison Operators

Operator	Function
=	Equal to. Limits the return to those records equaling this value.
>	Greater than. Limits the return to those records exceeding this value.
>=	Greater than or equal to. Limits the return to those records equaling or exceeding this value.
<	Less than. Limits the return to those records below this value.
<=	Less than or equal to. Limits the return to those records equal to or below this value.
<>	Not equal to. Limits the return to those records that are not equal to this value.

You can also use the Between And operator to specify a range of numerical values, just as you can with dates.

Using Or with multiple fields

Another way to use the Boolean operators, of course, is when you specify multiple criteria in the Or boxes in the query blank, as you did in the preceding step-by-step explanation. The interesting thing about this approach is that there's a hidden And operator involved in the query grid. Anytime you specify criteria for two fields, you're saying "This criterion And that criterion." As long as the criteria are on the same line, you're Anding them. There's one more quirk you can use, too. You already know that you can use the Or boxes to set up several possibilities, but you can use the Or boxes across more than one field as well. If you establish a criterion for one field and want to Or it with a criterion in another field, all you have to do is to put the criterion in the Or box of the second field. The query in Figure 36-7 shows this in action.

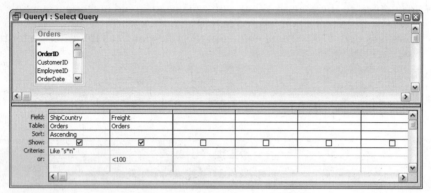

Figure 36-7: The Or criteria in action

The criterion in the first column would normally limit the output of the query to those records that have a ShipCountry beginning with "s" and ending with "n." The addition of the criterion in the second column, however, because it's in the Or box, changes the situation. If it were in the Criteria box—on the same line as the first criterion—it would be an And situation. Therefore, the response would be limited to records that have "s*n" countries and also have shipping costs less than $100.00. Because it's in the Or box, though, everything's different. Now, the response is limited to records that have either "s*n" countries or shipping costs less than $100.00.

Using Queries to Modify Records

When working with the results of a query, any changes you make to the information in the results also affect the underlying data from which the query is pulled. This means that queries are a great way to target specific information and make changes in that information, without affecting any information that doesn't meet your criteria.

Changing original table values

Figure 36-8 shows the results of a query that returns only the shipping carrier and the Order ID from the Orders table. It's limited by criteria that return those orders shipped via Speedy Express. When you click an entry in the Ship Via field, a drop-down list showing all the possible values of the field appears. (This is a result of the

Lookup property set in the Table's design; not all your fields might have this option.) Even though these query results don't reflect the values in the combo box, they're still all listed for your choosing. Clicking any of the options in the drop-down list changes the value in the original Orders table instantly, for that particular record. If you modify a field that is used for the query criteria (for example, you change the carrier to something other than Speedy), the record will not be removed immediately from the current query results and will continue to be displayed until something is done to refresh the query, like applying a filter or sorting the data.

Ship Via	Order ID
Speedy Express	10249
Speedy Express	10251
Speedy Express	10258
Speedy Express	10260
Speedy Express	10265
Speedy Express	10267
Speedy Express	10269
Speedy Express	10270
Speedy Express	10274
Speedy Express	10275
Speedy Express	10280
Speedy Express	10281
Speedy Express	10282
Speedy Express	10284

Record: 1 of 250

Figure 36-8: Changing a value in query results

Note You can't change all fields. For example, the Order ID values are generated by Access via AutoNumber and you won't be able to alter them. There are more restrictions regarding updating underlying tables in a query, especially when data permitted in the tables may be governed by a relationship.

Deleting groups of records

But what if you have lots of records you want to change? Suppose you're hiking all the prices of your products by 10 percent or you need to delete all the products under a certain price? It's possible to do this by hand, of course, but it's a tedious process fraught with opportunities for error. With action queries, such operations are a lot simpler. Action queries, you might recall, are queries that take some sort of action on the information in a database. For instance, an action query can be used to delete a number of records based upon criteria you specify. All you have to do is specify the criteria and let Access do the work for you.

Caution It is a good idea, prior to running an action query, to make a backup of any tables that the query will affect. This is because an action query can perform irreversible data changes.

To delete a group of records, follow these steps:

1. In the Database window under Objects, click Queries.

2. Double-click Create Query in Design View.

3. Click the tables or queries you want to add to your query blank in the Show Table dialog box, and then click the Add button (you can also just double-click the table or query to add it).

4. When you're done, click the Close button.

5. The table is added to the query window. By default, it's a select query. Choose Query ➪ Delete Query from the menus.

6. Put the asterisk field into the first Field box. To put it into the query, either select it from the table listing and drag it into the Field box or just double-click it. Alternatively, you can click in the first Field box and select the asterisk from the drop-down list (if you're using multiple tables in your query, you'll find multiple asterisks in the drop-down list, each in the form of "table-name.*"). The asterisk represents all the fields combined. Adding it is the same as adding all fields. It's necessary to put it in because a Delete Query deletes entire records and it needs to reference all the fields in the record.

7. Put the field you want to use for the deletion criteria into the next Field box.

8. Enter the criteria by which you are judging into the Criteria box. Figure 36-9 shows how the query looks at this stage. This example deletes all records in the Products table that have a price under $10.00, so we've entered the criterion "<10" under the UnitPrice field.

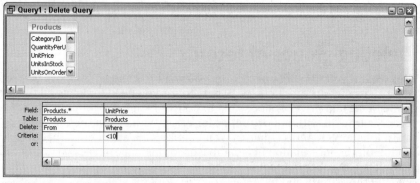

Figure 36-9: A delete query

9. Repeat Steps 7 and 8 for any other fields you need in order to establish your criteria.

10. Click the Run button on the toolbar to delete the records that fit the criteria.

Changing groups of records by updating

To simultaneously change the value of a group of records, you can use an update action query. Follow these steps:

1. In the Database Window under Objects, click Queries.

2. Double-click Create Query in Design View.

3. Click the tables or queries you want to add to your query blank in the Show Table dialog box, and then click the Add button (you can also just double-click the table or query to add it).

4. When you're done, click the Close button.

5. The table is added to the query window. By default, it's a select query. Choose Query ➪ Update Query from the menus.

6. Put the field you want to update into the query. To put a field into the query, either select it from the table listing and drag it into the Field box or just double-click it. Alternatively, you can click in the first Field box and select it from the drop-down list.

7. Enter the criteria, if any, into the Criteria box. It is not necessary to use criteria in an Update Query if you're going to be updating all the records, only if you intend to update some and not others.

8. Enter the expression or value to which you want to change the field in the Update To box. Figure 36-10 shows how the query looks at this stage. This example updates all records in the Products table that have a price under $10.00, so we've entered the criterion "<10" under the UnitPrice field. We're doubling the price of all those items, so we've entered the expression "[UnitPrice]*2." You don't have to use an expression. You can just as easily set a specific value instead.

9. Repeat Steps 6 through 8 for any other fields you need.

10. Click the Run button on the toolbar to update the records that fit the criteria.

Figure 36-10: An update query

Using the Query Wizards

The Query Wizards can simplify your life by taking the drudgery out of creating queries. Four built-in queries are available via this route: simple, crosstab, find duplicates, and find unmatched. The Simple Query Wizard is for a plain-vanilla select query with no criteria (you can add criteria later). The Crosstab Query Wizard is used to compare summarized values by two factors. The Find Duplicates Query Wizard searches a table for fields that have the same value. The Find Unmatched Query Wizard compares the same field in two different tables to determine whether there are no matching records in the two.

The Simple Query Wizard

To use the Simple Query Wizard, follow these steps:

1. In the Database Window under Objects, click Queries.

2. Double-click Create Query By Using Wizard to go directly to the first screen of the Simple Query Wizard (see Figure 36-11).

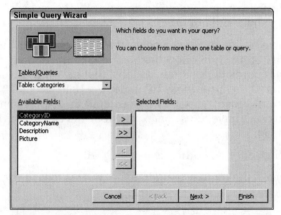

Figure 36-11: The Simple Query Wizard opening screen

3. Select the table or query on which you want to base your query. The fields from that table or query will show up under Available Fields.

4. To move a field from the Available Fields listing to the Selected Fields listing, select it and click the > button. To move all the fields at once, click the >> button instead.

5. At this point, the < and << buttons become active. You can use them to move either individual fields or all fields back into the Available Fields listing.

6. Repeat Steps 3 and 4 for any other tables or queries you want to use in this query.

7. Click the Next button.

8. The next screen (see Figure 36-12) asks if you want to see all the fields (Detail) or just a summary (depending on the fields you select, you might not get this screen).

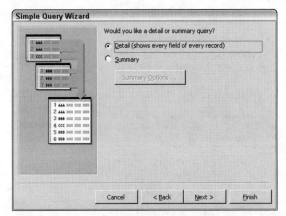

Figure 36-12: The Simple Query Wizard detail screen

9. If you chose a summary, click the newly activated Summary Options button. Otherwise, click the Next button to proceed.

10. In the Summary Options dialog box (see Figure 36-13), you can choose to have any or all of sum, average, minimum, or maximum values calculated for selected numeric fields, as well as to have a count of the records in the table. After you've made your selections, click the OK button to return to the Query Wizard and then click the Next button to proceed.

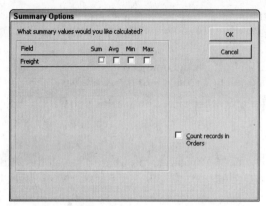

Figure 36-13: The Simple Query Wizard's summary options

11. The final screen of the Simple Query Wizard (see Figure 36-14) suggests a title for your query. You can accept the default title by doing nothing, or you can type another title over it.

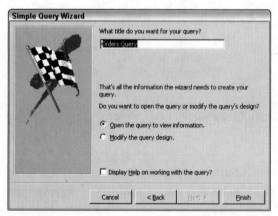

Figure 36-14: The Simple Query Wizard's final screen

12. The default option for viewing the query is to open it. If you intend to make changes to it, such as adding criteria, click the Modify option button instead so the query will show up in Design view.

13. Click the Finish button to complete the query.

The Crosstab Query Wizard

To use the Crosstab Query Wizard, follow these steps:

1. In the Database Window under Objects, click Queries.
2. In the Database Window, click the New button.
3. In the New Query dialog box (see Figure 36-15), select Crosstab Query Wizard.

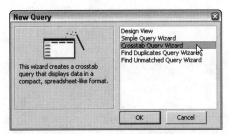

Figure 36-15: The New Query dialog box

4. Click the OK button.
5. The first screen of the Crosstab Query Wizard (see Figure 36-16) asks you to pick the table you want to use for the cross tabulation. Select one.

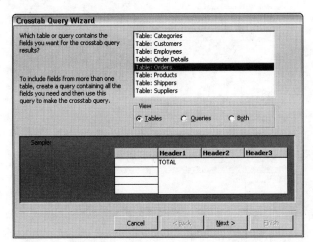

Figure 36-16: The Crosstab Query Wizard's Opening screen

6. Click the Next button to proceed.

7. The next screen (see Figure 36-17) asks you to pick the row headings for your crosstab. Select a field in the Available Fields listing and use the > button to move it to the Selected Fields listing. You can have up to three row headings.

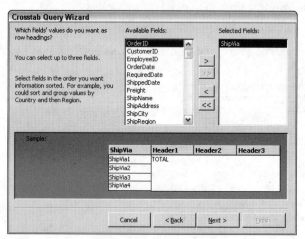

Figure 36-17: The Crosstab Query Wizard's row headings

8. Click the Next button.

9. Next, pick the column heading (see Figure 36-18). Select a single field.

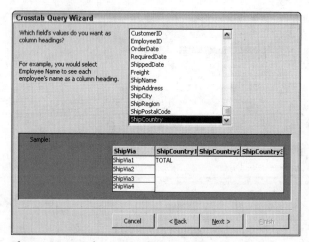

Figure 36-18: The Crosstab Query Wizard's column headings

10. Click the Next button.

11. The next screen (see Figure 36-19) asks you to decide which field's value will be cross-tabulated. Select a field and then select which function you want applied to it (for instance, you might want the field's value averaged or summed).

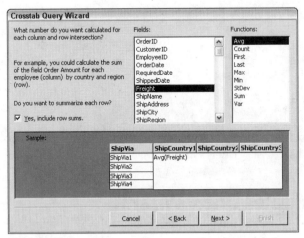

Figure 36-19: The Crosstab Query Wizard's crosstab calculation

12. Optionally, check the checkbox to have each row summed.

13. Click the Next button.

14. The final screen of the Crosstab Query Wizard (see Figure 36-20) suggests a title for your query. You can accept the default title by doing nothing, or you can type another title over it.

15. The default option for displaying the query is to view it. If you intend to make changes to it, such as adding criteria, click the Modify option button instead so the query will show up in Design view.

16. Click the Finish button to complete the query.

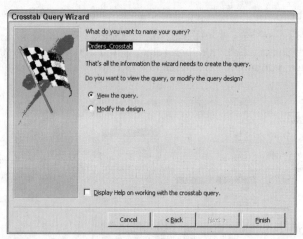

Figure 36-20: The Crosstab Query Wizard's final screen

The Find Duplicates Query Wizard

To use the Find Duplicates Query Wizard, follow these steps:

1. In the Database Window under Objects, click Queries.

2. In the Database Window, click the New button.

3. In the New Query dialog box, select Find Duplicates Query Wizard.

4. Click the OK button.

5. The first screen of the Find Duplicates Query Wizard (see Figure 36-21) asks you to pick the table you want to search for duplicates in. Select one.

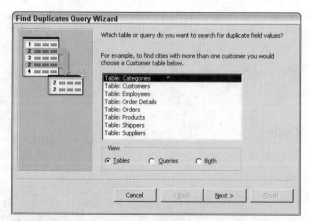

Figure 36-21: The Find Duplicates Query Wizard's opening screen

6. Click the Next button to proceed.

7. The next screen (see Figure 36-22) asks you to pick the fields you want to check for duplication. To move a field from the Available fields listing to the Duplicate-value fields listing, select it and click the > button. To move all the fields at once, click the >> button instead.

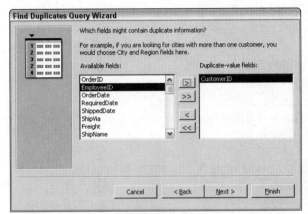

Figure 36-22: The Find Duplicates Query Wizard's field options

8. At this point, the < and << buttons become active. You can use them to move either individual fields or all fields back into the Available Fields listing.

9. Click the Next button.

10. Next, you can choose whether to show other fields in the query besides those on which you're performing the duplicate search (see Figure 36-23). This will help you to identify the records that show up as a result of the query. For instance, if you're looking for duplicate product IDs and you don't specify that you should also see the product name, you'll have a tougher time identifying the products in the completed query. As before, use the > and > buttons to move the selected fields.

11. Click the Next button.

12. The final screen (see Figure 36-24) suggests a title for your query. You can accept the default title by doing nothing, or you can type another title over it.

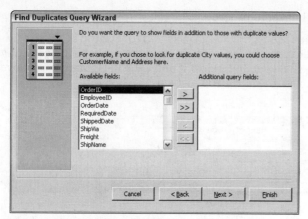

Figure 36-23: Additional visible fields in the Find Duplicates Query Wizard

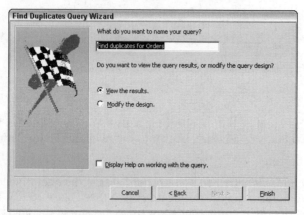

Figure 36-24: The Find Duplicates Query Wizard's final screen

13. The default option for displaying the query is to view it. If you intend to make changes to it, such as adding criteria, click the Modify option button instead so the query will show up in Design view.

14. Click the Finish button to complete the query.

The Find Unmatched Query Wizard

To use the Find Unmatched Query Wizard, follow these steps:

1. In the Database Window under Objects, click Queries.

2. In the Database Window, click the New button.

3. In the New Query dialog box, select Find Unmatched Query Wizard.

4. Click the OK button.

5. The first screen of the Find Unmatched Query Wizard (see Figure 36-25) asks you to pick the first table to compare. Select one.

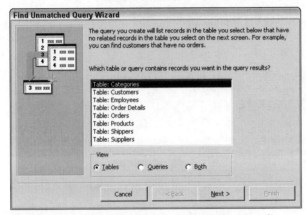

Figure 36-25: The Find Unmatched Query Wizard's opening screen

6. Click the Next button to proceed.

7. The next screen (see Figure 36-26) asks you to pick the table you want compared with the one you selected in the preceding screen. Select one.

8. Click the Next button.

9. The next screen (see Figure 36-27) is where you tell the Query Wizard how to compare the two tables. Select a field in the first table's field listing that is the same as one in the second table's listing. Select the second table's matching field as well, and then click the < = > button to equate the two.

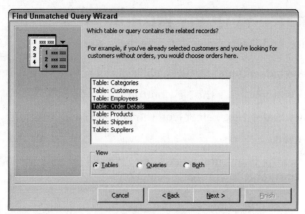

Figure 36-26: Selecting the second table in the Find Unmatched Query Wizard

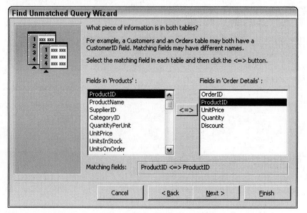

Figure 36-27: Linking tables in the Find Unmatched Query Wizard

10. Click the Next button.

11. Next, you can choose whether to show other fields in the query besides those on which you're performing the search (see Figure 36-28). This will help you to identify the records that show up as a result of the query. Use the > and > buttons to move the selected fields.

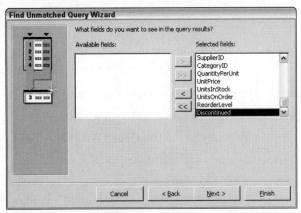

Figure 36-28: Additional visible fields in the Find Unmatched Query Wizard

12. Click the Next button.

13. The final screen (see Figure 36-29) suggests a title for your query. You can accept this title by doing nothing, or you can type another title over it.

Figure 36-29: The Find Unmatched Query Wizard's final screen

14. The default option for displaying the query is to view it. If you intend to make changes to it, such as adding criteria, click the Modify option button instead so the query will show up in Design view.

15. Click the Finish button to complete the query.

Summary

In this chapter, you learned how to use queries in Access. Highlights of the chapter include the following:

✦ Queries allow you to extract meaningful data from a database.

✦ The results of queries are dynamic and are shown in a datasheet.

✦ Queries can be created manually or via the Query Wizards.

✦ The three basic types of queries are select, action, and crosstab.

✦ Although you can change query results and thereby alter records in the underlying database, it's much easier to use action queries to change large numbers of records at once.

✦   ✦   ✦

Generating Reports

This chapter explains how to use Access reports. The
three basic types of reports are columnar, label, and tabular. Access's AutoReport feature can generate columnar or
tabular reports for you automatically. As is usual with Office
programs, you can also use a more complex wizard; in this
case, it's Report Wizard and Label Wizard, which give you
more control over the design of reports. If you want to create
reports from scratch, you can still do so, taking total control
over their content and appearance.

Types of Reports

There are three basic kinds of reports in Access (although
some would argue that there are really only two):

- ◆ **Columnar.** The first kind is the columnar report (see
  Figure 37-1), which lists records by showing the fields
  one by one from the top down in a single column until all
  the fields are listed, at which point the next record
  starts.

- ◆ **Label.** The second kind, the label report (see Figure
  37-2), is a variation of the columnar format, in which
  fields are listed in multiple columns, grouped as you
  specify, usually in a standard name-and-address format
  for mailing-label purposes.

- ◆ **Tabular.** The third report format is called tabular.
  Tabular reports are in a table format (see Figure 37-3),
  with each record listed on a single line and each field
  beginning in a separate column.

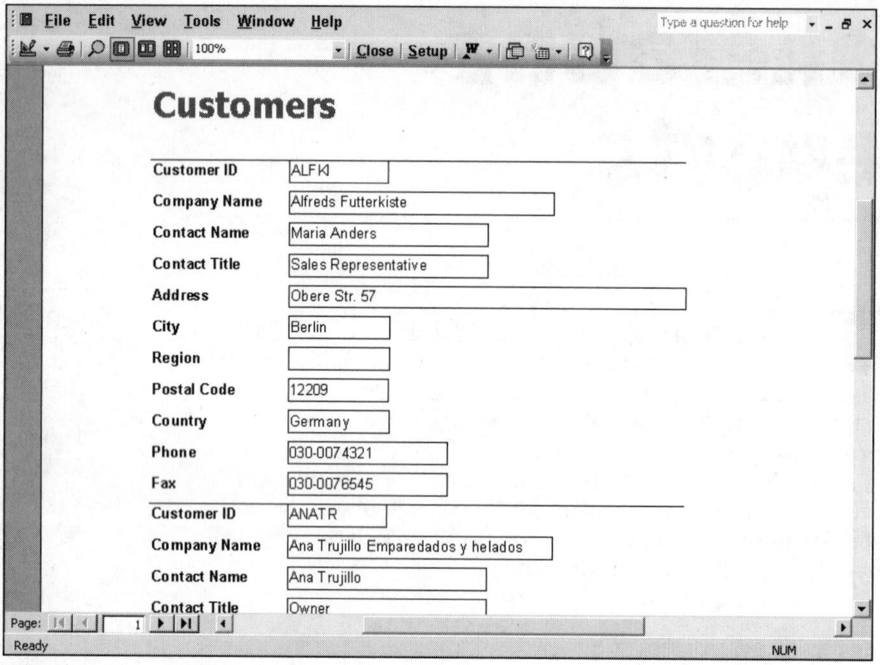

Figure 37-1: A columnar report

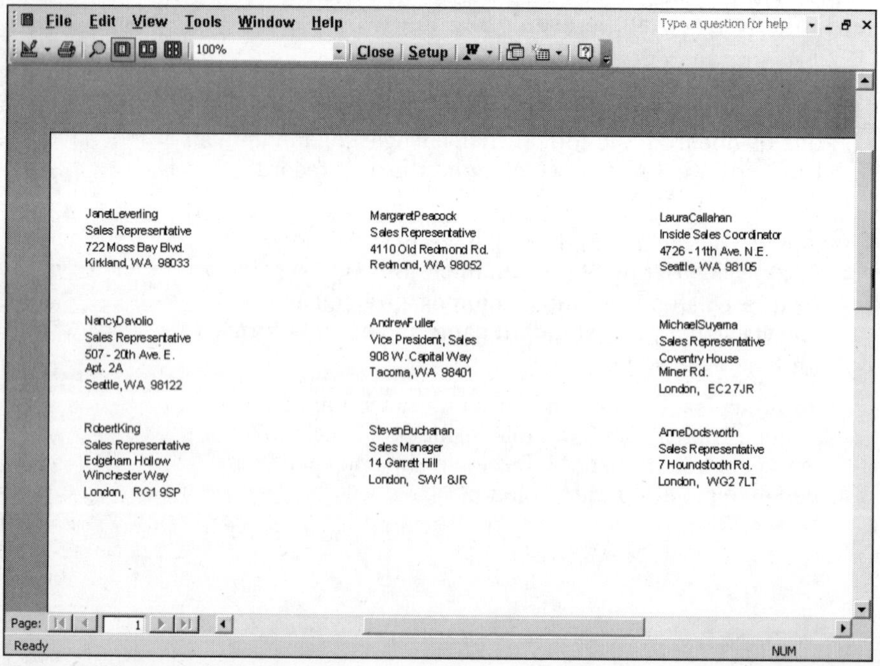

Figure 37-2: A label report

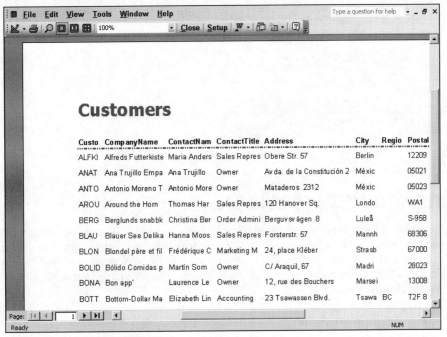

Figure 37-3: A tabular report

Using AutoReport

AutoReport is the fastest way to generate a report. Using AutoReport, you can quickly generate two of the three types of reports available in Access — the columnar and tabular report formats. To use AutoReport, follow these steps:

1. In the Database window, click Reports in the Objects list.

2. Click the New button.

3. In the New Report dialog box (see Figure 37-4), select either AutoReport: Columnar or AutoReport: Tabular.

4. Select a table or query from the drop-down list at the bottom of the dialog box.

5. Click the OK button to generate the report.

6. If you want to save the report, right-click it and select Save As from the pop-up menu. Either accept the suggested name for the report or type in your own and then click the OK button.

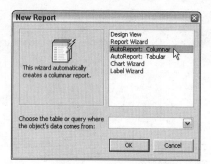

Figure 37-4: The New Report dialog box

Using the Report Wizard

The Report Wizard is an intermediary step between using AutoReport and working up your own report from scratch in Design view. Whereas AutoReport gives you no options at all but requires no input other than the table or query to base things on, Report Wizard asks more from you but delivers more control. To use Report Wizard, follow these steps:

1. In the Database window, click Reports in the Objects list.

2. Double-click Create Report By Using Wizard. Alternatively, click the New button in the Database window and, in the New Report dialog box, select Report Wizard.

3. If you opted for the New Report dialog box approach, you can select the table you want to base the report on from the drop-down list in the New Report dialog box (although you don't have to at this stage), and then click the OK button.

4. The first screen of Report Wizard (see Figure 37-5) is where you choose which fields from which tables are included in your report. If you came to this screen via the New Report dialog box and already selected a table in it, then that table will already be showing as the selected one here. Otherwise, the first table alphabetically will be the one that's showing. Either way, you can choose any table or query by selecting it from the drop-down list. When it's selected, its fields will appear under the Available Fields listing on the bottom left-hand side.

5. Next, you need to tell Report Wizard which fields to put on the report from those that are available. To move every field from the Available Fields listing to the Selected Fields listing, click the >> button. To move one particular field, select it and click the > button.

6. When there is at least one field in the Selected Fields listing, the < and << buttons become active. They work just like the > and >> buttons but in reverse, moving fields out of the Selected Fields listing back into the Available Fields listing.

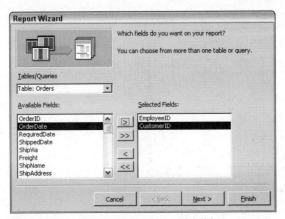

Figure 37-5: Choosing tables and fields in Report Wizard

7. If you want to select multiple tables to appear on your report, you have to select them one at a time, as the act of selecting a table replaces any fields in the Available Fields listing with the fields from the selected table. Fields already added to the Selected Fields listing are unaffected by selecting a new table.

8. If you change your mind and don't want a particular table to be included on the report, that's no problem. Although there is no button specifically designed to remove a table from the report once fields from it have been chosen, all you have to do to accomplish this is to move any field from that table out of the Selected Fields area. If you're not completely certain which fields belong to which tables, just clear them all out with the << button and start from scratch.

9. When you're satisfied with your field selections, click the Next button.

10. If you're using a single table on your report, skip to Step 12. If you've chosen more than one table, then you'll have to choose which table will be the main one. Select the main table from the listing on the upper-left-hand side (see Figure 37-6). The display area on the right side will show the basic structure of the report.

11. When you're satisfied with the report structure, click the Next button to proceed.

12. The next screen (see Figure 37-7) lets you establish groupings on your report. If you don't want to add any grouping levels, just click the Next button. Otherwise, select the field you want to group the report by and click the > button. Use the < button to remove a grouping. If you put in more than one grouping level, you can use the up and down arrow buttons to set grouping priority.

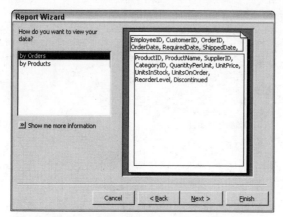

Figure 37-6: Report Wizard's multiple table options

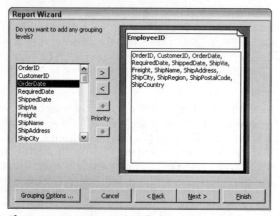

Figure 37-7: Report Wizard's grouping options

13. Click the Grouping Options button if you want to set the grouping intervals to a custom setting. In the Grouping Intervals dialog box (see Figure 37-8), choose the desired interval for each group-level field from the drop-down list, and then click the OK button to return to the Report Wizard.

14. Click the Next button.

15. Next, set the sort order for your report, if you want to. Click on the drop-down list (see Figure 37-9) to pick the field to sort by, and then click the Sort Order button to the right of the field name to select ascending or descending sort order. You can set up to four fields for sorting.

Figure 37-8: The Grouping Intervals dialog box

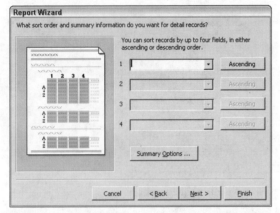

Figure 37-9: Setting sort order in Report Wizard

16. Click the Next button.

17. The next screen is where you choose the layout for your report, as shown in Figure 37-10. Click the radio button for the layout you want to use. The display area on the left side of the dialog box shows how each will look.

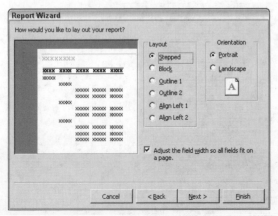

Figure 37-10: Report Wizard's report layout options

18. Click one of the radio buttons under Orientation to select either Portrait or Landscape orientation.

19. When you have the layout you want, click the Next button.

20. In the next screen (see Figure 37-11), choose the style of the report. Click on the various names of styles and observe the display area on the left-hand side of the dialog box to see what they look like.

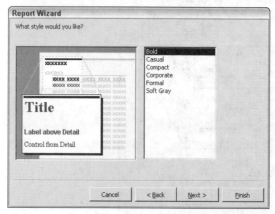

Figure 37-11: Report Wizard's report style options

21. When you have selected the style you want, click the Next button.

22. The final screen of Report Wizard (see Figure 37-12) lets you assign a title to the report (or you can just accept the wizard's suggested title) and choose whether to open the report in Design view or not.

23. When you're ready to complete your report, click the Finish button.

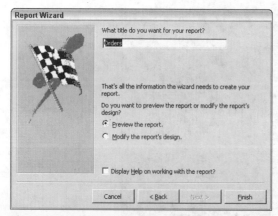

Figure 37-12: The Report Wizard's final screen

Creating Mailing Labels

One of the most common uses of databases is to generate mailing labels. Mailing labels can be generated from any table that has name and address information in it. Access provides an easy method for taking care of this important need. Label Wizard lets you set up the layout and format of mailing labels, taking into account the sizes and characteristics of major name-brand labels and even allowing you to create your own custom mailing-label templates. You can also set font characteristics and even sort the order in which your database records are fed to the labels in your printer.

To use Label Wizard, follow these steps:

1. In the Database window under Objects, click Reports.

2. Click the New button at the top of the Database window.

3. In the New Report dialog box, select Label Wizard.

4. From the drop-down list at the bottom of the dialog box, select the table or query you wish to use as the basis of your mailing labels.

5. Click the OK button.

6. The first screen of Label Wizard (see Figure 37-13) has a list of labels manufactured by Avery. If you use another manufacturer's labels, choose its name from the drop-down list next to Filter by manufacturer.

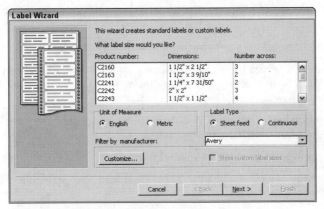

Figure 37-13: Label Wizard's opening screen

7. Under Unit of Measure, select either English or Metric.

8. Under Label Type, select either Sheet feed or Continuous.

9. If your labels aren't listed, and if none of the ones listed are the same size as your labels, click the Customize button. Otherwise, jump to Step 18.

10. After clicking on Customize (Step 9), you should now see the New Label Size dialog box. Since you want to add a new label, click the New button.

11. In the New Label dialog box (see Figure 37-14), enter a name for your labels.

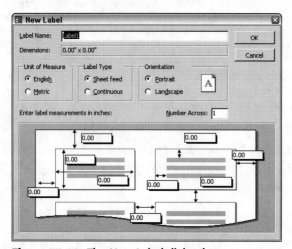

Figure 37-14: The New Label dialog box

12. Next, select the Unit of Measure, the Label Type, and the Orientation of your labels.

13. Enter the number of labels per row under Number Across.

14. In each of the edit boxes under Enter label measurements in inches (or centimeters, if you chose Metric), enter the dimensions for the spacing represented by the arrows.

15. When you're finished, click the OK button to return to the New Label Size dialog box, where your new label is now listed.

16. Click the Close button to return to Label Wizard.

17. If it is not already selected, click the Show Custom Label Sizes checkbox so your new label will be listed.

18. Click on the label you wish to use.

19. Click the Next button.

20. In the next screen (see Figure 37-15), you choose the font characteristics for your mailing labels. Choose the font name and font size from the drop-down lists at the top of the dialog box. The particular ones available will depend on what fonts you have installed on your system.

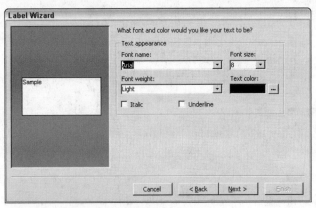

Figure 37-15: Label Wizard's font options

21. Select the font weight (ranges from thin to heavy). Experimenting on your printer will reveal the best settings for your particular system. It's recommended that you use plain paper for testing purposes to keep costs down.

22. If you're using a color printer and want to print in a color other than the default black, click the ellipsis button to the right of the Text Color window. This will bring up a standard color picker in which you can click on the desired color. Once you've chosen a color, click the OK button to return to Label Wizard.

23. If desired, select Italic or Underline for your fonts by clicking on the appropriate checkboxes.

24. Click the Next button.

25. In the next screen (see Figure 37-16), you construct the mailing label itself. Double-click on a field in the Available fields listing to move it to the Prototype label (or select the field and click the > button). This screen doesn't have a < button for removing a field from the label, but you can manually delete a field from the Prototype Label area. Be aware that if there are any fields to the right of the one you're deleting, they'll be deleted, too, unless they're separated by other characters like a space, or you select the field you want to delete before pressing the Delete key. However, because no field is actually removed from the Available fields listing at any time, you can simply put them right back in.

26. As you enter fields in the Prototype Label area, you can use normal editing and typing features to, for instance, put a comma or spaces between different parts of the address, so that the label will have a normal appearance. Make sure to press Enter at the end of each line of information, or you'll have all your data on a single line. There are no restrictions on what you may type into a mailing label, and you can enter any text you want to in addition to the fields.

27. When you're finished designing the label, click the Next button.

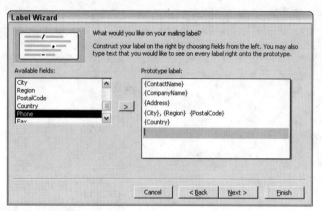

Figure 37-16: Label Wizard's label contents

28. In the next screen (see Figure 37-17), you have the option to sort the records before they're printed on the labels. The fields in the selected table are listed under Available fields. To move every field from the Available fields listing to the Sort by listing, click the >> button. To move one particular field, select it and click the > button.

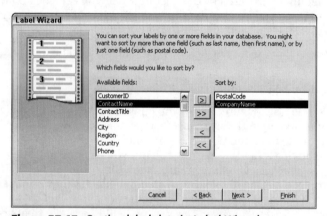

Figure 37-17: Sorting label data in Label Wizard

29. When at least one field is in the Sort by listing, the < and << buttons become active. They work just like the > and >> buttons but in reverse, moving fields out of the Sort by listing back into the Available fields listing.

30. When you're satisfied with your sort options, click the Next button.

31. The final screen of Label Wizard (see Figure 37-18) lets you assign a title to the label report (or you can just accept the wizard's suggested title), and choose whether to open the report in print preview or in Design view.

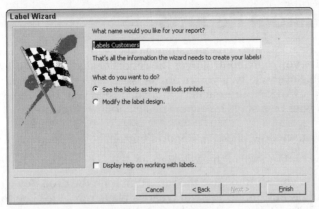

Figure 37-18: Label Wizard's final screen

32. When you've made your selections, click the Finish button. Figure 37-19 shows the finished mailing labels.

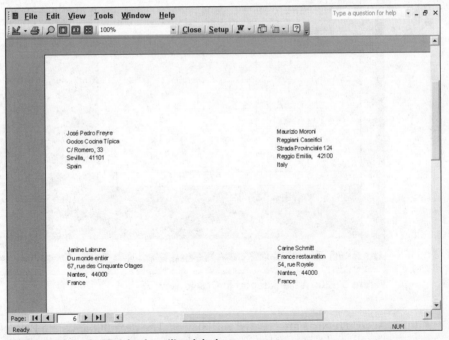

Figure 37-19: The finished mailing labels

Designing Custom Reports

Although the AutoReport approach can satisfy a quick-and-dirty report need, and the wizards can give you more control over the report design process, they don't cover every possible eventuality. If you're not satisfied with the results of either the AutoReport or Report Wizard approaches, you can design your own reports from scratch. To set up your own stage for report design, follow these steps:

1. In the Database window, click the Reports button.

2. Click the New button and, in the New Report dialog box, select Design View.

3. Select the table you want to base the report on from the drop-down list, and then click the OK button. Access will create a blank report for you to work on (see Figure 37-20).

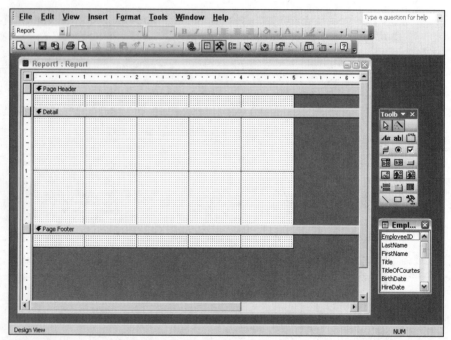

Figure 37-20: A blank report in Design view

4. Access reports are created with bands. The default bands are Page Header, Detail, and Page Footer. The Detail band is where the data goes in the report. To place a field in the Detail band, drag it from the field list and drop it in place. The Page header provides a space for items that you want to show up

at the top of every page of the report. You might want, for instance, to include the word "Confidential" or perhaps an image in this place. Some people use it to place labels showing the names of the fields that are shown underneath if they don't want the labels to take up precious space as a part of the Detail band. The Page footer is for items that you want to have at the bottom of every page. Generally, this is used for page numbers, although there is no requirement that you use it for that. You could, for example, put page numbers in the header and a confidentiality statement in the footer if you feel like it.

5. You can add another set of headers and footers to the report. These are the Report header and footer. They work just like the Page header and footer, but they print only once, on the very first page of the report. They're useful for such things as company logos and addresses. Right-click on the blank report and select Report Header/Footer from the pop-up menu to add them to the report (see Figure 37-21).

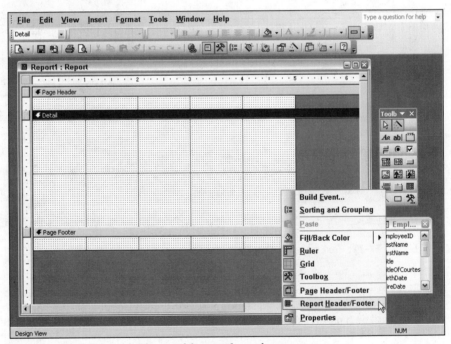

Figure 37-21: Select headers and footers from the pop-up menu.

6. Right-click on the blank report and select Toolbox so that you'll have access to the controls you'll be using in the Detail section.

At this point you are ready to add controls to the blank report, which is covered in the next section.

Placing Controls in Reports

The elements that go into the Detail band of a report are called controls. The most common control in a report is the text box and its associated label. Text boxes are linked to a data source in a table or query and display the data from the source field on the report. The report in Figure 37-22 shows some text boxes created by dragging fields from the Field List into the Detail band.

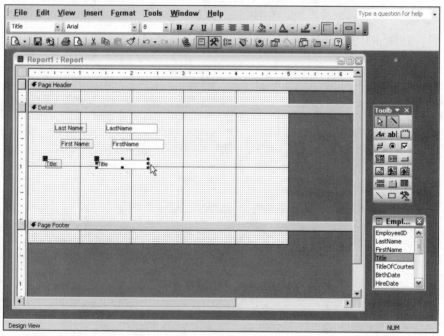

Figure 37-22: Text boxes in the Detail band

Note   As you can see, the automatic spacing of the labels and text boxes leaves a bit to be desired from a design standpoint. Don't worry about it at this stage; Every control on a report can be moved and resized, and you'll learn how to do it later in the chapter.

Bound and unbound text boxes

Text boxes created with Report Wizard or AutoReport are invariably *bound* to data in the associated table or query, as are those created by dragging a field from the Field List. Text boxes can also be *unbound*—that is, not linked to table data—and they can contain formulas much like a worksheet cell in Excel, in which case they are said to be *calculated* controls.

Creating calculated controls

Calculated controls are very useful in headers and footers—to add, for instance, the current date. To do this, simply drop an unbound text box in the header and put the value =[Date] into it. Likewise, the page number can be put into a footer by putting the value =[Page] into a calculated control. You can use the full range of Access expressions in calculated controls.

Placing text boxes in reports

There are two ways to place text boxes onto a report. Here's how they work:

✦ The first, which creates bound controls, is via the Field List. To add a text box that is bound to a field in the list, select the field and then drag it onto the report. You can add several fields at a time. To add a contiguous range of fields, select the first one. Then, while holding down the Shift key, select the last one. All the fields in between the two will be selected. Next, click within the selection and drag it onto the report. To add a noncontiguous range of fields, select the first one. Then, while holding down the Ctrl key, select the next one. Continue in this manner until you have selected all the fields you want to add. Next, click on any selected field and drag it onto the report; all the others will come along.

✦ The second way to add text boxes to a report is to use the Toolbox. This method adds unbound text boxes. Click the Text Box button in the Toolbox, and then click on the report at the point where you want to place the text box. The text box and a label will be created at that point.

Moving and Deleting Text Box Labels

Whenever you place a text box in your report, Access helpfully places a label in conjunction with that text box. In my opinion, the label is always too far away from the text box. It's also always on the left, while you may want it above the text box. In fact, you may not want a label at all. Fortunately, you don't have to accept the default placement. Following are some other options:

✦ If you don't want the label, just select it and press the Delete key; the text box will remain (if you select and delete the text box, though, the label will be deleted along with it).

✦ If you want to move the label in relation to the text box, select the text box and move the pointer to the upper-left corner of either the text box or its label. When the pointer changes to a pointing finger, press the mouse button and move the text box or the label until it's just where you want it.

✦ You also don't have to accept the label text that Access provides. To change it, select the label, click within it, and you'll be in normal editing mode for the label.

Note   The other controls are added in the same way as unbound text boxes. Just click on the button in the Toolbox, move the pointer to where you want to drop the control, and click on the report at that point.

Using the Toolbox

Other than dragging fields from the Field List, you put controls into a report by using the Toolbox. Although the Toolbox contains all the buttons used in form creation, many of the controls on it are pretty useless when you're working on a report. Remember that a report is not for data entry or alteration, just for display purposes. Table 37-1 shows the only controls in the Toolbox that you're likely to use in a report.

 Note   For more information on the Toolbox and the uses of all its tools, see Chapter 35.

	Table 37-1
	Toolbox Buttons Used in Reports

Button	*Purpose*
Select Objects	Switches back to the normal mouse pointer.
Control Wizards	Some controls (such as the Subform/Subreport button, which are covered in the section on relational reports) have wizards that can help you make selections regarding their properties. This toggle switch, when depressed, causes those wizards to be activated when the control is dropped onto the report.
Label	Adds a label to a report. These labels are unbound controls, not associated with any data.
Text Box	Adds an unbound text box and its associated label to a report.
Image	Adds an image (gif, jpg, pcd, etc.) to the report.
Unbound Object Frame	Frame used for objects not stored in tables.
Bound Object Frame	Frame used for objects stored in tables.
Page Break	Creates a page break for multipage reports.
Tab Control	Creates multiple pages in a report, which are accessible via tabs.
Subform/Subreport	Adds subreports to a report.
Line	Adds an unbound line to the report for design purposes.
Rectangle	Adds an unbound rectangle to the report for design purposes.
More Controls	Allows access to more controls, such as ActiveX objects.

Creating Relational Reports

Relational reports use multiple tables. The structure of a relational report is a master report and a subreport. The relationship between the data in the two reports is called a one-to-many relationship. One common example of such a relationship is a salesperson who sells to different clients. The salesperson is the "one" and the clients are the "many." You often find a need in such a situation to set up a report that shows which clients the one salesperson has dealt with (or you may wish to see the many sales the one salesperson has made, or the many products the one salesperson has sold).

The master report contains data relating to the "one" end of the relationship, and the subreport contains the information on the "many" end of it. The simplest way to create a relational report is to use Report Wizard (see the earlier section on this) and use multiple tables as your input. However, if you've already got a report and want to make it into a more complex relational report, then you'll be glad to know that it's an easy matter to add a subreport to it. All you have to do is use SubReport Wizard:

1. Make sure the Control Wizards button in the Toolbox is selected.

2. Click the Subform/Subreport button in the Toolbox.

3. Click on the report where you want the subreport to be placed. The Detail band will automatically expand to make room for it.

4. After a few moments, SubReport Wizard will appear (see Figure 37-23). You have two options in this step. You can use an existing table or query for your source, or you can use an existing report or form for it. Click the appropriate radio button. If you choose the existing report or form approach, then choose a report or form from the list in this dialog box.

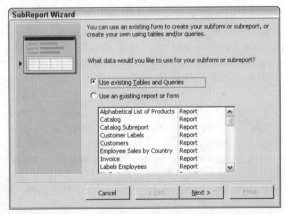

Figure 37-23: SubReport Wizard's opening screen

5. Click the Next button.

6. If you chose to use an existing table or query for your source, then you'll see the screen shown in Figure 37-24. Otherwise, skip this step and go on to Step 12. Choose any table or query by selecting it from the drop-down list. When it's selected, its fields will appear under the Available Fields listing on the bottom left-hand side.

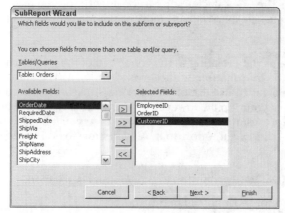

Figure 37-24: Choosing tables and fields in SubReport Wizard

7. To move every field from the Available Fields listing to the Selected Fields listing, click the >> button. To move one particular field, select it and click the > button.

8. Once at least one field is in the Selected Fields listing, the < and << buttons become active. They work just like the > and >> buttons but in reverse, moving fields out of the Selected Fields listing back into the Available Fields listing.

9. If you want to select multiple tables to appear on your report, you have to select them one at a time, as the act of selecting a table replaces any fields in the Available Fields listing with the fields from the selected table. Fields already added to the Selected Fields listing are unaffected by selecting a new table.

10. If you change your mind and don't want a particular table to be included on the report, that's no problem. Although there is no button specifically designed to remove a table from the report once fields from it have been chosen, all you have to do to accomplish this is to move any field from that table out of the Selected Fields area. If you're not completely certain which fields belong to which tables, just clear them all out with the << button and start from scratch.

11. When you're satisfied with your field selections, click the Next button.

12. The next screen (see Figure 37-25) is where you define the links between the master report and the subreport. The wizard will analyze the two reports and suggest fields to link them with. You can select one from the list suggested by the wizard, or you can click the Define my own radio button to choose others.

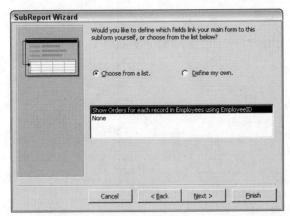

Figure 37-25: Linking the reports in SubReport Wizard

13. If you chose to define fields yourself, then the dialog box will change, as shown in Figure 37-26. Choose fields for the master report from the Form/report fields drop-down list, and for the subreport from the Subform/subreport fields drop-down list.

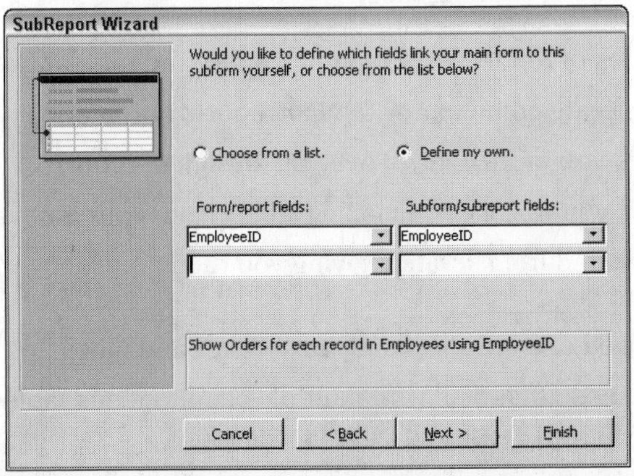

Figure 37-26: Manual linking in SubReport Wizard

14. Click the Next button.

15. The final screen of SubReport Wizard (see Figure 37-27) lets you assign a title to the report (or you can just accept the wizard's suggested title).

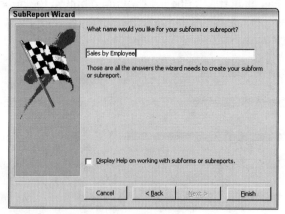

Figure 37-27: SubReport Wizard's final screen

16. When you're done, click the Finish button to complete the procedure.

Summary

In this chapter, you learned about the different types of reports Access can generate and the various methods of creating them.

✦ The three basic types of reports are columnar, label, and tabular.

✦ AutoReport can generate columnar or tabular reports automatically.

✦ Report Wizard gives you more control over the design of reports.

✦ Label Wizard allows you to generate mailing labels from your database.

✦ Reports can be designed from scratch, giving you total control over their content and appearance.

✦ Reports are composed of controls, mainly text boxes and labels.

✦ Relational reports, those that deal with multiple simultaneous tables, can be created with either Report Wizard or SubReport Wizard.

✦   ✦   ✦

Access and XML

In recent versions of its Office suite, Microsoft has been
highlighting its support for XML. Office 2003 is no exception; XML is supported very widely and very visibly.

Access supports XML well, as you discover in this chapter.
(This makes sense, really, because XML is used to define the
structure of data, and Access is a data-management program.)
This chapter introduces you to XML and to the ways in which
Access provides support for XML.

Note   Entire books have been written about the nuances of XML.
The purpose of this chapter is not to provide a definitive
treatise on XML in relation to Access but to give you the
information you need to start using the XML features of
Access. If you are looking for XML information that is devel-
oper- or programmer-oriented, you should refer to a book
written specifically for that audience. You might want to try
XML Bible, Gold Edition, by Elliotte Rusty Harold (Wiley,
2001) and *XML in Theory & Practice,* by Chris Bates (Wiley,
2003).

What Is XML?

XML is an abbreviation for eXtensible Markup Language, a
standards-based protocol governed by the World Wide Web
Consortium that establishes a set of rules and conventions for
designing data formats and structures. This is done in a manner such that the files containing XML-encoded data can be
easily read by different computer programs.

Like other markup languages (such as HTML, HyperText
Markup Language; and SGML, Standard Generalized Markup
Language), XML provides a way to "mark up" information so it
can be understood in a structured manner. Access understands information that has been marked up with XML, which
means that it can read XML *tags* and interpret them so that
information can be used in the way defined by those tags.

If you are familiar with HTML, you know that the language is used to define how a Web browser displays information. In other words, HTML defines, for the most part, the *format* of information. XML, on the other hand, defines the *structure* of information. It does not define how that information should be formatted or displayed, but it defines the way in which the content should be understood.

For instance, XML can be used to define the structure of your content. If you have an XML file that contains inventory records, the XML is used to define data elements such as `PartNumber`, `Quantity`, and `PurchaseDate`. After these elements are defined, programs such as Access can understand the characteristics of the data in the file. For instance, XML is used to define the characteristics of a `PartNumber` and then used to identify data that should be treated as a `PartNumber`. Access reads the XML tags, understands the definition, and therefore knows how to handle content subsequently defined as a `PartNumber`.

One thing that sets XML apart from other markup languages is that it is *extensible*. This means it is not static; it can evolve to meet the needs of different people or organizations. Whereas a language such as HTML has a set number of tags that perform a well-defined number of tasks, XML provides a limited number of tags and provides the means to define your own tags for your own special purposes.

Looking at an XML file

An XML file uses tags to mark up the contents of a file, just as HTML does. In fact, an XML file is nothing but a text file that contains data interspersed with tags that define the structure of that data. The tags follow the same pattern as used in HTML files, meaning that they are used in pairs. An opening tag is surrounded by angle brackets (as in `<unit>`), and a closing tag looks just the same, except that the tag name is preceded by a slash (as in `</unit>`). Because an XML file is a plain text file, you can easily open and edit it with a simple text editor, such as Notepad.

Consider the following data record, defined using XML:

```
<?xml version="1.0" ?>
<inventory-items>
   <item>
      <PartNumber>GN1039-24</PartNumber>
      <quantity>215</quantity>
      <unit>Spool</unit>
      <bin>NW-02-1</bin>
      <dates>
         <purchased>April 16, 2002</purchased>
         <stored>April 20, 2002</stored>
         <rotated>September 20, 2002</rotated>
         <expire>November 29, 2005</expire>
         <destroy>November 30, 2005</destroy>
      </dates>
```

```
    <prices>
        <purchase>5.7</purchase>
        <wholesale1>6.33</wholesale1>
        <wholesale2>7.58</wholesale2>
        <wholesale3>9.18</wholesale3>
        <retail>11</retail>
        <salvage>5.76</salvage>
    </prices>
  </item>
</inventory-items>
```

Notice the use of tags throughout the file. In this example, each pair of tags defines a component of an inventory record. For instance, the expiration date of the item is defined by the `<expire>` and `</expire>` tag pair. The tags used in an XML file can vary, depending on the specific needs of the data contained in the file. Access can read data formatted in this manner and import it into a database.

How Access uses XML

It seems that there are thousands of ways for data to be stored in a file. Every database-management program (Access included) has its own proprietary format for storing data. This can make exchanging data between applications extremely difficult and fraught with potential hazards, such as data loss or corruption. XML provides a way to easily import information into Access and a way to easily export information that can be readily used by other programs that understand XML. This can be a huge advantage in a business-computing environment.

Access considers XML to be one of its native formats. This means that Access can read XML-encoded data and convert it into the standard Access format. In the next section you learn how to import XML files into an Access database.

Caution

Access can read only *well-formed* XML files. This means that there must be no coding errors in the file being read. If there are coding errors and you attempt to load the file, Access displays a warning message and will not load the data in the file. If this occurs, you have no choice but to somehow get a version of the file that is correct. There are a number of ways you can do this. You can get a corrected copy of the XML file from whoever supplied it to you, or you can use a text editor to open the file and correct any formatting problems manually. There are also several on-line resources you can try—for example, `http://www.hcrc.ed.ac.uk/~richard/xml-check.html` and `http://www.w3.org/2001/03/webdata/xsv`.

Access can also create XML-encoded files based on information in a table, the results of a query, a datasheet, a form, or a report. Essentially, any of the Access objects that are used to extract and display information from a database can be used to create the output in an XML file. Access makes it as easy to export XML information as it is to export in other data formats.

Importing XML Data

Importing XML data into Access is very easy to do. In fact, if you have imported data from other sources before—such as from an Excel spreadsheet or a text file—you will find importing XML data to be very easy, indeed. When you import raw XML data created by a different program, Access analyzes the data during the import process and places the data into the number of tables necessary to adequately represent the data.

Start by opening (or creating) the database into which you want to import the XML data. Then, follow these steps:

1. From the main menu, select File ➪ Get External Data and then choose Import from the resulting submenu. Access displays the Import dialog box shown in Figure 38-1.

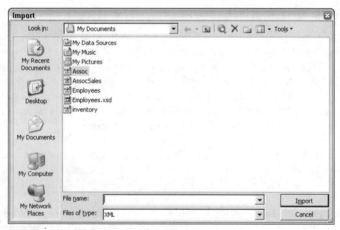

Figure 38-1: The Import dialog box

2. Use the Files of type drop-down list, at the bottom of the dialog box, to indicate you want to import XML files.

3. Use the controls in the dialog box to select the XML file you want to import.

4. Click the Import button. Access analyzes the data and displays its structure in the Import XML dialog box, as shown in Figure 38-2.

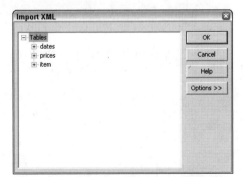

Figure 38-2: The Import XML dialog box

If desired, you can use the plus and minus signs in the dialog box to examine the structure of the data about to be loaded.

5. If you want to import all the XML information, as shown, click OK and proceed to Step 10.

6. Click Options to modify exactly how Access performs the import. The Import XML dialog box enlarges to show various import options, as shown in Figure 38-3.

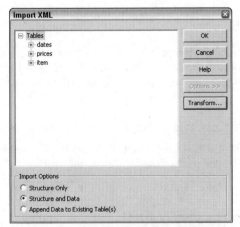

Figure 38-3: The enlarged Import XML dialog box

7. At the bottom of the dialog box, indicate exactly what you want imported by Access.

8. If you want to select an XML transform file, you can click Transform to display the Import Transforms dialog box (see Figure 38-4).

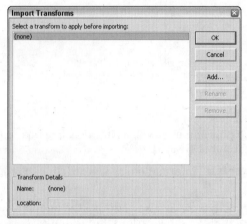

Figure 38-4: The Import Transforms dialog box

Select the transform file you want to use, or click Add to add a new transform file. When you are done, click OK.

Note   In Access, XML transform files are used to specify how imported data is to be "transformed" or processed during the import procedure. Unless you are dealing with heavy-duty XML data, chances are very good that you will never use a transform file.

9. In the Import XML dialog box, click OK to begin the actual import of the data.

10. When Access informs you that it has finished the import of your data, click OK. Your imported tables appear in the regular database window.

Exporting Access Data as XML

There might come a time when you need to export your Access data in a format that can be used by other programs. If the other program does not understand Access database tables, but it does understand XML files, you can easily export your Access information in that format.

To export your Access data as an XML file, open the database that contains the data you want to export and follow these steps:

1. Select the table, query, datasheet, form, or report you want to export.

2. From the main menu, select File ➪ Export. Access displays the Export Table As dialog box, as shown in Figure 38-5.

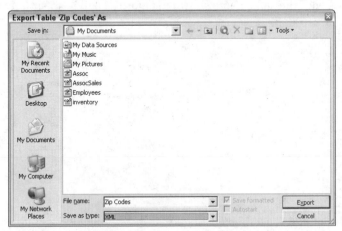

Figure 38-5: The Export Table As dialog box

3. Using the Save as type drop-down list (at the bottom of the dialog box), choose XML.

4. In the File name field, indicate the name for the file you are exporting.

5. Click the Export button. Access displays the Export XML dialog box, as shown in Figure 38-6.

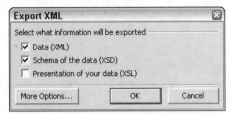

Figure 38-6: The Export XML dialog box

There are three things you can specify to be exported: the data, the schema for the data, and the presentation for the data. Each of these choices results in a different file's being created, as indicated within parentheses. (The letters in parentheses — XML, XSD, and XSL — indicate the filename extensions Access will use for the export files.)

6. Use the checkboxes beside each file type to indicate what type of export files you want to create.

7. Click the More Options button. Access displays another dialog box named Export XML, as shown in Figure 38-7. (This is not an expanded version of the dialog box with the same name shown in Figure 38-6; it is an entirely new dialog box.)

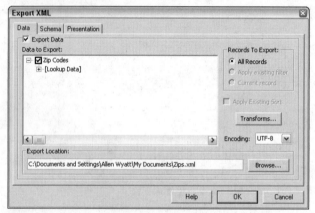

Figure 38-7: The Export XML dialog box

The tabs in this dialog box correspond to the export file types you could specify in Step 6 (and illustrated in Figure 38-6). Use the controls in the dialog box to specify exactly what you want exported by Access to each of the export files.

8. Click OK. Access creates the export files according to your specifications.

Summary

In this chapter, you learned how XML-encoded data is handled by Access, as well as how to export data in an XML format.

✦ XML is an abbreviation for eXtensible Markup Language, and it is used to define the structure and content of data.

✦ You can import XML-encoded data directly into an Access database.

✦ After XML data is loaded into Access, you can work with it just as you would any other data.

✦ You can export information in XML format from an Access table, a query, a datasheet, a form, or a report.

✦ When exporting information in XML format, you can also create schema files and presentation files.

✦ XML files can be loaded and viewed with a simple text editor, such as Notepad.

✦   ✦   ✦

Office and the Web

◆ ◆ ◆ ◆

◆ ◆ ◆ ◆

Designing Web Sites with FrontPage

Microsoft calls FrontPage "the leading Windows-based tool for developing Web pages and managing Web sites." You can create Web pages with all Office applications, some of them quite sophisticated, but even if you create a Web page using, say, Word or PowerPoint, you're likely to find FrontPage beneficial for some editing and formatting tasks. FrontPage's main appeal, however, is that it enables you to organize a set of pages, no matter how they're created, into a complete, coherent Web site, and publish the entire site to a server.

Note   Some of FrontPage's more advanced features work only on servers running the FrontPage Server Extensions. These are available for operating systems other than Windows, so you may have access to them even if the server you're publishing to is Unix- or Linux-based. Just be sure to check with your Web-site hosting service or system administrator before you start pumping your Web site full of FrontPage content.

What Is FrontPage?

Web pages differ from conventional documents in that they are designed to be interpreted by Web browsers. The most popular browsers (although there are many others) are Microsoft's own Internet Explorer (IE) and Netscape. Browsers take text, graphics, and even interactive elements, such as forms, sound, and video, and present them in the form that you're used to seeing when you visit a Web site.

The HyperText Markup Language (HTML)

Web browsers interpret and display Web page content by reading a markup language called HTML, which stands for HyperText Markup Language. A Web or HTML file is basically just a plain-text (i.e., sans formatting) file; markup languages enable Webmasters to "mark up" the text by inserting "tags" that Web browsers know how to interpret. Back in the Dark Ages, folks who wanted to create Web pages had to do so in a text editor, which required that they master the intricacies of HTML, memorizing hundreds of tags. FrontPage provides a graphical interface that enables you to create Web pages in an intuitive manner; the HTML tags are placed for you, and you needn't worry about knowing what they are or how they work.

Cross-Reference   Conversely, some people *prefer* to either hand-code their Web pages or at least insert specific bits of HTML code into the page's source code. FrontPage lets you do that, too; see the section "Experimenting with HTML" at the end of this chapter.

Publishing Web pages

The Web pages you create in FrontPage can be published (i.e., saved, along with all their accompanying images, sounds, and other associated files) on computers with Web server software and accessed by others. You can publish your Web pages to an internal server, or intranet, where they can be accessed by co-workers who have been given access to the server, or you can publish them to the Internet, where the whole world can access them. Finally, you can simply share Web files you create in FrontPage for others to view on their computers, by opening these files with IE or Netscape.

Navigating Through FrontPage Views

When you launch FrontPage and choose File ➪ New, the New task pane opens on the right (see Figure 39-1). The task pane gives you the opportunity to start a new blank page, start a new text file (useful if you want to add HTML tags manually), start a blank page based on an existing page, or start a one-page Web site, a SharePoint-based team Web site. You can also work from a template, either on your computer (Web package solutions and More Web site templates take you to different tabs of the Web Site Templates dialog box) or (as with all the Home task panes in Office) on Microsoft.com.

FrontPage offers several other views. If you're in Page view, you get to them from the View menu. If you're in any other view, you can easily move from view to view by clicking the color-coded buttons that appear at the bottom of the view, just above the status bar.

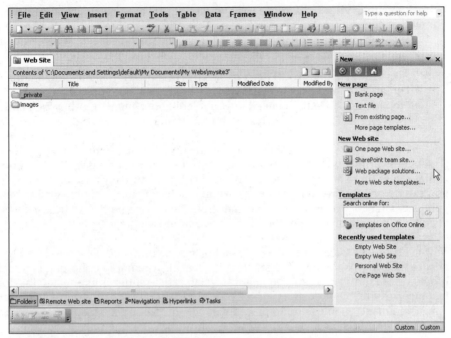

Figure 39-1: When you choose File ➪ New in FrontPage, this is what you see.

Note   Whenever you have a page open, it's indicated at the top of your workspace by a tab. You can maneuver from page to page just by clicking on the appropriate tab. Once you open an additional view, a new tab labeled Web Site appears on your workspace. You can thus toggle easily back and forth between Page view and the other views just by clicking the appropriate tab.

Before you start creating Web pages and organizing them into a Web site, it's a good idea to introduce yourself to these various views:

✦ **Folders view.** Think of Folders view as a directory of the files you create in FrontPage. After you start saving Web pages, you'll see them listed here.

✦ **Remote Web site view.** This view, new to FrontPage 2003, enables you to move files back and forth between local and remote Web sites easily, using FTP. It's ideal for working with other users on a site located on an FTP server.

✦ **Reports view.** FrontPage can generate reports that provide interesting information on the state and status of your Web site. Here's where you'll find them.

✦ **Navigation view.** Navigation view is going to be your second most frequently used view, after Page view. This is where you organize all your different Web page files into an integrated Web site.

✦ **Hyperlinks view.** *Hyperlinks* (or *links,* for short) are text or graphics that, when clicked, transport a visitor to some other location on the Web or on your Web site, or open an already-addressed e-mail message. When Web pages change, links can break or fall out of date; this view checks them for you.

✦ **Tasks view.** Finally, FrontPage enables the organizationally fixated among us to create lists of things to do. If you're designing a site yourself, a pocket notepad might be all you need. If you're collaborating with other Web authors, however, the Tasks view helps keep you all on the same page.

You should be aware of a few more commands on the View menu. View ⇨ Ruler and Grid offers various layout guides that you can turn on, including vertical and horizontal rulers that show you exactly how wide objects on your page are, in pixels, so you can be certain they'll fit within a certain resolution, and a visible grid to help you place objects precisely, which can even be made "magnetic" so that objects snap to it (particularly useful for aligning two or more objects).

New in FrontPage 2003 is the View ⇨ Tracing Image command. One good way to ensure that your Web page is aesthetically pleasing, or simply coherent, is to design it outside of FrontPage first. You might have an artist render it in pen and ink, for instance, or you might design it using your favorite graphics program. The Tracing Image command enables you to place an image into your design space to use as a reference. It's not a background — it won't show up when the page is published — but it can be an invaluable aid to design. When you choose the command, you're prompted to browse to the image you want to use. Then, you specify its placement on the page and its level of transparency — that is, whether it will appear with full color and contrast, or have a faded appearance.

Creating a Web Site

You have two ways to go about creating a Web site in FrontPage: You can start by creating individual pages or you can start by designing the site as a whole. Either way works; sometimes one approach works better than the other, depending on the situation. If you are creating a single Web page, for example, you need not worry about how it will connect with other pages at your Web site, because there aren't any. If you are designing a multipage Web site, often it works best to design the whole site first, and then provide page content.

To use an architectural analogy, if you were designing an office building, you would almost always want to start by laying out the design of the building, and then worry about furnishing the individual suites and offices. When you design Web sites with FrontPage, you also develop site-design skills.

Creating a new FrontPage Web site

You have two basic options in creating a FrontPage Web site. You can create your Web site on a Web server that is accessible to the Internet or an intranet, or you can create your Web site on a local computer drive (your hard drive). Web sites saved to your hard drive cannot have all the advanced features available in FrontPage, like the capability to collect data from input forms. In addition, of course, they can't be visited by anyone else. However, you can use your local drive to design a Web site, and then publish it to a Web server.

Starting from a template

To start a new Web site, choose One page Web site from the New task pane, which you open by choosing File ⇨ New. As in other Office applications, however, you can also choose to create a page or Web site from a template.

To create a Web site from a template, choose Web package solutions from the New Web site area of the New task pane or the More Web site templates link. (You can also search for templates on Office Online.) Both of these links open the dialog box shown in Figure 39-2; the only difference is that the Web package solutions link takes you to the Packages tab, whereas the More Web site templates link takes you to the General tab.

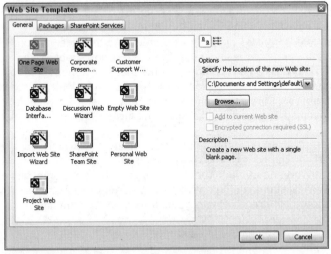

Figure 39-2: Starting a new FrontPage Web site from a template provides you with numerous options.

Under the General tab, you can find templates for other specialized Web sites — for example, an Issue Tracker, a Review Site, and a Web Log. You can read a description of any template by selecting it; the description is displayed in the lower-right-hand corner of the dialog box.

FrontPage offers both templates and wizards to help you create various kinds of Web sites. The templates include One Page Web Site, Personal Web Site, Customer Support Web Site, Empty Web Site, Personal Web Site, and Project Web Site. The wizards include a Corporate Presence Wizard, which enables you to quickly create a professional-looking Web site for any organization; a Database Interface Wizard, which enables you to create a site that can connect to a database and then be used to view, update, delete, or add records; a Discussion Web Wizard, which creates a discussion group, complete with message threads, a table of contents, and search capabilities; and the Import Web Site Wizard, which enables you to import an existing Web site into FrontPage as a new Web site. Finally, there's a template for a SharePoint Site. (There's also a tab in the Web Site Templates dialog box for templates for additional SharePoint Services Web sites.)

Cross-Reference   For details about SharePoint Services, see Chapter 47.

You're asked to specify the location of the new Web site — it can be on your computer or on another server. If you've already got a Web site open in FrontPage, you can simply integrate the pages from the template you've chosen into the current Web site, instead of starting a new one.

Note   Although the Web Site Templates dialog box doesn't make this clear, a FrontPage Web site's name is the same as the folder name or the URL you supply as the location of the new Web site. Be sure to choose a name that you want people to use for accessing your Web site. If you're planning to publish your Web site on the World Wide Web, observe the naming limitations in force there: Use only letters, numerals, and ordinary punctuation marks, and don't include spaces in the name.

Some of the Web site templates are quite complex, requiring a relatively high level of expertise with FrontPage in order to customize. These templates also require that you already have a Web site in place that's equipped with FrontPage Server Extensions. The Empty Web site, One Page Web site, and Personal Web site, however, all work well without FrontPage Server Extensions on a Web site server.

Starting from scratch

When you choose Empty Web site to create a new Web site, FrontPage sets up the Web site folders and support files and leaves you with the job of creating the Web site's pages. With any of the other templates and wizards, a new Web site contains at least one page to get you started. Either way, though, you're bound to need additional pages. To add a brand-new page to a Web site, you again open the New Page or Web Site task pane by choosing File ➪ New.

You can insert a blank page or you can create one from an existing page; the latter opens a copy of the page you select, which you can then edit. This is a great way to avoid having to re-create page elements from scratch or import elements you admire from other pages.

Note The other option in the task pane is Text file. This creates a new page with a .txt extension, rather than an .htm extension. You can use this page to edit or create text files, such as JavaScript or XML files, if you're adept at that level of hands-on programming.

Working with folders and files in Folders view

FrontPage's Folders view (see Figure 39-3) works like Windows Explorer, so you shouldn't have any trouble using it to navigate the constituent files and folders of your Web site. A few points merit comment, however.

Name	Title	Size	Type	Modified Date	Modified By	Comments
_borders						
_fpclass						
_kbas						
_overlay						
_private						
_reqdis						
_themes						
images						
archive.htm	Archive	7KB	htm	13/01/2003 1:58 PM	Edward Willett	
contact.htm	Contact Us	6KB	htm	13/01/2003 1:58 PM	Edward Willett	
discuss.htm	Discussions	7KB	htm	13/01/2003 1:58 PM	Edward Willett	
index.htm	Home	8KB	htm	13/01/2003 1:58 PM	Edward Willett	
kbaftr.htm	Included Article Footer for...	2KB	htm	13/01/2003 1:58 PM	Edward Willett	
kbahdr.htm	Included Article Header fo...	2KB	htm	13/01/2003 1:58 PM	Edward Willett	
kbcfrm.htm	Knowledge Base Confirma...	3KB	htm	13/01/2003 1:58 PM	Edward Willett	
kbfoot.htm	Included Footer for Knowl...	2KB	htm	13/01/2003 1:58 PM	Edward Willett	
kbhead.htm	Included Header for Know...	2KB	htm	13/01/2003 1:58 PM	Edward Willett	
kbpost.htm	Knowledge Base Submissi...	4KB	htm	13/01/2003 1:58 PM	Edward Willett	
kbsrch.htm	Knowledge Base Search F...	3KB	htm	13/01/2003 1:58 PM	Edward Willett	
kbtoc.htm	Knowledge Base TOC	2KB	htm	13/01/2003 1:58 PM	Edward Willett	
members.htm	Members	11KB	htm	13/01/2003 1:58 PM	Edward Willett	

Figure 39-3: FrontPage's Folders view helps you navigate the files and folders of your Web site.

You can select any arbitrary set of files to cut, copy, or delete; to find and replace text in the selected files; and to apply themes or specify shared borders. Press Shift while clicking to select a series of contiguous files, or Ctrl while clicking to select or deselect any file individually.

You can add a new page or new file folder by clicking the New Page and New Folder buttons in the upper-right-hand corner of the Folders view. The third button, Up One Level, moves you up in the hierarchy if you're currently looking inside a folder or subfolder.

Double-clicking a file opens it. By default, Web site pages created in another Office application open in that application; those created in FrontPage or stored in generic HTML open in FrontPage's Page view. Image files open in the application with which they're associated in Windows. You can change these defaults in the Configure Editors tab of the Options dialog box (Tools ➪ Options). All the editors you thus configure are available when you right-click a file and choose Open With.

Note that Folders view's icons for pages are informative. You can see at a glance which Office application created the page, because a mini-icon for the application is overlaid on each page's icon. Its title, size, type, the date it was modified, and who modified it are also displayed. In addition, when a page is open in the FrontPage editor, a little pencil is added to its icon in Folders view.

Finally, be aware that the Folder List navigation bar, a fixture of Folders view, is optionally available in the other views as well. It works a bit differently here, listing files and folders but not the additional information about when they were modified, who modified them, and so on. Use the View ➪ Folder List command to turn this list on or off.

Designing your Web site's navigation structure

When you've given your Web site its full complement of pages, it's time to organize those pages into a hierarchical structure for navigation purposes. Use Navigation view for this chore. As shown in Figure 39-4, Navigation view presents your Web site on a sort of pasteboard from which you can arrange and rearrange the pages to clarify their relationships.

You're supposed to use Navigation view in concert with link bars you insert in your pages. A link bar is a FrontPage component that automatically adds the appropriate navigation buttons to the page, based on the location of the page in the navigation structure. However, even if you eschew link bars, Navigation view can help you turn a vague concept of your site's organization into an unambiguous road map.

Note   Placing a page in the navigation structure does *not* automatically add links to any other pages in the structure. FrontPage creates links for you only if you add link bars to the page.

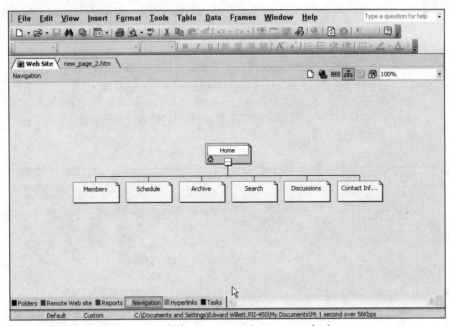

Figure 39-4: Navigation view helps you organize your Web site.

Working with pages in the navigation structure

A Web site's home page is the only one automatically included in its navigation structure. To add a page, open the Folder List by clicking the Toggle Pane button on the Standard toolbar, and then drag the pages from the Folder List to the location in the structure where you want them to reside.

Tip   By default, Navigation view is in Portrait orientation, with the Home page at the top and the subpages below. To toggle between Portrait and Landscape orientation (which places the Home page at the left side and extends the subpages to the right), click the Portrait/Landscape button in the upper-right corner of the Navigation view, or right-click the view and choose Portrait/Landscape from the shortcut menu.

To position the page where you want it, locate the ghostly line that connects the icon of the page you're adding to an existing icon on the structure (see Figure 39-5). Let the ghostly line guide you as follows:

✦ If you don't see the ghostly line, the page can't be added to the structure at the current location. Keep dragging until the line appears.

✦ To add a page to the top level of the Web site—the level of the home page—the ghostly line should extend to the left of the home page icon.

✦ To add a page at a subsidiary level to an existing page, drag the icon for the new page until the ghostly line connects it to the bottom (or right, in Portrait orientation) of the existing page's icon. You can add as many subsidiary pages as you like to an existing page.

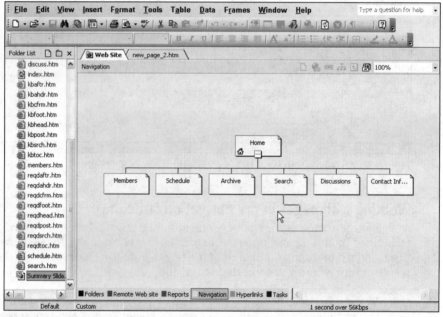

Figure 39-5: While you drag a page icon in the navigation structure, a ghostly outline shows you where the page will drop in.

You can add a page to the structure only once.

To revise the navigation structure, just drag page icons around on the screen. The ghostly line continues to serve as your guide to their placement. You can delete a page by clicking it to select it and pressing Delete, or via its shortcut menu. In the resulting dialog box, you can instruct FrontPage to delete the page from the navigation structure only, or to remove it from the Web site itself, erasing the page's file.

Caution   If the page you're deleting has subsidiary pages in the navigation structure, deleting it removes all subsidiary pages as well.

Using the Navigation tools

The Navigation tools are part of the Navigation view, appearing in the upper-right corner. I've already drawn your attention to the Portrait/Landscape button. From left to right, these Navigation tools include the following:

✦ **New page.** This adds a new blank page as a subsidiary page to the one currently selected. This command is not available if no pages are selected.

✦ **Add Existing Page.** To add to the navigation structure of a page or file located outside your Web site, select the page to which you want to connect the external item and click the Add Existing Page button. In the Insert Hyperlink dialog box that then appears, type in or navigate to a Web or intranet address or a disk file. When the existing page is part of your navigation structure, you can move it around just like any other page.

✦ **New Custom Link Bar.** This creates a Custom Link Bar, to which you can add any of the pages within your Web site or from outside it. A Custom Link Bar is separate from the link bars FrontPage will automatically add to your site for internal navigation; it can appear on only one page.

✦ **Included in Link Bars.** This button is selected to include a page in link bars. To exclude a particular page from your link bars, click the page to select it and then click this button to deselect it.

✦ **View Subtree Only.** Use this button to focus on a single branch of the navigation structure. Begin by clicking the page at the top of the branch, one that has subsidiary pages attached to it. When you then click the View Subtree Only button, you see only the chosen branch. Click the button again to see the entire navigation structure.

Note To hide the details of a given branch of the navigation structure, click the little white box containing a minus sign at the bottom or right side of the page at the top of the branch. All the subsidiary pages disappear. Clicking the box again (it now contains a plus sign) restores the hidden pages.

✦ **Zoom.** This drop-down list enables you to adjust the magnification by selecting one of several preset zoom factors.

Adding and Formatting Text

Whether you started your Web site using a template, or with a single blank page in Page view, or by laying out the structure in Navigation view, eventually you're going to want to add content to it, and probably the first content you're going to want to add is that workhorse of communication — text.

Adding text to a FrontPage Web site page is not hard. The basic text editing and formatting tools you already know from Word are available here, too. Type, cut, paste, or click the Spelling button to check your spelling. Click the Bold button on the Formatting toolbar to assign boldface to selected text, and so on.

One thing you might not have expected is how easy it is to take text, graphics, and even tables from other Office applications and add them to your Web site. This section shows you how to do that.

Getting text without typing

You can copy text from Word (or Excel, Access, and PowerPoint, for that matter) right into FrontPage's Page view. Simply select the text in another Office application and click the Copy button in that application's toolbar to save the text to the clipboard. Then, open or switch to FrontPage's Page view and paste the text at the cursor insertion point.

Much, but not necessarily all, of your formatting will be saved when you paste text. Your other application may use formatting that's not available in HTML pages, but FrontPage will do its best to keep your font type, size, color, and attributes when you paste in text from other applications.

Tip   If you don't want FrontPage to keep the original formatting, you can have it paste plain text only. A smart tag that appears when you paste text from the clipboard into FrontPage offers you two options: Keep Source Formatting (the default) and Keep Text Only. Choose the latter to remove the formatting. Since the formatting is typically only approximate because of the limited formatting options HTML offers, this is often the best choice.

Cross-Reference   For more information about Smart Tags in Office, see Chapter 1.

Editing text

The editing tools at your disposal in Page view include the following:

✦ Edit ➪ Find and Edit ➪ Replace enable you to find and/or replace text in Page view. Can you Find and Replace globally, for an entire Web site? Yes, you can — just select the All Pages radio button in the Replace dialog box. Of course, using this makes the most sense after you've created all your pages, so you have to do it only once.

✦ The Spelling tool in the Standard toolbar enables you to check the spelling for the open page in Page view. If you want to spellcheck your entire document, this too can be done. Click the Spelling tool while in any view except Page view and you have the option to select the Entire Web site radio button. The Add a task for each page with misspellings checkbox creates a link in Tasks view to each page that needs fixing, so you know exactly where you have to go to fix the problems.

Formatting text

All the formatting tools in FrontPage's Page view work much the same as they do in other Office applications. The main difference is that when you create Web site pages in FrontPage, the available options are different from those you get when you use other applications to create documents to print. Following are some general guidelines:

✦ **Font sizes.** When you select font sizes from the Font Size drop-down list, you'll notice a rather limited selection. This is because Web browsers don't interpret many font sizes.

✦ **Font colors.** On the plus side, you can assign font colors with the Font Color button, and every browser will interpret those colors. First, select the text; then, click the down arrow next to the Font Color button and choose a font color from the palettes that appear.

Formatting paragraphs

The following list details the general capabilities and restrictions you encounter when formatting paragraphs with FrontPage:

✦ **Indenting.** FrontPage lets you indent selected paragraphs using the Increase Indent tool.

✦ **Alignment.** You can left-align, center, right-align, or justify text.

✦ **Numbered and bulleted lists.** Automatic numbering or bullets are assigned by selecting text and clicking either the Numbering or the Bullets button. If you are adding to a numbered or bulleted list, each time you press Enter you create a new bulleted or numbered item. Remove bullet or numbering formatting from a selected paragraph by clicking the respective button again on the Formatting toolbar. Change the appearance of buttons or numbers by choosing Format ➪ Bullets and Numbering.

The Paragraph dialog box, shown in Figure 39-6, allows you some control over line and paragraph spacing. Although not all browsers will recognize the additional formatting features available in the Paragraph dialog box, you can apply them, and visitors using IE 4 and later will see them. To access the Paragraph dialog box, right-click selected paragraphs and choose Paragraph from the shortcut menu. The Preview area of the dialog box demonstrates the effect of the formatting you apply, assuming that your page is viewed by a visitor with a browser version current enough to recognize these formatting features.

 Tip
By default, most paragraphs have a line of spacing between them. You can create line breaks without vertical spacing by pressing Shift + Enter to create a forced line break (sometimes known as a soft return, whereas a new paragraph is indicated by a hard return).

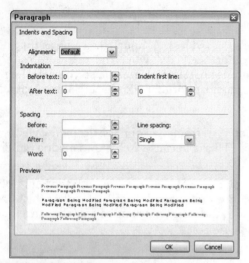

Figure 39-6: Options available in the Paragraph dialog box may or may not be viewable by your visitors' browsers.

Using Tables for Layout Purposes

Tables serve two purposes in Web page layout. One, you can create Excel- or Word-type tables to display information in rows and columns. Two, you can use tables to lay out text and graphics in newspaper-style columns.

In either case, the easiest way to create a table is to click the Insert Table tool on the Standard toolbar and click and drag in the Table grid to define the number of rows and columns in your table—just like creating a table with the Insert Table tool in other Office applications.

When you have finished creating a table, you can use it in a number of ways:

✦ **Add text.** You can add text to a table by clicking in a cell and typing.

✦ **Insert objects.** You can also insert any other object (such as a picture) into a table cell. You can apply the same editing and formatting techniques to table text as you do to text outside a table.

✦ **Select rows or columns.** You can select a row or column of a table by clicking in a cell and then choosing Table ➪ Select ➪ Column or Table ➪ Select ➪ Row.

✦ **Delete cells, rows, or columns.** You can delete selected cells (or rows or columns) by choosing Delete Cells from the Table menu.

Defining table properties

Formatting assigned to an entire table applies to all cells in the table and governs the overall appearance of the table. Right-click anywhere in a table, and choose Table Properties from the shortcut menu to open the Table Properties dialog box, shown in Figure 39-7.

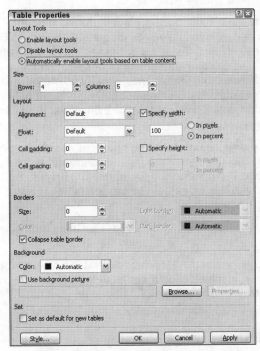

Figure 39-7: Define global table formatting in the Table Properties dialog box.

The main areas of this dialog box are as follows:

✦ **Layout tools.** Here you can activate layout tools for this table, disable layout tools, or leave it up to FrontPage to automatically activate layout tools as it sees fit. Layout tools are a special set of tools, new in FrontPage 2003, that let you more easily manipulate tables used for layout purposes. These tools are designed to create tables that work equally well in different types of browsers and different browser versions (more on these tools in the next section).

✦ **Size.** Defines the number of rows and columns in the table.

✦ **Layout.** Here you can set the alignment of the table (left, right or center), specify its width, determine the float (where text appears in relation to it), and specify cell padding (the space between the contents of a cell and the border) and cell spacing (the space between cells).

✦ **Borders.** Here you can set the size of any border placed around the table (a setting of 0 means no border is displayed). You can also assign colors to the table's border. There are three settings: Color, Light Border, and Dark Border. Use the Color setting to set a single color for the entire border. The Light Border and Dark Border settings enable you to specify colors for the top and left and bottom and right edges of the border, respectively. This can help you give your table a 3D look. Using either the Light or Dark Border setting overrides the Color setting for its respective area.

✦ **Background.** These options define the background color (or image) for your entire table. They work much the same as assigning a background to an entire page. Click the Use Background Picture checkbox and use the Browse button to locate an image to tile as the background for the table, or choose a background color from the Color drop-down list.

✦ **Set.** If you want to use the current settings as the default settings for future tables, click this checkbox.

✦ **The Style button.** Selecting this opens the Modify Style dialog box. Use the Format button in the Modify Style dialog box to assign default font, paragraph, border, or numbering styles to your table.

Defining cell properties

The Cell Properties dialog box, shown in Figure 39-8, provides quick access to all the formatting options available to individual cells within the table. To open this dialog box, select the cells to which you want to apply attributes, and then select Table ➪ Table Properties ➪ Cell, or right-click within the selected cells and select Cell Properties from the shortcut menu.

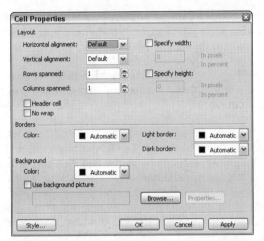

Figure 39-8: The Cell Properties dialog box offers formatting options for individual cells.

The Cell Properties dialog box provides the following capabilities:

✦ **Layout** enables you to set the horizontal alignment of whatever is placed in the cell, its vertical alignment, and the number of columns or rows the cell should span. Specify width and Specify height set the width and height for the cell. (Note that the greatest width setting in a column applies to all cells in that column, and the greatest height setting in a row applies to all cells in that row.) You can specify width or height either in pixels or as a percentage of the overall width or height of the row or column. Header cell formats the cell as a table header that appears in bold by default; No wrap forces text to remain on one line.

✦ **Borders** controls the look of the borders around cells. The Color setting sets the colors for the border of an individual cell, rather than the table as a whole. Light border refers to the bottom and right edges of the cell, and Dark border refers to the top and left edges of the cell; this is the opposite of their positions for the table's outline. If the table border is set to 0 width, these settings have no effect.

✦ **Background** is an option for assigning colors or images to the background of selected cells.

Using FrontPage's new Table Layout tools

FrontPage 2003 has an entirely new set of tools designed for use with tables that are being used specifically for layout purposes — tools you should use because tables created using them work equally well in different types of browsers and different versions of browsers.

To create one of these special tables, choose Table ⇨ Layout Tables and Cells. This opens the Layout Tables and Cells task pane (see Figure 39-9), where you'll see two links near the top: Insert Layout Table and Insert Layout Cell.

If you click Insert Layout Table, FrontPage inserts a default table into your current page; choose Insert Layout Cell, and a small dialog box opens that enables you to define the cell's width, height, and location.

Note   What's the difference between a layout cell and an ordinary table cell? You must insert a layout cell if you want to use FrontPage's new Cell Formatting tools, which enable you to add all sorts of graphical pleasantries to the cell. See the section "Using the Cell Formatting tools," later in this chapter.

Tip   Just as with other tables, you can draw a layout table or cell at any size you want; click the Draw Layout Table or Draw Layout Cell buttons in the Layout Tables and Cells task pane to activate that option.

The default table is a single big cell; however, FrontPage also offers several layouts at the bottom of the Layout Tables and Cells task pane that might suit your purposes better. In Figure 39-9, I've inserted one of these.

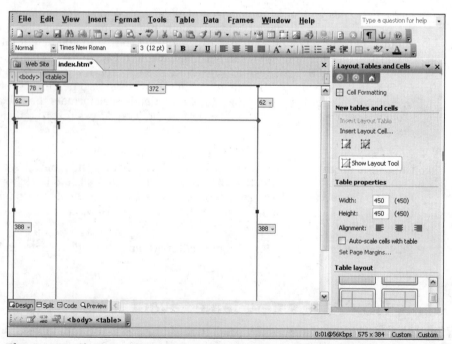

Figure 39-9: The new Layout Tables and Cells task pane gives you pixel-precise control over the tables you use to position elements on your Web pages.

The layout table, as you'll see, doesn't look much like the ordinary table you might have created in Word, but it still consists of rows and columns, and you can still set table properties and cell properties using the Table Properties and Cell Properties dialog boxes you've already seen. The big advantage of this new table, though, is the pixel-perfect control it gives you over the size and placement of objects.

Notice in Figure 39-9 that each row and column comes with little tags that specify its dimensions in pixels. Each of these tags is really a kind of Smart Tag; if you click the downward-pointing arrow at the right side of the tag, you'll see a shortcut menu that enables you to change that dimension, insert a spacer image to maintain the dimension no matter what changes are made to other parts of the table, and activate Autostretch, a new tool that prevents columns and rows from being distorted when someone views the page under unusual conditions, such as extremely low resolution or in a small window. If, for example, you created a table with the left column fixed at a certain width to accommodate a graphic, you could activate Autostretch in the right column, which contains text; that column would then automatically resize and wrap the text it contains to adjust to changing viewing conditions.

The Layout Tables and Cells task pane also offers you the option to set the table's width, height, and alignment.

Tip   Most pages, except for the most basic, make some use of tables as layout aids. Therefore, by default, FrontPage opens the Layout Tables and Cells task pane whenever you insert a new page. If you'd rather not have the task pane open, uncheck the Show when creating a new page checkbox at the bottom of the task pane.

Using the Cell Formatting tools

The Layout Tables and Cells task pane also provides access to another brand-new task pane, the Cell Formatting task pane (see Figure 39-10).

These tools enable you to change a layout cell's size and alignment and set its background, and apply a border to all or some of the cell's sides. Click the Header and Footer link to apply further formatting to a cell—adding a header or footer (sections of the cell, of any height, with different background colors). Click the Cell Corners and Shadows link to apply curved corners to a cell (or even a corner designed and saved as an image) and/or a drop shadow.

Note   The Cell Formatting tools work only on cells inserted using the Insert Layout Cell command in the Layout Tables and Cells task pane; they don't work on ordinary cells in regular tables, or even on ordinary cells in layout tables.

Note   Worried about changing the size or location of your cell after applying all this fancy formatting? Don't be. FrontPage will regenerate the corners, shadows, and other decorations you've applied to your cell as required.

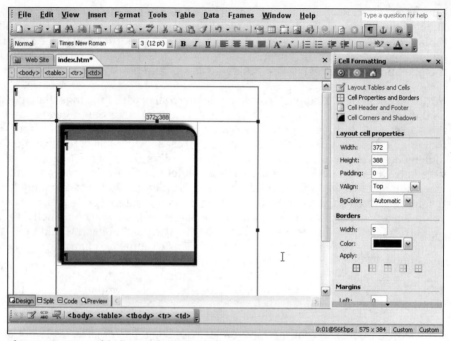

Figure 39-10: In this figure, I've used the Cell Formatting task pane to create a layout cell with borders, a header and footer, one rounded corner, and a shadow.

Converting tables to text

You can easily convert a table into text. You won't lose any of the objects (text, graphics, and so on) in the table, although you'll obviously lose the layout you created using that table. Those objects become normal page objects, laid out in paragraphs. To convert a table to text, click anywhere in the table and select Table ⇨ Convert ⇨ Table to Text.

Note   You can convert a layout table to text just as you can a regular table, but be aware that any layout cells you've inserted in that table will not be converted by the command; they'll remain as layout cells. Nor can you click inside the layout cell and use this command to convert it to text.

Tip   One of the most common uses of tables in Web design is to create columns on the page. The layouts included in the Choose Layout section of the Layout Tables and Cells task pane are designed with exactly that in mind.

Adding Graphics

Regardless of what you know about Web-compatible graphics, you'll like the way FrontPage handles pictures.

The easiest way to get pictures into your Web site page is to either insert them as files or copy them in through the clipboard. After you copy or insert a graphic of any file format, FrontPage handles the process of saving that image as a Web-compatible .gif, .png, or .jpg file (of course, if it already is in a Web-compatible format, it keeps its current format unless you choose to change it).

Inserting pictures

As in other Office applications, you insert a picture by placing your insertion point where you want the picture to go and choosing Insert ➪ Picture.

You have five options:

✦ **Clip Art.** This opens the Clip Organizer.

Cross-Reference

The Clip Organizer is discussed in detail in Chapter 43.

✦ **From File.** This option opens a standard Windows browsing box that enables you to navigate to the graphic file you want to insert.

✦ **From Scanner or Camera.** If you have a scanner or camera connected to your computer, this option enables you to scan in or download pictures from them, using whatever interface you normally use for those procedures.

✦ **New Photo Gallery.** This option enables you to insert multiple photographs using one of several preset layouts; this is unique to FrontPage (although it's somewhat similar to the Photo Album feature in PowerPoint), so it is covered in more detail in the following section.

✦ **Movie in Flash Format.** Use this command to insert a Shockwave Flash animation.

Inserting a Photo Gallery

When you choose Insert ➪ Picture ➪ New Photo Gallery, the Photo Gallery Properties dialog box opens. There are two tabs: Pictures and Layout. Figure 39-11 shows the Pictures tab; Figure 39-12 shows the Layout tab.

Choose the layout you want, based on the preview image and the description. The Horizontal and Vertical Layouts enable you to specify how many pictures you want per row.

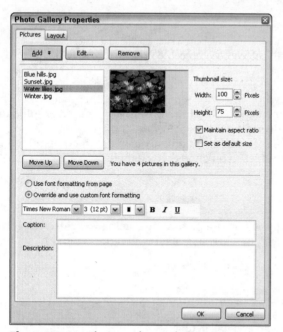

Figure 39-11: Choose a layout for your Photo Gallery from this dialog box.

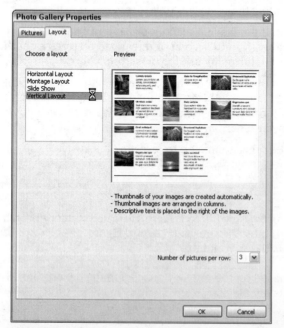

Figure 39-12: Insert pictures into your layout using this dialog box.

To add pictures, click Add. (To remove one added by accident, highlight it and click Remove.) You can add pictures from files, a scanner, or a camera. The pictures you choose are listed in the box at the upper left; you can reorganize them using the Move Up and Move Down buttons. You can also open another dialog box that lets you resize, rotate, and crop them by clicking Edit.

At the right, you can set the size of the thumbnail the gallery will display. Then, at the bottom, you can type in and format a caption and a description.

When you're done, click OK. FrontPage creates the Photo Gallery in Page view (see Figure 39-13; this is the Slide Show layout). If you press Shift while clicking any thumbnail, the full-size image appears.

Note   When the Web site is published and viewed through a browser, a regular click will display the full-size image. You use Shift+Click to follow any hyperlink in Page view in FrontPage because a regular click is used to select items for formatting, just as in other Office applications.

Figure 39-13: Here's one example of a FrontPage Photo Gallery, seen in Page view.

Copying a picture

You can copy a picture by creating or opening it (or a file that contains it) in any application. Copy the graphic to the clipboard, and then paste it into a Web site page open in Page view.

Saving graphics

When you save your Web site page, FrontPage will convert all the graphics on your page to Web-compatible formats and prompt you to save these embedded files. The Save Embedded Files dialog box will appear, as shown in Figure 39-14. Here you can rename or relocate files; clicking Picture File Type lets you set the format in which you want to save the picture (so you can convert a JPG to a GIF file, for instance) and set options specific to the format (e.g., image quality in a JPG file, transparency in a GIF file).

Figure 39-14: FrontPage prompts you to save all graphics on your page.

Editing pictures in FrontPage

FrontPage offers you some basic editing tools for any pictures you insert. You'll probably want to use a dedicated graphics program for any serious tweaking of pictures, but FrontPage's tools are still useful.

To see the tools, choose View ➪ Toolbars ➪ Pictures. Figure 39-15 shows the Pictures toolbar.

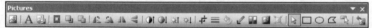

Figure 39-15: Edit pictures right in FrontPage with the Pictures toolbar.

The picture tools enable you to add images and text to, and change the appearance of, a picture. From left to right, the available tools are as follows:

✦ The Insert Picture From File button enables you to insert a new image.

✦ The Text button adds text to your image.

✦ Auto Thumbnail generates a small version of your image.

✦ Position Absolutely enables you to lock the position of your image to any spot on your page.

✦ Bring Forward and Send Backward move selected images in front of or behind other objects on the page.

✦ Rotate Left, Rotate Right, Flip Horizontal, and Flip Vertical rotate or flip your selected image.

✦ More Contrast, Less Contrast, More Brightness, and Less Brightness work like the contrast and brightness dials on your monitor or TV to change the brightness and contrast of your image.

✦ Crop puts movable corner and side handles on your picture. Click and drag on these handles to crop your picture, and then click the Crop button again to finalize your cut.

✦ Set Transparent Color displays an Eraser tool. Point and click at any one color in your image to make that color disappear, allowing the page background to show through.

✦ Color converts images from color to black-and-white and back again.

✦ Bevel adds a 3D frame around an image, suitable for navigation buttons.

✦ Resample saves your image as a smaller file if you've reduced the size of your image on the page.

✦ Select deselects other tools and displays the arrow pointer.

✦ Rectangular Hotspot, Circular Hotspot, and Polygonal Hotspot create clickable links called *image maps* (see the next section for a discussion of hyperlinks).

✦ Highlight Hotspots helps identify hotspots.

✦ Restore undoes changes to your picture, as long as you haven't saved the changes.

Changing image properties

Earlier, you were promised that you would like how FrontPage handles images. Up to now, we've relied on FrontPage to save images and assign a format. However, you can choose from the three widely recognized Web graphics formats (GIF, JPEG, or PNG). Moreover, you can assign other graphic properties to your pictures.

Note   Assigning attributes to Web graphics can get quite complex, but the basic picture tools and image properties you learn about in this chapter will give you the control you need to insert and format graphic images on your Web pages.

The General tab

To define image properties, right-click a picture and select Picture Properties from the shortcut menu. The General tab of the Picture Properties dialog box includes these options:

✦ Picture is the filename for the picture.

✦ The Picture File Type button lets you manually select a file type. Note that only the GIF file format allows you to apply transparency to an image. The PNG and GIF formats both allow for interlacing, which causes an image to fade in to a browser window (the advantage of this is that viewers can see what the image is before it has fully loaded—and decide if they want to wait for it to finish loading, or move on).

✦ The Alternative representations area enables you to provide a low-resolution image as an alternative for people whose browsers can't handle the regular image, and/or text that will display either (a) when a visitor has graphics turned off in his or her browser; or (b) when a visitor points at a picture.

The Appearance tab

Other formatting features are available in the Appearance tab of the Picture Properties dialog box, but you can do most of these things right in Design view. The Specify size option here is handy if you have a series of pictures that you want to ensure are all the same width or height. The Wrapping style options determine how the picture will be displayed relative to adjacent text—but for better control of that sort of thing, use tables (as described earlier in the chapter).

The Video tab

Interested in running a video on your Web page? Set that up here. Indicate the source of the video, and then choose how often to loop it and whether to start it running when the page is opened or when the mouse runs over it.

Among the video formats FrontPage allows you to add are:

✦ **Windows Video files (.avi)**, which are audio and video files;

✦ **Windows Media files (.asf)**, which is a streaming file format ("streaming" means that the sounds and video play as they're traversing the Internet, instead of having to be completely downloaded onto the computer first, and then played) for use with the Windows Media Player;

✦ **RealAudio files (.ram, .ra)**, a streaming file format designed for use with the RealNetworks RealAudio Player;

✦ **Moving Picture Experts Group (.mpeg)** files, digitally compressed video and audio files that provide high-quality images and sounds with smaller file formats; and

✦ **Apple QuickTime (.mov, .qt)** files, which can be played by any Macintosh computer and by Windows computers with a special QuickTime plug-in added.

Hyperlinks and Image Maps

Hyperlinks (or *links,* for short) are text or graphic images on your Web pages that provide links to something else — another, unrelated Web page, or perhaps another page within your Web site. The easiest way to create a link in Design view is to simply type a Web address or an e-mail address. FrontPage recognizes it as a URL or e-mail address and automatically links the text to that URL or e-mail address.

Note   The techniques described for assigning hyperlinks work in all Office applications, with slight variations. Master them here and you can master them anywhere.

Assigning links to text

Often, of course, in the interest of a cleaner, more professional look, you don't want the actual address to appear in your text; you just want a link from a bit of text to a Web page, an e-mail address, or maybe even somewhere farther down the current page. (This latter trick requires the insertion of bookmarks; see the section "Creating bookmarks," a little later in this chapter.)

To create a hyperlink, select the text you want to call up the link, and then click the Insert Hyperlink button on the Standard toolbar, or choose Insert ➪ Hyperlink, or (my favorite) press Ctrl+K (no, I don't know what the letter *K* has to do with hyperlinks). All these techniques open the Insert Hyperlink dialog box (see Figure 39-16).

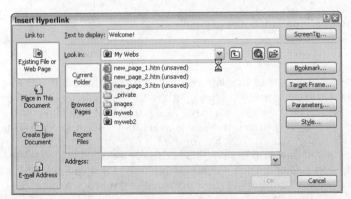

Figure 39-16: Use the Insert Hyperlink dialog box to define hyperlinks to Web sites, other Internet sites, and/or documents on a local or network drive.

The Text to display text box at the top of Figure 39-16 lets you enter or change the text of the hyperlink to be displayed in your document — it automatically contains any text you selected before opening the dialog box. (The traditional wording is "Click here," but these days most people can recognize a hyperlink when they see one, so an alternative is something like "For more information, check the XYZ site," with "XYZ" being the hyperlink.) Arranged vertically along the left side of the box, the large Link to bar contains buttons for selecting the type of hyperlink you want to create. When you click a button, the options in the main part of the box change accordingly. The Link to buttons are as follows:

✦ **Existing File or Web Page.** See the next section, "Creating hyperlinks to existing pages and documents," for details about this option.

✦ **Place in This Document.** This button's function is better expressed as *Create a hyperlink to another location in the current document* — not *Insert a hyperlink into the current document.*

✦ **Create New Document.** Click here if you want to start a new document as the destination for the hyperlink you're inserting.

✦ **E-mail Address.** Click this button if you want the hyperlink to start a new e-mail message using the viewer's default e-mail program.

Creating hyperlinks to existing pages and documents

Hyperlinks can jump to and activate any document file accessible on your system, your network, or the Internet. There are only two requirements: The application that opens that file type must be present on the viewer's system, and the file type must be associated in Windows with that application. For Web pages, of course, the requisite application is a browser.

Using the Insert Hyperlink dialog box, identify an existing Web page or document as the hyperlink's target by clicking the Existing File or Web Page button if necessary. Then use one of the following three techniques:

✦ Type a URL or a path and filename manually.

or

✦ Choose the target from one of the lists controlled by the three buttons just to the right of the Link to bar. Recent Files displays the files you've opened or inserted in Office. Browsed Pages displays Web pages that you've viewed in your browser recently (by title, if the title is available). (Because the HTML Help program is really just Internet Explorer with a different face, all the Help topics you've viewed show up here — this is usually a distracting nuisance.) Current Folder lists pages in the folder selected in the Look in field, which by default holds the folder containing the Web you're currently working in.

or

✦ Click one of the Browse for buttons, to the right of the Look in field, to locate
a filename or Web address. Clicking Browse for Web Page starts your browser.
When you find the page you're looking for, go back to the Insert Hyperlink dialog box; you'll find the address you browsed for ready to be inserted.

Use the Bookmark button to specify a named location in the target document as the
hyperlink's destination. See "Creating bookmarks," later in this chapter.

The ScreenTip button enables you to write a ScreenTip that will show up when a
viewer runs his or her mouse over a hyperlink. This can be a great aid to navigation
around a Web site.

Editing and removing hyperlinks

To edit an existing hyperlink, right-click over the link. Choose Hyperlink Properties
on the shortcut menu to open the Edit Hyperlink dialog box. Its controls are identical to those of the Insert Hyperlink dialog box.

Note　Clicking the Remove Link button doesn't delete the text or graphics that held the
link in your document; only hyperlink functionality is removed.

Creating image maps

Image maps divide sections of a graphic image into different links; these sections
(called *hotspots*) serve as hyperlinks. Therefore, for example, you could post pictures of your staff and let visitors connect with anyone on the staff by clicking the
images of each one's face.

To create an image map by assigning hotspot links to parts of a picture, follow
these steps:

1. Select the picture to which you want to add hotspots.

2. Open the Pictures toolbar by choosing View ➪ Toolbars ➪ Pictures.

3. Click the Rectangular Hotspot, Circular Hotspot, or Polygonal Hotspot button
on the Pictures toolbar.

4. If you selected the Rectangular or Circular Hotspot buttons, click and drag to
draw a rectangle or circle around part of your picture. Figure 39-17 shows a
rectangular hotspot being drawn. You can use the Polygonal Hotspot tool to
draw an outline around an irregularly shaped part of your picture. Do that by
clicking to set outline points, and double-clicking to end the outline.

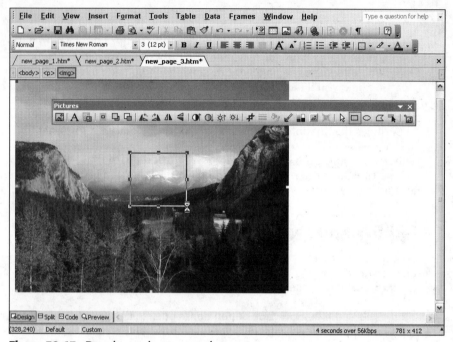

Figure 39-17: Drawing an image map hotspot

5. As soon as you complete your hotspot shape, the Insert Hyperlink dialog box opens. Create your hyperlink just as you did for text.

Creating bookmarks

The target of a link can be not only a specific Web page, but also a specific location on that Web page. These spots on a page are marked with *bookmarks*.

To create a bookmark, simply go to the spot on the page that you want visitors to be able to jump to and choose Insert ➪ Bookmark, or press Ctrl+G. If you've selected text, that text will be the default bookmark name. If you haven't, you can type a bookmark name into the Bookmark name field. Click OK, and the new bookmark is displayed as a small blue flag, or, if the bookmark is assigned to selected text, that text will be underlined with a dotted line. When a page includes bookmarks, you can link to them by selecting the page in your Insert Hyperlink dialog box and then clicking the Bookmark button. If there are bookmarks in the currently open page, clicking the Place in this Document button in the Insert Hyperlink dialog box displays a list of the bookmarks; just choose the one you want viewers to jump to when they click the hyperlink.

Inserting Special FrontPage Components

FrontPage offers tons of specialized prefab gadgets and gizmos that you can plug into a page to enhance its content, functionality, or looks. You can find the most frequently used elements by choosing Insert ➪ Web Component, Insert ➪ Form, or Insert ➪ Interactive Button.

Inserting Web components

Choosing Insert ➪ Web Component opens the dialog box shown in Figure 39-18, which contains a plethora of riches to spice up your Web site. Choose a component type from the list on the left, and then select from the Choose an effect list at right the specific component of that type that you want to insert.

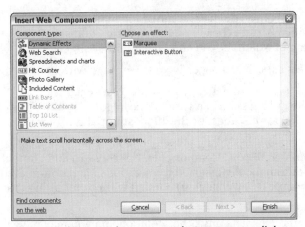

Figure 39-18: Use the Insert Web Component dialog box to add various useful items to your page.

Some especially interesting Web components include the following:

✦ **Dynamic Effects.** Want a button that changes in some way when a mouse pointer moves over it? Maybe you'd like to create an animated banner ad or a scrolling marquee. Those effects are all here.

Note   The Interactive Button option here can also be accessed by choosing Insert ➪ Interactive Button.

✦ **Web Search.** This lets visitors search your Web site using keywords.

Note

Like many other Web components, this one requires that you publish your Web site to a server with FrontPage Server Extensions in order for it to work. You can still design these FrontPage components without publishing them to a Web server with FrontPage Server Extensions, but they won't be functional. A couple of options also require a server that's running Microsoft SharePoint Services.

✦ **Spreadsheets and charts.** These are self-explanatory. You can insert a pivot table, too.

✦ **Hit Counter.** Ever popular, hit counters keep track of how often a particular page is visited.

✦ **Photo Gallery.** See the section "Inserting a Photo Gallery," earlier in this chapter.

✦ **Included Content.** Choose this to include author information, a description, and other such data automatically.

✦ **Link Bars.** These are navigation devices, some of which include only links to other pages within your Web site (based on the structure you specify in Navigation view), some of which let you add links to other sites, too.

✦ **Table of Contents.** This lists all the pages in your Web site, with links to them.

✦ **Top 10 List.** No, this doesn't automatically generate jokes for David Letterman; it lists the top 10 results in a variety of categories — the 10 most visited pages on the site, for instance, or the 10 most popular browsers used to visit the site.

✦ **bCentral, Expedia, MSN & MSNBC Components.** Use these to add content to your Web site that is automatically inserted from various Microsoft-related sites — giving you dynamic (ever-changing) content without requiring that you do the changing.

✦ **Additional Components.** This lists any other components you may have installed. You can download FrontPage components from many sources. Click Find components on the Web site in the lower-left corner to open a browser and do just that.

✦ **Advanced Controls.** Look here for Java applets and ActiveX controls, among other things. This is also where you'll find the option to include HTML code that you've written yourself (or copied from elsewhere), with the assurance that FrontPage won't modify it (see "Experimenting with HTML," the last section in this chapter).

Inserting Forms

Forms in FrontPage are interactive components designed to elicit a response from the viewer and generate information for you. You're already familiar with them to a certain extent from being on the receiving end of them as you use Windows programs of all sorts, and you've probably run across them in Web pages you've visited.

To insert a form, choose Insert ➪ Form, and then choose the type of form you want from the list provided.

Right-click the form after you've inserted it, and then choose Form Properties from the shortcut menu to open the Form Properties dialog box (see Figure 39-19). This will vary depending on what kind of form you've inserted. Here, you instruct FrontPage how you want to deal with the information generated by the form. You can instruct it to send information to a particular file, to an e-mail address, or to a database, for instance. If you click Options, you'll find even more details to specify about this process.

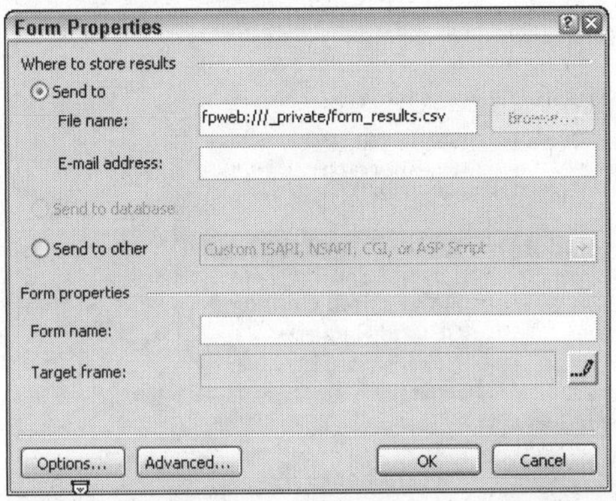

Figure 39-19: Use the Form Properties dialog box to specify how FrontPage should handle information gathered by forms.

Forms are a great way to gather information about visitors, compile an e-mail list of people interested in what you have to offer on your Web site, or just to keep people coming back. Take the time to familiarize yourself with them.

Experimenting with HTML

FrontPage automatically generates HTML tags when you create Web pages. The tags are interpreted by Web browsers. You don't need to know HTML to create Web pages in FrontPage. That's part of its appeal! However, you can enter your own HTML tags, or you can examine the tags FrontPage generates to teach yourself HTML.

You have a couple of ways to look at HTML tags. One is to look at the HTML in Design view. Click the Code button in the lower-left-hand corner to show the HTML, the whole HTML, and nothing but the HTML.

Alternatively—and an even better way to figure out what HTML goes with what part of the page—click the Split button to see both the Design view and the Code view at the same time (see Figure 39-20). This view is new to FrontPage 2003.

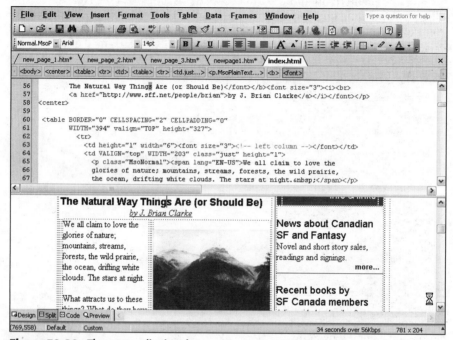

Figure 39-20: The new split view lets you compare HTML with the standard FrontPage Design view.

You can examine the HTML generated by FrontPage and probably figure out what some of the tags mean. For example, text turns boldface on () before the word "text" and then turns it off (). You can also edit your page's HTML directly in HTML view, although, if you want to be certain FrontPage won't alter your HTML coding as it goes about its own business, use the Insert ➪ Web Components ➪ Advanced Components ➪ HTML option (described in the "Inserting Web Components" section, earlier in this chapter).

If you prefer, you can stay in Design view but make HTML tags visible. To do that, while in Design view, select View ➪ Reveal Tags from the menu (you could also press Ctrl + /). The HTML tags are highlighted as shown in Figure 39-21. This is another great way to learn what HTML codes mean.

Tip   FrontPage 2003 offers another useful HTML tool you've probably already noticed. As you create a page, a list of HTML tags appears across the top of the Design view. Each time a new tag is created by FrontPage, it appears here. Clicking one of these tags highlights everything that's contained between it and its matching end tag. You can quickly edit the tag's properties by clicking the downward-pointing arrow at its right end and choosing Edit Tag; you can also quickly insert a bit of HTML at that specific location by choosing Insert HTML.

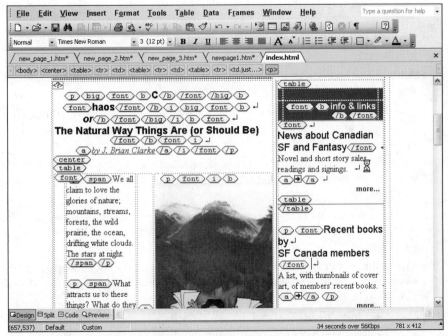

Figure 39-21: You can display HTML tags along with your formatted page on the Design tab in Page view.

Cross-Reference   HTML is a subject for an entire book in its own right. Wiley's own *HTML 4 For Dummies,* Fourth Edition, by Ed Tittel and Natanya Pitts, is a good place to start.

No need to dip a toe any farther into that particular ocean in this chapter. In addition to other books, you can find tons of information online about coding HTML. (If there's one topic the Internet covers particularly thoroughly, it's its own inner workings!)

Summary

All Office documents can be used to create Web pages, but FrontPage specializes in it, with tools that make it easier than ever to create a top-notch Web site using techniques you're already familiar with from other Office applications. Some of the FrontPage topics discussed in this chapter included the following:

✦ FrontPage offers you numerous views. Design view is the one you'll use for editing pages; Navigation view enables you to control the structure of your Web site.

✦ You can start a Web site from scratch, or choose to use one of many different templates.

✦ Adding and formatting text and inserting pictures are both very similar to the same operations in other Office documents.

✦ Learning how to use tables effectively is the key to creating well-laid-out Web pages, and FrontPage 2003 offers new tools to make creating and formatting tables easier than ever.

✦ FrontPage's handy Photo Gallery feature does a lot of the work of formatting pages of photos for you, creating thumbnails that link to full-size versions of the images.

✦ Hyperlinks can link text, pictures, or specific areas of pictures to other Web sites, other pages on your own site, e-mail addresses, or other areas on the same page.

✦ The commands Insert ➪ Web Components and Insert ➪ Forms open up a world of interactive components for your Web sites. It is highly recommended that you learn to use them.

✦ You don't have to know HTML to use FrontPage — but FrontPage makes it easy to use if you already know it, and can help you learn it if you don't.

✦   ✦   ✦

Managing Your Web Site with FrontPage

In Chapter 39, you learned techniques that will help you create quite an attractive Web site. You learned how to use one of FrontPage's templates to design a Web site, how to create and edit Web pages, how to add text and graphics, and how to add advanced elements such as hit counters. You've come a long way. In this chapter, you'll learn to use FrontPage to manage your Web site, and how to customize it to give it a unique look and feel.

Themes, Shared Borders, and Link Bars

In Chapter 39, you added elements to your Web site one page at a time. Some elements can be added globally, however. They include themes, which assign a universal color and design scheme to a Web site, shared borders, and link bars.

Selecting and assigning a theme

Themes are collections of design elements that are assigned to every page in a FrontPage Web site. You can remove a theme from a page, or even use different themes for different pages in a Web site. Generally, however, the point is to use the same theme throughout a site to give it a consistent look and feel.

Themes include background colors, font size, style, and color, and graphic elements. They are assigned in the Theme task pane.

Follow these steps to assign a theme:

1. With your Web site open, select Format ⇨ Theme. You can do this from any view. This opens the Theme task pane (see Figure 40-1).

2. If you want to apply a theme to only some of the pages in your Web site, open or select them in either Folders or Navigation view.

3. Scroll through the displayed themes. They're categorized as the Web site default theme (if you're working with a template), Recently used themes (if any), and All available themes.

4. When you see a theme you'd like to use, point at the preview to reveal a downward-pointing arrow along its right border. Click on the arrow to bring up a shortcut menu.

5. Choose from the shortcut menu how you'd like to apply the theme: as the default theme (in which case it will be applied to all pages in the site) or just to pages you selected in Step 2.

6. Use the checkboxes at the bottom of the task pane to toggle on or off Vivid colors, Active graphics, and the Background picture.

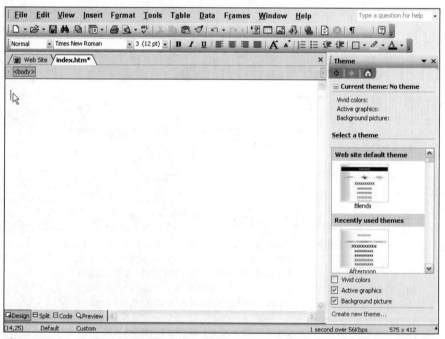

Figure 40-1: Choose themes for your Web site from the Theme task pane.

Adding shared borders

Shared borders are actually separate Web pages that are attached to a border of every page in a Web site. As with themes, shared borders are most effective when applied to every page in a site. Shared borders most often hold link bars, but they can also contain any other object, such as graphics or text.

To apply shared borders to your Web site you first have to turn support for Shared Borders on in FrontPage. To do so, choose Tools ➪ Page Options, then click the Authoring tab and check the Shared Borders checkbox.

With that done, you can follow these steps to add Shared Borders:

1. Select Format ➪ Shared Borders from the FrontPage menu (you can be in any view).

2. In the Shared Borders dialog box (see Figure 40-2), select either the All pages or Selected page(s) radio button to apply the shared borders to either only selected pages, or to the entire Web site. (If you choose Selected pages and later change your mind about the shared borders you've assigned them, you can reset their borders to the default for the rest of the Web site by checking the Reset borders for current page to web default checkbox at the bottom of the Shared Borders dialog box.)

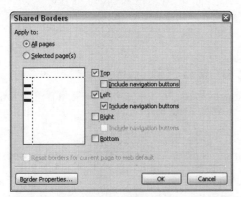

Figure 40-2: Use the Shared Borders dialog box to add borders, complete with navigation links, to your Web site's pages. Here I've chosen to add a left border with navigation links and a top border without to all the pages in my site.

3. Top and Left shared borders are the most widely used. Start experimenting by selecting them. Later, you can elect to deselect one or both of these shared borders, and apply bottom or even right shared borders.

Tip

Most Web site designers shy away from right-side shared borders. Visitors tend to look up, left, or possibly down for navigational links. Moreover, the right side of a Web page is sometimes out of the browser window and requires horizontal scrolling to view.

4. If you select Top and/or Left shared borders along with the All pages option, you can select the Include navigation buttons checkboxes for one or both of these shared borders. (If you're applying shared borders only to selected pages, you don't have the option of including navigation buttons.)

5. Click the Border Properties button to set a background color and/or image for any of the borders you've activated; in the Border Properties dialog box, choose a color from the palette provided or browse for a background picture, and then click OK to return to the Shared Borders.

6. When you have selected shared borders and set their background colors or images, click the OK button.

Tip

Shared borders can include any Web page element, including text and graphics. Shared borders act as a consistent element of each page in your Web site. To edit the content of a shared border, click in the border, and edit as you would any other Web page. When you save the Web page, the embedded shared border page is saved as well.

Inserting and editing link bars

You can change the way links are presented in link bars. You can define link bars by selecting Insert ➪ Navigation. This opens the Insert Web Component dialog box, with Link Bars selected.

Cross-Reference

For more information about inserting Web Components in FrontPage, see Chapter 39.

You can choose from three link bar options: Bar with custom links, Bar with back and next links, and Bar based on navigation structures.

The bar with custom links displays a separate button for each hyperlink, and can point to pages both within and outside the Web site. The bar with back and next links is designed to point to a sequence of pages inside the Web site, and shows only Back and Next buttons. The bar based on navigation structure is just what it sounds like; you determine the links that appear on the bar by altering the structure of the Web site in Navigation view.

Cross-Reference   For more information about using Navigation view, see Chapter 39.

All three of these types of link bars can be edited. If you choose Bar with custom links or Bar with back and next links and click Next, you're first asked to define a style for the bar (a wide variety of styles, including one in the style of each theme, is provided), and then to choose an orientation (horizontal or vertical). If you click Finish at that point, you're given the opportunity to name your new link bar, and then you'll find yourself in the Link Bar Properties dialog box (see Figure 40-3), where you can add a hyperlink, remove a link, and modify existing links on the bar. You can also add links to the home page (the one saved with the name index.htm) or the parent page (based on your navigation structure). The Style tab enables you to change the look and orientation of the link bar again.

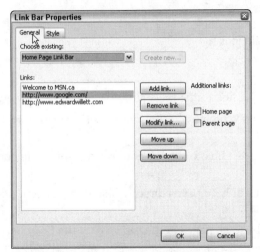

Figure 40-3: Edit your link bars using the Link Bar Properties dialog box.

If you choose Bar based on navigation structure, you select a style and orientation just as you do with the other link bars, but then you are presented with an entirely different Link Bar Properties dialog box (see Figure 40-4).

If you've ever seen or designed a family tree, you can follow the metaphor here. Parent pages are pages one step up on the flowchart hierarchy of Navigation view. Child pages are one step below in the flowchart.

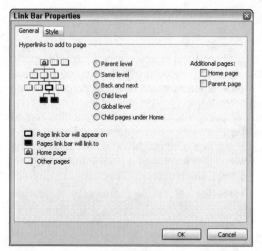

Figure 40-4: Link bar options are analogous to the branches of a family tree.

✦ **Parent level** links display only a link to the page above the page being viewed.

✦ **Same level** links display other Web pages on the same level of the Navigation view site flowchart.

✦ **Back and next** display the nearest link to the left and to the right of the current page.

✦ **Child level** links generate links only to pages directly below the current page in the Navigation view flowchart.

✦ **Global level** links display links to all pages in the top level of the flowchart.

✦ **Child pages under Home** links display the child pages of the home page.

✦ The **Home page** checkbox adds a link to the site's home page on every page in the site. This is a very useful option. Enabling visitors to navigate directly to your home page is usually the most-appreciated navigational link you can provide.

✦ The **Parent page** checkbox adds a link to the parent page on each page. This is redundant if you selected the Parent level radio button, but if you're using other linking logic, it can be helpful.

Tip   Which type of navigational link is best? Probably the most useful navigation links for many sites are generated by selecting the Child level radio button and both the Parent page and Home page checkboxes.

Tip Why can't you assign Link bars to the right or bottom shared borders? Actually, you can. You just have to do it manually, by clicking in the generated border and using the Insert ➪ Navigation command.

Customizing Themes

Just because you've chosen a theme for your Web site doesn't mean you're stuck with it. You can choose to use it as a starting point, and then modify it to suit your aesthetic sense — and practical needs — better. To do so, start by choosing Format ➪ Theme to open the Theme task pane shown in Figure 40-1. Click on one of the themes to bring up the downward-pointing arrow, click on the arrow, and choose Customize from the shortcut menu. This opens the Customize Theme dialog box shown in Figure 40-5, which features three buttons under the question "What would you like to modify?"

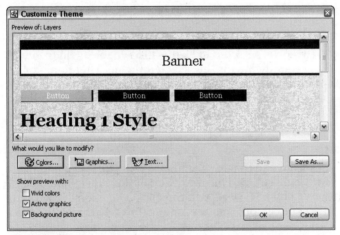

Figure 40-5: If you wish, you can use an existing theme as a starting point for creating your own unique theme.

Modifying theme colors

Clicking the Colors button opens the dialog box shown in Figure 40-6, which features three tabs, providing three different ways to change the colors in your theme.

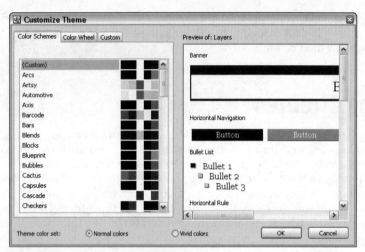

Figure 40-6: You can customize the color scheme in your theme.

The Color Schemes tab

The Color Schemes tab (which is selected in Figure 40-5) enables you to substitute the color scheme of a different theme for the selected theme. Therefore, for example, if you like the graphics and fonts of the Citrus Punch theme, but you prefer the color scheme in the Cactus theme, you can assign the Citrus Punch theme, but select the Cactus color scheme.

The Color Wheel tab

Switching color schemes from one theme to another gives you some, but not complete, control over your theme colors. For even more options, click the Color Wheel tab in the Modify Theme dialog box. Here, you can click a location in the Color Wheel to generate a new set of colors that are color-coordinated with the color you clicked in the wheel.

You can also adjust the colors in your theme color scheme by moving the Brightness slider, and you can toggle between intense colors and muted colors by using the Normal colors or Vivid colors radio buttons at the bottom of the dialog box.

The Custom tab

Finally, you can modify the colors of different text elements in the Custom tab of the Modify Theme dialog box. First, pull down the Item list and select the item to which you want to assign a color. Then, click the Color drop-down list and select a color to assign to that text element.

When you have finished modifying the color scheme of your customized theme, click OK. If you decide not to modify the color scheme after all, click Cancel.

Modifying theme graphics

Themes assign many graphics to your Web pages — for example, a background image, a graphic to use for bullets, another to use for banners, and navigational icons. You can substitute your own graphics for those that come with a theme, and you can customize the font of the text that is added to these images. To do all this, click the Graphics button shown in Figure 40-5. The dialog box shown in Figure 40-7 appears.

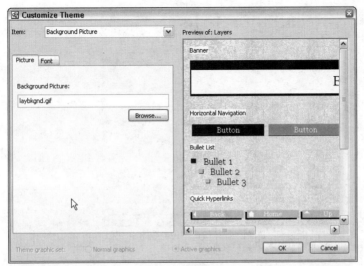

Figure 40-7: Use the Customize Theme dialog box to substitute your own graphics for theme elements.

The Picture tab

You can assign new graphics to the various elements of the theme that use them by selecting the name of the element you want to modify from the Item list and then browsing for a new picture (or, in some cases, more than one picture — Vertical Navigation, for example, requires a graphic image for the normal picture, for the picture after it has been selected, and for the picture when the mouse pointer simply hovers over it).

The Font tab

The Font tab, similarly, enables you to assign fonts, font styles, font sizes, and horizontal and vertical alignment to various items, pulled down from the Item list. (Remember, you already assigned font colors in the Colors tab.)

Changing theme styles

You can assign fonts to any of the HTML styles available in the Style drop-down list in Page view. To do this, click the Text button in the Customize Theme dialog box. Select a style from the Item drop-down list, and then choose a font from the Font list (see Figure 40-8).

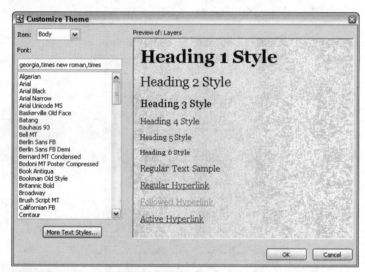

Figure 40-8: Redefining style fonts the easy way

You can see additional styles by clicking the More Text Styles button. After you've assigned custom fonts to different styles, click the OK button to close this dialog box and return to the Theme task pane.

Saving a custom theme

By now, you've assigned custom graphics, custom color schemes, and custom text, so you've actually defined a brand-new theme of your own. To save this new theme, and add it to the list of available themes, click the Save As button in the Theme task pane.

The Save Theme dialog box appears. Enter a new descriptive theme name and click OK.

After you have saved a theme, it appears in the Select a theme area of the Theme task pane.

Organizing Office Documents into a Web Site

Every Office application can save some files as Web pages. FrontPage can turn many Office documents into Web pages automatically.

Cross-Reference For more information about creating Web pages in other Office applications, see Chapter 41.

You can incorporate all these files into a FrontPage Web site. Here's how:

1. Choose File ⇨ New and select the More Web site templates link in the New task pane. This opens the Web Site Templates dialog box; find the Empty Web Site template, select it, and click OK. A new empty Web site is created in Front Page.

2. Select File ⇨ Import to open the Import dialog box.

3. Click Add File to begin to add files to your Web site. Navigate to the file you want to include in your Web site in the Add File to Import List dialog box.

4. Click Open to add the file to the list of files you will import into your Web site.

5. Add additional files to your site.

   The list of files to import appears in the Import dialog box, as shown in Figure 40-9.

Note You can add an entire folder to your Web site by clicking the Add Folder button. When you add a folder, all files in the folder are included, and the URL given to each file includes the name of the folder and any subfolders. This directory structure is also added to your Web site. You can also add files from an existing Web site by clicking From Site; this starts a wizard that guides you through that process.

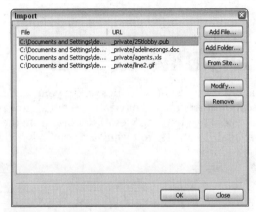

Figure 40-9: You can add all sorts of Office-generated files to your Web site.

6. When you've completed your list of files (you can always add more later), click the OK button.

Your selected files are imported into your Web site.

7. Use Navigation view to organize the new files in your Web site. Click and drag files from the Folder list in Navigation view into the flowchart to connect them to the Web site, as shown in Figure 40-10.

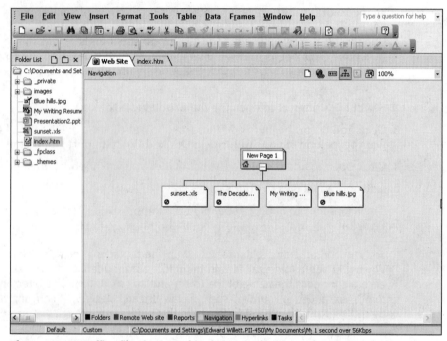

Figure 40-10: Office files imported into your Web site can be arranged using the Navigation view.

Generating Usage and Other Reports

The Reports view provides a list of many useful statistics about your Web site. Additional reports update you about the status of navigational links, slow pages, and new files. You can select a report by choosing View ➪ Reports from the menu, and then selecting one of the available reports. Following are brief descriptions of how you can use these reports:

✦ The Site Summary report gives you an overview of your site. The rows in the Site Summary are themselves links to other views. One of the most useful things about the Site Summary report is that it provides you with the size of your Web site, which is helpful when you are looking for server space for your site.

✦ The All Files report (from the Files submenu of the Reports menu) is shown in Figure 40-11. This report shows you detailed information about each file in your Web site.

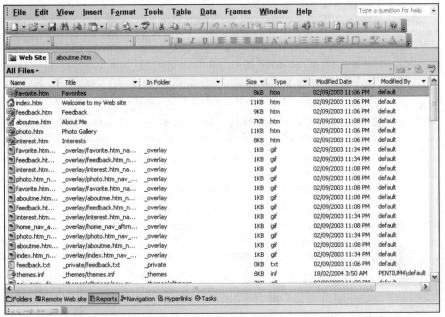

Figure 40-11: The All Files report tells you everything you need to know about files in your Web site.

✦ Recently Added Files, Recently Changed Files, Older Files, and Slow Pages (the first three are on the Files submenu of the Reports menu, the latter on the Problems submenu) are obviously subjective categories. What's recent? What's old? What's slow? You define the criteria for these reports by selecting Tools ➪ Options and selecting the Reports View tab.

✦ The Unlinked Files report (Problems submenu) shows files in your Web site to which there are no links. These stranded Web pages are sometimes called orphan pages.

✦ The Hyperlinks (Problems submenu) report shows you hyperlinks in your Web site that are either broken (so-called because they point to a site or document that doesn't exist) or untested. You can right-click one of these untested hyperlinks and choose Verify from the context menu to test the link. If the link is to an Internet or intranet site, you must be logged on to the Internet or your intranet to test the link. After an unverified link is tested and FrontPage determines that the link works, you'll see an OK mark in the Status column.

✦ The Component Errors report (Problems submenu) tests FrontPage Web components and forms.

✦ The Review Status and Assigned To reports (Workflow submenu) are for workgroups collaborating on a Web site. The Review Status report enables you to log pages that need to be reviewed and track whether pages have been reviewed. The Assigned To report is similar to the Review Status report, but it tracks who is assigned to which page.

✦ The Categories report (Workflow submenu) sorts components of your Web site by category, such as Business, Competition, Expense Report, and so on.

✦ The Publish Status (Workflow submenu) report lists which pages are marked to be published to your Web server when you publish your Web site.

✦ The Checkout Status report (Workflow submenu) tells you whether someone else on your network has already checked out certain files for editing. You can still open those files, but only as read-only.

✦ The various reports under Usage show you not only how many times your pages have been visited but also what operating systems your visitors were using, what browsers they were using, what domains they were referred from, what URLs they were referred from, and even what searches were performed.

Note   Usage reports are available only if your Web site has been published to a server that supports this kind of analysis.

Global Site Editing

Most of the work you do to edit the content of your Web site takes place in Page view and is done on a page-by-page basis. However, FrontPage provides editing tools that work across an entire Web site. Here, we'll look at two of them: Spellchecking and Find and Replace.

Spellchecking your entire site

To spellcheck your entire Web site, select Tools ⇨ Spelling from a view other than Page view (if you're in Page view, this command will allow you to check only the open page for spelling errors). Here's how it works:

✦ The Spelling dialog box has two radio buttons: Selected page(s), and Entire Web site.

✦ You can also select the Add a task for each page with misspellings checkbox. This handy option creates a list of pages that need their spelling corrected, which you can check in Tasks view.

✦ After you've selected these options, click the Start button to begin the check of your spelling. After FrontPage checks all your pages for spelling problems, it produces a list in the Spelling dialog box, as shown in Figure 40-12.

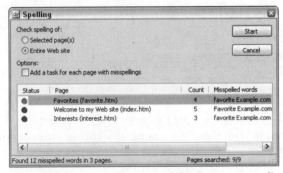

Figure 40-12: FrontPage's spellchecker creates a list of pages with apparent spelling mistakes.

✦ Double-click any page in the list to open that page as well as a conventional spelling box like the one in other Office applications. Use it to correct (or ignore) questionable spellings.

Tracking tasks for your entire site

In the previous section, you learned that you can add pages that require spelling corrections to your Tasks list. To see this Tasks list, click Tasks in the view bar (the bottom-left-hand corner of the workspace, just above the status bar). Figure 40-13 shows a Tasks view.

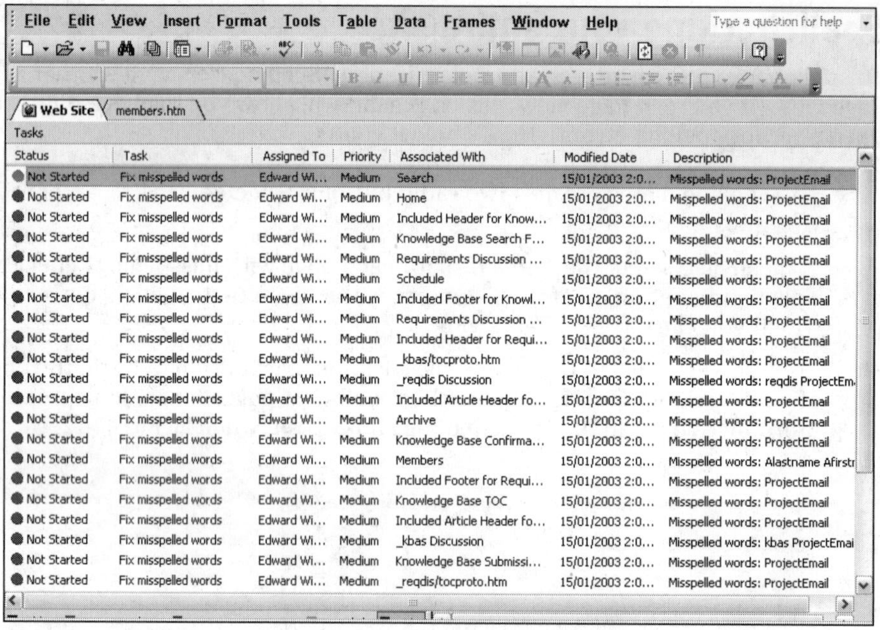

Figure 40-13: Pity the Web site designer with this Tasks view!

You can also add your own tasks to the Tasks view list. Select Edit ➪ Tasks ➪ Add Task to define a new task. The New Task dialog box appears, as shown in Figure 40-14.

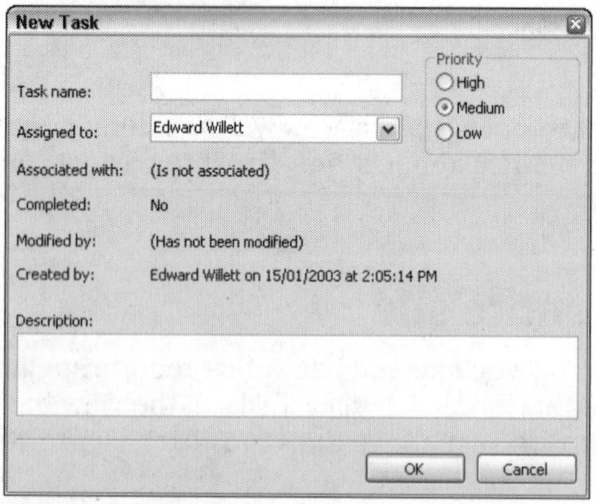

Figure 40-14: You can add your own tasks to the Tasks view list.

As you complete tasks, you can click them in the Tasks view list, and select Edit ➪ Tasks ➪ Mark Complete. Use the command Edit ➪ Tasks ➪ Show History to toggle between showing and hiding completed tasks. Tasks that were generated automatically by FrontPage, like correcting spelling, can be launched by selecting Edit ➪ Tasks ➪ Start Task.

Replacing throughout a site

You can use Find and Replace throughout your site. This comes in very handy when the corporate president you gushed over on every single Web page is replaced. Here's how it works:

1. To replace text throughout a site, select Edit ➪ Replace in any view.

2. In the Find and Replace dialog box, select the Replace tab, and then enter text to find in the Find what text box, and replacement text in the Replace with box.

3. Choose the All pages radio button under Find where to replace the text in every page.

4. Under Direction, you can choose to search either up or down through a single Web page, or simply to search All. (If you've selected the All pages radio button under Find where, the Direction option isn't available.)

5. Under Advanced, the Find whole word only and Match case options work as they do in the Find and Replace dialog box in Word and other Office applications. However, the Find in source code checkbox enables you to find and replace HTML code if you are so inclined. The HTML Rules button enables you to create complex conditions for your search of the code. You can specify text to search for, and specify whether you're searching for text inside a tag or outside a tag — and even specify which type of tag to look under. Be careful that you don't replace text that's part of the URL a link points to, or you'll end up with broken links (unless you also change the name of the targets to match the new links, which, in fact, you might want to do, using my example, if you have Web pages whose names are based on that of the dearly departed president — e.g., smith.htm).

Tip

If you're conversant with HTML and need to replace an HTML tag, note that the HTML Tags tab in the Find and Replace dialog box provides a drop-down list of possible HTML tags to search for and a complete list of possible replacement actions for them.

6. After you define your replace options, if you are replacing in an entire Web site, click the Find in Site button (or the Find Next button if you're searching only the current page). FrontPage will generate a list of pages at the bottom of the Replace tab with the text to be replaced (see Figure 40-15).

Figure 40-15: Replacing for an entire site generates a list of pages that need fixing.

7. Double-click a page to make the changes in that page. Alternatively, select a page in the list and click the Add Task button to add a task for the selected page to your task list.

Publishing Your Site

Whenever you start working on Web pages in FrontPage, it's best to begin by creating a new Web site, rather than a single blank page, if you want to use the program's full power to manage your files.

Publishing your Web site is a breeze. Just follow these steps:

1. Select File ➪ Publish Site; in the resulting view, click the Remote Web Site tab to set up the site to which you want to publish (see Figure 40-16).

2. Enter the type of server to which you're publishing. The default — and certainly the preferred type, if you want to make use of all of FrontPage's bells and whistles, such as Web Components — is one that supports FrontPage Server Extensions or SharePoint Services.

Figure 40-16: Prepare for publishing your Web site in this dialog box.

Cross-Reference

For more information about SharePoint Services, see Chapter 47.

However, you have other options, including Web DAV (Distributed Authoring and Versioning) and FTP (File Transfer Protocol — the most common option of all). Finally, you can choose to publish your Web site to a folder on your computer or onto a network, which might work fine for you if it's meant to be viewed only locally.

3. Once you've selected a server type, enter in the Remote Web site location box the location of the server or folder to which you're publishing.

4. Before you click OK, you may want to specify exactly what you want to publish. Choose the Publishing tab in the Remote Web Site Properties dialog box (see Figure 40-17). Here, you can choose to publish only pages that have changed since the last time you published (which saves time, especially if you have a dial-up or other slow connection), or all pages, overwriting those already on the server. You can also specify whether or not to include subsites (these are separate sites installed in folders within your main Web site), and how to determine which pages have changed — by comparing the actual contents of the source and destination files or by simply comparing the time stamps on the two sets of files. You can also choose to log any changes made during the publishing operation to a log file, which you can view the next time you publish your site by clicking the View log file button.

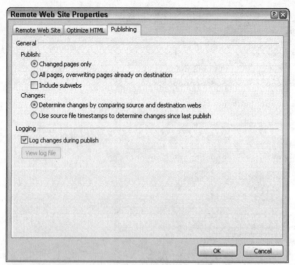

Figure 40-17: Specify the rules for publishing your
Web site here.

Tip   If you're particularly concerned about making your source file as small as possible,
choose the Optimize HTML tab in the Remote Web Site Properties dialog box. You
can choose to remove a number of unnecessary elements, including comments,
extra white space, and some HTML coding generated by FrontPage.

5. Click OK. FrontPage attempts to contact the server you specified. For any
option other than publishing to a folder on your own computer, you'll probably see a dialog box prompting you for a username and password at this
point.

Once FrontPage has contacted the target server, you'll see a display something like
the one shown in Figure 40-18. On the left is your Local Web site; on the right is
your Remote Web site. You can modify the view of your Local Web site by choosing
an option from the View drop-down list just above it: Folder Contents, Files to
Publish, Files not to Publish, and Files in Conflict are the options.

Files that are currently selected to be published are marked with an arrow. You can
publish one file at a time, or a small group of files, by selecting them and clicking
the top button in the middle of the display, the one with the arrow pointing to the
right. You can also publish all the pages that have changed since the last time you
published by selecting the Local to remote radio button in the lower-right corner
and clicking the Publish Web site button.

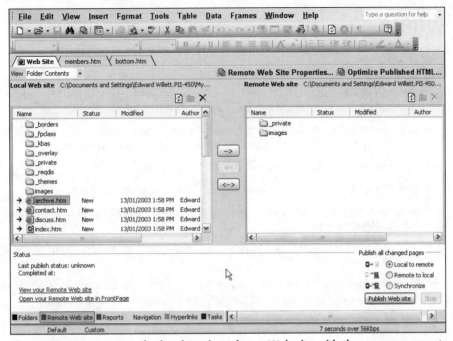

Figure 40-18: Compare the local version of your Web site with the one on a remote server and choose which files to update.

Tip Publishing works both ways; if the Web site you're publishing to is one that other people may have updated, you can move changed files from it to your computer by choosing the Remote to local radio button and clicking Publish Web site. Choosing the Synchronize option ensures that both your local and remote Web sites have the latest versions of all files.

Getting More Information

FrontPage is a very complex program in its own right, and I've been able to touch on only a few basics in this chapter and the preceding one. You can find numerous good books about FrontPage that will help you to get the most out of the program.

Tip For further information, consult *FrontPage 2003 Bible,* by Curt Simmons (Wiley, 2003).

Summary

This chapter presented some of the ways you can manage your entire Web site, including the following:

✦ You can create customized themes, save them, and apply them to your Web site to create a unique atmosphere for your entire Web site.

✦ You can edit the content of shared borders to create embedded pages in the top, bottom, left, or even right side of all pages in your Web site.

✦ You can assign customized link bars.

✦ You can add pages created in other Office applications.

✦ You can check the status of your Web site using the selection of reports available in Reports view.

✦ You can globally spellcheck your Web site and find and replace throughout your Web site.

✦ You can publish your site to another Web server. The best options are servers that support FrontPage Server Extensions or SharePoint Services.

✦　　✦　　✦

Creating Web Pages in Other Office Applications

FrontPage, of course, is the application Microsoft specifically designed for creating and managing Web pages, but you can also create Web pages using any of the other Office applications. All Office applications enable you to save your documents as Web pages — which means you can draw on Office's plethora of sophisticated text-editing, graphics-design, and document-layout features.

Saving Documents as Web Pages

Turning an Office document into a Web page is as easy as choosing File ➪ Save as Web Page and supplying a filename. As much of the content and formatting as possible is preserved in the resulting HTML file, and even if some elements don't appear correct when you display the page in a browser, if you open the file in the originating application again, everything should still be there.

The role of XML

As is discussed throughout this book, Office now lets you save documents in XML format as well as HTML format — but even when you save an Office document as HTML, XML plays a role. Office uses XML to supply the data necessary for the re-creation of formatting and other elements that can't be converted into conventional HTML code. When a browser that doesn't understand XML opens one of these Office-generated Web pages, it ignores these elements — meaning some of that formatting might be lost.

For that reason, Word offers you the option of removing this Office-specific XML (Word calls it WordML) from documents you save as Web pages. This makes the file smaller and gives you a chance to see how your page will look in browsers that don't understand the embedded XML. Choose File ➪ Save as Web Page, and then, in the File of Type drop-down list, choose Web Page, Filtered.

Cross-Reference See Chapter 11 for information on using XML in Word, Chapter 20 for a discussion of using XML in Excel, and Chapter 38 for a detailed look at using XML in Access.

Previewing documents in your browser

In Excel, Word, and PowerPoint, you can view any open document in your browser to see how it will look as a Web page. You don't need to save the document first. Choose File ➪ Web Page Preview to start the browser and load it with a temporary Web page version of the document.

Word also offers a Web Layout view that gives you an approximate idea of what your Web page will look like while you work on it.

Changing Web page titles

The title of a Web page appears in the browser's title bar while the page is being viewed; it's also stored in the History and Favorites folders. That being the case, it's worth giving this title some thought. (If you don't assign a title of your own, Office uses the document's filename.)

To change the title, click the Change Title button in the Save As dialog box that appears when you choose File ➪ Save as Web Page. Choose File ➪ Properties and click the Summary tab; you'll see the title at the top of the dialog box. You can also click the Change Title button on the Summaries tab of the File ➪ Properties dialog box.

Setting Web page options

In each Office application, a number of settings control the way documents are converted into Web pages. You can decide where to store supporting files, for instance, select a format for graphics, and more. You'll find these settings by choosing Tools ➪ Options, clicking the General tab, and then clicking the Web Options button. Figure 41-1 shows the Web Options dialog box in Excel, with the Files tab selected.

Note   Although some settings on the Web Options dialog box vary from application to application, many are common to more than one program—in which case, changing the settings in one application changes them throughout Office.

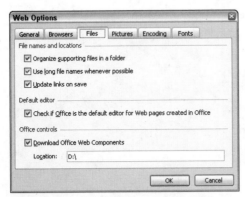

Figure 41-1: The Web Options dialog box controls numerous settings for Web pages created in each Office application.

Making allowances for browser capabilities

Each new version of HTML has new tags providing new display capabilities. Only the latest versions of browsers can make use of these new possibilities—but not everyone uses the latest version of the available browsers.

This might not be a problem on a corporate network, where everyone probably has the same browser, but it can be for Web pages intended for viewing on the Internet.

One way to avoid problems is to avoid using some of the latest tags. Office can help you do that. One of the Web Options tabs is labeled Browsers (see Figure 41-2). You can use it to allow or disallow certain formatting options that might cause problems, and choose from a list of browsers—from Internet Explorer/Netscape versions 3.0 all the way up to Internet Explorer version 6.0 or later—that you expect most viewers to be using. Office will allow or disallow certain features based on your choices.

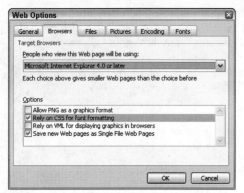

Figure 41-2: The Web Options dialog box includes a tab that lets you specify what kind of browser most viewers of your page will be using.

Dealing with Office's automatic support folders

When you save a document as a Web page, Office automatically creates a subfolder for the page's supporting files and automatically writes the `<image>` tag in the page's HTML so that it references the files appropriately — graphics, sound clips, video clips, and so on. The subfolder is placed inside the folder where you save the page and is named after the page's filename: in other words, a page called MyPage.htm would have a support folder called MyPage_files. Located in the folder where you save the page itself, the subfolder is named after the page's filename. If you save the page as HomePage.htm, the support folder will be called HomePage_files. Files in the subfolder are named automatically (if they don't already have names).

Tip   If you would rather store support files in the same folder as the page, instead of using a subfolder, go to the Files tab of the Web Options dialog box and uncheck Organize supporting files in a folder.

Office keeps track of these supporting files for you. If you delete a picture from your Web page, the corresponding file is automatically deleted from your disk when you save the page.

On the other hand, if you move the page, Office doesn't move the support files for you; you have to look after the subfolder and its contents manually — so it's best not to move the page if you can avoid it.

Note   This automated system of creating subfolders might cause trouble if you want to use Office-generated pages in a larger site, combined with other pages created by other programs. There are likely to be graphics that appear on many other pages besides the one you made in Office; instead of assigning the graphics for each page to a subfolder closely linked to that page, most sites put all the graphics for all the pages in one folder, so any page that needs it can "call" it from there. Office doesn't let you specify alternative locations for supporting files for the pages it generates, however; nor will it let you choose the names you want for those supporting files. So if you want to integrate Office-generated Web pages into a larger site, you'd better either be able to write HTML by hand or use a dedicated Web-site design and management program like FrontPage.

Cross-Reference   For an introduction to using FrontPage, see Chapters 39 and 40.

Saving Web pages as single files

Office 2003 offers you a new wrinkle in Web-page creation: One of the choices when you choose Save as Web Page is Single File Web Page. This eliminates the support folders; everything on the page is instead encapsulated in a single file using a variation on HTML called MHTML (for MIME Encapsulation of Aggregate HTML Documents). This format is ideal for sending Web pages and all their contents as e-mail attachments, because it boils everything down to a single page. It also simplifies the file structure of your Web page, but it gives up some flexibility; you can't easily replace an image with an updated version, for example, whereas when your images are saved in support folders you can do so simply by saving a new version of an image over top of the version you want to replace by using the same name for the new version as the old one.

Tip   You can turn your MHTML Web page back into a standard HTML Web page with accompanying support folders by opening the Single File Web Page in the program you used to create it, and then choosing File ➪ Save As ➪ Save as Web Page and selecting Web Page instead of Single File Web Page in the Save as type drop-down list.

Working with Hyperlinks

In all Office applications, you insert Hyperlinks by selecting what you want to apply the link to and choosing Insert ➪ Hyperlink or pressing Ctrl+K.

Cross-Reference   For additional details on using the Insert Hyperlink dialog box, see the section on hyperlinks and image maps in Chapter 39.

You can insert hyperlinks in any Office document, even it isn't going to be saved as a Web page, and those links can be to other ordinary Office documents (a capability most useful if the document with the links in it and the documents it links to are all available on the same network, obviously). You'll look at those capabilities in this chapter as well.

Jumping to specific locations in documents

Most hyperlinks take you to the beginning of a Web page or document, but they can jump you to specific places within those files instead. You can also create a link to a specific location in the current document.

There are three ways to do this: dragging and dropping the Office content you want to create the link to into your document, copying and pasting it, or using the Insert Hyperlink dialog box.

Note   Before you can create a hyperlink to a specific location in a document, you must save the target document.

Dragging Office content to create hyperlinks

The drag-and-drop method of creating a hyperlink within an Office document or from one document to another is the easiest. Here's how:

1. Open the document in which you want to place the link.

2. Create or open the target document; if it hasn't been saved, save it.

3. Tile the documents on your screen so you can see both of them.

4. Select the text or graphics you want to link to.

5. Click and hold the right mouse button, and drag the selected text or graphics to the document where you want to place the link.

6. When you get where you want the hyperlink to go, release the mouse button.

7. On the shortcut menu that appears, choose Create Hyperlink Here or Insert Hyperlink (it varies).

Creating a hyperlink via the Clipboard

To use the Office Clipboard to create a hyperlink to a specific location, open the target document (or create and save it), select the destination text or graphics there, copy the selection to the Clipboard, switch to the document that is to contain the hyperlink, place your cursor where you want it, and choose Edit ➪ Paste as Hyperlink.

Creating location-specific hyperlinks using a dialog box

If you use the Insert Hyperlink dialog box to create a hyperlink to a particular spot in an Office document or Web page, the target document doesn't have to be open.

Place your cursor wherever you want the hyperlink to be inserted, and then choose Insert ➪ Hyperlink. Then:

✦ If the hyperlink's destination is in the same document, click the Place in This Document button (in Access, the button is Object in This Database). You'll see a list of locations in the current document (see Figure 41-3).

✦ If the destination is in a different document, stay with the default Existing File or Web Page instead. Locate the target Web page or Office document and click Bookmarks. A dialog box lists linkable locations in the document.

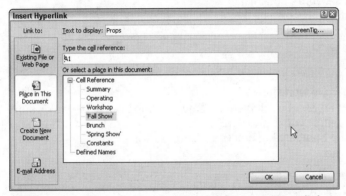

Figure 41-3: Here's the Excel version of the Insert Hyperlink dialog box with the Place in This Document button clicked.

This technique works well, as long as the location you want to jump to appears in the list of bookmarks. In Word and Excel, you can create your own bookmarks.

Bookmarks in Word documents

To create a bookmark in a Word document, place the insertion point where you want the bookmark to go and choose Insert ➪ Bookmark to open the Bookmark dialog box (see Figure 41-4).

Figure 41-4: Use Word's Bookmark dialog box to insert a bookmark that is then available as a hyperlink destination.

Bookmarks in Excel worksheets

A bookmark in an Excel worksheet is really a named range of one or more cells. Highlight the cell(s) you want to mark and then choose Insert ⇨ Name ⇨ Define to open the Define Name dialog box (see Figure 41-5).

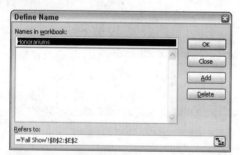

Figure 41-5: After naming a range of cells in this dialog box, you can set up a hyperlink that jumps to the named range.

Controlling the look of hyperlinks

Office gives you varying degrees of control over the appearance of hyperlinks (color, font, underlining styles), depending on the application.

Formatting hyperlinks in Word and Excel

Use styles to format your hyperlinks in a Word document or throughout an Excel workbook.

In Word, choose Format ➪ Styles and Formatting, or click the Styles and Formatting button on the Formatting toolbar, to open the Styles and Formatting task pane. Choose All Styles from the Show list box at the bottom of the pane. In the list of styles, the ones you want are Hyperlink, for links that haven't been followed yet, and FollowedHyperlink. Choose Modify from the menu that opens when you click the downward-pointing arrow to the right of the style name. All Word text effects are available.

Cross-Reference

Themes provide an alternative to styles for formatting Web pages that include hyperlinks. See "Working with themes," later in this chapter.

In Excel (by contrast), you must first insert a hyperlink, and then choose Format ➪ Style. The Style dialog box opens (see Figure 41-6). Choose Hyperlink from the list and click Modify to make your changes to it. To change the style of a followed hyperlink, you must first follow a hyperlink; FollowedHyperlink then becomes available in the list of styles in the Format ➪ Style dialog box.

Figure 41-6: Use Excel's Style dialog box to set the formatting for hyperlinks and followed hyperlinks.

Setting hyperlink appearance in PowerPoint

In PowerPoint, the text color of your hyperlinks is determined by each slide's color scheme. To change or customize the color scheme, choose Format ➪ Slide Design to open the Slide Design task pane, and then click the Color Schemes link to open the menu of available color schemes. Each scheme includes its own rules for hyperlinks and followed hyperlinks. Click the Edit Color Schemes list at the bottom of the task pane to change the preset rules; choose Accent and hyperlink or Accent and followed hyperlink from the Custom tab of the Edit Color Scheme dialog box, and then choose the color you want (see Figure 41-7).

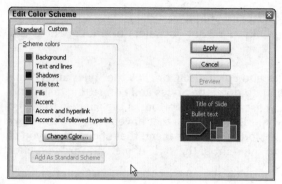

Figure 41-7: PowerPoint lets you alter the preset colors for hyperlinks and followed hyperlinks by editing color schemes.

Changing hyperlink options in Access

To set the color of hyperlinks in an Access database, open the Tools ➪ Options dialog box. There, switch to the General tab and click Web Options. In Access, this dialog box is devoted entirely to the appearance of your hyperlinks.

Automatic hyperlinks in Word

By default, Word automatically converts URLs and filenames into hyperlinks as you type them. This is fine if you plan to save the document as a Web page or send it to someone who might then want to follow those links, but if you're trying to write something that has a lot of links it in it that you just want to print, it can be disconcerting. You can turn this behavior off by selecting Tools ➪ AutoCorrect Options, choosing the AutoFormat As You Type tab, and clearing the box labeled Internet and network paths with hyperlinks.

To convert any Internet or network paths in an existing document's text into live hyperlinks, choose the AutoFormat tab and turn on the Internet and network paths with hyperlinks option there. Then click OK to return to Word. Then choose Format ➪ AutoFormat, select the other options you want, and click OK.

Access and hyperlinks

You can store hyperlinks as data directly in an Access database table using a Hyperlink data field, or you can insert hyperlinks directly into forms.

Storing hyperlinks in fields

To keep track of hyperlinks in a table, create a field and choose Hyperlink as the Data Type. After the hyperlinks have been entered into the table, you can access any hyperlink by clicking it in the table itself. In addition, just as with any Access field, you can display a hyperlink field on a form by binding it to a text box so that the hyperlink associated with the current record is always visible.

Creating hyperlink buttons

To insert a label containing a hyperlink into a form in Design View (see Figure 41-8), click the Insert Hyperlink button or choose Insert ➪ Hyperlink.

Figure 41-8: A hyperlink inserted into an Access form; by default, it displays the URL, but you can edit the text without changing the link.

After creating a hyperlink control, you can edit the text displayed on the control without affecting the underlying hyperlink. To change the text, you can click the text directly so a blinking insertion point appears, or use the control's Caption property.

When a hyperlink on a form is clicked, Access displays the Web toolbar.

PowerPoint and hyperlinks

Hyperlinks are active in a PowerPoint presentation only when it's being viewed as a slide show. To follow the hyperlink on a slide that you're editing, right-click it and choose Open Hyperlink from the shortcut menu.

Tip   You can also assign hyperlinks to action buttons using the Action Settings dialog box that appears at the time you insert it or when you right-click the button and choose Hyperlink from the shortcut menu.

About Graphics in Office-created Web Pages

When you save an Office document as a Web page, each graphic in the document is stored in a separate file. The format used depends on the type of image, the number of colors it contains, and the settings you've established in the Web Options dialog box. Because the file format affects image quality and file size, you need to know the differences among the different types.

Working with .gif and .jpg images

The main image formats on the Web continue to be .gif and .jpg files. Both are bitmap formats, which means that they're made up of individual pixel elements or pixels. Both compress the original image, but in different ways; they have other differences as well. To whit:

✦ The .gif format compresses files by finding and recording where large blocks of the same color are located; with that information, it can avoid mapping every individual pixel within those elements. Images in .gif format can be interlaced, which means the browser displays every other line of dots to begin with, and then goes back and fills in the missing lines — in a browser, that means the user sees the entire image sooner, though fuzzily, and then clearer as the image finishes loading. The .gif format also allows you to specify a transparent color and supports simple animation by storing multiple images and displaying them in quick succession.

✦ The .jpg format compares the colors of adjacent pixels and records the difference. It can be adjusted to ignore different degrees of difference. The greater the difference it ignores, the less information it records; this makes the files smaller but affects image quality at the same time.

What it all boils down to is that .gif is best for logos and icons or any image containing text, whereas .jpg is best for photographs and other images that contain smooth gradations of color.

If you insert an image that is already in either format, Office keeps the image in that format when you save the page. If the image you insert is in a different format, however, Office chooses the format it thinks best suits the image.

Saving graphics in .png format

Portable Network Graphics .png, a relatively new bitmap format, produces high-quality images that are smaller than even .jpg or .gif files. Older browsers can't display .png files, though, so be aware that you could be limiting your page's viewership if you use .png.

If you want to use .png files in your Office document, go to the Web Options dialog box, click the Browsers tab, and check the Allow PNG as a graphics format checkbox.

Using vector graphics in Web pages

In a bitmap image, every pixel in the image is mapped individually. In a vector graphic, images are described mathematically as a series of lines, or vectors, with color fills inside the shapes described by those lines. Vector graphics are smaller (and thus download faster) than bitmap images, and they look just as sharp when they're blown up to humongous size as they do when displayed in a much smaller size. (A TrueType font is really a kind of vector graphic; that's why you can use it at 72-point size and it will still look as good as it does at 12-point.)

Office supports the use of vector graphics in Web pages through its Vector Markup Language (VML), which allows the description of the image to be part of the Web page itself, and not a separate file. That means you can use the many vector graphics Office supplies in the Clip Organizer in documents you save as Web pages; Office can generate the necessary VML code when you save the page.

Again, though, be aware that not all browsers support VML, which is why the checkbox labeled Rely on VML for displaying graphics in browsers is normally unchecked in the Web Options dialog box, and rather than use VML, Office turns vector graphics into .gif images when you save your page. If you're confident that most or all of your viewers use the latest browsers, you can check this box and tell Office not to generate bitmaps for any images it can represent using VML.

 Note This option will be turned on automatically if you choose Microsoft Internet Explorer 5.0 or later from the list of browsers.

Editing HTML Code in Office

You can use Office applications to view and edit the HTML representing a document, if you're so inclined. After you've saved or opened an HTML document, you can choose View ➪ HTML Source. This opens the page's HTML in the Microsoft Script Editor (see Figure 41-9), which displays the HTML tags in the main part of its display. You can close the Project Explorer pane at the right to see more. HTML tags are displayed in various colors, so you can easily distinguish the tags from your text and see at a glance their attributes and values. You can edit the tags as you can in Notepad or any other text editor.

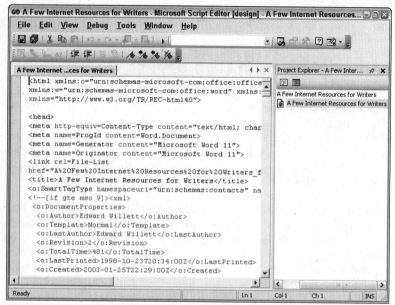

Figure 41-9: The Microsoft Script Editor offers you tools to edit HTML manually, if you're so inclined.

Note   By default, the HTML Source command shows up only in Word, but it's available in other applications from the Commands tab of the Tools ➪ Customize dialog box. Select View in the Categories list, and then scroll down to find HTML Source in the Commands list. Scroll the Commands list until you find the HTML Source command. Drag it to the View menu or wherever else you want it.

Web Page Authoring with Word

Word makes a terrific Web page editor, because the editing of text and graphics and the pleasing layout of all these elements are the goal of the word processor — whether for paper or the screen is only a minor consideration. In addition, Word has many special features just for Web page authors.

As noted at the beginning of the chapter, all you need to do to turn any Word document into a Web page is choose Files ➪ Save as Web Page. But if you're setting out from the very beginning to create a Web page, Word can provide additional help, in the form of templates.

Basing new Web pages on templates

To create a new blank Web page, choose File ➪ New to open the New Document task pane, and then choose Web page from the New section. This opens a blank Web page — which is just another way of saying a new empty document based on the Normal template and displayed in Web Layout view. However, you can also turn any other Word template into a Web page.

Cross-Reference For more on using Word's templates, see Chapter 8.

Choose File ➪ New to open the New Document task pane, and click the On my computer link in the Other templates section. This opens the Templates dialog box (see Figure 41-10). The Preview section to the right gives you a miniature glimpse of what a document created using one of these templates will look like.

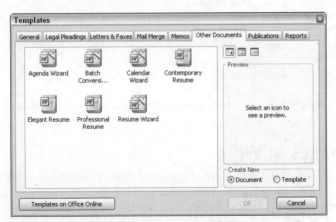

Figure 41-10: The Web Pages tab of the Templates dialog box offers you a number of templates for various types of documents.

Once you've opened the template, choose View ➪ Web Layout to see what it will look like as a Web page (see Figure 41-11). You can now edit it however you like (see the next section of this chapter, "Editing Web pages in Word," for details.

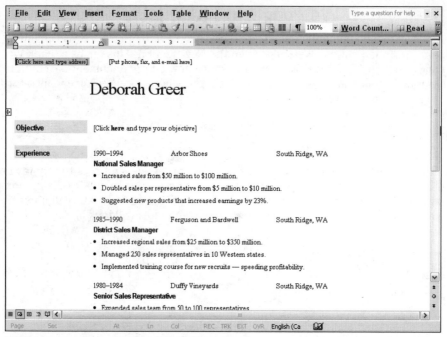

Figure 41-11: A new Web page based on the Contemporary Resume Word template

Editing Web pages in Word

Although you can save a Word document from any view, Word's Web Layout is the view to work in if you're designing for the Web; what you see there is pretty much what you'll see in a browser. This view disables features that don't work in Web pages and enables Web-specific components such as frames — but otherwise, all of Word's standard editing and layout capabilities are at your disposal.

Tip   If you specify a browser type in the Browsers tab of the Web Options dialog box, Word disables formatting that won't display properly in the target browser.

Adding tables to your Word Web page

You create and modify Word tables for a Web page just as you do in any other Word document, as detailed in Chapter 5. Tables can be used not only to display information but also as layout tools to keep text, graphics, and other elements where you want them on the page (otherwise, they tend to get moved around by individual browsers depending on their own settings). Tables also allow you to create columns, necessary because HTML doesn't have tags to create true columns.

Cross-Reference For more on using tables in Web pages, see the "Using tables as layout tools" section in Chapter 39.

Inserting horizontal lines

Horizontal dividing lines are often used to separate blocks of text in Web pages. To add one in Word, place the insertion point where you want the line and choose Format ➪ Borders and Shading. Click the Horizontal Line button in the resulting dialog box to open a gallery of graphical lines from the Clip Organizer (see Figure 41-12). After you've chosen a line, you can insert it over and over simply by clicking the Horizontal Line button on the Tables and Borders toolbar.

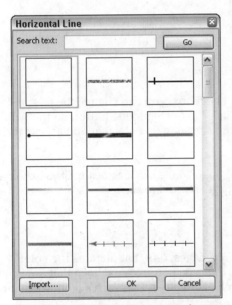

Figure 41-12: Office offers several types of horizontal lines.

Adding scrolling text

Would you like text to scroll across your page as though it were a marquee sign? Click the Scrolling Text button. (Be aware, though, that not all browsers necessarily support this option effect.) To have text scroll across your page like a marquee sign, first activate the Web Tools toolbar by checking it off on the View ➪ Toolbars menu. Next, click the Scrolling Text button on the Web Tools toolbar. Enter the text in the dialog box that appears (see Figure 41-13) and set some other options such as direction, background color, and how often the text should loop.

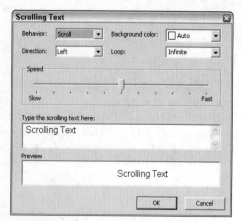

Figure 41-13: You can add scrolling text with this dialog box.

After you've accepted the Scrolling Text checkbox, you can change the font and other formatting for the scrolling text. Click the Design Mode button on the Web Tools toolbar; this allows you to select the scrolling text element and access the relevant commands on the Format menu.

Note   You might not see the formatting you apply to the scrolling text until you choose File ➪ Web Page Preview to see your page in your browser.

Working with themes

A theme is a comprehensive design for Web pages, one that dictates the color scheme, the background color or image, the type of horizontal lines that are used, the type of bullets, the fonts used for each element, and so on. It's a bit like a paragraph style in Word.

Applying a theme to a Web page sets all of these variables in one easy step, and if you use the same theme for every page in your site, all of your pages will share a consistent look.

Themes are available in Access and FrontPage as well as Word, and PowerPoint's Slide Designs echo the themes, so they're essentially in that program, too.

Cross-Reference   In FrontPage, you can customize themes; see Chapter 40 for details.

To apply a theme in Word, choose Format ➪ Theme. The Theme dialog box (see Figure 41-14) lists and previews the available themes. Options for each theme include vivid colors, active graphics, and background image.

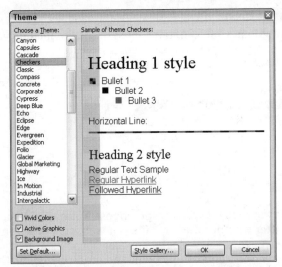

Figure 41-14: Choose a theme for your Word Web page here.

Note Don't be confused by the Style Gallery button. The Style Gallery lists and shows samples of Word templates, not themes.

In Access, you can assign themes only to data access pages, described later in this chapter in the section "Working with data access pages."

Working with frames in Word

Frames divide browser windows into independent sections. For example, you might place a header containing information you always want visible—such as your company logo or a link back to the home page—in a frame at the top of the window, a list of navigation hyperlinks down the left side of the window in another frame, and the page currently being visited in a third frame. Each frame actually displays a separate Web page.

A frames page is an additional special page that you don't see directly; instead, it serves as a container for the displayed frames.

Caution Be aware that some people hate frames in Web pages; you might get negative feedback if you choose to use them.

Using the Frames toolbar and menu

Figure 41-15 shows the Frames toolbar, which contains most of the commands you need to create frames in Word. It appears automatically when you start or open a frames page.

Figure 41-15: Word's Frames toolbar contains the tools necessary to create and edit frames.

Creating a frames page

To create a new frames page for your current document, choose Format ➪ Frames ➪ New Frames Page. It doesn't matter whether the open file is a Web page or an ordinary Word document; the frames page is a new document that opens in Web Layout view, although because it has only one frame at this point and nothing in it, that's not immediately apparent.

You use standard editing and formatting techniques to edit any document displayed in a frame. Save the frames page as you would any other Word document; Word saves the frames page and the documents its frames contain.

Tip   If you want to give the document contained in an individual frame a different name or store it in another location, so you can work on it by itself later, save it by itself: Right-click in the frame and choose Save Current Frame As from the shortcut menu. The standard Save As dialog box appears.

Adding and deleting frames

Add frames to a frames page left, right, above, or below by clicking the appropriate New Frame button on the Frames toolbar. Word creates a new document for each new frame; these documents will be automatically assigned names when you save the frames page. To delete a frame, click inside it, and then click the Delete Frame button.

Working with frame properties

You control formatting options and other settings in frames with the Frame Properties dialog box (see Figure 41-16). Right-click the frame you're concerned with and choose Frame Properties from the shortcut menu.

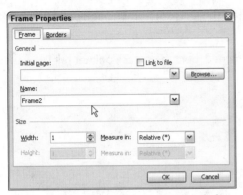

Figure 41-16: The Frame Properties dialog box lets you control the content and format of Web page frames.

Specifying a frame's name and initial Web page

Word assigns each frame a name, but you can change the assigned names on the Frame tab. As well, the Initial page field lists the page or document currently displayed; you can change that to a different page by entering its URL or filename here. (Frames have names so you can direct documents to appear in them; see "Inserting hyperlinks in frames" a little later in this chapter.)

Formatting frames

You can resize adjacent frames by dragging the frame border. If it's not visible, or for more precise control, use the Width and Height settings on the Frame tab of the Frame Properties dialog box. Settings for the borders themselves are on the Borders tab. You can choose visible or invisible borders, their width, and their color. Clear the Frame is resizable in the browser box to prevent users from changing frame sizes. Scrollbar options are also offered; you can show them always, never, or only when needed.

Inserting hyperlinks in frames

When you insert a hyperlink in a frames page, you're given one more option in the Insert Hyperlink dialog box than usual: a button labeled Target Frame.

Click this button to open the Set Target Frame dialog box (see Figure 41-17). Here you're asked to select the frame where you want the document to appear; a small representation of the current frames page is shown at left. You can choose a frame from the drop-down list; besides names for the individual frames, there's the Page Default (none) option, which opens the new page on its own, and the Same frame option, which opens it in the frame in which you clicked the hyperlink. Click the Set as default for all hyperlinks checkbox if you want all hyperlinks to open in the selected pane by default.

You can also click the frame you want in the Current frames page preview; the frame you select will be shaded, as it is in the figure.

Tip   If you're not sure what a frame is named, hold the mouse pointer briefly over the corresponding part of the preview. The name will appear in a ScreenTip.

Figure 41-17: Choose which frame a hyperlink will open in using the Set Target Frame dialog box.

Web Presentations with PowerPoint

Saving a PowerPoint presentation in a format that can be viewed over the Internet is as easy as choosing Save as Web Page. PowerPoint converts your presentation into a set of linked Web pages. Figure 41-18 shows a sample presentation saved in Web format and displayed in Internet Explorer.

The browser window is divided much like the Normal view in PowerPoint, with the main part of the window displaying the slide and a navigation frame. The navigation frame on the left carries links to all the other pages, identified by their titles. An area under the slide displays Note, if there are any. Running across the entire window at the bottom are the viewing controls, which, from the left, are:

- ✦ **Outline button.** Hides or displays the outline frame.

- ✦ **Expand/Collapse Outline button.** Expands the outline to show subsidiary points under the slide titles (each of which is also a link to that slide), or collapses it again.

- ✦ **Notes button.** Hides or displays the Notes frame.

- ✦ **Previous and Next buttons.** Take you to other slides in order.

- ✦ **Full Screen Slide Show button.** Displays the presentation on the entire screen, as you would usually see it from within PowerPoint. This hides the outline and notes frames.

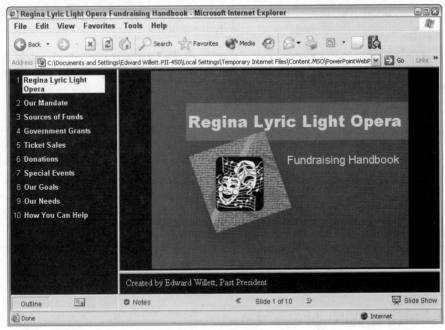

Figure 41-18: A PowerPoint presentation saved in Web format looks like this.

Saving a Web presentation

Converting an ordinary PowerPoint presentation to one for the Web is as simple as choosing the File ➪ Save as Web Page command, supplying a filename, and clicking Save. Additional options are available by clicking the Publish button in the Publish as Web Page dialog box (see Figure 41-19).

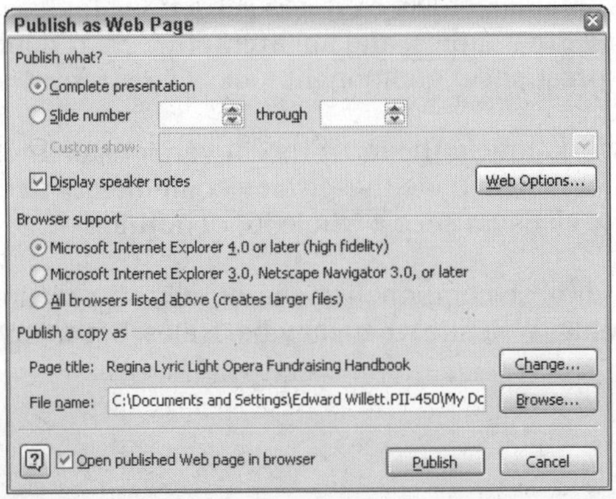

Figure 41-19: Use this dialog box to set options governing your Web presentations in PowerPoint.

This dialog box includes a handy button to open the Web Options dialog box discussed earlier in this chapter. Other options include:

✦ **Which slides to include.** You can include the entire presentation, select a series of slides, or choose from among the custom slide shows you've defined for the presentation, if any.

✦ **Whether to include speaker notes.** To exclude notes, clear the Display speaker notes box on the Publish dialog box.

✦ **Which browser(s) to support.** You can select a target browser or select the All browsers listed above option.

✦ **Where to publish a copy.** Enter the location to which you want to publish a copy of the presentation; typically, even if you're publishing to a server somewhere else on the Internet, you'd publish the presentation to your own computer for archival and for troubleshooting purposes.

✦ **Whether to open the published Web page in a browser immediately upon publishing.** That's really the only way you can make sure everything looks OK, so why not?

Editing a Web presentation

You can open the Web version of a presentation in PowerPoint, edit it, and save the changes; but remember that not all slides in the original document may have been published. If you didn't include the entire presentation, you might be better off opening the original PowerPoint document and going through the Web-page creation process again.

Creating Interactive Pages in Office

Office Web components include a spreadsheet like a mini-Excel; a PivotTable component for viewing and manipulating PivotTables, and an interactive chart control. (Figure 41-20 shows you what the spreadsheet component looks like in a browser.)

Unfortunately, these components work only in the most recent versions of Internet Explorer, and they work only for people who have these same components already installed on their systems. Everyone else just sees a whole lot of nothing.

In other words, the best place to use these components is internally, in a setting where everyone has Office. On a public Web site, they may be useless for many of the people who visit.

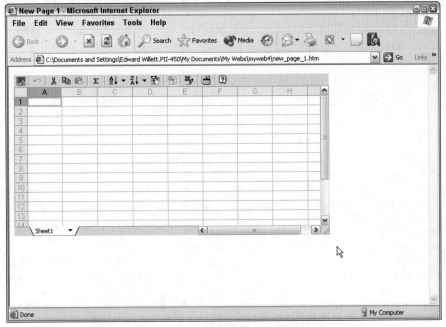

Figure 41-20: An interactive Office spreadsheet in a Web page

Publishing Spreadsheets on the Web

You can convert any part of an Excel workbook to a Web page simply by choosing File ➪ Save as Web Page. You just have to tell Excel whether to convert the entire workbook or only a section of it, and whether to make the resulting Web page static or interactive.

That much you can decide in the Save As dialog box itself. For more options, though, click the Publish button to open the Publish as Web Page dialog box (see Figure 41-21).

Caution   Excel workbooks can lose some functionality or formatting when you convert them to Web pages. Although Excel can open the resulting HTML files again, they might not look the way they used to. For this reason, always save your workbooks in the standard .xls format before saving them as Web pages.

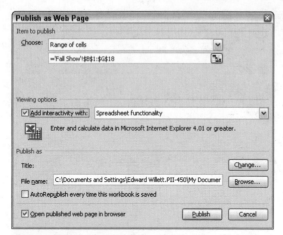

Figure 41-21: The Publish as Web Page dialog box gives you control over which part of your workbook to convert to a Web page and how to make the conversion.

Choosing workbook elements to convert

In the Choose area of the Publish as Web Page dialog box, you can convert nearly every discrete element of the workbook. The drop-down list offers you all the worksheets by name, as well as the Previously published items and Range of cells as options. If your selection has more than one element that can be saved, you can then select the element you want in the list box just below the drop-down list. If you selected a Range of cells, you must type in a range or click the button to the right of the list box to select the range with the mouse.

Publishing interactive data

In most Web pages, data just sits there. In an interactive page, visitors get to manipulate that data — they can modify values, sort or filter the information, enter formulas and perform calculations. In the case of PivotTables, users can reorganize the component fields and choose the level of detail to see in grouped fields. Users can alter interactive charts by changing the values of the data they represent.

To save a workbook element as an interactive Web page, just click the Add Interactivity checkbox in either the Save as Web Page or Publish as Web Page dialog box. The Save as Web Page dialog box automatically determines the type of interactive page you saved (spreadsheet, PivotTable, or chart). The Publish as Web Page dialog box gives you more control, allowing you to choose from a list of possibilities, so that you can save worksheets or ranges as interactive PivotTables, or to save PivotTables as interactive spreadsheets.

Tip You can't turn an entire workbook into an interactive Web page. However, you can save each sheet individually in interactive format and then create a frames page in Word (see earlier in this chapter) to display the sheets in one frame under the control of a navigation button in another frame.

Preparing to publish interactive workbook data

Things to keep in mind as you prepare to publish an interactive spreadsheet include:

✦ If the worksheet or data range you're converting contains external data, saving it as a Web page "freezes" the data. To allow the Web page to retrieve current data each time it's opened, incorporate the data into a PivotTable, and then save the PivotTable in interactive form.

✦ If you're saving an interactive PivotTable, remove custom calculations and set the data fields to use Sum, Count, Min, or Max. You can save an interactive PivotTable that you've already formatted, but don't bother reformatting it for the Web — all custom character and cell formatting you apply vanishes.

✦ In interactive charts (see Figure 41-22), limit yourself to the types that translate properly to Web pages. Surface and 3-D charts are off limits. If the chart comes from a worksheet, save it separately rather than as part of the sheet, because charts are removed when you save sheets with interactivity.

Note In interactive Web pages, changes in the data provided are reflected in the displayed items only when the Refresh button is clicked.

Formatting interactive pages

Cell and text formatting is retained in interactive spreadsheets but not in PivotTables. If you open a page containing an interactive spreadsheet in Excel, changes you make to cell formatting are retained when you save the page and will appear in the browser. However, you have to use the spreadsheet control's property toolbox to apply formatting to the cells in the control — Excel's usual formatting commands don't work.

You're better off applying formatting to any parts of the page that aren't part of the interactive control using Word, Access, or FrontPage, all of which are superior to Excel as page-layout tools.

Working with interactive data in a browser

Opened in a browser, an interactive spreadsheet behaves like a scaled-down version of Excel. Users can edit cell data, type new values or formulas, and so on. Most built-in Excel functions are available.

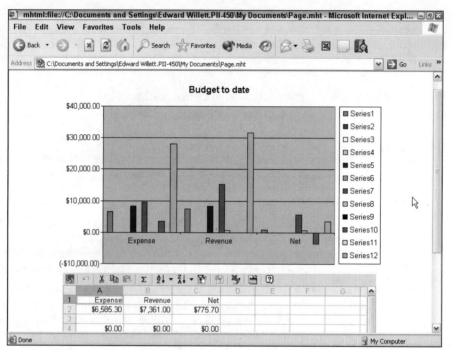

Figure 41-22: Here's an interactive chart as it appears in a browser. The chart can be altered by changing the entries in the data table at the bottom, which is saved as a spreadsheet Web component.

The toolbar across the top of the spreadsheet (visible at the top of the data table in the lower part of Figure 41-22) provides some of the usual buttons for sorting and filtering information, among other tasks.

Tip   Click the Command and Options button, second from the right, to see a plethora of additional controls, including several for formatting font, color, and other cell properties.

Interactive PivotTables work much like PivotTables in Excel, except that you can't change their formatting.

Interactive charts can't be reformatted, but their underlying data can be altered as the users see fit in the spreadsheet that appears below them.

Database Publishing on the Net with Access

Access provides several ways to distribute information over the Internet or an intranet. The easy way is to export database objects such as tables and queries as ordinary HTML documents, which you can then post to the Web. However, you can also (with a bit more work) make live Web pages that display current information from your database.

Exporting data to static Web pages

You can export any database object to the Web in Access by choosing File ⇨ Export. In the Export dialog box, select HTML Documents in the Save as Type box. Check the AutoStart box if you want Access to open the exported document in your browser right away so you can check your results.

After you choose Export, a diminutive HTML Output Options dialog box appears. You can merge the exported data with an HTML template you specify (which can spruce up what would otherwise be a minimalist page). Click OK.

Note   An HTML template is a text file that specifies the location and appearance of common elements in an Access-based Web page.

Access exports each selected datasheet and each printed page of a report as a separate HTML file, adding the page number to the end of each filename. If you save a report with multiple pages, Access supplies basic navigation controls in the form of First, Previous, Next, and Last text buttons and generates the appropriate hyperlinks.

Using report snapshots on the Web

Formatting won't survive the export procedure. If you want your Web page to look a bit more like that report you spent so many hours making pretty, and it's displaying static data, consider using a report snapshot instead — a file that displays an Access report as it appears in print preview. Even people without Access can view these snapshots (provided they install the Snapshot Viewer program that comes with Access and is available free from Microsoft).

You create a report snapshot by selecting the report, and then choosing File ⇨ Export and selecting Snapshot Format from the Save as type list. Access will ask you for any parameters required by the report. It will then create the snapshot and display it in the Snapshot Viewer, so you can proofread it before distributing it.

The easiest way to include a snapshot in a Web page is to insert a hyperlink to it; when the user clicks the link, the snapshot opens in the browser or in a separate window.

Cross-Reference You might get better results by publishing your Access reports, forms, tables, or queries as XML files, which include an associated XSL file for presentation. For more information about using XML in Access, see Chapter 38.

Creating server-side dynamic database pages

If you want users to be able to interact with your database through their browsers, you have to export database information in a dynamic data format such as Microsoft Active Server Pages (ASP). In this format, your Web server software is told to query the database as required, generate an HTML file containing the requested file, and send that file to the browser. This ensures that the data displayed by the browser is always current. You can export tables, queries, and form datasheets, but not reports.

Of course, because ASP relies on enhancements to standard HTML, it works only when published to a compatible server — so make sure the server you're publishing to is compatible with ASP beforehand.

Exporting dynamic database pages

It's only slightly more complicated to export a database object in ASP format than it is in static format. Again, choose File ➪ Export. Select Microsoft Active Server Pages from the Save as type list; click Export All.

This opens the Output Options dialog box shown in Figure 41-23, which prompts you for a number of additional entries.

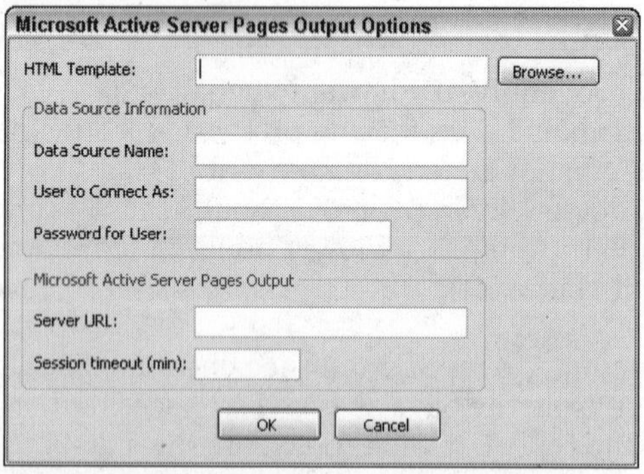

Figure 41-23: Fill out this dialog box when you export in ASP format.

In addition to the path to an HTML template, you must specify the data source name (obviously, so the server knows where to look for the database), along with user connection information (a username and password). Finally, you have to provide a URL for the server that will store the exported ASP page during Web access.

Working with data access pages

Access's data access pages also enable users to work with live, formatted data in their browsers — as long as they're using Internet Explorer 5 or later. Users can change the way data is displayed in their browsers without affecting the data access page; changes to the data itself, on the other hand, are posted to the database.

You can create data access pages that function as:

✦ **Interactive reports.** Unlike a printed report, a data access page lets users determine how much detail they want to see and lets them sort and filter the data.

✦ **Data entry forms.** When you add, edit, or delete a record on a data access page, the changes are entered in the underlying database.

✦ **Data analysis tools.** Data access pages can include interactive spreadsheets, PivotTables, and charts that summarize data and help you identify trends.

Creating data access pages

The easiest way to create a data access page is to create a form or report as you normally would, and then save it as a data access page. Simply open the form or report you want to save as a data access page, and then choose File ➪ Save As. In the small Save As dialog box, assign a name to the file, and then choose Data Access Page from the As list. Click OK.

Figure 41-24 shows a data access Page created from an Access form.

You can also create data access pages as you can other Access database objects. Switch to the Pages button in the Objects bar. There, your options include:

✦ **Create a page (semi)automatically.** Click New and choose AutoPage: Columnar in the resulting dialog box. Select a table or query on which to base the page, and click OK.

✦ **Double-click Create data access page by using wizard.** A wizard will guide you through the process of choosing, grouping, and sorting records.

✦ **Double-click Create data access page in Design view.** This starts a new data access page from scratch; you use the same basic techniques for laying out a data access page as you use when designing an Access form or report.

✦ **Double-click Edit Web page that already exists to convert an existing Web page into a data access page.** When Access opens the page you specify, tell it what database you want to connect it to. You can then add interactive elements. Saving the page creates a corresponding shortcut in the Database window.

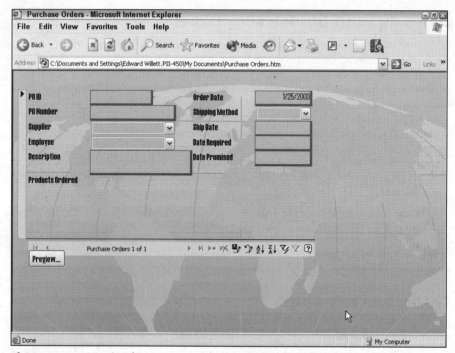

Figure 41-24: Here's what an Access data access page looks like in a browser.

Designing data access pages

Figure 41-25 shows a new data access page opened in Design view. You place all the visible elements in the blank area of the page, called the body, which adjusts its size to fit into the browser window when viewed online. Note that it contains a preformatted text area for typing a title. You can place labels, buttons, checkboxes and other controls in the body, but they usually go into the gridded rectangular area, or section, that's intended to help you with form design.

To add controls to the form, drag them from the Field list at right, which lists all the tables and queries in the database and their fields, or use the Toolbox. When you add a field from the Field List, it produces a text box control linked to that field.

Cross-Reference   Chapter 35 describes Access forms in detail.

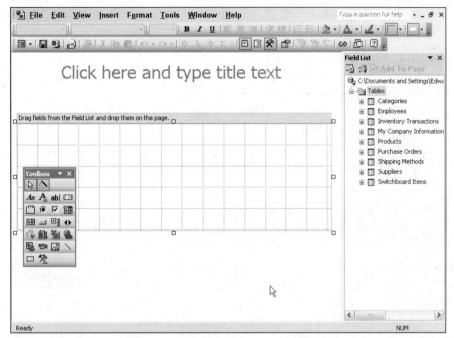

Figure 41-25: When you start a new data access page in Design view, it looks like this.

Working with grouping levels and sections

A new, blank data access page like the one shown in Figure 41-20 isn't linked to any table or query in the database. As soon as you bind a database object, sections are defined by the way you group the data. For example, if your data access page displays sales data grouped by week and then by store location, you have two group levels, each with its own sections. Four sections are available in each group level (although you only use the ones you need):

✦ **Header.** This section is used to display individual records as well as elements you might expect to see in a header.

✦ **Footer.** Displayed directly above the navigation section, the footer displays calculated totals for the group.

✦ **Navigation.** This section automatically displays the record navigation control for the group level and appears after the group header section. You can add unbound controls to it as well.

✦ **Caption.** This section, above the group header, is open to text boxes, labels, and other unbound controls; bound controls are off-limits.

Note   In data access pages used for data entry, you can have only one group level, and the Group footer section isn't available.

Setting up group levels

You can create as many nested group levels as you need. The Page Wizard helps you set up grouping levels if you make use of it; otherwise, you have to do it manually.

You create the first group level in a new blank page by binding a database object to the unbound section. Drag a field that belongs to the desired table or query from the Field List to the section; this creates a field on the page and binds the section to the table or query containing the field (see Figure 41-26).

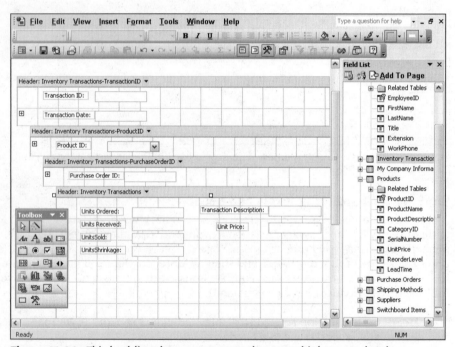

Figure 41-26: This budding data access page shows multiple group levels.

The technique for adding additional group levels depends on whether you're grouping by an individual field in the same table or query, or by one of two separate tables or queries.

Here are the details on setting up each type of group:

✦ **Grouping by a field in the same table or query.** A field that contains the same data in many records makes a useful "group-by" field. In a table of addresses, for example, you might want to group by the state fields, because the database probably contains multiple records from each state. To group by an individual field, add it to the section, select it, and then click the Promote button on the Page Design toolbar.

✦ **Grouping by a table or query.** You can add fields from more than one table or query to the same data access page. When two tables or queries have a one-to-many relationship, you can group the item on the "one" end of the relationship. For example, if the database has a Type table and a Sales table related by a shared SalesID field, you would group by Sales, producing a page that shows the sales that fall into each type. Add the fields you want to display from both tables, and then select any field from the table you want to group by and click the Group by Table button on the Page Design toolbar.

When you create a new group level, Access automatically adds new sections to the page for that group. You can see and modify the settings for each group level by right-clicking the title bar for that group level and choosing Group Level Properties.

Creating data entry data access pages

There's one essential rule you must obey to create a data access page for entering and editing data: Create only one group level for the page.

Tip

You can't use group levels to work with two related tables in a single data entry data access page, but you can work around that problem by using two pages. Bind each page to one of the tables, and then place a hyperlink from the page on the "one" side of the "one-to-many" relationship to the other page. Next, create a frames page in Word or FrontPage, and load each of the pages into a different frame. The result should look like a single page that enables you to see and edit data from either table.

Using data access pages within Access

A data access page is live in the Access database where you create it — you don't have to view it in Internet Explorer. In other words, data access pages can serve essentially the same functions as forms and reports — so you might consider using an existing data access page rather than going to the trouble of building a comparable form or report from scratch.

Publishing Your Web Pages

When you're finished creating all of your Web pages, it's time to post them to a server. There are a number of ways to do this, and the preferred method will depend on the server you're posting to.

The most important thing is to make sure that all the files wind up in the proper locations. Unless you've used Office's capability to save documents as single-file Web pages, your Web page might actually consist of several files — not just the HTML page itself, but all the associated pictures, buttons, lines, sounds, video, and so on. These files have to be exactly where the HTML page expects them to be, relative to itself. If they're not, they won't load into browsers for viewing.

To be sure everything works properly, be sure to test all the pages in a Web browser after they've been published to a server. Make sure all the graphics are visible, all the links work, all the sounds load, and so on. Double-check by refreshing each page after it's loaded.

If the server you're publishing to has SharePoint Services running, you might have been able to transfer your files using Web Folders. If so, you might have direct access to the page in Office, which has a tool to help you correct any problems. Open the page in the originating application, choose Tools ➪ Options, choose the General tab, and click the Web Options button. Go to the Files tab, and make sure the box labeled Update links on save is checked. With that option enabled, simply saving the page back to the server should fix the problem.

If you cannot use Web Folders, you'll have to double-check the locations of all the support files manually and republish.

Cross-Reference   For more detailed information about using SharePoint Services, see Chapter 47.

Summary

You can create complex and beautiful Web pages in Office's core applications without worrying about buying a specialized authoring tool or even learning how to use FrontPage. You can even incorporate interactive spreadsheets and databases. As you saw in this chapter:

✦ You can save most Office documents as Web pages with all their formatting intact — and bring them back again.

✦ You can tell your Office applications how you want them to save documents as Web pages by choosing Tools ➪ Options, going to the General tab, and clicking Web Options.

✦ Hyperlinks can carry you not only to Web pages but also to other Office documents.

✦ Of all the Office applications (apart from FrontPage, of course), Word is the best at creating Web pages. It offers several Web site and Web page templates, a Web page wizard, and numerous themes to get you started.

✦ Word's frames tools are ideal for creating Web pages that use this useful design feature some people love to hate.

✦ PowerPoint presentations can be turned into Web presentations simply by saving them as Web pages.

✦ You can create interactive pages on the Web using Microsoft Web components, Excel, and/or Access. All offer powerful tools.

✦   ✦   ✦

Collaborating in Office

◆   ◆   ◆   ◆

◆   ◆   ◆   ◆

Building Integrated Documents

Each Office application is so powerful in its own right that
you can usually find some way to make it do whatever
you want it to. Forcing Excel to print a letter, however, or trying to make a Word table work like a spreadsheet isn't very
efficient. That's where linked and embedded objects come in:
You can use them to create an Office document in one application that contains objects you created in other applications.
Not only that, you can configure Office so that changes made
to objects in their original applications are automatically
reflected in the document in which they all appear together.

First, a couple of definitions:

+ A linked object is one that appears in your Office document but isn't really part of it: It's stored somewhere
else. All that's really included in your document is the
object's name and location; when you display or print
the page that includes the linked object, Office fetches
the object from wherever it is and dutifully includes it.
One advantage of linking over embedding is that any
changes made to the object in the original program
(e.g., Excel or Word) will automatically be reflected in
the Office document in which it is included.

+ An embedded object is created and edited with another
program, but all the data for it is contained within your
publication. Whereas a linked object has little effect on
the amount of disk space your publication takes up, an
embedded object may have a much greater effect.

Inserting Objects from Other Applications

There's more than one way to insert an object created in another application into your current Office document.

Copy and paste

One simple method to move an object from application to application is simply to copy and paste it. For example, if you highlight a range of cells in an Excel spreadsheet, select Edit ➪ Copy, go to Word, and select Edit ➪ Paste, the spreadsheet will be pasted into Word as a Word table. The trouble with this is that you don't actually have an Excel spreadsheet in the Word document, which means you can't manipulate the information in that object the way you could before.

Tip   In Word, the Standard toolbar includes a button for creating an Excel spreadsheet. Click it and choose the number of rows and columns you want it to display, just as if you were adding a Word table. (It's really a full spreadsheet, by the way; if you decide later you need more rows and columns, you can simply drag its corner or side handles to reveal more.)

Using Paste Special in Word

A better choice is to select Edit ➪ Paste Special in Word. This opens the dialog box shown in Figure 42-1. Choose the format in which you want to paste the object from the clipboard, and then click OK. By default, Paste Special creates an embedded object, but you can make it a linked object by choosing Paste Link.

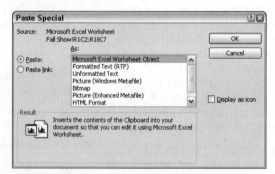

Figure 42-1: The Paste Special dialog box lets you choose how an object created in another application is pasted into the current one.

Choosing a paste method

You have several ways to paste your copied object into the new application:

✦ **Object.** This creates an embedded or linked object, depending on whether you have the Paste or Paste link radio button selected. If you want to be able to edit the object using the tools of the application that created it, this is the choice to make.

✦ **Text.** You can insert many objects as either formatted (RTF) or unformatted text. If it's primarily the words in the object you're interested in, choose one of these options.

✦ **Picture.** You can insert the object as a high-quality picture—the equivalent of a screenshot—of itself, in Picture (Windows Metafile) (the best choice for high-quality printers and also the one that takes up the least disk and memory space), Bitmap, or Picture (Enhanced Metafile) format. The only editing you'll be able to do to the object if you make this choice is the kind of editing you can do to an inserted piece of clip art: resizing, recoloring, and so on.

✦ **HTML.** This inserts the object in HTML format—extremely useful if you're building a Web page.

Using the Insert Object command

You can also insert objects into Office applications by choosing Insert ➪ Object from the menu. This opens a dialog box similar to the one shown in Figure 42-2, from Word.

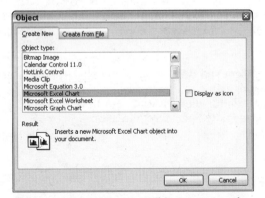

Figure 42-2: The Insert ➪ Object command lets you insert a variety of objects created in other programs into an Office application.

By default, the Create New tab is selected. Choose the type of object you want to insert from the Object type list. Check the Display as icon box if you want to indicate the object with an icon (which users must double-click in order to view the object). When you've made your selection, click OK, and a new object of the type specified is embedded in your Office document.

Clicking the Create from File tab changes the look of the dialog box to that shown in Figure 42-3.

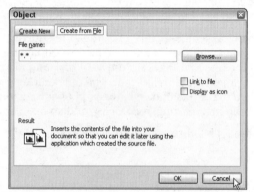

Figure 42-3: Use these tools in your Office application to create an embedded or linked object that already exists as a separate file elsewhere.

Click Browse to locate the file you want to insert as a new object. By default, this will create an embedded object, but you can make it a linked object by checking the Link to file box.

Although Paste Special and Insert Object can be used to accomplish the same ends, Insert Object has the advantage of being able to create new objects of specific types as well as create objects from existing files without your having to first open those files and copy their contents, as Paste Special requires.

Working with Embedded Objects

Once you've inserted an embedded object into an Office document, it appears to be part of the document. But there's a big difference: If you click the object once, you can move it around and possibly resize it, but you can't edit it. To do that, you have to double-click it. When you do, the menus and controls of the current application change to those of the application that created the object, so you can use the controls of the object's native application to edit it.

Figures 42-4 and 42-5 illustrate this concept. Figure 42-4 shows an embedded object, part of an Excel worksheet, as it looks embedded in a Word document; Figure 42-5 shows what it looks like when you double-click the embedded worksheet to edit it.

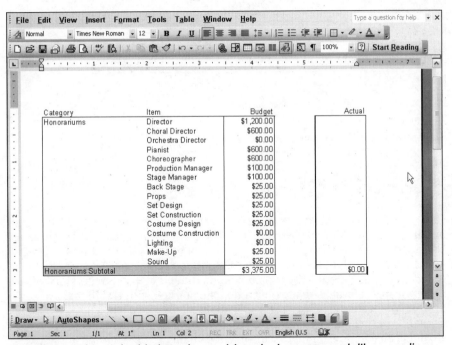

Figure 42-4: This embedded Excel spreadsheet looks pretty much like an ordinary Word table . . .

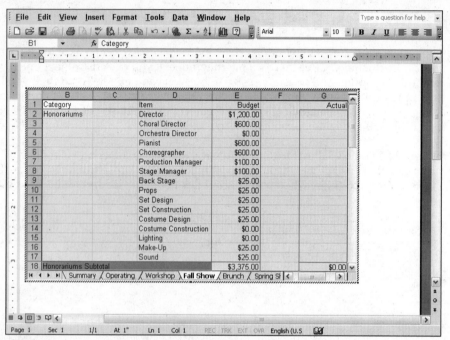

Figure 42-5: . . . but double-clicking it reveals its Excel roots—and Excel controls.

Working with Linked Objects

Linked objects, like embedded objects, look like they're part of your Office document—but they really aren't. They're simply displayed in it. They really still live somewhere else, associated with the program that created them. (They're a bit like graphics displayed on a Web page in that regard; what you really see is a graphic that's been called up from a different location, not something that's an integral part of the Web page, which, after all, is really only a text file marked with HTML tags.)

If you're working with dynamic data that changes all the time, linked objects are great, because it doesn't matter if someone changes some figures in the Excel spreadsheet you've linked to on page three of your report—the link, which, by default, is updated every time you open the document, ensures that your report reflects those changes.

Note   Linked objects require two documents in two different files—the source document and the destination document. If you want to send a document containing linked objects to someone else, you also have to send the source document for those objects—and make sure that the recipient stores the source document in exactly the same drive and file folder as you had it stored. If the source document isn't where the destination document expects it to be, the link won't work.

Moving and resizing linked objects

You can move or resize a linked object just as you can move or resize an embedded object. You can also edit it in its source application by double-clicking it, with one difference: When you double-click an embedded object, the menus and toolbars of the originating program are displayed in the destination document's application. Double-clicking a linked object opens the source document in the originating application: In the case of the previous example, it would open the source document in Excel in a new window.

Editing and updating links

If you have a lot of linked objects in the same document, the easiest way to work with them is to choose Edit ⇨ Links. This opens a dialog box similar to the one shown in Figure 42-6. (Its appearance varies slightly among the various Office applications.)

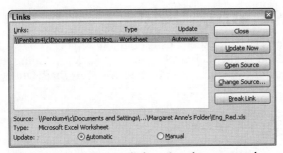

Figure 42-6: Edit your links using these controls.

The list box includes all the linked objects in the current document (in this case, only one). Down the right side are additional controls:

- ✦ Update Now updates the linked object in the destination document to match the source.

- ✦ Open Source opens the source file in its originating application.

- ✦ Change Source lets you browse your computer for a different source file. Obviously, changing source files is likely to completely change the appearance of your current document. You can also use Change Source to find a source file that has been relocated, thus repairing the severed link.

- ✦ Break Link turns the linked object into a picture, severing its connection with the source file.

You can also choose to either automatically update the linked object whenever you open the destination document or whenever the source file changes, or you can choose to update the linked object only when you click Update Now.

Using the Locked and Save picture options

Some applications include two additional options in this dialog box: Locked and Save Picture in Document. If Locked is available, you can select it to deactivate the Update Now button and prevent the linked object from being updated automatically. You might do this to freeze the data in your document at a particular point in time.

Save picture in document is normally checked. If you uncheck it, you can save a graphic as a linked object instead of inserting it into your document. This can save disk space.

Other Methods of Sharing Data

The four main Office applications (Word, Excel, PowerPoint, and Access) offer additional ways to share data. You'll look at collaborating on a network (including the Internet) in a separate chapter, but there are several other ways in which Office applications work together.

For a full explanation of how you can collaborate on a network with Office applications, see Chapter 46.

Sending a Word document to PowerPoint

Word lets you send the currently active document to PowerPoint as the basis of a new presentation. It automatically turns each paragraph of the document into a new PowerPoint slide (see Figures 42-7 and 42-8), which you can then edit and format as you wish in PowerPoint. To send a document to PowerPoint, choose File ➪ Send To ➪ Microsoft PowerPoint.

You can reduce the amount of formatting you'll have to do in PowerPoint by using styles. PowerPoint will interpret each Heading 1 style as a title slide, each Heading 2 style as the next level of text, and so on. For that reason, a Word outline actually makes a better PowerPoint presentation than a Word document consisting of long paragraphs of text.

For more information on using outlines in Word, see Chapter 7. For more information on how PowerPoint uses outlines, see Chapter 26.

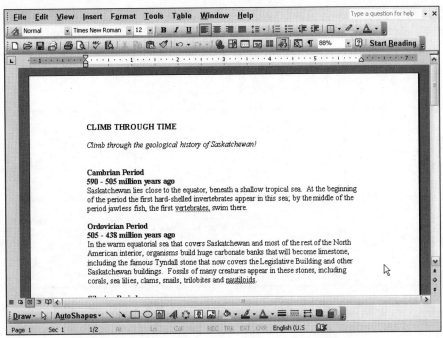

Figure 42-7: This ordinary Word document can be sent to PowerPoint . . .

Analyzing Access data in Excel

Access is a great application for storing and retrieving, but when you want to analyze data, Excel wins out. For that reason, Office makes it easy to analyze Access databases in Excel.

To do so, open the Access table you want to analyze, and then choose Tools ➪ Office Links ➪ Analyze it with MS Excel. Excel opens the table and converts it into a spreadsheet, where you can play with the data to your heart's content.

Publishing Access reports with Word

Access has a disadvantage when it comes to designing reports for its data: Its tools can seem awkward if you aren't thoroughly familiar with it. But one advantage of Office's integration is that you can usually use data from any application in another application with which you're more comfortable. For that reason, Access also makes it easy to publish reports in Word.

Open the report you want to publish in Word in Access, and then choose Tools ➪ Office Links ➪ Publish it with MS Word. Access opens Word and converts the report into a new document in RTF format.

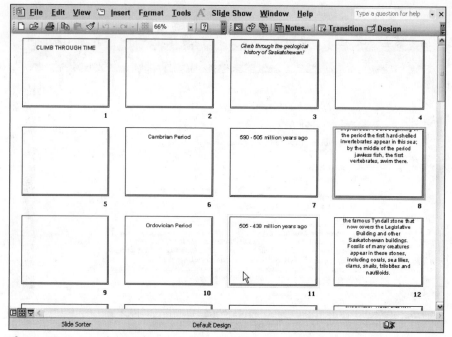

Figure 42-8: . . . where it becomes a presentation in which each paragraph forms a new slide (although obviously some formatting work is needed!).

Merging Access data in Word

Access also lets you easily merge data from a database table with a Word document. To do so:

1. In Access, open the table you want to merge, and then choose Tools ⇨ Office Links ⇨ Merge it with Microsoft Word. This opens the wizard shown in Figure 42-9.

2. Choose either to link your data to an existing Microsoft Word document — a form letter, for instance — or to create a new document and then link the data to it. If you choose to use an existing document, you'll be asked to select it.

3. Access opens Word and either displays the existing document you chose or a blank document that you can create and format. You can't see it, but the Word document and the Access document are linked.

4. From here on, the process of using the Access data is the same as creating any other mail-merged document in Word.

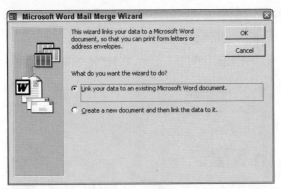

Figure 42-9: Use this wizard to merge Access data in Word.

Cross-Reference   To review mail-merging procedures, see Chapter 6.

Sending a PowerPoint presentation to Word

Just as you can turn a Word document into the basis of a PowerPoint presentation, you can turn a presentation into a Word document which you can then edit and format. This can be a great way to create a hard-copy version of it.

To do so, open the presentation you want to turn into a Word document, and choose File ➪ Send To ➪ Microsoft Office Word. This opens the dialog box shown in Figure 42-10.

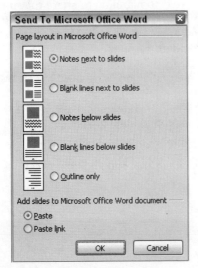

Figure 42-10: Turn your PowerPoint presentation into a Word document, laid out just the way you like it.

Choose how you want to lay out the pages (you can position slides two to a page, with notes or blank lines beside them; one to a page, with notes or blank lines below them; or send the outline only, without any slide images), and whether you want to paste (embed) the presentation into Word or paste it as a linked object.

Click OK. PowerPoint creates a new document in Word and pastes the presentation into it.

Sharing Data with XML

As has been pointed out several times already in this book, Office 2003 offers XML (eXtensible Markup Language) as a native file format—meaning you can save your files as XML files instead of as Office files.

XML is described in greater detail elsewhere (see the cross-references that follow), but it's worth reiterating what I think is the clearest definition of differences between HTML (the markup language used to create Web pages) and XML: XML was designed to describe data, focusing on what data is, whereas HTML was designed to display data, focusing on how data looks.

That makes XML an ideal format in which to exchange data between applications, especially between Office and non-Office applications (provided they, too, support XML to the extent Office does).

However, because Office applications do a fine job of interacting with each other with their standard file formats, there's no particular reason to use XML instead when sharing data between them—unless you're also planning to share that data with non-Office applications. In which case you'll find the techniques for inserting linked and embedded files work with Office documents saved in XML format just as they do for Office documents saved in their standard formats.

For an overview of XML and more detailed information on using Word to edit XML documents, see Chapter 11.

For information on making use of XML with Excel, see Chapter 20.

For information on exporting and importing data in XML into and from Access, see Chapter 38.

Summary

In this chapter, you learned ways to build documents using more than one Office application at a time. Key points included the following:

✦ There's more than one way to insert an object from one application into another. You can copy it and select Paste Special, choose Insert ➪ Object from the menu, or, in some applications, use built-in tools.

✦ When you use Paste Special, you can choose to insert an object in a number of formats, which vary depending on what kind of object you copied. Typical options include inserting the object as text, as a picture, as a linked or embedded object, or as HTML.

✦ Embedded objects can be edited using the program that created them by double-clicking them.

✦ Linked objects can be edited in the same way. The difference is that linked objects are created from a source file, and if that source file is changed in the originating program, the display in the destination document also changes. This is useful for keeping documents up-to-date when data is changing rapidly.

✦ You can edit all the linked objects in your document by choosing Edit ➪ Links. You can choose to update links automatically or manually.

✦ Other ways to share data in Office include sending Word documents to PowerPoint presentations (and vice versa) and sending Access data to Excel for analysis or to Word for publication or mail merging.

✦ You can integrate Office documents saved in XML format exactly the same way as those saved in standard Office formats — useful if you need to keep your documents in XML format for sharing with non-Office users.

✦   ✦   ✦

Universal Drawing and Graphics Features

Not all the embedded objects (described in Chapter 42) you may place in your Office documents are created by one of the main Office applications. In fact, the most commonly embedded objects are those you insert using one of the subprograms that come with Office: subprograms that you call up whenever you want to insert a picture or a bit of WordArt. Separate from the main applications, yet integrated with them, these subprograms enhance Office's capabilities and provide you with numerous highly useful tools for making better documents.

This chapter examines some of these programs — and, because they mostly deal with graphics, we'll revisit the process of inserting and editing pictures that's common to almost all the Office applications.

Inserting and Editing Pictures

Office uses the term *picture* to mean any type of graphical image you acquire from a source, as opposed to those you create with the built-in drawing tools.

Pictures are also *objects* (the general term Office uses for anything from an external source inserted into an Office document in its original form).

Inserting pictures

The standard way to add pictures created in other software is to choose Insert ➪ Picture and then choose either From File or Clip Art. Choosing Insert ➪ Picture ➪ Clip Art opens the Insert Clip Art task pane, through which you access the Clip Organizer, described in the section "Managing clip art (and other content) with the Clip Organizer," later in this chapter.

Note   It's worth remembering that the only real difference between clip art and other pictures is where you find them. Once they're in your document, you handle them all the same.

Selecting Insert ➪ Picture ➪ From File brings up the Insert Picture dialog box (see Figure 43-1), with the Thumbnails viewing option selected so you can preview the available images.

Figure 43-1: The Insert Picture dialog box gives you a preview of the images you might want to place in your document.

Select the picture you want to insert and click Insert. Or, simply double-click the picture you want.

Managing clip art (and other content) with the Clip Organizer

The second option under the Insert ➪ Picture menu in Office Applications, Clip Art, opens the Clip Art task pane. This is linked to a separate program, the Clip Organizer, which is used by all the Office applications. Figure 43-2 shows the Clip Art task pane in Word, displaying the results of a search for sports pictures.

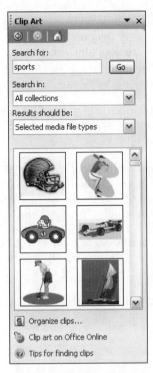

Figure 43-2: Microsoft Clip Organizer displays its wares in the Clip Art task pane.

Use Search for at the top of the task pane to search the Clip Organizer for images that match the keywords you enter — *sports*, in Figure 43-2.

Search in enables you to select a location in which to search for clip art collections. (Pictures have to be in a collection before the Clip Organizer recognizes them — see the section "Organizing your clips" to learn how to put other pictures on your computer into collections that the Clip Organizer can recognize.) Use the Results should be list box to choose what kind of objects you want to search for: clip art, photographs, movies, or sounds.

Using content items in Clip Organizer

When you've conducted a search, the Clip Organizer displays thumbnail images of the items it has found. Inserting a clip-art image or other content item from the Clip Organizer couldn't be easier: just double-click the thumbnail.

Clicking the down-pointing arrow to the right of the object opens a shortcut menu with several other options. Not only can you insert the item, you can also copy it to the Office clipboard, delete it from the Clip Organizer, copy or move it to a different collection, edit its associated keywords, find other items of a similar style, and preview it and check out its properties (size, graphic format, and so on).

Organizing your clips

A collection of clip art, sounds, and video clips can quickly become overwhelmingly difficult to manage. The Clip Organizer helps you keep track of all the content and arrange it so you can find it in the Clip Art task pane in any of your Office applications.

To organize your clips, click the Organize clips link at the bottom of the Clip Art task pane or, alternatively, open the Clip Organizer directly; you'll find it in the Microsoft Office Tools folder in your main Windows program list.

The first time you open the Clip Organizer, whichever way you do it, a message appears asking you if you want to organize your clips now or later. If you choose Now, Organizer immediately starts searching your hard drive and organizing your clips into collections — one collection for each folder in which clips are found.

If you'd prefer to specify exactly how the Clip Organizer should organize your content, click Options; you can select the exact folders in which the Clip Organizer should look.

If you'd prefer to get acquainted with the Clip Organizer before you do anything at all, click Later. The Clip Organizer itself opens (see Figure 43-3).

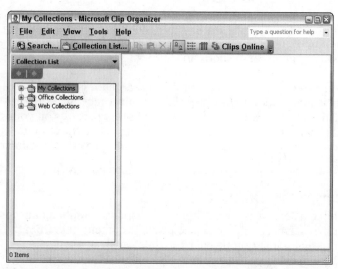

Figure 43-3: The Clip Organizer organizes the various types of media on your computer for use in Office applications.

On the left is your Collection List; this shows you the content that has already been organized into collections, either by you or by Office (Office comes with a number of collections). Clicking a collection name brings up thumbnail previews of all the images in that collection, on the right. Each image provides the same menu you've already seen in the Insert Clip Art task pane.

To add content already on your computer to the Clip Organizer, choose File ➪ Add Clips to Organizer. You can choose to do so automatically (in which case, the Clip Organizer searches your hard drive for all the media types it recognizes and collects them all); to input images from a scanner or camera; or to choose which specific images you want to add to the organizer. If you choose the last option, called On My Own you'll be presented with a pretty standard Office browsing window; choose the clip or clips you want to add to a collection and click Add To to choose the collection to which the clip should be added. In the resulting Import to Collection dialog box, you can also start a new collection by clicking New.

The thumbnail images in the Clip Organizer work exactly the same as the thumbnail images in the Insert Clip Art task pane. The menu associated with them is the same, too. If you choose one and then choose Edit Keywords from the attached menu, you'll see the dialog box shown in Figure 43-4.

Figure 43-4: Use the Keywords dialog box to add a caption and keywords to content items.

For any content item, type a caption that will jog your memory. Your description appears in the Clip Organizer when you hover the mouse over the item for a second or so. You may want to include technical information such as the number of colors the image contains or the file format. By default, the caption you see includes the current file name; the keyword list automatically contains the image type ("jpg" in Figure 43-4), taken from the filename extension.

Type keywords that the Clip Organizer will match when you initiate a search. To apply the same keyword to several different clips in a collection, select them in the main Clip Organizer window. Open the menu attached to any of the selected clips and choose Edit Keywords; then choose the All Clips at Once tab. This looks just like the Clip by Clip tab showing in Figure 43-4, but any captions and keywords you add will be attached to all of the selected clips.

You can create a new collection at any time by choosing File ⇨ New Collection. You're asked to supply a name and then a location for the new collection.

Finding clips online

You're not limited to choosing clips from the collections included with Office or the other pictures you may already have on your computer. Whenever the Clip Art pane is open, you can click the Clip art on Office Online link to open the Office Clip Art and Media Home Web site. (You can also get there by clicking the Clips Online button on the Clip Organizer toolbar).

Here you'll find tips and tricks, news, featured clips of the day, a search function, and links to hundreds of clips, divided into categories.

Figure 43-5 shows what a search of Clip art using the keyword "sports" turned up. Just like the clips in the Clip Art task pane, the clips here show a downward-pointing arrow if you point at them; clicking the arrow opens a small shortcut menu that lets you Copy the clips to your clipboard or add them to your Selection Basket (whence you can later download them all at once). You can also add them to your Selection Basket simply by checking the checkbox under each one. The Web page shows you how many items you've selected and the current size of the file you'll be downloading. You can click Review basket to review what you've selected; when you're ready to download, click one of the Download items links. By default, the pictures are saved into your My Pictures\Microsoft Clip Organizer folder.

Inserting pictures from a scanner or camera

The third way to insert pictures is to choose From Scanner or Camera on the Insert ⇨ Picture menu. This opens a small dialog box in which you choose the device from which you want to import the picture, choose Web quality or Print quality, and then click either Insert or Custom Insert (the latter provides additional options, which vary depending on the hardware from which you're importing pictures). You also have the option to automatically add the picture you're scanning to the Clip Organizer — a good option, as it saves you the trouble of adding it later!

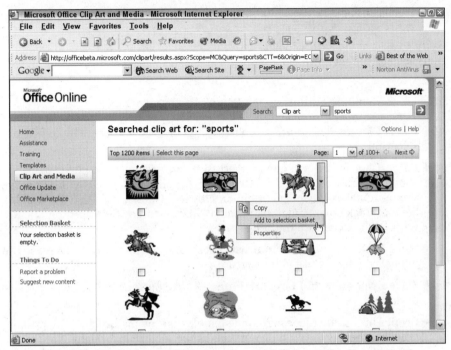

Figure 43-5: Microsoft's Art and Media Home Web site provides hundreds of additional clips from which to choose.

Modifying pictures

When you've inserted a picture, you aren't limited to its current appearance. Office lets you fuss with all sorts of picture characteristics, depending on the type of picture you're working with, but the most basic option available to you is to resize or move the picture. Click on it to bring up a set of grab handles; click and drag as you see fit to resize it (or even to reshape it; its aspect ratio isn't locked in, so you can squeeze it or stretch it). To move it, just click in the middle of it and drag it wherever you want.

Tip

> To resize a picture without distorting it, hold down Shift while you click and drag one of its corner handles.

Using the Picture toolbar

The Picture toolbar (see Figure 43-6) has most of the controls you need for modifying your digital art. You can turn it on by right-clicking a selected picture and choosing Show Picture toolbar, or by choosing it from the View ➪ Toolbars menu. Once you've turned it on for one picture, it pops open automatically whenever you click on a picture.

Figure 43-6: Use the Picture toolbar to manipulate images.

From left to right, the buttons on the Picture toolbar work as follows:

✦ **Insert Picture.** This button duplicates the Insert ⇨ Picture ⇨ From File menu selection.

✦ **Color.** Choose Grayscale to convert the picture's colors to corresponding shades of gray, or Black & White to convert all colors to either black or white. Washout makes the image bright and low-contrast; if you then use the Draw ⇨ Send to Back command, it can simulate a watermark. Select Automatic if you want Office to choose the settings.

✦ **More Contrast and Less Contrast.** These buttons increase or decrease the intensity of the colors in the picture.

✦ **More Brightness and Less Brightness.** These buttons make the picture lighter or darker.

✦ **Crop.** This button places cropping handles on the picture; by clicking and dragging them, you can hide portions of the picture from sight. Note that when you crop a picture, the entire picture is still there; part of it is just hidden.

✦ **Rotate Left.** This rotates the image 90 degrees left. (Click it twice, and you've turned the picture upside down.)

✦ **Line Style.** This is a duplicate of the button on the Drawing toolbar (discussed in the section "Controlling line options," later in this chapter). It applies a border around the picture itself (or in Word, around the picture boundary).

✦ **Compress Pictures.** This tool ensures that the size of the image file is as small as possible. Clicking it opens a dialog box that enables you to change the resolution of the picture to Web/Screen (96 dots per inch, or dpi), Print (200 dpi), or No Change (its original resolution). You can also choose to delete cropped areas. You can compress only the selected picture, or all pictures in the document.

Caution   If you choose to delete the cropped areas of a cropped picture, you won't be able to return the picture to its original appearance later; you'll have to re-insert it.

✦ **Text Wrapping.** This button, available only in Word, controls the flow of text around the picture.

✦ **Recolor Picture.** This button, available only in PowerPoint, lets you change the fill color and line colors of clip art and some drawings.

Transparent Pitfalls

The Set Transparent Color tool on the Picture toolbar is handy for removing one color from a bitmapped image. Images with transparent areas are often used in Web pages; they make the graphics look more at home on the background and less as if they'd been stuck on as an afterthought.

Note some caveats, however. For one thing, some bitmapped images already include transparent areas, and if these are present, you can't use the tool. Many bitmapped images use large palettes of dozens or even hundreds of colors — which means you'll rarely find one area that's all one color. As a result, you end up with a ragged image that looks like a T-shirt that's been through the washer a few dozen too many times — with rocks. Finally, you may find the background color in the foreground, which means you end up with holes in the foreground, too.

✦ **Format Picture.** This button displays the Format Picture dialog box. See the section "Formatting Objects: The Master Control Center," later in this chapter.

✦ **Set Transparent Color.** This tool, available only for bitmapped images, makes one color transparent. Click the button, then click the color you want to make transparent. (See the sidebar "Transparent Pitfalls" for additional information.)

✦ **Reset Picture.** This button restores the picture to its original condition, canceling out any changes you may have applied to it.

Drawing Your Own Art

In four of the Office applications — Word, Excel, PowerPoint, and Publisher — you can use Office's drawing tools to create your own graphics. Don't assume that because Office's drawing tools are built-in, they aren't powerful. They may not be as full-featured as, say, those in Corel Draw, but when you delve into them, you may be surprised by what they enable you to do.

You can draw simple lines, rectangles, and ovals, sure, but you can also insert complex AutoShapes, or draw complex freehand shapes. Moreover, once you've created an object, you can modify it in more ways than you've probably ever considered modifying a drawing before.

All of these tools are accessible from the Drawing toolbar, one of the standard toolbars that look the same in all the applications in which it is available; in Figure 43-7, you can see it at the bottom of the PowerPoint screen. If for some reason it's not visible in an application, you can turn it on by choosing View ➪ Toolbars ➪ Drawing.

Figure 43-7: Use the Drawing toolbar to add your own graphics and edit imported clip art.

Inserting basic shapes

To insert one of the basic shapes (line, arrow, rectangle, or oval), click the button for that shape on the Drawing toolbar. The mouse pointer changes to a simple cross; place it approximately where you think you want the shape, and then click. This produces the shape at a default size and with a default fill. Click in the document to produce the shape at the predetermined size. Alternatively, you can click and drag to draw the shape the exact size you want it.

If you hold down Shift while you draw a shape, its boundary remains perfectly proportioned — which enables you to draw squares, circles, or other perfectly proportioned shapes. Holding down Shift while you draw a line or arrow keeps the line or arrow angles divisible by 15 — e.g., 90 degrees, 180 degrees, 300 degrees, etc. This is particularly useful for drawing true horizontal or vertical lines.

If you hold down the Ctrl key while you draw the shape, it expands symmetrically in the opposite direction as you draw, like a mirror image. You can use this technique to center an object in a particular spot; just start drawing from that spot while you hold down the Ctrl key.

Tip   By default, the mouse pointer reverts to normal as soon as you've finished drawing a shape — but that's annoying if you want to draw multiple shapes of the same type. To avoid having to reactivate the tool each time, double-click the button for the shape. To toggle off this repeat-shape mode, click the button once more, or press Esc.

Inserting AutoShapes

To insert an AutoShape, choose AutoShapes on the Drawing toolbar and select from one of the submenus, or choose Insert ⇨ Picture ⇨ AutoShapes to open the AutoShapes toolbar; click the button that describes the type of AutoShape you want, and you'll see the same selection of shapes. Figure 43-8 shows both the AutoShapes menu and the submenus on the AutoShapes toolbar.

Tip   You can't double-click the AutoShapes buttons. To draw an AutoShape repeatedly, tear off its submenu to make it a floating toolbar; then you can double-click any of its buttons to enter repeat-shape mode.

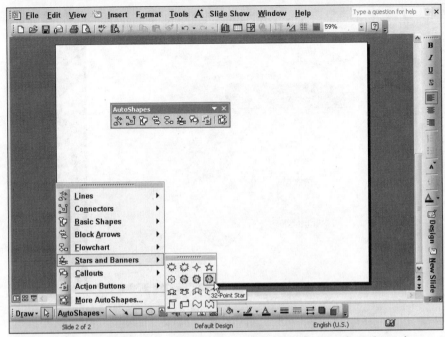

Figure 43-8: Place AutoShapes in your documents by selecting them from the AutoShapes menus on the Drawing toolbar, or from the AutoShapes toolbar.

More AutoShapes?

At the bottom of the AutoShapes menu, and at the far right of the toolbar, lies the option More AutoShapes. The shapes available by clicking this option aren't really AutoShapes at all; they're ordinary pictures in the Clip Organizer, which means you can't use the techniques described above to size them as you insert them, you can't add text to them, and you can't reshape them the way you can most AutoShapes, unless you ungroup them first.

Cross-Reference See the section "Organizing and aligning graphics" later in this chapter for more on grouping and ungrouping.

Connectors and action buttons

The available AutoShapes include *connectors,* special shapes that you use to connect two objects; once you've done so, you can move the two objects and they'll stay connected. Figure 43-9 shows a curved connector joining a rectangle and a star.

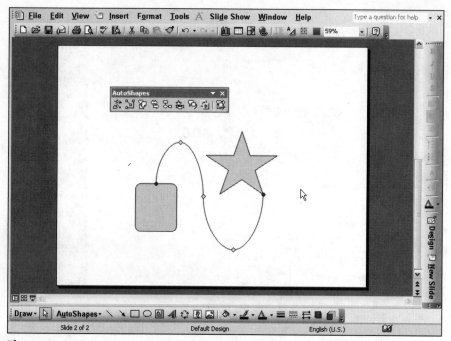

Figure 43-9: Connectors are special AutoShapes used to join two objects.

When you choose a connector and point at an existing object, blue dots appear around the edge of the object, indicating the points to which a connector can be attached. Point at one of these, and then click and drag to the second object to which you want to connect the first object. Dots will appear on it, too, when you reach it; select the one you want to attach the connector to on that end and release the mouse button. You can then adjust the connector's shape by clicking and dragging on the yellow diamonds that appear along it (the curved connector in Figure 43-9 has three of them, as you can see).

Once objects are connected, they remain connected even if you move one of the objects. The connector changes shape and stretches or shrinks as necessary to maintain the connection.

In PowerPoint alone, the AutoShapes menu includes action buttons, which are buttons that do something, such as display another slide, when you click them during a PowerPoint slide show.

Cross-Reference   Creating actions in PowerPoint is covered in detail in Chapter 30.

Action buttons are resizable, beveled rectangles (to make them look like they pro-trude from the surface of the screen). Each contains an icon indicating what it's for — for example, a right-pointing arrow to indicate "next slide," or a lowercase "i" to indicate "click here for more information." You can rotate action buttons just like any other shape; a yellow diamond control lets you change the apparent depth of the beveling.

Moving, resizing, rotating, and duplicating graphics objects

Office provides numerous methods to alter the size or location of a drawing (or a picture you inserted some other way, for that matter). They're summarized in Table 43-1.

Table 43-1
Keyboard and Mouse Actions with Graphics Objects

To Do This	Use This Mouse Action	Or This Keyboard Action
Select an object	Click the object	After first selecting an object with the mouse, press Tab or Shift+Tab to select the next or previous object.
Move an object	Drag over the shape (or its outline), or drag with the right button to the new location and choose Move Here from the shortcut menu that appears when you release the button.	Select the object, then press the arrow keys (Ctrl+arrow lets you move objects in smaller increments.) Note that this may not work in Word, where graphics have to interact with text; in particular, it doesn't work if inline text wrapping has been selected.
Move an object horizontally or vertically only	Hold down Shift while dragging.	
Duplicate an object, moving the new copy	Hold down Ctrl while dragging the object, or drag with the right button to the new location and select Copy Here from the shortcut menu.	Select the object; press Ctrl+C and then Ctrl+V; and move the copy.
Resize an object	Drag a handle.	

Continued

Table 43-1 *(continued)*

To Do This	Use This Mouse Action	Or This Keyboard Action
Resize an object, preserving its proportions	Hold down Shift while dragging a corner handle.	
Resize an object from the center outward	Hold down Ctrl while dragging a handle.	
Resize an object from the center outward, preserving its proportions	Hold down Ctrl+Shift while dragging a corner handle.	
Resize an object without the grid or guides active	Hold down Alt while dragging a sizing handle.	
Specify a new location or size precisely	Double-click the object; use the Format Shapes dialog box.	Select the object. Then choose Format, followed by the type of object (at the bottom of the Format menu); or display the shortcut menu and choose Format at the bottom.
Rotate an object	Select the object and then drag over any of the circular green rotation handles.	Select the object; then choose Draw ➪ Rotate or Flip. Choose a flipping option from the menu.

Reshaping AutoShapes

Many shapes you draw, both the basic ones and AutoShapes, show yellow diamonds when selected. Experiment with dragging them. They'll change the shape of the object in various ways, depending on the object in question, without affecting its overall size (see Figure 43-10).

Tip
You can transform almost every AutoShape into any other AutoShape if you change your mind about which one to use—for example, if you decide to use a different shape of arrow or a five-point star instead of a four-point star. Select the shape, choose Draw ➪ Change AutoShape, and pick the new shape you want. This works for text boxes and other shapes containing text, but not if the shape was drawn freehand using the AutoShapes ➪ Lines menu. (Text boxes and freehand drawing are discussed later in this chapter.)

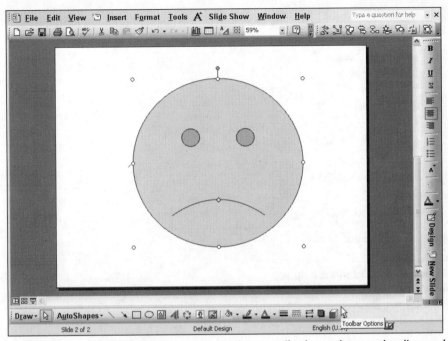

Figure 43-10: This was a Smiley Face AutoShape until I dragged up on the diamond handle at the center of its mouth.

Using the grid

Word and PowerPoint offer you additional help with drawing, moving, and resizing objects in the form of an evenly spaced grid to which objects snap. When the grid is on, you can't place an object between adjacent gridlines—it's as if a magnet pulls the object to the nearest line. (Excel doesn't need a grid because the cells of each worksheet already form a grid—and yes, you can snap objects to the cell walls.)

Another option makes objects automatically align with one another, so that the boundary of any object you move or resize clings to the boundary of any object it passes over.

Choose Draw ➪ Grid on the Drawing toolbar in Word, or Draw ➪ Grid and Guides in PowerPoint, to turn on these tools. In the resulting dialog box (the Word version is shown in Figure 43-11), check the Snap objects to grid checkbox to turn on the grid. You can then define the grid's spacing and origin. The Snap objects to other objects option makes objects stick to one another as you draw.

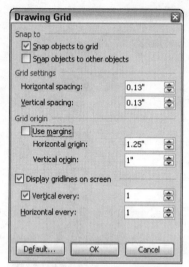

Figure 43-11: Detail the help you want from the drawing grid in this dialog box.

Tip   You can disable snap-to features — which, even if you like them most of the time, occasionally turn into a real pain — on the fly by holding down Alt while you work.

Working with text boxes and callouts

Text boxes, as the name implies, are onscreen boxes into which you type characters. You can place a text box anywhere you want in a document, regardless of where the application usually places text.

To create a text box, click the Text Box button on the Drawing toolbar, then insert the text box just as you would any other drawing.

You can also insert text into most enclosed AutoShapes (but not to lines and free-hand drawings). To do so, right-click the shape and choose Add Text from the shortcut menu. This causes a rectangle (representing an attached text box) to enclose the shape. A flashing cursor shows where your text will appear. Figure 43-12 shows a text box attached to an irregular shape.

Note   Text added to an AutoShape has to stay within the attached rectangular text box.

Tip

Another way to add text to an AutoShape is to draw a text box, then move it over the AutoShape and group the two together. This allows greater flexibility in where the text appears. See the section "Organizing and aligning graphics" later in this chapter for more on grouping and ungrouping.

Figure 43-12: You can add text to most enclosed AutoShapes.

Using callouts

A *callout* is just a text box with a line (or leader) connecting it to another location. Callouts typically comment on another item, as in Figure 43-13. The AutoShapes menu offers callouts in many different shapes and with many different lines.

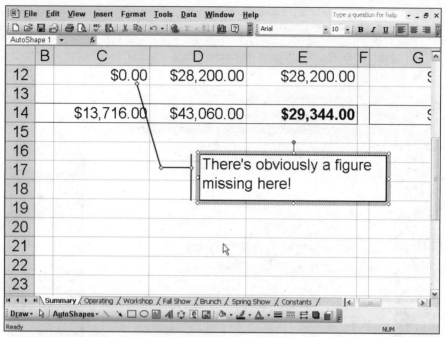

Figure 43-13: A callout in action in Excel

Formatting text boxes and the text inside them

You can format the text in text boxes just as you do text anywhere else. Excel and PowerPoint enable you to apply character formatting; PowerPoint also lets you apply paragraph alignment and line and paragraph spacing, and create bulleted and numbered lists, while Excel lets you apply paragraph alignment, but not spacing. Word also gives you control over paragraph alignment and line and paragraph spacing, and enables you to apply paragraph styles and create bulleted or numbered lists, just as with text in the main body of the document. You can also link Word text boxes together, so that text that overflows one box can flow automatically into the next.

Because text boxes are also drawings, most of the Drawing toolbar's additional formatting options (detailed later in this chapter) are also available.

To format a text box itself, as opposed to the text inside it, click on the rectangle that defines it. If you want to work with the text, click the text area to display the insertion point; if you have trouble making that work, then right-click and choose Edit Text.

Cross-Reference The section "Formatting Objects: The Master Control Center" at the end of this chapter offers more text-formatting tips.

In Word, Excel, and PowerPoint, you can rotate the text in a text box, but the method differs a little from application to application, thusly:

✦ **To rotate text in Word:** Select the text box and then click the Change Text Direction button on the Text Box toolbar. (If the Text Box toolbar isn't visible, choose View ➪ Toolbars ➪ Text Box to display it.)

✦ **To rotate text in Excel:** Select the text box and choose Format ➪ Text Box. Then click the appropriate orientation on the Alignment tab.

✦ **To rotate text in PowerPoint:** Rotate the text box just as you would any other drawing, by dragging the circular, green rotation handle at its top.

Drawing and editing freehand shapes

Office's three powerful freehand drawing tools—curve, freeform, and scribble—are sufficient to create freehand sketches (see Figure 43-14).

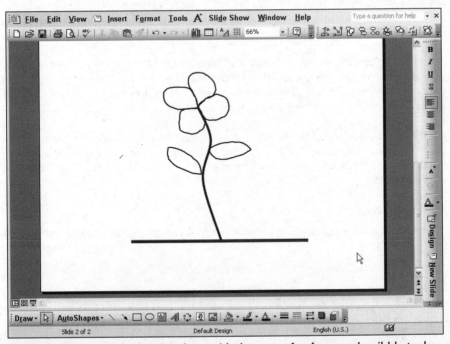

Figure 43-14: A simple drawing done with the curve, freeform, and scribble tools: the flower petals were created with the scribble tool, the stem with the curve tool, and the leaves with the freeform tool.

These tools are available from the AutoShapes ⇨ Lines menu. They're the three tools on the bottom. Here's how they work:

✦ **Curve.** Drawing a curve is like playing with a long rubber band you can pin down wherever you want. Click and release the mouse button to set the starting point; move the mouse pointer to extend the line; click again at every point where the line should change direction; double-click to set the final anchor point. If you change your mind about a bend point, you can remove it (and others before it, in reverse order) by pressing the Backspace key.

✦ **Freeform.** This tool is for drawing shapes that include both straight and curving lines. To define the endpoints of straight segments, click and release the mouse button. If you also drag the mouse, the Freeform tool becomes the Scribble tool, allowing you to add curves. As with lines, you can hold down the Shift key to constrain your straight portions of the freeform to 15-degree increments.

✦ **Scribble.** Drag with this tool to draw freehand shapes just as you draw with a pencil — an incredibly awkward pencil.

Editing freehand shapes

It's not easy drawing with a mouse (as my flower in Figure 43-14 should prove; believe it or not, I studied art in college!). However, Office lets you go back to your drawing and push recalcitrant lines into space.

To do so, right-click on the drawing and choose Edit Points from the shortcut menu (it's also available from the main Draw menu). Figure 43-15 shows the flower portion of the drawing in the previous figure with the edit points activated and the line made thinner so you can see them more easily.

Each black square along the shape's outline indicates a change in direction. Each of these points is called (by Microsoft, anyway) a *vertex*. You can manipulate these vertices (or *vertexes*, as Microsoft pluralizes them), and the lines attached to them, in several ways:

✦ Click and drag a vertex to move it.

✦ Ctrl+Click on a point to remove it; this can smooth out a particularly squiggly stretch.

✦ Add a new point using Ctrl+Click anywhere on the line where no point exists.

✦ Change the degree and direction of deflection for the segment passing through a point. Click the point to select it, and then drag its *tangent handles*, described in the following section.

Figure 43-15: Use the edit points to fine-tune your freehand drawing.

Working with tangent handles and tangent lines

Tangent handles, shown in Figure 43-16, appear whenever you select a vertex. Drag them to control the pair of blue tangent lines to which each handle is attached. The angle of one tangent line to the other determines the direction in which the curve is stretched; the length of the tangent line determines how far that part of the curve is stretched. If you see only one handle, the segment on the other side of the point is a straight line and can't be bent (but see the section "Changing a segment's type"). Experiment by dragging the tangent handles and you'll soon see how powerful a tool they can be. (The dashed lines show you where you're dragging the tangent line to so you can position it precisely before releasing the mouse button.)

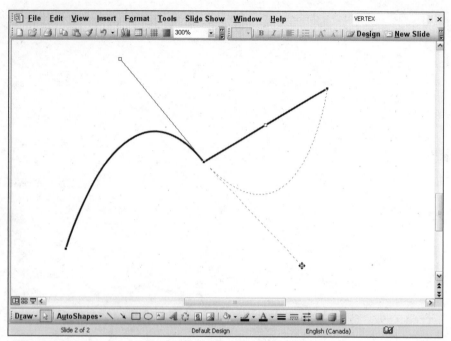

Figure 43-16: You can reshape a freehand line by dragging a point's tangent handle; when I release the mouse, the flat part of the line will become curved.

Changing point and segment types

With Edit Points turned on, to further refine the contour at a specific point, right-click along the outline to display a shortcut menu. The options listed in the second menu group of the shortcut that appears vary, depending on whether you right-clicked directly over a point or elsewhere along the outline.

On the shortcut menu for a specific point, the important option is the type of point. Four point types are available:

✦ **Auto Point.** Creates a smooth curve through the point automatically. Office decides how to bend the outline; no tangent handles are available.

✦ **Corner Point.** Creates a sharp corner at the junction of the two segments that meet at the point. You can vary the length and angle of each tangent line independently.

✦ **Smooth Point.** The outline curves smoothly through the point. You can bend the outline by dragging either tangent handle, but the two tangent lines always extend equally in opposite directions (you can't vary the angle at which they meet).

✦ **Straight Point.** This makes the segment on one side of the point flatter than the segment on the other, without creating a sharp corner. You can stretch the two tangent lines by different amounts, though they always extend in opposite directions.

Changing a segment's type

Right-click on any line segment between two edit points, and the shortcut menu offers you two options for the segment:

✦ **Straight Segment.** This connects two points with a straight line that can't be bent, no matter what kind of point lies on either end.

✦ **Curved Segment.** Although this type of segment sometimes *looks* perfectly straight, you can deform it by pulling on the tangent handles of the points at either end of the segment.

To convert one type of segment to the other, just choose the other option on the menu.

Closing and opening freehand shapes

Note one more option from the shortcut menu when you're editing the edit points of a freehand drawing: you can break apart a closed shape by choosing Open Path. This breaks the shape at the direction-change point nearest to where you right-clicked. If the shape is already an open line with a definite beginning and end, choosing Close Path will connect the two endpoints.

WordArt: designer text

Next on the Drawing toolbar is the WordArt button; WordArt is discussed in its own section later in this chapter.

Adding a diagram

Next to WordArt is the insert Diagram or Organization Chart button, which opens the Diagram Gallery dialog box (see Figure 43-17). This offers you six different types of diagrams: an organization chart, a cycle diagram, a radial diagram, a pyramid diagram, a Venn diagram (overlapping circles that depict the relationship among various elements), and a target diagram.

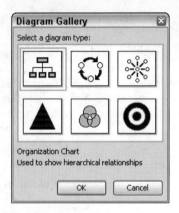

Figure 43-17: Insert an organization chart or diagram from this dialog box.

Cross-Reference   You can find a detailed description of the process for inserting an organization chart or diagram in the PowerPoint section of this book, specifically in Chapter 29.

Working with color, line, and texture

You can control the width and color of the line defining any drawing object, and you can fill most objects with a color, simple pattern, textured background, or picture.

Most of the objects you can draw are closed — they have a continuous outline. Of course, you can also open lines with two free ends.

Tip   In addition to the techniques covered in this section, you can also control fill and line options from the Format dialog box, described in the section "Formatting Objects: The Master Control Center," later in this chapter.

Filling objects

To fill an object, select it, and then click the Fill Color button on the Drawing toolbar. Click the main portion of the button to fill the object with the currently selected color. To change colors or apply a pattern or texture, click the vertical bar at the right of the button to display a pop-up menu of colors. You can choose from these, but if you want an even fancier fill, select More Fill Colors or Fill Effects.

Tip   The More Fill Colors dialog box has a slider in it for setting transparency. Transparent or semi-transparent fill colors are useful for letting text or other objects peek through a drawing object. This slider is also available on the Format dialog box, described in the section "Formatting Objects: The Master Control Center," later in this chapter.

The Fill Effects option brings up the Fill Effects dialog box, shown in Figure 43-18.

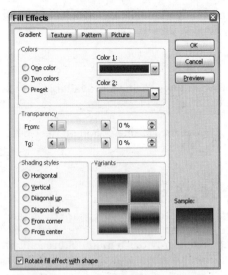

Figure 43-18: Use the Fill Effects dialog box to apply fancy fills, textures, patterns, or pictures to drawing objects.

Here, select from the tabs to create four different types of fills:

✦ **Gradient.** This creates a fill with a gradual transition between two or more colors. The One Color option blends the chosen color into black or white, depending on the setting of the Dark/Light slider. You can select the colors and pattern and set the transparency of the start point and the end point.

✦ **Texture.** This option fills the shape with a pattern designed to imitate a textured surface. Several textures are already available; you can also choose Other Texture to use a texture image you may have stored elsewhere on your computer. Office tiles the image until the shape is filled.

✦ **Pattern.** Selecting this fills the shape with one of 48 simple preset patterns. You can select foreground and background colors.

✦ **Picture.** This option fills the shape with an imported picture, scaled as necessary.

Controlling line options

You can also use techniques similar to those described in the previous section to change the color, width, or pattern of a shape's outline. Click the main part of the Line Color button on the Drawing toolbar to apply the line color shown on the button. Click the downward-pointing arrow beside the button to select a different color or to choose a patterned outline.

Use the menu that is displayed when you click the Line Style button to select the line width and whether you see a single, double, or triple line.

To create a broken line, click the Dash Style button.

The Arrow Style menu, which applies arrow endings to lines, is available only if you're working on a line and not a closed shape.

Tip   To remove the outline from an object, choose the No Line option on the Line Color menu.

Adding shadow and 3-D effects

Some of the most striking effects Office's Drawing tools can apply are the shadow and 3-D effects. To apply them, select the object and click either the Shadow Style or 3-D Style button on the Drawing toolbar. Each provides a menu of present effects, which appear as graphical examples. Click one of these, and your shape takes on the settings of the chosen preset.

Of course, you aren't limited to the presets. Click the Shadow Settings option at the bottom of the Shadow Style pop-up menu or the 3-D Settings option at the bottom of the 3-D Style pop-up menu to open the Shadow Settings or 3-D Settings toolbars, respectively.

Tip   You can add shadows to just about any object — even multimedia placeholders. However, you *can't* add the Drawing toolbar's 3-D and shadow effects to selected text. When you add 3-D to a text box, the text itself remains flat. For 3-D text effects, you need to use WordArt instead of a text box.

Both the 3-D and Shadow toolbars have On/Off buttons at the left, which toggle their effects on and off. The object retains its most recent settings, so you can turn an effect on or off or switch back and forth between 3-D and shadow effects without losing previous work.

Customizing shadow and 3-D effects

The Shadow Settings toolbar has buttons for moving the shadow relative to the object itself, as well as one for changing the shadow's color. The 3-D Settings tool-bar (see Figure 43-19) includes many more options:

✦ **Tilt.** These four buttons rotate the object on its horizontal and vertical axes — but only through 180 degrees.

✦ **Depth.** Use this to set how far, in points, the 3-D effect extends from the original drawing. When available, the Infinity setting extends the 3-D effect toward the horizon.

✦ **Direction.** This determines which way the 3-D effect extends from its object. Select Perspective to make all the lines converge toward a vanishing point on the horizon; choose parallel to keep all lines parallel (the usual choice for technical drawings, as opposed to artistic ones).

✦ **Lighting.** Use this to select the brightness and direction of the imaginary lighting source. Click the center cube to light the object directly from the front.

✦ **Surface.** Select from four options controlling how reflective the surface of your 3-D shape appears. Matte gives it a dull look, Metal makes it look like polished metal, Plastic is somewhere in between, and Wire Frame removes the surface.

✦ **3-D Color.** This determines the color of the 3-D effect. Select Automatic to have Office base the effect's color on the original object's color.

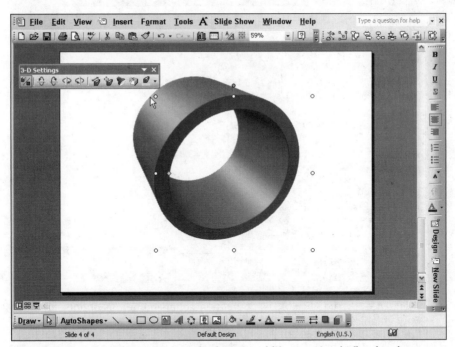

Figure 43-19: This impressive metal tube started life as a simple flat doughnut.

Organizing and aligning graphics

Office provides many options for working with groups of objects. These options fall into three basic categories: alignment, grouping, and ordering.

Aligning multiple objects

Trying to line up two or more graphics on a screen using a mouse is worse than trying to hang a picture straight without using a level. For help, choose Draw ➪ Align or Distribute (see Figure 43-20).

First, select the objects you want to align, either relative to each other or to the page. Then display the Align or Distribute menu. In Word or PowerPoint, if you want to align or distribute the objects relative to the whole page, rather than to one another, turn on the Relative To option at the bottom of the menu (to Page in Word, to Slide in PowerPoint).

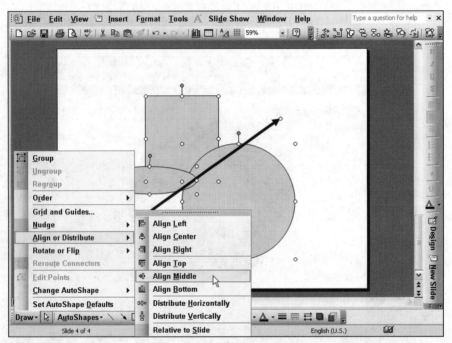

Figure 43-20: The Align or Distribute menu offers numerous options for placing your graphics.

The alignment options are self-explanatory, but you should know that objects are moved so they line up with the one that's already located farthest in the selected alignment direction. For example, if you select three objects and choose Align Left, the object that is farthest left remains in place, while Office moves the other two objects to it. In addition, remember that Office aligns the objects based on the imaginary rectangles that surround them, not necessarily on what's visible.

The distribution options arrange three or more selected objects at equal distances from one another. The two objects at the top and bottom (or left and right) of the page remain in place, while the ones in between divide the intervening space evenly. If the Relative to Page option is on, distributing two or more objects moves them all so they're evenly spaced on the page.

Grouping objects

You can and should group objects together to preserve their relative positions and sizes during moving and resizing operations. Grouping them also enables you to apply the same effects to all the objects in the group.

Select the objects (the easiest way is to draw an imaginary box around them with your mouse pointer), and then choose Draw ⇨ Group. The selection handles are removed from the individual objects but appear around the entire group, which you can now move, size, or apply effects to as a unit.

You can still apply some attributes to objects in a group by selecting the group and then clicking again on the individual object to select it. You will see small, gray circles with Xs inside; these indicate that an individual object within a group is selected. You can now change the color, line thickness, 3-D settings, font face, etc., for that individual object.

To work with some individual attributes, select the group and choose Draw ⇨ Ungroup. After making any changes you need to individual objects (perhaps you needed to edit the Edit Points of a freehand drawing), you can reform the last group you ungrouped by choosing Draw ⇨ Regroup. This works even if you have moved the objects onto different pages.

The grouping commands are also available from the Grouping menu on any object's shortcut menu.

You can group smaller groups of objects into larger groups for as many levels of organization as you like. The Ungroup command breaks apart the top-level group only. If a drawing is composed of groups of groups, you have to use the Ungroup command repeatedly to get to the individual shapes.

Ordering objects

If two or more graphics overlap, they're arranged in a stack, one on top of the next in a theoretical sequence of layers. Use the Draw ⇨ Order menu (see Figure 43-21) to change a selected object's position in the stack (this menu is also available from an object's shortcut menu).

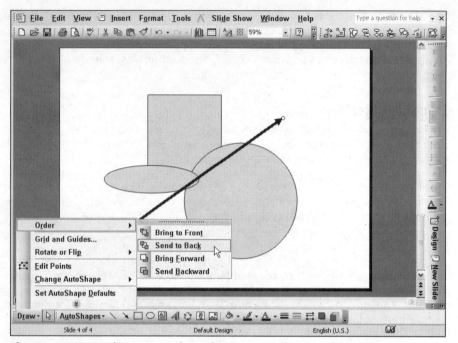

Figure 43-21: Use the commands on this menu to place an object beneath something else or to switch its position again.

The Bring to Front and Send to Back commands move the selected object to the very top or bottom of the pile. The Bring Forward and Send Backward options promote or demote it by one level. In Word, the menu also offers commands to move the object in front of or behind the document text, which is initially at the bottom of the theoretical stack.

Formatting Objects: The Master Control Center

Whether you're working with an object you created with the Office drawing tools or a picture you imported, the Format dialog box consolidates a comprehensive assemblage of tools for controlling your object's appearance.

Select an object and choose Format ➪ Object to open the Format dialog box. Exactly what settings it will contain varies from object to object and application to application, but Figure 43-22 shows a representative sample.

Figure 43-22: The Format Picture dialog box
is typical of Format dialog boxes.

Tabs on this key dialog box include the following:

✦ **Colors and Lines.** This tab duplicates the Fill Color, Line, and Arrow Style buttons from the Drawing toolbar.

✦ **Size.** This tab enables you to specify size in absolute units or as a percentage of the object's current size. For pictures, check Relative to original picture size to scale the picture based on its original size, rather than its current size. Whether you use the Size or Scale settings, check Lock aspect ratio to maintain the object's original proportions as you change either height or width.

✦ **Position.** In PowerPoint, use this tab to specify the object's position on a slide. Use the From settings to indicate the starting point for the measurements you enter. Word doesn't have the Position tab. Instead, you must switch to the Layout tab and then click the Advanced button to bring up the Advanced Layout dialog box. From there, switch to the Picture Position tab.

✦ **Properties.** In Excel, you can select one of three options governing how the object changes as its underlying cells move or change size (handy for sorting tables containing pictures).

✦ **Layout.** In Word, this tab specifies how text wraps around the object.

✦ **Picture.** Use this tab to crop a picture object and set brightness and contrast.

✦ **Text Box.** In Word, this tab enables you to set the margins between the boundaries of a text box and the text it contains. PowerPoint adds controls for finetuning the look of your text boxes.

Using WordArt

WordArt is a program, used primarily in Word, PowerPoint and Excel, for creating fancily formatted text — text with 3-D effects, for example, or text made to look like a brick wall or some other texture.

Creating a WordArt object

To create a WordArt object in Word, PowerPoint, or Excel:

1. Choose Insert ➪ Picture ➪ WordArt, or click the WordArt button on the Drawing toolbar. This opens the WordArt Gallery dialog box shown in Figure 43-23.

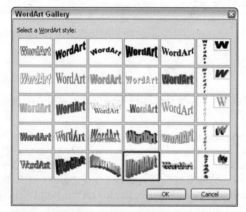

Figure 43-23: From this dialog box, choose the style of WordArt object that's closest to what you want.

2. Choose the style of WordArt object that appeals to you and click OK.

3. In the Edit WordArt Text dialog box (see Figure 43-24), type your text. Choose the font you want to use from any of those available in the Font drop-down list, and choose a size and style (bold, italic, or both).

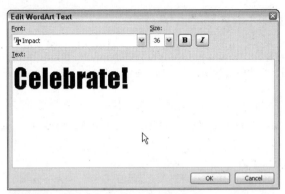

Figure 43-24: Type the text you want to make into a WordArt object into this dialog box.

4. Click OK. Your text appears in the style of the WordArt object you chose (see Figure 43-25).

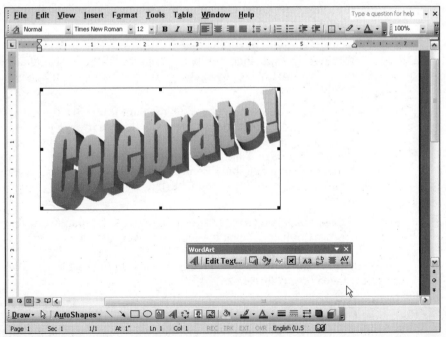

Figure 43-25: A WordArt object. Notice the WordArt toolbar, which opens whenever you select a WordArt object.

Editing and formatting WordArt

You can edit the WordArt object further using the WordArt toolbar that has also appeared. (Exactly which tools you see depends on which application you're using.) This toolbar features a number of commands:

✦ **Insert WordArt.** This inserts a new WordArt object.

✦ **Edit Text.** This reopens the Edit WordArt Text dialog box shown in Figure 43-24.

✦ **WordArt Gallery.** This opens the dialog box that displays all the WordArt styles, so you can apply a different style to your text if you wish.

✦ **Format WordArt.** This opens the Format WordArt dialog box, a version of the Format dialog box described in the previous section, which has several tabs. (Again, which tabs you'll see depends on which application you're using.)

  • Colors and Lines contains controls for changing the appearance of the WordArt characters' fill. You can apply a solid color; choose a preset one- or two-color gradient (or create one); choose from a variety of textures ranging from stone to wood grain; or even use a picture. In addition, you can change the color, weight, and dash of the lines (if any) outlining the letters in the WordArt object.

  • Size enables you to set the height and width of the WordArt object and rotate it by a specified number of degrees. You can also change the size of the WordArt object by scaling it to a certain percentage of normal height or width.

  • Layout determines how the object will interact with the Office document: should it be In line with text (as though it were just one large text character itself), or should text wrap itself Square to the edges of the WordArt frame or Tight to the image itself (rather than the frame)? Should the object appear Behind text or In front of text? Layout also enables you to set the alignment (left, right, or center) of the WordArt frame.

  • Web enables you to enter alternative text to be displayed while the WordArt object is being loaded into a Web browser.

✦ **WordArt Shape.** This lets you change the shape the text in your WordArt object takes (see Figure 43-26).

✦ **Text Wrapping.** Like the Layout tab of the Format WordArt dialog box, this enables you to set the way surrounding text will interact with your WordArt object. Clicking Edit Wrap Points enables you to manually adjust the normally invisible border around the image that text wraps to when Tight is selected.

✦ **WordArt Same Letter Heights.** This makes all letters in your WordArt object the same height and aligns the tops and bottoms of all letters — in other words, lowercase letters will be exactly the same height as uppercase letters.

✦ **WordArt Vertical Text.** This makes letters appear vertically, stacked one over the top of the other and reading from top to bottom. Clicking this button again returns the WordArt text to its horizontal format.

✦ **WordArt Alignment.** This determines how text is positioned within the WordArt frame. It can be aligned left, right, or center, like ordinary text. Three types of justification are also possible: word justify, which justifies the text by adding space between words; letter justify, which justifies the text by adding space between letters; and stretch justify, which justifies text by making the letters wider.

✦ **WordArt Character Spacing.** This determines the spacing between letters in the WordArt text. You can set it for very tight, tight, normal, loose, or very loose; or set a percentage of normal. You can also change kerning (the amount of space between pairs of letters).

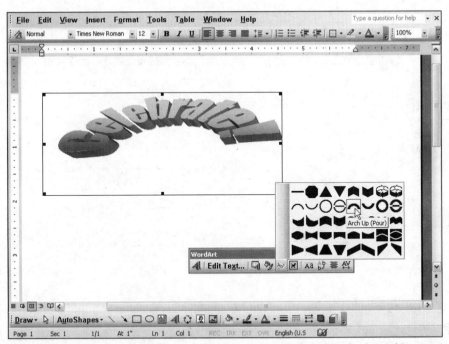

Figure 43-26: Choose the shape you want your WordArt text to take from this menu.

Once you're satisfied with your WordArt object, click anywhere outside its frame to deselect it. After that, you can move it and resize it anytime by clicking on it once, and then dragging it from place to place (or clicking and dragging on its handles); you can edit it by double-clicking on it.

Using Microsoft Equation Editor

Microsoft Equation Editor is a fairly esoteric program, in that its use is primarily limited to those who work with complex mathematical equations. Equation Editor enables you to create equations using a wide range of mathematical symbols and can be used in Word, PowerPoint, and Excel.

To open Microsoft Equation Editor, choose Insert ➪ Object and select Microsoft Equation 3.0 as the object type. This creates an object frame in your document and opens the Equation toolbar (see Figure 43-27). (It's a fairly safe bet that if you recognize only two or three symbols on this toolbar, you're unlikely to ever need to use Microsoft Equation Editor!)

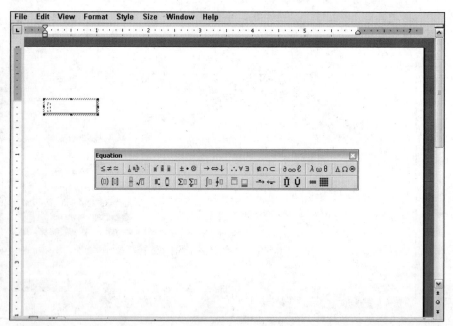

Figure 43-27: The Microsoft Equation Editor toolbar has 19 function buttons.

This toolbar consists of an upper and lower row. The upper row contains mathematical symbols, while the lower row contains mathematical templates. Each template consists of a predetermined set of symbols and unfilled slots. Once you choose a template, the insertion point automatically moves to the slot that would ordinarily be filled first. Equation Editor adjusts spacing, formatting, and so on, to adhere to standard mathematical layout. Once you've created the equation, you can use the Format, Style, and Size menus to adjust its appearance.

Click anywhere outside the equation's frame to close Microsoft Equation Editor and return to your Office application.

Summary

In this chapter, you learned how to use some of the supplemental programs that provide added functionality to all Office applications, in particular those that involve graphics. Highlights included the following:

✦ The Clip Organizer helps you find just the right picture, no matter where it's located, and tuck it away so you can always find it again.

✦ You can create your own line objects from scratch using the Drawing bar — even add shadows and 3-D effects.

✦ Any drawing object you create you can fine-tune, line by line.

✦ The Format ➪ Picture command provides a master control center for any picture you've inserted into your document.

✦ WordArt is a powerful tool for creating eye-catching text that features 3-D effects, unusual shapes, and colorful fills.

✦ Once you've chosen the type of WordArt you like from the WordArt Gallery, you can easily customize it using the WordArt toolbar.

✦ Microsoft Equation Editor is likely to be of use to you only if you're a mathematician, but if you need mathematical symbols to construct equations, you'll find it invaluable.

✦   ✦   ✦

Using Microsoft Office Document Imaging and Scanning

This book has described working with documents at length, with the understanding that the documents we're talking about are Office documents. However, the most common type of office document isn't an Office document at all. Instead, it's the kind of document all documents were before computers came along: a paper document, received in the mail, or by fax, or through a courier service. These days it's known as a "hard copy."

To bring that kind of document into your Office application, you have to first turn it into a file that a computer can handle—that is, digitize it. That's where Microsoft Office Document Imaging (MODI), a tool provided with Office, comes in. Once documents are digitized, Microsoft Office Document Imaging lets you perform optical character recognition (OCR) on them, and copy and export text and images from them into Word; search for text within scanned documents; reorganize scanned pages just as you would papers in a folder, annotate scanned documents, send them to other users via e-mail or fax, and more.

Scanning Documents

When you first open Microsoft Office Document Imaging, most of its tools are unavailable because you don't have any documents loaded into it. Although you can open existing documents in MODI, the usual way to get a document into the program is to scan it in.

To do so, choose File ➪ Scan New Document. This opens the dialog box shown in Figure 44-1.

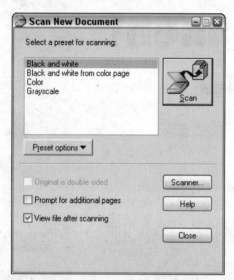

Figure 44-1: Use the Scan New Document dialog box to specify settings for the document you're about to scan into Microsoft Office Document Imaging.

Choosing a scanner

The first step is to choose your scanner (if you have more than one installed); click the Scanner button in the Scan New Document dialog box. In the resulting Choose Scanner dialog box, you can choose your scanner from a list of installed scanners, choose to use an automatic document feeder if your scanner has one (in which case MODI expects the pages to keep coming one after the other, instead of just one page at a time) and, optionally, Show scanner driver dialog before scanning.

Note This last option turns over control of your scanner to the scanner's own software, rather than leaving it in the hands of MODI. It means that any changes you want to make to MODI's preset scanner settings have to be done within that software, rather than in MODI. Conversely, your scanner software may provide more options than MODI, so it's your call.

Managing presets

MODI offers you four preset settings for scanning:

✦ **Black and white.** This preset scans in monochrome at 300 dots per inch (i.e., the number of pixels generated per inch of image, abbreviated dpi); it's the one to use when scanning ordinary text (black ink on white paper) or line art. It's the preset that provides the best Optical Character Recognition, too.

✦ **Black and white from color page.** This scans in grayscale at 300 dpi, saving the results in monochrome format. It's designed to give you the best possible text resolution for OCR when you're scanning from documents that have colored backgrounds or colored text.

✦ **Color.** This scans in color at 200 dpi; it's the preset for scanning full-color documents such as a page from a magazine. The somewhat lower resolution than the black-and-white presets means that small text may not be legible enough for OCR to accurately handle. Also, because color scans contain the most information, the resulting image files can be quite large.

✦ **Grayscale.** This scans in grayscale at 200 dpi, which is a good setting for documents that contain black-and-white, continuous-tone images such as black-and-white photographs. It handles text and colored text reasonably well.

If for some reason these presets don't offer exactly what you need, you can edit them or create a new one by clicking Preset options and choosing Edit selected preset or Create new preset.

Caution If you edit an existing preset, make sure you make note of the original settings before you save it; no command is provided that lets you reset presets to their original settings, so if you want the original preset back, you'll have to re-create it manually.

Either option opens the Preset Options dialog box shown in Figure 44-2; the only difference is that the Create new preset option asks you to first name your new preset.

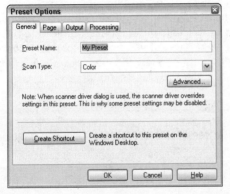

Figure 44-2: You can edit MODI's built-in scanning presets here, or create new presets.

This dialog box has four tabs:

✦ **General.** Here you can change the preset's name, choose a scan type (the same four types that are represented in the built-in presets), and create a shortcut to the preset on your desktop. Click the Advanced button to gain additional control. Use the resulting Advanced Scan Settings dialog box (see Figure 44-3) to set the resolution at which you want to scan; to set the scan type (monochrome, 8-bit gray [equivalent to 256 shades of gray] or 24-bit color [equivalent to 16.8 million colors]); to turn on Auto-contrast and save the resulting file in monochrome (this is the option for scanning color text for OCR); and to set the file format you want the scan to produce. TIFF with either LZW or JPEG compression (LZW, or *lossless compression,* results in larger files but greater detail; JPEG compression results in smaller color files and can be adjusted for better quality or smaller file size using a slider); and MDI, MODI's own format, which also offers a slider that can adjust the image output for better quality or smaller file size.

✦ **Page.** Here you can set the page size. By default, MODI saves multipage scans as a single document; you can change that here by checking the Save each page as a separate document checkbox. Note, however, that this will make OCR more difficult, because you'll have to run it on each document separately.

✦ **Output.** Choose the folder in which you want scanned files to be saved, and choose how you want to name the file: automatically, based on the first words on the page; using an automatically generated number; or with the date and time, in the format of your choice. (Whichever option you choose, you'll probably want to rename the files later to something more meaningful to you.)

✦ **Processing.** By default, MODI launches OCR immediately upon completion of the scan to recognize the text in the document. You can turn that option off here. You can also turn off the Auto rotate and Auto straighten functions, designed to make OCR more successful, and choose the OCR language (it defaults to your existing Office language setting).

Back in the Scan New Document dialog box, there are three more options. Check Original is double sided if the original is double-sided and if you have a scanner equipped with an automatic document feeder (ADF), which allows automatic scanning of multiple pages; this ensures that both the front and back of multiple pages will be scanned. Check Prompt for additional pages if you want to be prompted each time a page has finished scanning; and check View file after scanning (which is checked by default) if you want to view the file once it's scanned.

Finally, click Scan.

Figure 44-4 shows an example of what you see at the completion of a one-page scan.

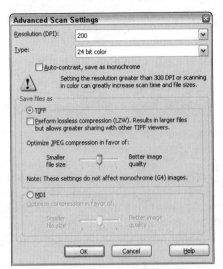

Figure 44-3: Set scanner resolution and output file type in the Advanced Scan Settings dialog box.

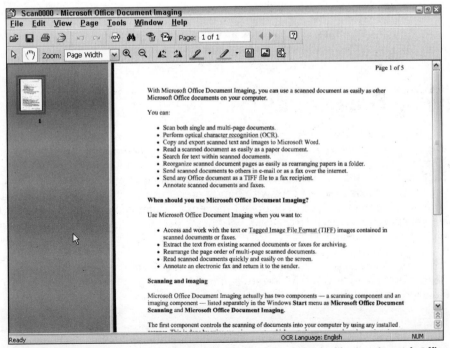

Figure 44-4: Here's what a scanned document typically looks like in Microsoft Office Document Imaging.

Opening and importing files

You don't have to scan a document in order to work with one in Microsoft Office Document Imaging; it can work with files that already exist in digital format, provided that format is either TIFF or MDI.

There are two ways to get such a document into MODI: you can open it or import it.

Opening it is done via the File ⇨ Open command, which simply opens a standard Open dialog box; choose the file you wish to work with and click Open.

Importing is a little different. Importing can take an image in one format, change it into another format, and save it in that format for editing. Choose File ⇨ Import to open the Import dialog box, which looks just like the Open dialog box except for the Preferences button. Clicking that opens a dialog box in which you choose whether to output the file as MDI or TIFF (and which resolution of TIFF — 100, 200, or 300 dpi), and the folder in which you want the new file saved.

Select MDI - Compressed Document Format when you want the final document to be saved in color or grayscale; check the Compress images in the document option if you want a smaller file size (however, this will degrade the quality of any pictures somewhat). Choose the Tiff - Monochrome Fax format to save the file in black and white and keep the file size small.

Tip   If you're importing a document in order to annotate it, make the document monochrome and use color for your annotations, for greater legibility.

Viewing Documents

MODI provides a number of tools for viewing documents, most of them located on the View toolbar (underneath the Standard toolbar). The Pan tool, which looks like a little hand, can be used to drag the document around in its view window. This is particularly useful in close-up views — which brings us to the Zoom tools. You can set the Zoom using the list box, with handy presets such as Entire Page, Text Width, Page Width and Page Height, or preset percentages of full-size (from 25 percent to 500 percent), or you can zoom in and out using the Zoom In and Zoom Out tools, or type in a percentage.

If the document was scanned in sideways for some reason, you can rotate it 90 degrees left or right using the Rotate Left and Rotate Right tools. (You'll have to save it to maintain the new orientation.)

Use the View menu to set the size of thumbnails (Tiny, Small, Medium, or Large), and specify whether the view in the main pane should be of a single page, a continuous page (where, if there are multiple pages, you view them like one long roll of paper), or Two Pages (two pages at once side by side; the others scroll up from below in pairs).

Tip You can rearrange multipage documents you've scanned in by simply clicking and dragging the thumbnails in the thumbnail pane. This changes the original file, so in order to keep the new order, you'll have to save.

Finally, MODI offers a special Reading view for documents, which removes the extraneous toolbars and lets you concentrate on simply reading the document. Click the Reading View button on the Standard toolbar or choose View ➪ Reading View (see Figure 44-5).

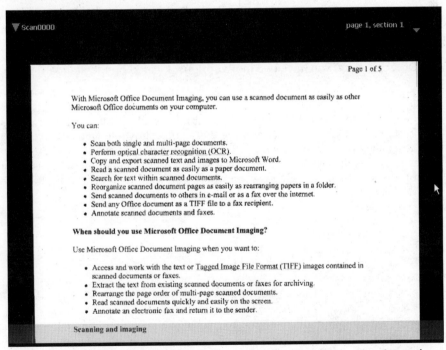

Figure 44-5: Reading view enables you to ignore the program you're using and simply concentrate on the document.

You can scroll through the document using the wheel on your mouse, the minimalist arrows in the upper-right corner, or your arrow keys. To return to Page view, press Esc.

Using Optical Character Recognition (OCR)

Optical Character Recognition (OCR) recognizes the shapes of letters in a digital image and exports that information as a text or word-processor file.

Caution OCR is reasonably accurate, but I've never yet seen an OCR-generated document that didn't need additional editing, so make sure you review the result carefully.

As noted, MODI applies OCR by default to any document you scan. You can also use it on documents you've opened or imported by clicking the Recognize Text Using OCR button on MODI's Standard toolbar, or choosing Tools ➪ Recognize Text Using OCR.

Once OCR is complete, you won't see much difference in the document's appearance, except that any thumbnails to which OCR has been applied have a tiny image of an eye in the lower-right corner, and the ScreenTip you see if you hover your mouse pointer over the thumbnail informs you that it "Contains OCR information."

With OCR complete, you have two more options, located on the Standard toolbar:

✦ **Find.** You can now search for specific text in the document.

✦ **Send Text to Word.** This does just what it says; click this button, or choose Tools ➪ Send Text to Word, and the dialog box shown in Figure 44-6 opens. You can choose which available recognized text you wish to send (the current selection, selected pages, or all pages), whether to maintain pictures in output or remove them, and the location where you want to save the resulting Word document.

Figure 44-6: The Send Text To Word dialog box lets you set options for sending the text you retrieved from a scanned document using OCR to Word.

Note   Maintaining pictures when sending OCR text to Word does not mean that any graphics in the scanned document will also show up in the Word document. If you select the option to Maintain pictures in output, your Word document will contain the text that was scanned both as new text and also as an image of that text. In other words, your new Word document will contain text and a picture of the text.

 Note   Remember that only basic formatting (paragraph marks, bullets, bold, and italics) gets sent along to Word. Expect to do quite a bit of additional formatting to get the file to look the way you want it.

Annotating Documents

MODI provides several annotation tools that enable you to make notes, circle and underline, highlight, and even add pictures to scanned documents. These options are available from the Annotations toolbar, which is to the right of the View toolbar.

Five options are available from this toolbar:

✦ **Pen.** Use this to hand-draw circles, lines, or whatever you like (and can draw with a mouse) on the document. Click the downward-pointing arrow to the right of the Pen button to select the size of point you want and the color. If you don't see one you like, click Pen Settings to set the thickness, color, and tip style (round or chisel).

✦ **Highlighter.** Unlike the pen, the highlighter overlays the text with a wash of color without hiding what's underneath. You can set its width, color, and whether it uses a round or chisel point, too.

✦ **Insert Text Box.** This inserts a resizable box into which you can type text; it has a colored background to distinguish it from the text of the document itself. To format the text in the box, select the text, right-click, and choose Format Text from the shortcut menu. Alternatively, select the text and choose Edit ➪ Format Text from the menu. To format the text box itself (fill color and transparency, as well as position on the page and visible borders), right-click on the box and choose Format Text Box.

✦ **Insert Picture.** Use this to insert a resizable picture from a file.

✦ **Select Annotations.** Click this to turn your mouse pointer into a selection tool, so you can select annotations by pointing and clicking (or by drawing a box around several at once).

Figure 44-7 shows a document annotated (in rather unlikely fashion, I admit) with pen markings, highlighting, a text box, *and* a picture.

Initially, annotations are not permanent parts of the document, and you can hide them by choosing Tools ➪ Annotations ➪ Hide Annotations. You can choose to make annotations permanent, however, by choosing Tools ➪ Annotations ➪ Make Annotations Permanent.

Note   You may be prompted to save your document before the annotations can be made permanent. Also be aware that if you are working with a black-and-white or grayscale document, your nicely colored annotations will be saved in black and white or grayscale.

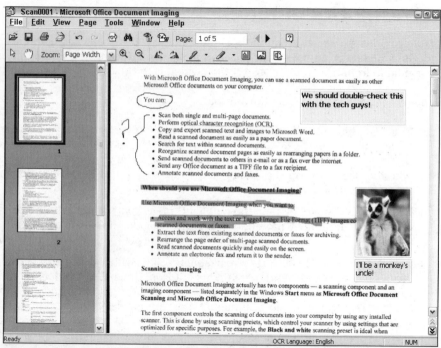

Figure 44-7: You can annotate a digitized document in many different ways.

Customizing Microsoft Office Document Imaging

You can readily customize many of the MODI features that are otherwise scattered among many different tools and dialog boxes by choosing Tools ➪ Options. This opens the Options dialog box shown in Figure 44-8.

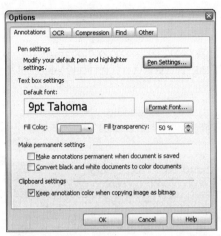

Figure 44-8: Customize Microsoft Office Document Imaging here.

This dialog box offers five tabs:

✦ **Annotations.** Here you can modify the default pen and highlighter settings and the default font and formatting for text boxes, including the fill color and its transparency. In addition, you can choose to make annotations permanent when the document is saved, and to convert black-and-white documents to color documents. There's also an option to keep annotation color when you copy the image as a bitmap; you can turn this option off if you wish.

✦ **OCR.** Use this tab to deactivate Auto rotate and Auto straighten, which otherwise turn pages and straighten them as needed to help OCR perform its work; you can also change the language setting (this doesn't affect your default language setting for other Office applications). The Indexing service button controls how the TIFF and MDI files that MODI creates are indexed by the Windows Indexing Service (Fast Search). You have to be logged on as a system administrator to change these indexing service settings, however.

✦ **Compression.** Here you can set the TIFF color compression and MDI compression levels, optimizing for file size or quality.

✦ **Find.** Use this tab to specify how the Find command works, including whether or not to ignore white space characters (with this checked, if you entered "check box" in Find, Find would also bring up "checkbox"; with this unchecked, it wouldn't). The other three options here relate only to searches in Japanese.

✦ **Other.** This tab provides a Reset button to return MODI to its place as default program for opening TIFF files, if you've changed that somewhere else (e.g., in an Explorer window under Tools ➪ Folder Options ➪ File Types). It also lets you set your File Import preferences, choosing what format to save imported files in and where.

Distributing Documents

Once you've scanned and saved a document in MODI, you can distribute it to others by saving it to an accessible location on the network, or by sending it via e-mail or fax.

To e-mail a scanned document as an attachment, choose File ➪ Send To ➪ Mail Recipient (as Attachment). This opens a blank message in your default e-mail client, with the scanned image already attached.

To fax a scanned document, choose File ➪ Send To ➪ Fax Service.

Summary

Microsoft Office Document Imaging enables you to bring non-Office documents in old-fashioned paper form into the Office environment by scanning them into your computer. With Microsoft Office Document Imaging, you can perform numerous useful tasks:

✦ Scan documents using a variety of presets, or specify your own scanner settings.

✦ Open or import existing documents in TIFF or MDI format.

✦ View documents using a variety of zoom levels or read documents in a special Reading mode that eliminates the distraction of toolbars and menus.

✦ Rearrange multipage documents by clicking and dragging thumbnails.

✦ Turn the text from a scanned document into an editable file.

✦ Annotate documents, either temporarily or permanently, with pen marks, highlighting, text, and/or pictures.

✦ E-mail or fax documents to others.

✦   ✦   ✦

Using Microsoft Office Picture Manager

I've mentioned several times in the course of this book that although the various Office applications contain some basic picture-editing tools, you can usually improve pictures more by working with them in a dedicated graphics program.

As it happens, Office 2003 contains a tool specifically designed for working with your pictures—not just editing them and touching them up, but helping you find and organize them.

It's called Microsoft Office Picture Manager, and this chapter provides a quick overview of its features and capabilities.

Adding Picture Shortcuts

When you first open Microsoft Office Picture Manager, it doesn't look too exciting (see Figure 45-1), because it doesn't have any pictures in it. By default, it shows you three panes: one called Picture Shortcuts; one in which the pictures you work with will be displayed once you've established some picture shortcuts; and a task pane that contains links to basic commands, and where the various tools Picture Manager offers will be displayed in more detail (as buttons, sliders, etc.) as you make use of them.

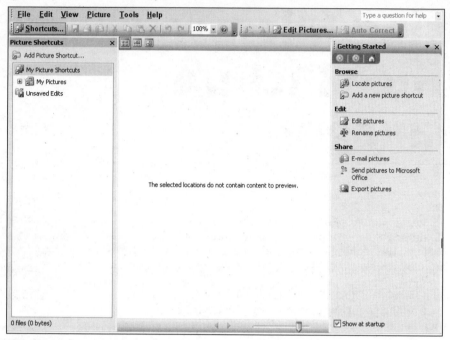

Figure 45-1: Here's what Picture Manager looks like on startup.

Before you can work with a picture in Picture Manager, you have to add a shortcut to that picture. You can do this folder by folder, or you can have Picture Manager scan your computer for pictures and add shortcuts to those it finds.

Adding shortcuts to individual folders

To add shortcuts to the pictures in an individual folder, click either the Add Picture Shortcut link in the Picture Shortcuts pane or the Add a new picture shortcut in the Getting Started task pane. Browse to the folder whose contents you want to create shortcuts to, and click Add. The folder is added to the Picture Shortcuts list, and the pictures the folder contains appear as thumbnails in the main viewing pane (see Figure 45-2).

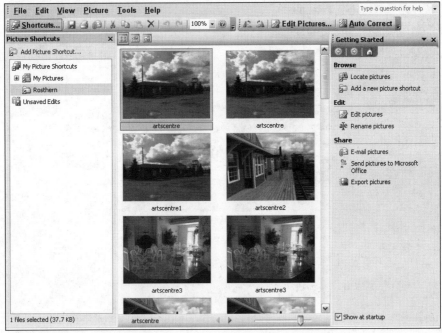

Figure 45-2: When you add a folder containing images to Picture Manager's Picture Shortcuts, the pictures it contains are displayed in the main viewing pane.

By default, pictures are displayed in Thumbnail view. You have two other views from which to choose: either from the View menu or by clicking one of the three icons above the view pane. Single Picture View is self-explanatory; it displays a single picture, perforce bigger than the pictures in Thumbnail view.

The other option, Filmstrip view (see Figure 45-3), displays the currently selected picture at a size that fills the available space. You can move through the pictures in the folder one at a time by using the arrow buttons below the currently displayed picture (similar to the Forward and Back buttons in Internet Explorer) or use the horizontal scrollbar at the bottom of the pane.

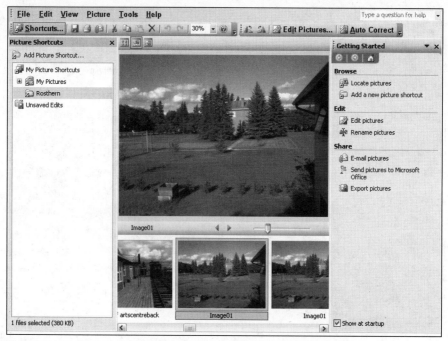

Figure 45-3: Filmstrip view offers an alternative way to look at your pictures.

In all views, you can adjust the current zoom with the slider just to the right of the arrow buttons shown in Figure 45-3. In Single Picture view and Filmstrip view, this zooms the currently selected picture in and out; in Thumbnail view, it zooms all the thumbnails in and out, so you can see more of them on the page at one time, or fewer if you prefer.

If you zoom into a picture so close that you can't see all of it, you can adjust its placement in the view pane simply by clicking and dragging anywhere inside the

...ly locating pictures and adding shortcuts

...e Picture Manager scan your drives and automatically
...ny pictures you may have saved. To do so, either click
...Getting Started task pane or choose File ➪ Locate
...asked to specify which drive you want to search (or
...lick OK, and Picture Manager takes care of the rest.

Tip

Picture Manager can recognize and work with numerous different picture types, including .jpg, .gif, .bmp, .png, .tif, .wmf, and .emf files. If you want, you can make Picture Manager your default viewer for any of these types of picture files. To do so, choose Tools ➪ File Types and select from the list provided the file types you want to open with Picture Manager. (This list also appears the first time you run Picture Manager.)

Caution

Picture Manager looks for folders containing at least five images, each of which is at least 300 pixels × 300 pixels in size. (It was likely designed this way to avoid adding shortcuts to folders containing large numbers of tiny images.) Because of this, Picture Manager may not find all of your image files when you use the Locate pictures links; in those cases, you will need to add the shortcuts manually to the appropriate folders.

If you think that Picture Manager has found too many image folders and you're swimming in shortcuts, you may want to remove some of them from the Picture Manager shortcut pane. To do this, simply right-click the folder and choose Remove as Shortcut. Be careful not to click Delete; this will not only delete the shortcut from Picture Manager, it will also delete that folder completely from your drive!

Editing Pictures

After you've added picture shortcuts to the pictures you want to work with, you can manipulate those pictures in a variety of useful ways, as detailed in the following sections.

Renaming pictures

The easiest way to rename a picture is to simply double-click on the name (it's displayed underneath any thumbnail image in Thumbnail or Filmstrip view), and then type the new name.

Cropping pictures

One thing I quickly learned in my years as a newspaper photographer is that almost any photo can be improved in the darkroom by simply cropping out extraneous material, to focus attention on the photo's main subject.

Stray limbs from passers-by, unnecessary trees and buildings, cluttered backgrounds — all can be ruthlessly removed, making the final image much more eye-catching an informative.

To crop a picture in Picture Manager, select it in one of the views and click the Edit Pictures button on the toolbar, choose Edit ⇨ Edit Pictures, or right-click on a thumbnail and choose Edit Pictures from the shortcut menu. This opens the Edit Pictures task pane, shown on the right in Figure 45-4.

Figure 45-4: Picture Manager's editing tools are readily available from the Edit Pictures task pane.

Now click Crop. If you are in Filmstrip or Single Picture view, black crop marks like ~~~es shown in Figure 45-5 will appear around the picture. (If you are in ~~~ew, you'll be automatically switched over to Filmstrip view.) At the ~~~op task pane opens.

~~~ quickly by clicking and dragging the crop handles. (Hold ~~~ing so if you want the cropped area to maintain the orig-~~~ finer control, use the Crop handles controls in the ~~~ move the left, right, top, and bottom crop handles

Figure 45-5: When you want to crop a picture, black crop marks enable you to quickly accomplish the task.

Tip One of the most useful innovations in Picture Manager is the Aspect ratio control in the Crop settings area of the Crop task pane. This locks the cropping you do into the correct aspect for the four most common sizes of photographs: 3 × 5, 4 × 6, 5 × 7, and 8 × 10. This is great if you plan to print digital photos using Photo Library for use in a standard photo album or frame; the images from digital cameras don't necessarily have the same proportions as images from a conventional camera. You can also select either Landscape or Portrait orientation for the cropped area.

When you click OK, the cropped image replaces the original image in your view pane—and your Picture Shortcuts pane indicates that you now have an Unsaved Edit (more on that in the section "Saving Your Edited Pictures" later in this chapter).

Tip To return to the Edit Pictures task pane and continue editing pictures, either click the Back to Edit Pictures link at the bottom of the Crop task pane or use the Back button at the top to move back through the task panes you've recently opened until you reach the Edit Pictures pane again.

Using Rotate and Flip

Another option in the Edit Pictures task pane is Rotate and Flip. This opens the Rotate and Flip task pane, with the basic controls you would expect: You can rotate the picture left 90 degrees with one link, rotate it right 90 degrees with another, or rotate it left or right a precise number of degrees (rotate it right by entering a positive number, left by entering a negative number).

You can also flip the picture horizontally (creating a mirror image) or vertically.

 Note What's the difference between flipping and rotating? Think of the picture as being transparent, so that you can see it by looking through either side A or side B. When you rotate a picture, you keep the current side up and simply turn the picture right or left. When you flip a picture, you turn it over so you're looking through it from the opposite side. The big difference is that flipping a picture reverses everything in it; text, for example, will become a mirror image.

Resize

The Resize option in the Edit Pictures task pane opens the Resize task pane, shown in Figure 45-6. At the bottom, this pane shows you the original size of your picture. You have four options, selected by radio buttons and additional controls:

✦ **Original Size.**

✦ **Predefined width × height.** This drop-down list provides several standard sizes for various purposes: document, large and small; Web, large and small; and Email, large or small. The precise dimensions in pixels are also listed.

✦ **Custom width × height.** Here you can enter the exact width or height you want to apply to the picture. You don't have to worry about distorting the picture's proportions as you do so; when you click OK, Picture Manager takes the last dimension you enter here in either box and adjusts the other dimension to maintain the picture's original proportions. (In other words, you can't deliberately distort a picture in Picture Manager; to get that kind of effect, you'll need to edit the picture in a different program.)

✦ **Percentage of original width × height.**

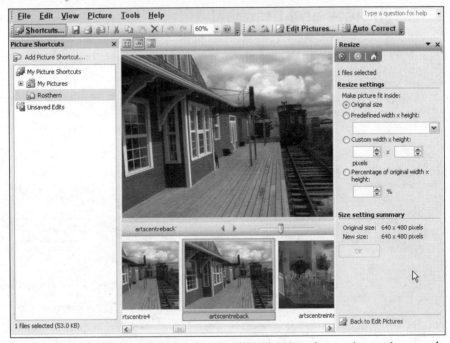

Figure 45-6: Use the Resize task pane to adjust the size of your pictures in several different ways.

Touching Up Pictures

In addition to manipulating the name, size, shape, and orientation of your pictures, Picture Manager enables you to alter their brightness, contrast, and color. It can even help you eliminate *red-eye,* the demonic glowing eyes that show up in flash photographs taken in a dark room because the subjects' wide-open pupils allow light to reflect off of their blood-rich retinas.

You'll find these touch-up tools on the Edit Pictures task pane (refer to Figure 45-4).

Auto Correct

This is the easiest touch-up tool of all; it lets Picture Manager make all the decisions about brightness, contrast, and color. If one of your pictures looks too light or dark, washed out or too contrasty, or if the colors don't look right, select it and click the Auto Correct button in the Edit Pictures task pane.

Brightness and Contrast

Click the Brightness and Contrast link in the Edit Pictures task pane to open the Brightness and Contrast task pane (see Figure 45-7). Use the brightness slider to make the picture either brighter or darker, and the Contrast slider to increase or decrease the difference between dark and light areas in the picture. Alternatively, you can enter a specific number, from -100 (minimum brightness or contrast) to 100 (maximum brightness or contrast).

Figure 45-7: Adjust brightness and contrast with these handy sliders.

Three controls are available under Advanced settings, although only the Midtone: adjust midtones only slider is visible unless you click the More link to the right of Advanced settings. If you do, you'll also discover the Highlight: adjust light colors only and Shadow: adjust dark colors only sliders. Both of these options do exactly what they suggest, and they can help you turn a picture with too little detail to be useful into one much more aesthetically pleasing (and a few words closer to the proverbial thousand that every picture is supposed to be worth). You can hide the Highlight and Shadow controls again by clicking Less.

Color

Click the Color link in the Edit Pictures task pane to open the Color task pane (see Figure 45-8). Here you'll find an additional automatic correction button, labeled Enhance Color. If you click it, your mouse pointer changes to a targeting symbol (which you can also see in the figure) when you move it over the picture. Center this on an area that should be white and click; Picture Manager automatically adjusts the color of the entire picture to make that area white.

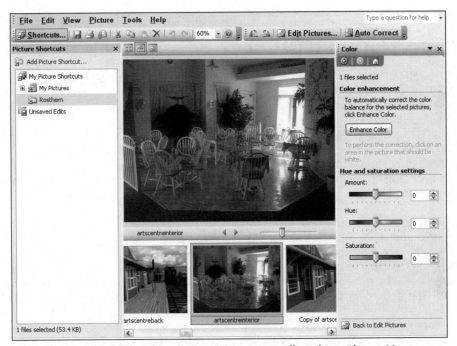

Figure 45-8: Adjust the color of your pictures manually or have Picture Manager automatically enhance it.

Alternatively, you can adjust hue and saturation yourself. The top area adjusts hue: The colored Hue slider lets you choose the color you want to increase; the Amount slider lets you adjust how much of the chosen hue should be added. Slide it to the far right, and the picture will take on that hue exclusively; slide it to the far left, and that hue will be removed from the picture entirely.

Saturation increases the color intensity of the entire picture. This can make colors stand out in an otherwise drab picture — one, for example, that was taken on a cloudy day.

Red Eye

To fix red eyes in a photo, click the Red Eye Removal link on the Edit Pictures task pane to open the Red Eye Removal task pane.

When you move your mouse pointer over the selected picture, it turns into a targeting symbol. Aim this at the red eyes you want to correct, and click; a tiny picture of a red eye appears. Click as many red eyes in the picture as you want to fix, then click OK. Picture Manager gets the red out.

Compressing Pictures

Picture Manager's other major function is to compress pictures. If you're planning to print a picture and want it as close to photo quality as possible, then compression is *not* something you want to do; even the best compression results in some loss of information.

However, if you're planning to simply use pictures in an ordinary document in which they should look good but not photo-perfect, compression can save you time by speeding up the printing process. In addition, of course, smaller files are always better when they're going to be displayed by a Web page or e-mailed.

To compress a picture, select it in either Thumbnail or Filmstrip view, and then click the Compress Pictures link in the Edit Pictures task pane to open the Compress Pictures task pane (see Figure 45-9). Compressed pictures are saved in the Unsaved Edits folder, so you can preview them before saving them; the original picture is untouched by the operation. You can also undo the Compress Pictures operation with the Undo command, just as you can other picture-editing operations.

Compress Pictures offers you four radio buttons. As you select one, you can refer to the Estimated total size figures at the bottom of the task pane to see how much smaller the new file will be.

- ✦ **Don't compress.** Uncompressed, the original picture selected in Figure 45-8 is 380 KB in size.

- ✦ **Documents.** This is intended for pictures that will illustrate documents, where photo-quality reproduction isn't needed. If you choose this, the picture is saved in a compressed file format and resized to fit within a window of 1024 × 768 pixels. My 380 KB picture would be reduced to 229 KB by this option.

✦ **Web pages.** Onscreen pictures don't need the high resolution of printed pictures, because even the best monitor can't match the resolution of a good printer. Moreover, it's best to use pictures that can be viewed in their entirety, obviating the need to scroll. If you choose this, the picture is saved in a compressed file format and resized to fit within a window of 448 × 336 pixels. My 380 KB picture would shrink to a mere 44 KB with this option.

✦ **E-mail messages.** Essentially, this turns the picture into a thumbnail, suitable for inserting into an HTML-format e-mail (perhaps with a link to the full-size image on a Web site somewhere). It saves the picture in a compressed file format and resizes it to fit within a window of 160 × 160 pixels. If this is selected, my 380 KB picture would shrink to 5.61 KB.

Click OK when you've made your selection.

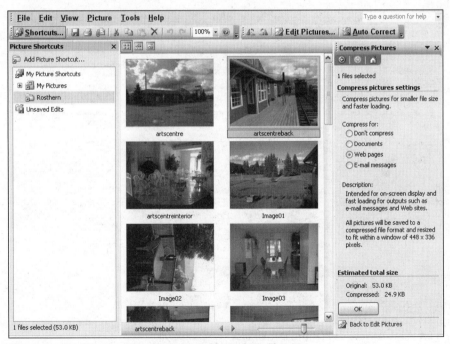

Figure 45-9: Compressing pictures reduces their file size.

Tip   Pay attention to the picture's KB sizes when you select each of these options. If your image has already been optimized — for example, for Web use — "compressing" for documents can actually cause the picture's file size to increase. As well, compressing a picture that has already been compressed will usually result in an unacceptable loss of quality.

Sharing Pictures

Picture Manager offers you an easy way to share your pictures: You can simply right-click on a thumbnail (or select several thumbnails and right-click on any one of them) and choose Send To ⇨ Mail Recipient.

This opens the E-mail task pane shown in Figure 45-10. You first have to set a few parameters. Decide whether you want to send the picture as a preview in the body of an HTML message, as an attachment, or as both. (If you're going to send it in the body of an HTML message, be sure that the recipient's e-mail client is set up to display HTML messages; if the recipient is seeing e-mail as plain text only, the picture won't appear for him or her.)

Figure 45-10: Here's what the E-mail task pane looks like.

If you're including a preview in the body of the message, you have to choose the Preview size (Thumbnail, Postcard, or Large Postcard) from the Preview size drop-down list. You can also choose a Preview layout: Table or 1 per line.

Note The Send to ⇨ Microsoft Office option in the shortcut menu opens a small dialog box you can use to insert the picture either into an open Office file or into a new Outlook message, Word document, PowerPoint presentation, or Excel worksheet; the Options link lets you set the size of the picture, among other things.

When you've made your decisions, click the Create Message button. Picture Manager opens your default e-mail editor, with the pictures previewed and/or attached. If they're included as attachments, an Attachment Options task pane opens, which offers you the options for resizing pictures again (see Figure 45-11); choose small (448 × 336 pixels), Medium (640 × 480), or Large (1024 × 768) from the drop-down list.

Caution Don't try to blow up a picture to a size much larger than its original. It will quickly start to look grainy, or "pixilated," because you're not increasing the number of pixels in the picture, just making the existing ones bigger.

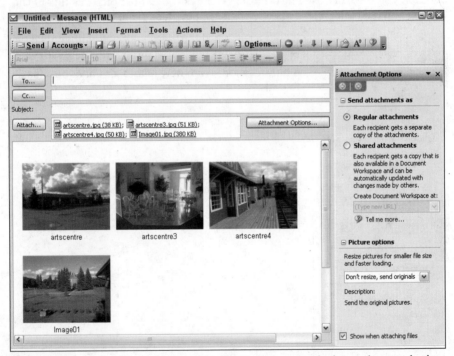

Figure 45-11: Here's the message Picture Manager created when I chose to both preview and attach four pictures to an e-mail message and selected the Table layout for previews.

In the Send attachments as area of the task pane, you have two options: Regular attachments (each recipient gets a separate copy of the attachments) and Shared attachments (each recipient gets a copy that is also available in a Document Workspace, a feature of SharePoint Services, and can be automatically updated as recipients make changes).

Cross-Reference   For more information about SharePoint Services, see Chapter 47.

Add any text you want, enter the address and subject line, and click the Send button, and your pictures are on their way.

Exporting Pictures

You can also use Picture Manager to change pictures from one picture format to another. To do so, choose File ➪ Export or click the Export pictures link in the Getting Started task pane. This opens the Export task pane shown in Figure 45-12.

Figure 45-12: Use the Export task pane to send files to a new location — with new names, or under new file formats.

Choosing a location

Choose the location to which you want to export the files. You can export them to their original location, or you can export them to some other location on your computer or network, or to external media.

Renaming your files

You can rename your pictures by unchecking the Original file names box and clicking the Rename link. This opens the Rename task pane shown in Figure 45-13.

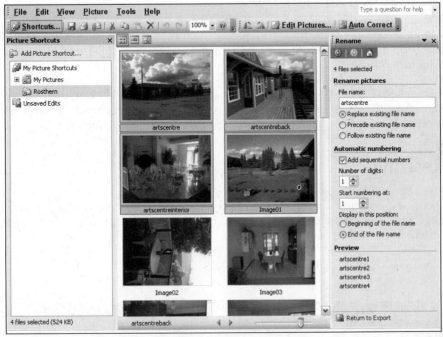

Figure 45-13: Rename your exported pictures here.

In the Rename task pane, you can either completely rename pictures or alter their names with additional identifying information. Type text into the File name field, and then choose either Replace existing file name, Precede existing file name, or Follow existing file name. If you choose Replace existing file name, then the files will be exported under the new file name. All the selected files will have the same name, but by default the second file will be named filename1, the third file filename2, and so on.

You can change the format of these identifying numbers by using the controls at the bottom of the Rename task pane. You can use one, two, three, or four digits, and you can set the starting number.

Another option is to not enter a new file name and instead choose Precede existing file name or Follow existing file name. This keeps the existing file names, but assigns numbers to them. Or, you can not enter a new file name and choose Replace existing file name; this assigns numbers only, no names, to the pictures.

These options may sound confusing, but you can see exactly what effect your choices will have (i.e., what the new filenames will be) by looking at the preview at the bottom of the task pane.

Choosing a file format

You can use Picture Manager to change pictures from one file format to another by using the Export command and changing the format in the Export with this file format drop-down list. Your options are Original File Format, JPEG, PNG, TIF, GIF, and Windows Bitmap.

If you choose JPEG, the JPEG options link becomes active; click on this, and you can adjust the compression level of the resulting file. Increasing the compression level makes the file smaller, but it will also result in a loss of quality.

Resizing

You can automatically resize the pictures you're exporting from the Export using this size drop-down list (again, your options are Document, Web, and Email, with large and small options for each), or you can click the Resize link to open the Resize task pane discussed earlier.

When you've made all your selections, click OK.

Understanding Picture Formats

Here's a brief description of the various file formats Picture Manager lets you use for pictures:

✦ **JPG (Joint Photographic Experts Group).** Pronounced "jay-peg" and also known as JPEG, this popular format is designed specifically for the display of photographic images in full color. You can control the amount of compression involved, which means you can control the quality of the final image.

✦ **TIF (Tagged-Image File Format).** TIF files are uncompressed or slightly compressed bitmap files, which tends to make them rather large but of very high quality. They can be read by pretty much all graphics software but not by Web browsers.

✦ **GIF (Graphics Interchange Format).** GIF is the format most often used for non-photographic images such as cartoons and icons. GIF images are limited to 256 colors, so they aren't as good for photographs.

✦ **PNG (Portable Network Graphic).** This format is growing in popularity. It has a higher rate of compression than either GIF or JPEG, with less loss of detail.

✦ **BMP (Windows Bitmap).** This is an uncompressed format: large, but high-quality.

Saving Your Edited Pictures

The changes you make to pictures in Picture Manager aren't final until you save them. Whenever you alter a picture, the changed version is placed in the Unsaved Edits folder in the Picture Shortcuts list on the left. If you click that folder, the saved pictures are displayed.

If you decide you don't want to save the changes you've made to a picture in the Unsaved Edits folder, right-click on it and choose Discard Changes. (Since you aren't affecting the original picture, you won't get a warning message when you choose this option.) If you do want to keep it, you have to save it.

Choose File ⇨ Save to save the changed picture and replace the original picture. This saves your changes, all right; it also permanently removes the original picture, so use this with caution.

Save As opens a standard Save As dialog box, which enables you to save the picture under a new name or with the same name in a different location.

Tip   If you're completely certain you want to keep all the changed pictures in your Unsaved Edits folder and replace the originals with them, right-click the Unsaved Edits folder and choose Save All. Conversely, choose Discard All Changes to clear out the Unsaved Edits folder and leave the original versions of the pictures unchanged.

Printing

To print a picture from Picture Manager, select it and choose File ⇨ Print. This opens the Photo Printing Wizard, which takes you step by step through the process of printing your picture (see Figure 45-14). After you choose a printer and a layout (the wizard offers several, and a preview to show you how your picture will look in each one), you're ready to print. Piece of cake!

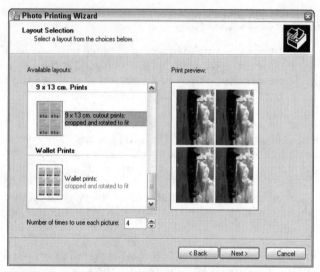

Figure 45-14: Here is the first screen of the Photo Printing Wizard, which offers numerous layouts from which to choose.

Summary

Microsoft Office Picture Manager is a new tool included with Office 2003 to help you organize, find, edit, and touch up your collection of pictures. It enables you to perform countless tasks, including the following:

✦ Manually or automatically establish Picture Shortcuts to the pictures on your computer

✦ Rename, crop, rotate, flip, and resize pictures

✦ Adjust the brightness, contrast, and color of pictures, automatically or manually, and eliminate red-eye

✦ Compress pictures to reduce their file size

✦ E-mail pictures

✦ Export pictures to new locations, and automatically rename, resize, and change their file formats at the same time

✦ Print pictures in a variety of layouts

✦   ✦   ✦

Collaborating on a Network

I n most business environments, very few things are done solely by individuals. Projects are planned, discussed, dissected, and carried out by teams of people working together. If one of the final products of a project is to be an Office document, it's helpful if all members of the team can share information, files, and ideas online—either via the company's internal computer network or (if team members are more far-flung) via the Internet.

Office makes it possible!

Resource Sharing and Security

If your computer is hooked up to a local network of some type, chances are good you have a choice of saving your files either to your own computer or to a location somewhere on the network.

Access to various folders on the network is overseen by whoever looks after the network; it's quite likely that many people not in your workgroup have access to a particular folder. However, in most Office applications you can control who has access to files you place in network folders. You can also allow or deny access by network users to your own computer's hard drive.

Setting file-sharing options when saving

Whenever you save a Word or Excel document, you have the option of restricting access to it.

In Word's standard Save or Save As dialog box, choose Tools ⇨ Security Options. This opens the Security dialog box shown in Figure 46-1.

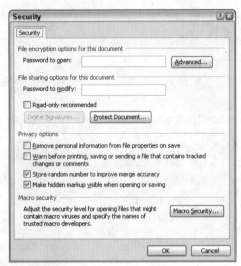

Figure 46-1: The Security dialog box in Word lets you restrict access to any file.

Three levels of file-sharing security are provided here:

✦ **Password to open.** If you enter a password here, only someone who knows the password can open the file. (Passwords can be up to 15 characters long and can contain letters, numbers, and symbols. They are case-sensitive. As you type them in, only asterisks are displayed.)

Caution

Password protection isn't as secure as you might think; there are utilities available on the Internet that claim to be able to crack open protected documents (in fact, a common question in Office-related newsgroups is "I've forgotten my password; how do I get in?").

✦ **Password to modify.** If you enter a password here, anyone can open the file, but only someone who knows the password can modify it. Users who don't know the password can open the file only as read-only—and that includes you if you forget your password, so don't!

✦ **Read-only recommended.** If you check this, users opening this file will get a message suggesting they open it as a read-only file. If they do, they can't change the original document; instead, any changes they make must be saved as a new document, under a different name.

In Excel, you have the same options, but you get to them by choosing Tools ➪ General Options in the Save or Save As dialog box.

In PowerPoint, you have only the password-protection options; you don't have the Read-only recommended option. You get to the password-protection options by choosing Tools ➪ Security Options in the Save or Save As dialog box.

Word offers additional Privacy options: You can choose to remove personal information (e.g., the document author's name and the names of people who have added comments) from the file before it is saved; have Word warn you before printing, saving, or sending a file that contains tracked changes or comments; and stop Word's usual practice of generating random numbers during merge activities to indicate to itself that two documents are related. Even though those numbers are hidden in the files, they could conceivably be used to show that two documents were related. Be aware, however, that removing this option will reduce the accuracy of merging operations.

Protecting documents

In addition, you can fine-tune the level of access you want to allow people to have to a particular file by applying protection to it.

Protecting documents in Word

To protect a document in Word:

1. Choose Tools ➪ Protect Document (or click the Protect Document button in the Security Options dialog box from the previous section). This opens the Document Protection task pane shown in Figure 46-2.

2. Under Formatting restrictions, check the checkbox if you want to limit formatting to a selection of styles, and then click Settings to open the Formatting Restrictions dialog box (see Figure 46-3).

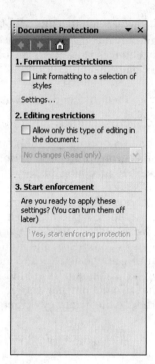

Figure 46-2: Protect Word documents using this task pane.

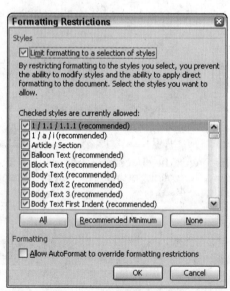

Figure 46-3: Specify formatting restrictions on a shared document here.

3. Uncheck any styles you don't want to allow in the document, or click the Recommended Minimum button to have Office automatically select what it considers to be a minimum number of styles. Click All to check all styles and None to uncheck them all.

4. If you want to allow AutoFormat to override these formatting restrictions, check that box at the bottom of the dialog box, and then click OK.

5. Back in the Document Protection task pane, if you want to allow only certain types of editing in the document, check the Editing restrictions box. This activates a drop-down list with four options: Tracked changes (all changes are permitted, but they're automatically tracked), Comments (no changes are permitted, but comments can be inserted), Filling in forms (no changes are permitted, but data can be entered into forms), and No changes (no changes are permitted—the document is read-only).

6. Next, enter any exceptions to the editing rules. If you have established user groups, they're listed; otherwise, click More users and enter the user names for those to whom you want to give greater editing access in the Add Users dialog box that appears.

7. Finally, back in the Document Protection task pane, click the Yes, start enforcing protection button if you're ready to apply the protection settings to your document.

Protecting documents in Excel

To protect an Excel worksheet or workbook:

1. Choose Tools ➪ Protection.

2. From the submenu, choose which part of your Excel document you want to protect: a particular worksheet or the workbook. You can also choose to protect and share your workbook (more on sharing workbooks a little later in this chapter).

3. If you choose Protect Sheet, you'll see the dialog box shown in Figure 46-4. Here you can enter a password to unprotect the sheet, and then choose from the long list provided which actions you're willing to allow users of the worksheet to perform.

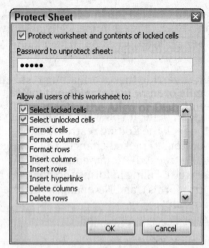

Figure 46-4: Set protection for Excel worksheets here.

4. If you choose Protect Workbook, you'll see the dialog box shown in Figure 46-5, which contains three options:

- **Structure** prevents users from adding, deleting, moving, hiding, or unhiding worksheets.

- **Windows** prevents users from moving, hiding, unhiding, resizing, or closing workbook windows.

- **Password** allows you to enter a password that users must have before they can unprotect the workbook.

Figure 46-5: Protect elements of your workbook here.

5. Protect and Share Workbook brings up a dialog box with only one box you can check, to prevent those sharing the workbook from turning off change tracking. You can enter a password that they'll have to know before they can do so.

6. Allow Users to Edit Ranges opens the dialog box shown in Figure 46-6. Here you can apply passwords to specific ranges within your worksheet. Even if the worksheet as a whole is protected, users who have the password can edit the ranges you specify. You can also click Permissions to specify which users are allowed to edit the range without a password, and just so you don't forget, you can even paste permissions information into a new workbook so you can refer to it easily.

Figure 46-6: You can make ranges available for editing to those with the correct password even if the rest of the sheet is protected.

Protecting files in Access and PowerPoint

You'll learn about protecting Access files in detail later in this chapter. You need to use file system features to protect PowerPoint files; talk to your system administrator.

Using Information Rights Management tools

In previous versions of Office, the only way to protect sensitive information was to limit access to it, as described in the preceding sections. That didn't necessarily prevent the people who were granted access from copying the information and/or sending it to someone who wasn't supposed to have access to it.

Information Rights Management (IRM) is a new feature in Office 2003 that gives you greater control over files even when they're no longer on your computer or network. No matter where the file goes, the permissions you've assigned go with it, so that only those users you've approved can read or change it; you can also restrict printing and forwarding.

Note In order to use IRM, you must have access to a computer running Windows Server 2003, with Windows Rights Management activated. If you are working in a net-worked environment, consult your network administrator for details. As of this writing, Microsoft offers a trial Internet-based service for individuals based on the .NET passport system; follow the prompts the first time you attempt to use the fea-ture to sign up for that service if it's available (because it's just a trial service at this writing, it may not be by the time you read this book). Undoubtedly other providers of public IRM servers will come forward as well.

Whenever you create a document in Word, Excel, or PowerPoint, you can set IRM policies for it by choosing File ➪ Permission to open the Permission dialog box (see Figure 46-7).

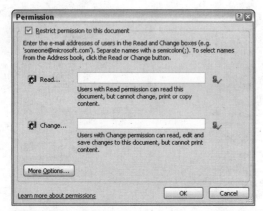

Figure 46-7: The Permission dialog box allows you to enter the e-mail addresses of users you'd like to be able to read or change a document's content.

Check the Restrict permission to this document box to activate the Read and Change options. Enter the e-mail addresses of users you want to give Read permis-sion to (they can read the document but can't change, print, or copy its content) and those you want to give Change permission to (they can read, edit, and save changes to the document but can't print it). Click the Read and/or Change buttons to access e-mail addresses in your Address book.

To fine-tune permission, click More Options. This opens the dialog box shown in Figure 46-8.

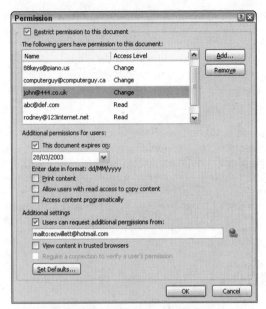

Figure 46-8: Fine-tune the permissions you
grant with these controls.

At the top is a list of all the users you've given permission to access the document
and the access level they currently have (your name shows up at the top of the list
with Full Control). Highlight the user whose permissions you'd like to fine-tune, and
then choose from the options in the Additional permissions for users area. You can:

✦ Set an expiration date for the user's permission.

✦ Allow users to print content.

✦ Allow a user with read access to also copy content.

✦ Give specific users permission to read a document, print a document, copy a
document, or edit a document, or any combination of those; you can also set
an expiration date.

✦ Allow users to access the content programmatically — that is, to open the file
in the same program that created it and edit its content.

Under Additional settings, you can enter a link to an e-mail address (or other hyperlink) that will pop up whenever a document with restricted permission is forwarded
to an unauthorized individual, so that that individual can request permission to view
it. If you leave this blank, unauthorized individuals simply see an error message.

You can also choose to allow users to view the content in a browser; a Rights-Management Add-on for Internet Explorer makes this possible. Otherwise, IRM-protected files can be opened in Office 2003 only.

Tip   If you generally provide the same permissions to many different users, click Set Defaults to make those permissions the default set.

Note   Network administrators can create permission policies that define who can access documents, workbooks, and presentations and what editing capabilities (if any) they have. For example, a company might define a policy called "Confidential" that allows documents to be opened only by users whose e-mail addresses use the company's domain name. Once these policies have been defined, they appear in alphabetical order on a submenu under File ➪ Permission; authors simply choose the one they want to use.

Sharing Excel Workbooks

One of the most common types of Office documents shared on a network is an Excel workbook because workbooks frequently contain budgetary or sales information that is constantly being updated by a variety of users. Excel lets multiple users share a workbook so they can all work on it at the same time; it also lets you combine several workbooks into a single workbook.

Creating a shared workbook

To create a shared workbook:

1. Choose Tools ➪ Share Workbook. This opens the dialog box shown in Figure 46-9.

2. If you want more than one person to be able to edit the workbook at the same time, or to combine several workbooks into one shared workbook, check the box at the top of the dialog box.

3. To fine-tune the way the workbook is shared, click the Advanced tab (see Figure 46-10). In the Track changes section, choose the number of days you want to track changes — if at all.

4. In the Update changes section, choose when you want changes made to the workbook to be updated: whenever the file is saved, or automatically how ever often you specify. If you choose to automatically update changes, you can choose to save your changes and see everyone else's changes at the specified interval, or just see everyone else's changes at the specified interval without saving yours.

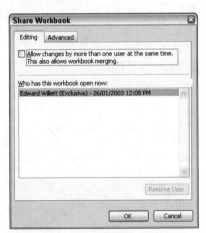

Figure 46-9: The Editing tab of the Share Workbook dialog box shows you who currently has the workbook open.

Figure 46-10: The Advanced tab lets you choose your method of tracking, updating, and dealing with conflicting changes.

5. Sometimes two or more users will make conflicting changes to the workbook—changes that are mutually exclusive. You can decide here how to deal with those changes either by having Excel ask you which change should take effect or by replacing any conflicting changes with your own changes every time you save.

6. Click OK.

Here's one example of a shared workbook being useful: A sales group could share a common workbook, with each salesperson in the group recording his or her sales as they occur; that would give the sales manager the ability to monitor their sales, and the progress of the group as a whole, in "real time."

Reviewing changes

Once a workbook is being shared, you can review changes in it by choosing Tools ⇨ Track Changes ⇨ Accept or Reject Changes. Choose the changes you want to review in the Select Changes to Accept or Reject dialog box shown in Figure 46-11. You can filter the changes you want to look at by using the three fields. The When field lets you look for changes made on a specific date; the Who field lets you look at changes made by everyone, everyone but you, only you, or only any other user who has made changes; and the Where field lets you specify a range of cells in which to look for changes.

Any changes found are brought to your attention in the Accept or Reject Changes dialog box (see Figure 46-12). You can choose to accept or reject any or all of the changes brought to your attention.

Tip   Choose Tools ⇨ Highlight Changes to highlight any changes made throughout the workbook.

Figure 46-11: Use this dialog box to select the changes you want to review.

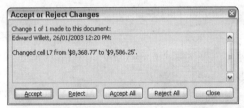

Figure 46-12: Changes made to the workbook are brought to your attention here.

You can merge different versions of the same shared workbook into a single workbook by choosing Tools ➪ Compare and Merge Workbooks. Track Changes must be turned on (and the workbook must be shared) for this to work.

Collaborating in PowerPoint

You can send your PowerPoint presentation to others for comment and revision, and then combine all the reviewed presentations into one for easy review.

Note The easiest way to send a presentation for review is to choose File ➪ Mail Recipient (for Review). This feature, common to most Office applications, is discussed later in this chapter.

To do so, open the presentation you want to combine reviewed presentation with and choose Tools ➪ Compare and Merge Presentations. Browse for the presentations you want to merge, and then click Merge.

PowerPoint opens the Revisions Pane and the Reviewing toolbar to allow you to sort through all the suggested revisions and decide whether you want to apply them (see Figure 46-13).

PowerPoint points out the suggested revisions in several ways. In the Revisions Pane, you can see graphical representations of the altered slides, or you can view them as a list. You can choose whether to look at the changes suggested by all reviewers, or just those made by specific reviewers. The names of reviewers who made changes to a particular slide appear above the thumbnail of the slide, color-coded. Click the name of any reviewer whose changes you want to accept.

You can also call up a shortcut menu by pointing at the thumbnail and then clicking the downward-pointing arrow that appears beside it. The shortcut menu also lets you apply changes by the current reviewer, show only that reviewer's changes, preview animation (in case there was a change to an animation) and, finally, finish off your review of that reviewer's changes by clicking Done With This Reviewer.

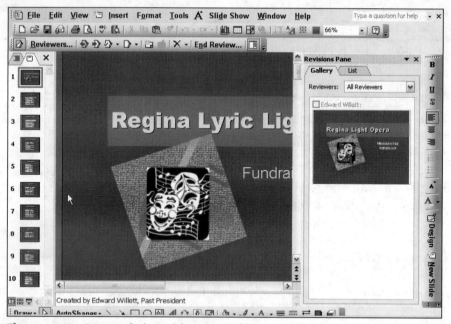

Figure 46-13: PowerPoint's Revisions Pane shows you all the changes reviewers have made to your presentation.

The list version of the changes in the Revisions Pane is a little different; it shows a list of changes to the slide (text edits, new graphics, etc.), and a separate list of Presentation changes (slide transitions, for instance). The Previous and Next buttons at the bottom of the task pane take you from slide to slide.

The Reviewing toolbar, also visible in Figure 46-13, is very similar to Word's Reviewing toolbar. You can step from item to item, choose to apply or unapply, edit and delete comments, choose which reviewers' changes you want to see, end the review, and toggle the Revisions pane off and on.

 Caution   Clicking End Review discards all unreviewed changes in the merged presentation, so don't click it until you're certain you're done.

You can also toggle markup on and off. The Markup feature shows callouts detailing changes made to the presentation without obscuring the presentation or affecting its layout (see Figure 46-14). Accepting a change is as simple as checking it off in the markup callout.

Figure 46-14: PowerPoint's Markup feature provides a way to see changes in the context of the slide they're on.

Sharing Access Databases

The information in the typical Access database is valuable not only to people working in Access but also to people working in all other Office applications. Typically, the Access database changes constantly as changes are made to the data in it; by drawing on it, network users can ensure that their own Office projects always contain the most up-to-date information.

If you don't need any extra security on your Access database, you can share it just as you can any other file in Office (see the first part of this chapter). If you do need extra security, however, Access can provide it in several ways: passwords, permissions, user groups and accounts, and encryption.

Using passwords

A password is the easiest way to protect a database. Every time a user tries to access a password-protected database, he or she is asked to provide a password. Without it, the database can't be opened.

To set a password for a particular Access database:

1. Choose File ➪ Open.

2. In the Open dialog box, find the database you want to assign the password to and select it.

3. Click the down arrow next to the Open button and choose Open Exclusive. This ensures that no one else can open the database while you are assigning a password to it.

4. The database opens. Now choose Tools ➪ Security ➪ Set Database Password.

5. In the Set Database Password dialog box, enter the password once in the Password field and then enter it again in the Verify field (all you'll see are asterisks).

Note   Remember, passwords are case-sensitive, are limited to 15 characters, and can contain letters, numbers, and/or symbols.

6. Click OK.

Once the password is set, it doesn't matter if you're the user who created the database and assigned the password to it: If you forget or lose the password, you can't open the database (at least, not without the use of a third-party password-cracking tool like the ones available at www.lostpassword.com—the existence of which is why a password provides only low-level security).

To remove the password, open the file exclusively again, and then choose Tools ➪ Security ➪ Unset Database Password. Enter the password and click OK.

Creating user and group accounts

If a password doesn't provide enough security, you might want to set up user accounts and groups, which will require users to supply both an account name and a password before they can access a database. This is called user-level security.

To set up user and group accounts:

1. Open a database.

2. Choose Tools ➪ Security ➪ User and Group Accounts. This opens the dialog box shown in Figure 46-15.

Figure 46-15: Add new users and new user group accounts here.

3. By default, Access creates two groups: Admin and Users. Admin users can perform administrative functions such as adding users and groups; users can access only the database itself.

4. By default, Access creates an Admin user called, unimaginatively, Admin. Choose it from the Name drop-down list, and then click the Change Logon Password tab. Type the password you want to use in the New Password and Verify fields. (Once you've closed the database and Access, the next time you open it you'll have to log on using this account name and password.)

5. Click the Users tab.

6. To create a new account, enter the name of the user in the Name box, and then select the group you want to add him or her to; click the New button.

7. Enter the name of the user and the personal ID—a string of four to 20 characters of your choice that Access combines with the user's name to identify that user in the group.

8. Click OK to create the new account.

9. To create a new group, click the Groups tab, click the New button, and enter a name and personal ID for the new group.

10. To delete a user, click the group he or she is a member of in the Available Groups list; then locate the name in the Name list and click Delete. To delete a group, click the Groups tab, highlight the group you want to delete, and click Delete.

Securing the database

Access makes securing the database easy by providing a wizard. Choose Tools ⇨ Security ⇨ User-Level Security Wizard, and then follow the instructions, providing information as needed. At one point you're asked to choose which objects in the database should be secured. All secured objects will thereafter be accessible only by users in the Admin group until you grant other users permissions.

The Wizard makes a backup copy of your database and then encrypts the original.

Note   You can't run this wizard if the database is open in exclusive mode.

Assigning permissions

To assign permissions, choose Tools ⇨ Security ⇨ User and Group Permissions. This opens the dialog box shown in Figure 46-16.

Figure 46-16: You can limit the access of certain users or groups of users to specific databases and objects by setting permissions.

To assign permissions from this dialog box:

1. Click the Users radio button if you want to assign permissions to individual users, or the Groups radio button if you want to assign permissions to groups.

2. Select the name of the user or group you want to assign permissions to.

3. Select the object you want to assign permissions for from the list of objects, and select the object type from the drop-down list.

4. Use the checkboxes to set permissions for that user or group: Check boxes to grant permission for the action described to be performed; uncheck boxes to deny that permission.

5. When you've set permissions for all the users and groups, click OK. You'll have to close and open the database again for the permissions to fully take effect.

6. Click the Change Owner tab to assign ownership for the database or objects in it to someone other than the Admin user.

Encryption

Encryption makes it impossible to view a database file in any other program except Access, and even in Access you have to decrypt it first. It's usually used in conjunction with a password or user-level security (remember, the User-Level Security wizard encrypts the database as part of securing it).

To encrypt a database:

1. Choose Tools ➪ Security ➪ Encrypt/Decrypt Database.

2. Locate the database you want to encrypt in the Encrypt/Decrypt Database dialog box, which looks just like a Save As dialog box.

3. Click OK.

4. Another dialog box opens that looks much like the first; in this one, specify the name and location of the encrypted file.

5. Click Save.

You can save the encrypted file over the original by specifying the same filename and location.

To decrypt a file, follow the same procedure, but choose an encrypted file to be decrypted in Step 2.

Distributing Office Documents

Group collaboration on documents requires the capability to save Office documents somewhere where they are available to everyone in the group. Office provides plenty of help to that end; the latest development in this process is SharePoint Services.

Cross-Reference
For more information on SharePoint Services, see Chapter 47.

Even if your organization isn't running STS, though, you can readily share documents and link them together by placing hyperlinks in them.

In Windows, any accessible network site shows up in your file-related dialog boxes and in My Computer, just like local disks and folders.

In Office dialog boxes such as Open and Save As, click the My Network Places icon to navigate to computers on the network and their folders (or else click on shortcuts you may have made to those locations, if you've gone that route). Once you've opened the right folder, you can store and retrieve documents on another computer exactly as you do those on your own PC.

Sharing documents via e-mail

Instead of sharing your documents over a network, you can share them via e-mail. This not only makes it possible for someone who isn't on your organization's network to view the document, it also enables you to more tightly control who sees the document, and when.

To do so, choose File ➪ Send To and choose an option from the resulting menu:

✦ Choose one of the Mail Recipient options to send the document to a single person, or to several people at once. The disadvantage is that if you're sending a document to several reviewers for comments, they'll all get their own copy of the file. This means you'll have multiple copies of the document returned to you, which can be a nuisance.

✦ To avoid that, choose Routing Recipient to specify a series of recipients who will receive the document one at a time. This allows each of them to see the comments of previous reviewers, ensures that only one copy of the document is in circulation, and ensures that you get only a single copy of the document back, one that contains all the comments from all of the reviewers. You can also set up routing so that you're notified by e-mail each time the document is forwarded to a new recipient, and so that the document is automatically returned to you when the last reviewer on the list is done with it.

Sending a document (without routing it)

There are three versions of the Send To ➪ Mail Recipient command:

✦ **Send To ➪ Mail Recipient** sends the document in the body of the e-mail.

✦ **Send To ➪ Mail Recipient (for Review)** sends the document as an attachment and fills in the Subject line and body with brief messages asking for the document to be reviewed.

✦ **Send To ➪ Mail Recipient (as Attachment)** attaches the document to a blank message, which you then fill in as you want.

Routing a document

To route a document to a series of recipients, choose File ⇨ Send To ⇨ Routing Recipient. In the Routing Slip dialog box (see Figure 46-17), select recipients for the routing list by choosing Address (Outlook will pop up its security dialog box and ask you for permission to access the Address book). The order of recipient names in the To list determines the order in which they receive the document. You can change the order by selecting a name and clicking the Move buttons at right.

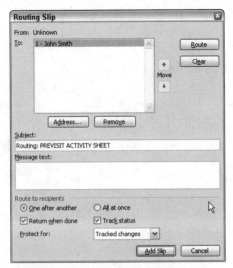

Figure 46-17: Route a document to a series of recipients using this dialog box.

Supply a subject and any text you want in the accompanying message, and then, at the bottom of the dialog box, specify whether you want the document to be sent to each recipient in sequence or to all of them at once. The difference between this option and simply sending out the document using the Send To ⇨ Mail Recipient command is that the Routing Slip option enables you to track the document's status and, in Word, protect the document from unauthorized changes.

Check Return when done if you want to get the document back automatically after the last reviewer is done with it, and check Track status if you want e-mail notification as it reaches each recipient

In Word, choose from among the following options in the Protect for list:

✦ **Comments.** This allows recipients to add comments but prevents them from changing the document's contents.

✦ **Tracked Changes.** This toggles the Track Changes command. By default it is on, so you can see all changes the reviewers make.

✦ **Forms.** Use this if the document you're sending around is a form that you want the recipients to fill in. They can then fill in the form but not alter the form itself.

✦ **(none).** This allows recipients to change the document as they want, and there's no automatic tracking of the alterations they make, although they can turn Track Changes on manually if they want.

To send the document to the first recipient immediately, choose Route. If you prefer, however, you can close the dialog box without sending the document by choosing Add Slip. When you've decided to send the document, choose File ➪ Send To ➪ Next Routing Recipient.

Sending documents that aren't already open

You don't have to open an Office document (or any other file, for that matter) to e-mail it to someone. Start from within an Office Open or Save dialog box — or in My Computer, Windows Explorer, or Outlook's own file manager. Right-click the document and choose Send To ➪ Mail Recipient. Outlook creates an e-mail message containing the document as an attachment; you enter the message text and address.

Posting documents to Exchange folders

If you prefer not to e-mail your document to a large number of recipients, an alternative is to place it in an Exchange public folder, where it will be available to anyone who has access. Of course, this works only if your group is using Exchange Server.

With the document open, choose File ➪ Send To ➪ Exchange Folder. A list of Exchange public folders appears. Specify the destination folder and click OK.

Sending documents to online meeting participants

If you're participating in an online meeting, you can send an open document to someone else participating in the meeting by choosing File ➪ Send To ➪ Online Meeting Participant and choosing from the list provided the participant to whom you want to send the document.

Summary

In this chapter you learned some of the ins and outs of sharing Office information over a network. Highlights included the following:

✦ You can add a level of protection to Word and Excel documents when you're saving them by specifying passwords for opening and/or modifying the file.

✦ You can add protection to Word and Excel files by choosing Tools ➪ Protect Document in Word and by choosing Tools ➪ Protection in Excel.

✦ You can create a shared workbook in Excel by choosing Tools ➪ Share Workbook.

✦ PowerPoint lets you merge presentations altered by reviewers with your copy and then provides a Revisions pane and onscreen markup features to help you accept or refuse the suggested changes.

✦ Access databases are one of the most commonly shared types of Office files. You can make them freely available or create very tight security for them by using the commands under Tools ➪ Security on the menu.

✦ E-mail is another way to share Office documents. You can send documents to individuals or to a sequential group of recipients for review.

✦　　✦　　✦

Windows SharePoint Services with Office System

Windows SharePoint Services is a Web-based service that provides a collaboration and information presentation environment that integrates with Microsoft Office 2003 applications such as Word 2003, Outlook, Excel, PowerPoint, and Access.

Windows SharePoint Services (WSS) is an evolution of SharePoint Team Services (STS), which shipped with Microsoft Office XP. If you have previously used SharePoint Team Services, you will find the new and improved features offered by WSS much more helpful. Windows SharePoint Services has the potential to become an integral and extremely useful part of your everyday Office experience.

Note Windows SharePoint Services requires installation on Microsoft Windows Server 2003, Standard Edition, Enterprise Edition, or Datacenter Edition. This chapter assumes you have access to a server running Windows SharePoint Services. If you don't have such access, you might still find the information in this chapter informative. Visit www.microsoft.com/sharepoint/ to locate a SharePoint hosting partner if you don't have access to your own SharePoint site.

In this chapter, you learn how to access and use the features of Windows SharePoint Services to collaborate on your Office 2003 documents. You learn how to create, share, and access Web-based contacts and calendars. You learn how to work with lists and how to use the powerful Datasheet list view and calculated columns to bring the power of Excel to SharePoint lists.

Working with SharePoint Sites and SharePoint Lists

One of the central features of Windows SharePoint Services is its use of lists. Lists include such items as Announcements, Contacts, Events, Links, and Tasks and Issue Tracking. The placement of these items on a Windows SharePoint Services Web page is up to the site designer. You can create, access, and modify lists and add new list items via your Web browser.

> **Note** Although you can access and use many of the features of Windows SharePoint Services sites online using Web browsers such as Netscape, it's better to use Internet Explorer 6 or later when working with WSS sites. Support for browsers such as Netscape is improved with WSS, but IE 6 and later offer the highest level of support and compatibility.

Many of the features available with lists on Windows SharePoint Services sites are common to other Windows SharePoint Services items and views. Document Libraries, for example, are presented in a list-type view.

Accessing SharePoint Services sites

One of the advantages of Windows SharePoint Services is that SharePoint sites can be accessed via any Web browser that can access the server that hosts the SharePoint site. In some cases, site access can be restricted to local network users, whereas, in other cases, SharePoint sites can be accessed over the Internet from any location that can access the Internet. The capability to access Windows SharePoint Services sites over the Internet makes WSS a powerful and flexible collaboration environment.

> **Note** Although you can, and do, perform many tasks with Windows SharePoint Services sites using a Web browser, such as Internet Explorer, you can more successfully work with Office 2003 documents on SharePoint sites if the Office 2003 application that is associated with those documents is also installed.

Access methods depend on your administrator and how the site and server that support the site are configured. In most cases, in order to access a Windows SharePoint Services site, you need an account on the server that hosts that site. An exception to this is when the site is configured for anonymous access. Anonymous users have basic read-only access to SharePoint sites. If you have any difficulty accessing your Windows SharePoint Services site, contact your SharePoint administrator or the Windows SharePoint Services documentation if you are the administrator.

When you first receive an account on a Windows SharePoint Services site, you will usually receive an e-mail similar to that shown in Figure 47-1. Save the e-mail for future reference.

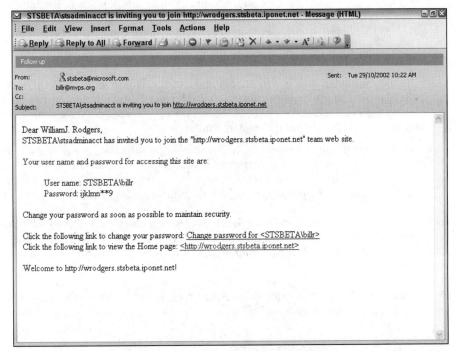

Figure 47-1: Your invitation to Windows SharePoint Services

You might also receive a separate e-mail specifying the site group you belong to. Site groups are dealt with in the section of this chapter entitled "Windows SharePoint Services site permissions."

The content of the introductory e-mail you receive might differ depending on whether the e-mail is from a server located on your LAN or on a server on the Internet. The e-mail shown in Figure 47-1 was generated from a WSS server located on the Internet and contains a username and randomly generated password in addition to a link to the SharePoint site.

Tip   If you receive a welcome e-mail, such as is shown in Figure 47-1, with a randomly generated password, take advantage of the Change Password link in the e-mail to change your password to one you can more easily remember.

Regardless of how you obtain your Windows SharePoint Services V2 login information, there are three basic pieces of information you will usually need in order to access and work with SharePoint sites:

✦ The location of the Windows SharePoint Services site. This is in the familiar form of a URL such as `http://Lindy`, `http://STS.Wigletco.net`, or `http://STS.Wigletco.net/mysite/`. The form of the URL depends on the location of the Server hosting the site and the location of the site on that server.

✦ The username you will use to access and use the Windows SharePoint Services site. Usernames are usually entered in the format `SERVERNAME\username`, where `SERVERNAME` is the name of the server or domain you are connecting to and `username` is, of course, your username.

✦ The password you will use to access and use the Windows SharePoint Services site. This can be a password generated by SharePoint, or, in some cases, it may be the password for the account you have on the server that hosts the site or the password of your domain user account.

To connect to a Windows SharePoint Services site you simply open the URL of the site in your Web browser. You can do this by entering the URL of the site in the address bar of your browser or by clicking the link provided in your welcome e-mail.

When accessing a SharePoint site, you might be presented with a login dialog box similar to that shown in Figure 47-2.

Figure 47-2: Use this dialog box to authenticate your username and password with the SharePoint server.

If presented with a login prompt, as shown in Figure 47-2, enter your username and password and then press OK to log on to the site. Refer to the preceding list if you have any difficulties.

If you are not presented with a login prompt similar to that shown in Figure 47-2 when you attempt to access your site, don't despair. You might later be presented with the login prompt or your network might be configured in such a way that you automatically authenticate with the server.

Note   The login prompt you see when accessing your Windows SharePoint Services site might be slightly different than the one shown in Figure 47-2, depending on the operating system installed on the machine you are using. The basic login information you need to provide, however, remains essentially the same.

Windows SharePoint Services site permissions

The operations you can perform on Windows SharePoint Services sites depend on the site group you are a member of. Although most site group names and permissions are configurable by the site administrator, there are five default site groups. The five default groups and a description of their rights are shown in Table 47-1. Users can also be given limited access rights to a particular page, Document Library, list, or item in a list without being specifically assigned to a group.

Table 47-1
Default SharePoint Site Group Permissions

Group Name	Description
Guest	Users who are given only limited rights to a particular page, Document Library, list, or item in a list are automatically assigned to the Guest group. This group cannot be deleted or customized.
Reader	Readers are given basic read-only access. They cannot add content and cannot personalize main sites. They can, however, create their own top-level sites using Self-Service Site Creation (SSSC) and can personalize and customize such sites. When a Reader creates their own site using SSSC, they become the Administrator and owner of that site without affecting their Reader group membership for any other site.
Contributor	Has all the rights of a Reader but can also manage list permissions, manage personal groups and views, personalize Web Part Pages, and add content to existing lists and Document Libraries. A Contributor can personalize Web parts. A Contributor cannot create new lists or Document Libraries.

Continued

Table 47-1 *(continued)*	
Group Name	**Description**
Web designer	Has all the rights of Contributor but can also manage lists, delete items, define and apply themes and borders, link style sheets, and cancel checkout. Web designers can create new lists and Document Libraries and can modify the structure of the site.
Administrator	Has all the rights of other site groups, plus rights to manage site groups and view usage analysis data. An Administrator has complete control over the site. The Administrator group cannot be customized or deleted.

Note   In order for a Reader, or any other user with adequate permissions, to be able to create a top-level site using Self-Service Site Creation (SSSC), the site administrator needs to have first enabled SSSC. When SSSC is first enabled, a new announcement is automatically made on the Announcements list of the home page of the root Web site. This announcement contains a link to the SSSC tool. SSSC sites are usually contained in the `sites` directory. A site created using SSSC is like your own personal little SharePoint site of which you are the administrator.

If, during use of your SharePoint site, you cannot perform the operations you want to, contact your site administrator and ask for your permissions or group membership to be changed.

Exploring the Windows SharePoint Services site

Figure 47-3 shows the start page of a typical Windows SharePoint Services site. Your site might look different but will still contain the same basic elements. The SharePoint main home page usually contains a Quick Launch Bar and a "main" Web part zone. The Quick Launch Bar provides quick and easy access to many of the Windows SharePoint Services features.

Provided you have adequate permissions, you can customize the site layout to suit your own personal preferences. You can, for example, minimize existing Web parts or add Web parts to the main page frame. In Figure 47-3, the drop-down menu for customizing the Announcements list is expanded, whereas the MSNBC Stock News Web part is minimized. The Modify this page drop-down menu (shown at the top right in Figure 47-3) is available on some pages. This allows you to add Web parts and change the design of the main page. Changes you make are stored in the server database. Log on to the site from another computer and you see your own personalized pages. Users with adequate permissions can apply changes made to pages to all other users.

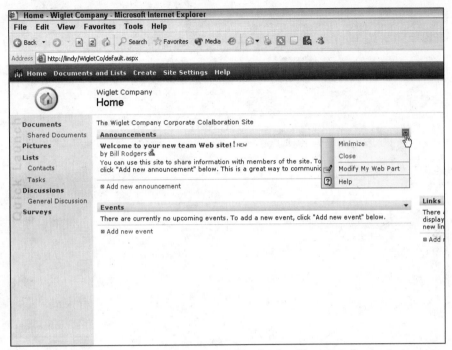

Figure 47-3: SharePoint sites are presented in the familiar HTML format in Internet Explorer.

Adding items to existing lists

Links, Announcements, Contacts, Events, Tasks, and the Issue Tracking feature are all examples of SharePoint lists. Lists provide a place to store and present data in a convenient, standardized format with some level of customization available. You can add and remove columns in lists and change the order of fields in a list.

The information stored in lists is available for export to many Office 2003 applications.

Figure 47-4 shows the default view for a Contacts list with an item's drop-down menu expanded. The drop-down menu shown in Figure 47-4 allows you to view, edit, or delete the item. By selecting the Alert Me entry in the drop-down menu, you can choose to receive an e-mail alert when changes are made to the item or the item is deleted. The default list style and layout for all lists are similar to that shown in Figure 47-4.

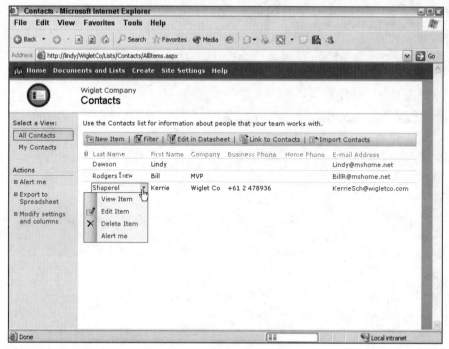

Figure 47-4: You can use the drop-down menu available with selected items to work with that item.

Tip   You will find the Actions submenu, shown in the left pane in Figure 47-4, in the views of many SharePoint libraries. Use the Alert me link to obtain an e-mail notification when items are added, changed, or deleted. This is particularly useful for new announcements and to keep your eye on documents, stored in a Document Library, that are modified by other users. The Export to spreadsheet link allows you to export the list to Excel. You can use the Modify settings and columns link to customize the display of the library and control many aspects of the library (including specific permissions for the library, general library settings, saving the list as a template, and modifying the list template). Explore what options are available to you. Note that here the term "library" includes all WSS views that are presented in a list format.

To add new items to an existing list, follow these steps:

1. Select the list by clicking its entry in the Quick Launch bar. You are presented with a view similar to that shown in Figure 47-4. For Events, Announcements, Links, and other lists shown in a Web part zone, you can select the item header in the Web part zone to give a view as shown in Figure 47-4 (to work with Announcements, for example, select Announcements by clicking the bold Announcements heading).

2. Select the New Item icon. You are presented with a New Item form customized to the particular type of list you are working with. For Events, Announcements, Links, and other lists shown in a Web part zone, you can skip Step 1 and go directly to the New Item form by selecting the relevant Add new link in the Web part zone (refer to Figure 47-3).

3. Complete the New Item form with relevant data. Fields marked with a red asterisk are required. You can also attach a file to the new item via the attach file icon.

Note For security purposes, Windows SharePoint Services, by default, blocks the saving and retrieving of a number of file types. The SharePoint site administrator can configure the types of files that are blocked. Consult your administrator if you want to work with blocked file types.

4. Select Save and Close.

Note Picture Libraries are a special type of list with unique features intended to suit the presentation of pictures and to integrate with Microsoft Picture Library. You can apply the same skills you use to create and work with SharePoint lists to Picture libraries. Unique features of Picture Libraries include the capability to edit pictures in the library directly with Microsoft Picture Library; the capability to send pictures from the library directly to Outlook, Word, Excel, or PowerPoint; the capability to download Full Size, Preview, or Thumbnail versions of the pictures; and a new View Slide Show feature for a stunning presentation of your pictures.

Creating new Windows SharePoint Services lists and libraries

Creating new Windows SharePoint Services lists and libraries is easy.

To create a new SharePoint list, follow these steps:

1. Click the bold Lists heading in the Quick Launch bar.

2. In the new Documents and Lists view, click Create List.

3. Choose the type of list you want to create by clicking it. You are presented with six types of lists to choose from by default: Links, Announcements, Contacts, Events, Tasks, and Issue Tracking.

4. In the New List Web form, enter a name and description for the list and choose whether to include the list in the Quick Launch bar. A list description is not mandatory.

5. Select Create.

New Document Libraries, Form Libraries, Picture Libraries, Discussions, and Surveys can be created using steps similar to the previous ones. Just replace "Lists" with the type of library you want to create in the previous steps and choose from the available library templates for that library type in Step 3.

Note   Libraries of any type can also be created via the Create link in the top bar of the Windows SharePoint Services home page (see Figure 47-3). The Create link additionally allows you to create a blank Web page, a Web Part Page, or a WSS Subweb. You can also create a custom list via the Create link. Custom lists can be created from a basic list that you can add columns to either using provided templates or in Datasheet view, or can be based on an existing Excel spreadsheet that already contains the data you want in your list. A Web Part Page is a special customized SharePoint page, composed from Web parts, that you can create to consolidate dynamic information into one central location. Datasheet views are discussed later in this chapter.

Working with Datasheet views and linking lists to Excel and Access

The Windows SharePoint Services Datasheet view brings the power and familiarity of Excel to list-type SharePoint libraries. The Datasheet view brings such features as Cut, Copy, Paste, Fill, and AutoComplete to list-type libraries. Column and row resizing is implemented, and you can sort and filter data in Datasheet view. Data analysis is available, and you can chart the list with Excel, export and link the list to Excel, export the list to Access, or create an Access or Excel PivotTable report from the list all from within Datasheet view.

You work with the Datasheet view in much the same way you work with Excel. Cells can be filled with data, and right-clicking areas of the Datasheet provides context-specific actions for a single cell, an entire row or column, or the whole list.

To explore the power and some of the features of the lists Datasheet view and the high level of integration with Excel, this section works through an example.

The example begins by opening Excel and creating a row of header information named Month, Expenses, and Approved. In the first cell of the Month column, enter January. In the first cell of the Expenses column, enter a currency such as $2687.43. Leave the first cell of the Approved column blank. Next, save the Excel spreadsheet with an appropriate name.

You are now ready to create a new list from the Excel spreadsheet. In this example, you'll create the list from within Excel and link the WSS list to Excel so that updates made in either the WSS list or the Excel spreadsheet can be synchronized with the other.

To create a new list from an Excel spreadsheet and link the spreadsheet to the new list, follow these steps:

1. Open the Excel spreadsheet.

2. Select the cells with data.

3. From the Excel Data menu, select List ⇨ Create List.

4. In the new Create List dialog box, ensure the My List Has Headers checkbox is selected and then press OK.

5. From the Excel Data menu or the List and XML toolbar, select List ⇨ Publish List. If not already visible, the List and XML toolbar can be displayed by right-clicking a toolbar and selecting it.

6. In the new Publish List to SharePoint - Step 1 of 2 dialog box, enter the location of the SharePoint server, give the list a name, and enter a description (optional).

7. To ensure that a link is established between Excel and the new list, select the Link to the new SharePoint list checkbox in the Publish List to SharePoint - Step 1 of 2 dialog box.

8. Select Next. The next Publish List to SharePoint - Step 2 of 2 dialog box gives you the opportunity to review the data types that SharePoint Team Services V2 will use for each column.

9. Select Finish.

Your new list can be accessed at any time by opening the original Excel spreadsheet, selecting the list in Excel, and choosing Data ⇨ List ⇨ View List on Server from the Excel main menu or by choosing List ⇨ View List on Server from the List and XML toolbar.

Tip   You can also create a new Windows SharePoint Services list from an Excel spreadsheet by selecting Create from the site Home page and then selecting Import spreadsheet from the Custom section of the Create Page Web page.

Now that you have the basis of your list created on the server, you are ready to work with the Datasheet view of the list. You can view and edit any list in Datasheet view by selecting the Edit in Datasheet link in the view of that list if it is provided.

First, let's take a look at the Fill feature implemented with Datasheets. The Month column in the Datasheet example is a prime candidate for demonstrating the Fill feature.

To use the Datasheet Fill feature, follow these steps:

1. Open the existing SharePoint list in Datasheet view.

2. Select the cell you want to use as the basis of the Fill and position your mouse at the lower-right corner of that cell until the mouse pointer turns into a cross.

3. Left-click and drag the mouse cursor vertically down until you have filled the number of cells you want.

4. Release the mouse button.

Figure 47-5 illustrates the procedure for using the Fill features with this example. Once the cursor is released, the enclosed cells are filled with incremented months. Cells are incremented only if SharePoint can predict some sort of pattern to the cells. If SharePoint cannot predict a pattern, the Fill method duplicates the initial cell over the range of selected cells.

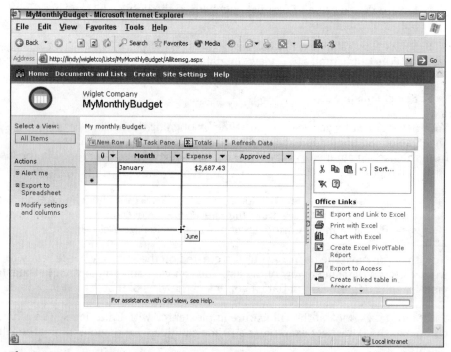

Figure 47-5: Drag and release to apply the fill to the Datasheet's columns.

Note The Datasheet task pane is shown in Figure 47-5. The Office Links section of the task pane allows you to export and report a list with Excel or Access. Use the Export and Link to Excel option if you want to export and link an existing list to Excel. The task pane can be toggled on and off via the Task Pane link in the top bar in Datasheet view or by clicking the Show Task Pane arrow on the right side of the Datasheet component.

Next, you'll change the format of the Approved column in the example to display a drop-down menu with two options: Approved and Not Approved. Columns can be formatted in Windows SharePoint Services in a number of formats. The complete list of formatting that can be applied to columns is: Single line of text, Multiple lines of text, Choice (menu to choose from), Number, Currency, Date and Time, Lookup (information already on this site), Yes/No (checkbox), Hyperlink or Picture, and Calculated (calculation based on other columns).

Note that the format that can be applied to a column depends on the type of list you are working with and whether you are modifying an existing column or adding a new column.

To format a list column, follow these steps:

1. Open the list in Internet Explorer.

2. In the Actions submenu in the left pane, select Modify settings and columns by clicking it.

3. In the new Customize page, in the Columns section, select the column you want to modify by clicking its link.

4. In the Name and Type section of the new page, select the radio button for the type of format you want to apply to the column. The page updates to provide options specific to the type of formatting you want to apply.

5. Make any other changes that are required or appropriate. In the case of the Choice (menu to choose from) format you enter each of your choices, on a separate line, in the space provided, and can also choose a default value and whether the choice appears as a Drop-Down menu, Radio Buttons, or Checkboxes that allow multiple selections.

6. Press OK to return to the Customize page and then select the Go Back link to return to the newly formatted list.

You can use the same basic procedure to add an existing column to a list. To add a new column to a list, in the Columns section of the Customize page (Step 3), select Add a new column instead of the column you want to modify. Adding a new column consisting of calculations based on other columns is a particularly powerful feature of WSS.

Figure 47-6 shows the completed example with the drop-down menu of Approved and Not Approved demonstrated. Additional expenses have been entered in the example to complete the list.

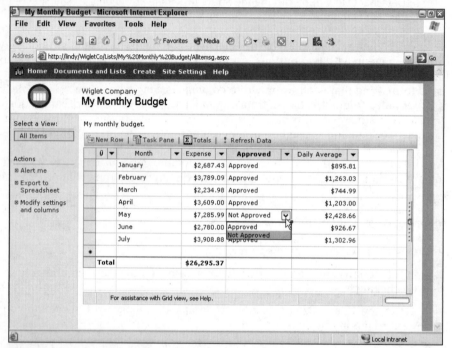

Figure 47-6: A custom choice and calculated column implemented in Datasheet view

Note the additional calculated column, called Daily Average, in the list shown in Figure 47-6. The Daily Average is simply Expense/30.

Calculated columns are added to lists using the same basic method you use to add any column. When creating a calculated column, you are required to enter a formula for that column and select the data type returned by that formula. In the above example, the formula for the daily average was entered as =[Expenses]/30 and the data type returned was set to number. The formula was entered by typing = into the Formula text box, selecting Expense in the Insert Column list, clicking Add to Formula from below the Insert Column list, and then typing /30 after [Expense] in the Formula text box.

Calculated columns support formulas using data in other columns and any Excel function with the exception of the following: Now(), Today(), Me(), and Rand(). Select any cell in a calculated column and the formula used is displayed in the status bar of the Datasheet view. When you hover your cursor over a cell in a calculated column in Datasheet view, the formula applied to that column is displayed as a ToolTip. Double-clicking in a cell in a calculated column in Datasheet view displays the formula for that column, in the cell, and allows you to edit it right there. The power of Excel is available with SharePoint lists.

Note also the Totals row in the list (shown in Figure 47-6). Totals can be calculated simply by selecting the Totals link in the top bar of the Datasheet view. The type of Totals that can be performed depends on the format of the columns in the list. In the case of the Month column in this example, all you can do is to count the months or leave that cell blank. For the Expense column, the Totals options available are None, Average, Count, Maximum, Minimum, Sum, Standard Deviation, and Variance.

To select the Totals expression to use in a Totals row, select the cell in the Total row where the Total will appear and select the type of calculation to be used from the drop-down menu displayed (by pressing the arrow in the left of that cell).

Figure 47-7 shows the options available for the Totals on the Expense column of the Budget example.

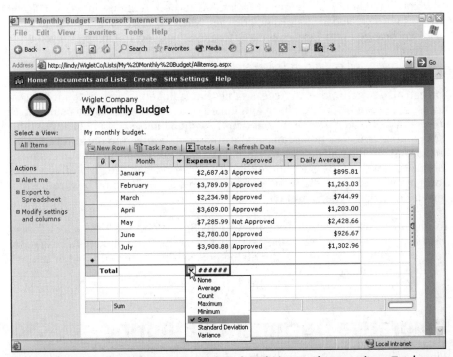

Figure 47-7: You can perform basic statistical analysis on columns using a Totals row.

Tip   To update the value in a calculated cell, simply select another cell.

Now that you have an Excel spreadsheet linked to a SharePoint list, you can add data to the list from within SharePoint or within Excel and easily synchronize those changes.

To synchronize a linked Excel spreadsheet with the SharePoint list it is linked to, follow these steps:

1. Open the linked Excel spreadsheet with Excel.

2. Select the list in the Excel spreadsheet.

3. From the Data menu in Excel, select List ➪ Synchronize List.

The preceding procedure applies for all Excel spreadsheets that are linked to SharePoint lists and not just lists created from an Excel spreadsheet.

Tip   When a SharePoint list is created from an Excel list that contains a calculated column, WSS converts all cells with individual formulas to values. Such converted columns cannot be reformatted into calculated columns in WSS. Calculated columns created in SharePoint, however, when exported to and linked to Excel or synchronized with Excel retain their formulas for direct use in Excel. If you want to work with a calculated column in both Excel and SharePoint, you need to create the calculated column in SharePoint.

You can also synchronize an Access table that is linked to a SharePoint list. An Access table can be created from and linked to a SharePoint list by using the Create Linked Table in Access option (found in the Office Links section of the Datasheet task pane). An Access table can also be created and linked to data stored on a SharePoint server via File ➪ Get External Data ➪ Link Tables in the Access menu. In this case, you need to select SharePoint Team Services in the Files of Type drop-down menu in the Link dialog box. Doing so opens a new dialog box from which you can enter or select the SharePoint site.

To synchronize a linked Access table with its SharePoint list, first select Tools ➪ Database Utilities ➪ Linked Tables Manager from the open, linked, Access database. Next, in the Linked Table Manager dialog box, select the linked table or tables to be updated and then select OK.

Collaborative Document Authoring

Windows SharePoint Services provides two features that facilitate collaborative document authoring: Document Libraries and Shared Workspaces. Both provide the means in SharePoint where workers, from any location able to access the SharePoint site, can share documents in real time.

Document Libraries provide a central location intended to store and present almost any type of file. The exceptions are those file types blocked by SharePoint and your administrator. A Shared Workspace further enhances a Document Library by adding its own Tasks, Links, and Members lists. A Shared Workspace is like its own little SharePoint site that focuses exclusively on collaborative document authoring. Think of a Document Library like you would the presentation area for your finished product, whereas a Shared Workspace is like the back office where you do the majority of your work and collaboration. Although some level of collaboration is supported in a Document Library, a Shared Workspace is specifically tailored to document collaboration and provides a high level of integration with supported Office 2003 applications.

Exploring Document Libraries and Shared Workspaces

Figure 47-8 shows a typical Document Library containing both an Excel spreadsheet and a Word document.

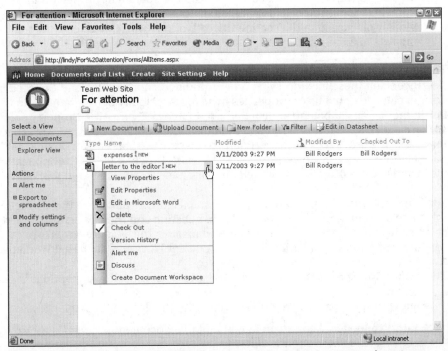

Figure 47-8: Use a Document Library to store and present important documents.

A Document Library has a default appearance similar to SharePoint lists. The left bar in Figure 47-8 contains an Actions submenu that can be used in the same manner as discussed earlier for lists.

The uppermost bar in Figure 47-8 has the following options:

✦ **New Document.** Allows you to create a new document in the library using the default template for that library. The default template for a library is usually specified when a library is first created. Default Document Library templates can be set to blank Microsoft Word, FrontPage, Excel, PowerPoint, Blank Page (.aspx Web page), or Web Part Page documents.

✦ **Upload Document.** Allows you to upload any supported file to the library. You can upload multiple files in an Explorer-like view by selecting Upload Multiple in the Upload Document page that appears after selecting this option.

✦ **New Folder.** Allows you to create a new folder in the Document Library.

✦ **Filter.** Enables you to filter columns by adding drop-down filter choices next to the properties column headings.

✦ **Edit in Datasheet.** Permits editing of editable document properties in Datasheet view. You can also access the same features of Datasheet view previously discussed in the section titled "Working with Datasheet views and linking lists to Excel and Access."

The list-type layout of a Document Library provides columns of document properties. By default these include Type, Name, Modified, Modified By, and Checked Out To. You can add columns of properties by using the Modify Settings and Columns link in the Actions submenu shown in the left pane in Figure 47-8. Property columns that are added appear in the Document Information tab of the Shared Workspace task pane in Word, Excel, or PowerPoint. To display the Shared Workspace task pane in Word, Excel, or PowerPoint, select View ⇨ Task Pane from the application's menu and use the drop-down menu in the task pane to select Shared Workspace.

You can display the drop-down menu shown in Figure 47-8 by selecting the cell in the Name column of the document or file in question and then selecting the arrow at the right side of that cell. This drop-down menu is the same regardless of whether you are working with a file in a Document Library or a Shared Workspace.

The drop-down menu, shown in Figure 47-8, provides the following options:

✦ **View Properties.** Provides a new view with the document properties.

✦ **Edit Properties.** Allows you to edit editable document properties including the filename and custom properties.

✦ **Edit in.** Allows you to open the file for editing in the application associated with it. You can also open a file for editing by simply clicking it. The Edit in option is available only for Microsoft Word, Excel, and PowerPoint documents.

✦ **Delete.** Allows you to delete a file if permissions allow.

✦ **Check Out.** Allows you to "check out" a document. A document can be checked out from a Document Library in a similar way that a book is checked out from a regular library. When you check out a document, you provide a long-term lock on the file that prevents others from making changes to it while you want to work on it. This options changes to Check In when a document is already checked out.

✦ **Version History.** When file versioning is enabled, this allows you to View, Restore, or Delete specific versions of that file. You can view comments on the file and enable file versioning for the Document Library that file is in via the Modify Versioning Settings link that appears in the new page when you select this option.

Note   Versioning is not enabled by default when new Document Libraries or Shared Workspaces are created.

✦ **Alert me.** You can use this to receive an e-mail alert when the specific document is changed or deleted or when a Web discussion on the document has changed.

✦ **Discuss.** Displays a discussion bar in Internet Explorer where you can comment on and discuss the document with your colleagues. Inline discussions can be inserted in HTML documents only. You can create a discussion about any type of document.

✦ **Create Document Workspace.** Allows you to create a Document Workspace "around" a document in an existing Document Library. When working with a document in a Shared Workspace created from a source file in a Document Library, this option becomes Publish to Source Location and allows synchronization between the file copy in the Document Workspace and the original source file.

Figure 47-9 shows a typical Shared Workspace containing a central Word document and other supporting files.

A Shared Workspace has an appearance similar to a SharePoint site. You can customize the site and work with the features just as you would with a regular SharePoint home page. From within the Shared Workspace you can add members, assign tasks, upload related documents, add hyperlinks contacts and events, and create and participate in discussions and surveys all from within Internet Explorer.

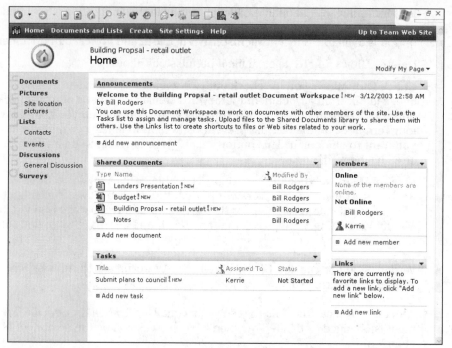

Figure 47-9: A Shared Workspace is specifically suited to collaborative document authoring.

The high level of integration between a Shared Workspace and Office 2003 also allows you to perform many of these tasks, and more that aren't available via the Web interface, from within the supported Office 2003 application.

Before delving into working with a Shared Workspace from within Office 2003 applications, the next section takes a look at how to create your own Shared Workspace.

Creating Shared Workspaces

You can create a Shared Workspace using any of the following methods:

To create a Shared Workspace for an existing document in a Document Library, follow these steps:

1. Connect to the SharePoint site with Internet Explorer and open the Document Library containing the document you want to create a workspace from.

2. Hover your mouse over the Name cell in the name column for the document in question and select Create Document Workspace from the drop-down menu (see Figure 47-8).

Use this method when you want to retain a copy of the document in a Document Library while collaborating on it in a Shared Workspace. You can work behind the scenes on a document using this method and then publish the final, completed document back to the original Document Library. To publish a document in a Shared Workspace back to its original Document Library, select Publish to Source Location from the drop-down menu in the Name column associated with that file in the Shared Workspace. Users can open the document from the workspace and work with it as if were saved on their machines. Users will need to open and then save the document to have their own local copy of the document that is dynamically linked to the copy in the Shared Workspace.

To create a Shared Workspace from an existing document in Word, Excel, or PowerPoint, follow these steps:

1. Open the file in its associated application.

2. From the Tools menu in Word, Excel, or PowerPoint, select Shared Workspace to display the Shared Workspace task pane. If a task pane is already visible in the application, you can simply select Shared Workspace from the drop-down menu at the top right of that task pane.

3. In the Document Workspace Name section of the Shared Workspace pane, change the name for the new Document Workspace if you desire. This field will already contain the name of the open file.

4. In the Location for New Workspace section of the Shared Workspace pane, use the drop-down menu to select the SharePoint site where the Document Workspace will be created or enter the location of the SharePoint site.

5. Click the Create button in the Shared Workspace pane.

Use this method when you want to create a Shared Workspace from an existing supported Office 2003 file type and have your own local copy of the file dynamically linked to the copy in the Shared Workspace. Other users of the Shared Workspace will need to visit the workspace and open and save the file to have their own local copies.

To create a Shared Workspace using Outlook, follow these steps:

1. Create a new e-mail message in Outlook addressed to yourself and others you want to collaborate with on the document. Users can be added in the To, CC, or BCC fields.

2. Attach the file you want to use as the basis of the Shared Workspace via the Insert File paperclip icon in the Outlook toolbar.

3. If the Attachment Options pane is not displayed in Outlook, display it by selecting the Attachment Options button to the right of the attached file.

4. Select the Shared Attachments option in the Attachment Options pane.

5. In the Create Document Workspace At text box, use the drop-down arrow to select a SharePoint server to create the workspace on. You can also simply enter the location of the SharePoint server.

6. Choose the account you want to send the e-mail from and click the Send button in Outlook to send the e-mail.

Outlook creates a Shared Workspace on the specified server of the same name as the attached file and sends a hyperlink to the workspace in the sent e-mail. If the attached file is a Word, Excel, or PowerPoint file, the copy of the file received by the recipient is linked directly to the newly created Shared Workspace. The recipient can save and work on the file locally and synchronize changes with the copy stored in the Shared Workspace. Use this method when you want to create a Shared Workspace and distribute a copy of the document dynamically linked to the copy in the workspace.

Regardless of which method you use to create a Shared Workspace, the file is available in the workspace to all users with appropriate access permissions. Users can simultaneously open and work on a document in a Shared Workspace and update the copy they are working on with the centrally stored copy in the workspace.

Working with Shared Workspaces inside Office 2003 applications

Now that you have some familiarity with Document Libraries and Shared Workspaces, and understand how to create them, you can focus exclusively on document collaboration from solely *within* supported Office 2003 applications. Although Document Libraries support collaboration, this section focuses on using a Shared Workspace. From the applications covered in this book, Word, Excel, and PowerPoint support the Shared Workspace task pane with the capability to not only create a Shared Workspace but to also work with the Shared Workspace from within the Shared Workspace task pane.

Note   Some Office 2003 applications not covered in this book also utilize the Shared Workspace task pane. The skills you learn here to work with the Shared Workspace task pane can be applied to any Office 2003 application that implements it.

Figure 47-10 shows the Shared Workspace task pane, displayed in Word, for a local copy of a document that is linked to a shared copy in a Shared Workspace.

Regardless of whether you are collaborating on a Word, Excel, or PowerPoint file, the options and tabs in the Shared Workspace task pane are the same.

Before taking a closer look at how to work with the Shared Workspace task pane, let's consider the updating of linked files saved locally when you open and close them and discuss how to deal with conflicts between local file copies and those on the server.

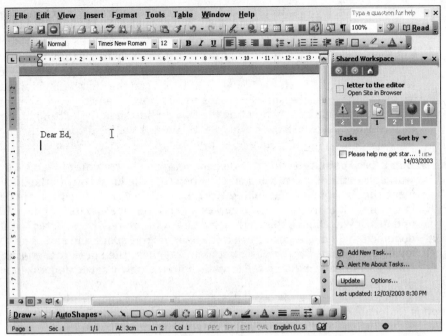

Figure 47-10: You can create and manage a Shared Workspace using the Shared Workspace task pane.

The first thing you might notice when opening a local copy of a document linked to a central copy in a Shared Workspace is that the Office 2003 application will ask you whether you want to check the Shared Workspace for updates to the document. You can choose from among any of the following options:

✦ **Update.** Selecting Update immediately checks the Shared Workspace for updates to the document. If changes are made to the local copy that is in conflict with changes made to the central copy, you are prompted to review and resolve the conflicts. Selecting Yes opens the Document Updates pane from which you can choose to merge copies, open the workspace copy for comparison, or select one copy to replace the other.

Note

If, at any time, SharePoint detects conflicts between a local copy and the copy in the Shared Workspace, those conflicts can be resolved via the Document Updates task pane. When conflicts between copies exist, they are reported in the Status tab (the first tab) of the Shared Workspace pane. The content of and options available in the Document Updates pane depends on the current status of conflicts between documents. Use of the Document Updates task pane, when required, is pretty much self-explanatory.

+ **Don't Update.** If you select this option, the document remains linked to the central copy but many of the Shared Workspace task pane tabs that require a connection with the server are unpopulated. The Office 2003 application will not then periodically check the server to determine whether any updates are available. Select Don't Update at those times when you want to solely work on a local copy of the file for a period of time or when the SharePoint site that hosts the file is inaccessible or access to it is slow. At any time, you can manually check for updates by pressing the Update button at the bottom of the Shared Workspace task pane. This will reconnect the local copy to the workspace copy and repopulate empty tabs in the Shared Workspace pane.

+ **Don't Ask Again.** Selecting this disconnects the file from the Shared Workspace, thereby removing any link between the local copy of the document and the copy on the Shared Workspace. Select this only if you are certain you want to unlink the two copies and not receive any further document updates. If you choose this option and later want to receive updates to the document, you might need to visit the Shared Workspace and save a new linked copy of the file to your computer. You might then need to merge any changes you have made to the local file into the newly saved and linked file.

When you close the local copy of a linked file, you are presented with only the option to update the workspace copy with your changes. If conflicts between copies are determined, you can resolve them using the Document Updates task pane.

You can control how the Office 2003 application checks for updates on opening and closing the document and the period of automatic update checking via the Options button at the bottom of the Shared Workspace task pane. Options include the capability to automatically update on opening and closing (and thereby disable any dialog box prompts) and to globally turn off automatic updating.

To demonstrate how to use the Shared Workspace task pane, this section works through an example. In this case, an existing Word document is used. This document can be opened directly from a Shared Workspace or from a local copy linked to a Shared Workspace. Remember that the same techniques also apply to Excel and PowerPoint.

Note   The following operations assume you are working with an open document linked to a Shared Workspace and that the Shared Workspace task pane is displayed. The document can be opened directly from the workspace or can be a local copy of the document that is linked to the workspace. If the Shared Workspace task pane is not displayed, display it via Tools ➪ Shared Workspace in the application's main menu.

First, you need to assign members to the Shared Workspace.

To assign members to a Shared Workspace, follow these steps:

1. Select the Members tab in the Shared Workspace task pane.

2. From towards the bottom of the Members tab, select Add New Members to open the new Add New Members dialog box.

3. In the Choose Members section of the Add New Members dialog box, enter the e-mail address or usernames of the new members separated by a semicolon.

4. In the Choose Site Group section of the Add New Members dialog box, select the group you want those new members to be assigned to. If you want to assign new members to different site groups, you need to add those new members individually.

5. Select Next and then, in the new dialog box that opens, select Finish.

Note

If SharePoint cannot properly identify any users you are trying to add with the host server, you might be presented with the requirement to enter additional information or to correct existing information after pressing Next in Step 5. If then, after pressing Finish and confirming that you do indeed have the correct details entered, you are presented with a new dialog box stating that the usernames are not valid, you should contact your SharePoint administrator to determine whether the users you are trying to add have access to the SharePoint site.

6. In the next new dialog box that opens, you can choose to send an e-mail to the newly added members. To send an e-mail to the new members informing them of their new membership and their workspace's location, ensure the Send E-Mail Invitation to the New Members checkbox is checked.

7. Click OK.

The E-Mail All Members option at the bottom of the Members tab of the Shared Workspace task pane allows you to send an e-mail to all members at once.

Members are grouped into categories in the Members tab of the Shared Workspace task pane according to whether they are Online or Offline; you are listed separately at the top of that pane.

Figure 47-11 shows the Members tab of the Shared Workspace task pane with newly added members.

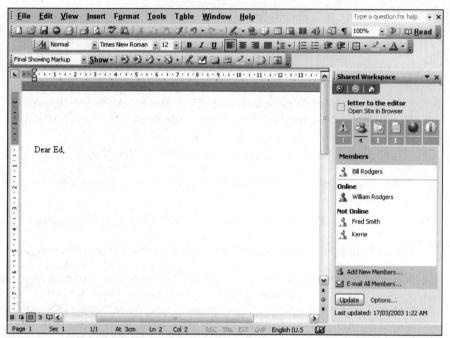

Figure 47-11: Use the Members tab to manage and communicate with workspace members.

You can use the drop-down arrow at the right of the member entry (shown in Figure 47-11 but not expanded) to manage Shared Workspace members. Among the options available, you can choose to remove the member, edit the member's group membership, send an Instant Message to the member (provided that member and you are online), add a member to Messenger Contacts, edit the member's user information, schedule a meeting with the member using Outlook, and add the member to your Outlook Contacts. Additional actions are available. Explore the Member-entry menu to see which options are available to you. The online/offline status of members is refreshed when you select the Update button at the bottom of the Shared Workspace task pane.

Now that you have added members to your Shared Workspace and are aware of how to manage your members, you're ready to assign tasks and work with assigned tasks.

To assign a task to a Shared Workspace member, follow these steps:

1. Select the Tasks tab in the Shared Workspace task pane.

2. Select Add New Task from the Tasks tab to open the new Task dialog box.

3. In the Task dialog box, enter a Title, Status, Priority, and a task Description, and assign the Task as shown in Figure 47-12. Only a Title is compulsory.

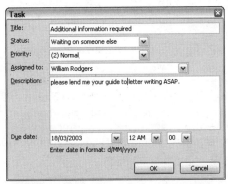

Figure 47-12: Create, use, and assign tasks with the Tasks tab.

4. Select OK.

Completed tasks are displayed with a green tick in the checkbox next to the task in the task tab of the Shared Workspace pane, whereas tasks not yet started are shown with no fill in that checkbox. Tasks with any other status are shown with a partly filled checkbox. High Priority tasks are also marked with a red exclamation mark. You can mark a task as complete or change the status of a task from complete to incomplete by selecting the checkbox next to that Task.

You can open the Task dialog box to edit a task simply by double-clicking the task in the Task tab of the Shared Workspace pane. Alternatively, open the task for editing via the menu available to the right of the task when that task is selected. This menu also contains options to delete a task and to create an alert about a task. The capability to create an alert for a task is also available at the bottom of the Task pane. All options that are available to you when you create a task are available when you edit the task provided you have adequate permissions in the Shared Workspace.

Now that you know how to assign tasks, you're ready to learn how to work with documents and folders using the Shared Workspace pane.

To add a new document to a Shared Workspace, follow these steps:

1. Select the Documents tab in the Shared Workspace pane.

2. From the bottom of the Documents tab, select Add New Document.

3. In the new Add New Document dialog box, use the Browse button to select a file to upload. Only single files can be selected. To link the newly uploaded documents to the local copy of that document ensure the Make Workspace Updates Available When I Open My Copy checkbox is selected.

4. Press OK.

To create a new folder, simply select Add New Folder in Step 2, enter the folder name in the Add New Folder dialog box, and press OK. To view the contents of a folder, click it or select View Contents from the menu available to the right of that folder. You can also delete a folder *and* its contents via the available menu on the right of its entry. Be sure you don't delete a folder without first checking that it doesn't contain important files. To return to the main view after a folder is in its contents view simply select the folder again. Documents are added to a folder using the same method as before, but with that folder's contents in view.

The menu available to the right of a documents entry in the Documents pane allows you to delete the document or to obtain an alert when changes are made to the document. Alerts are also available via the Alert Me About Documents link at the bottom of the Documents pane. When a document is not the currently open document, the menu to the left of that document allows you to open the document in its associated application. You can also open a document in its associated application by clicking its entry in the Documents pane.

Entries in the Tasks tab are refreshed when you press the Update button at the bottom of the Shared Workspace pane.

You can easily add links to the Shared Workspace by using the Links tab of the Shared Workspace pane. Links are added by selecting the Add New Link hyperlink from the bottom of the Links pane, entering the location, description, and any Notes relevant to the link in the new Link dialog box, and then pressing OK. From the menu available to the right of the link in the Links tab, you can choose to edit or delete the link or to receive an alert when that item is changed.

The Document information tab in the Shared Workspace displays information about the currently open document. From the Alert me link towards the bottom of the Document information tab you can choose to receive an e-mail alert when changes are made to the item or when Web discussions on the item have changed.

The Restrict Permissions link towards the bottom of the Document information tab allows you to set permissions on the file in the same way that you can via the Permissions button on the standard toolbar.

Cross-Reference For more information on document permissions, see Chapter 46.

You can open, restore, delete, and view comments for versions of the document stored in the Shared Workspace via the Version History link at the bottom of the Information tab of the Shared Workspace pane. Versioning can be enabled via the Modify Settings for Document Versions link in the new Versions Saved For dialog box that opens after selecting the Version History link. The Version History is also accessible via File ⇨ Versions ⇨ In a Document Library from the standard toolbar.

Figure 47-13 shows the Versions Saved For dialog box opened from the Version History link in the Information tab in the Shared Workspace pane in Word.

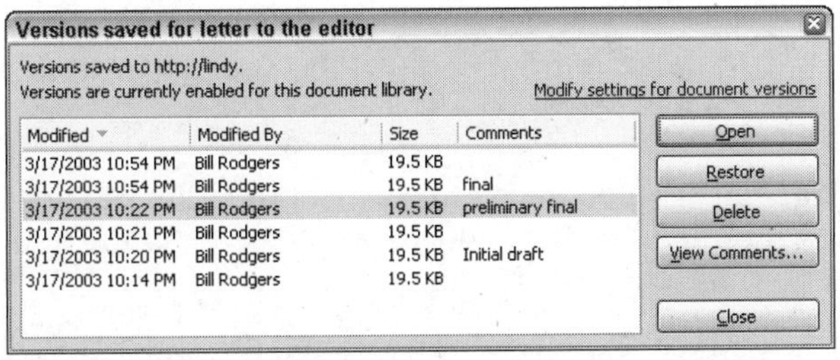

Figure 47-13: Enable and work with versions via the Document Information tab.

To open, restore, delete, or view comments on a document version, simply select that version in the Versions Saved for dialog box, choose the appropriate action from the options available on the right, and respond appropriately to any subsequent prompts. Restoring a document does not delete it but, instead, makes it the current and active available document. You cannot restore or delete the currently open and active document. Use the Open button to view the contents of document versions prior to deleting or restoring them unless comments you have added to the version adequately describe that version.

Comments can be added to a document only when it is checked in. To check in a document you, naturally, need to have first checked it out. Checking out a document, as covered previously, provides a long-term lock on the file that prevents others from making changes to it while you want to work on it. The Check Out and alternate Check In links in the Document Information tab of the Shared Workspace pane are available only when you are working with a writeable copy of the file opened directly from the Shared Workspace.

Tip Check the Status tab (the first tab of the Shared Workspace pane) to determine whether a document has been checked out and to whom it is checked out.

To check out a document, follow these steps:

1. Open the document from the Shared Workspace by clicking it.

2. If the document opens as a read-only file, select the Save button on the standard toolbar and select Save in the new Save As dialog box to overwrite the Workspace copy. This makes the currently open file writeable. This then makes Check Out and the alternate Check In available in the Document Information tab of the Shared Workspace task pane. If a Word document was opened from the Workspace in Reading Layout, for editing purposes, select the Close button on the standard Word toolbar to change to your preferred editing layout.

3. Select the Check Out link from the bottom of the Document Information pane (see Figure 47-13).

To check a document back in and add comments to it, select the Check In link from the bottom of the Document Information pane, add your comments in the new Check In Comments dialog box, and then select OK.

A checked-out document can also be checked in, and comments added, when the file is closed. When closing a checked-out document that is opened directly from a Shared Workspace, you are prompted to check in the file, keep the file checked out, or to discard changes and undo the check out. Respond accordingly to your requirements at that time.

Note   To provide a lock on a copy of a document in a Shared Workspace while you work on a local copy of that file that is linked to the workspace copy, you need to visit the workspace using Internet Explorer and check out the document using the menu available to the right of that file. The file remains synchronized to the workspace copy, but only you can make changes that can be updated to the workspace copy. When you want to check the file back in, simply visit the workspace again and use the same menu to, this time, check the file in. Comments can then be added to the file version in the Check In Web page in Internet Explorer.

SharePoint as a Central Contacts and Calendar Server

Two of the useful features available with Windows SharePoint Services are the capability to act as a central server for calendars and contacts. You can maintain a central database of contacts and events that can be linked directly to Outlook and are accessible by anyone with access to the Contacts and Events folders on the SharePoint site. These features, although not as powerful as those available with

Microsoft Exchange, provide an alternative to comparable Exchange features when that server is not available.

Linking a SharePoint Events folder (which is essentially a calendar) to Outlook is particularly useful when you want to compare events in the SharePoint calendar with another calendar in your Outlook profile.

Figure 47-14 shows a linked SharePoint calendar opened side by side with an Outlook calendar. Multiple SharePoint calendars can also be opened side by side for comparison.

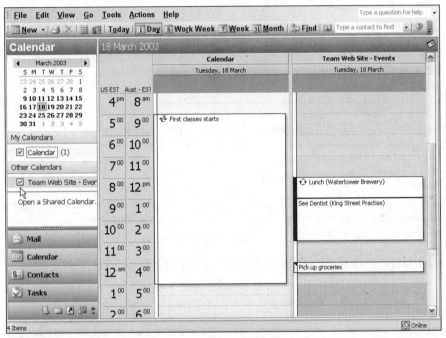

Figure 47-14: View a SharePoint calendar in Outlook.

In Figure 47-14, my girlfriend has access to a SharePoint events folder and uses it to remind me of certain appointments I am "required" to do. You can use this feature for many imaginable scenarios. Perhaps you want to maintain a SharePoint calendar of company meetings and events and make that available to all employees from within Outlook.

SharePoint calendars are listed in the Other Calendars section of the Calendar view in the Outlook Navigation pane. Linked SharePoint calendars are cached for offline use in Outlook when the SharePoint server is inaccessible. To view a linked

SharePoint calendar in Outlook, simply select its checkbox in Other Calendars. When connected to the SharePoint server, you can refresh the SharePoint calendar by deselecting and then selecting its entry in Other Calendars.

Linking a SharePoint Events folder to Outlook (regardless of where it is located on the SharePoint server), and therefore making its information available in Outlook, is as easy as opening that Events folder in Internet Explorer, selecting the Link To Outlook link in the top bar of that folder's view, and selecting Yes when you receive the prompt from Outlook to add it.

SharePoint calendars are opened in Outlook as read-only. You need to edit the SharePoint calendar and add events at the SharePoint site. You can, however, add events from the SharePoint calendar to your default Outlook from within Outlook. The reverse, unfortunately, doesn't apply.

To add an event from a SharePoint calendar opened in Outlook to your default Outlook calendar, open the calendars side by side and drag and drop the event from the SharePoint calendar to the Outlook one. You can drag and drop the event into any time slot you choose.

Tip

You might need to compensate for differing time zones when adding events from the linked SharePoint calendar to one of your other available non-SharePoint calendars. Check with your SharePoint administrator to determine the time zone used on the SharePoint server.

To remove a linked Calendars folder from Other Calendars, right-click its entry in Other Calendars and select Remove from Other Calendars.

Making SharePoint contacts available to Outlook

The integration of SharePoint with Outlook also includes the capability to open a SharePoint Contacts folder as a read-only Contacts folder in Outlook and the capability to import Outlook contacts into a SharePoint Contacts folder. This is particularly useful when you want to maintain a shared, central global address list accessible from Outlook to all who have access to the SharePoint Contacts folder. You can add contacts from your Outlook address book to the SharePoint Contacts folder and make them available to all others with access to the SharePoint Contacts folder. SharePoint Contacts folders that are linked to Outlook can be made available in the Outlook address book and are also available to Outlook as an address list for checking purposes when Outlook sends e-mail. Linked SharePoint contacts are cached in Outlook so the information is available offline or when the server is not accessible.

SharePoint Contacts folders that are linked to Outlook are opened as read-only, and, therefore, you have to edit the SharePoint Contacts folder at the SharePoint server.

You can drag and drop the contacts from the linked SharePoint Contacts folder to other non-SharePoint Outlook Contact folders.

To import Outlook contacts into a SharePoint Contacts folder, follow these steps:

1. Connect to the SharePoint site in Internet Explorer.

2. Locate and then open the Contacts folder by clicking its entry. In the case of the default SharePoint Contacts folder, the link to the folder is found in the Quick Links section of the main SharePoint Home Page.

3. Select the Import Contacts link in the top bar of the Contacts Web page to open the Select Users to Import dialog box. This dialog box is a representation of the Outlook address book.

4. In the Show Names From The drop-down menu of the Select Users to Import dialog box, select the address list you want to import from.

5. Select the entries you want to import from the main pane in the Select Users to Import dialog box (a modification of the Outlook address book) and press Add to add them to the list of contacts to be imported. Use Ctrl+Click to select multiple entries. Contiguous entries can be selected using Shift+Click. You can resize the Select Users to Import dialog box to more easily locate contacts by dragging the bottom-right corner of that dialog box. You can also begin typing a contact's name in the Type Name or Select From List text boxes to assist in locating a contact.

6. Press OK to finalize the import and to add the selected contacts to the SharePoint Contacts folder.

Note Outlook contacts with multiple e-mail addresses and fax numbers are listed in the Select Users to Import dialog box as separate entries (one entry for each e-mail address and one for each fax number). When these entries are imported into SharePoint and subsequently viewed as a linked Outlook contacts folder, each e-mail address and fax number is displayed as a separate contact.

To link a SharePoint Contacts folder to Outlook, simply select Link To Outlook in Step 3 and then select Yes when prompted by Outlook to add the link.

Contacts folders linked to Outlook are available in the Other Contacts section of the Contacts view in the Outlook navigation pane. Select the linked SharePoint Contacts folder from Other Contacts to view its entries. Contacts folders in other Contacts can be enabled or disabled as an Outlook address book via the Outlook Address Book tab in the Properties dialog box, which becomes available when you right-click on the entry in Other Contacts and select Properties. Other options in the right-click menu include the capability to remove the link from Other Contacts.

Conducting an Online Meeting with the Meeting Workspace

A Meeting Workspace is a special type of workspace designed specifically to centralize all the information needed to conduct a meeting. The Meeting Workspace can be used to publish the attendee list, agenda, and documents you plan to discuss prior to the meeting. After the meeting, you can use the workspace to track tasks and to publish information gathered during the meeting. You work with Meeting Workspaces using Internet Explorer in much the same way as you do with other SharePoint sites. The familiarity you have gained using SharePoint sites in the rest of this chapter can be easily extended a to Meeting Workspace.

Outlook includes the capability to create a Meeting Workspace and simultaneously invite attendees while checking on their availability to attend the meeting.

To create a schedule and invite attendees to a Meeting Workspace using Outlook, follow these steps:

1. Select Meeting request from the drop-down menu next to the New button in the standard Outlook toolbar.

2. In the To field of the Meeting Request form, enter the e-mail addresses of attendees separated by semicolons. You can use the To button to select attendees from Outlook address lists.

3. In the Subject text box of the Meeting Request form, enter a Subject for the meeting.

4. Complete the Start Time and End Time for the meeting. You can use the Scheduling tab in the Meeting request form to check the availability of attendees who have published Free/Busy times and to auto-pick a time for the meeting.

5. Add any notes about the meeting in the Notes area of the form, give the Meeting a label, set the Show Time As, and link to any Contacts and Categories as required.

6. In the Outlook Meeting request form, select the Meeting Workspace button to display the Meeting Workspace task pane. You can choose to use the workspace setting given in the Create a Workspace section of the Meeting Workspace task pane or customize the Meeting Workspace. If you choose to use the displayed settings, skip ahead to Step 11.

7. To customize the Meeting Workspace, select Change Settings in the Create a Workspace section of the Meeting Workspace task pane. This allows you to reformat the Meeting Workspace pane as shown in Figure 47-15.

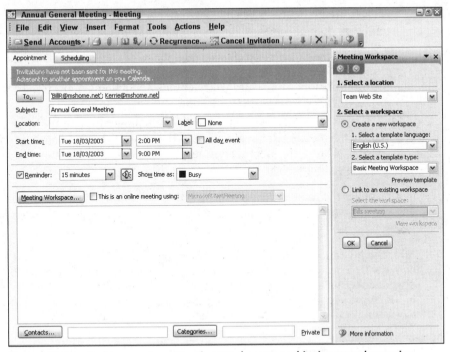

Figure 47-15: Create a custom Meeting Workspace and invite attendees using Outlook.

8. In section 1 of the Meeting Workspace pane, Select a Location, you can use the displayed server or select another server to host the Meeting Workspace. Use the adjacent drop-down menu to select another server. If the server you want to create the Meeting Workspace on is not listed, select Other from the drop-down menu and enter the location of the server in the new Other Workspace Server dialog box.

9. In section 2 of the Meeting Workspace pane, Select a Workspace, you can choose to create a new workspace or to link to an existing Meeting Workspace. To create a new workspace, select the Create a New Workspace button. You can choose a template language for a new workspace from the available templates using the Select a Template Language drop-down menu. You can choose a template type for a new workspace from the Select a Template Type drop-down menu. Available templates include Basic Meeting Workspace, Blank Meeting Workspace, Decision Meeting Workspace, Social Meeting Workspace, and Multipage Meeting Workspace.

10. Select OK to refresh the meeting Workspace pane with a similar view as seen in Step 6.

11. Select Create to create the new workspace. If you chose to link to an existing workspace, select Link. Outlook will either create a new workspace or link to an existing workspace depending on your choice in Step 9. The location of the meeting is automatically entered into the Notes field in the Outlook Meeting Request form. The Meeting Workspace task pane is updated to provide a link to the workspace for your own reference and a Remove button from which you can remove the workspace link.

12. If desired, select an account using the Accounts button in the standard toolbar of the Meeting Request form and then click the Send button in the standard toolbar of the Meeting Request form to send the Meeting Request to addressed attendees.

Recipients of the request receive the meeting invitation with a link to the meeting and can respond to it in the same way that they do to any other Outlook Meeting request.

After the invitation has been sent, the meeting is added to your default Outlook calendar with a designation of "M" for, of course, Meeting. The Tracking tab on the opened meeting allows you to track responses to your invitation. Use the hyperlink in the Notes section or in the Meeting Workspace task pane of the opened Meeting to customize and prepare the workspace for your meeting.

Summary

In this chapter, you learned how to access a Windows SharePoint Services site and about site permissions. You learned how to create lists using SharePoint and Excel, how to use the powerful Datasheet view to present data in an Excel-like view and perform Excel-like calculations, and how to dynamically link lists to Excel and Access. You learned how to create and use a Shared Workspace to collaborate on documents from within Office 2003, and how to add new workspace members and assign tasks using the Shared Workspace pane. You learned how to view and use SharePoint contacts and events in Outlook, and how to create a Meeting Workspace with Outlook.

✦ SharePoint provides the powerful Datasheet list view that allows you to perform Excel-like calculations and dynamically link lists to Excel and Access.

✦ You can create and manage a Shared Workspace from within Word, Excel, and PowerPoint, allowing you to collaborate on documents with anyone who can access the workspace.

✦ SharePoint provides default Web pages and event, contacts, announcements, tasks, and shared document components that are highly flexible and customizable to suit your needs or personal preferences.

✦ SharePoint allows you to share central calendar and contacts databases with any user who can access the SharePoint site and to access and use those databases in Outlook.

✦ SharePoint site permissions can restrict user groups to have specific rights on the SharePoint server.

✦ You can send a meeting request with Outlook and simultaneously create a specialized Meeting Workspace to help facilitate the meeting.

✦ SharePoint provides a high level of security such that access to the server can be restricted. You might need to log on to the server to use it.

✦ ✦ ✦

Customizing and Automating Office

Customizing Office Applications

Office applications are powerful and flexible, sure, but they don't always think the way you do. Fortunately, you can tweak them in a number of ways to bring them more in line with your way of approaching day-to-day tasks.

The most powerful customization tool you have, of course, is the ability to move commands to different toolbars, create new toolbars and menus, and even change the appearance of the icons that represent the various commands. How to do all that is spelled out in Chapter 2, "Using Office's Menus and Toolbars."

This chapter looks at some additional tips for customizing Office applications.

Customizing Tips for Word

Word is probably the most customizable of all Office applications, and the way to start is to choose Tools ➪ Options. This dialog box (see Figure 48-1) contains more than 100 options that control all facets of Word.

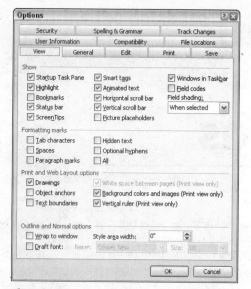

Figure 48-1: Here's Word's Options dialog box, with the View tab (one of 11) selected.

That's too many options to cover in detail; besides, most of them are very straight-forward, and others are useful to very few people. In any event, most of the most useful options were mentioned in the chapters on Word as they came up. However, I suggest you take a few minutes to check through all of these tabs. Use the Help tool to explain any choices whose functions aren't clear.

Using the entire screen in Full Screen view

Word has a view you might not even know exists, in addition to Normal, Web Layout, Print Layout, Outline, and the new Reading view. It expands your workspace by hiding pretty much everything except for the document.

To access it, choose View ➪ Full Screen.

Tip   There's a Full Screen view in Print Preview, too; there's a toggle button on the toolbar — you can add this button to other toolbars using the standard customization methods covered in Chapter 2.

Full Screen view hides the menu, the toolbars, the status bar, the scroll bars, the title bar, and even the Windows taskbar (assuming you have it showing), leaving only a tiny floating Full Screen toolbar (see Figure 48-2). This toolbar has exactly one button on it: Close Full Screen.

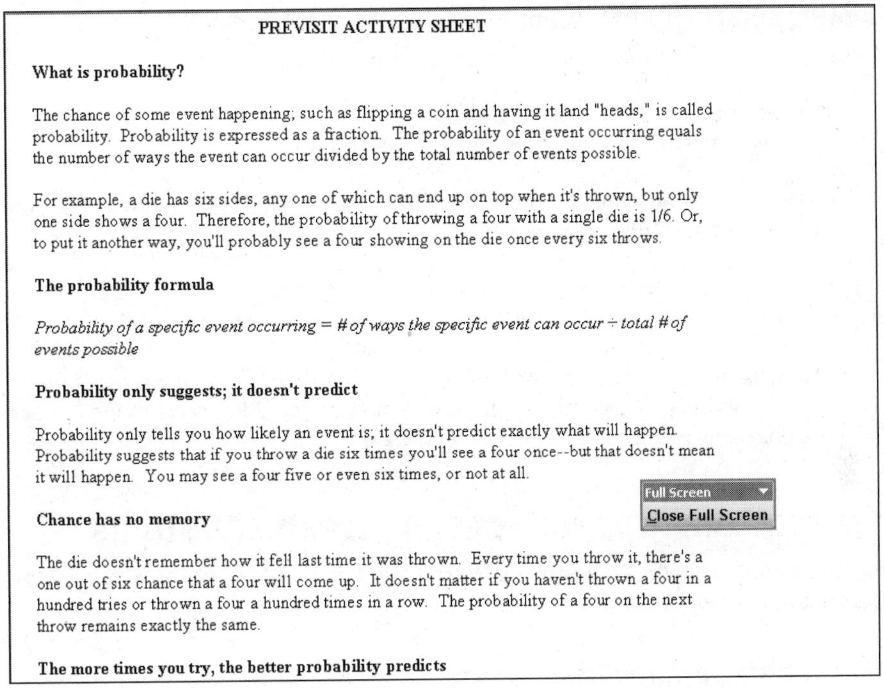

PREVISIT ACTIVITY SHEET

What is probability?

The chance of some event happening; such as flipping a coin and having it land "heads," is called probability. Probability is expressed as a fraction. The probability of an event occurring equals the number of ways the event can occur divided by the total number of events possible.

For example, a die has six sides, any one of which can end up on top when it's thrown, but only one side shows a four. Therefore, the probability of throwing a four with a single die is 1/6. Or, to put it another way, you'll probably see a four showing on the die once every six throws.

The probability formula

Probability of a specific event occurring = # of ways the specific event can occur ÷ total # of events possible

Probability only suggests; it doesn't predict

Probability only tells you how likely an event is; it doesn't predict exactly what will happen. Probability suggests that if you throw a die six times you'll see a four once--but that doesn't mean it will happen. You may see a four five or even six times, or not at all.

| Full Screen |
| Close Full Screen |

Chance has no memory

The die doesn't remember how it fell last time it was thrown. Every time you throw it, there's a one out of six chance that a four will come up. It doesn't matter if you haven't thrown a four in a hundred tries or thrown a four a hundred times in a row. The probability of a four on the next throw remains exactly the same.

The more times you try, the better probability predicts

Figure 48-2: Full Screen view provides maximum space for your document.

How do you access Word commands? Here are three ways:

✦ Aim your mouse pointer at the top edge of the screen and the Menu bar appears (move your mouse pointer away and the Menu bar disappears again).

✦ Use keyboard shortcuts instead of mouse-clicks.

✦ Right-click to open the shortcut menu. This menu will vary depending on where your cursor is in the document, but by default, it includes the Cut, Copy, and Paste commands and links to the Font, Paragraph, and Bullets and Numbering dialog boxes.

Tip   As described in Chapter 2, you can customize shortcut menus just as you can toolbars and regular menus. That means you can add all the commands you normally use to the shortcut menu for use in Full Screen view—e.g., Save, Print, Find, Replace. You can also add any macros you may have created. Construct your shortcut menu carefully, and you'll never have to exit Full Screen view if you don't want to.

Adding select window elements to Full Screen view

If you prefer a few other elements in your Full Screen view, you can add them individually from the Menu bar. To display the task pane, choose View ➪ Task Pane from the Menu bar. Looking for the ruler? Choose View ➪ Ruler. And you can turn on any toolbar you want from the View ➪ Toolbar menu.

Note   Word remembers which toolbars you unhide and will display them again the next time you enter Full Screen view.

If it's the scroll bars you miss, or the status bar, you can display them by choosing Tools ➪ Options and checking the appropriate boxes on the View tab.

Tip   Looking for only certain commands? Add them to the Full Screen toolbar by choosing Tools ➪ Customize — but note that you can add buttons to the Full Screen toolbar only while you're in Full Screen view.

Customizing tips for special screen situations

Here are some tips for customizing Word from the View tab of the Tools ➪ Options dialog box, shown in Figure 48-1.

Maximizing performance

Using these tips can make Word run faster:

✦ **Picture placeholders.** Checking this box makes Word display placeholders in place of pictures in your document; sometimes displaying pictures can slow down less powerful systems. When you want to see the pictures during the final proofing, return to the View tab and uncheck this box.

✦ **Draft font.** Choose this option to display all text in the same font (which you can choose from a list of all the fonts installed on your system) and size. Again, while using this option might speed up Word's performance on a low-end system, it won't make much difference to more powerful systems. You may also find your document easier to edit this way.

Maximizing screen space without using Full Screen view

If you don't want to use Full Screen view but you could still use some more screen room for your text, consider these options in the View tab:

✦ **Status bar.** Unselecting this hides the status bar at the bottom of the screen.

✦ **Horizontal scroll bar and Vertical scroll bar.** If you prefer using the keyboard for navigation, turn off the scrollbars by unselecting these boxes. This will also hide the buttons for the various views that reside to the left of the horizontal scroll bar, but you've still got the View menu.

✦ **Style area.** The style area is a vertical region along the left edge of the window where Word displays paragraph style names. Although it can be useful when you want to see how various styles look in your document, most people don't use it — in fact, I doubt most Word users even know it exists. If by some chance it's turned on, though, it cuts significantly into your screen real estate. Return its width to the default 0 with the Style area width option.

Cross-Reference

For a more detailed description of the style area, and styles in general, see Chapter 8.

Using Word effectively in a small window

We've just talked about maximizing space for your text, but sometimes you need to work with other applications alongside Word and have to shrink the window to the point that your text feels uncomfortably cramped — in fact, if your window is smaller than the width of your text, some of your text can disappear and you'll have to use the horizontal scroll bar to find it.

If you're stuck working in a too-small window like this, check the Wrap to window checkbox in the View tab. Now Word displays each paragraph so that text does not continue off the "page," thus obviating the need for horizontal scrolling back and forth (see Figure 48-3).

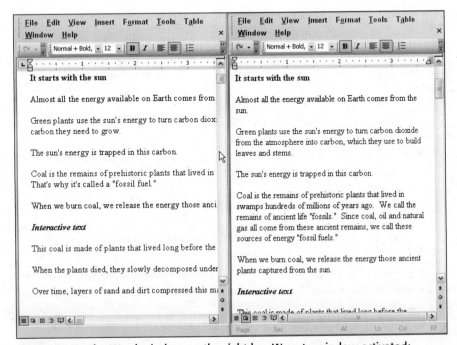

Figure 48-3: The Word window on the right has Wrap to window activated; the one on the left doesn't.

Note   Only the display of your text has changed, not the actual formatting. If you want to check line wrapping on certain styles, make sure you turn off the Wrap to window option to see an accurate representation of your formatting, or switch to Print Layout view, in which the Wrap to window option is not available.

Customizing Outlook

Just as in Word (and the other Office applications), you can find most of Outlook's customizing settings on the Tools ➪ Options dialog box (see Figure 48-4).

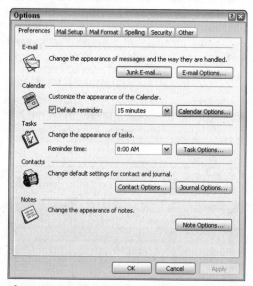

Figure 48-4: The Preferences tab on Outlook's Options dialog box

Your choices in the Options dialog box occupy six tabs, as follows:

✦ **Preferences.** This tab offers basic settings controlling the look of Outlook items and includes options governing contact and journal items; I'll look at this one in more detail in a moment.

✦ **Mail Setup and Mail Format.** The settings on these tabs pertain mostly to e-mail and are covered in Chapters 21 and 22.

✦ **Spelling.** Options governing Outlook's spellchecker reside on this tab, including an option to edit the custom dictionary.

✦ **Security.** This tab has controls that can help protect you and your organization from unauthorized access to mail and sensitive data, and are covered in Chapter 23.

✦ **Other.** This tab houses some key Outlook settings; I'll mention one or two of them in detail in a moment, as well.

Changing preferences

There are too many options in the Options dialog box, and even on the Preference tab alone, to describe in detail, but here are a few things I like to tweak:

✦ **E-mail Options.** Clicking this button on the Preferences tab opens the dialog box shown in Figure 48-5; at the bottom are the controls for changing the way message replies and forwards look. For each, you have the option of not including the original message, attaching the original message, including the original message text, including and indenting the original message text, or including the original message text and prefixing each line of the message with a particular character — by default, the symbol >.

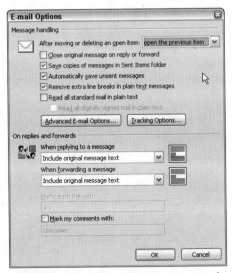

Figure 48-5: Change the appearance of e-mail messages, and their handling options, here.

 The second button in the E-mail area of the Options dialog box, Junk E-mail, is discussed in detail in Chapter 23.

✦ **Calendar Options.** Don't like the way the calendar looks? This dialog box (see Figure 48-6) lets you change the starting day of your work week and even your work year, the start time and end time of your day, the background color, and even (by clicking the Add Holidays button) which country's holidays you want noted. If you click the Enable alternate calendar button, you can even choose an entirely different calendar, such as the Gregorian or the Hebrew Lunar.

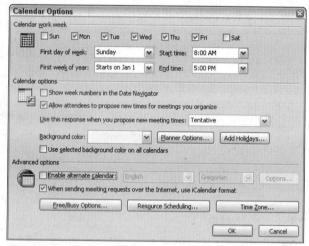

Figure 48-6: Customize your calendar in this dialog box.

✦ **Task Options.** Here you can set the colors for overdue and completed tasks and deactivate some default options.

✦ **Contact Options.** Change the format you want Outlook to use for new names—Last First instead of First (Middle) Last, for instance—and the default setting for how new contacts should be filed (such as by company instead of by last name, first name). You can also choose to display an additional contacts index in a different language, for your international contacts.

✦ **Note Options.** Change the appearance of Notes, setting their color, size, and font.

Other options

Under the Other tab of the Tools ➪ Options dialog box in Outlook is an option to customize reading options for the Preview Pane. By default, an item in the Preview Pane is marked as read as soon as you go on to another item; however, you can change that to Mark messages as read after they've been open for a certain amount of time, in seconds.

Customizing forms

One of Outlook's most powerful customization features is the capability to customize the forms it supplies for inputting information. If you don't like the default forms, change them!

Opening a form for customizing

To customize a form, open it, and then choose Tools ➪ Forms ➪ Design this Form. This changes the form window so that it shows new menu items, toolbars, and tabs for designing forms (see Figure 48-7), plus the Field Chooser.

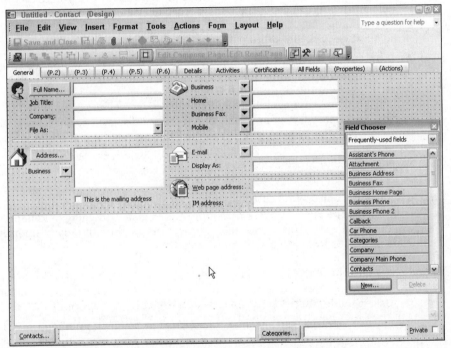

Figure 48-7: The standard contact form, ready to be customized

Working with form pages in design mode

Besides its standard pages, every Outlook form also has several blank pages, labeled in design mode as P.2, P.3, and so on; you can see the tabs that activate them in Figure 48-7. The parentheses around the names indicate that these pages are normally hidden when you open this form; the pages that are normally available, such as (in the case of the contact form) Details, Activities, and Certificates, do not have parentheses around their names.

To work with a blank page, click its tab. The page takes the form of an empty grid onto which you place fields and buttons.

No matter which type of form you're working with, you'll see a tab for All Fields. This displays fields in a big table, and it can be an easier view in which to enter information.

Working with special design mode pages

The last two tabs on the right are for pages used exclusively when designing forms. They are:

✦ **Properties.** You define the custom form's properties here. If you're creating lots of forms, you can organize them hierarchically with the Category and Sub-Category fields. Click the Contact button to add the name of the form's designer or anyone else whom users should contact if they have a problem.

✦ **Actions.** Use this page to add commands to the form that automatically open another form. Add, modify, and remove actions with the New, Properties, and Delete buttons at the bottom of the page.

Tip   To hide a page from the normal view of a form — or display it again — choose the Form ⇨ Display This Page toggle. You can tell when a page is hidden because its name appears in parentheses in design mode. To rename a page, choose Form ⇨ Rename Page and type the new name.

Adding fields and controls to a custom page

Add content from the Field Chooser by simply clicking and dragging field names. The drop-down list at the top of the Field Chooser offers you not only frequently used fields but fields from other folders as well.

To add radio buttons, checkboxes, and other controls, choose Form ⇨ Control Toolbox to display a selection of useful controls. However, be aware that making these controls useful requires knowing how to write code in VBScript (not VBA). Fields, on the other hand, are ready to go as soon as they're inserted.

Use the toolbar buttons or Layout menu commands to align, group, and order the fields and controls you add. To modify characteristics of an individual field or control, right-click it and select Properties from the shortcut menu; the Advanced Properties choice displays properties in a table.

Adding default information to a custom form

Because information typed into the fields of a custom form is saved with the form, you can supply yourself (or other users) with default content by adding it in just before saving.

Saving forms

Once you've customized a form, you have three choices for saving the new version:

✦ Save it as an individual item in the corresponding Outlook folder.

✦ Save it as a separate template or message file.

✦ Save it in an Outlook forms library.

Or, if you can't make up your mind, you can save it all three ways.

Saving a form as an information item

Choose File ➪ Save to save a custom form as a single item in the Outlook folder associated with that type of form.

Saving a form as a separate file

Use File ➪ Save As to save a form and its accompanying information in a separate file outside the Outlook folders.

There are several formats in the Save as Type list for you to choose from. Text only and Rich text format are useful if you want to transfer the information to a non-Outlook user.

To save the form itself, as well as its contents, save it as an Outlook template or in message format. Either allows you to send a copy of the form to someone who isn't on your network.

Another way to save a custom form for reuse is to click the Publish Form button on the Forms toolbar. In the dialog box shown in Figure 48-8, you supply a name for the new form and tell Outlook where the form should be stored by choosing a location from the Look In drop-down list. Options include:

✦ **Personal Forms library.** This stores the form for your use only as a choice in the Forms Library drop-down list.

✦ **Organization Forms library.** If your computer is on a network, this library might be available; it resides on a network server and makes forms available to the entire organization.

✦ **Outlook folders.** You can also choose a specific Outlook folder in which to store the form. If you can't find the one you want, look for it by clicking Browse.

Using Outlook forms

To use a custom form or template, choose File ➪ New ➪ Choose Form. In the Choose Form dialog box (see Figure 48-9), use the Look In drop-down list to search the available form libraries, Outlook folders, and template locations.

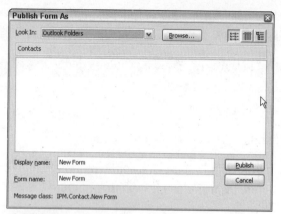

Figure 48-8: Store custom forms using the Publish Form As dialog box.

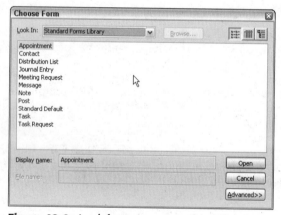

Figure 48-9: Look for your custom forms here.

Customizing Excel

Excel offers fewer customization options, but you still have extensive control over the way the program operates, how it looks on the screen, and what information, formatting, and special features are added automatically to new workbooks.

Startup options

Do you routinely use one or more specific workbooks? Have Excel open them for you whenever you start the program by placing shortcuts to them (or the workbooks themselves) into the XL Start folder. Use Windows' Search function, available from the Start menu, to track it down.

Another option is to go to the Tools ➪ Options dialog box, choose the General tab, and type the full path for a folder holding the files you want to start automatically into the At startup, open all files box.

Caution   Excel will attempt to open *every* file it finds in the startup folders, so be sure the only files you place there are workbooks or their shortcuts.

Setting Excel options

There are many other options in the Tools ➪ Options dialog box (shown in Figure 48-10), just as with other Office applications. Many of the 13 tabs are almost identical to the ones in Word, and other options are covered as they come up elsewhere in the book, but I'll mention a few specifically.

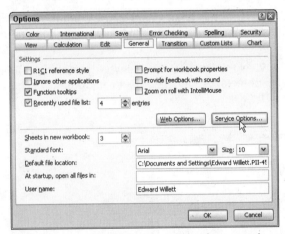

Figure 48-10: Excel's Options dialog box contains many ways to customize Excel.

The General tab's settings affect overall program operation:

   ✦ You might want to boost the recently used file list to its maximum of 9; I always find that being able to open a file with a quick click beats going through the Open dialog box.

   ✦ Consider changing the number of sheets in a new workbook to 1, instead of the default 3. (You can also boost it all the way to 255.) You can always add extra sheets if you need them.

   ✦ If you change your user name here, you change it for other Office applications, too.

On the Transition tab, the Save Excel files as setting lets you set a new default for saving files — as an XML spreadsheet, for instance, or as a Web page.

Customizing the screen

The View tab (see Figure 48-11) contains most of the controls you need to change Excel's looks. Most are self-explanatory, but I do have a few comments:

✦ Use the settings under Show and Window options to control which elements of Excel's user interface appear on the screen. You can turn off the Startup task pane or the Status bar, for instance. The four Show choices apply throughout Excel, whereas the Window options settings apply only to the current document.

✦ Select the Page breaks box under the Windows options if you want to see dotted lines to indicate the current page breaks for printing.

✦ By default, the Zero values box is checked; this puts a 0 in each cell containing a zero value. Uncheck this if you'd rather see the cell displayed as empty.

✦ The drop-down menu labeled Gridlines color changes the color of the worksheet gridlines. (Note that it doesn't change the color of the workbook gridlines, just the worksheet ones.)

✦ The Objects section of the View tab lets you choose whether to show objects, show only placeholders for objects, or hide all objects, including charts, drawings, clip art, and text boxes.

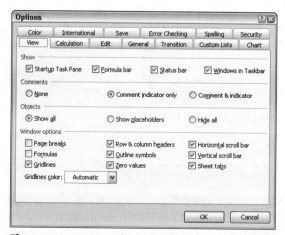

Figure 48-11: Control Excel's appearance with the settings in the View tab.

Working with the color palette

Use the color palette on the Color tab of the Options dialog box (see Figure 48-12) to change the selection of 56 colors Excel makes available for coloring all the various elements that can appear in a worksheet.

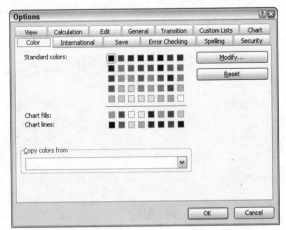

Figure 48-12: Modify the color palette in the Color tab of the Options dialog box.

To replace one of the colors in the existing palette, select it and choose Modify. The colors set apart as Chart fills and Chart lines are the first eight colors Excel automatically applies to these chart elements, so by changing these, you can alter the look of future charts dramatically. Click Reset to restore all colors to their defaults.

The modified color palette is stored with the current workbook; you can copy the palette from any open workbook by choosing it from the Copy colors from drop-down list. To create a new default palette, you have to modify the palette in your default template.

Using Full Screen view

Like Word, Excel has a Full Screen view (see Figure 48-13); unlike Word, it doesn't hide the Menu bar.

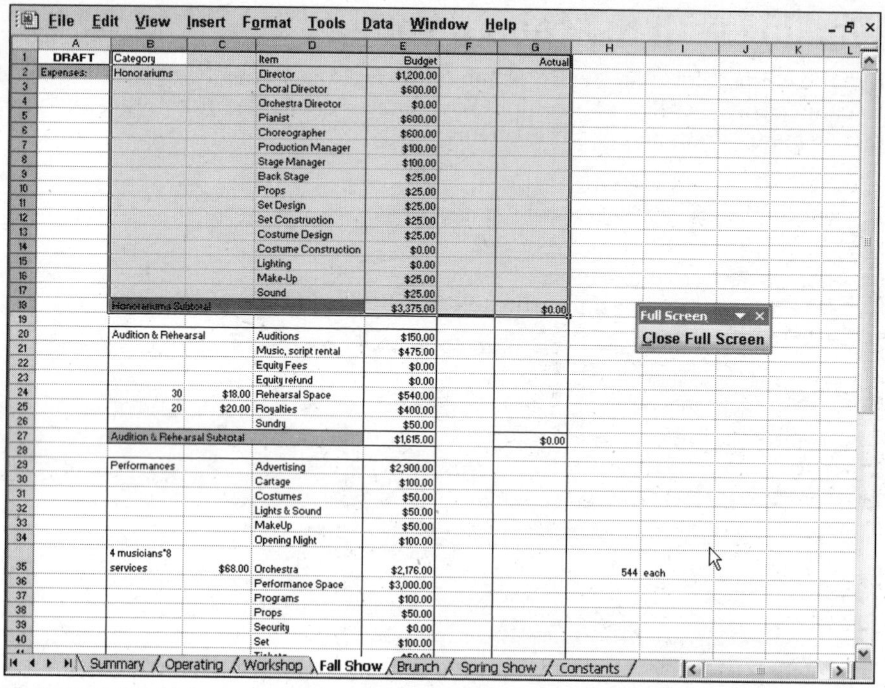

Figure 48-13: Make room for more data by using Excel's Full Screen view.

Storing a view of the current workbook

To record a worksheet's current look so you can return it to those settings later, you have to save a view. Choose View ➪ Custom Views. Click Add to create a new custom view, and in the dialog box that appears, give the view a name and choose whether to include Print settings and Hidden rows, columns, and filter settings. The next time you open that worksheet, the custom view is automatically displayed; if you have created more than one custom view for a worksheet, you can move among them by choosing View ➪ Custom Views, selecting the view you want, and clicking Show.

Customizing PowerPoint

PowerPoint has fewer customizable features than some of the other Office applications, and most of the ones of note I've already mentioned in other chapters in this book. But here are a few things to look for in (where else?) the Tools ➪ Options dialog box (see Figure 48-14):

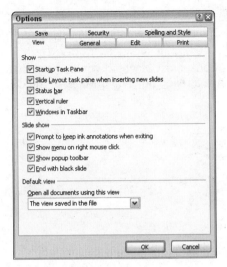

Figure 48-14: PowerPoint doesn't offer as many customization options as other Office applications, but it offers enough.

✦ **Change the default view.** On the View tab, there's a section called Default view, with a list box labeled Open all documents using this view. The default view is the one saved with the file you're opening, but you have other choices, from various variations on normal to Outline Only, Slide Sorter, and even Notes.

✦ **Disable new features.** If you're using the latest version of PowerPoint but some of the people who will be reviewing your presentation aren't, using some of the latest features can cause trouble. On the Edit tab, you can disable those potentially troublesome features: New animation effects, Multiple masters, and Password protection. If someone you've shared the presentation with runs into difficulty with one of these features, try turning it off.

✦ **Always save as a Web page.** Change the default form in which you save your PowerPoint presentations with the Save PowerPoint files as drop-down list under the Save tab. Both Web Page and Single File Web Page are options.

✦ **Activate the Check style option.** This is a checkbox under the Spelling and Style tab. If it's active, PowerPoint will automatically check and correct style inconsistencies in your presentation, from differences in capitalization to differences in formatting among similar elements, to the use of too many fonts (which affects clarity) or fonts that are too small. Click the Style Options button to specify what PowerPoint should check.

Customizing Access

Just like the other Office applications, Access has an extensive Tools ⇨ Options dialog box (see Figure 48-15) chock-full of options, most of which you'll probably never be concerned with, and many of which have already been mentioned in the chapters on Access.

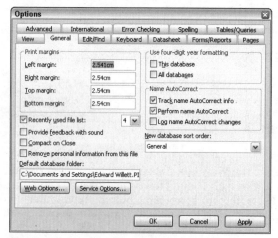

Figure 48-15: Access's Options dialog box is as busy as any of them.

However, just as with PowerPoint, there are a few that are worth pointing out:

✦ **Recently used file list.** This option on the General tab is set to 4, but again, I see no reason not to boost it all the way to its maximum of 9; it's a great convenience to have your recently used files ready to be opened from the File menu.

✦ **Four-digit year formatting.** Okay, I admit that the next time we run into a problem like the Y2K "bug" is thousands of years away, but it still seems good form to me to use four-digit year formatting in all databases (i.e., 2001, 2010, 2020, as opposed to just 01, 10, 20). Besides, the new millennium is still young enough that many databases will have 1900s dates in them; why risk confusing things? This option, too, is on the General tab.

✦ **Maximize your work space.** Access doesn't offer a Full Screen view, but you can still maximize the amount of space you have to work in by deselecting unneeded items in the View tab.

✦ **Customize keyboard behavior.** The Keyboard tab in Access lets you specify what move should be made after you press Enter (Next field is the default, but you can also choose Don't move and Next record), as well as arrow key behavior (next field or next character). You can also specify what the behavior should be when you do press Enter or an arrow key and enter a new field: select it (the default), go to the start of the field, or go to the end of a field.

✦ **Change your default colors.** The Datasheet tab offers you the opportunity to change the default colors, font, gridlines, and cell effect (i.e., whether your cells appear flat, raised, or sunken) of your datasheets.

Summary

Microsoft Office applications are almost infinitely customizable. This chapter introduced just a few of the many customizing options that are available in each of the main Office programs:

✦ Full Screen view in Word removes all those distracting toolbars and scrollbars and such — you can restore just the ones you want.

✦ The View tab of Word's Tools ➪ Options dialog box contains useful options for customizing Word for a variety of screen conditions.

✦ Outlook lets you change preferences for just about everything — and even allows you to create custom forms to create new Outlook items.

✦ You can set Excel to open the same worksheets every time you start it.

✦ Excel also has many options for customizing the look of worksheets, including a way to alter the menu of colors used for everything from gridlines to charts.

✦ You can save the view you create for a worksheet for use the next time around.

✦ PowerPoint has fewer customization possibilities, but among those it does have is a powerful option to check your presentation against a set of style options you define — and automatically correct problems.

✦ Access, too, offers customization possibilities, from changing keyboard behavior to altering color schemes.

✦   ✦   ✦

Working with Macros

Macros can help make you more productive by automating tasks that you perform frequently. Suppose, for example, you've developed a procedure to change the formatting of a document from what's standard for interoffice memos to what's standard for documents released to the public on business letterhead. You could create a macro for that procedure and even assign it to a button on a toolbar or to a menu item, so all you have to do is click once and all the tasks you used to have to perform step by step are carried out for you—faster than you originally did them.

Recording Macros

The simplest way to create a macro is by recording it: You turn on the macro recorder, perform the procedures you want to make part of the macro, and then turn the macro recorder off.

Caution If your macro is designed to do something to selected text, you have to select the text first, before recording the macro; you can't select text once the recorder is going. Also, if your macro involves pasting something (e.g., Paste as text), make sure there's something on the clipboard to paste or the macro will fail because when the clipboard is empty, the Paste button and command are grayed out.

The first step in creating such a macro is to think very carefully about what you want to do and the sequence of commands you'll have to carry out in order to achieve that end. You might want to jot them down on a piece of paper.

The precise procedures for recording a macro vary from program to program, as outlined below.

Recording a macro in Excel

Suppose that you want to create a macro that will automatically apply a green fill and an 18-point bold italic, Times New Roman font in blue to Excel cells. Here's how you do it:

1. Open an Excel worksheet.

2. Choose Tools ⇨ Macro ⇨ Record New Macro. This opens the dialog box shown in Figure 49-1.

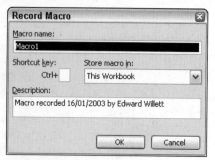

Figure 49-1: You need to make a few administrative decisions about your macro before you begin recording it.

3. In the Record Macro dialog box, enter a name for your macro (one that's meaningful to you) and choose where it should be stored: in the currently open workbook, in a new workbook, or in a personal macro workbook, which is a workbook that is created when you choose this option just to store your macros, ensuring that they're available every time you run Excel (otherwise, they're available only when you open the workbook in which they're stored). You can also choose a shortcut key that when pressed with the Ctrl key will run the macro. (You can't assign the macro to a menu command or button just yet.) Finally, you can add additional information about the macro to the description field.

Tip   If you're recording a lot of macros for use in a specific project, name them in such away that they'll all show up together in the list of macros — start them all with the same couple of letters, for instance.

4. When you click OK, recording begins immediately, and the Stop Recording toolbar opens. It has just two buttons: The one on the left stops recording, and the one on the right lets you choose whether you want to use absolute or relative cell references when recording.

Tip

By default, Excel uses absolute references, which means that, if you record cells being selected, the next time you run the macro those exact same cells will automatically be selected. If you click this button and switch to relative references and record cells being selected, the next time you run the macro the cells that are selected will be based on whatever cell is currently active and will have the same position relative to it as the cells you originally selected had to the active cell at the time of recording, even if the absolute location within the worksheet is completely different. If your macro doesn't involve cell selection, you don't need to worry about this button.

5. Carry out the actions you want to record. (Take your time and be methodical; no matter how long you take to record the macro, it will play back lickety-split, ignoring any pauses.) In this case, you'd click Fill Color and choose green from the color palette, click Font and choose Times New Roman, choose size 18 from the Font Size list, click the Bold and Italic buttons, and then click the Font Color button and choose blue from the color palette. (In this particular case, the sequence is arbitrary—the macro will work just as well regardless of the order in which these steps are recorded.)

6. Click the Stop Recording button.

Recording macros in other applications

Although the procedure is basically the same as in Excel, recording a macro is slightly different in Word and PowerPoint, and creating a macro in Access is a whole different ballgame.

Word

In Word, the Record Macro dialog box looks like the one shown in Figure 49-2. Instead of simply assigning a shortcut key, you're given the option to assign your macro to either the keyboard or a menu (we'll look at how to do both of those later in the chapter). The macro can be saved to either the normal.dot template, which means it will be available to all documents based on the Normal template (the default template), or just to the current document.

Figure 49-2: Word's Record Macro dialog box differs slightly from Excel's.

The Stop Recording toolbar looks a little different, too. Although, like the Excel one, it has two buttons, the second one is Pause Recording. This enables you to halt recording temporarily while you carry out steps you don't want to record — maybe you need to open another document temporarily and check on a style used there, or something like that — and then resume recording.

Note   As an aid to the absentminded, while you're recording a macro in Word, your mouse pointer changes: A small image of a tape cassette is attached to it.

PowerPoint

In PowerPoint, things are even simpler. The Record Macro dialog box has only three fields: one for naming the macro, one for choosing which of the open presentations it should be stored in, and one for providing a description (see Figure 49-3). There's no provision at the time of recording for assigning the macro to a shortcut key or toolbar. The Stop Recording toolbar is simpler, too: it consists only of a Stop Recording button.

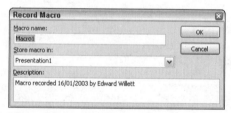

Figure 49-3: PowerPoint's Record Macro dialog box is particularly straightforward.

Access and Outlook

Access and Outlook don't allow you to record a macro as the other applications do; Outlook macros must be created in the Visual Basic Editor (see the introduction to Visual Basic later in this chapter), while Access macros can be created in the Visual Basic Editor or using an entirely different method. Access macros are also covered later in this chapter.

Running a macro

To run any macro, especially one that hasn't been assigned a shortcut key, toolbar button, or menu item (see the next section of this chapter), choose Tools ➪ Macro ➪ Macros. This opens a Macros dialog box similar to the one shown in Figure 49-4. (This is the Word version, but Excel and PowerPoint's dialog boxes are similar.) Highlight the macro you want to run, and then click Run, or simply double-click the macro's name.

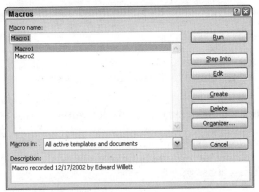

Figure 49-4: Choose the macro you want to run from this list.

You can look for macros in more than one place. Open the Macros in drop-down list at the bottom of the Macros dialog box, and you can look for macros in a variety of locations, which vary from application to application but generally include the option to look for macros just in the current document, workbook, presentation, etc., or in all open documents, workbooks, presentations, etc.

Tip   Word's built-in commands are really permanent macros, and one of the places where you can look for macros in Word is Word commands. You can find any command Word has to offer and run it from the Macros dialog box, just as you would any other macro.

Assigning Macros to Keyboard Combinations, Toolbars, and Menus

A successfully recorded macro is really just another command — and, just like other commands, it can be assigned to a shortcut key, toolbar button, or menu item.

Assigning macros to shortcut keys

As noted earlier, you're given the opportunity to assign a shortcut key to macros in Excel before you even record them, in the Record Macro dialog box. You can do the same thing in Word, but the procedure is a little different.

To assign a macro to a shortcut key in Word before you record it:

1. Choose Tools ➪ Macro ➪ Record New Macro.

2. In the Record Macro dialog box, click the Keyboard button in the Assign Macro to area. This opens the Customize Keyboard dialog box shown in Figure 49-5.

3. Click inside the Press new shortcut key text box, and then enter the key combination you'd like to use as a keyboard shortcut for your new macro. If you choose a combination that's already assigned to a command, Word tells you that. You can overwrite the existing keyboard shortcut if you wish, or you can find another shortcut that's not yet assigned.

Note   Your shortcut key must be either a function key or a key combination that begins with either Alt or Ctrl. You can't use a single ordinary key such as A (for obvious reasons: You'd end up setting off macros right and left while you typed!).

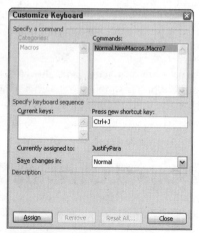

Figure 49-5: You can assign a Word macro to a keyboard shortcut in this dialog box.

4. When you're happy with your shortcut, click Assign, and then record your macro as usual. Once it's recorded, you can run it at any time by pressing the assigned shortcut keys.

PowerPoint does not let you assign a shortcut key to a macro.

Assigning macros to toolbars and menus

Once you have recorded macros in Excel, Word, or PowerPoint, the process of attaching them to toolbars and menus is straightforward: It's exactly the same procedure you follow for customizing any other tools.

In all three applications:

1. Choose Tools ➪ Customize. This opens the Customize dialog box, which is almost identical in Word, Excel, and PowerPoint.

2. If you want to create a brand-new toolbar to contain your macros, click the Toolbars tab, and then click New. Enter a name for the toolbar. In Word, you can also specify which documents you want to have access to the new toolbar (documents based on a particular template or just the current document). Click OK. A tiny floating toolbar with no buttons on it appears.

3. To place your macro on the new toolbar or on an existing toolbar, click the Commands tab and scroll down through the Categories list until you find Macros. Highlight that, and all the macros you've created will be displayed. (Again, this is easier if you've given all your related macros names that start with the same couple of letters, so they show up together in the list.)

4. Click on the macro you want to assign to a toolbar and drag it to the toolbar to which you want it added. In Figure 49-6, for instance, one macro has been dragged onto the new toolbar created in Step 2, and a second is on its way.

5. Once you've installed a macro onto a toolbar, and as long as you still have the Customize dialog box open, you can customize its appearance by clicking it, and then clicking Modify Selection (see Figure 49-7).

Note Each time you want to customize a different tool, you have to click on it, and then click Modify Selection again.

Here, you can change the command's name; choose whether you want the new command displayed as text only in both toolbars and menus, as an image on toolbars and text on menus, or as both an image and text; or assign a new button image, edit the current one pixel by pixel or paste in a new one you've copied from another command (click the button you want to copy, click Copy Button Image; click the button you want to use the copied button's image with; and click Paste Button Image). You can also make the macro button the first command of a new group of commands on the toolbar you've dragged it onto.

Cross-Reference For more information about customizing toolbars, see Chapter 2.

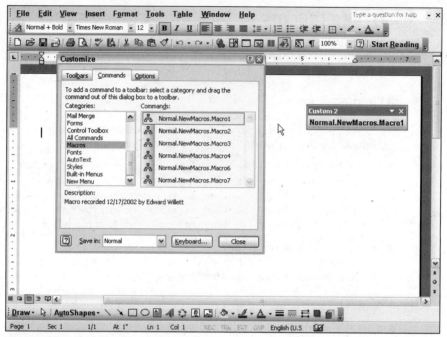

Figure 49-6: Add your recorded macros to toolbars or menus from here.

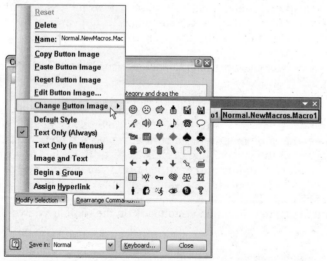

Figure 49-7: Modify the way your macro's button is displayed from this menu; here, the Change Button Image submenu is displayed.

6. In Word only, you can click Keyboard to reopen the Customize Keyboard dialog box and assign a new shortcut key to the macro.

7. Adding a macro to a menu follows exactly the same procedure as adding it to a toolbar; simply drag it onto any menu in the location you want (see Figure 49-8), and then modify its appearance using the Modify Selection button.

8. When you've successfully installed your macros onto their toolbars and menus, click Close.

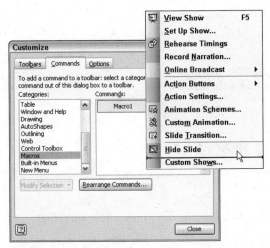

Figure 49-8: You can drag a macro onto a menu just as you can drag it onto a toolbar.

Using Macros in Access

As already noted, you can't record macros in Access the same way you can in other Office applications. That's because Access macros are typically more complex than those in other applications — which is why macros get their own button under Objects in the database window (see Figure 49-9).

Figure 49-9: Click the Macros button under Objects to see a list of all macros created for the current database.

Creating an Access macro

Rather than record macros in Access, you create them by assembling a list of actions from a list. To create an Access macro:

1. In the database window, click Macros, and then click New. This opens the window shown in Figure 49-10.

2. Choose the first action you want to perform as part of the macro from the drop-down list in the Action column, and click on it.

3. In the Action Arguments section, enter any additional information that is required.

4. Enter any comments you want to make about the action in the Comment column. You don't have to enter comments, but they make macro maintenance easier.

5. Move to the second row of the Action column and choose the second action you want to perform.

6. Repeat Steps 2–5 until you've finished your macro.

7. When you're done creating your macro, close the Macro window. Access asks if you want to save changes; click Yes.

8. Provide a descriptive name for your macro and click OK.

9. Click the Macros button under Objects in the database window again, and you'll see your new macro listed with the others in the database.

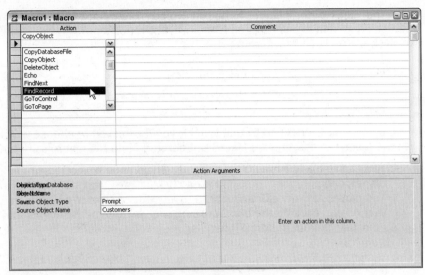

Figure 49-10: This is where you assemble your Access macros.

Tip

You can also create macros that perform actions on specific objects in the database: Arrange your windows so you can see both the Macro window and the database window and then drag objects from the database window to the Action column.

Creating macro groups

If you have a lot of macros, grouping similar ones together can help you keep them organized. To create a macro group instead of a single macro, follow the steps just outlined, but click the Macro Names button on the toolbar when the Macro window is open. This adds another column to the Macro window. You can enter a name for a macro and then select a list of actions for that macro to perform, and then enter a name for a new macro, selecting another list of actions for that macro to carry out, etc. When you save, you'll be specifying the name for a macro group, instead of a single macro.

Running an Access macro

Once you've created your macro, you can run it directly by clicking the Macros button under Objects in the database window and then double-clicking the name of your macro or clicking it once and clicking Run. If the database window isn't visible, you can run a macro from anywhere in Access by choosing Tools ➪ Macro ➪ Run Macro, choosing the name of the macro you want to run in the Macro Name dialog box.

It's rather unusual for a macro to be run directly, however, except to test it; most macros created in Access are run from forms or reports or even from other macros. To run a macro from a form or report:

1. Open the form or report in Design view.

2. Right-click on the object that you want to use to activate the macro, and choose Build Event.

3. If no event is attached to that object, you'll be asked to choose which builder you want to use; choose Macro Builder and build the macro as before.

4. You can also add a macro that already exists to an object. Right-click on the object, choose Properties, and then click on the Event tab (see Figure 49-11). You can assign any existing macro to any one of several possible events for that object; click on the box to the right of any one of the events and choose your macro from the drop-down list.

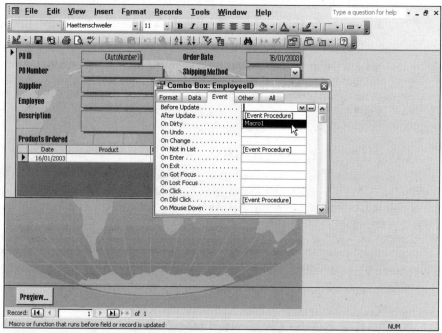

Figure 49-11: Make a form or report run a macro by entering the macro in this builder.

You can add Access macros to toolbars and menus just as you can in other Office applications. For instance, you could create a macro that opens a particular form or report, assign it to a button, and attach it to a toolbar so you can get to that form or report with a single click.

Introduction to Visual Basic for Applications

Visual Basic for Applications (VBA) is a powerful programming language that you can use to create new procedures for all of your Office applications — once you learn how to use it. Learning to use it effectively is outside the scope of this book — entire books are devoted just to that — but what follows is a brief introduction to some of the basic concepts behind VBA.

VBA is an object-oriented programming language, which means that you program in it by scripting a series of events, each of which is triggered by something that happens to an object (such as text boxes, command buttons, or sections of a form). This is consistent with all programming under Windows, which also involves responding to a series of events.

VBA offers you considerably more control than regular macros do, especially in such areas as handling program errors, creating new functions, and performing applications at the level of the operating system. VBA programming consists of units called *procedures,* each of which consists of a group of statements and methods that perform a desired operation; procedures, in turn, are grouped into modules.

That's about as far as we're going to delve into VBA in this book. For more detailed information, consult a book like *VBA For Dummies, Fourth Edition*, by John Paul Mueller (Wiley, 2003).

To get a taste of VBA, open Word, Excel, PowerPoint, or Outlook and choose Tools ➪ Macro ➪ Macros, choose a Macro, and then click Edit. You'll see a window something like the one shown in Figure 49-12.

Examining the innards of macros to see how they're put together is one good way to begin to grasp how VBA programs are constructed.

If you're the hands-on type, note that VBA enables you to tweak Office to your heart's content; but if you're a more typical user, you'll probably never go near it.

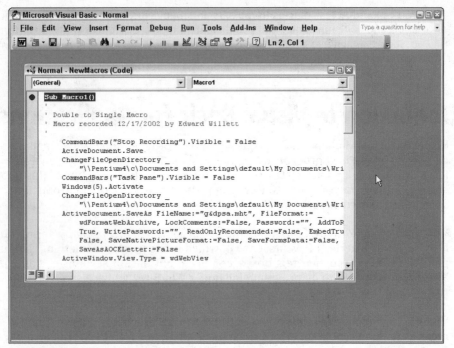

Figure 49-12: The Visual Basic Editor is a powerful application for creating programs in Visual Basic.

Summary

In this chapter, you learned procedures for creating macros in Office applications. Highlights included the following:

✦ You can automate procedures you perform regularly by choosing Tools ➪ Macro ➪ Record New Macro (in Word, Excel, and PowerPoint) and then performing the series of actions you want to automate.

✦ Recorded macros are essentially identical to any other command in Office and can be added to toolbars and menus by using the Customize dialog box (Tools ➪ Customize). Word and Excel also enable you to create keyboard shortcuts for macros.

✦ You can run a macro either by clicking the toolbar button or menu command you created for it (or pressing the keyboard shortcut) or by choosing Tools ➪ Macro ➪ Macros, selecting the macro you want to run, and clicking Run.

✦ You can't record a macro in Access; instead, you have to build it. Choose Objects ➪ Macros in the database window, and then click New. From a series of available actions, you can create a macro that does what you want it to.

✦ Macros in Access can be run from toolbars or menus as in other Office applications; they can also be activated from forms or reports.

✦ Macros in Access and in other Office applications can also be created using Visual Basic for Applications, a powerful programming language included with Office. You can access the Visual Basic Editor by choosing Tools ➪ Macro ➪ Visual Basic Editor, but you might want to get a good reference book on the topic first.

✦   ✦   ✦

What's on the CD-ROM

This appendix provides you with information on the contents of the CD that accompanies this book. For the latest and greatest information, please refer to the ReadMe file located at the root of the CD.

Here you'll find information on the following topics:

♦ System requirements

♦ Using the CD

♦ Files and software on the CD

♦ Troubleshooting

System Requirements

Make sure that your computer meets the minimum system requirements listed in this section. If your computer doesn't match up to most of these requirements, you may have a problem using the contents of the CD.

For Windows 9x, Me, XP, Windows 2000, Windows NT4 (with SP 4 or later):

♦ PC with a Pentium processor running at 120 Mhz or faster

♦ At least 32MB of total RAM installed on your computer; for best performance, we recommend at least 64MB

♦ Ethernet network interface card (NIC) or modem with a speed of at least 28,800 bps

♦ A CD-ROM drive

Office 2003–specific requirements:

- ✦ PC with Pentium 133 MHz or higher processor; Pentium III recommended
- ✦ Microsoft Windows 2000 with Service Pack 3 or Windows XP or later operating system

Using the CD

To install the items from the CD to your hard drive, follow these steps:

1. Insert the CD into your computer's CD-ROM drive.

2. A window appears displaying the License Agreement. Press Accept to continue. Another window appears with the following buttons (which are explained in greater detail in the next section):

   Office 2003 Bible: Click this button to view an eBook version of the book as well as any author-created content specific to the book, such as templates and sample files.

   Super Bible: Click this button to view an electronic version of the *Office 2003 Super Bible*, along with any author-created materials from the *Super Bible*, such as templates and sample files.

   Bonus Software: Click this button to view the list and install the supplied third-party software.

   Related Links: Click this button to open a hyperlinked page of Web sites.

   Other Resources: Click this button to access other Office-related products that you might find useful.

Files and Software on the CD

The following sections provide more details about the software and other materials available on the CD.

eBook version of *Office 2003 Bible*

The complete text of the book you hold in your hands is provided on the CD in Adobe's Portable Document Format (PDF). You can read and quickly search the content of this PDF file by using Adobe's Acrobat Reader, also included on the CD.

eBook version of *Office 2003 Super Bible*

The *Super Bible* is an eBook PDF file made up of select chapters pulled from the individual Office 2003 *Bible* titles. This eBook also includes some original and exclusive content found only in this *Super Bible*. The products that make up the Microsoft Office 2003 suite have been created to work hand in hand. Consequently, Wiley has created this *Super Bible* to help you master some of the most common features of each of the component products and to learn about some of their interoperability features. This *Super Bible* consists of over 500 pages of content to showcase how Microsoft Office 2003 components work together.

Bonus software

The CD contains software distributed in various forms: shareware, freeware, GNU software, trials, demos, and evaluation versions. The following list explains how these software versions differ:

✦ **Shareware programs:** Fully functional, trial versions of copyrighted programs. If you like particular programs, you can register with their authors for a nominal fee and receive licenses, enhanced versions, and technical support.

✦ **Freeware programs:** Copyrighted games, applications, and utilities that are free for personal use. Unlike shareware, these programs do not require a fee or provide technical support.

✦ **GNU software:** Software governed by its own license, which is included inside the folder of the GNU product. See the GNU license for more details.

✦ **Trial, demo, or evaluation versions:** Software usually limited either by time or functionality, such as not permitting you to save projects. Some trial versions are very sensitive to system date changes. If you alter your computer's date, the programs may time out and will no longer be functional.

Software highlights

Here are descriptions of just a few of the programs available on the CD:

✦ **ACDSee:** ACDSee 5.0 digital camera software from ACD Systems makes it easy to get, view, organize, print, enhance, and share your digital photographs super fast. Whether you're a digital photography beginner or a graphics professional, this picture viewer of choice for millions of people will make your digital photography experience more rewarding.

✦ **Power File Gold, Drag and Zip, Drag and View:** Power File Gold from Canyon Software is a powerful file management utility; Drag and Zip zips and unzips files and even checks them for viruses; and Drag and View lets you view the contents of many different types of files without opening them!

✦ **Fontlister:** With this program from Conquerware, you'll never have trouble finding a font for a special task. Now you'll be able to browse all your fonts without first installing them. If you decide to install or remove a font, you have to press only one button and it's done. Furthermore, Fontlister is able to print complete samples of all fonts before they're installed.

✦ **HyperCam:** From Hyperionics Technology comes this powerful video capture software that records AVI movies directly from your monitor, for software presentations, software training, demos, tutorials, and fun! HyperCam supports text annotations, sound, and screen notes (great for creating automated software demos!).

✦ **Debt Analyzer, Keyboard Express, ZipExpress:** Three great programs from Insight Software Solutions! Debt Analyzer analyzes and helps you reduce, eliminate, or consolidate up to 50 debts. Keyboard Express allows you to issue just about any series of keystrokes to your Windows applications with the touch of a key. And Zip Express provides easy look-up of U.S. Zip codes and their associated cities, states, counties, area codes, time zones, and current time.

✦ **WS_FTP Pro:** WS_FTP Pro from Ipswitch is nothing less than the world's most popular FTP client for Windows.

✦ **PaintShop Pro:** Paint Shop Pro from Jasc Software is a complete image creation and manipulation program that enhances the imaging power of business and home users with unrivaled ease of use, speed, and affordable functionality.

✦ **Judy's TenKey:** Judy's TenKey from Judy's Applications is an award-winning Windows calculator that includes nearly every feature imaginable, including a scrolling tape that automatically recalculates when you edit it. You can control the appearance of your personal calculator, from choosing the types of buttons to showing negative numbers in red. More important, you can set Judy's TenKey to behave like a standard calculator, an adding machine, or a scientific calculator.

✦ **Power Utility Pak:** Power Utility Pak from Jwalk and Associates is a collection of Excel add-ins, consisting of general-purpose utilities, custom worksheet functions, enhanced shortcut menus, and even games!

✦ **WinZip:** WinZip from WinZip Computing makes opening zip files and other archive and compression formats easier than ever before. WinZip features built-in support for most popular Internet file formats, and interfaces to most virus scanners.

✦ **PlanMagic Business:** PlanMagic Business from PlanMagic Corporation is one of the finest programs available for generating business plans, from starting to running a business. It features all aspects of a professional plan (forecasts, ratios, marketing, goals, strategies, etc.), and a complete online business guide.

Comprehensive list of software

Here is a list of all the products available on the CD. For more information and a description of each product, see the Interface CD or Bonus Software sections of the CD.

3D Charts for Excel

4TOPS Data Analysis

4TOPS Document Management

4TOPS Excel Import Assistant

4TOPS Excel Link

4TOPS Filter Builder

4TOPS Screen Capture

4TOPS Summary Wizard

4TOPS Word Link

Acc Compact v1.10

Access Form Resizer 2.3

Access Image Albums 2.1

Access Property Editor 2.0

Access to VB Object Converter v5.0

AccessBooks

AccessBooks Updater

AccessViewer, Version 2

AccVerify for FrontPage v5.0

ACDSee 5.0

Acrobat Reader 5.x

AcroWizard v2.0

Action Process Automator v.4.2

ActiveConverter Component

ActiveDocs 2002

Addsoft StoreBot 2002

Advanced Disk Catalog

Advanced Office Password Recovery

All-in-1 Personal Organizer

Analyse-It

Apache Axis Beta 3

Apache Batik

Apache FOP (Formatting Objects Processor)

Attach for Microsoft Outlook

Attachment Options

Auscomp eNavigator Suite V7.5

Auscomp Fort Knox V4.0

Auscomp IT Commander V3.0

Auscomp Smart Login V4.0

AutoSpell for Microsoft Office

B2BDataBus

BadBlue Personal Edition v2.0

Barcode ActiveX Control & DLL demo

BoilerPlate_addin

Business Card Creator

c:JAM - Central Jet Accounts Manager

CaBook v1.1

Camtasia Studio

Capture Express v1.1a

CD Case & Label Creator

CD Player

Change Management System

Charset Decoding

Classify for Outlook v8.7.15.12

ClipMate

Code 128 Fonts demo with VBA

Code Critter

Collage Complete v2.0

Colored Toolbar Icons

COM Explorer

CompareDataWiz 2002 version 10.03

CompareWiz 2002 version 10.03

Configuration Manager's Workbench

CONTACT Sage

Convert Cell Reference Utility

Crossword Compiler

CS School

CSE HTML Validator Lite

CSE HTML Validator Professional

Data Flow Manager

Data Flow Manager

Data Loader

Database Browser Plus v3.0

Database for Microsoft Excel

Database Password Sniffer

Datahouse v2

DataMoxie

DataPrompter_addin

DataWiz 2002 version 10.01

DB Companion

DBSync

Debt Anaylzer

DeskTop.VBA

Dialgo Personal Call Center App v1.3

Dictation 2002 v3.3

Digital Juice v2.0 (or later)

DinkIT Listbar ActiveX

Directory Lister

DoctoHtml 1.2

Drag and View v4.5

Drag and Zip v3.0

Drag-N-Dropper for MS Access - v4

dtd2xs

Dubit

DynaZIP-Max

EasyT 2000

eForms Word templates & forms

El Scripto 2

Eliminate Spam!

Excel Tetris v1.1

Executive Accounting

ExLife

expat - XML Parser Toolkit

ExSign v1.21

EZDetach v1.2

EZ-ROM Presentation Pro Edition

Fax4Outlook

FileBox eXtender

Filter Assistant

Fontlister 3.4.9

Free templates

FrontLook Chameleon Demo

FrontLook Component Effects

FrontLook Java Effects

FrontLook Page Effects Sampler

FrontLook Screen Capture

FrontLook Super Themes Sampler

Fundraising Mentor

Gantt Chart Builder (Access)

Gantt Chart Builder (Excel)

GFI FAXmaker for Networks/SMTP

GFI MailSecurity 8.2

GFI MailSecurity for SMTP 8.2

Gif Construction Set

Gif Movie Gear

GraphicsButton

GuruNet

HiddenFileDetector_addin

HP EzMath v1.1

HTML Tidy

HtmlIndex v2.2.4

HyperCam

HyperSnap-DX 5

IdiomaX Office Translator v2.2

InspireApps.com Manager

IntelligentApps 4excel 3.5

JAU:Jeff-Net Access Utility v1

Judy's TenKey v4.5

JustAddCommerce

Keyboard Express v3.0d

King James Access Bible

Lark v1.0

Larval

LASsie for MS Access - v2.1

List & Label v9.0

LiveMath Maker and LiveMath Plug-in v3.0

Loan Assistant

Mach5 Mailer

Macro Express 3 v3.2

Mail Administrator

Mail Washer

Maillist Deluxe

Math Easy for Excel

Mathematical Summary Utility

MathEQ 4.0 Expression Editor

MathPlayer 1.0

MathType

Mdb2txt

Micro Eye ZipOut 2003

Microsoft Publisher Tips and Tricks

Milori Training Tools 2001

Moe (Mouse Over Effects) v2.4

Mozilla

MultiNetwork Manager v6.3

Name Splitter for Microsoft Access

NetAdvantageSuite

NewsGator v1.0

OfficeBalloonX (ActiveX Control)

OfficeRecovery Enterprise

OfficeSpy v1.0

OutBooks

Outcome XP

OutlookConnect

OutlookSpy v2.6

Paint Shop Pro 7.x

PDF Plain Text Extractor v2.3

Pendragon Forms v3.2

People's Choice Premier Accounting Version 4.4

PerformX Author 2

PerformX Designer

PERT Chart EXPERT v. 2

PivotTable Assistant

PlanMagic Business 5.3

PlanMagic Finance Pro 6.0

PlanMagic Marketing 6.0

PlanMagic WebQuestPro 2.002

PocketKnife v2.5

Polar Crypto Component 2.5

Polar Draw Component 2.0

Polar Spellchecker Component 4.0

Polar Zip Component 5.0

Power File Gold v1

Power Utility Pak v5

PowerFinish sample templates

PowerPak for PowerPoint

PowerPoint Backgrounds

Powerpointed

PrettyCode.Print v1.60

Print Assistant

PrintDirect Anywhere v.2.0

PrintDirect Utility v.1.6

PROMODAG StoreLog V2 (freeware)

Quick Charts

Recover My Files

Registry Crawler

ReplaceWiz 2002 version 10.01

Report Runner

Response Time Logger v4 (demo)

RFFlow 4.09 Trial Version

RnR PPTools Starter Set, Version 2

SafeCard v1.03

Scan to Outlook

Schedule XP

ScreenTime for Flash v2

Secrets Keeper v3.0

Selector for MS Access 2002 - v3.2

SendMail

Sensitivity Analyzer

SetClock v.2.4

SetFileDate v.1.1

Sheet Navigator

ShortKeys 2 v2.0b

ShrinkerStretcher v9.2

Signature995 v4.1

SimpleRegistry Control

SmartBoardXP

SmartDraw 5

SnagIt v6.2

Soft Graphics Buttons

SP SGML parser

SPEED Ferret v4.1

Style Builder

Style XP

SuperFax

TagGen Office 2003

TeeChart Pro ActiveX Control v5.0

TelePort Pro v1.29

The <WebSite> Promotion SuiteT 2003

The Spreadsheet Assistant

"The Wonderful World of Excel" clip art

Toolbar Doubler

Turbo Browser v9.0

TX Text Control, Version 8

Ulead Gif Animator

UltraPdf

VBAcodePrint v6.13.65

VBToolBox v1.01

VendAbility System 7

Virtual Check Solutions for Word v3.0

Visual Staff Scheduler PRO

V-Tools

Wave To Text v2.2

WBS Chart Pro v. 4

WebCompiler

WebEQ

WebMerge v2.2

WebSpice Animation sampler

WebSpice Objects

WinACE

WinFax Pro Automator

WinRAR

WinSell Express Version 3.1.0

WinSell Pro Version 2.2

WinZIP 8.1

Word Report Builder

Wordware 2002

Wordware PIM

WordWeb

WorkgroupMail 7.1

WS_FTP Pro

WS_Ping Propack

X2Net WebCompiler v2.04

Xalan

Xbooks

Xerces

XLSTAT-Pro v4.6

XlToHtml 1.3

XSBROWSER

XT

Zip Code Companion v3.00

ZIP Disk Jewel Case and Label Creator

Zip Express

Zip Repair

Related Links

Check out this page for links to all the third-party software vendors included on the CD, plus links to other vendors and resources that can help you work more productively with Office 2003.

Other Resources

This page provides you with some additional handy Office-related products.

ReadMe file

The ReadMe contains the complete descriptions of every piece of bonus software on the CD, as well as other important information about the CD.

Troubleshooting

If you have difficulty installing or using any of the materials on the companion CD, try the following solutions:

✦ **Turn off any anti-virus software that you may have running.** Installers sometimes mimic virus activity and can make your computer incorrectly believe that it is being infected by a virus. (Be sure to turn the anti-virus software back on later.)

✦ **Close all running programs.** The more programs you're running, the less memory is available to other programs. Installers also typically update files and programs; if you keep other programs running, installation may not work properly.

✦ **Reference the ReadMe:** Please refer to the ReadMe file located at the root of the CD-ROM for the latest product information at the time of publication.

If you still have trouble with the CD, please call the Customer Care phone number: (800) 762-2974. Outside the United States, call 1 (317) 572-3994. You can also contact Customer Service by e-mail at techsupdum@wiley.com. Wiley Publishing, Inc. will provide technical support only for installation and other general quality control items; for technical support on the applications themselves, consult the program's vendor or author.

✦   ✦   ✦

Optimizing Your Office Installation

Office Setup should run automatically when you put the first Office CD in the computer. If Office 2003 isn't already installed, you'll be walked through the steps required. These are straightforward, so I won't detail them here; the purpose of this appendix is to provide a few tips to help you configure Office optimally after the initial installation.

Note Just a couple of reminders about the initial installation: You'll be asked, before anything else happens, to provide the Product Key (a 25-character code on the back of the CD case or on the Certificate of Authority); you cannot install Office without this key. That's not the only security measure Microsoft has put into Office to prevent software piracy: Even after you have successfully installed Office, it must be activated before it has been used a set number of times or else it will lose functionality. Office will warn of the need to do this repeatedly; you can do it over the Internet with just a few mouse clicks if you have an Internet connection. If you prefer, you can do it by phone.

Tip You can run the installer whenever you want to examine or change your current configuration.

On most systems, AutoPlay will start the installer as soon as you insert the CD. If the CD is already in the drive, or if AutoPlay didn't start the installers, the easiest way to run it is simply to go to My Computer and double-click the Office CD icon. The installer starts up and displays the Office Setup screen in maintenance mode. To see how Office is currently installed, click the Add or Remove Features radio button, and then click Next.

In the next panel of the installer, Custom Setup, all office applications are checked by default. Leave them checked unless you want to uninstall one of them.

Check the Choose advanced customization of applications checkbox at the bottom of the panel, and then click Next. This opens the installer's Advanced Customization panel, which lets you see and change the parts of Office that are available on your computer, and where their files reside. To modify the setting for any component, click the graphic beside the component name and pick from the list of options for that component. The components are organized in hierarchical groups. To work with components individually or as a group, expand or collapse the hierarchy by clicking the boxes that contain plus or minus signs.

You'll get the fastest performance from the Run from My Computer choice, which copies all the necessary files to your hard disk. Run from the CD saves space on your hard drive but slows file operation, and also means you have to have the Office CDs at hand all the time. Still, this option is worthwhile for features you rarely use, or for content like clip art that might take up too much space on your computer. (Today's hard drives have enormous amounts of data-storage space, but even the biggest hard drive can be so nearly full that you want to save as much space as possible.)

There's also a kind of compromise option, Installed on First Use, which tells the Windows installer to put off copying the necessary files to your hard disk until the first time you try to use the feature. But while this saves time initially, it can be very annoying to suddenly discover that the feature you want hasn't been installed yet — and again, you must have your CD at hand to install it before you can use it. (Which makes it doubly annoying if you're using a laptop, you're on the road some-where, and you didn't take your Office CD with you.)

Manually Repairing Your Office Installation

Whenever you run Setup, it verifies that your Office installation matches the config-uration you specified during setup. If something seems to have stopped working properly, though, you can perform the examination whenever you like by choosing Help ➪ Detect and Repair in any Office application.

An alternative choice is to open Office Setup and select the Repair Office option. If you have to, you can even reinstall Office entirely — although that's pretty drastic (*most* of your settings *should* carry on into the reinstalled version . . .).

Tip   If you do have to do reinstall and you've modified the Normal template in Word, be aware that the new version of Office will overwrite it. If you want to keep your modified version of the Normal template, save it in a non-Office folder some-where so you can load it back in after the reinstall.

Preserving Settings from a Previous Version of Office

Office features what Microsoft calls Intelligent Setup — which means that when you upgrade from a previous version of Office, Setup analyzes your current configuration and automatically installs the same components.

In addition, you can save your settings directly to a file where you can easily access them and apply them to another machine. That means you no longer have to laboriously re-create your settings on a second Office-equipped computer. (This also makes it quicker and easier for administrators to move settings from machine to machine.)

To save your settings, run the Save My Settings Wizard, which you can find in the Microsoft Office Tools folder in your Programs list in Windows.

Note It's possible to install Office without installing the Save My Settings Wizard, so if you can't find it, you may have to run your old version of Office's Setup an install the wizard first.

✦　　✦　　✦

International Support and Accessibility Features

In Office, core software functions are completely separate from the language-specific portions of the code, which plug into the core as needed. Because Office comes complete with these plug-in language components, you don't need to buy any add-ons — or, worse, a whole different edition of Office — when you want to work in another language, even if you want to change the language in which Office displays its menus and Help system on-screen.

Office's support for multiple languages includes:

✦ Compatibility with Unicode, a standard system for encoding language characters.

✦ Fonts for languages such as Chinese and Arabic that don't use European alphabets, and multilanguage versions of commonly used fonts such as Arial, Courier New, Garamond, and Times New Roman.

✦ Proofing tools such as spelling and grammar checkers, as well as their supporting dictionaries, thesauri, AutoCorrect lists, and hyphenation algorithms.

✦ Templates and wizards customized for the supported languages.

✦ Utilities for editing in (and converting between) various Asian languages.

✦ Components for displaying the user interface in any supported language.

✦ A translation feature that lets you translate words and phrases between various languages.

The Office applications include commands unique to particular languages that appear automatically when you enable a given language. Word has the greatest support for multiple languages among the Office applications. Even more impressively, Word can figure out automatically which language you're typing in!

Note Despite these features, Office is still available in localized versions, because the language components provided with the English version don't cover every Office feature.

Tip If you want to use different languages to label the Office user interface and switch between them, be sure to turn off the Windows Active Desktop first. If you leave Active Desktop on, the user interface appears only in the default language that comes with your version of Windows.

Installing the MultiLingual User Interface Pack

Office's language-related plug-in components are packaged as the MultiLingual User Interface Pack on two separate CDs.

To activate the capability to change language settings, install the MultiLingual User Interface Pack by running its own Setup program. After you've installed the pack, the main Windows installer takes over, installing any needed components when you change language settings in Office. Note that your Office CDs don't include files for every supported language — you may have to download files from Microsoft's Web site or order supplemental disks.

Note Language-specific components that have the same filename in every language are installed in folders named according to Microsoft's locale ID number for the language in question. That's why you have those folders named 1033: 1033 is the locale ID number for U.S. English.

When you no longer need to work in a particular language, you may want to remove its files to free up space on your hard disk, if it's close to being full. To do so, run the MultiLingual User Interface Pack's Setup program again. When the installer's dialog box appears, click Add or Remove Features to get to the list of installed languages; set the ones you don't want anymore to Not Available.

Turning on Language-related Features

The control panel for Office's language-related features is the Microsoft Office Language Settings dialog box, accessible from the Windows taskbar via the Start ➪ All Programs ➪ Microsoft Office Tools folder. The dialog box has three tabs: User Interface, Enabled Languages, and About Microsoft Office Language Settings. You use the first two tabs to change language settings; the third tab simply provides information about which version of the language settings you're using and whom it's licensed to.

The settings on the User Interface tab determine the language that Office displays to the user to label its features (for example, text on menus, in dialog boxes, and in the Help system). You won't see this tab until you've actually installed language-specific user interface components from the MultiLingual User Interface Pack. When the tab does appear onscreen, the only choices offered are those of the installed languages.

Use the Enabled Languages tab to specify the languages in which you want to edit documents. All languages supported by Office are shown, regardless of whether or not you've installed them on your system. However, be aware that commands unique to each selected language appear on menus and in dialog boxes (for example, with Japanese enabled, you'll see a Japanese Consistency Checker command under Tools ➪ Language, and an Asian Layout submenu appears on the Format menu), an annoyance if you're not actually using that language.

Turning on keyboard support for other languages in Windows

All Windows versions let you switch among different languages at the operating-system level. When you do so, Office adjusts itself accordingly. The Windows language setting also determines the layout of your keyboard. Although Windows provides a default keyboard layout for each locale, you can choose any layout you like for any locale.

In Windows 2000, open Regional Settings, and then click the Add button on the Input Locales tab; in Windows XP, open Regional and Language Options and click the Languages tab.

Using other languages in your documents

After you've installed and enabled the language features in Windows and Office, you can start using them to view and edit documents. You don't have to do anything special to view documents — just open them in the appropriate Office application. Entering new information in a different language requires more work, however.

Editing with alternative keyboard layouts

Often, the language chosen as the active language offers more characters than fit on the standard and shifted keys — the accented characters in European languages, for instance. In such cases, you typically enter accented characters by pressing a two-key sequence that starts with the accent key. In some layouts, still more characters are available when you hold down the right Alt key.

Using the onscreen keyboard

Included with Windows (it's in the Accessibility subfolder of the Accessories folder in your Program list), the On-Screen Keyboard utility (see Figure C-1) lets you see the keyboard layout for the language that's currently active in Windows.

Figure C-1: The On-Screen Keyboard shows which keys to type to enter the characters available to you in the active keyboard layout.

If you're working with a Windows keyboard layout that differs from the one shown on your real-life keyboard, the On-Screen Keyboard shows you which key you must type to enter any given character into your document, or you can use the mouse to "type" on the On-Screen Keyboard instead of on your regular keyboard. Pressing Shift (or clicking the onscreen Shift key) shows you the shifted version of the character set. To use characters that must be entered via a two-key sequence, press or click the key that starts the sequence.

Editing documents in Asian languages

Although you can view documents created in an Asian language when you turn on support for that language, you can't enter new ideographic characters directly. Instead, you need a special tool called an Input Method Editor (IME). Versions of Windows localized for a language include the corresponding IME, of course, but only the one for that language. However, Office's MultiLingual User Interface Pack comes with limited IMEs for Japanese, Korean, and two versions of Chinese (Simplified and Traditional); these work in the English version of Office.

Translating documents in Word

Not only does Word allow you to use multiple languages, but it can also provide translation between two languages for single words or short phrases. Choose Tools ➪ Language ➪ Translate. The Research task pane (see Figure C-2) opens, with Translation chosen in the Show results from list. You can enter text you want translated in the box at the top of the pane or choose to translate text highlighted in the currently open document, as I've done in the figure (highlight the text before choosing the Translate command; you can also right-click highlighted text and choose Translate from the shortcut menu).

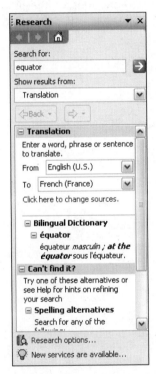

Figure C-2: Word's Translate command can provide basic translation between installed languages.

Understanding Unicode

The text-handling features of Office support Unicode, an international standard for numerically encoding the characters used in major languages. While conventional Windows fonts can hold only about 200 different characters, Unicode can handle more than 65,000. Unicode numbers have already been assigned to about 40,000 letters, numerals, ideograms, punctuation marks, and other features unique to particular languages. With Unicode, text prepared in any major language can be displayed accurately by other applications and on other computers, as long as the necessary fonts are installed.

About the Unicode fonts included with Office

Office comes with a complete 40,000-character-or-so (I didn't count) Unicode font called Arial Unicode MS. This font enables the display of multilanguage text in Unicode-aware applications that don't support font changes.

For example, Access allows only one font in each database table. If you happen to have an Access table that lists translations for words from many languages, you'll need a Unicode font that contains all the characters required in order to display the table accurately.

Word's Insert ⇨ Symbol dialog box and the Windows Character Map utility (in the System Tools subfolder of the Accessories folder on your Program list; see Figure C-3) both recognize Unicode fonts.

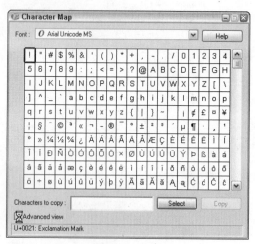

Figure C-3: Use Character Map to select and view a subset of Unicode characters.

Other Unicode fonts

Office also includes a number of Unicode updates for some scalable TrueType fonts that you most likely already have on your system. These fonts don't contain all the Unicode characters, but they do offer multiple character sets that cover many non-English languages. Among these fonts are Arial, Arial Black, Arial Bold, Arial Narrow, Bookman Old Style, Courier New, Garamond, Impact, Tahoma, Times New Roman, Trebuchet, and Verdana.

Accessibility Features

Office has several tools that can make it easier for visually and physically impaired individuals to work with Office applications:

✦ **Zoom.** All Office applications except Outlook have, on the Standard toolbar, a list box labeled Zoom. You can choose to view documents at any percentage of full size, either by selecting one of the percentages in the list (which range from 10 percent to 500 percent) or by typing a percentage into the box. For those who find it difficult to read fine print on a computer screen, Zoom can be a major help. (To avoid having to scroll horizontally back and forth to see your text, turn on the Wrap to Window option; choose Tools ⇨ Options, click on the View tab, and then check the Wrap to window checkbox in the Outline and Normal options area, at the bottom of the dialog box.)

✦ **Large icons.** Another helpful feature in Office applications is the ability to enlarge the icons on the toolbars. Choose Tools ⇨ Customize, click the Options tab, and then check the Large Icons checkbox. The change takes effect immediately (see Figure C-4).

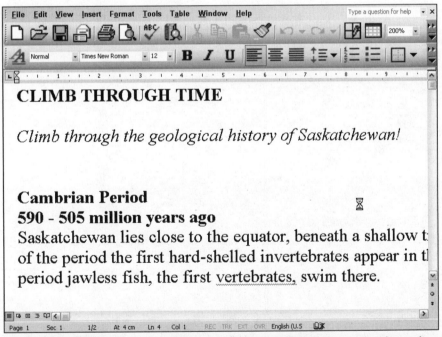

Figure C-4: Enabling the large icons option makes it much easier to see the tools on Office's toolbars.

✦ **Microsoft IntelliMouse.** If you have difficulty operating a mouse, you might want to consider the Microsoft IntelliMouse pointing device, which Office supports and which lets you scroll and zoom more easily, thanks to the addition of a wheel. (Other mice with wheels will usually give you most of the same functionality as an IntelliMouse.) For example, you can scroll to the end of the document with a single click, and without using keys. Another option is to use a trackball instead of a mouse.

✦ **Keyboard shortcuts.** Many Office features and commands can be activated with the keyboard alone. For a complete list of keyboard shortcuts for each application, refer to that application's Help files.

✦   ✦   ✦

Finding Office Information on the Web

The following sites provide additional useful information about using Office, as well as additional macros, templates, themes, and other useful add-ons. As well, many of these sites offer links to additional sites that I haven't listed.

The Microsoft Office Home Page

At the official Microsoft Office Home Page, you'll find the latest Office news, plus product information, demos, and more.

```
http://www.microsoft.com/office
```

Microsoft Office Tools on the Web

Another site run by Microsoft focuses on the Office suite. Here you'll find templates, clip art, program updates, articles, converters, viewers, and more. Office Help sends you to this site if it can't answer your question.

```
http://office.microsoft.com
```

Element K Journals

This site offers several monthly journals for Office users; be aware, though, that you have to subscribe to them, and they aren't cheap.

```
http://www.elementkjournals.com
```

CNET.com Office Sites

CNET is an excellent source for information about all aspects of computers, including Microsoft Office. Do a search for "Microsoft Office."

```
http://www.cnet.com
```

Woody's Office Portal

Another source of Office tips and trivia is Woody's Office Portal, the companion Web site to a free weekly newsletter ("Woody's Office Watch") that Woody Leonhard distributes via e-mail. Subscribe at

```
http://www.wopr.com
```

Smart Solutions

Smart Solutions is the home page for a magazine focusing on "Business Productivity with Microsoft Technology." You'll find lots of articles, reviews, and Office-related downloads.

```
http://www.mssmartsolutions.com
```

Outlook and Exchange Solutions Center

Here you can find news and articles about and downloadable tools for Outlook from computer-book author Sue Mosher.

```
http://www.slipstick.com
```

The Spreadsheet Page

Here you can find great Excel information and add-ins from computer-book author John Walkenbach.

```
http://j-walk.com/ss/
```

Smart Access Online

This is the online version of the *Smart Access* newsletter, with tons of information about how to get the most out of Access.

```
http://www.smartaccessnewsletter.com
```

MVPs.org

This site is a jumping-off point to dozens of other sites created by some of the people associated with the Microsoft Most Valuable Professional program—which means they're acknowledged by their peers and by Microsoft for their active participation in Microsoft technical communities around the globe. In other words, they know what they're talking about!

```
http://www.mvps.org
```

FrontPage Talk

Here you'll find a collection of forums focusing on FrontPage. If you have a question you can't find an answer to anywhere else, you can probably get it answered here.

```
http://www.frontpagetalk.com
```

Office Zealot.com

This site focuses on the needs of higher-end Office developers, providing tons of news and offering a free electronic newsletter.

```
http://www.officezealot.com
```

✦   ✦   ✦

Index

Continued

Continued

Continued

Continued

Continued

Continued

Continued

Continued

Continued

Continued